Research Methods in
EDUCATION

For my wife Angela, my loving supporter and most honest advisor, always.

—Joseph Check

To my wife, Elizabeth.

—Russell Schutt

Research Methods in
EDUCATION

Joseph **CHECK** ▪ Russell K. **SCHUTT**

University of Massachusetts Boston

Los Angeles | London | New Delhi
Singapore | Washington DC

Los Angeles | London | New Delhi
Singapore | Washington DC

FOR INFORMATION:

SAGE Publications, Inc.
2455 Teller Road
Thousand Oaks, California 91320
E-mail: order@sagepub.com

SAGE Publications Ltd.
1 Oliver's Yard
55 City Road
London EC1Y 1SP
United Kingdom

SAGE Publications India Pvt. Ltd.
B 1/I 1 Mohan Cooperative Industrial Area
Mathura Road, New Delhi 110 044
India

SAGE Publications Asia-Pacific Pte. Ltd.
33 Pekin Street #02-01
Far East Square
Singapore 048763

Acquisitions Editor: Jerry Westby
Editorial Assistant: Erim Sarbuland
Production Editor: Catherine M. Chilton
Copy Editor: Gillian Dickens
Typesetter: C&M Digitals (P) Ltd.
Proofreader: Annette R. Van Deusen
Indexer: Sheila Bodell
Cover Designer: Candice Harman
Marketing Manager: Katherine Winter
Permissions: Karen Ehrmann

Printed in the United States of America

Library of Congress Cataloging-in-Publication Data

Check, Joseph W., 1947-
Research methods in education / Joseph Check, Russell K. Schutt.

p. cm.
Includes bibliographical references and index.

ISBN 978-1-4129-4009-2 (pbk.)
1. Education—Research—Methodology. I. Schutt, Russell K. II. Title.

LB1028.C523 2012
370.72—dc232011032014

This book is printed on acid-free paper.

11 12 13 14 15 10 9 8 7 6 5 4 3 2 1

Brief Contents

Detailed Contents

3. Ethics in Research   45

4. Conceptualization and Measurement   65

5. Sampling   91

Preface

This is an exciting time to begin learning about educational research. For many years, the study of education was slow to change and regularly criticized—by practitioners for not being practical enough, by researchers from other disciplines for not being theoretical enough (Lagemann, 2000). Research that met rigorous "scientific" standards was accused of staying on library shelves and being of little use to teachers. Research that documented the daily life of students and teachers was derided as mere storytelling and "not scientific enough" (Walters & Lareau, 2009, pp. 1–2). Overall, education research was characterized by "continuing contests among different groups, especially scholars of education, scholars in other fields and disciplines, school administrators, and teachers" (Lagemann, 1997, p. 5).

Despite criticisms and contention, in the early years of the new century—the 2000s—it became clear that things were changing, that we were seeing "an explosion of new methodologies and approaches to inquiry" (Biesta & Burbules, 2003, p. 1) that could make educational research an evolving and exciting field, both practical *and* theoretical, both rigorous *and* context sensitive.

Educational research today is marked by three qualities. It is eclectic, dynamic, and essential. By *eclectic,* we mean that many disciplines and schools of thought contribute to educational research. By *dynamic,* we mean rapidly evolving, with new philosophies and methods emerging on a regular basis. By *essential,* we mean necessary, and recognized as necessary, for the optimal development of schooling.

▣ Eclectic

Eclectic means coming from many sources. Because learning is affected both by schooling and by factors outside schooling, educational research must be interdisciplinary, meaning that it involves more than one academic discipline or field of study. An "educational researcher" might be a professor of education, a sociologist, an anthropologist, an economist, a psychologist, or a medical doctor. In some forms of educational research, teachers are themselves researchers of their own classrooms.

Many common techniques in educational research originated outside the field of education. Anthropology gave us ethnography, the study of culture and cultural processes, now used to study classrooms and the culture of schools. Sociology gave us survey research; survey techniques are now used throughout education to study large populations of teachers and students. Psychology gave us tools for understanding the intellectual and emotional development of children. Quantitative disciplines such as mathematics and economics contribute multiple tools based on statistical analysis, including recent work in areas such as effect sizes, which measure the strength of relationships between variables. Many academic disciplines have scholarly journals that deal specifically with the intersection between their discipline and education, including *Anthropology and Education, Education Economics, Sociology of Education,* and the *Journal of Educational Psychology.*

▣ Dynamic

Educational research is a continually developing field. New theoretical approaches and data-gathering techniques emerge regularly. This is due in part to education's dynamic relationship with other fields of study, mentioned above. Examples of techniques that have been developed or refined in recent years include multilevel analysis and narrative inquiry. Multilevel analysis is an advanced statistical technique that enables a researcher to accurately analyze "nested" or "hierarchical" data sets at different levels, such as an individual student, a classroom of students, and a whole school (Hox, 2010). Narrative inquiry concentrates on collecting and telling the life stories of a single individual (Clandinin, Pushor, & Orr, 2007). A second kind of dynamic tension is created by the current federal push for scientifically based research and the simultaneous questioning of what that means in a naturalistic setting such as a classroom, particularly in classrooms with culturally diverse and disadvantaged populations.

Education researchers also have their own energetic and up-to-date professional organization, the American Educational Research Association (AERA), which provides a platform for discussion and new inquiry techniques and is open to participation from anyone involved in educational inquiry, whatever their philosophical or methodological approach.

▣ Essential

Accountability-based school reform efforts, particularly federal and state legislation, have made test scores, dropout rates, and other measurements an essential component of life in schools. Regular data collection, one of the key elements of research, is now the norm. New professional standards in fields such as school counseling and special needs teaching stress the importance of evidence-based practice. In addition, the growing popularity of formats such as teacher research and action research means that teachers are no longer just subjects of research conducted by others. Classroom teachers now have the tools to become researchers of their own practice and change agents in their own buildings. Taken together, these developments make research an essential dimension of life in schools today, both for the students, teachers, and administrators inside them and the parents, legislators, and policy makers outside.

At its heart, research starts with questions; every chapter of this book begins with a research question. Examples of published research studies related to the opening question are then used as examples throughout the chapter. By the end of the book, you will have encountered more than 30 published research studies that take different theoretical approaches and use many different methods to gather and interpret data.

Acknowledgments

Our thanks to Jerry Westby, Acquisitions Editor, SAGE Publications. Jerry has encouraged and supported this project continuously from the idea stage through final production. His patience, confidence, and human touch have smoothed the rough spots and helped us always keep the final goal in view. No author could ask for a better publisher.

We also thank the personable and highly creative SAGE professionals who turned a typescript into a scrupulously edited, highly attractive book: editor Denise Simon, production manager Catherine Chilton, copy editor Gillian Dickens, marketing manager Katharine Winter, associate editor Megan Krattli, editorial assistant Erim Sarbuland, and assistant editor Rachael Leblond. Kathryn Stoeckert Sabella did a superb job of developing the online exercises, and Gina Cook and Michelle Turner Mangan developed the fine set of ancillary materials.

We feel gratitude and friendship for the unique, cross-disciplinary support group of SAGE authors of related methods texts who have extended their wisdom and expertise: Ronet Bachman (University of Delaware), Dan Chambliss (Hamilton College), Ray Engel (University of Pittsburgh), and Paul Nestor (University of Massachusetts, Boston).

We are also indebted to the first-rate group of reviewers whose thoughtful suggestions and cogent insights have helped improve every chapter. They are Kimberly Alkins, Queens College; Maureen Angell, Illinois State University; Scott Bauer, George Mason University; Calvin Brown, Tennessee State University; Elaine Bukowiecki, Bridgewater State College; Laurie Carlson, Colorado State University; Dick M. Carpenter II, University of Colorado; Stephen E. Cramer, University of Georgia; Patrick Dilley, Southern Illinois University; Paul Erickson, Eastern Kentucky University; Chester Fuller, Central Michigan University; Gerry Giordano, University of North Florida; Carol Ann Gittens, Santa Clara University; Kristine Hogarty, University of South Florida; John Huss, Northern Kentucky University; Richard M. Jacobs, Villanova University; Lori Kim, California State University, Los Angeles; Lydia Kyei-Blankson, Illinois State University; Marie Kraska, Auburn University; Maria K. E. Lahman, University of Northern Colorado; Brian Lawler, California State University San Marcos; Alar Lipping, Northern Kentucky University; Jeffrey Lorentz, University of Houston, Clear Lake; Crystal Machado, Indiana University of Pennsylvania; Jerry R. McMurtry, University of Idaho; Steven Miller, Loyola University Chicago; Ralph Mueller, George Washington University; Victor Nolet, Western Washington University; Jeffrey Oescher, Southeastern Louisiana University; Gary W. Ritter, University of Arkansas; Charles Thomas, George Mason University; Jacqueline Waggoner, University of Portland; Scott Walter, Washington State University; Carol Wickstrom, University of North Texas; Diane Wilcox, James Madison University; and Nadia Zabtcheva, Montclair State University.

Joe thanks Russ greatly for the opportunity to co-create this book and for his constant concern not just for high-quality content but for straightforward writing to make the content accessible to students. Joe also thanks Karen Daniels and Margo Moore, the two hard-working graduate assistants who helped with this project; departmental administrative staffer Molly Pedriali, who was always needed and always there; his faculty colleagues, for their invaluable expertise not just as researchers but as teachers; and his students, on whom many of the approaches in this book were tried out. Finally, Joe thanks his wife Angela for her constant and unstinting encouragement and support, both emotional and editorial, and his children, Joe and Pietra, for their suggestions and support, and for enriching his life just by being who they are.

Russ thanks Joe for his skill, dedication, and good cheer throughout this project, and he thanks his wife Elizabeth for her love and support, and his daughter Julia, for the joy she brings to his life and for all that she contributes to the social world.

PART I
Foundations of Research

CHAPTER 1

Science, Schooling, and Educational Research

Research Question: *How Do Early Childhood Experiences Affect Schooling?*

Chapter Contents

- **Learning About the Educational World**
- **The Educational Research Approach**
- **Educational Research Philosophies**

C an watching too much television hurt toddlers, putting some children at a disadvantage before they enter preschool? Are preschool children whose mothers work outside the home academically behind when they go to school? Understanding early childhood influences is a key task for educational researchers and forms the research focus for this chapter. Dimitri A. Christakis, Frederick J. Zimmerman, David L. DiGiuseppe, and Carolyn A. McCarty (2004, pp. 708–713) studied more than 1,200 children and found that 1- and 3-year-olds who watched more than 3 hours of television daily had a substantially increased risk of developing attention problems by age 7. This was one of the first large-scale, systematic investigations that linked difficulty concentrating, restlessness, and impulsive behavior to watching television as a young child.

The Christakis et al. (2004) study appeared in the medical journal *Pediatrics*, yet it deals with an educational question that parents and early childhood teachers face every day. The study took a scientific, research-based approach to a complex, emotional question: Does too much TV harm very young children?

Have you thought about TV's effects on your own learning or that of children you have contact with? No one wants to feel that children are threatened by television, yet TV is widely used as an "electronic babysitter." In this chapter, you will learn how the Christakis et al. (2004) study and other, more recent investigations are helping to answer important questions about early childhood learning.

▣ Learning About the Educational World

Just one research question about learning raises so many more questions about education. Take a few minutes to read each of the following questions and jot down your answers. Don't worry about your responses: *This is not a test;* there are no "wrong" answers.

1. Do you think you watched too much television as a child?

2. How has television watching affected your learning?

3. How many hours of television does the average American child watch every day?

4. Does the content of what young children watch make a difference? Is educational programming such as *Sesame Street* better for a 3-year-old than Saturday cartoons?

5. How much does quality of early child care in general affect learning?

6. Most television viewing takes place outside school, but its effects show up in the classroom. How do you think other forces outside school affect how children will perform in school?

We'll bet you didn't have too much trouble answering the first two questions, about your own experiences, but what about the others? These four questions concern "the educational world"—the educational experiences and orientations of people in addition to ourselves. Usually, when we answer such questions, we combine information from many different sources. We may also recognize that our answers to the last four questions will be shaped by our answers to the first two—that is, what we think about the educational world will be shaped by our own experiences and by the ways we have learned about the experiences of others. Of course, this means that different people will often come up with different answers to the same questions. Studying research methods will help you learn what criteria to apply when evaluating these different answers and what methods to use when seeking to develop your own answers.

Take a bit of time in class and share your answers to the six questions. Why do some of your answers differ from those of your classmates? Now, let's compare your answers to Questions 3 through 6 to the findings of researchers using educational research methods.

Question 3: Preschool children in general watch anywhere from 0 to 30 hours of television a week, but the average is more than 4 hours per day. Four-year-olds average 50 to 70 minutes of viewing daily, most of which is cartoons (Huston, Wright, Rice, Kerkman, & St. Peters, 1990).

Exhibit 1.1 shows the amount of television watched by 18-month-olds in the Christakis et al. (2004) study mentioned earlier. Notice that the highest bar is at the zero level—no TV watching—and that more than half of the children studied watched 0 to 2 hours per day of television.

Question 4: Television viewing at an early age affects learning in school at a later age, but the connection is not a simple one. Important considerations include the type of programs viewed (commercial or educational), whether parents talk with children about what they're seeing, and how well children understand the difference between cartoon-type fantasies and real life (Peters & Blumberg, 2002).

Question 5: Conditions of child care, particularly the amount and quality of adult attention, can make a large difference in how television viewing affects later learning. Researchers at the National

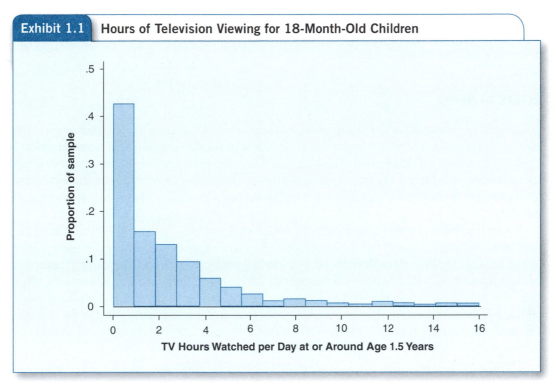

Exhibit 1.1 Hours of Television Viewing for 18-Month-Old Children

Source: Christakis et al. (2004, p. 711).

Institute of Child Health and Human Development (2002) studied the effects of early child care on more than 1,000 children. The study found that "children's development was predicted by early child-care experience" (p. 133). Educational development was connected to quantity, quality, and type of child care just prior to the child going to school. Higher quality care was associated with better language skills for 4½-year-olds, and after a certain point, the more hours children spent in care, the more behavior problems they showed.

Question 6: Many factors outside school affect learning in school. Physical and cognitive disabilities, for example, affect in-school learning for many children. Later in this chapter, you will learn of research on a legally blind preschool child in a classroom with 13 physically normal students. You will also learn of research that looks at cognitive effects on children when mothers work during the first year of the child's life. Economic and social factors play a large role in educational success or failure, and the federal government has created "compensatory" programs to level the educational playing field. One such program, Early Head Start, seems to be succeeding, and you will also learn of this research.

How do these answers compare with the opinions you recorded earlier? Do you think your personal experiences have led you to different answers than others might have given? Do you see how different people can come to such different conclusions about educational issues?

We cannot avoid asking questions about our complex educational world or trying to make sense of our position in it. In fact, the more that you begin to "think like an educational researcher," the more such questions will come to mind. But as you've just seen, our own prior experiences and orientations, particularly our own experiences as learners and teachers, can have a major influence on what we perceive and how we interpret these perceptions. As a result, one person may see television as a way to extend learning to millions of children, another person may think television for preschoolers should be completely banned, and others may think the entire issue is overblown. In this chapter, you will begin to look at research results in an analytic way, asking what questions have been researched, what the results of these studies are and what they mean, and how much confidence we can place in them.

Errors to Avoid

Educational research relies on analytic thinking, and one important element of analytic thinking is avoiding errors in logic. As readers and consumers of educational research, we have a right to expect rigorous thinking in research articles. Errors in thinking can occur in the way a research question is constructed, the methods used to carry it out, or the conclusions the researcher draws. Becoming aware of some of the most common errors in thinking will give you a head start on becoming a smart reader of educational research.

Four common errors in reasoning occur in the nonscientific, unreflective talk and writing about education that we encounter daily. Our favorite examples of these "everyday errors in reasoning" come from a letter to Ann Landers. The letter was written by someone who had just moved with her two cats from the city to a house in the country. In the city, she had not let her cats outside and felt guilty about confining them. When they arrived in the country, she threw her back door open. Her two cats cautiously went to the door and looked outside for a while, then returned to the living room and lay down. Her conclusion was that people shouldn't feel guilty about keeping their cats indoors—even when they have the chance, cats don't really want to play outside.

Do you see this person's errors in reasoning? She was guilty of the following:

- *Selective observation.* She observed the cats at the outside door only once.

- *Overgeneralizing.* She observed only two cats, both of which previously were confined indoors. Yet she drew a conclusion about cats in general.

- *Illogical reasoning.* She assumed that others feel guilty about keeping their cats indoors and that cats are motivated by feelings about opportunities to play.

- *Resistance to change.* She was quick to conclude that she had no need to change her approach to the cats.

If you recognize these errors for what they are and make a conscious effort to avoid them, you can improve your own reasoning. You will guard against stereotyping people, avoid jumping to conclusions, and look at the big picture. These are errors in observing, generalizing, reasoning, and reevaluating that the methods of educational research help us avoid.

Observing

One common observing mistake is **selective observation**—choosing to look only at things that are in line with our preferences or beliefs. When we are inclined to criticize individuals or institutions, it is all too easy to notice their every failing. For example, if we are convinced in advance that all television viewing by children is harmful, we can find many confirming instances. But what about educational programs such as *Sesame Street* and educational software games that use television to teach basic concepts in language and arithmetic? If we acknowledge only the instances that confirm our predispositions, we are victims of our own selective observation.

Our observations can also simply be inaccurate. If a child says she is "hungry" and we think she said she is "hunted," we have made an **inaccurate observation.** If we think five students are standing in a hallway when seven actually are, we have made an inaccurate observation.

Such errors occur often in casual conversation and in everyday observation of the world around us. In fact, our perceptions do not provide a direct window onto the world around us, for what we think we have sensed is not necessarily what we have seen (or heard, smelled, felt, or tasted). Even when our senses are functioning fully, our minds have to interpret what we have sensed (Humphrey, 1992). The optical illusion in Exhibit 1.2, which can be viewed as either two faces or a vase, should help you realize that perceptions involve interpretations. Different observers may perceive the same situation differently because they interpret it differently.

| Exhibit 1.2 | An Optical Illusion |

Generalizing

Overgeneralization occurs when we conclude that what we have observed or what we know to be true for some cases is true for most or all cases. We are always drawing conclusions from our experience, but sometimes we forget that our experiences are limited. The educational world is, after all, a complex place. We have the ability to interact with just a small fraction of the individuals who inhabit the educational world, especially in a limited span of time. Some people feel that television watching can't hurt young children because it exposes them to ideas and information they would never have otherwise encountered. Would their experience generalize to yours? To others?

Exhibit 1.3 depicts the difference between selective observation, which we have already discussed, and overgeneralization.

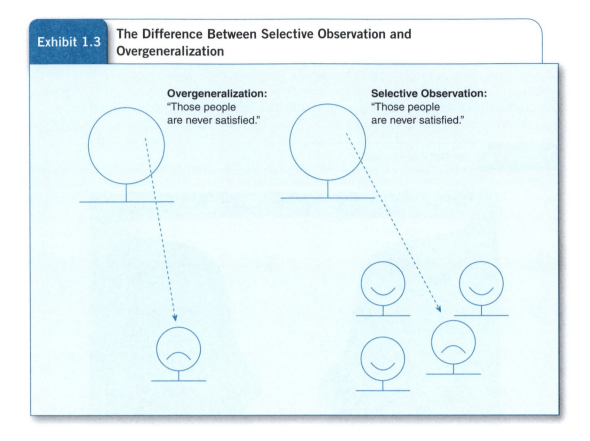

Exhibit 1.3 The Difference Between Selective Observation and Overgeneralization

Reasoning

When we prematurely jump to conclusions or argue on the basis of invalid assumptions, we are using **illogical reasoning.** For example, it is not reasonable to propose that children who watch no television will have no attention problems in school because there are sources of attention problems other than television. On the other hand, an unquestioned assumption that every child who watches television will have some attention problems overlooks some important considerations, such the type of programs that are being watched and the amount of parent interaction around the child's TV viewing. Logic that seems impeccable to one person can seem twisted to another—the problem usually is reasoning from different assumptions rather than just failing to "think straight."

Reevaluating

Resistance to change, the reluctance to reevaluate our ideas in light of new information, may occur for several reasons:

Ego-based commitments. We all learn to greet with some skepticism the claims by leaders of companies, schools, agencies, and so on that people in their organization are happy, that revenues are growing, and that services are being delivered in the best possible way. We know how tempting it is to make statements about education that conform to our own needs rather than to the observable facts. It can also be difficult to admit that we were wrong once we have staked out a position on an issue.

Excessive devotion to tradition. Some degree of devotion to tradition is necessary. Learning both in and out of school can be traditional in many ways, both open and hidden. Some skepticism about the effects of television on children can be a healthy antidote to panic about media's effects, which neither parents nor teachers can control. But too much devotion to tradition can stifle adaptation to changing circumstances. When we distort our observations or alter our reasoning so that we can maintain beliefs that "were good enough for my grandfather, so they're good enough for me," we hinder our ability to accept new findings and develop new knowledge.

Uncritical agreement with authority. If we do not have the courage to evaluate critically the ideas of those in positions of authority, we will have little basis for complaint if they exercise their authority over us in ways we don't like. And if we do not allow new discoveries to call our beliefs into question, our understanding of the educational world will remain limited.

Now take just a minute to reexamine the opinions about learning that you recorded earlier. Did you grasp at a simple explanation even though reality is far more complex? Were your beliefs influenced by your own ego and a tendency to overgeneralize your own learning experiences? Did you weigh carefully both the positive and negative effects that television has on learning? Do you see some of the challenges faced by educational researchers?

▣ The Educational Research Approach

Educational research is designed to reduce potential sources of error in reasoning about the educational world. Educational research builds on the methods of **science,** so it relies on logical and systematic methods to answer questions, and it does so in a way that allows others to inspect and evaluate its methods. In the realm of educational research, these methods are not so unusual. After all, they involve asking questions, observing social groups, and counting people, which we often do in our everyday lives. However, educational researchers develop, refine, apply, and report their understanding of the educational world more systematically, or "scientifically," than the general public does.

Science and Educational Research

What is "scientific" about educational research methods? Consider this:

- Educational research methods reduce the likelihood of overgeneralization by using systematic procedures for selecting individuals or groups to study that are representative of the individuals or groups to which we wish to generalize.

- Educational researchers use explicit criteria for identifying causes and for determining whether these criteria are met in a particular instance to avoid illogical reasoning.

- Educational research methods reduce the risk of selective or inaccurate observation by requiring that we measure and sample phenomena systematically.

Science: A set of logical, systematic, documented methods for investigating nature and natural processes; the knowledge produced by these investigations.

Educational research: The use of scientific methods to investigate teaching and learning, both inside and outside school—the educational world; the knowledge produced by these investigations.

- Because they require that we base our beliefs on evidence that can be examined and critiqued by others, educational research methods lessen the tendency to develop answers about the educational world from ego-based commitments, excessive devotion to tradition, and/or unquestioning respect for authority.

Motives for Educational Research

Research begins with questions—in this chapter, questions about television viewing and early childhood development. What motivates selection of a research question or focus? Usually it's one or more of the following reasons:

Personal motivations. Some educational researchers who explore early childhood learning feel that by doing so, they can help to improve the lives of children, the effectiveness of schooling, or the conditions of disadvantaged groups in their communities or countries. Educational researchers may become interested in early childhood as a result of watching their own children or grandchildren or after teaching or working with young children. A teacher-researcher who teaches second graders might want to find out how much television the children in her class watch and what kinds of programs they spend the most time on. Many research questions spring from the researcher's own life, experiences, and values.

Academic motivations. Academic questions about influences on educational processes have stimulated much educational research. Early childhood researchers want to understand the strength and meaning of family and other outside influences on the school performance of young students. Do lower income, family disintegration, or other factors that often lead to increased day care mean that some children enter school at a large disadvantage? Can public interventions in the early years help to equalize this disadvantage? The desire to gain a better understanding of questions such as these is motivation enough for many educational researchers.

Policy motivations. Many government agencies, elected officials, and private organizations seek better descriptions of the effects of television so they can advocate for policies that use television for the public good. School officials may need information for planning curriculum, teaching approaches, and media awareness programs. Parent groups may want to inform their members to limit television viewing in the best interests of their children. These policy and program management needs can stimulate numerous research projects.

Quantitative methods: Methods such as surveys and experiments that record variation in educational life in terms of categories that vary in amount. Data that are treated as quantitative are either numbers or attributes that can be ordered in terms of magnitude.

Qualitative methods: Methods such as participant observation, intensive interviewing, and focus groups that are designed to capture educational reality as participants experience it, rather than in categories predetermined by the researcher. Data that are treated as qualitative are mostly written or spoken words or observations that do not have a direct numerical interpretation.

Quantitative and Qualitative Orientations

One of the most common divisions in educational research is the distinction between quantitative research and qualitative research. Both quantitative and qualitative researchers collect data and then use them to tell a meaningful story—data analysis and findings, in research terms—but the data they collect and the methods they use to analyze them differ substantially. Here's a very basic way of understanding the difference. Quantitative researchers collect numbers and quantities as basic data and employ a whole array of statistical procedures to analyze those data. Qualitative researchers record words, pictures, or video as data and identify patterns and themes in those data that result in narrative interpretations that create meaning.

The distinction between quantitative and qualitative data is not always sharp. Qualitative data can be converted to quantitative data, when we count the frequency of particular words or phrases in a text or measure the time elapsed between different observed behaviors. Surveys that collect primarily quantitative data may also include questions asking for written responses, and these responses may be used in a qualitative, textual analysis. Qualitative researchers may test explicit explanations of educational phenomena using textual or observational data. We'll examine such "mixed method" possibilities in Chapter 11.

Educational researchers often combine these methods to enrich their research. The use of multiple methods to study one research question is called **triangulation.** The term suggests that a researcher can get a clearer picture of the educational situation being studied by viewing it from several different perspectives. Each will have some liabilities in a specific research application, and all can benefit from combination with one or more other methods (Brewer & Hunter, 1989; Sechrest & Sidani, 1995).

> **Triangulation:** The use of multiple methods to study one research question.

The distinction between quantitative and qualitative methods involves more than just the type of data collected. Quantitative methods are most often used when the motives for research are explanation, description, or evaluation. Exploration is most often the motive for using qualitative methods, although researchers also use these methods for descriptive, explanatory, and evaluative purposes. Chapters 9 and 14 present qualitative methods in much more detail, and most other chapters include some comparison of quantitative and qualitative approaches. The next section discusses four primary types of educational research and their relationship to qualitative and quantitative orientations.

Types of Educational Research

There are four types of educational research projects. This section illustrates each type with examples from educational research about early childhood:

Descriptive research. Defining and describing education-related phenomena is a part of almost any research investigation, but **descriptive research** is often the primary focus of the first research about some issue. One of the early descriptive questions researchers asked about the extent of television viewing by young children was, "What patterns of viewing do children have in early childhood and how do they differ from the viewing habits of older children?" (Huston et al., 1990). **Measurement** (the topic of Chapter 4) and sampling (Chapter 5) are central concerns in descriptive research. Survey research (Chapter 8) is often used for descriptive purposes.

Exploratory research. **Exploratory research** seeks to find out how people get along in the setting under question, what meanings they give to their actions, and what issues concern them. The goal is to learn "What is going on here?" and to investigate educational phenomena without explicit expectations. This purpose is associated with the use of methods that capture large amounts of relatively unstructured information. For example, researchers investigating young children's learning have had to look closely at the educational effects of social context and peer interaction. Exploratory research frequently involves qualitative methods.

Explanatory research. Many consider explanation the premier goal of any science. **Explanatory research** seeks to identify causes and effects of educational phenomena, to predict how one phenomenon will change or vary in response to variation in some other phenomenon. Early childhood researchers adopted explanation as a goal when they began to focus on factors that influence children's development and behavior. Their explanatory questions have included "Is maternal employment in the first year of life associated with negative child outcomes in the first three years of life?" and "Are these effects . . . mediated by the quality of child care or the home environment?" (Brooks-Gunn, Han, & Waldfogel, 2002, p. 1052). We focus on ways of identifying causal effects in Chapter 6. Explanatory research often involves experiments or surveys (see Chapter 8), both of which are most likely to use quantitative methods.

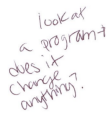

Evaluation research. Seeking to determine the effects of an educational program or other type of intervention is a type of explanatory research because it deals with cause and effect (see Chapter 7). However, **evaluation research** differs from other forms of explanatory research because evaluation research considers the implementation and effects of educational policies and programs. These issues may not be relevant in other types of explanatory research. For example, concern over the impact of Early Head Start, an extensive federal early childhood program, provided the impetus for a major federal evaluation study that involved more than 3,000 families (U.S. Department of Health and Human Services, 2002).

Certain types of research are often used with certain research methods because those methods yield a kind of data that are helpful for answering that type of question. Exhibit 1.4 shows some common correspondences between type of research, the goal of the research, and methods and techniques that match. The correspondence between types and methods should not be regarded as a hard-and-fast rule—it's possible to find exploratory research that uses some quantitative techniques, for example—but the chart gives a handy way of thinking about relationships between types and methods.

Exhibit 1.4 **Types of Research and Their Relation to Goals and Methods**

Research Category	Goal	Method	Possible Techniques	Comments
Descriptive	What is the scope or shape of the issue or problem?	Quantitative	Survey research	Often used for early research on an issue
Exploratory	"What's going on here?" (often about processes or relationships)	Qualitative	Observations, narrative description, interviews	Captures large amounts of unstructured information; often leads to more questions
Explanatory	Identify causes and effects, predict how one variable will change in relation to another	Quantitative	Experiments, statistical analysis of large data sets	Difficult when there are many variables or strong "context effects"
Evaluation	Determine implementation and effects of policies and programs	Quantitative and qualitative	Measure program processes and outcomes using statistics, test scores, rating scales, interviews, focus groups, on-site observations	Can be considered a special type of explanatory research.

We'll now summarize four actual early childhood research projects that exemplify these four types of research.

Description: What Types of TV Programs Do Young Children Watch?

In the 1980s, when this research was conducted, researchers knew that children watched a lot of television but knew little about what types of programs they were actually watching. A team of researchers followed 326 children for 2 years to determine how much television and what kind of programming the children were watching. The children were in two age groups, 3 to 5 and 5 to 7 years old.

The researchers found that the children watched, on average, 2 to 3 hours of television per day. Children's viewing changed with age, and boys tended to watch more cartoon and action programs than girls. Boys were also more interested in adult informational programs. As they grew older, children of both sexes began watching more comedies meant for general audiences. As the children matured, they moved from informative programs aimed at children to entertainment programs for a general audience (Huston et al., 1990).

Exploration: How Does Classroom Social Context Affect a Disabled Preschool Child?

Elizabeth Erwin, Elizabeth Alimaras, and Nikki Price (1999) knew that research going back to the 1930s shows the importance of social context and peer interaction to learning. They also knew that there was little research on peer interactions in early childhood settings that included children with disabilities. They designed a small pilot study of socialization experiences in a preschool class that included Ryan, a 3-year-old with identified disabilities (Ryan had detached retinas in both eyes with no light perception in his right eye and a visual acuity of 20/600 in his left eye, no cognitive impairments, but other medical complications, including kidney disease). To conduct the study,

> qualitative methods (i.e. participant observations and semi-structured personal interviews) were used . . . in an effort to provide a rich portrait of events, experiences, and perspectives. Data were gathered across daily classroom routines and natural settings within the school such as the music room, playground, hallways, and classrooms. (p. 57)

Observations began in September and were conducted approximately once a month until school closed in June. Observational data were supplemented by 1-hour personal interviews with the classroom teacher, the teacher assistant, and Ryan's mother and father. Because this was an exploratory study, the findings included narrative descriptions of the types of interactions that occurred between Ryan and other children. Overall, the authors felt that their exploratory study, rich in description, resulted in more questions than answers, and they urged other researchers to further explore the skills and knowledge practitioners needed to successfully support disabled students. This type of conclusion, which points the way for further research, is not uncommon in exploratory studies, which are typically undertaken when a question or research area is just starting to be investigated.

Explanation: When Mothers Work During the Child's First Year, Do Children Suffer Cognitively?

One of the large changes in our society over the past 40 years has been the increasing number of mothers who work outside the home. Questions have been raised about whether this helps or harms young children as they prepare to begin formal schooling. Researchers at the U.S. National Institute of Child Health and Human Development (Brooks-Gunn et al., 2002) tried to find out if maternal employment during a child's first year had positive or negative cognitive effects later, when the child was almost ready to go to school. They used quantitative methods to analyze a large body of information (called a "data set") that the agency had already collected.

The researchers studied 900 European American children. The number of hours that mothers worked was compared to their children's scores on a standard test of cognitive skills. They concluded that

> maternal employment by the ninth month was found to be linked to lower Bracken School Readiness Scores at 36 months, with the effects more pronounced when mothers were working 30 hours or more per week and with effects more pronounced for certain subgroups (i.e., children whose mothers were not sensitive, boys, and children with married parents). (Brooks-Gunn et al., 2002, p. 1052)

The researchers were careful to note limitations of their study. These included the fact that they had studied only one population, European Americans, and the idea that factors other than working also made a difference. These factors included "quality of child care, home environment, and maternal sensitivity." However, even when these additional factors were taken into account, "the negative effects of working 30 or more hours per week in the first 9 months were still found" (Brooks-Gunn et al., 2002, p. 1052).

The researchers also made policy recommendations based on their findings, which is not unusual in explanatory research in education. They recommended, for instance, that "it would be prudent for policy makers to go slow on measures . . . that would require mothers to enter the labor force (full-time) early in the first year of life and to consider measures (such as the proposed Family and Maternal Leave Act extensions) that would allow more mothers to choose to delay their return to the labor force and/or to work part-time until late in the first year of life" (p. 1068).

Evaluation: Is the Early Head Start Program Working?

Because large- and small-scale programs are a common feature of schools, many educational research studies try to measure program effectiveness. In 1995, Congress created Early Head Start, which was the only federal program specifically designed to improve the early education experiences of low-income babies and toddlers. In August 2002, the federal government published the first full evaluation study of the program, which aims to improve infants' and toddlers' later school success by supporting prenatal health and improving children's cognitive, social, and emotional development (U.S. Department of Health and Human Services, 2002).

The researchers used a large, randomly assigned sample—more than 3,000 families—in 17 sites across the country and a wide range of evaluation measures of cognitive, language, and social-emotional development. Evaluation results showed that the program was working across the whole range of indicators. These included cognitive functioning, interaction with parents, movement toward self-sufficiency, child-father interactions, and greater school readiness (U.S. Department of Health and Human Services, 2002).

Exhibit 1.5 shows some of the indicators used in the Early Head Start study to measure parents' knowledge of and involvement with their children. The last three items refer to a hypothetical scenario presented to parents in which their child's behavior required parental intervention. Unfortunately, one of the other findings of the evaluation was that the program currently reached only 3% of those eligible to receive services (Stark, 2003).

Exhibit 1.5 — **Parenting Knowledge and Discipline Strategies Measured by Early Head Start Study (2002)**

- Knowledge of Infant Development Inventory
- Use Guards or Gates for Windows
- Always Use a Car Seat for Child
- Spanked Child in Previous Week
- Responses to Hypothetical Situation with Child: Prevent or Distract
- Responses to Hypothetical Situation with Child: Talk and Explain
- Responses to Hypothetical Situation with Child: Physical Punishment

Source: U.S. Department of Health and Human Services (2002, p. 16).

▣ Educational Research Philosophies

Different educational researchers are guided by different research philosophies. A philosophy, in this case, means a viewpoint on what constitutes educational reality. Naturally, how you think about reality has implications for what methods you use to investigate that reality. In this section, we will describe and explain two alternative research philosophies that are prevalent in educational research, positivism and interpretivism. **Positivism**—and its descendent postpositivism—is more closely linked to quantitative research approaches. Interpretivism—and its descendent **constructivism**—is more closely linked to qualitative approaches.

Positivism and Postpositivism

Researchers with a positivist philosophy believe that an objective reality exists apart from the perceptions of those who observe it and that the goal of research is to better understand this reality. This is the philosophy traditionally associated with natural science (e.g., biology, chemistry, physics), with the expectation that there are universal laws of human behavior and with the belief that scientists must be objective and unbiased to see reality clearly (Weber, 1949, p. 72). Positivists believe that a well-designed test of a theoretically based prediction can move us closer to understanding actual educational processes.

The philosophy of **postpositivism** is closely related to positivism. Postpositivists believe that there is an external, objective reality, but they are very sensitive to the complexity of this reality and to the limitations and biases of the scientists who study it (Guba & Lincoln, 1994, pp. 109–111). As a result, they do not think we can ever be sure that scientific methods allow us to perceive objective reality. Instead, postpositivists believe that the goal of science is to achieve intersubjective agreement among scientists about the nature of reality (Wallace, 1983, p. 461). For example, postpositivists may worry that researchers' predispositions bias them in favor of a certain theory. Therefore, they remain skeptical of research results that support that theory until a number of researchers report such evidence. A postpositivist has much more confidence in the community of researchers than in any individual researcher (Campbell & Russo, 1999, p. 144).

> **Positivism:** The belief, shared by most scientists, that there is a reality that exists quite apart from our own perception of it, that it can be understood through observation, and that it follows general laws.
>
> **Postpositivism:** The belief that there is an empirical reality, but that our understanding of it is limited by its complexity and by the biases and other limitations of researchers.
>
> **Intersubjective agreement:** An agreement by different observers on what is happening in the natural or educational world.

Interpretivism and Constructivism

Qualitative educational research is often guided by a different, interpretivist philosophy. Interpretivist approaches have become increasingly influential in educational research, and their growing prevalence since the 1990s, sometimes referred to as the "interpretive turn," has changed the educational research landscape (Howe, 1998). Interpretivist researchers believe that educational reality is socially constructed and that the goal of educational research is to understand what meanings people give to reality, not to determine how reality works apart from these interpretations. This philosophy rejects the positivist belief that there is a concrete, objective reality that scientific methods help us to understand (M. Lynch & Bogen, 1997). Instead, interpretivists believe that people construct an image of reality based on their own prefer-

> **Interpretivism:** The belief that reality is socially constructed and that the goal of social scientists is to understand what meanings people give to that reality.
>
> **Constructivist paradigm:** A perspective that emphasizes how different stakeholders in educational settings construct their beliefs.

ences and prejudices and their interactions with others and that this is as true of scientists as it is of everyone else. This means that we can never be sure that we have understood reality properly, that "objects and events are understood by different people differently, and those perceptions are the reality—or realities—that social science should focus on" (Rubin & Rubin, 1995, p. 35).

The constructivist paradigm extends interpretivist philosophy by emphasizing the importance of exploring how different stakeholders in a social setting construct their beliefs (Guba & Lincoln, 1989, pp. 44–45). It gives particular attention to the different goals of researchers and other participants in a research setting and seeks to develop a consensus among participants about how to understand the focus of inquiry. From this standpoint, "Truth is a matter of the best-informed and most sophisticated construction on which there is consensus at a given time" (Schwandt, 1994, p. 128).

Taking a Balanced Approach

It is tempting to think of positivism as representing an opposing research philosophy to interpretivism and constructivism. Then it seems that we should choose the one philosophy that seems closest to our own preferences and condemn the other as "unscientific," "uncaring," or perhaps just "unrealistic." But there are good reasons to prefer a research philosophy that integrates some of the differences between these philosophies (J. Smith, 1991). Researchers influenced by a positivist philosophy should be careful to consider how their research approaches and interpretations are shaped by their own social and educational background—just as we are cautioned to do by interpretivist researchers. Researchers influenced more by an interpretivist philosophy should be careful to ensure that they use rigorous procedures to check the trustworthiness of their interpretations of data (Reissman, 2008, pp. 185–199). If we are not willing to ask "hard questions" about our projects and the evidence we collect, we are not ready to investigate the educational world (Reissman, 2008, p. 200). The educational phenomena we study are often complex, and we must take this complexity into account when we choose our methods and interpret our results.

But even in areas of research that are fraught with controversy, the quest for new and more sophisticated research has value. What is most important for improving understanding of the educational world is not the result of any particular study but the accumulation of evidence from different studies of related issues. By designing new studies that focus on the weak points or controversial conclusions of prior research, educational researchers contribute to a body of findings that gradually expands our knowledge about the educational world and resolves some of the disagreements about it.

Conclusions

We began this chapter with the question, "How do early childhood experiences affect schooling?" Throughout the chapter, you saw examples of ways in which researchers approached this topic, including looking at the effects of television on attention span and aggressive behavior; the effects of social dynamics in a preschool classroom with 14 students, one of whom was severely disabled; the possible cognitive effects on very young children when mothers work; and the evaluation of Early Head Start, a federal preschool program. Each study examined the question from a different perspective, used different methods, and reached different conclusions. Taken together, though, they begin to build a research-based answer to the original question. They show, in a small way, how the aggregation of individual studies can eventually help us to attain big answers.

We hope this first chapter has given you an idea of what to expect in the rest of the book. Our aim is to introduce you to educational research methods by describing what educational researchers have learned about the educational world as well as how they have learned it. The substance of educational research inevitably is more interesting than its methods, but the methods become more interesting when they're linked to substantive investigations.

This book's first six chapters deal with Foundations of Research. We have focused attention on early childhood research in this chapter; in Chapter 2, we use studies of reading instruction to illustrate the research process. Chapter 2 outlines the research process as a whole and also presents specific techniques for becoming a savvy reader and user of educational research. We also introduce the process of writing research proposals, which is then continued in special end-of-chapter exercises throughout the book. Chapter 3 explains research ethics, particularly the importance of the ethical treatment of human subjects.

To complete our overview of the foundations of research, in Chapters 4, 5, and 6, we introduce a variety of measurement approaches, different ways of sampling larger populations, and specific techniques to maximize the validity of causal assertions. Methods of designing research and collecting data are the focus of the book's second section (Chapters 7–12). Evaluation research and educational assessment, the subjects of Chapter 7, are conducted to identify the impact of educational programs or to clarify educational processes involving such programs. Experimental methods are often part of evaluation research, and so they are discussed in this chapter. Survey research (Chapter 8) can be used to collect data from a large population of students, teachers, or community members.

Chapter 9 shows how qualitative methods can uncover aspects of the educational world that we are likely to miss in experiments and surveys and sometimes result in a different perspective on educational processes.

Chapters 10, 11, and 12 introduce data collection approaches that can involve several methods. Chapter 10 focuses on single subject designs, which can be extremely useful in investigations in the classroom and in counseling, where a single student can be studied. Chapter 11 covers mixed methods. As you might suspect, mixed-method approaches combine two or more of the other methods. Chapter 12 gives special attention to methods of inquiry—teacher research and action research—that emphasize the concerns and insights of practitioners—classroom teachers and others directly involved in education.

The third section of this book, comprising the final three chapters, deals with Analyzing and Reporting Data. Chapter 13 is not a substitute for an entire course in statistics, but it gives you a basic idea of how to use statistics when analyzing research data and reporting or reviewing research results. In Chapter 14, we examine in some detail the logic and procedures of qualitative data analysis. You will be struck by the differences between qualitative data analysis techniques and the quantitative data analysis techniques of Chapter 13. Chapter 15 deals with reporting research; our research efforts are really only as good as the attention we give to our research reports. In Chapter 15, we finish the discussion of research proposals started in Chapter 2.

Each chapter ends with several helpful learning tools. Lists of key terms and chapter highlights will help you to review. Discussion questions and practice exercises will help you to apply and deepen your knowledge. Special exercises guide you in developing your first research proposal and finding information on the World Wide Web.

Key Terms

Constructivism 15	Inaccurate observations 6	Resistance to change 8
Descriptive research 11	Measurement 11	Science 9
Evaluation research 12	Qualitative methods 10	Selective observation 6
Explanatory research 11	Quantitative methods 10	Triangulation 11
Exploratory research 11	Positivism 15	
Illogical reasoning 8	Postpositivism 15	

Highlights

- Educational research cannot resolve value questions or provide permanent, universally accepted answers.

- Empirical data are obtained in educational research investigations from either direct experience or others' statements.

- Four common errors in reasoning are overgeneralization, selective or inaccurate observation, illogical reasoning, and resistance to change. These errors result from the complexity of the educational world, subjective processes that affect the reasoning of researchers and those they study, researchers' self-interestedness, and unquestioning acceptance of tradition or of those in positions of authority.

- Educational research is the use of logical, systematic, documented methods to investigate individuals, processes, contents, and educational systems, as well as the knowledge produced by these investigations.

- Educational research can be motivated by personal preferences, academic issues, and policy concerns.

- Educational research can be descriptive, exploratory, explanatory, or evaluative—or some combination of these.

- Quantitative and qualitative methods structure research in different ways and are differentially appropriate for diverse research situations.

- It is possible to mix **qualitative** and **quantitative methods** to gain accurate knowledge of particular questions.

Student Study Site

To assist in completing the web exercises, please access the study site at www.sagepub.com/check, where you will find the web exercise with accompanying links. You'll find other useful study materials such as self-quizzes and e-flashcards for each chapter, along with a group of carefully selected articles from research journals that illustrate the major concepts and techniques.

Discussion Questions

1. Select an educational issue that interests you, such as television watching or charter schools. List at least four of your beliefs about this phenomenon. Try to identify the sources of each of these beliefs.

2. Find a report of an educational research in an article in a daily newspaper. What were the major findings? How much evidence is given about the methods the researcher used? What additional design features might have helped to improve the study's validity?

Practice Exercises

1. Review letters to the editor and opinion pieces in your local newspaper. Identify any errors in reasoning: overgeneralization, selective or inaccurate observation, illogical reasoning, or resistance to change.

2. Read the abstracts (initial summaries) of each article in a recent issue of a major educational research journal.

(Ask your instructor for some good journal titles.) On the basis of the abstract only, classify each research project represented in the articles as primarily descriptive, exploratory, explanatory, or evaluative. Note any indications that the research focused on other types of research questions.

Web Exercises

1. Prepare a 5- to 10-minute class presentation on the ERIC System. Go to the ERIC site at http://www.eric.ed.gov/ to view some of the research. Pick a study listed on ERIC and write up a brief outline for your presentation, including information on study design, questions asked, and major findings.

2. Is the *Pediatrics* study's perspective representative of other researchers? Check out the research reports on early childhood and television for the last 5 years at ERIC. How many studies did you find? Write up some information regarding the research and its goals, methods, and major findings. What do the researchers conclude about the impact of television on young children? How do these conclusions compare to each other and to those of the *Pediatrics* study?

Developing a Research Proposal

Will you develop a research proposal in this course? If so, you should begin to consider your alternatives.

1. Think of three or four topic areas you might like to study. What are your motives for studying each topic?

2. Develop four questions that you might investigate about two of the topics you just selected. Each question should reflect a different research motive: description, exploration, explanation, or evaluation. Be specific.

3. Which question most interests you? Would you prefer to attempt to answer that question with quantitative or qualitative methods? Why?

CHAPTER 2

The Process and Problems of Educational Research

Research Question: *How Does a Child Learn to Read?*

Chapter Contents

- **Educational Research Questions**
- **Educational Research Basics**
- **The Role of Educational Theory**

- **Educational Research Goals**
- **Educational Research Proposals, Part I**

eading has formed the core of the elementary school curriculum since the beginning of public education in the United States. In this chapter, we will examine different educational research strategies and how they have been used to answer questions about reading. We will consider in some detail the techniques required to begin the research process: formulating research questions, finding information, reviewing prior research, and writing a research proposal. Appendices A, B, and C provide more details on these key techniques. By the chapter's end, you should be ready to formulate a research question, design a general strategy for answering this question, critique previous studies that addressed this question, and begin a proposal for additional research on the question.

▣ Educational Research Questions

An educational research question is a question about the educational world that you seek to answer through the collection and analysis of firsthand, verifiable, empirical data. It is not a question about who did what to whom but a question about individual cases, people in groups, general educational processes, or tendencies in school change. What kinds of responses does a disabled preschooler get from classroom peers? Is language development innate or environmental? How much have techniques for teaching reading changed over the past 40 years? So many research questions are possible that it is more of a challenge to specify what does *not* qualify as an educational research question than to specify what does.

But that doesn't mean it is easy to specify a research question. In fact, formulating a good research question can be surprisingly difficult. We can break the process into three stages: identifying one or more questions for study, refining the questions, and then evaluating the questions.

Identifying Educational Research Questions

Educational research questions may emerge from your own experience—from your "personal troubles," as C. Wright Mills (1959) put it. One experience might be based on your own learning to read, another on your son's or daughter's preschool experiences, a third on a show about high schools you saw on television. You may find yourself asking a question such as, "In what ways do students tend to transfer home reading experiences to school?" or "Do 3-year-old boys play differently than 3-year-old girls?" or "Does the high school day begin too early for effective learning by adolescents?"

The research literature is often the best source for research questions. Every article or book will bring new questions to mind. Even if you're not feeling too creative when you read the literature, most research articles highlight unresolved issues and end with suggestions for additional research. For example, Anderson, Hiebert, Scott, and Williamson (1985, p. 23) reviewed a large body of previous research and concluded that reading aloud to children was the most important thing parents could do to ensure their children's reading success in school. However, later researchers challenged this conclusion, particularly in regard to family literacy practices in nonmainstream homes (Auerbach, 1995; Moll, Amanti, Neff, & Gonzalez, 1992). A new study could focus on the effects of social context on a child's emergent literacy: How do home literacy activities in widely different settings influence future school literacy performance? Any research article in a journal in your field is likely to have comments that point toward unresolved issues.

Many educational researchers find the source of their research questions in educational theory. For example, you may have concluded that children who have been read aloud to at home have a big advantage in learning to read in school, so you may ask whether reading theory can explain how listening affects reading.

Finally, some research questions have very pragmatic sources. You may focus on a research question posed by someone else because it seems to be to your advantage to do so. Some educational scientists conduct research on specific questions posed by a funding source in what is termed an RFP, a request for proposals. (Sometimes the acronym RFA is used, meaning request for applications.) Or you may learn that the action research team in the school where you work needs help with a survey to learn about parents' home reading practices, which becomes the basis for another research question.

Refining Educational Research Questions

It is even more challenging to focus on a problem of manageable size than it is to come up with an interesting question for research. We are often interested in much more than we can reasonably investigate with limited time and resources. In addition, researchers may worry about staking a research project (and thereby a grant or a grade) on a single problem, and so they may address several research questions at once. Also, it might seem risky to focus on a research question that may lead to results that conflict with our own cherished assumptions about the educational world. The prospective commitment of time and effort for some research questions may seem overwhelming, resulting in a certain degree of paralysis.

The best way to avoid these problems is to develop the research question one bit at a time. Don't keep hoping that the perfect research question will just spring forth from your pen. Instead, develop a list of possible research questions as you go along. At the appropriate time, you can look through this list for the research questions that appear more than once. Narrow your list to the most interesting, most workable candidates. Repeat this process as long as it helps to improve your research questions.

Evaluating Educational Research Questions

In the third stage of selecting a research question, we evaluate the best candidate against the criteria for good educational research questions: feasibility, given the time and resources available; educational importance; and scientific relevance (King, Keohane, & Verba, 1994).

Feasibility

We must be able to conduct any study within the time and given the resources we have. If time is short, questions that involve long-term change may not be feasible. Another issue is what people or groups we can expect to gain access to. Observing educational interaction in Tahiti may be impractical if you are a student in Maine. Next we must consider whether we will have any additional resources, such as research funds or other researchers to collaborate with. Remember that there are severe limits on what one person can accomplish. On the other hand, we may be able to piggyback our research onto a larger research project. We also must take into account the constraints we face due to our schedules and other commitments, as well as our skill level.

Educational Importance

Educational research is not a simple undertaking, so it is hard to justify the expenditure of effort and resources unless we focus on a substantive area that is important. Besides, you need to feel motivated to carry out the study. Nonetheless, "importance" is relative, so for a class assignment, university students' memories of learning to read and write might be important enough.

For most research undertakings, we should consider whether the research question is important to other people. Will an answer to the research question make a difference for society or for educational relations?

Educational researchers are not wanting for important research questions. A typical recent issue of the journal *American Educational Research* (2009) included studies of the role of courts in educational policy; of college students majoring in disciplines related to science, technology, and math; of the study habits of academic versus vocational track high school students; and of the use of grade-level teaching teams in elementary schools. All of these articles addressed research questions about important educational issues, and all raised new questions for additional research.

Scientific Relevance

Every research question should be grounded in the educational research literature. Whether we formulate a research question because we have been stimulated by an academic article or because we want to investigate a current educational problem, we should first turn to the educational research literature to find out what already has been learned about this question. You can be sure that some prior research is relevant to almost any research question you can think of.

Different studies of reading aloud to children and other home literacy practices have led to contradictory conclusions about the impact of home life on learning to read. This particularly has been the case in studying students from nonmainstream families or families where English is not the home language. Exploring the educational research literature on a given topic will not usually tell you that someone has already found "the answer." It will inform you, though, about who has begun to ask good questions, how they have attempted to answer those questions, and what areas have and haven't been explored. So you always need to connect new research questions to prior research investigations.

⊞ Educational Research Basics

How do we find prior research on questions of interest? You may already know some of the relevant material from prior coursework or your independent reading, but that won't be enough. When you are about to launch an investigation of a new research question, you must apply a very different standard than when you are studying for a test or just seeking to "learn about how kids learn to read." You need to find reports of previous investigations that sought to answer the same research question that you wish to answer, not just those that were about a similar topic. If there have been no prior studies of the same research question on which you wish to focus, you should seek to find reports from investigations of closely related research questions. Once you have located reports from prior research similar to the research you wish to conduct, you may expand your search to include investigations about related studies that used similar methods.

Sometimes you'll find that someone else has already reviewed the literature on your research question in a special review article or book chapter. For example, Melanie R. Kuhn and Steven A. Stahl (2003) published an excellent review of the research on fluency in reading instruction in the *Journal of Educational Psychology*. They began with two basic questions: "How do children become fluent readers?" and "What instructional strategies are effective in promoting literacy among beginning readers?" (p. 3). Their article summarizes a range of literature in these areas, covering both theoretical and practical approaches.

You will not always be lucky enough to find a recent, comprehensive literature review article in the area of your question, but most of the research articles you find will include a literature review. These reviews can help a lot, but they are no substitute for reviewing the literature yourself. No one but you can decide what is relevant for your research question and the research circumstances you will be facing—the setting you will study, the timing of your study, the new issues that you want to include in your study, and your specific methods. And you can't depend on any published research review for information on the most recent work. New research results about many questions appear continually in scholarly journals and books, in research reports from government agencies and other organizations, and on websites all over the world; you'll need to check for new research such as this yourself.

Finding Information

Conducting a thorough search of the research literature and then reviewing critically what you have found is an essential foundation for any research project. Fortunately, much of this information can be identified online, and an increasing number of published journal articles can be downloaded directly to your own computer (depending on your particular access privileges). But just because there's a lot available online doesn't mean that you need to find it all. Keep in mind that your goal is to find reports of prior research investigations; this means that you should focus on scholarly journals that choose articles for publication after they have been reviewed by other educational researchers—"refereed journals." Newspaper and magazine articles and Wikipedia entries just won't do, although you may find some that raise important issues or even that summarize educational science research investigations.

Every year, the Web offers more and more useful material, including indexes of the published research literature. You may find copies of particular rating scales, reports from research in progress, papers that have been presented at professional conferences, and online discussions of related topics. We will review in this section the basic procedures for finding relevant research information in both the published literature and on the Web, but keep in mind that the primary goal is to identify research articles published in refereed journals. Appendix C provides more detailed instructions.

Searching the Literature

The educational research literature should be consulted at the beginning and end of an investigation. Even while an investigation is in progress, consultations with the literature may help to resolve methodological problems or facilitate supplementary explorations. As with any part of the research process, the method you use will affect the quality of your results. You should try to ensure that your search method includes each of the following steps:

Specify your research question. Your research question should be neither so broad that hundreds of articles are judged relevant nor so narrow that you miss important literature. "Does building vocabulary improve reading comprehension?" is probably too broad. "Does weekly vocabulary testing strengthen word attack skills for second-grade boys?" is probably too narrow. "Does the vocabulary level of early childhood students affect their growth as readers?" provides about the right level of specificity.

Identify appropriate bibliographic databases to search. The Educational Resources Information Center (ERIC) may meet many of your needs. Sponsored by the U.S. Department of Education, ERIC is a comprehensive, searchable, digital library of education-related resources, including both abstracts and full-text articles, going back to 1966. However, if you are studying a question about education and disability, you should also search in Medline, the database for searching the medical literature. If your focus is on counseling or mental health, you'll also want to include a search in the online psychological abstracts database, PsycINFO, or the version that also contains the full text of articles since 1985, PsycARTICLES. There are a wide variety of other specialized databases you may wish to investigate, such as Ebsco Business Source Complete, which covers research pertaining to adult learners in the workplace.

In addition, the search engine Google now offers "Google Scholar" (which indexes journal articles) and "Google Print" (which indexes books) for anyone with Web access.

Choose a search technology. For most purposes, an online bibliographic database that references the published journal literature will be all you need. In addition to the databases already mentioned, your college library can probably give you access to scholarly databases covering education such as Academic Search Premier, Educator's Reference Complete, Expanded Academic ASAP, and JSTOR. However, searches for obscure topics or very recent literature may require that you also search websites or bibliographies of relevant books.

Create a tentative list of search terms. List the parts and subparts of your research question and any related issues that you think are important: "reading comprehension," "vocabulary instruction," "emergent literacy," and perhaps "early childhood reading." List the authors of relevant studies. Specify the most important journals that deal with your topic.

Narrow your search. The sheer number of references you find can be a problem. Depending on the database you are working with and the purposes of your search, you may want to limit your search to English-language publications, journal articles rather than conference papers or dissertations (both of which are more difficult to acquire), and materials published more recently, say, in the past 5 years.

Refine your search. Learn as you go. If your search yields too many citations, try specifying the search terms more precisely. If you have not found much literature, try using more general terms. Whatever terms you search first, don't consider your search complete until you have tried several different approaches and have seen how many articles you find. A search for *reading research* in ERIC on June 2, 2010, yielded 59,424 hits, but searching *quantitative reading research* and then *qualitative reading research* reduced the number of hits to 1,892 and 1,351, respectively.

Use Boolean search logic. It's often a good idea to narrow your search by requiring that abstracts contain combinations of words or phrases that include more of the specific details of your research question. Using the Boolean connector AND allows you to do this, while using the connector OR allows you to find abstracts containing different words that mean the same thing. (This is explained further in Appendix C.) Exhibit 2.1 provides an example of a Boolean search using AND plus keywords *reading* and *qualitative* in the Advanced Search option in ERIC.

Use appropriate subject descriptors. Once you have found an article that you consider appropriate, take a look at the "descriptors" field in the citation (see Exhibit 2.2). You can then redo your search after requiring that the articles be classified with some or all of these descriptor terms.

Check the results. Read the titles and abstracts you have found and identify the articles that appear to be most relevant. If possible, click on these article titles and generate a list of their references. See if you find more articles that are relevant to your research question but that you have missed so far. You will be surprised (we always are) at how many important articles your initial online search missed.

Read the articles. Now it is time to find the full text of the articles of interest. If you're lucky, some of the journals you need will be available to patrons of your library in online versions, and you'll be able to link to the full text just by clicking on a "full text" link. But many journals, specific issues of some journals, or both will be available only in print; in this case, you'll have to find them in your library or order a copy through interlibrary loan.

Refer to a good book for even more specific guidance. Arlene Fink's (2005) *Conducting Research Literature Reviews: From the Internet to Paper* is an excellent guide.

Exhibit 2.1   Boolean Connectors in ERIC

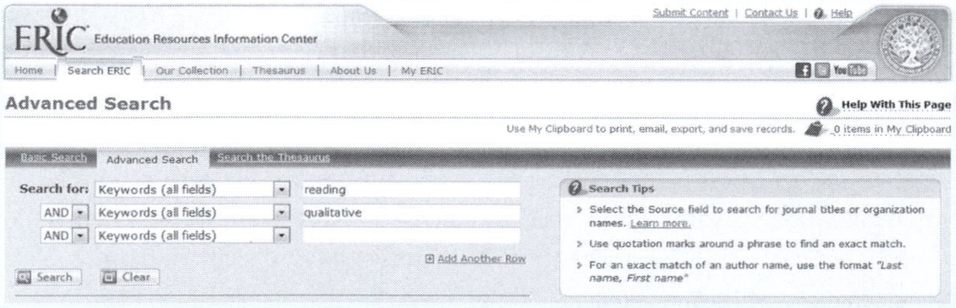

| Exhibit 2.2 | **ERIC Search Result With Descriptors** |

1. Poor Readers-Good Learners: A Study of Dyslexic Readers Learning with and without Text ⬛ Share 📁 Add
(EJ875384)

Author(s): Braten, Ivar; Amundsen, Anita; Samuelstuen, Marit S.

Source: Reading & Writing Quarterly, v26 n2 p166-187 2010

Pub Date: 2010-00-00
Pub Type(s): Journal Articles; Reports - Research
Peer-Reviewed: Yes

Descriptors:
Reading Difficulties; Comprehension; Qualitative Research; Independent Study; Economically Disadvantaged; Interviews; Decoding (Reading); Inferences; Junior High School Students; Foreign Countries; Language Processing; Task Analysis; Learning Strategies

Abstract:
Our purpose was to examine how high-achieving dyslexic readers compensated for their poor decoding skills both during independent learning from text and in the broader learning context of home and school. The participants were 8 Norwegian junior high school students who had performed well in school despite diagnosed difficulties with single word decoding and phonological processing. Through a com ⭕Show Full Abstract

Related Items: Show Related Items

Full-Text Availability Options:

You may be tempted to write up a "review" of the literature based on reading the abstracts or using only those articles available online, but you will be selling yourself short. Many crucial details about methods, findings, and theoretical implications will be found only in the body of the article, and many important articles will not be available online. To understand, critique, and really learn from previous research studies, you must read the important articles, no matter how you have to retrieve them.

If you have done your job well, you will now have more than enough literature as background for your own research, unless it is on a very obscure topic (see Exhibit 2.3). At this point, your main concern is to construct a coherent framework in which to develop your research question, drawing as many lessons as you can from previous research. You may use the literature to identify a useful theory and hypotheses to be reexamined, to find inadequately studied specific research questions, to explicate the disputes about your research question, to summarize the major findings of prior research, and to suggest appropriate methods of investigation.

| Exhibit 2.3 | **A Search in ERIC on "Early Childhood Reading" on May 26, 2011, Showing the First of 13 Items** |

1. Phonological and Non-Phonological Language Skills as Predictors of Early Reading Performance (ED514629) ⬛ Share 📁 Add

Author(s): Batson-Magnuson, LuAnn

Source: ProQuest LLC, Ph.D. Dissertation, University of Medicine and Dentistry of New Jersey

Pub Date: 2010-00-00
Pub Type(s): Dissertations/Theses - Doctoral Dissertations
Peer-Reviewed: N/A

Descriptors:
Reading Comprehension; Intervention; Early Reading; Program Effectiveness; Grade 1; Screening Tests; Language Skills; Phonology; At Risk Students; Disability Identification; Validity; Reading Skills; Student Placement; Reading Programs; Elementary School Students; Suburban Schools; Statistical Analysis; Correlation; Vocabulary Development; Age Differences; Gender Differences; Preschool Education; Nonverbal Communication; Cognitive Ability; Memory

Abstract:
Accurate prediction of early childhood reading performance could help identify at-risk students, aid in the development of evidence-based intervention strategies, and further our theoretical understanding of reading development. This study assessed the validi ⭕Show Full Abstract

Related Items: Show Related Items

Full-Text Availability Options:

Help Finding Full Text | Find in a Library | Publisher's Web Site

Be sure to take notes on each article you read, organizing your notes into standard sections: theory, methods, findings, and conclusions. In any case, write the literature review so that it contributes to your study in some concrete way; do not feel compelled to discuss an article just because you have read it. Be judicious. You are conducting only one study of one issue; it will only obscure the value of your study if you try to relate it to every tangential point in related research.

Do not think of searching the literature as a one-time-only venture—something that you leave behind as you move on to your *real* research. You may encounter new questions or unanticipated problems as you conduct your research or as you burrow deeper into the literature. Searching the literature again to determine what others have found in response to these questions or what steps they have taken to resolve these problems can yield substantial improvements in your own research. There is so much literature on so many topics that it often is not possible to figure out in advance every subject you should search the literature for or what type of search will be most beneficial.

Another reason to make searching the literature an ongoing project is that the literature is always growing. During the course of one research study, whether it takes only one semester or several years, new findings will be published and relevant questions will be debated. Staying attuned to the literature and checking it at least when you are writing up your findings may save your study from being outdated.

Searching the Web

The World Wide Web provides access to vast amounts of information of many different sorts (Ó Dochartaigh, 2002). You can search the holdings of other libraries, download the complete text of government reports, and find descriptions of particular research projects. It is also hard to avoid finding a lot of information in which you have no interest, such as commercial advertisements, third-grade homework assignments, or college course syllabi.

After you are connected to the Web with a browser such as Microsoft Internet Explorer, Firefox, or Chrome, you can use three basic strategies for finding information: direct addressing—typing in the address, or URL, of a specific site; browsing—reviewing online lists of websites; and searching—the most common approach. Google is currently the most popular search engine for searching the Web. For some purposes, you will need to use only one strategy; for other purposes, you will want to use all three. Appendix C contains information on all three methods.

Exhibit 2.4 illustrates the first problem that you may encounter when searching the Web: the sheer quantity of resources that are available. It is a much bigger problem than when searching bibliographic databases. On the Web, less is usually more. Limit your inspection of websites to the first few pages that turn up in your list (they're ranked by relevance). See what those first pages contain and then try to narrow your search by including some additional terms. Putting quotation marks around a phrase that you want to search will also help to limit your search—searching for "early childhood reading" on Google (on May 25, 2011) produced 105,000 sites, compared to the more than 13 million retrieved when the quotes were omitted—so Google searched "early" *and* "childhood" *and* "reading." Notice also in Exhibit 2.4 that the first two results, as well as all of the entries down the right-hand side of the page, are labeled "ads," meaning that Google was paid to list them. Almost all of the time, ads should be ignored because they are paid promotions for commercial products or services rather than scholarly contributions. Many other Google entries, such as most of those shown in Exhibit 2.4 (a YouTube video, commercial reading booklets), are also of little or no value for your purposes. When using Google, you must always separate legitimate scholarly contributions from the "background noise" that your search will inevitably pull up. Using Google Scholar or Google Print rather than regular Google will address this problem but will also reduce the number of results considerably.

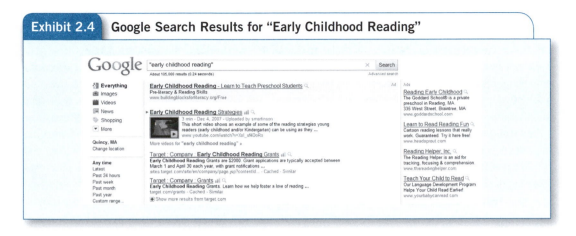

Exhibit 2.4 Google Search Results for "Early Childhood Reading"

Remember the following warnings when you conduct searches on the Web:

Clarify your goals. Before you begin the search, jot down the terms that you think you need to search for as well as a statement of what you want to accomplish with your search. This will help to ensure that you have a sense of what to look for and what to ignore.

Quality is not guaranteed. Anyone can post almost anything, so the accuracy and adequacy of the information you find are always suspect. There's no journal editor or librarian to evaluate quality and relevance.

Anticipate change. Websites that are not maintained by stable organizations can come and go very quickly. Any search will result in attempts to link to some URLs that no longer exist.

One size does not fit all. Different search engines use different procedures for indexing websites. Some attempt to be all-inclusive, whereas others aim to be selective. As a result, you can get different results from different search engines (such as Google or Yahoo) even though you are searching for the same terms.

Be concerned about generalizability. You might be tempted to characterize district reading policies by summarizing the documents you find at school district websites. But how many school districts are there? How many have posted their policies on the Web? Are these policies representative of all school districts? To answer all these questions, you would have to conduct a research project just on the websites themselves.

Evaluate the sites. There is a lot of information out there, so how do you know what's good? Some websites contain excellent advice and pointers on how to differentiate the good from the bad.

Avoid Web addiction. Another danger of the enormous amount of information available on the Web is that one search will lead to another and to another and so on. There are always more possibilities to explore and one more interesting source to check. Establish boundaries of time and effort to avoid the risk of losing all sense of proportion.

Cite your sources. Using text or images from Web sources without attribution is plagiarism. It is the same as copying someone else's work from a book or article and pretending that it is your own. Record the Web address (URL), the name of the information provider, and the date on which you obtain material from the site. Include this information in a footnote to the material that you use in a paper.

Reviewing Research

Effective review of the prior research you find is an essential step in building the foundation for new research. You must assess carefully the quality of each research study, consider the implications of each article for your own plans, and expand your thinking about your research question to take account of new perspectives and alternative arguments. It is through reviewing the literature and using it to extend and sharpen your own ideas and methods that you become a part of the educational science community. Instead of being just one individual studying an issue that interests you, you are making your own small contribution to an ever-growing body of knowledge that is being constructed by the entire community of scholars.

The research information you find on various websites comes in a wide range of formats and represents a variety of sources. *Caveat emptor* (buyer beware) is the watchword when you search the Web; following review guidelines such as those we have listed will minimize, but not eliminate, the risk of being led astray. By contrast, the published scholarly journal literature that you find in databases such as ERIC and Psychological Abstracts follows a much more standard format and has been subject to a careful review process. There is some variability in the contents of these databases—some journals publish book reviews, comments on prior articles, dissertation abstracts, book reviews, and conference papers. However, most literature you will find on a research topic in these databases represents peer-reviewed articles reporting analyses of data collected in a research project. These are the sources on which you should focus. This section concentrates on the procedures you should use for reviewing these articles. These procedures also can be applied to reviews of research monographs—books that provide much more information from a research project than that which can be contained in a journal article.

Reviewing the literature is really a two-stage process. In the first stage, you must assess each article separately. This assessment should follow a standard format such as that represented by the "Questions to Ask About a Research Article" in Appendix A. However, you should keep in mind that you can't adequately understand a research study if you just treat it as a series of discrete steps, involving a marriage of convenience among separate techniques. Any research project is an integrated whole, so you must be concerned with how each component of the research design influenced the others—for example, how the measurement approach might have affected the causal validity of the researcher's conclusions and how the sampling strategy might have altered the quality of measures.

The second stage of the review process is to assess the implications of the entire set of articles (and other materials) for the relevant aspects of your research question and procedures and then to write an integrated review that highlights these implications. Although you can find literature reviews that consist simply of assessments of one published article after another—that never get beyond stage one in the review process—your understanding of the literature and the quality of your own work will be much improved if you make the effort to write an integrated review.

In the next two sections, we will show how you might answer many of the questions in Appendix A as we review a research article about reading. We will then show how the review of a single article can be used within an integrated review of the body of prior research on this research question. Because at this early point in the text you will not be familiar with all the terminology used in the article review, you might want to read through the more elaborate article review in Appendix B later in the course.

A Single-Article Review: Home Literacy Activities and Signs of Children's Emerging Literacy

Christine Winquist Nord, Jean Lennon, Baiming Liu, Westat, and Kathryn Chandler (1999) of the National Center for Education Statistics (NCES) analyzed data from 1993 and 1999 concerning family literacy practices in the home and their effects on emerging literacy in young children. In this section, we will examine the article that resulted from that analysis, which was published by the Office of Educational Research and

Improvement of the U.S. Department of Education. This type of report is very common in education, where large-scale survey data sets gathered by state or federal agencies produce mountains of statistics that require analysis integrating the survey outcomes with important questions in the field and with previous research.

The research question. The data used were from the 1993 and 1999 administrations of the National Household Education Survey for 3-, 4-, and 5-year-olds not enrolled in kindergarten, in which "the parent most knowledgeable about the child, usually the child's mother" was asked a standard set of questions about literacy practices in the home and "school readiness skills" (Nord et al., 1999, p. 2). Literacy practices surveyed included reading to the child; telling a story; teaching letters, words, or numbers; teaching songs or music; doing arts and crafts; and visiting a library in the past month. School readiness skills surveyed included "recognizes all letters," "counts to 20 or higher," "writes name," and "reads or pretends to read storybook" (p. 7).

There is no explicit discussion of ethical guidelines in the article, although reference is made to a more complete unpublished report. Clearly, important ethical issues had to be considered, given the focus on what is going on in the private space of the home across a wide range of income, racial, and ethnic groups, but the adherence to standard survey procedures suggests attention to these issues.

The research design. Asking the same set of questions of statistically similar groups (e.g., mothers with 3-, 4-, and 5-year-olds) at periodic intervals (in this case, 6 years) is a standard way of measuring change over time. The survey design was careful to match the 1993 and 1999 groups of mothers in such important areas as race/ethnicity, home language, education level, employment status, family type (one, two, or no parents present in home), and poverty status. The analysis acknowledged some unavoidable limitations in the design, including the fact that "parents may overestimate both their involvement in home literacy activities and their children's skills because they recognize that such activities and skills are socially desirable" as a source of non-sampling error (Nord et al., 1999, p. 2).

The article's discussion embedded the survey findings in a theoretical framework drawn from other research studies on emerging literacy that have shown, for instance, that "children begin the process of learning to read long before they enter formal schooling" and "families, and parents in particular, play an important role in this process" (Nord et al., 1999, p. 1). The choice of literacy activities surveyed comes in part from research showing that "reading to children, telling them stories, and singing with them" helps them to learn (p. 1).

The research findings and conclusion. The article's report on findings was framed in the context of Goal One of the National Education Goals—"the importance of family-child engagement in literacy activities to children's learning and readiness for school" (Nord et al., 1999, p. 1). Overall, the analysts felt that survey data showed that "families have gotten the message about the importance of reading to their young children. Eighty-two percent of children ages 3 to 5 years in 1999 who were not yet enrolled in kindergarten were read to three or more times in the last week by a family member" (p. 1). Many families also engaged in other literacy activities. Of course, readers of this analysis who are skeptical about this high figure may wonder about parents' acknowledged tendency to overestimate their involvement. The report also outlines differences in families' engagement by the children's race and ethnicity but found "no statistically significant differences" in results for "black, non-Hispanic children and white, non-Hispanic children. . . . Hispanic children, though, are significantly less likely than either white, non-Hispanic or black, non-Hispanic children" to have done the specified literacy activities with their families (pp. 2, 5).

Overall, this NCES study represents an important contribution to understanding the changing dynamics of families and literacy. Although there are certainly limitations to what can be discovered through such a survey, the national scope of the data and the fact that it was repeated at a regular interval under controlled sampling conditions give it a high level of usefulness. It is not the last word, by any means, but forms an important contextual background to more close-up, detailed studies by other researchers of individual classrooms, students, and families. It is not hard to understand why such studies continue to stimulate further research and ongoing policy discussions.

An Integrated Literature Review: Home and School Factors in Reading

The goal of the second stage of the literature review process is to integrate the results of your separate article reviews and develop an overall assessment of the implications of prior research. The integrated literature review should accomplish three goals:

1. Summarize prior research.

2. Critique prior research.

3. Present pertinent conclusions. (Hart, 1998, pp. 186–187)

We'll discuss each of these goals in turn.

Summarize prior research. Your summary of prior research must focus on the particular research questions that you will address, but you also may need to provide some more general background. Jeanne R. Paratore (2002) begins her research review of home and school effects on early readers with a section labeled "Early Beliefs About Parents and Children's Literacy." In this section, she first describes the evolution of, then questions, the belief that what parents do or don't do has a large role in whether their children succeed in school. She then reviews different theories and supporting research studies on parent and school roles that have influenced classroom instruction, school district policies, and construction of basal reader textbook series.

Ask yourself three questions about your summary of the literature:

1. *Have you been selective?* If there have been more than a few prior investigations of your research question, you will need to narrow your focus to the most relevant and highest quality studies. Don't cite a large number of prior articles "just because they are there."

2. *Is the research up-to-date?* Be sure to include the most recent research, not just the "classic" studies.

3. *Have you used direct quotes sparingly?* To focus your literature review, you need to express the key points from prior research in your own words. Use direct quotes only when they are essential for making an important point (Pyrczak, 2005, pp. 51–59).

Critique prior research. Evaluate the strengths and weaknesses of the prior research. In addition to all the points you develop as you answer the "article review questions" in Appendix A, you should also select articles for review that reflect work published in peer-reviewed journals and were written by credible authors who have been funded by reputable sources. Consider the following questions as you decide how much weight to give each article:

1. *How was the report reviewed prior to its publication or release?* Articles published in academic journals go through a rigorous review process, usually involving careful criticism and revision. Top "refereed" journals may accept only 10% of submitted articles, so they can be very selective. Dissertations go through a lengthy process of criticism and revision by a few members of the dissertation writer's home institution. A report released directly by a research organization is likely to have had only a limited review, although some research organizations maintain a rigorous internal review process. Papers presented at professional meetings may

have had little prior review. Needless to say, more confidence can be placed in research results that have been subject to a more rigorous review.

2. *What is the author's reputation?* Reports by an author or team of authors who have published other work on the research question should be given somewhat greater credibility at the outset.

3. *Who funded and sponsored the research?* Major federal funding agencies and private foundations fund only research proposals that have been evaluated carefully and ranked highly by a panel of experts. They also often monitor closely the progress of the research. This does not guarantee that every such project report is good, but it goes a long way toward ensuring some worthwhile products. On the other hand, research that is funded by organizations that have a preference for a particular outcome should be given particularly close scrutiny (Locke, Silverman, & Spirduso, 1998, pp. 37–44).

Present pertinent conclusions. Don't leave the reader guessing about the implications of the prior research for your own investigation. Present the conclusions you draw from the research you have reviewed. As you do so, follow several simple guidelines (Pyrczak, 2005, pp. 53–56). Distinguish clearly your own opinion of prior research from conclusions of the authors of the articles you have reviewed (Fink, 2005, pp. 190–192).

- Make it clear when your own approach is based on the theoretical framework you are using rather than on the results of prior research.

- Acknowledge the potential limitations of any empirical research project. Don't emphasize problems in prior research that you cannot avoid either.

- Explain how the unanswered questions raised by prior research or the limitations of methods used in prior research make it important for you to conduct your own investigation.

A good example of how to conclude an integrated literature review is provided by Paratore (2002), who begins her closing section by posing and then addressing the provocative question, "So, what have we learned about parents and their role in children's literacy learning that we did not know or understand 10 or 20 years ago?" (p. 56). This approach gives her a chance to look back at the studies she has reviewed, then forward to new studies, concluding with, "When all is said and done, the teacher makes the difference" (p. 65).

🔲 The Role of Educational Theory

With a research question formulated and a review of the pertinent literature taking shape, we are ready to consider the process of conducting our research.

When we conduct educational research, we are attempting to connect theory with empirical data—the evidence we obtain from the educational world. Researchers may make this connection by starting with an educational theory and then testing some of its implications with data. This is the process of deductive research; it is most often the strategy used in quantitative methods. Alternatively, researchers may develop a connection between educational theory and data by first collecting the data and then developing a theory that explains patterns in the data (see Exhibit 2.5). This inductive research process is more often the strategy used in qualitative methods. As you'll see, a research project can draw on both deductive and inductive strategies.

We have already pointed out that educational theory can be a source of research questions and that it plays an important role in literature reviews. What deserves more attention at this point is the larger role of

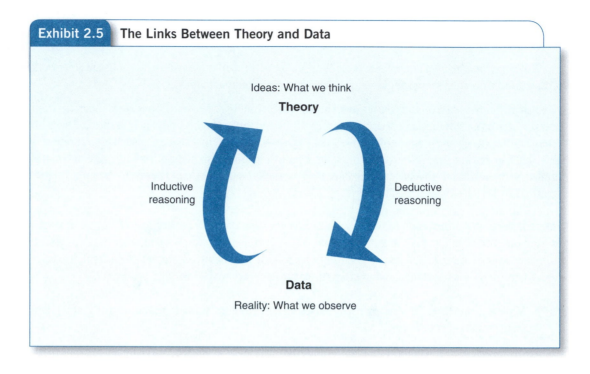

Exhibit 2.5 The Links Between Theory and Data

educational theory in research. Theories are logically interrelated sets of propositions that help us make sense of many interrelated phenomena and predict behavior or attitudes that are likely to occur when certain conditions are met; they help educational scientists to know what to look for in a study and to specify the implications of their findings for other research. Building and evaluating theory is therefore one of the most important objectives of educational research.

Most educational research is guided by some theory, although the theory may be only partially developed in a particular study or may even be unrecognized by the researcher. Educational theories do not provide the answers to the questions we pose as topics for research. Instead, educational theories suggest the areas on which we should focus and the propositions that we should consider for a test. Educational theory makes us much more sensitive to the possible directions for research and so helps us to design better research and draw out the implications of our results. Before, during, and after a research investigation, we need to keep thinking theoretically.

In Chapter 1, we discussed and showed examples of three types of research: explanatory, exploratory, and descriptive. Exhibit 1.4 in that chapter showed relationships between these types of research and their goals and methods. We will now look at a different relationship, the one between the three types of research and theoretical approaches—specifically, deductive and inductive methods of looking at a research question.

Explanatory Research

The process of conducting research designed to test explanations for educational phenomena involves moving from theory to data and then back to theory. This process can be characterized with a **research circle** (Exhibit 2.6).

Deductive Research

As Exhibit 2.6 shows, in **deductive research,** a specific expectation is deduced from a general theoretical premise and then tested with data that have been collected for this purpose. We call the specific expectation

Exhibit 2.6   The Research Circle

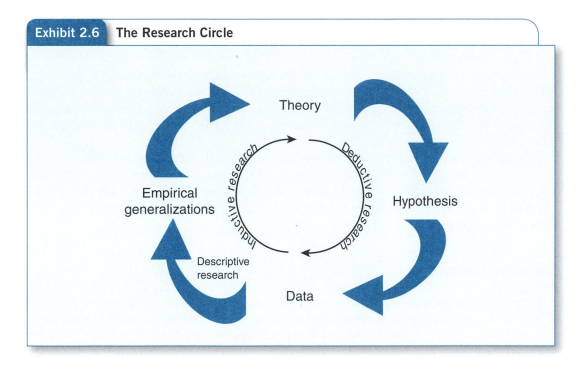

deduced from the more general theory a **hypothesis.** It is the hypothesis that researchers actually test, not the complete theory itself. A hypothesis proposes a relationship between two or more **variables**—characteristics or properties that can vary. Variation in one variable is proposed to predict, influence, or cause variation in the other variable. The proposed influence is the **independent variable;** its effect or consequence is the **dependent variable.** After the researchers formulate one or more hypotheses and develop research procedures, they collect data with which to test the hypothesis.

Hypotheses can be worded in several different ways, and identifying the independent and dependent variables is sometimes difficult. When in doubt, try to rephrase the hypothesis as an "if-then" statement: "*If* the independent variable increases (or decreases), *then* the dependent variable increases (or decreases)."

Both explanatory and evaluative studies are types of deductive research. Rachel Brown, Michael Pressley, Peggy Van Meter, and Ted Schuder (1996) were aware of the "seminal discovery" in earlier, descriptive research that "American students received little instruction about how to comprehend text" (p. 19). They designed a study to test the hypothesis that formal instruction in comprehension would improve the reading of "low-achieving" second graders more than traditional approaches that lacked comprehension instruction.

They recruited five teachers willing to use a specially designed "transactional strategies" instructional package, called SAIL, and five "comparison" teachers who would use their regular instructional methods (p. 19). The study lasted the entire instructional year. The researchers collected four types of data: a "strategies interview" with students, a set of "retelling questions" to assess change in retelling and sequencing skills, a "think-aloud task," and standardized measures of comprehension and word skills (p. 20). Overall, the researchers found that the impact of SAIL was positive in both the short and long term. In the short term, SAIL students were

Hypothesis: A tentative statement about empirical reality, involving a relationship between two or more variables.

Example of a hypothesis: Students who receive instruction in specific reading comprehension strategies will improve their reading more than students who do not receive such instruction.

Variable: A characteristic or property that can vary (take on different values or attributes).

Example of a variable: grade level of students.

Independent variable: A variable that is hypothesized to cause, or lead to, variation in another variable.

Example of an independent variable: type of reading comprehension strategy.

Dependent variable: A variable that is hypothesized to vary depending on, or under the influence of, another variable.

Example of a dependent variable: amount of reading improvement.

better than control group students in acquiring information from what they read and having a deeper understanding. In the long term, SAIL students knew more reading strategies and had higher scores on standardized tests at the end of the year.

In both explanatory and evaluative research, the statement of expectations for the findings and the design of the research to test these expectations strengthen the confidence we can place in the test. The deductive researcher shows her hand or states her expectations in advance and then designs a fair test of those expectations. Then, "the chips fall where they may"—in other words, the researcher accepts the resulting data as a more or less objective picture of reality.

The relationship between hypothesis, independent variable, and dependent variables in the Brown et al. (1996) study is shown in Exhibit 2.7. The patterns Brown and her colleagues found in their data, or their **empirical generalizations,** were consistent with the hypothesis that the researchers deduced from their theoretical assumptions and from previous research showing a lack of comprehension instruction (Exhibit 2.7). The theory thus received support from the experiment.

Inductive Research

In contrast to deductive research, **inductive research** begins with specific data, which are then used to develop (induce) a general explanation (a **theory**) to account for the data. One way to think of this process is in terms of the research circle: Rather than starting at the top of the circle with a theory, the inductive researcher starts at the bottom of the circle with data and then develops the theory. Another way to think of this process is represented in Exhibit 2.8, using social context theory—the theory that a child's language development is heavily influenced by the social context in which the child grows up. Specific predictions about language

---

Exhibit 2.7   Hypothesis and Variables in the Brown et al. (1996) Study

	Hypothesis	Independent Variable	Dependent Variables
Comparison group	Instruction in comprehension strategies improves reading.	New comprehension strategies instructional package	At end of year, more understanding, better reading scores than control group
Control group	Instruction in comprehension strategies improves reading.	No independent variable (no new instructional package)	At end of year, less growth in understanding and reading scores than comparison group

---

Exhibit 2.8   Deductive and Inductive Reasoning

Deductive

Premise 1: All children's language development is influenced by their social context.
Premise 2: Sophia is a child.
Conclusion: Sophia's language development will be influenced by her social context.

Inductive

Evidence 1: Sophia grew up in a Spanish-speaking home and speaks Spanish.
Evidence 2: Jorge grew up in a Spanish-speaking home and speaks Spanish.
Evidence 3: Jennifer grew up in an English-speaking home and speaks English.
Conclusion: Children will grow up speaking the language that is spoken at home.

development are *deduced* from general theories about development. In deductive research, reasoning from specific premises results in a conclusion that a theory is supported, while in inductive research, the identification of similar empirical patterns results in a generalization about some educational process.

An inductive approach to changes in reading instruction. In 2000, James F. Baumann, James V. Hoffman, Ann M. Duffy-Hester, and Jennifer Moon Ro published a modern-day **replication** of a classic reading study from the 1960s (Austin & Morrison, 1963). Data from the 2000 study showed many similarities in reading instruction to the 1960s, including significant amounts of time devoted to reading at the elementary level, explicit instruction in phonics, the administration of standardized tests, and difficulties in meeting the challenges posed by underachieving readers. The new survey also showed significant differences: a balanced and eclectic approach among teachers rather than strict skills instruction, more whole-class instruction, and much greater use of trade books than in the 1960s. Many teachers had adopted an emergent literacy perspective, there were more and better classroom libraries in use, and schools were much more likely to make changes in their reading programs than they were in the 1960s.

Many of the major changes described have roots in theoretical approaches such as social context theory, emergent literacy, whole language, and balanced phonics instruction. The Baumann team's research thus offers some evidence of the extent to which such reading theories are actually being adopted in schools.

Exploratory Research

Qualitative research is often exploratory and, hence, inductive from beginning to end. The researchers begin by observing educational interaction or interviewing educational actors in depth and then developing an explanation for what has been found. The researchers often ask questions such as, "What is going on here?" "How do people interpret these experiences?" or "Why do people do what they do?" Rather than testing a hypothesis, the researchers are trying to make sense of some educational phenomenon. They may even put off formulating a research question until after they begin to collect data—the idea is to let the question emerge from the situation itself (Brewer & Hunter, 1989, pp. 54–58).

Of course, the research questions that serve as starting points for qualitative data analyses do not simply emerge from the setting studied but are shaped by the investigator. As Harry Wolcott (1995) explains,

> [The research question] is not embedded within the lives of those whom we study, demurely waiting to be discovered. Quite the opposite: *We instigate the problems we investigate.* There is no point in simply sitting by, passively waiting to see what a setting is going to "tell" us or hoping a problem will "emerge." (p. 156)

Our focus on the importance of the research question as a tool for guiding qualitative data analyses should not obscure the creative nature of the analytic process. The research question can change, narrow, expand, or multiply throughout the processes of data collection and analysis.

Explanations derived from qualitative research will be richer and more finely textured than they often are in quantitative research, but they are likely to be based on fewer cases from a limited area. We cannot assume that the people studied in this setting are like others or that other researchers will develop explanations similar to ours to make sense of what was observed or heard. Because we do not initially set up a test of a hypothesis according to some specific rules, another researcher cannot come along and conduct the same test.

Descriptive Research

You learned in Chapter 1 that some educational research is purely descriptive. The study on emergent literacy discussed earlier in this chapter is an example. Such research does not involve connecting theory and data, but it is still a part of the research circle—it begins with data and proceeds only to the stage of making empirical generalizations based on those data (see Exhibit 2.6).

Valid description is important in its own right—in fact, it is a necessary component of all investigations. Much important research for the government and public and private organizations is primarily descriptive: What percentage of parents surveyed read to their children at least three times per week? Were there more or fewer home literacy practices in 1999 than there were in 1993? Do single-parent homes report as many literacy practices as two-parent homes? Simply put, good description of data is the cornerstone of the scientific research process and an essential component for understanding the educational world.

Good descriptive research can also stimulate more ambitious deductive and inductive research. Descriptive research showing performance differences on achievement tests based on race has fueled a great many "achievement gap" studies in recent years. This research has helped to establish priorities for both public policy and additional research.

▣ Educational Research Goals

Educational researchers strive to fulfill three goals: **validity, authenticity,** and **practical significance.**

Validity

We have reached the goal of validity when our conclusions about empirical reality are correct. In the chapters that follow, we will be concerned with three aspects of validity: measurement validity, generalizability, and causal validity (also known as internal validity). We will learn that invalid measures, invalid generalizations, or invalid causal inferences result in invalid conclusions.

Measurement validity: Exists when a measure measures what we think it measures.

Generalizability: Exists when a conclusion holds true for the population, group, setting, or event that we say it does, given the conditions that we specify.

Causal validity (internal validity): Exists when a conclusion that A results in B is correct.

Measurement Validity

Measurement validity is our first concern in establishing the validity of research results, because without having measured what we think we measured, we really don't know what we're talking about. Measurement validity is discussed further in Chapter 4.

Problems with measurement validity can result for many reasons. In studies of TV viewing and learning such as those discussed in Chapter 1, relying on parents' reports of TV viewing by their children results in underestimates. Instead, researchers have used timing devices connected to the family TV(s). It is also difficult to obtain valid measures of the amount of time parents or other caregivers spend interacting with children. Some researchers question people repeatedly over a period of time to avoid inaccuracies that can occur when respondents are asked to recall what they did at some time in the past.

We must be very careful in designing our measures and in subsequently evaluating how well they have performed. We cannot just *assume* that measures are valid.

Generalizability

The **generalizability** of a study is the extent to which it can be used to inform us about persons, places, or events that were not studied. We rarely have the resources to study the entire population that is of interest to us, so we have to select a sample of cases so that our findings can be generalized to the population of interest. When many studies using different cases or in different settings produce similar results, conclusions can have a high level of generalizability. Generalizability is a key concern in research design and is the focus of Chapter 5.

Causal Validity

Causal validity, also known as internal validity, refers to the truthfulness of an assertion that A causes B. Educational researchers frequently must be concerned with causal validity. As we have seen, much educational research focuses on causal questions such as, "What influence does television watching have on aggressive behavior?" and "What impact does direct teaching of reading comprehension strategies have on children's reading development?"

You'll learn more about these different aspects of validity in Chapters 4 and 5. The main take-away message about validity for now is that the goal of educational research is not to come up with conclusions that people will like or conclusions that suit our own personal preferences but to figure out how and why some aspect of the educational world operates as it does.

Authenticity

You already know that the educational world is complex. You may have wondered whether investigations can really be objective, because no matter how you look at educators and educational practices, you are doing so through your *own* eyes and developing interpretations that invariably will draw on your *own* life and prior experiences. Many educational researchers share your skepticism about the possibility of achieving a valid understanding of the educational world—of finding out how the educational world *really* operates. These researchers do not accept validity, as it is commonly defined, as the goal for research.

For researchers who feel that attempts to understand the educational world are inevitably subjective and cannot give us much confidence that we have learned the reality of that world, authenticity is an alternative research goal. An *authentic* understanding of an educational process or educational setting is one that reflects fairly the various perspectives of participants in that setting (Gubrium & Holstein, 1997). In fact, authenticity is a worthy goal for all educational research endeavors.

Authenticity is often the goal for qualitative research investigations, and it reflects the belief that those who study the educational world can hope to understand only how others view that educational world. From this perspective, every observer sees the educational world from his or her own vantage point; there is no basis for determining that one perspective is the "valid" one. "The conception of knowledge as a mirror of reality is replaced by knowledge as a linguistic and social construction of reality" (Kvale, 2002, p. 306).

> **Authenticity:** When the understanding of an educational process or educational setting is one that reflects fairly the various perspectives of participants in that setting.

Practical Significance

Researchers have an obligation to ask questions and produce conclusions that are in some way useful to others, particularly to moving forward the collective enterprise of teaching and learning. The goal of practical significance must be addressed in both the design and conclusions of good educational research.

In recent years, two developments have raised awareness of practical significance as a goal for researchers. First, the federal No Child Left Behind legislation has placed pressure on the states to raise student test

> **Practical significance:** When research answers the "So what?" question and affects the everyday practice of teachers, administrators, and policy makers.

scores and to find and use only "research-proven" methods to make schools better. Second, participatory research methods that are school based and classroom based have become increasingly popular. Using these methods, teachers are investigating their own practice and using the results to modify instruction and curriculum in their own classrooms and schools.

▣ Educational Research Proposals, Part I

Be grateful for those people or groups who require you to write a formal research proposal (as hard as that seems), and be even more grateful for those who give you constructive feedback. Whether your proposal is written for a professor, a thesis committee, an organization seeking practical advice, or a government agency that funds basic research, the proposal will force you to set out a problem statement and a research plan. So even in circumstances when a proposal is not required, you should prepare one and present it to others for feedback. Just writing your ideas down will help you to see how they can be improved, and almost any feedback will help you to refine your plans.

Each chapter in this book includes "Developing a Research Proposal" exercises that will guide you through the process of proposal writing. This section presents an overview of the process of proposal writing that also serves as an introduction to these special end-of-chapter exercises. The last chapter in the text (Chapter 15) contains a wrap-up discussion of the entire proposal preparation process.

Every research proposal should have at least five sections. The following list is adapted from Locke, Spirduso, and Silverman (2000, pp. 8–34):

1. *An introductory statement of the research problem,* in which you clarify what it is that you are interested in studying

2. *A literature review,* in which you explain how your problem and plans build on what has already been reported in the literature on this topic

3. *A methodological plan,* detailing just how you will respond to the particular mix of opportunities and constraints you face

4. *An ethics statement,* identifying human subjects issues in the research and how you will respond to them in an ethical fashion

5. *A statement of limitations,* reviewing weaknesses of the proposed research and presenting plans for minimizing their consequences

You will also need to include a budget and project timeline, unless you are working within the framework of a class project.

If your research proposal will be reviewed competitively, it must present a compelling rationale for funding. It is not possible to overstate the importance of the research problem that you propose to study (see the first section of this chapter). If you propose to test a hypothesis, be sure that it is one for which there are plausible alternatives. You want to avoid focusing on a "boring hypothesis"—one that has no credible alternatives, even though it is likely to be correct (Dawes, 1995, p. 93).

A research proposal also can be strengthened considerably by presenting results from a pilot study of the research question. This might have involved administering the proposed questionnaire to a small sample, conducting a preliminary version of the proposed experiment with a group of students, or making observations over a limited period of time in a setting such as that proposed for a qualitative study. Careful presentation of the methods used in the pilot study and the problems that were encountered will impress anyone who reviews the proposal.

Don't neglect procedures for the protection of human subjects. You will learn much more about this in our next chapter, "Ethics in Research." But even before you begin to develop your proposal, you should find out what procedure your university's institutional review board (IRB) requires for the review of student research proposals. Follow those procedures carefully, even if they require that you submit your proposal for an IRB review. No matter what your university's specific requirements are, if your research involves human subjects, you will need to include in your proposal a detailed statement that describes how you will adhere to these requirements.

You have learned in this chapter how to formulate a research question, review relevant literature, consider ethical issues, and identify some possible research limitations, so you are now ready to begin proposing new research. If you plan to do so, you can use the proposal exercises at the end of each subsequent chapter to incorporate more systematically the research elements discussed in those chapters. By the book's end, in Chapter 15, you will have attained a much firmer grasp of the various research components. At that point, we will return to the process of proposal writing.

Conclusions

We began this chapter with the question, "How does a child learn to read?" In the course of the chapter, you saw widely different approaches researchers have taken to studying this question. These included a review of research on fluency in reading (Kuhn & Stahl, 2003), ERIC and Google searches on topics in early childhood reading, a review of research on home and school effects on early readers (Paratore, 2002), a deductive research study on the effects of instruction in reading comprehension (Brown et al., 1996), and a replication, 40 years later, of a classic study of the types of reading instruction used in American elementary schools (Baumann et al., 2000).

Selecting a worthy research question does not guarantee a worthwhile research project. The simplicity of the research circle presented in this chapter belies the complexity of the educational research process. Of course, our answers to research questions will never be complete or entirely certain. Thus, when we complete a research project, we should point out how the research could be extended and evaluate the confidence we have in our conclusions. The elaboration of knowledge about complex research topics requires recognizing research difficulties, carefully weighing evidence, and identifying unanswered questions.

Ethical issues, one of the main topics of Chapter 3, also must be considered when evaluating research proposals and completed research studies. Ethical issues in educational research are no less complex than the other issues that researchers confront. It is inexcusable to jump into research on people without any attention to ethical considerations.

We hope that you will return often to this chapter as you read the subsequent chapters, when you criticize the research literature, and when you design your own research projects. To be conscientious, thoughtful, and responsible—this is the mandate of every educational researcher. If you formulate a feasible research problem, ask the right questions in advance, adhere to the research guidelines, and steer clear of the most common difficulties, you will be well along the road to fulfilling this mandate.

Key Terms

Authenticity   38
Deductive research   34
Dependent variable   35
Empirical generalization   36
Generalizability   38

Hypothesis   35
Independent variable   35
Inductive research   36
Institutional review board (IRB)   41
Practical significance   38

Replication   37
Research circle   34
Theory   36
Validity   38
Variable   35

Highlights

- Research questions should be feasible (within the time and resources available), educationally important, and scientifically relevant.

- Building educational theory is a major objective of educational research. Investigate relevant theories before starting educational research projects, and draw out the theoretical implications of research findings.

- The type of reasoning in most research can be described as primarily deductive or inductive. Research based on deductive reasoning proceeds from general ideas, deduces specific expectations from these ideas, and then tests the ideas with empirical data. Research based on inductive reasoning begins with specific data and then develops general ideas or theories to explain patterns in the data.

- The research process can be represented as circular, with a path from theory to hypotheses, to data, and then to empirical generalizations. Research investigations may begin at different points along the research circle and traverse different portions of it. Deductive research begins at the point of theory, inductive research begins with data but ends with theory, and descriptive research begins with data and ends with empirical generalizations.

- Valid knowledge is the central concern of scientific research. Authenticity can also be a concern for qualitative researchers. Practical significance is also an important goal for educational researchers.

- Replications of a study are essential to establishing its generalizability in other situations. An ongoing line of research stemming from a particular research question should include a series of studies that, collectively, traverse the research circle multiple times.

- Writing a research proposal is an important part of preparing for research.

Student Study Site

To assist in completing the web exercises, please access the study site at www.sagepub.com/check, where you will find the web exercise with accompanying links. You'll find other useful study materials such as self-quizzes and e-flashcards for each chapter, along with a group of carefully selected articles from research journals that illustrate the major concepts and techniques.

Discussion Questions

1. Find a research journal article that is cited in another source. Compare the cited source to what was said about it in the original article. Was the discussion of it accurate? How well did the authors of both articles summarize their work in their abstracts? What important points would you have missed if you had relied only on the abstracts?

2. Classify five research projects you have read about, either in previous exercises or in other courses, as primarily inductive or deductive. Did you notice any inductive components in the primarily deductive projects? How much descriptive research was involved? Did the findings have any implications that you think should be investigated in a new study? What new hypotheses are implied by the findings?

Practice Exercises

1. Search the journal literature for three studies concerning some educational program or policy. Several possibilities are research on the Head Start project, the effects of phonics versus whole language, No Child Left Behind, and poverty's effects on student achievement. Would you characterize the findings as largely consistent or inconsistent? How would you explain discrepant findings?

2. Using a research project you have read about, either in previous exercises or in another course, identify the stages of the research project corresponding to the points on the research circle. Did the research cover all four stages? Identify the theories and hypotheses underlying the study. What data were collected? What were the findings (empirical generalizations)?

Web Exercises

1. Using education topics that interest you, practice using ERIC and ERIC Advanced Search. Make sure you try using Boolean connectors, using descriptors to expand your search, and learning how to access the full text of articles.

2. Pick a topic and run the same search three times, once on Google, once on Google Scholar, and once on Google Scholar Advanced Search.

Developing a Research Proposal

Now it's time to start writing the proposal. These next exercises are very critical first steps.

1. State a problem for research. If you have not already identified a problem for study, or if you need to evaluate whether your research problem is doable, a few suggestions should help to get the ball rolling and keep it on course:

   a. Jot down questions that have puzzled you in some area having to do with people and educational relations, perhaps questions that have come to mind while reading textbooks or research articles or even while hearing news stories, or from your own experience with education. Don't hesitate to jot down many questions, and don't bore yourself—try to identify questions that really interest you.

   b. Now take stock of your interests, your opportunities, and the work of others. Which of your research questions no longer seem feasible or interesting? What additional research questions come to mind? Pick out a question that is of interest and seems feasible and that your other coursework suggests has been the focus of some prior research or theorizing.

   c. Write out your research question in one sentence, and elaborate on it in one paragraph. List at least three reasons why it is a good research question for you to investigate. Then present your proposal to your classmates and instructor for discussion and feedback.

2. Search the literature (and the Web) on the research question you identified. Refer to Appendix C for more guidance on conducting the search. Copy down at least 10 citations to articles (with abstracts from ERIC and other resource sites) and five websites reporting research that seems highly relevant to your research question; then look up at least five of these articles and three of the sites. Inspect the article bibliographies and the links in the website, and identify at least one more relevant article and website from each source. Write a brief description of each article and website you consulted, and evaluate its relevance to your research question. What additions or changes to your thoughts about the research question are suggested by the sources?

CHAPTER 3

Ethics in Research

Research Question: *How Do We Conduct Research Validly and Ethically?*

Chapter Contents

- **Historical Background**
- **Ethical Principles**

I magine this: One spring morning as you are drinking coffee and reading the newspaper, you notice a small ad for a psychology experiment at the local university.

WE WILL PAY YOU $45 FOR ONE HOUR OF YOUR TIME

Persons Needed for a Study of Memory

"Earn money and learn about yourself," it continues. Feeling a bit bored, you call and schedule an evening visit to the lab.

You are about to enter one of the most ethically controversial experiments in the history of social science.

You arrive at the assigned room at the university, ready for an interesting hour or so, and are immediately impressed by the elegance of the building and the professional appearance of the personnel. In the waiting room, you see a man dressed in a lab technician's coat talking to another visitor—a middle-aged fellow dressed in casual attire. The man in the lab coat turns and introduces himself and explains that as a psychologist, he is interested in whether people learn things better when they are punished for making a mistake. He quickly convinces you that this is a very important question for which there has been no adequate answer; he then explains that his experiment on punishment and learning will help answer this question. Then he announces, "I'm going to ask one of you to be the teacher here tonight and the other one to be the learner."

The Experimenter, as we'll refer to him from now on, says he will write either "Teacher" or "Learner" on small identical slips of paper and then asks both of you to draw out one. Yours says "Teacher."

The Experimenter now says, in a matter-of-fact way, "All right. Now the first thing we'll have to do is to set the Learner up so that he can get some type of punishment."

He leads you both behind a curtain, sits the Learner down, attaches a wire to his left wrist and straps both his arms to the chair so that he cannot remove the wire (Exhibit 3.1). The wire is connected to a console with 30 switches and a large dial on the other side of the curtain. When you ask what the wire is for, the Experimenter says he will demonstrate. He then asks you to hold the end of the wire, walks back to the control console, flips several switches, and focuses his attention on the dial. You hear a clicking noise, see the dial move, and then feel an electric shock in your hand. When the Experimenter flicks the next switch, the shock increases.

Exhibit 3.1 **Learner Strapped in Chair With Electrodes**

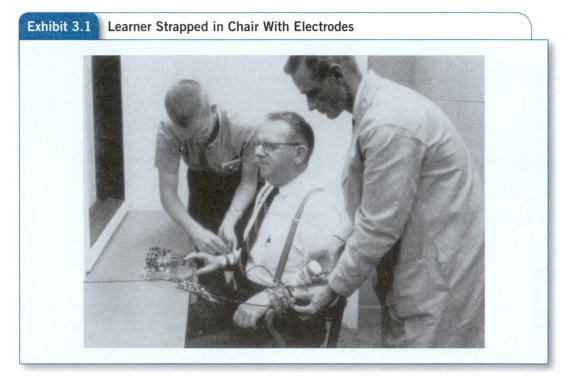

Source: From the film *OBEDIENCE* © 1968 by Stanley Milgram, © Renewed 1993 by Alexandra Milgram, and distributed by Penn State, Media Sales.

"Ouch!" you say. "So that's the punishment. Couldn't it cause injury?" The Experimenter explains that the machine is calibrated so that it will not cause permanent injury but acknowledges that when it is turned up all the way, it is very, very painful.

Now you walk back to the other side of the room (so that the Learner is behind the curtain) and sit before the console (Exhibit 3.2). The experimental procedure has four simple steps:

1. You read aloud a series of word pairs, like *blue box, nice day, wild duck,* and so on.

2. You read one of the first words from those pairs and a set of four words, one of which contains the original paired word. For example, you might say, "blue: sky ink box lamp."

3. The Learner states the word that he thinks was paired with the first word you read (*blue*). If he gives a correct response, you compliment him and move on to the next word. If he makes a mistake, you flip a switch on the console. This causes the Learner to feel a shock on his wrist.

| Exhibit 3.2 | Milgram's "Shock Generator" |

Source: From the film *OBEDIENCE* © 1968 by Stanley Milgram, © Renewed 1993 by Alexandra Milgram, and distributed by Penn State, Media Sales.

4. After each mistake, you are to flip the next switch on the console, progressing from left to right. You note that a label corresponds to every fifth mark on the dial, with the 1st mark labeled "slight shock," the 5th mark labeled "moderate shock," the 10th "strong shock," and so on through "very strong shock," "intense shock," "extreme intensity shock," and "danger: severe shock."

You begin. The Learner at first gives some correct answers, but then he makes a few errors. Soon you are beyond the 5th mark ("moderate shock") and are moving in the direction of more and more severe shocks. As you turn the dial, the Learner's reactions increase in intensity: from a grunt at the 10th mark ("strong shock") to painful groans at higher levels, to anguished cries to "get me out of here" at the "extreme intensity shock" levels, to a deathly silence at the highest level. When you protest at administering the stronger shocks, the Experimenter tells you, "The experiment requires that you continue." Occasionally he says, "It is absolutely essential that you continue."

This is a simplified version of the famous "obedience" experiments by Stanley Milgram (1963), begun at Yale University in 1960. Outside the laboratory, Milgram surveyed Yale undergraduates and asked them to indicate at what level they would terminate their "shocks" if they were in the study. Before reading further, look at the picture of the meter in Exhibit 3.3 (p. 48). Mark on this meter the most severe shock that you would agree to give to the Learner.

The average (mean) maximum shock level predicted by the Yale undergraduates was 9.35, corresponding to a "strong" shock. Only one student predicted that he would provide a stimulus above that level, at the "very strong" level. Responses were similar from nonstudent groups.

But the actual average level of shock administered by the 40 New Haven adults who volunteered for the experiment was 24.53, higher than "extreme intensity shock" and just short of "danger: severe shock." Twenty-five of Milgram's original 40 subjects (62.5%) complied entirely with the experimenter's demands, going all the way to the top of the scale (labeled simply as "XXX"). Judging from the subjects' visibly high stress and their subsequent reports, they believed that the Learner was receiving physically painful shocks.

We introduce the Milgram experiment not to discuss obedience to authority but instead to introduce research ethics. We want to encourage you to think about research from the standpoint of the people who are the subjects of research. We will refer to Milgram's obedience studies throughout this chapter since they ultimately had as profound an influence on researchers' thinking about ethics as on how to understand obedience to authority.

Exhibit 3.3 Shock Meter

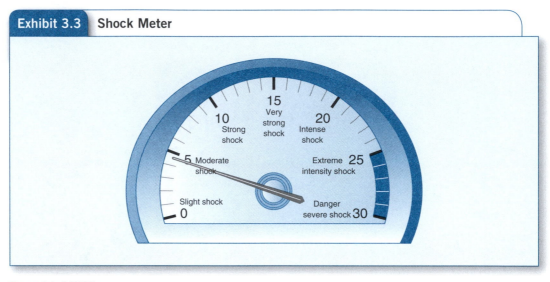

Source: Schutt (2009).

Throughout this book, we discuss ethical problems common to various research methods: in this particular chapter, we present in more detail some of the general ethical principles that educational researchers use in monitoring their work.

Historical Background

Formal procedures for the protection of participants in research grew out of some widely publicized abuses. A defining event occurred in 1946, when the Nuremberg War Crime Trials exposed horrific medical experiments conducted by Nazi doctors and others in the name of "science." In the 1970s, Americans were shocked to learn that medical researchers funded by the U.S. Public Health Service had, for decades, studied 399 low-income African American men diagnosed with syphilis in the 1930s to study the "natural" course of the illness. In the Tuskegee Syphilis Study, many participants were not informed of their illness (Exhibit 3.4) and were denied treatment until 1972, even though a cure (penicillin) was developed in the 1950s (Jones, 1993).

Such egregious violations of human rights similar to these resulted, in the United States, in the creation of a National Commission for the Protection of Human Subjects of Biomedical and Behavioral Research. The commission's 1979 "Belmont Report" established three basic ethical principles for the protection of human subjects (Exhibit 3.5):

1. *Respect for persons:* Treating persons as autonomous agents and protecting those with diminished autonomy

2. *Beneficence:* Minimizing possible harms and maximizing benefits

3. *Justice:* Distributing benefits and risks of research fairly

The Department of Health and Human Services and the Food and Drug Administration then translated these principles into specific regulations that were adopted in 1991 as the Federal Policy for the Protection of

Exhibit 3.4 **Tuskegee Syphilis Experiment**

Source: Tuskegee Syphilis Study Administrative Records. Records of the Centers for Disease Control and Prevention. National Archives–Southeast Region (Atlanta).

Human Subjects. This policy has shaped the course of research in the United States ever since, and you will have to take it into account as you design your own research investigations. Some professional associations, such as the American Psychological Association, the American Sociological Association, and the American Educational Research Association, as well as university review boards and ethics committees in other organizations, also set standards for the treatment of human subjects by their members, employees, and students; these standards are designed to comply with the federal policy.

Federal regulations require that every institution that seeks federal funding for biomedical or behavioral research on human subjects have an **institutional review board (IRB)** that reviews research proposals. IRBs at universities and other agencies apply ethical standards that are set by federal regulations but can be expanded or specified by the IRB itself (Sieber, 1992, pp. 5, 10). To promote adequate review of ethical issues, the regulations require that IRBs include members with diverse backgrounds. The Office for Protection From Research Risks in the National Institutes of Health monitors IRBs, with the exception of research involving drugs (which is the responsibility of the U.S. Food and Drug Administration).

Exhibit 3.5 **Belmont Report Principles**

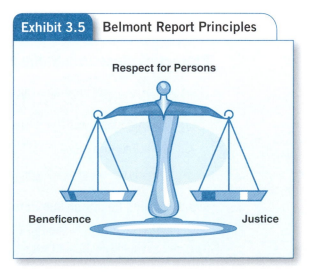

Respect for Persons

Beneficence

Justice

▣ Ethical Principles

The American Educational Research Association (AERA), like other professional organizations, has adopted, for practicing educational researchers, ethical guidelines that are more specific than the federal regulations. The statement on Ethical Standards of the AERA (2000) is available on the AERA website (http://www.aera .net), where it is described as "an educational document to stimulate collegial debate and to evoke voluntary compliance by moral persuasion."

To give more concrete guidance on ethical questions, the AERA has published two books, *Ethical Standards of the American Educational Research Association: Cases and Commentary* (Strike et al., 2002) and *Standards for Educational and Psychological Testing* (1999). The AERA also has taken a leadership role in the Social and Behavioral Sciences Working Group on Human Research Protections funded by the National Institutes of Health, serving as the scientific society that provides the institutional home for the group.

Mostly, ethical issues in research are covered by five guidelines:

1. Research should cause no harm to subjects.

2. Participation in research should be voluntary, and therefore subjects must give their informed consent to participate in the research.

3. Researchers should fully disclose their identity.

4. Anonymity or confidentiality must be maintained for individual research participants unless it is voluntarily and explicitly waived.

5. Benefits from a research project should outweigh any foreseeable risks.

Each of these guidelines became a focus of debate about Milgram's experiments, to which we will refer frequently. Did Stanley Milgram respect the spirit expressed in these principles? You will find that there is no simple answer to the question: What "is" (or "isn't") ethical research practice? But we do promise that by the time you finish this chapter, you will be aware of the major issues in research ethics and be able to make informed, defensible decisions about the ethical conduct of educational research.

Protecting Research Subjects

This guideline, our most important, can be divided into three specific directions:

1. Avoid harming research participants.

2. Obtain informed consent.

3. Maintain privacy and confidentiality.

Avoid Harming Research Subjects

This standard may seem straightforward but can be difficult to interpret in specific cases. Does it mean that subjects should not be at all harmed, even mentally or emotionally? That they should feel no anxiety or distress?

The most serious charge leveled against the ethics of Milgram's study was that he had harmed his subjects. A verbatim transcript of one session will give you an idea of what participants experienced when the "shock generator" made it appear they were delivering increasingly severe shocks to the Learner (Milgram, 1965, p. 67):

150 volts delivered.   You want me to keep going?

165 volts delivered.   That guy is hollering in there. There's a lot of them here. He's liable to have a heart condition. You want me to go on?

180 volts delivered.   He can't stand it! I'm not going to kill that man in there! You hear him hollering? He's hollering. He can't stand it. . . . I mean who is going to take responsibility if anything happens to that gentleman?

[The experimenter accepts responsibility.] All right.

195 volts delivered.   You see he's hollering. Hear that. Gee, I don't know. *[The experimenter says: "The experiment requires that you go on."]* I know it does, sir, but I mean—Hugh— he don't know what he's in for. He's up to 195 volts.

210 volts delivered.

225 volts delivered.

240 volts delivered.

The experimental manipulation generated "extraordinary tension" (Milgram, 1963, p. 377):

Subjects were observed to sweat, tremble, stutter, bite their lips, groan and dig their fingernails into their flesh. . . . Full-blown, uncontrollable seizures were observed for 3 subjects. One . . . seizure so violently convulsive that it was necessary to call a halt to the experiment [for that individual]. (Milgram, 1963, p. 375)

An observer (behind a one-way mirror) reported, "I observed a mature and initially poised businessman enter the laboratory smiling and confident. Within 20 minutes he was reduced to a twitching, stuttering wreck, who was rapidly approaching a point of nervous collapse" (Milgram, 1963, p. 377).

Milgram's "Behavioral Study of Obedience" was published in 1963 in the *Journal of Abnormal and Social Psychology*. In the next year, the *American Psychologist* published a critique of the experiment's ethics by psychologist Diana Baumrind (1964, p. 421). From Baumrind's perspective, the emotional disturbance in subjects was "potentially harmful because it could easily effect an alteration in the subject's self-image or ability to trust adult authorities in the future" (p. 422). Stanley Milgram (1964) quickly countered that

momentary excitement is not the same as harm. As the experiment progressed there was no indication of injurious effects in the subjects; and as the subjects themselves strongly endorsed the experiment, the judgment I made was to continue the experiment. (p. 849)

Milgram (1963) also attempted to minimize harm to subjects with postexperimental procedures "to assure that the subject would leave the laboratory in a state of well being" (p. 374). A friendly reconciliation was arranged between the subject and the victim, and an effort was made to reduce any tensions that arose as a result of the experiment.

In some cases, the "dehoaxing" (or "**debriefing**") discussion was extensive, and all subjects were promised (and later received) a comprehensive report (Milgram, 1964, p. 849). Baumrind (1964) was unconvinced: "It would be interesting to know what sort of procedures could dissipate the type of emotional disturbance just described" (p. 422).

When Milgram (1964, p. 849) surveyed the subjects in a follow-up, 83.7% endorsed the statement that they were "very glad" or "glad" "to have been in the experiment," 15.1% were "neither sorry nor glad," and just 1.3% were "sorry" or "very sorry" to have participated. Interviews by a psychiatrist a year later found no evidence "of any traumatic reactions" (Milgram, 1974, p. 197). Subsequently, Milgram argued that "the central moral justification for allowing my experiment is that it was judged acceptable by those who took part in it" (Milgram, as cited in Cave & Holm, 2003, p. 32).

In a later article, Baumrind (1985, p. 168) dismissed the value of the self-reported "lack of harm" of subjects who had been willing to participate in the experiment—although noting that still 16% did NOT endorse the statement that they were "glad" they had participated in the experiment. Many researchers, ethicists, and others concluded that Milgram's procedures had not harmed the subjects and so were justified for the knowledge they produced; others sided with Baumrind's criticisms (A. G. Miller, 1986, pp. 88–138).

How does a 50-year-old argument between two psychologists apply to educational research? Consider the possible harm to subjects in a study of "peer stigmatization" (what we would today call "bullying") in kindergarten conducted by Amos Hatch (1993). Hatch spent 6 months in a half-day kindergarten, observing child-to-child social interactions. He took the role of a "passive participant observer" and made daily field notes, collected classroom artifacts, and interviewed both the teacher and the students (p. 5). As time went on, he began to focus on a student named Lester, who was being stigmatized by his classmates as "less than normal." Other students regularly made hurtful comments toward Lester and excluded him from group activities. Hatch continued in his observer role until the end of the school year and then wrote up his results. When he presented his work at a conference, a member of the audience challenged him with the question, "If you knew Lester was being stigmatized by his classmates, why didn't you intervene on his behalf?" (p. 5). Hatch immediately realized his ethical dilemma. As a researcher, wasn't his role to observe and record, not to affect or influence what he was seeing? But if he didn't intervene, wasn't he failing to protect from harm the very student who had emerged as his primary research subject? This type of ethical question comes up frequently in education research. What do you think Hatch should have done? If you were in this situation, what would you do? Hatch's conclusion was that he should have taken his data, however tentative and incomplete, to the teacher and initiated a discussion about the best course of action. Feelings of guilt stayed with him, because while the research was going on, he had "never recognized (he) was dealing with an ethically paradoxical situation" (Hatch, 1993, p. 16).

Even well-intentioned researchers may fail to foresee all the potential problems. Hatch did not realize there were ethical issues in his study until he presented the details at a conference. Milgram (1974, pp. 27–31) reported that he and his colleagues were surprised by the subjects' willingness to carry out such severe shocks. If these risks were not foreseeable, was it acceptable for the researchers to presume in advance that the benefits would outweigh the risks? And are you concerned, like Arthur Miller (1986, p. 138), that real harm "could result from *not doing* research on destructive obedience," stigmatization, and other troubling human behaviors?

In later chapters, we will consider such ethical questions as they arise in relation to different research methods.

Obtain Informed Consent

Just defining informed consent may also be more difficult than it first appears. To be informed, consent must be given by persons who are competent to consent, have consented voluntarily, are fully informed about the research, and have comprehended what they have been told (P. D. Reynolds, 1979). Yet you probably realize, like Diana Baumrind (1985), that due to the inability to communicate perfectly, "full disclosure of everything that could possibly affect a given subject's decision to participate is not possible, and therefore cannot be ethically required" (p. 165).

Obtaining informed consent creates additional challenges for researchers. The language of the consent form must be clear and understandable to the research participants and yet sufficiently long and detailed to explain what will actually happen in the research.

There are many different types of consent forms, depending on the project. Sample consent forms that can be used as models are widely available on the Internet. Many universities have offices of research that post model consent forms on their websites. You should consult with your professor or visit your university's website to see if that is the case on your campus.

Exhibit 3.6 shows a sample consent form adapted from one posted on the website of California State University at Fresno. It illustrates the basics of informed consent: (1) The consent form must be written in

---

Exhibit 3.6	**Sample Short Consent Form**

Sample Consent Form

The following sample is provided as a skeleton from which a consent form can be developed. It is not provided with the intention that it be precisely emulated. The detailed description of the basic elements of the consent form is presented in the CPHS Policy and Procedures manual. **REMINDER: The consent form should be written in terms comprehensible to the intended subject.**

You are invited to participate in a study conducted by [name of investigator and affiliation]. We hope to learn [state what the study is designed to discover or establish]. You were selected as a possible participant in this study because [state why the subject was selected].

If you decide to participate, we [or: Dr. (blank space) and his associates] will [describe the procedures to be followed, including their purposes, how long they will take, and their frequency]. [Describe the risks, discomforts, inconveniences, and benefits reasonably to be expected. If benefits are mentioned, add:] We cannot guarantee, however that you will receive any benefits from this study.

[Describe appropriate alternative procedures that might be advantageous to the subject, if any. Any standard treatment that is being withheld must be disclosed.]

Any information that is obtained in connection with this study and that can be identified with you will remain confidential and will be disclosed only with your permission or as required by law. If you give us your permission by signing this document, we plan to disclose [state the persons or agencies to whom the information will be furnished, the nature of the information to be furnished, and the purpose of the disclosure].

[If the subject will receive compensation, describe the amount or nature.] [If there is a possibility of additional cost to the subject because of participation, describe it.] (If there are risks to the subjects, state them explicitly.)

Your decision whether or not to participate will not prejudice your future relations with California State University, Fresno [and the named cooperating agency or institution, if any]. If you decide to participate, you are free to withdraw your consent and to discontinue participation at any time without penalty. The Committee on the Protection of Human Subjects at California State University, Fresno has reviewed and approved the present research.

If you have any questions, please ask us. If you have any additional questions later, Dr. (state name) [give a phone number or address] will be happy to answer them. Questions regarding the rights of research subjects may be directed to xxxxxxxx, Chair, CSUF Committee on the Protection of Human Subjects, (559) xxx-xxxx.

You will be given a copy of this form to keep.

YOU ARE MAKING A DECISION WHETHER OR NOT TO PARTICIPATE. YOUR SIGNATURE INDICATES THAT YOU HAVE DECIDED TO PARTICIPATE, HAVING READ THE INFORMATION PROVIDED ABOVE.

_____   _____
Date   **Signature**

_____
Relationship to Subject [This line should not appear on forms that will be given to subjects consenting for themselves.]

_____   _____
Signature of Witness (if any)   **Signature of Investigator**

Source: Retrieved from California State University, Fresno, Institutional Review Board Web site (http://www.csufresno.edu/humansubjects/resources/informed_consent.shtml).

such a way as to be understood by the person signing it. For example, if the research population includes speakers of languages other than English, the researcher must prepare forms in every language included in the target population. (2) The consent form must state clearly who is doing the research, including affiliation with a university or other sponsoring organization if that applies. (3) The consent form must briefly describe the research, including any anticipated risks to the research subjects and the benefits expected to flow from it, and any compensation that will be offered. (4) The consent form should describe how confidentiality will be maintained, including what will happen to records (tapes, transcripts) at the completion of the project. (5) Consent must be freely given and can be withdrawn at any time without consequences.

Exhibit 3.7 shows an actual, IRB-approved consent form for a school-based interview study conducted in 2009 by graduate student Esta Montano under the direction of one of the authors. Montano's study investigated White teachers' attitudes toward METCO (Metropolitan Council for Educational Opportunity), a long-established, voluntary, urban-suburban desegregation program funded by the Commonwealth of Massachusetts.

Finally, some participants can't truly give informed consent. College students, for instance, may feel unable to refuse if their professor asks them to be in an experiment. Legally speaking, children cannot give consent to participate in research; a child's legal guardian must give written informed consent to have the child participate in research (Sieber, 1992). Then the child must, in most circumstances, be given the opportunity to give or withhold *assent* to participate in research, usually by a verbal response to an explanation of the research. The need for two levels of protection for children—consent and assent—is a particularly important consideration for educational researchers, who do much of their work in K–12 schools. Exhibit 3.8 shows two short model assent forms posted on the university website by the Research, Grants, and Contracts Office of the University of Tennessee at Martin.

Special protections exist for other vulnerable populations—prisoners, pregnant women, mentally disabled persons, and educationally or economically disadvantaged persons.

In general, the researcher's sensitivity to possible consent risks for participants should be in direct proportion to the difference in power or authority—the power relationship—between researcher and subjects. Research subjects with the least power need the most protection, the highest level of informed consent. If a classroom teacher is interviewing other classroom teachers, adults over whom she has little authority, the power relationship is virtually equal. If the same teacher wishes to interview special needs students in a school where most of the children qualify for free and reduced lunch, the power relationship is quite unequal, and most IRBs would expect a detailed statement, in the research proposal, of how students, staff, and families will be safeguarded and how informed consent will be gained.

Maintain Privacy and Confidentiality

Maintaining privacy and confidentiality during and after a study is another way to protect subjects, and the researcher's commitment to that standard should be included in the informed consent agreement (Sieber, 1992). Procedures to protect each subject's privacy, such as locking records, creating special identifying codes or pseudonyms, and destroying interview tapes after a set period of time, must be created to minimize the risk of access by unauthorized persons. Exhibit 3.9 shows the separate consent form that Esta Montano used for the tape-recorded portion of her project. Note how careful she is to describe exactly what will happen to the tapes at every stage of the process to safeguard the subjects' privacy, up to and including the point at which the tapes are destroyed. Also, because she had previously taught an anti-bias course in the Edwardsville district and so had a previous relationship with some of her subjects, she employs a substitute interviewer, a "proxy," to interview those subjects.

Educational researchers often deal with highly confidential material such as school records, medical or psychological evaluations, and teachers' assessments of students. The Health Insurance Portability and

Accountability Act (HIPAA), passed by Congress in 1996, created much more stringent regulations for the protection of health care data. As implemented by the U.S. Department of Health and Human Services in 2000 (and revised in 2002), the HIPAA Final Privacy Rule applies to oral, written, and electronic information that "relates to the past, present or future physical or mental health or condition of an individual." The HIPAA rule requires that researchers have valid authorization for any use or disclosure of "protected health information" (PHI) from a health care provider. Waivers of authorization can be granted in special circumstances (Cava, Cushman, & Goodman, 2007).

Exhibit 3.10 shows a consent form related to student medical records. It was posted on the website of the U.S. Department of Education in October 2009, when an H1N1 flu epidemic was widely predicted, and was intended to help "answer questions that school officials may have concerning the disclosure of personally identifiable information from students' education records to outside entities when addressing an H1N1 flu outbreak" (http://www2.ed.gov/policy/gen/guid/fpco/pdf/ferpa-h1n1.pdf).

However, statements about confidentiality also need to be realistic: Laws allow research records to be subpoenaed and may require reporting child abuse; a researcher may feel compelled to release information if a health- or life-threatening situation arises and participants need to be alerted. The National Institutes of Health can issue a "Certificate of Confidentiality" to protect researchers from being legally required to disclose confidential information. Researchers who are focusing on high-risk populations or behaviors, such as crime, substance abuse, sexual activity, or genetic information, can request such a certificate. Suspicions of child abuse or neglect must still be reported, and in some states, researchers may still be required to report crimes such as elder abuse (Arwood & Panicker, 2007). The standard of confidentiality does not apply to observation in public places and information available in public records.

Maintaining Honesty and Openness

Protecting subjects, then, is the primary focus of research ethics. But researchers have obligations to other groups, including the scientific community, whose concerns with validity require that researchers be open to disclosing their methods and honest in presenting their findings. To assess the validity of a researcher's conclusions and the ethics of his or her procedures, you need to know how the research was conducted. The scientific concern with validity requires in turn that scientists be open in disclosing their methods and honest in presenting their findings. This means that articles or other reports must include a detailed methodology section, perhaps supplemented by appendices containing the research instruments or websites or other resources where contact information can be obtained. Biases or political motives should be acknowledged since research distorted by political or personal pressures to find particular outcomes is unlikely to be carried out in an honest and open fashion.

The act of publication itself is a vital element in maintaining openness and honesty since then others can review procedures and debate with the researcher. Although Milgram disagreed sharply with Diana Baumrind's criticisms of his experiments, their mutual commitment to public discourse in journals widely available to other researchers resulted in a more comprehensive presentation of study procedures and a more thoughtful discourse about research ethics. Almost 50 years later, this commentary continues to inform debates about research ethics (Cave & Holm, 2003).

Achieving Valid Results

It is the pursuit of impartial knowledge—the goal of validity—that justifies our investigations and our claims to the use of human subjects. We have no business asking people to answer questions, submit to

Exhibit 3.7 Consent Form for a School-Based Interview Study

Consent Form for Participation

University of Massachusetts Boston
Graduate College of Education
Leadership in Urban Schools
100 Morrissey Boulevard
Boston, MA 02125-3393

Principal Investigator: Esta Montano

Introduction and Contact Information

You are asked to take part in a dissertation research project that is investigating the perspectives of METCO and race on the part of white educators who work at Edwardsville High School. My name is Esta Montano, and I am the principal researcher. I am a doctoral candidate in the Leadership in Urban Schools Program at the University of Massachusetts, Boston.

Please read this form and feel free to ask questions. If you have further questions, I will discuss them with you. I can be reached at any time at the above address, via telephone, at xxx-xxx-xxxx, or via email at emontano@xxx.

As a doctoral candidate, I am required to conduct research as part of the requirements for a Doctorate of Education (Ed.D.). My research is being conducted under the supervision of Joseph Check, Ph.D., Associate Professor, Leadership in Urban Schools Program, University of Massachusetts, Boston. You may contact Dr. Check at the above address, via telephone at 617-287-7655, or via email at joseph.check@umb.edu.

Description of the Project

This study, which will be conducted at Edwardsville High School during 2008, attempts to understand the manner in which white educators make sense of the METCO program at their school. It also attempts to understand how white educators who are employed at Edwardsville High School perceive of race, which is the most significant factor of the METCO program.

If you are an Edwardsville High School educator and you decide to participate in this study, you will be asked to fill out an introductory questionnaire, participate in two audio-taped interviews (the duration of which will not exceed one hour each), engage in one short email correspondence with me following each interview, and complete a short final reflection. If you choose to participate in this study, you will be compensated with a one-time stipend of $150.00 (one hundred and fifty dollars).

If you are a member of the METCO faculty at Edwardsville High School, you will be asked to participate in one interview with me, the length of which will not exceed one hour. You will be compensated in the amount of $30.00 (thirty dollars) for your participation.

Risks or Discomforts

This is considered to be a minimal risk study, meaning that the research risk to you is no greater than that ordinarily encountered in daily life activities. The primary risk that may be associated with this study is the emergence of negative or distressful feelings in completing the research materials. You may speak with me at any time to discuss any distress or other issues related to study participation.

Benefits

This study is essentially about educators' thinking on the subject of METCO and race in their district; it is not about the educators as individuals. The potential benefits of your participation in this research include substantial benefits to the Edwardsville Public Schools district, as findings will be shared with upper management and will be used to improve professional development for faculty in the area of race and relationships with METCO students. This study may also help the district to realign the mission of METCO.

This study may also be beneficial to you as a participant in that it may help you to delve into your own thinking and thereby improve your practice. Research of this type is important because to date, there are several studies that have been conducted about METCO, but none have studied the perspectives of white educators who work with METCO students. Therefore, this study has the potential to be instructive to all school systems that participate in METCO.

Confidentiality and Anonymity

Your participation in this research is confidential. That is, the information gathered for this study will not be published or presented in a way that would allow anyone to identify you. Your high school will be known as "Edwardsville," a town in Massachusetts. You will be asked to choose a pseudonym, which will be used in place of your name. To the best of my ability, I will also omit or alter any details that might identify a specific person. All research materials and data that I collect will be stored in a locked file cabinet in my home that only I have access to. You will have access to these materials at any time. At the end of my study and at such time that my dissertation has been accepted, all research materials, including questionnaires, field notes, audio-tapes, transcriptions, emails, and reflections, will be destroyed.

Voluntary Participation

The decision whether or not to take part in this research study is voluntary. If you do decide to take part in this study, you may terminate participation at any time without consequence. Withdrawal from the study or electing to skip or omit questions that are included in the questionnaire or interviews will have no bearing whatsoever on your job standing or employment status with Edwardsville Public Schools. If you wish to terminate your participation in this study, please telephone me immediately. If you do choose to terminate your participation before the study is completed, however, you will not receive the $150.00 stipend.

Rights

You have the right to ask questions about this research before you sign this form and at any time during the study. You can reach my research supervisor, Dr. Joseph Check, or me at any time. If you have any questions or concerns about your rights as a research participant, please contact a representative of the Institutional Review Board (IRB), at the University of Massachusetts, Boston, which oversees research involving human participants. The IRB may be reached at the following address: IRB, Quinn Administration Building -2-080, University of Massachusetts, 100 Morrissey Boulevard, Boston, MA 02125-3393. You can also contact the Board by telephone or email at 617/287-5370 or at human.subjects@umb.edu.

Signatures

I HAVE READ THE CONSENT FORM. MY QUESTIONS HAVE BEEN ANSWERED. MY SIGNATURE ON THIS FORM INDICATES THAT I CONSENT TO PARTICIPATE IN THIS STUDY.

_____

Printed Name of Participant

_____   _____

Signature of Participant   **Date**

_____

Printed Name of Researcher

_____   _____

Signature of Researcher   **Date**

Source: Montano (2010, p. 459).

Exhibit 3.8   Two Sample Assent Forms for Students Who Are Minors

Following are two sample assent forms. They are included as guides to you in construction of a child's assent to be used in your project. Fill in the appropriate information and adjust to the specifics of your research.

NOTES:

*Do not include a statement to the effect that "your parent has agreed to allow you to take part in the study." This implies the possibility of parental pressure for the child's participation. Instead use "your parent is aware of this project."

*Make sure you use age-appropriate language. For example, do not use the same language for a third-grade student as you would a graduate student.

Sample Minor Assent Document 1

Your parent knows we are going to ask you to *[participate in this project/fill out this survey]*. We want to know about kids' *[attitudes/ experiences about topic of research]*. It will take *[amount of time]* to complete the task. Your name will not be written anywhere on the *[research instrument]*. No one will know these answers came from you personally.

If you don't want to participate, you can stop at any time. There will be no bad feelings if you don't want to do this. You can ask questions if you do not understand any part of *[the study]*.

Do you understand? Is this OK?

Name (Please print): _____

Signature: _____

Date: _____

Investigator's Signature: _____ **Date:** _____

Sample Minor Assent Document 2

Project Title: _____

Investigator: _____

We are doing a research study about *[purpose in simple language]*. A research study is a way to learn more about people. If you decide that you want to be part of this study, you will be asked to *[description, including time involved]*.

There are some things about this study you should know. There are *[procedures, things that take a long time, other risks, discomforts, etc.]*.

Not everyone who takes part in this study will benefit. A benefit means that something good happens to you. We think these benefits might be *[description]*.

If you do not want to be in this research study, we will tell you what other kinds of treatments there are for you. *[This statement applies to research projects that offer treatment or intervention.]*

When we are finished with this study, we will write a report about what was learned. This report will not include your name or that you were in the study.

You do not have to be in this study if you do not want to be. If you decide to stop after we begin, that's okay too.

If you decide you want to be in this study, please sign your name.

I, _____, want to be in this research study.

  (Print your name here)

_____   Date: _____

  (Sign your name here)

Parts in italics should be modified for your specific project. Other parts may need to be modified as well depending on your research methods.

Source: Retrieved from the University of Tennessee, Martin, Research, Grants, and Contracts website: http://www.utm.edu/departments/rgc/_pdf/ irbminorassent.pdf

---

Exhibit 3.9 Tape Consent Form

University of Massachusetts Boston
Graduate College of Education
Leadership in Urban Schools
100 Morrissey Boulevard
Boston, MA 02125-3393

TAPE CONSENT FORM

Oral Interview and Transcription

White Educators and the METCO Program:
Perspectives of METCO and Race

Principal Researcher: Esta Montano

This portion of my study involves the audio taping of your interview with me. If you are an educator who was previously in a course that I facilitated in the district entitled Effective Anti-Bias Teaching and Mentoring for All Students, you will be interviewed and audio taped by a proxy, TBD, who is an associate of mine. **Neither your name nor any other identifying information will be associated with the audiotape or the transcript.** I am the only individual who will be able to listen to the tapes or read the transcriptions following the interview.

After the interview, the audio tapes will be transcribed by a professional transcription agency, but the transcriber will not know who you are or what district you are from. Transcripts of your interview may be reproduced in whole or in part for use in my dissertation. **However, neither your name nor any other identifying information (such as your voice) will be used in presentations or in written products resulting from the study.**

Immediately following the interview, you will be given the opportunity to have the tape erased if you wish to withdraw your consent to taping or participation in this study. I would like to remind you that only I have access to your tapes and transcriptions and all of these materials will be kept in a locked file cabinet in my home.

By signing this form you are consenting to *[Include only those options that are being used]*

- ☐ having your interview taped
- ☐ to having the tape transcribed
- ☐ use of portions of the written transcript in my dissertation

By checking the box in front of each item, you are consenting to participate in that procedure.

This consent for taping is effective until the following date: <u>May 30, 2009</u>. On or before that date, the tapes will be destroyed.

Participant's Printed Name_____

Participant's Signature _____

Source: Montano (2010, p. 469).

---

observations, or participate in experimental procedures if we are simply seeking to verify our preexisting prejudices or convince others to take action on behalf of our personal interests. If, on the other hand, we approach our research projects impartially, setting aside our personal predilections in the service of learning a bit more about human behavior, we can honestly represent our actions as potentially contributing to the advancement of knowledge.

Exhibit 3.10 Sample Consent Form for Student Medical Records

Sample Consent Form for Disclosures by *[Name of School District]* to *[Name of Health Department]*

The *[school district]* will seek to keep students healthy and safe this fall and through the school year. As part of this effort, we will be collaborating with the *[local]* Health Department to help track student absences. This effort will enable us to identify unusual clusters of disease and provide information to the school community, and particularly students at high risk, about illnesses. These efforts will also help the health community assess the spread of disease and potentially allocate scarce medical resources.

Pursuant to the Family Educational Rights and Privacy Act (FERPA), 20 U.S.C. § 1232g, parental consent is required before personally identifiable information from your child's education records may be disclosed to *[the health department]*, absent a health or safety emergency or another exception to the requirement of consent. If your child is age 18 or over, he or she is an "eligible student" and has to provide consent for disclosures of information from his or her education records.

Please note that information about your child may be shared with the Health Department without your consent if school officials determine that there is a significant and articulable threat to the health or safety of your child or other individuals and that the Health Department needs to know the information to protect the health or safety of your child or other individuals.

I, _____, hereby agree to allow *[school district name]* to disclose *[specify records]* on *[student name]* to *[name of health department]* for the purpose of *[state purpose of disclosure]*.

You may withdraw your consent to share this information at any time. This request should be submitted in writing and signed.

_____

Signature of Parent, Guardian, or Eligible Student

Date: _____

Source: U.S. Department of Education website: http://www2.ed.gov/policy/gen/guid/fpco/pdf/ferpa-h1n1.pdf

---

The details in Milgram's 1963 article and 1974 book on the obedience experiments make a compelling case for his commitment to achieving valid results—to learning how and why obedience influences behavior. In Milgram's (1963) own words,

> It has been reliably established that from 1933–45 millions of innocent persons were systematically slaughtered on command. . . . Obedience is the psychological mechanism that links individual action to political purpose. It is the dispositional cement that binds men to systems of authority . . . for many persons obedience may be a deeply ingrained behavior tendency. . . . Obedience may [also] be ennobling and educative and refer to acts of charity and kindness, as well as to destruction. (p. 371)

Milgram (1963) then explains how he devised experiments to study the process of obedience in a way that would seem realistic to the subjects and still allow "important variables to be manipulated at several points in the experiment" (p. 372). Every step in the experiment was carefully designed to ensure that the subjects received identical stimuli and that their responses were measured carefully.

However, not all psychologists agreed that Milgram's approach could achieve valid results. Baumrind's (1964, p. 421) critique begins with a rejection of the external validity—the generalizability—of the experiment. Because "the laboratory is unfamiliar as a setting and the rules of behavior ambiguous," the laboratory is not the place to study degree of obedience or suggestibility, as a function of a particular experimental condition. And so, "the parallel between authority-subordinate relationships in Hitler's Germany and in Milgram's laboratory is unclear" (p. 423).

Milgram (1974, pp. 169–178) also pointed out that his experiment had been replicated in other places and settings with the same results, that there was considerable evidence that the subjects had believed that they actually were administering shocks, and that the "essence" of his experimental manipulation—the request that subjects comply with a legitimate authority—was shared with the dilemma faced by people in Nazi Germany, soldiers at the My Lai massacre in Vietnam, and even cultists who drank poison in Jonestown, Guyana, at the command of their leader, Jim Jones (A. G. Miller, 1986, pp. 182–183).

But Baumrind (1985) was still not convinced. In a follow-up article in the *American Psychologist,* she argued that "far from illuminating real life, as he claimed, Milgram in fact appeared to have constructed a set of conditions so internally inconsistent that they could not occur in real life" (p. 171).

Milgram assumed that obedience could fruitfully be studied in the laboratory; Baumrind disagreed. Both, however, buttressed their ethical arguments with assertions about the external validity (or invalidity) of the experimental results. They agreed, in other words, that a research study is in part justified by its valid findings—the knowledge to be gained. If the findings aren't valid, they can't justify the research at all. It is hard to justify any risk for human subjects, or even any expenditure of time and resources, if our findings tell us nothing about human behavior.

If you were to serve on your university's IRB, would you allow this research to be conducted? Can students who are asked to participate in research by their professor be considered to be able to give informed consent? Do you consider "informed consent" to be meaningful if the true purpose or nature of an experimental manipulation is not revealed?

Would you allow research on prisoners, whose ability to give "informed consent" can be questioned? What special protections do you think would be appropriate?

Encouraging Appropriate Application

Finally, researchers must consider the uses to which their work is put. Although many researchers believe that personal values should be left outside the research setting, some feel that it is proper—even necessary—to concern themselves with the way their research is used.

Educational researchers who conduct research on behalf of specific organizations—a school, a school system, a funding agency implementing a new program—may face additional difficulties when the organization, instead of the researcher, controls the final report and the publicity it receives. If organizational leaders decide that particular research results are unwelcome, the researcher's desire to have findings used appropriately and reported fully can conflict with contractual obligations. Researchers can often anticipate such dilemmas in advance and resolve them when the contract for research is negotiated—or simply decline a particular research opportunity altogether. But often, such problems come up only after a report has been drafted, or the problems are ignored by a researcher who needs to have a job or needs to maintain particular personal relationships. These possibilities cannot be avoided entirely, but because of them, it is always important to acknowledge the source of research funding in reports and to consider carefully the sources of funding for research reports written by others.

Conclusions

Different kinds of research produce different kinds of ethical problems. Most survey research, for instance, creates few ethical problems and can even be enjoyable for participants. In fact, researchers from Michigan's Institute for Survey Research interviewed a representative national sample of adults and found that 68% of those who had participated in a survey were somewhat or very interested in participating in another; the more times respondents had been interviewed, the more willing they were to participate again (P. D. Reynolds, 1979, pp. 56–57). On the other hand, some experimental studies in the social sciences that have put people in uncomfortable or embarrassing situations have generated vociferous complaints and years of debate about ethics (P. D. Reynolds, 1979; Sjoberg, 1967).

Research ethics should be based on a realistic assessment of the overall potential for harm and benefit to research subjects. In this chapter, we have presented some basic guidelines, and special ethics sections in other chapters suggest applications for specific types of research, but answers aren't always obvious. For example, full disclosure of "what is really going on" in an experimental study is unnecessary if subjects are unlikely to be harmed. In one student observation study on cafeteria workers, for instance, that institution's IRB didn't require consent forms to be signed. The legalistic forms and signatures, they felt, would be more intrusive or upsetting to workers than the very benign and confidential research itself.

Nevertheless, researchers should make every effort to foresee possible risks and to weigh the possible benefits of the research against these risks. They should consult with individuals with different perspectives to develop a realistic risk-benefit assessment, and they should try to maximize the benefits to, as well as minimize the risks for, subjects of the research (Sieber, 1992, pp. 75–108).

Ultimately, these decisions about ethical procedures are not just up to you, as a researcher, to make. Your university's IRB sets the human subjects' protection standards for your institution and will require that researchers—even, in most cases, students—submit their research proposal to the IRB for review. So the ethical propriety of your research will be guarded by an institutional committee, following professional codes and guidelines; but still, that is an uncertain substitute for your own conscience.

Key Terms

Debriefing 51	Institutional review board (IRB) 49

Highlights

- Stanley Milgram's obedience experiments led to intensive debate about the extent to which deception could be tolerated in social science research and how harm to subjects should be evaluated.

- Egregious violations of human rights by researchers, including scientists in Nazi Germany and researchers in the Tuskegee Syphilis Study, led to the adoption of federal ethical standards for research on human subjects.

- The 1979 Belmont Report developed by a national commission established three basic ethical standards for the protection of human subjects: respect for persons, beneficence, and justice.

- The Department of Health and Human Services adopted in 1991 a Federal Policy for the Protection of Human Subjects. This policy requires that every institution seeking federal funding for biomedical or behavioral research on human subjects have an institutional review board to exercise oversight.

- The AERA's standards for the protection of human subjects require avoiding harm, obtaining informed consent, avoiding deception except in limited circumstances, and maintaining privacy and confidentiality.

- Educational research should maintain high standards for validity and be conducted and reported in an honest and open fashion.

- Effective debriefing of subjects after an experiment can help reduce the risk of harm due to the use of deception in the experiment.

Student Study Site

To assist in completing the web exercises, please access the study site at www.sagepub.com/check, where you will find the web exercise with accompanying links. You'll find other useful study materials such as self-quizzes and e-flashcards for each chapter, along with a group of carefully selected articles from research journals that illustrate the major concepts and techniques.

Discussion Questions

1. Why does unethical research occur? Is it inherent in science? Does it reflect "human nature"? What makes ethical research more or less likely?

2. Does debriefing solve the problem of subject deception? How much must researchers reveal after the experiment is over as well as before it begins?

Practice Exercises

1. Pair up with one other student and select one of the research articles you have reviewed for other exercises. Criticize the research in terms of its adherence to each of the ethical principles for research on human subjects, as well as for the authors' apparent honesty, openness, and consideration of educational consequences. Be generally negative but not unreasonable in your criticisms. The student with whom you are working should critique the article in the same way but from a generally positive standpoint, defending its adherence to the five guidelines but without ignoring the study's weak points. Together, write a summary of the study's strong and weak points, or conduct a debate in the class.

2. Investigate the standards and operations of your university's IRB. Interview one IRB member and one researcher whose research has been reviewed by the IRB (after receiving the appropriate permissions!). How well do typical IRB meetings work to identify the ethical issues in proposed research? Do researchers feel that their proposals are treated fairly? Why or why not?

Web Exercises

1. The Collaborative Institutional Training Initiative (CITI) offers an extensive online training course on the basics of human subjects protections issues. Go to the public access CITI site at https://www.citiprogram.org/rcrpage and complete the course on social and behavioral research. Write a short summary of what you have learned.

2. The U.S. Department of Health and Human Services maintains extensive resources concerning the protection of human subjects in research. Read several documents that you find on its website, www.hhs.gov/ohrp, and write a short report about them.

Developing a Research Proposal

Now it's time to consider the potential ethical issues in your proposed study and the research philosophy that will guide your research. The following exercises involve very critical "Decisions in Research":

1. List the elements in your research plans that an IRB might consider to be relevant to the protection of human subjects. Rate each element from 1 to 5, where 1 indicates no more than a minor ethical issue and 5 indicates a major ethical problem that probably cannot be resolved.

2. Draft a consent form to be administered to your subjects when they enroll in your research. Use underlining and marginal notes to indicate where each standard for informed consent statements is met. Start by checking to see if your university posts a sample consent form on its website. It will probably be under either the institutional review board (IRB) or the office of Research, Grants, and Contracts.

CHAPTER 4

Conceptualization and Measurement

Research Question: *What Do We Mean by "At Risk"?*

Chapter Contents

- **Concepts**
- **Measurement Operations**
- **Levels of Measurement**
- **Evaluating Measures**

"At-risk" students are an educational concern of large proportions. By one definition, 46% of U.S. children are at risk for one reason or another (Kominski, Jamieson, & Martinez, 2001, p. 4). Compared to other students, at-risk students can be in greater danger of having low academic performance, dropping out of school, abusing drugs or alcohol, and displaying antisocial behavior such as participation in gangs.

Teachers, counselors, administrators, coaches—practically anyone involved in education—work with at-risk students at some point. They often find they need to learn more about at-risk students by reading the research or perhaps even conducting research of their own. To read intelligently or to design a study, one must answer two questions: "What is meant by *at risk* in this research?" (the conceptualization issue) and "How was at-riskness measured?" (the operationalization issue). Both types of questions must be answered when we evaluate prior research, and both types of questions must be kept in the forefront when we design new research. It is only when we conclude that a study used valid measures of its key concepts that we can have some hope that its conclusions are valid.

In this chapter, we first address the issue of **conceptualization,** using at-riskness and related concepts as examples. We then focus on measurement, reviewing first how measures of at risk have been constructed using operations such as available data, questions, observations, and less direct and obtrusive measures.

We then discuss the different possible levels of measurement and methods for assessing the validity and reliability of measures. The final topic is to consider the unique insights that qualitative methods can add to the measurement process. By the chapter's end, you should have a good understanding of measurement, the first of the three legs on which a research project's validity rests.

回 Concepts

Although the statistics on at-risk students sound scary, we need to be clear about what they mean before we jump in and try to solve the problem. Here are three different definitions of *at risk*:

1. Researchers often use the socioeconomic status of students' homes and of the schools they attend as an indicator of academic risk. Using this definition, in addition to low economic status, students identified as most at risk in a study by Finn (2006, pp. iii–iv) shared these characteristics: were minority status, attended urban or rural public schools, were from non-English-speaking homes, and were not living with both biological parents.

2. The federal government's Educational Resources Information Clearinghouse (ERIC, 2008) defines at-risk students as "students considered in danger of not graduating, being promoted, or meeting other education-related goals. Risk factors may include, but are not limited to, socioeconomic status; academic background; behavior, cognitive, or physical problems; family or community environment; and school capacity to meet student needs."

3. The U.S. Department of Education's National Institute on the Education of At-Risk Students (2002) states that its mission is "to improve the education of students at risk of educational failure because of limited English proficiency, poverty, race, geographic location, or economic disadvantage."

Conceptualization: The process of specifying what we mean by a term. In deductive research, conceptualization helps to translate portions of an abstract theory into specific variables that can be used in testable hypotheses. In inductive research, conceptualization is an important part of the process used to make sense of related observations.

Notice that these definitions largely overlap but that each contains at least one element that is not included in the other two. The first definition includes minority status; the second contains specific mention of behavior, cognitive, or physical problems; and the third mentions geographic location. There is no single definition that everyone agrees with. This means that "at risk" is a concept—a mental image that summarizes a set of similar observations, feelings, or ideas. To make that concept useful in research (and even in ordinary discourse), we have to define it.

This will become obvious once you realize that many concepts are used without consistent definition, that definitions are themselves often the object of intense debate, and that the meanings of concepts may change over time.

Concepts such as "at risk," "behavior problem," and "poverty" require an explicit definition before they are used in research because we cannot be certain that all readers will share a particular definition or that the current meaning of the concept is the same as it was when previous research was published. It is especially important to define clearly concepts that are abstract or unfamiliar. When we refer to concepts such as "at risk," "behavior problem," or "poverty," we cannot count on others knowing exactly what we mean. Even experts may disagree about the meaning of frequently used concepts if they base their conceptualizations on different theories. That's okay. The point is not that there can be only one definition of a concept but that we have to specify clearly what we mean when we use a concept, and we must expect others to do the same.

Conceptualization in Practice

If we are to do an adequate job of conceptualizing, we must do more than just think up some definition, any definition, for our concepts. We have to turn to educational theory and prior research to review appropriate definitions. We may need to distinguish subconcepts, or dimensions, of the concept. We should understand how the definition we choose fits within the theoretical framework guiding the research and what assumptions underlie this framework.

At-Risk Students

What observations or images should we associate with the concept "at risk"? A 10th grader giving up on a state assessment test because he knows he'll fail? A middle school student passing out on Saturday night from too much to drink? A high school freshman constantly suspended for acting out and not paying attention? Do all of these images share something in common that we should define as "at-riskness" for the purposes of a particular research study? Should we take into account cultural and linguistic differences? Social situations? Medical conditions?

Many researchers would agree with the North Central Regional Educational Laboratory (1996):

> The question of what it means to be "at risk" is controversial. When children do not succeed in school, educators and others disagree about who or what is to blame. Because learning is a process that takes place both inside and outside school, an ecological approach offers a working description of the term *at risk*. In this view, inadequacies in any arena of life—the school, the home, or the community—can contribute to academic failure when not compensated for in another arena.

We should recognize that this definition reflects a particular theoretical orientation, the "ecological approach." The ecological approach emphasizes an all-around view that looks not just at what happens to the student in school but at the home and the community as well. How we conceptualize reflects how we theorize.

Just as we can connect concepts to theory, we also can connect them to other concepts. What this means is that the definition of any one concept rests on a shared understanding of the other terms used in the definition. So if our audience does not already have a shared understanding of a term such as *academic failure,* we must also define that term before we are finished with the process of defining at-riskness.

Poverty

One factor closely associated with at-riskness is poverty. But what exactly does this mean? What is the effect of poverty on America's schoolchildren? We know that "children represent a disproportionate share of the poor in the United States; they are 25 percent of the total population, but 35 percent of the poor population. In 2008, 15.45 million children, or 20.7 percent, were poor." (National Poverty Center, 2009). We also know that child poverty rates vary widely depending on race and ethnicity (see Exhibit 4. 1).

By any definition, family poverty is an academic risk factor: A correlation between poverty and school performance has long been accepted as fact. But there are various ways to define and calculate poverty, each with its own consequences. Exhibit 4.1 gives the results of the standard method used by the U.S. Census Bureau. But in education, "School poverty rates are defined as the percentage of students eligible to receive free or reduced-price lunches" (Roosa, Deng, Nair, & Burrell, 2005, p. 971). This conception makes it fairly simple to calculate whether a school is "high poverty" or not, an important factor in federal reimbursement formulas. High-poverty schools are more likely to have negative characteristics such as fewer resources, less qualified teachers, and lower academic achievement even among students who have a family income above the poverty line. But the "free or reduced-lunch" definition does little to explain the mechanisms by which poverty affects

Exhibit 4.1	Child Poverty in the United States, 2008

Children Younger Than Age 18 Living in Poverty, 2008		
Category	Number (in Thousands)	Percentage
All children younger than age 18	15,451	20.7
White only, non-Hispanic	4,850	11.9
Black	4,480	35.4
Hispanic	5,610	33.1
Asian	531	13.3

Source: U.S. Census Bureau (2009, pp. 62–67).

student performance or what the relationship is between family and neighborhood dynamics and school attitudes related to poverty. Because poverty can be viewed in so many ways—as family centered, neighborhood centered, or job centered, for instance—many conceptualizations of it exist.

Decisions about how to define a concept reflect the theoretical framework guiding the researchers. Different conceptualizations of poverty lead to different estimates of its prevalence and different educational policies for responding to its effects on schooling.

Most of the statistics that you see in the newspaper about the poverty rate reflect a conception of poverty that was formalized by Mollie Orshansky of the Social Security Administration in 1965 and subsequently adopted by the federal government and many researchers (Putnam, 1977). Orshansky (1977) defined poverty in terms of what is called an *absolute* standard, based on the amount of money required to purchase an emergency diet that is estimated to be nutritionally adequate for about 2 months (see Exhibit 4.2). The idea is that people are truly poor if they can just barely purchase the food they need and other essential goods. This poverty standard is adjusted for household size and composition (number of children and adults), and the minimal amount of money needed for food is multiplied by three because a 1955 survey indicated that poor families spend about one-third of their incomes on food (Orshansky, 1977). The graph in Exhibit 4.2 shows a relative standard of poverty, with the *x*-axis showing a distribution of annual incomes that goes from 0 to $120,000. Using a relative standard, the number of people in poverty (the area shown under the curve on the graph) varies at each income level.

Some researchers disagree with the absolute standard and have instead urged adoption of a *relative* poverty standard. They identify the poor as those in the lowest 5th or 10th percentile of the income distribution or as those having some fraction of the average income. The idea behind this relative conception is that poverty should be defined in terms of what is normal in a given society at a particular time.

Some researchers prefer yet another conception of poverty. With the *subjective* approach, poverty is defined as what people think would be the minimal income they need to make ends meet. Of course, many have argued that this approach is influenced too much by the different standards that people use to estimate what they "need" (Ruggles, 1990, pp. 20–23).

The conceptualization of poverty is still very much an open question. In the 1990s, some researchers proposed increasing the absolute standard for poverty so that it reflects what a low-income family must spend to maintain a "socially acceptable standard of living" that allows for a telephone, house repairs, and decent

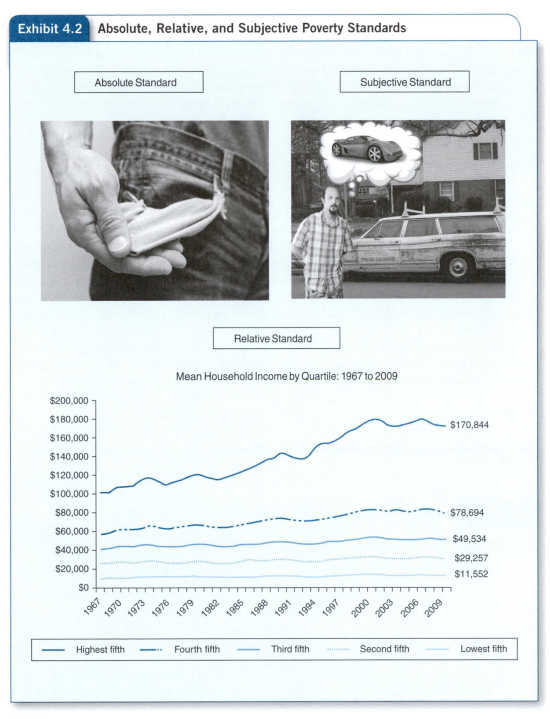

Exhibit 4.2 Absolute, Relative, and Subjective Poverty Standards

Absolute Standard

Subjective Standard

Relative Standard

Mean Household Income by Quartile: 1967 to 2009

$170,844

$78,694

$49,534

$29,257

$11,552

Highest fifth — Fourth fifth — Third fifth — Second fifth — Lowest fifth

Source: Schutt (2012).

clothes (Uchitelle, 1999). In 2009, in response to perceived limitations in the official measure, the U.S. Census Bureau began developing the Supplemental Poverty Measure, an experimental alternative method of calculating poverty (Short, 2011).

Which do you think is a more reasonable approach to defining poverty: some type of absolute standard, a relative standard, or a subjective standard? Be careful here: Conceptualization has consequences! Research using the standard absolute concept of poverty indicated that the percentage of Americans in poverty declined by 1.7% in the 1990s, but use of a relative concept of poverty led to the conclusion that poverty increased by 2.7% (Mayrl et al., 2004, p. 10). No matter which conceptualization we decide to adopt, our understanding of the concept of poverty will be sharpened after we consider these alternative definitions.

From Concepts to Observations

Operationalization: The process of specifying the operations that will indicate the value of cases on a variable.

Identifying the concepts we will study, specifying dimensions of these concepts, and defining their meaning only begins the process of connecting our ideas to concrete observations. If we are to conduct empirical research involving a concept, we must be able to distinguish it in the world around us and determine how it may change over time or differ between persons or locations. **Operationalization** is the process of connecting concepts to observations. You can think of it as the empirical counterpart of the process of conceptualization. When we conceptualize, we specify what we mean by a term (see Exhibit 4.3). When we operationalize, we identify specific observations that we will take to indicate that concept in empirical reality.

Exhibit 4.3 illustrates conceptualization and operationalization by using the concept of "social control," which Donald Black (1984) defines as "all of the processes by which people define and respond to deviant behavior" (p. xi). What observations can indicate this conceptualization of social control? Billboards that condemn drunk driving? Proportion of persons arrested in a community? Average length of sentences for crimes? Should we distinguish formal social control such as laws and police actions from informal types of social control such as social stigma? If we are to conduct research on the concept of social control, we must identify empirical indicators that are pertinent to our theoretical concerns.

Exhibit 4.3	**Conceptualization and Operationalization of Social Control**

Concept	Definition	Types	Possible Operational Indicators
Social Control	The normative aspect of social life[a]	Law	Legal rules; punishments; police stops
		Etiquette	Handbooks
		Customs	Gossip; aphorisms
		Bureaucracy	Official conduct rules; promotion procedures
		Psychiatric treatment	Rules for dangerousness; competency hearings

Source: Based on Black (1976).

a. Specifically, "the definition of deviant behavior and the response to it" (Black, 1976, p. 2).

Concepts vary in their level of abstraction, and this, in turn, affects how readily we can specify the indicators pertaining to the concept. We may not think twice before we move from a conceptual definition of "age" as time elapsed since birth to the concrete indicator "years since birth." "Binge drinking," a phenomenon associated with risk of academic failure at the high school and college levels, is also a relatively concrete concept, but it requires a bit more thought (see Exhibit 4.4). Most researchers define binge drinking conceptually as heavy episodic drinking and operationally as drinking five or more drinks in a row (for men) (Wechsler et al., 2002, p. 205). That's pretty straightforward, although we still need to specify the questions that will be used to determine frequency of drinking.

A very abstract concept such as social status may have a clear role in educational theory but a variety of meanings in different social settings. Clearly, at the lower end of the spectrum, poverty frequently translates to low social status. Indicators that pertain to social status may include level of esteem in a group, extent of influence over others, level of income and education, or number of friends. It is very important to specify what we mean by an abstract concept such as social status in a particular study and to choose appropriate indicators to represent this meaning.

You have already learned in Chapter 2 that variables are phenomena that vary. Usually, the term *variable* is used to refer to some specific aspect of a concept that varies and for which we then have to select even more concrete indicators. For example, in a study on poverty, research on the *concept* of social support might focus on the *variable* level of perceived support, and we might then select as our *indicator* the responses to a series of statements about social support, such as this one from the "Interpersonal Support Evaluation List" by Cohen, Mermelstein, Kamarck, and Hoberman (1985): "If I needed a quick emergency loan of $100, there is someone I could get it from" (p. 93). Identifying the variables we will measure is a necessary step on the road to developing our specific measurement procedures.

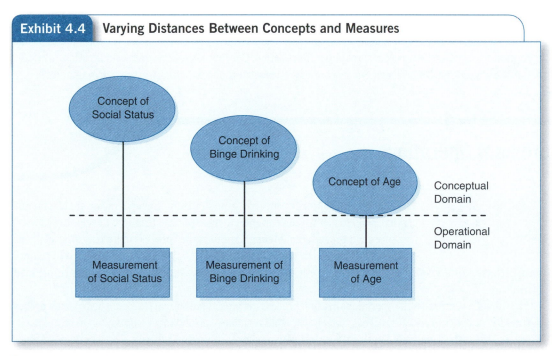

Exhibit 4.4 Varying Distances Between Concepts and Measures

Source: Adapted from Viswanathan (2005, p. 7).

Bear in mind that concepts don't necessarily vary. For example, gender may be an important concept in a study of influences on school attendance, but it isn't a variable in a study of students on the boys' volleyball team. When we explain school attendance patterns for the team, we might attach great importance to the all-male team subculture. However, because gender doesn't vary in this setting, we won't be able to study differences in attendance between male and female students. So, gender will be a **constant,** not a variable, in this study (unless we expand our sample to include both the boys' volleyball and girls' volleyball teams).

How do we know what concepts to consider and then which variables to include in a study? It's very tempting to simply try to measure everything by including in a study every variable we can think of that might have something to do with our research question. This haphazard approach will inevitably result in the collection of some data that are useless and the failure to collect some data that are important. Instead, a careful researcher will examine relevant theories to identify key concepts, review prior research to learn how useful different indicators have been, and assess the resources available for measuring adequately variables in the specific setting to be studied.

From Observations to Concepts

Qualitative research projects usually take an inductive approach to the process of conceptualization. In an inductive approach, concepts emerge from the process of thinking about what has been observed, as compared to the deductive approach that just described, in which we develop concepts on the basis of theory and then decide what should be observed to indicate that concept. So instead of deciding in advance which concepts are important for a study, what these concepts mean, and how they should be measured, if you take an inductive approach, you will begin by recording verbatim what you hear in intensive interviews or see during observational sessions. You will then review this material to identify important concepts and their meaning for participants. At this point, you may identify relevant variables and develop procedures for indicating variation between participants and settings or variation over time.

Qualitative researchers often develop key concepts inductively, in the course of the research, and continue to refine and evaluate the concepts throughout the research. Conceptualization, operationalization, and validation are ongoing and interrelated processes. You will learn more about qualitative research in Chapter 9.

▣ Measurement Operations

Operation: A procedure for identifying or indicating the value of cases on a variable.

The deductive researcher proceeds from defining concepts in the abstract (conceptualizing) to identifying variables to measure and finally to developing specific measurement procedures. **Measurement** is the "process of linking abstract concepts to empirical indicants" (Carmines & Zeller, 1979, p. 10). The goal is to achieve measurement validity, so the measurement **operations** must actually measure the variables they are intended to measure.

Exhibit 4.5 represents the operationalization process in three hypothetical studies. The first researcher defines his or her concept, at-riskness, and chooses one variable—attendance (truancy)—to represent it. This variable is then measured with a single indicator: school attendance records. The second researcher defines his or her concept, poverty, as having two aspects or dimensions: subjective poverty and absolute poverty. Subjective poverty is measured with responses to a survey question: "Would you say that you are poor?" Absolute poverty is measured by comparing family income to the poverty threshold. The third

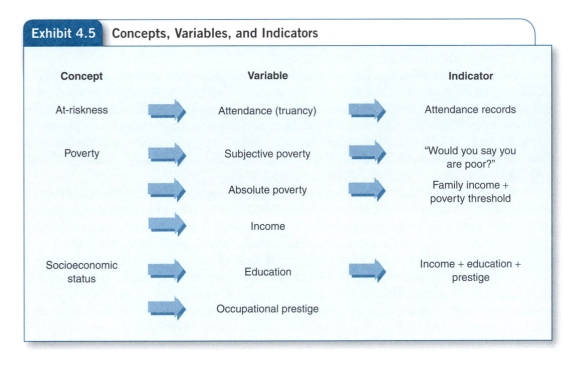

Exhibit 4.5   Concepts, Variables, and Indicators

researcher decides that her concept, social class, is defined by a position on three measured variables: income, education, and occupational prestige.

Educational researchers have many options for operationalizing concepts. Measures can be based on activities as diverse as asking people questions, observing classroom interactions, coding words in student work or policy documents, checking census data tapes, or analyzing test scores. Experimental researchers may operationalize a concept by manipulating its value. For example, to operationalize the concept of "exposure to antidrug messages," some subjects may listen to a talk about the evils of drug use while others do not. We will focus here on the operations of using published data, asking questions, observing behavior, and using unobtrusive means of measuring people's behavior and attitudes.

The variables and particular measurement operations chosen for a study should be consistent with the research question. If we ask the evaluative research question, "Are peer mediation groups more effective than out-of-school suspension in reducing fights in high schools?" we may operationalize "school antiviolence programs" in terms of the effect of these two types of approaches. However, if we are attempting to answer the explanatory research question, "What influences the success of peer mediation programs?" we should probably consider what it is about these programs that is associated with successful prevention of violence. Prior theory and research suggest that peer mediation provides students with negotiation strategies that help them to control their behavior and short-circuit violence before it starts, resulting in fewer overall suspensions from school (D. W. Johnson & Johnson, 1996).

Time and resource limitations also must be taken into account when we select variables and devise measurement operations. For many sociohistorical questions (such as "How has the poverty rate varied since 1950?"), census data or other published counts must be used.

Using Available Data

Government reports are rich and readily accessible sources of educational data. Organizations ranging from nonprofit service groups to private businesses also compile a wealth of figures that are often available for research purposes. In addition, the data collected in many educational evaluations and surveys, such as the National Assessment of Educational Progress (NAEP), are archived and made available for researchers who were not involved in the original assessment or survey project.

Before we assume that available data will be useful, we must consider how appropriate they are for our concepts of interest. We may conclude that some other measure would provide a better fit with a concept or that a particular concept simply cannot adequately be operationalized with the available data. For example, family poverty is an important component of at-riskness. But definitions and methods for measuring poverty vary widely. One study of this definitional problem concluded that "most family scholars take the concept of poverty for granted. [But] the variety of ways people have chosen to measure this concept . . . makes it difficult to interpret or compare research results" (Roosa et al., 2005, p. 971).

We also cannot assume that available data are accurate, even when they appear to measure the concept in which we are interested in a way that is consistent across communities. "Official" counts of school dropouts at the local and state levels over time may be less than accurate because school systems can change the way they measure "dropping out" from year to year. This makes cross-state comparisons unreliable (P. Kaufman, Alt, & Chapman, 2001).

Online resources such as the *Basic Family Budget Calculator* of the Economic Policy Institute (http://www.epi.org/content/budget_calculator/) and the *Kids Count Online Data Snapshot Series* of the Annie E. Casey Foundation (http://www.aecf.org/kidscount/) present public statistics from a variety of state and federal sources in highly accessible, user-configurable formats. Poverty rates, relative family income measures, childhood obesity statistics, and a plethora of other information on the well-being of children and families are instantly available on these and other websites.

Constructing Questions

Asking people questions is the most common and probably the most versatile operation for measuring educational variables. Most concepts about individuals can be defined in such a way that measurement with one or more questions becomes an option. We associate questions with survey research, but questions are also often the basis of measures used in educational experiments and in qualitative research. In this section, we'll introduce some options for writing single questions; in Chapter 8, we'll explain why single questions can be inadequate measures of some concepts, and then we'll examine measurement approaches that rely on multiple questions to measure a concept.

In practice, questions can sometimes yield misleading or inappropriate answers. Memories and perceptions of events can be limited, and some respondents may intentionally give misleading answers. All questions proposed for a study must be screened carefully for their adherence to basic guidelines and then tested and revised until the researcher feels some confidence that they will be clear to the intended respondents and likely to measure the intended concept (Fowler, 1995). Specific guidelines for reviewing questions are presented in Chapter 9; here our focus is on the different types of questions used in educational research.

Measuring variables with single questions is very popular. Public opinion polls based on answers to single questions are reported frequently in newspaper articles and TV newscasts: "Do you favor or oppose U.S. policy in. . . ?" "If you had to vote today, for which candidate would you vote?" Educational research surveys also rely on single questions to measure many variables: "Overall, how satisfied are you with teaching as a career?" "How would you rate your current principal?"

Single questions can be designed with or without explicit response choices. The question that follows is a **closed-ended (fixed-choice) question** because respondents are offered explicit responses to choose from. It deals with an important educational and personal risk factor for college students, alcohol abuse. It has been selected from the Core Alcohol and Drug Survey distributed by the Core Institute, Southern Illinois University, for the Fund for the Improvement of Postsecondary Education (FIPSE) Core Analysis Grantee Group (Presley, Meilman, & Lyerla, 1994).

Compared to other campuses with which you are familiar, this campus's use of alcohol is . . . (*Mark one*)

____ Greater than other campuses

____ Less than other campuses

____ About the same as other campuses

Most surveys of a large number of people contain primarily fixed-choice questions, which are easy to process with computers and analyze with statistics. With fixed-choice questions, respondents are also more likely to answer the question that the researcher really wants them to answer. Including response choices reduces ambiguity and makes it easier for respondents to answer. However, fixed-response choices can obscure what people really think if the choices do not match the range of possible responses to the question; many studies show that some respondents will choose response choices that do not apply to them simply to give some sort of answer (Peterson, 2000, p. 39).

Most important, response choices should be **mutually exclusive** and exhaustive, so that every respondent can find one and only one choice that applies to him or her (unless the question is of the "Check all that apply" format). To make response choices exhaustive, researchers may need to offer at least one option with room for ambiguity. For example, a questionnaire asking college students to indicate their school status should not use freshman, sophomore, junior, senior, and graduate student as the only response choices. Most campuses also have students in a "special" category, so you might add "Other (please specify)" to the five fixed responses to this question. If respondents do not find a response option that corresponds to their answer to the question, they may skip the question entirely or choose a response option that does not indicate what they are really thinking.

Researchers who study small numbers of people often use **open-ended questions,** which don't have explicit response choices and allow respondents to write in their answers. The next question is an open-ended version of the earlier fixed-choice question:

How would you say alcohol use on this campus compares to that on other campuses?

An open-ended format is preferable when the full range of responses cannot be anticipated, especially when questions have not been used previously in surveys or when questions are asked of new groups. Open-ended questions also can allow clear answers when questions involve complex concepts. In the previous question, for instance, "alcohol use" may cover how many students drink, how heavily they drink, if they drink in public or not, if drinking affects levels of violence on campus, and so on.

Just like fixed-choice questions, open-ended questions should be reviewed carefully for clarity before they are used. For example, if respondents are just asked, "When did you move to Boston?" they might respond with a wide range of answers: "In 1944," "After I had my first child," "When I was 10," "20 years ago." Such answers would be very hard to compile. A careful review should identify potential ambiguity. To avoid it, rephrase the question to guide the answer in a certain direction, such as, "In what year did you move to Boston?" or provide explicit response choices (Center for Survey Research, 1987).

Making Observations

Observations can be used to measure characteristics of individuals, events, and places. The observations may be the primary form of measurement in a study, or they may supplement measures obtained through questioning.

Direct observations can be used as indicators of some concepts, such as disability. For example, you may recall the study cited in Chapter 1, in which Erwin et al. (1999) studied interactions between 3-year-old Ryan, a physically disabled student, and his classmates. The research team observed the classroom once a month for a full year, developing a coding form with notations for frequently observed behaviors such as how many contacts occurred between Ryan and other students, who initiated the contacts, and whether they were verbal, physical, or both.

Observations may also supplement data collected in an interview study. This approach was used in a study of school satisfaction among 61 poor, at-risk African American third- through fifth-grade students in a large urban district in the southeast United States (Baker, 1999). Each student filled out a self-report survey and participated in a 15-minute structured interview by a trained researcher to try to judge their satisfaction with the school. The same researcher then observed the students in a classroom setting, coding teacher-student interaction into four categories: (1) student initiated contact regarding academic work, (2) teacher initiated contact regarding academic work, (3) teacher-initiated contact regarding behavior, and (4) procedural contact (Baker, 1999). The researcher concluded that the findings indicated that "although much previous research has focused on adolescents, in this study clear distinctions were evident in school satisfaction by third grade" (p. 67).

Direct observation is often the method of choice for measuring behavior in natural settings, as long as it is possible to make the requisite observations. Direct observation avoids the problems of poor recall and self-serving distortions that can occur with answers to survey questions. It also allows measurement in a context that is more natural than an interview. But observations can be distorted, too. Observers do not see or hear everything, and what they do see is filtered by their own senses and perspectives. When the goal is to observe behavior, measurement can be distorted because the presence of an observer may cause people to act differently from the way they would otherwise (Emerson, 1983). We will discuss these issues in more depth in Chapter 9, but it is important to consider them whenever you read about observational measures.

Collecting Unobtrusive Measures

Unobtrusive measures allow us to collect data about individuals or groups without their direct knowledge or participation. In their classic book (now revised), Webb, Campbell, Schwartz, and Sechrest (2000) identified four types of unobtrusive measures: physical trace evidence, archives (available data), simple observation, and contrived observation (using hidden recording hardware or manipulation to elicit a response). These measures can provide valuable supplements or alternatives to more standard, survey-based measures because they lessen the possibility that respondents will make different statements to an interviewer than when they are not being studied and because they are unaffected by an interviewer's appearance or how he or she asks questions. We have already considered some types of archival data and observational data, so we will focus here on other approaches suggested by Webb et al.

The physical traces of past behavior are one type of unobtrusive measure that is most useful when the behavior of interest cannot be directly observed (perhaps because it is hidden or occurred in the past) and has not been recorded in a source of available data. To measure the prevalence of drinking in college dorms or fraternity houses, we might count the number of empty bottles of alcoholic beverages in the surrounding dumpsters. Student interest in the college courses they are taking might be measured by counting the number of times that books left on reserve as optional reading are checked out or by the number of class handouts left in trash barrels outside a lecture hall.

Unobtrusive measures can also be created from such diverse forms of media as newspaper archives or magazine articles, historical documents, policy reports, or e-mail messages. Qualitative researchers may read and evaluate text. Quantitative researchers use content analysis to measure aspects of media such as the frequency of using particular words or ideas or the consistency with which authors convey a particular message in their stories.

Combining Measurement Operations

Using available data, asking questions, making observations, and using unobtrusive indicators are interrelated measurement tools, each of which may include or be supplemented by the others. The choice of a particular measurement method is often determined by available resources and opportunities, but measurement is improved if this choice also takes into account the particular concept or concepts to be measured. Responses to questions such as, "How engaged are you in class?" or "How many days were you absent last year?" are unlikely to provide information as valid as, respectively, direct observation or school records. On the other hand, observations in class may not answer our questions about why some students do not participate; we may have to ask them. However, questioning can be a particularly poor approach for measuring behaviors that are very socially desirable, such as voting or attending church, or that are socially stigmatized or illegal, such as abusing alcohol or drugs.

Triangulation—the use of two or more different measures of the same variable—can strengthen measurement considerably (Brewer & Hunter, 1989, p. 17). We will see several school-based examples of triangulation used by teacher researchers in Chapter 12. When we achieve similar results with different measures of the same variable, particularly when they are based on such different methods as survey questions and field-based observations, we can be more confident in the validity of each measure. If results diverge with different measures, it may indicate that one or more of these measures are influenced by more measurement error than we can tolerate. Divergence between measures could also indicate that they actually operationalize different concepts.

▣ Levels of Measurement

When we know a variable's **level of measurement,** we can better understand how cases vary on that variable and so understand more fully what we have measured. Level of measurement also has important implications for the type of statistics that can be used with the variable, as you will learn in Chapter 13. There are four levels of measurement: nominal, ordinal, interval, and ratio. Exhibit 4.6 depicts the differences among these four levels.

> **Level of measurement:** The mathematical precision with which the values of a variable can be expressed. The nominal level of measurement, which is qualitative, has no mathematical interpretation; the quantitative levels of measurement—ordinal, interval, and ratio—are progressively more precise mathematically.

Nominal Level of Measurement

The **nominal level of measurement** (also called the categorical or qualitative level) identifies variables whose values have no mathematical interpretation; they vary in kind or quality but not in amount. In fact, it is conventional to refer to the values of nominal variables as "attributes" instead of values. "State" (referring to the United States) is one example. The variable has 50 attributes (or categories or qualities). We might indicate specific states with numbers, so that California might be represented by the value 1 and Oregon with the value 2 and so on, but these numbers do not tell us anything about the difference between the states except that they are different. California is not one unit more of "state" than Oregon, nor is it twice as much "state." Nationality, occupation, religious affiliation, and region of the country are also measured at the nominal level. A person may be Spanish or Portuguese, but one nationality does not represent more nationality than another—just a different nationality (see Exhibit 4.6). A person may be a doctor or a truck driver, but one does not represent three units more occupation than the other.

Exhibit 4.6 Levels of Measurement

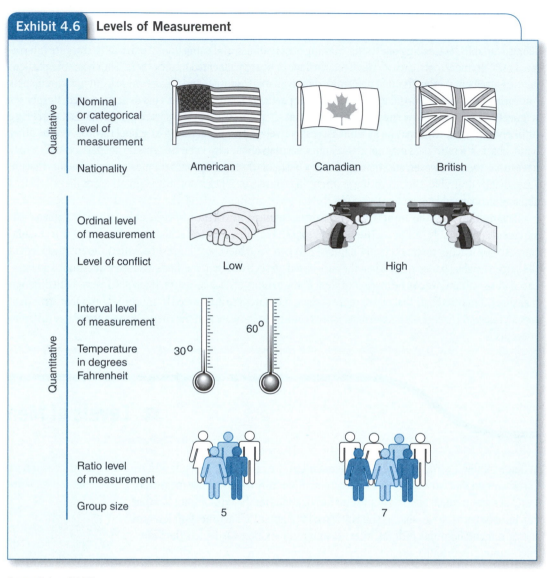

Source: Schutt (2009).

Although the attributes of categorical variables do not have a mathematical meaning, they must be assigned to cases with great care. The attributes we use to measure, or categorize, cases must be mutually exclusive and exhaustive:

- A variable's attributes or values are mutually exclusive if every case can have only one attribute.

- A variable's attributes or values are exhaustive when every case can be classified into one of the categories.

When a variable's attributes are mutually exclusive and exhaustive, every case corresponds to one, and only one, attribute.

Ordinal Level of Measurement

The first of the three quantitative levels is the **ordinal level of measurement.** At this level, you specify only the order of the cases in "greater than" and "less than" distinctions. At the coffee shop, for example, you might choose between a small, medium, or large cup of decaf—that's ordinal measurement.

The properties of variables measured at the ordinal level are illustrated in Exhibit 4.6 by the contrast in the level of conflict in two groups. The first group, symbolized by the people shaking hands, has a low level of conflict. The second group, symbolized by two people pointing guns at each other, has a high level of conflict. To measure conflict, we could put the groups "in order" by assigning 1 to the low-conflict group and 2 to the high-conflict group, but the numbers would indicate only the relative position, or order, of the cases.

As with nominal variables, the different values of ordinal variables must be mutually exclusive and exhaustive. They must cover the range of observed values and allow each case to be assigned no more than one value.

Interval Level of Measurement

At the **interval level of measurement,** numbers represent fixed measurement units but have no absolute zero point. This level of measurement is represented in Exhibit 4.6 by the difference between two Fahrenheit temperatures. Note, for example, that 60 degrees is 30 degrees hotter than 30 degrees, but 60 is not "twice as hot" as 30. Why not? Because heat does not "begin" at 0 degrees on the Fahrenheit scale. The numbers can therefore be added and subtracted, but ratios of them (2 to 1 or "twice as much") are not meaningful.

Sometimes, though, researchers will create indexes by combining responses to a series of variables measured at the ordinal level and then treat these indexes as interval-level measures. An **index** of this sort could be created with responses to the Core Institute's (1994) questions about friends' disapproval of substance use (see Exhibit 4.7). The survey has 13 questions on the topic, each of which has the same three response choices. If "Don't disapprove" is valued at 1, "Disapprove" is valued at 2, and "Strongly disapprove" is valued at 3, the summed index of disapproval would range from 12 to 36. A score of 20 could be treated as if it were four more units than a score of 16. Or the responses could be averaged to retain the original 1 to 3 range.

Ratio Level of Measurement

A **ratio level of measurement** represents fixed measuring units and an absolute zero point. Zero, in this situation, means absolutely no amount of whatever the variable indicates. On a ratio scale, 10 is 2 points higher than 8 and is also 2 times as great as 5. Ratio numbers can be added and subtracted, and because the numbers begin at an absolute zero point, they can be multiplied and divided (so ratios can be formed between the numbers). For example, people's ages can be represented by values ranging from 0 years (or some fraction of a year) to 120 or more. A person who is 30 years old is 15 years older than someone who is 15 years old (30 − 15 = 15) and is also twice as old as that person (30/15 = 2). Of course, the numbers also are mutually exclusive and exhaustive, so that every case can be assigned one and only one value. Age (in years) is clearly a ratio-level measure.

Exhibit 4.6 displays an example of a variable measured at the ratio level. The number of people in the first group is 5, and the number in the second group is 7. The ratio of the two groups' sizes is then 1.4, a number that mirrors the relationship between the sizes of the groups. Note that there does not actually have to be any group with a size of 0; what is important is that the numbering scheme begins at an absolute zero—in this case, the absence of any people.

Exhibit 4.7 | **Example of Interval-Level Measures: Core Alcohol and Drug Survey**

26. **How do you think your close friends feel (or would feel) about you...**
    (mark one for each line)

    | | Don't disapprove | Disapprove | Strongly disapprove |

    a. Trying marijuana once or twice . . . . ○ ○ ○
    b. Smoking marijuana occasionally . . . . ○ ○ ○
    c. Smoking marijuana regularly . . . . ○ ○ ○
    d. Trying cocaine once or twice . . . . ○ ○ ○
    e. Taking cocaine regularly . . . . ○ ○ ○
    f. Trying LSD once or twice . . . . ○ ○ ○
    g. Taking LSD regularly . . . . ○ ○ ○
    h. Trying amphetamines once or twice . . . . ○ ○ ○
    i. Taking amphetamines regularly . . . . ○ ○ ○
    j. Taking one or two drinks of an alcoholic beverage (beer, wine, liquor) nearly every day . . . . ○ ○ ○
    k. Taking four or five drinks nearly every day . . . . ○ ○ ○
    l. Having five or more drinks in one sitting . . . . . . ○ ○ ○
    m. Taking steroids for body building or improved athletic performance . . . . ○ ○ ○

Source: Core Institute (1994, p. 3).

Note: Responses could be combined to create an interval scale (see text).

Exhibit 4.8 | **Properties of Measurement Levels**

Examples of Comparison Statements	Appropriate Math Operations	Relevant Level of Measurement			
		Nominal	Ordinal	Interval	Ratio
A is equal to (not equal to) *B*	= (≠)	✓	✓	✓	✓
A is greater than (less than) *B*	> (<)		✓	✓	✓
A is three more than (less than) *B*	+ (−)			✓	✓
A is twice (half) as large as *B*	× (÷)				✓

Source: Schutt (2009).

Comparison of Levels of Measurement

Exhibit 4.8 summarizes the types of comparisons that can be made with different levels of measurement, as well as the mathematical operations that are legitimate. All four levels of measurement allow researchers to assign different values to different cases. All three quantitative measures allow researchers to rank cases in order.

Researchers choose levels of measurement in the process of operationalizing variables; the level of measurement is not inherent in the variable itself. Many variables can be measured at different levels, with different procedures. Age can be measured as "young" or "old"; as 0–10, 11–20, 21–30, and so on; or as 1, 2, or 3 years old. We could gather the data by asking people their age, by having an observer guess (Now *there's* an old guy), or by searching through hospital records for exact dates and times of birth. Any of these approaches could work, depending on our research goals.

It usually is a good idea to try to measure variables at the highest level of measurement possible. The more information available, the more ways we have to compare cases. We also have more possibilities for statistical analysis with quantitative than with qualitative variables. Even if your primary concern is only to compare teenagers to young adults, you should measure age in years rather than in categories; you can always combine the ages later into categories corresponding to "teenager" and "young adult."

Be aware, however, that other considerations may preclude measurement at a high level. For example, many people are very reluctant to report their exact incomes, even in anonymous questionnaires. So asking respondents to report their income in categories (such as under $10,000, $10,000–19,999, $20,000–29,999) will result in more responses, and thus more valid data, than asking respondents for their income in dollars.

🔲 Evaluating Measures

Do the operations developed to measure our variables actually do so—are they valid? If we have weighed our measurement options, carefully constructed our questions and observational procedures, and selected sensibly from the available data indicators, we should be on the right track. But we cannot have much confidence in a measure until we have empirically evaluated its validity. What good is our measure if it doesn't measure what we think it does? If our measurement procedure is invalid, we might as well go back to the starting block and try again. As part of evaluating the validity of our measures, we must also evaluate their reliability because reliability (consistency) is a prerequisite for measurement validity.

Measurement Validity

Measurement validity refers to the extent to which measures indicate what they are intended to measure. For instance, a good measure of a person's age is the current year minus the year given on that person's birth certificate. Very probably, the resulting number accurately represents the person's age. A less valid measure would be for the researcher to ask the person (who may lie or forget) or for the researcher to simply guess. Measurement validity can be assessed with four different approaches: face validation, content validation, criterion validation, and construct validation.

Face Validity

Researchers apply the term **face validity** to the confidence gained from careful inspection of a concept to see if it is appropriate "on its face." More precisely, we can say that a measure is face valid if it obviously pertains to the meaning of the concept being measured more than to other concepts (Brewer & Hunter, 1989, p. 131). For example, a count of the number of drinks people had consumed in the past week would be a face-valid measure of their alcohol consumption.

Although every measure should be inspected in this way, face validation in itself does not provide convincing evidence of measurement validity. The question "How much beer or wine did you have to drink last week?" looks valid on its face as a measure of frequency of drinking, but people who drink heavily tend to underreport the amount they drink. So the question would be an invalid measure, at least in a study of heavy drinkers.

Content Validity

Content validity establishes that the measure covers the full range of the concept's meaning. To determine that range of meaning, the researcher may solicit the opinions of experts and review literature that identifies the different aspects, or dimensions, of the concept.

Criterion Validity

Criterion validity is established when the scores obtained on one measure can be accurately compared to those obtained with a more direct or already validated measure of the same phenomenon (the "criterion"). A measure of blood alcohol concentration, for instance, could be the criterion for validating a self-report measure of drinking. In other words, if Jason says he hasn't been drinking, we establish criterion validity by giving him a "breathalyzer" test. Observations of drinking by friends or relatives could also, in some limited circumstances, serve as a criterion for validating a self-report.

The criterion that researchers select can be measured either at the same time as the variable to be validated or after that time. Concurrent validity exists when a measure yields scores that are closely related to scores on a criterion measured at the same time. A store might validate a test of sales ability by administering it to sales personnel who are already employed and then comparing their test scores to their sales performance. Or a measure of walking speed based on mental counting might be validated concurrently with a stopwatch. With predictive validity, a measure is validated by predicting scores on a criterion measured in the future—for instance, SAT scores are validated when they predict a student's college grades.

Criterion validation greatly increases our confidence that a measure works, but for many concepts of interest to educational researchers, it's difficult to find a criterion. If we are measuring subjective states, such as feelings of loneliness, what *direct* indicator could serve as a criterion? How do you know he or she is lonely? Even with variables for which a reasonable criterion exists, the researcher may not be able to gain access to the criterion—as would be the case with a tax return or employer document that we might wish we could use as a criterion for self-reported income.

Construct Validity

Measurement validity can also be established by showing that a measure is related to a variety of other measures as specified in a theory. This validation approach, known as **construct validity,** is commonly used in social and educational research when no clear criterion exists for validation purposes. For example, in one study of the validity of the Addiction Severity Index (ASI), A. Thomas McLellan and his associates (1985) compared subject scores on the ASI to a number of indicators that they felt, from prior research, should be related to substance abuse: medical problems, employment problems, legal problems, family problems, and psychiatric problems. They could not use a criterion validation approach because they did not have a more direct measure of abuse, such as laboratory test scores or observer reports. However, their extensive research on the subject had given them confidence that these sorts of problems were all related to substance abuse, and, indeed, they found that individuals with higher ASI ratings tended to have more problems in each of these areas.

Two other approaches to construct validation are convergent validation and discriminant validation. **Convergent validity** is achieved when one measure of a concept is associated with different types of measures of the same concept (this relies on the same type of logic as measurement triangulation). Discriminant validity is a complementary approach to construct validation. In this approach, scores on the measure to be validated are compared to scores on measures of different but related concepts. Discriminant validity is achieved if the measure to be validated is not associated strongly with the measures of different concepts.

The distinction between criterion validation and construct validation is not always clear. Opinions can differ about whether a particular indicator is indeed a criterion for the concept that is to be measured. What both construct validation and criterion validation have in common is the comparison of scores on one measure to scores on other measures that are predicted to be related. It is not so important that researchers agree that a particular comparison measure is a criterion rather than a related construct. But it is very important to think critically about the quality of the comparison measure and whether it actually represents a different view of the same phenomenon. For example, correspondence between scores on two different self-report measures of alcohol use is a much weaker indicator of measurement validity than the correspondence of a self-report measure with an observer-based measure of substance use.

Reliability

Reliability means that a measurement procedure yields consistent scores (or that the scores change only to reflect actual changes in the phenomenon). If a measure is reliable, it is affected less by random error, or chance variation, than if it is unreliable. Reliability is a prerequisite for measurement validity: We cannot really measure a phenomenon if the measure we are using gives inconsistent results. Let's say, for example, that you would like to know your weight and have decided on two different measures: the scale in the bathroom and your best friend's estimate. Clearly, the scale is more reliable, in the sense that it will show pretty much the same thing from one day to the next unless your weight actually changes. But your best friend may say, "You're so skinny!" on Sunday, but on Monday, when he or she is in a bad mood, say "You look terrible! Have you gained weight?" Your friend's estimates may bounce around quite a bit. The bathroom scale is not so fickle; it is *reliable*.

This doesn't mean that the weight given by the scale is *valid*—in fact, if the scale is spring-operated and old, it might be off by quite a few pounds. But it will be off by the same amount every day—hence not valid but *reliable* nevertheless.

There are four possible indications of unreliability. For example, a test of your knowledge of research methods would be unreliable if every time you took it, you received a different score even though your knowledge of research methods had not changed in the interim, not even as a result of taking the test more than once. This is test-retest reliability. Similarly, an index composed of questions to measure knowledge of research methods would be unreliable if respondents' answers to each question were totally independent of their answers to the others. The index has interitem reliability if the component items are closely related. A measure also would be unreliable if slightly different versions of it resulted in markedly different responses (it would not achieve alternate-forms reliability). Finally, an assessment of the level of at-riskness in a group of students would be unreliable if ratings of the level of at-riskness by two observers were not related to each other (it would then lack interobserver reliability).

Test-Retest Reliability

When researchers measure an unchanging phenomenon at two different times, the degree to which the two measurements are related to each other is the **test-retest reliability** of the measure. If you take a test of your math ability and then retake the test 2 months later, the test is reliable if you receive a similar score both times—presuming that your math ability stayed constant. Of course, if events between the test and the retest have changed the variable being measured, then the difference between the test and retest scores should reflect that change.

Interitem Reliability (Internal Consistency)

When researchers use multiple items to measure a single concept, they must be concerned with **interitem reliability** (or internal consistency). Suppose a 10th grader who has always had good attendance and a strong academic record suddenly shows a major change. She becomes withdrawn, begins to miss school frequently, and has trouble concentrating. The school counselor suspects depression based on a recent death in the family but wants some reliable, quantifiable data to support this assessment. The counselor may use a rating scale, but it must be reliable and quantifiable. For example, if we are to have confidence that a set of questions (such as those in Exhibit 4.9) reliably measures depression, the answers to the

Exhibit 4.9	**Examples of Indexes: Short Form of the Center for Epidemiologic Studies (CES-D) and "Negative Outlook" Index**		

At any time during the past week . . . (Circle one response on each line)	Never	Some of the Time	Most of the Time
a. Was your appetite so poor that you did not feel like eating?	1	2	3
b. Did you feel so tired and worn out that you could not enjoy anything?	1	2	3
c. Did you feel depressed?	1	2	3
d. Did you feel unhappy about the way your life is going?	1	2	3
e. Did you feel discouraged and worried about your future?	1	2	3
f. Did you feel lonely?	1	2	3
Negative outlook			
How often was each of these things true during the past week? (Circle one response on each line)	A Lot, Most, or All of the Time	Sometimes	Never or Rarely
a. You felt that you were just as good as other people.	0	1	2
b. You felt hopeful about the future.	0	1	2
c. You were happy.	0	1	2
d. You enjoyed life.	0	1	2

Source: Adapted from Radloff (1977, p. 387). Copyright 1977 by West Publishing Company/Applied Psychological Measurement, Inc.; reproduced by permission. Material also used from Hawkins et al. (2007).

questions should be highly associated with one another. The stronger the association is among the individual items and the more items that are included, the higher the reliability of the index will be.

Alternate-Forms Reliability

When researchers compare subjects' answers to slightly different versions of survey questions, they are testing alternate-forms reliability (Litwin, 1995, pp. 13–21). A researcher may reverse the order of the response choices in an index or modify the question wording in minor ways and then readminister that index to subjects. If the two sets of responses are not too different, alternate-forms reliability is established.

A related test of reliability is the **split-halves reliability** approach. A survey sample is divided in two by flipping a coin or using some other random assignment method. These two halves of the sample are then administered the two forms of the questions. If the responses of the two halves of the sample are about the same, the measure's reliability is established.

Interobserver Reliability

When researchers use more than one observer to rate the same people, events, or places, **interobserver reliability** is their goal. If observers are using the same instrument to rate the same thing, their ratings should be very similar. If they are similar, we can have much more confidence that the ratings reflect the phenomenon being assessed rather than the orientations of the observers.

Assessing interobserver reliability is most important when the rating task is complex. Consider the observation-of-play scale shown in Exhibit 4.10. The rating task seems straightforward, with clear descriptions of the subject characteristics that are supposed to lead to high or low scores. However, the judgments that the rater must make while using this scale are complex. They are affected by a wide range of subject characteristics, attitudes, and behaviors as well as by the rater's reactions. As a result, interobserver agreement can be low on complex scales, unless the raters are trained carefully.

▣ Can We Achieve Both Reliability and Validity?

The reliability and validity of measures in any study must be tested after the fact to assess the quality of the information obtained. But then, if it turns out that a measure cannot be considered reliable and valid, little can be done to save the study. Hence, it is supremely important to select, in the first place, measures that are likely to be reliable and valid.

Finding methods that are both reliable and valid can be challenging. Don't just choose the first measure you find or can think of: Consider the different strengths of different measures and their appropriateness to your study. Conduct a pretest in which you use the measure with a small sample, and check its reliability. Provide careful training to ensure a consistent approach if interviewers or observers will administer the measures. In most cases, however, the best strategy is to use measures that have been used before and whose reliability and validity have been established in other contexts. But the selection of "tried-and-true" measures still does not absolve researchers from the responsibility of testing the reliability and validity of the measure in their own studies.

Remember that a reliable measure is not necessarily a valid measure, as Exhibit 4.11 illustrates. This discrepancy is a common flaw of self-report measures of substance abuse. People's answers to the questions are consistent, but they are consistently misleading. A number of respondents will not admit to drinking, even though they drink a lot. The multiple questions in self-report indexes of substance abuse, a crucial issue for

Exhibit 4.10 The Challenge of Interobserver Reliability

Play Skills Rating Scale: Sample Checklist

Child's name: _____

Observation date: _____

Child's age: _____

Observation time: _____

Observed by: _____

Location: _____

Circle the number which most closely describes the child's play skills during this observation.

	(Circle One)				
	Never	←		→	**Always**
1. Appears to enjoy interacting with peers.	1	2	3	4	5
2. Able to enter play groups successfully.	1	2	3	4	5
3. Uses peer's name.	1	2	3	4	5
4. Communicates effectively with peers.	1	2	3	4	5
5. Able to lead play effectively.	1	2	3	4	5
6. Able to follow directions of others.	1	2	3	4	5
7. Able to share materials appropriately.	1	2	3	4	5
8. Able to solve social problems appropriately.	1	2	3	4	5
9. Able to get attention from other children.	1	2	3	4	5
10. Is accepted into play groups.	1	2	3	4	5
11. Plays with a variety of children.	1	2	3	4	5
12. Sought out by other children.	1	2	3	4	5
13. Able to choose play activity.	1	2	3	4	5
14. Appears engaged, involved.	1	2	3	4	5
15. Play is appropriately complex.	1	2	3	4	5
16. Shows enjoyment.	1	2	3	4	5
17. Adds to play, has ideas about activity.	1	2	3	4	5
18. Is creative in play.	1	2	3	4	5
19. Appears comfortable playing.	1	2	3	4	5
20. Interacts with make-believe activities.	1	2	3	4	5
21. Shows interest in different activities.	1	2	3	4	5
22. Sustains play for appropriate period.	1	2	3	4	5

Source: Greater Essex County School District, Ontario, Canada. Retrieved from http://www.gecdsb.on.ca/d&g/onlinepd/onlinepd.htm

| Exhibit 4.11 | The Difference Between Reliability and Validity: Drinking Behavior |

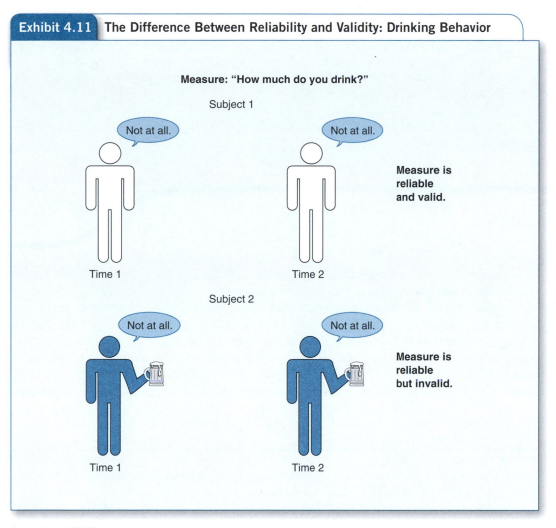

Source: Schutt (2009).

some at-risk students, are answered by most respondents in a consistent way, so the indexes are reliable. As a result, some indexes based on self-report are reliable but invalid. Such indexes are not useful and should be improved or discarded.

If the research focuses on previously unmeasured concepts, new measures will have to be devised. Researchers can use one of three strategies to improve the likelihood that new question-based measures will be reliable and valid:

1. Engage potential respondents in group discussions about the questions to be included in the survey. This strategy allows researchers to check for consistent understanding of terms and to hear the range of events or experiences that people will report.

2. Conduct cognitive interviews. Ask people a test question, then probe with follow-up questions about how they understood the question and what their answer meant.

3. Record, using either audio or video, test interviews during the pretest phase of a survey. The researchers then review these recordings and systematically code them to identify problems in question wording or delivery (Fowler, 1995, pp. 104–129).

In these ways, qualitative methods help to improve the validity of the fixed-response questions used in quantitative surveys.

回 Conclusions

We began this chapter by asking, "What do we mean by 'at risk'?" The three conceptualizations of "at-riskness" introduced demonstrated the importance of defining the concepts we use. Definition often requires subconcepts, and we examined several definitions of "poverty," a concept in its own right but also a subconcept in definitions of at-riskness. The methods for defining poverty led us to the issue of operationalization, "the process of specifying the operations that will indicate the value of cases on a variable." Operationalization is the necessary link between conceptualization and measurement. Only when we know how a concept or subconcept is operationalized can we begin figuring out a valid way to measure it. Remember always that measurement validity is a necessary foundation for educational research. Gathering data without careful conceptualization or conscientious efforts to operationalize key concepts often is a wasted effort.

The difficulties of achieving valid measurement vary with the concept being operationalized and the circumstances of the particular study. The examples in this chapter of difficulties in achieving valid measures of at-risk behavior and associated concepts and subconcepts (poverty, social status, drug and alcohol abuse, depression) should sensitize you to the need for caution.

Planning ahead is the key to achieving valid measurement in your own research; careful evaluation is the key to sound decisions about the validity of measures in others' research. Statistical tests can help to determine whether a given measure is valid after data have been collected, but if it appears after the fact that a measure is invalid, little can be done to correct the situation. If you cannot tell how key concepts were operationalized when you read a research report, don't trust the findings. And if a researcher does not indicate the results of tests used to establish the reliability and validity of key measures, remain skeptical.

Key Terms

Closed-ended (fixed-choice) question 74
Conceptualization 65
Constant 72
Construct validity 82
Content validity 82
Convergent validity 83

Criterion validity 82
Face validity 82
Idiosyncratic errors 89
Index 79
Interitem reliability 84
Interobserver reliability 85
Interval level of measurement 79

Level of measurement 77
Measurement 72
Mutually exclusive 75
Nominal level of measurement 77
Open-ended question 75
Operation 72
Operationalization 70

Highlights

- Conceptualization plays a critical role in research. In deductive research, conceptualization guides the operationalization of specific variables; in inductive research, it guides efforts to make sense of related observations.

- Concepts may refer to either constant or variable phenomena. Concepts that refer to variable phenomena may be very similar to the actual variables used in a study, or they may be much more abstract.

- Concepts are operationalized in research by one or more indicators, or measures, which may derive from observation, self-report, available records or statistics, books and other written documents, clinical indicators, discarded materials, or some combination of these.

- Indexes and scales measure a concept by combining answers to several questions and thus reducing **idiosyncratic error** variation. Several issues should be explored with every intended index: Does each question actually measure the same concept? Does combining items in an index obscure important relationships between individual questions and other variables? Is the index multidimensional?

- If differential weighting is used in the calculation of index scores, then we say that it is a scale.

- Level of measurement indicates the type of information obtained about a variable and the type of statistics that can be used to describe its variation. The four levels of measurement can be ordered by complexity of the mathematical operations they permit: nominal (least complex), ordinal, interval, and ratio (most complex). The measurement level of a variable is determined by how the variable is operationalized.

- The validity of measures should always be tested. There are four basic approaches: face validation, content validation, criterion validation (either predictive or concurrent), and construct validation. Criterion validation provides the strongest evidence of measurement validity, but there often is no criterion to use in validating social science measures.

- Measurement reliability is a prerequisite for measurement validity, although reliable measures are not necessarily valid. Reliability can be assessed through a test-retest procedure, in terms of interitem consistency, through a comparison of responses to alternate forms of the test, or in terms of consistency among observers.

Student Study Site

To assist in completing the web exercises, please access the study site at www.sagepub.com/check, where you will find the web exercise with accompanying links. You'll find other useful study materials such as self-quizzes and e-flashcards for each chapter, along with a group of carefully selected articles from research journals that illustrate the major concepts and techniques.

Discussion Questions

1. If you were given a questionnaire right now that asked you about your use of alcohol and illicit drugs in the past year, would you answer truthfully and disclose details fully? How do you think others would respond? What if the questionnaire were anonymous? What if there was a confidential ID number on the questionnaire so that the researcher could keep track of who responded?

2. Are important concepts in educational research always defined clearly? Are they defined consistently? Search the literature for four to six educational research articles that focus on "at-riskness," "poverty," or some other concept suggested by your instructor. Is the concept defined clearly in each article? How similar are the definitions?

Practice Exercises

1. Now it's time to try your hand at operationalization with survey-based measures. Formulate a few fixed-choice questions to measure variables pertaining to one or more of the concepts in this chapter, such as what factors place students at risk, how poverty should be defined, or what effects drug or alcohol abuse has on school attendance and performance. Arrange to interview one or two other students with the questions you have developed. Ask one fixed-choice question at a time, record your interviewee's answer, and then probe for additional comments and clarifications. Your goal is to discover what respondents take to be the meaning of the concept you used in the question and what additional issues shape their response to it.

   When you have finished the interviews, analyze your experience: Did the interviewees interpret the fixed-choice questions and response choices as you intended? Did you learn more about the concepts you were working on? Should your conceptual definition be refined? Should the questions be rewritten, or would more fixed-choice questions be necessary to capture adequately the variation among respondents?

2. Now try index construction. You might begin with some of the questions you wrote for Practice Exercise 1. Try to write about four or five fixed-choice questions that each measures the same concept. Write each question so it has the same response choices. Now conduct a literature search to identify an index that another researcher used to measure your concept or a similar concept. Compare your index to the published index. Which seems preferable to you? Why?

Web Exercises

1. What are some of the research questions you could attempt to answer with available statistical data? Visit your library and ask for an introduction to the government documents collection. Inspect the U.S. Census Bureau website (http://www.census.gov) and find the population figures broken down by city and state. List five questions you could explore with such data. Identify four variables implied by these research questions that you could operationalize with the available data.

2. Using ERIC, Google Scholar, and Google, find at least three reports or scholarly articles on the Web that you could use to educate a school faculty about the effects of poverty on student learning. Write a brief summary for the faculty based on these sources. Start with the website of the National Poverty Center at the University of Michigan: http://www.npc.umich.edu/.

Developing a Research Proposal

At this point, you can begin the processes of conceptualization and operationalization. You'll need to assume that your primary research method will be conducting a survey.

1. List at least 10 variables that will be measured in your research. No more than two of these should be sociodemographic indicators such as race or age. The inclusion of each variable should be justified in terms of theory or prior research that suggests it would be an appropriate independent or dependent variable or will have some relation to either of these.s

2. Write a conceptual definition for each variable. Whenever possible, this definition should come from the existing literature—either a book you have read for a course or the research literature that you have been searching. Ask two class members for feedback on your definitions.

3. Develop measurement procedures for each variable. Several measures should be single questions and indexes that were used in prior research (search the Web and the journal literature in ERIC, JSTOR, Google Scholar, or some other database of scholarly articles). Make up a few questions and one index yourself. Ask classmates to answer these questions and give you feedback on their clarity.

4. Propose tests of reliability and validity for four of the measures.

CHAPTER 5

Sampling

Research Question: *How Can We Take a Valid Sample in an Educational Setting?*

Chapter Contents

- **Sample Planning**
- **Sampling Methods**
- **Sampling Distributions**

A common technique in journalism is to put a "human face" on a story. For instance, a *Boston Globe* correspondent (MacDonald, 2005) interviewed the mother of a 3-year-old daughter for a story about pre-kindergarten students being expelled from their schools for behavioral problems. Lisa Mathey of Ashburn, Virginia, was frustrated because her child, who has attention deficit and oppositional defiant disorders, was asked to leave one pre-K program, and this raised liability concerns at the next program she went to. Eventually, Lisa was able to get her daughter into a federally mandated program for children with disabilities. The reporter included a second similar story and also interviewed several educators and "experts."

The story provides a compelling rationale for not giving up on these particular "at-risk" children, for providing more consultant services to preschools, and for legislation to address this issue. However, we do not know if the children mentioned in the story are like most children in nursery schools or like most children who are expelled from their nursery schools—or if they are just two compelling stories that caught the eye of one reporter. In other words, we don't know how generalizable their stories are, and if we don't have confidence in generalizability, then the validity of this account of expulsion of preschool students is suspect. Because we don't know whether their situation is widely shared or unique, we cannot really judge what the account tells us about the educational world.

Sampling techniques tell us how to select cases that can lead to valid generalizations about a **population,** or the entire group you wish to learn about. In this chapter, we define the key components of sampling strategy and then present the types of sampling one may use in a research study, with the strengths and weaknesses of each.

By the chapter's end, you should understand which questions you need to ask to evaluate the generalizability of a study as well as what choices you need to make when designing a sampling strategy. You should also realize that it is just as important to select the "right" people or objects to study as it is to ask participants the right questions.

回 Sample Planning

You have encountered the problem of generalizability in many of the studies you have read about in this book. Whether we are designing a sampling strategy or evaluating someone else's findings, we have to understand how and why researchers decide to sample and what the consequences of these decisions are for the generalizability of the study's findings.

Define Sample Components and the Population

Let's say that we are designing a survey about families of kindergarten children in a large city. We don't have the time or resources to study the entire kindergarten family population of the city, even though it comprises the set of individuals or other entities to which we wish to be able to generalize our findings. Even the school department, which closely tracks kindergarten enrollment because it predicts upper grade enrollment for subsequent years, does not have the resources to actually survey the families of the children they count. So instead, we resolve to study a **sample,** a subset of this population. The individual members of this sample are called **elements,** or elementary units.

In many studies, we sample directly from the elements in the population of interest. We may survey a sample of the entire population of students at a school, based on a list obtained from the principal's office. This list, from which the elements of the population are selected, is termed the **sampling frame.** The students who are selected and interviewed from that list are the elements.

In some studies, the entities that can easily be reached are not the same as the elements from which we want information, but they include those elements. For example, we may have a list of households but not a list of the kindergarten-age children of a town, even though the children are the elements that we actually want to sample. In this situation, we could draw a sample of households so that we can then identify the kindergarten-age children in these households. The households are termed **enumeration units,** and the children in the households are the elements (Levy & Lemeshow, 1999, pp. 13–14).

Sometimes, the individuals or other entities from which we collect information are not actually the elements in our study. For example, a researcher might sample schools for a survey about educational practices and then interview a sample of teachers in each sampled school to obtain further information. Both the schools and the teachers are termed **sampling units** because we sample from both (Levy & Lemeshow, 1999, p. 22). The schools are selected in the first stage of the sample, so they are the *primary sampling units* (in this case, they are also the elements in the study). The teachers are *secondary sampling units* (but they are not elements, because they are used to provide information about the entire school) (see Exhibit 5.1).

Population: The entire set of individuals or other entities to which study findings are to be generalized.

Elements: The individual members of the population whose characteristics are to be measured.

Sampling frame: A list of all elements or other units containing the elements in a population.

Enumeration units: Units that contain one or more elements and that are listed in a sampling frame.

Sampling units: Units listed at any stage of a multistage sampling design.

Exhibit 5.1 | **Sample Components in a Two-Stage Study**

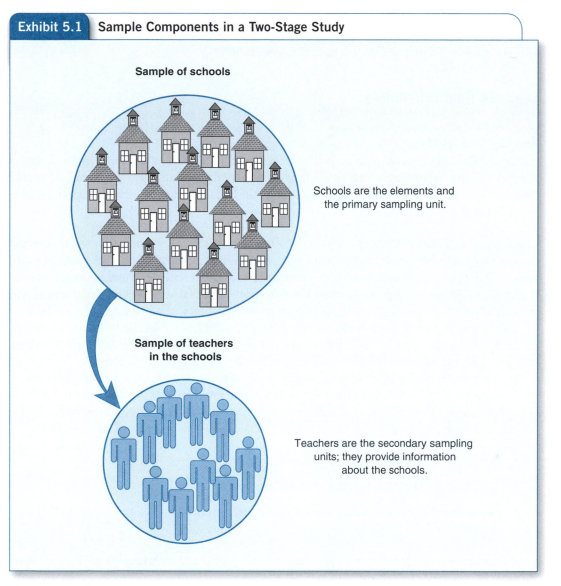

Sample of schools

Schools are the elements and the primary sampling unit.

Sample of teachers in the schools

Teachers are the secondary sampling units; they provide information about the schools.

Source: Schutt (2009, p. 151). Based on information from Levy and Lemeshow (1999).

It is important to know exactly what population a sample can represent when you select or evaluate sample components. The population for a study is the aggregation of elements that we actually focus on and sample from, not some larger aggregation we really wish we could have studied. If we sample students in one high school, the population for our study is the student body of that school, not all high school students in the city or the state in which that high school is located.

Some populations, such as at-risk students, are not identified by a simple criterion such as a geographic boundary or an organizational membership. Clear definition of such a population is difficult (as we saw in the previous chapter) but quite necessary. Anyone should be able to determine just what population was actually studied, so we would have to define clearly the concept of "at-risk students" and specify how we determined their status.

A clear definition allows researchers in other locations or at other times to develop procedures for studying a comparable population. The more complete and explicit the definition is of the population from which a sample was selected, the more precise our generalizations can be.

Evaluate Generalizability

Once we have defined clearly the population from which we will sample, we need to determine the scope of the generalizations we will make from our sample.

Can the findings from a sample of the population be generalized to the population from which the sample was selected? Do a certain study's findings and theory apply to all the students in a given school? To the entire school population of a given state? Of all the students in the United States? This type of generalizability is defined as *sample generalizability.*

Can the findings from a study of one population be generalized to another, somewhat different population? Are the students of a small-town school system similar to students in other small towns? To students in large urban areas as well? To students across the United States? Do findings from a study of reading development in a large northeastern city differ from those that would be obtained in a rural area in the Southwest? This type of generalizability question is defined as cross-population generalizability.

This chapter focuses attention on the problem of sample generalizability: Can findings from a sample be generalized to the population from which the sample was drawn? This is really the most basic question to ask about a sample, and educational research methods provide many tools with which to address it.

Sample generalizability depends on sample quality, which is determined by the amount of **sampling error**— the difference between the characteristics of a sample and the characteristics of the population from which it was selected. The larger the sampling error, the less representative the sample—and thus the less generalizable the findings. To assess sample quality when you are planning or evaluating a study, ask yourself these questions:

- From what population were the cases selected?

- What method was used to select cases from this population?

- Do the cases that were studied represent, in the aggregate, the population from which they were selected?

But researchers often project their theories onto groups or populations much larger than, or simply different from, those they have actually studied. The population to which generalizations are made in this way can be termed the **target population**—a set of elements larger than or different from the population that was sampled and to which the researcher would like to generalize any study findings. When we generalize findings to target populations, we must carefully consider the validity of claims that the findings can be applied to other groups, geographic areas, cultures, or times. Because the validity of cross-population generalizations cannot be tested empirically, except by conducting more research in other settings, we will not focus much attention on this problem here.

Assess the Diversity of the Population

Sampling is unnecessary if all the units in the population are identical. Physicists don't need to select a representative sample of atomic particles to learn about basic physical processes. They can study a single atomic particle because it is identical to every other particle of its type.

What about people? Certainly all people are not identical (nor are other animals, in many respects). Nonetheless, if we are studying physical or psychological processes that are the same among all people, sampling is not needed to achieve generalizable findings. Psychologists and social psychologists often conduct experiments on college students to learn about processes that they think are identical across individuals. They believe that most people would have the same reactions as the college students if they experienced the same experimental conditions. But we must always bear in mind that we don't really know how generalizable our findings are to populations we haven't actually studied. This is particularly important when studying diverse school populations, where variables such as cultural background, language, income level, and family expectations can have strong effects on students' behavior and academic performance.

So we usually conclude that we must study the larger population in which we are interested, if we want to be able to make generalizations about it. For this purpose, we must obtain a **representative sample** of the population to which generalizations are sought (see Exhibit 5.2). The educational world and the people in it are just too diverse to be considered "identical units."

> **Representative sample:** A sample that "looks like" the population from which it was selected in all respects that are potentially relevant to the study. The distribution of characteristics among the elements of a representative sample is the same as the distribution of those characteristics among the total population. In an unrepresentative sample, some characteristics are overrepresented or underrepresented.

| Exhibit 5.2 | **Representative and Unrepresentative Samples** |

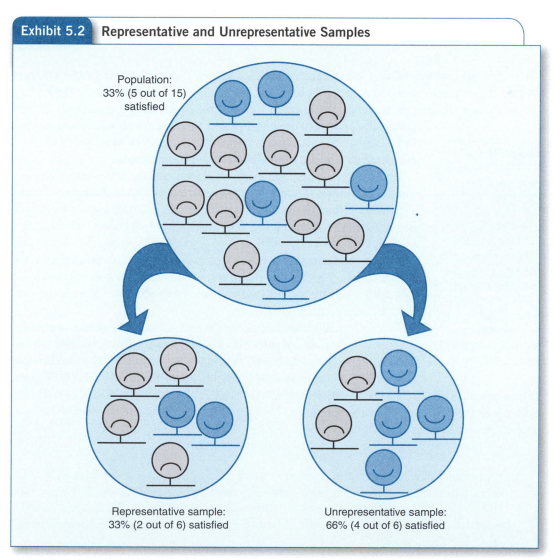

Population:
33% (5 out of 15) satisfied

Representative sample:
33% (2 out of 6) satisfied

Unrepresentative sample:
66% (4 out of 6) satisfied

Source: Schutt (2009, p. 155).

Consider a Census

Census: Research in which information is obtained through the responses that all available members of an entire population give to questions.

In some circumstances, it may be feasible to skirt the issue of generalizability by conducting a **census**—studying the entire population of interest—rather than drawing a sample. This is what the federal government tries to do every 10 years with the U.S. census. Censuses also include studies of all the employees in small organizations, all the students in a class, or all the teachers in a school. Researchers don't often attempt to collect data from all the members of some large population because doing so would be too expensive and time-consuming. But fortunately, a well-designed sampling strategy can result in a representative sample of the same population at far less cost and in far less time.

In most survey situations, it is much better to survey only a limited number from the total population so that there are more resources for follow-up procedures that can overcome reluctance or indifference about participation.

Sampling Methods

Certain features of samples make them more or less likely to represent the population from which they are selected; the more representative the sample, the better. The crucial distinction about samples is whether they are based on a probability or a nonprobability sampling method. **Probability sampling methods** allow us to know in advance how likely it is that any element of a population will be selected. Sampling methods that do not let us know in advance the likelihood of selecting each element are termed **nonprobability sampling methods.**

Probability of selection: The likelihood that an element will be selected from the population for inclusion in the sample. In a census of all the elements of a population, the probability that any particular element will be selected is 1.0. If half of the elements in the population are sampled on the basis of chance (say, by tossing a coin), the probability of selection for each element is one half, or .5. As the size of the sample as a proportion of the population decreases, so does the probability of selection.

Probability sampling methods rely on a random, or chance, selection procedure, which is, in principle, the same as flipping a coin to decide which of two people "wins" and which one "loses." Heads and tails are equally likely to turn up in a coin toss, so both persons have an equal chance to win. Their **probability of selection** is 1 out of 2, or .5.

Flipping a coin is a fair way to select one of two people because the selection process harbors no **systematic bias.** You might win or lose the coin toss, but you know that the outcome was due simply to chance, not to bias. For the same reason, a roll of a six-sided die is a fair way to choose one of six possible outcomes (the odds of selection are 1 out of 6, or .17).

There is a natural tendency to confuse the concept of **random sampling,** in which cases are selected only on the basis of chance, with a haphazard method of sampling. On first impression, "leaving things up to chance" seems to imply not exerting any control over the sampling method. But to ensure that nothing but chance influences the selection of cases, the researcher must proceed very methodically, leaving nothing to chance except the selection of the cases themselves. The researcher must follow carefully controlled procedures if a purely random process is to occur.

Two problems are often cause for concern when drawing random samples:

1. If the sampling frame is incomplete, a sample selected randomly from that list will not really be a random sample of the population. You should always consider the adequacy of the sampling frame. Even for a simple population such as a university's student body, the registrar's list is likely to be at least a bit out of date at any given time. For example, some students will have dropped out, but their status will not yet be officially recorded.

2. Nonresponse is a major hazard in survey research because **nonrespondents** are likely to differ systematically from those who take the time to participate. If the response rate is low (say, below 65%), you should not assume that findings from even a random sample will be generalizable to the population from which the sample was selected.

Probability Sampling Methods

Probability sampling methods are those in which the probability of selection is known and is not zero (so there is some chance of selecting each element). These methods randomly select elements and therefore have no systematic bias; nothing but chance determines which elements are included in the sample. This feature of probability samples makes them much more desirable than nonprobability samples when the goal is to generalize to a larger population.

> **Bias:** Sampling bias occurs when some population characteristics are over- or underrepresented in the sample because of particular features of the method of selecting the sample.

Even a randomly selected sample will have some sampling error—some deviation from the characteristics of the population—due to chance. The probability of selecting a head is .5 in a single toss of a coin and in 20, 30, or however many tosses of a coin you like. But it is perfectly possible to toss a coin twice and get a head both times. The random "sample" of the two sides of the coin is selected in an unbiased fashion, but it still is unrepresentative. In general, both the size of the sample and the homogeneity (sameness) of the population affect the degree of error due to chance. Despite what you might think, the proportion of the population that the sample represents does not affect the sample representativeness, unless that proportion is very large—it is the number of cases in the sample that is important. To elaborate:

*   The larger the sample, the more confidence we can have in the sample's representativeness. If we randomly pick 5 people to represent the entire population of our city, our sample is unlikely to be very representative of the entire population in terms of age, gender, race, attitudes, and so on. But if we randomly pick 100 people, the odds of having a representative sample are much better; with a random sample of 1,000, the odds become very good indeed.

*   The more homogeneous the population, the more confidence we can have in the representativeness of a sample of any particular size. That's why blood testing works—blood is homogeneous in any specific individual's body. Or let's say we plan to draw samples of 50 people from each of two communities to estimate mean family income. One community is very diverse, with family incomes varying from $12,000 to $85,000. In the other, more homogeneous community, family incomes are concentrated in a narrow range, from $41,000 to $64,000. The estimated mean family income based on the sample from the homogeneous community is more likely to be representative than is the estimate based on the sample from the more heterogeneous community. With less variation to represent, fewer cases are needed to represent the homogeneous community.

*   The fraction of the total population that a sample contains does not affect the sample's representativeness unless that fraction is large. This isn't obvious, but it is mathematically true. The raw number of cases matters more than the proportion of the population. Other things being equal, a sample of 1,000 from a population of 1 million (with a sampling fraction of 0.001, or 0.1%) is much better than a sample of 100 from a population of 10,000 (although the sampling fraction is 0.01, or 1%, which is 10 times higher). The larger size of the samples makes representativeness more likely, not the proportion of the whole that the sample represents. We can regard any sampling fraction under 2% with about the same degree of confidence (Sudman, 1976, p. 184). In fact, sample representativeness is not likely to increase much until the sampling fraction is quite a bit higher.

Because they do not disproportionately exclude or include particular groups within the population, random samples that are successfully implemented avoid systematic bias. Random error can still be considerable, however, and different types of random samples vary in their ability to minimize it. The four most common types of random samples are simple random sampling, systematic random sampling, cluster sampling, and stratified random sampling.

Simple Random Sampling

Simple random sampling identifies cases strictly on the basis of chance. As you know, flipping a coin or rolling a die can be used to identify cases strictly on the basis of chance, but these procedures are not very efficient tools for drawing a sample. A **random number table** simplifies the process considerably. The researcher numbers all the elements in the sampling frame and then uses a systematic procedure for picking corresponding numbers from the random number table. (Practice Exercise 1 at the end of this chapter explains the process step-by-step.) Alternatively, a researcher may use a lottery procedure. Each case number is written on a small card, and then the cards are mixed up and the sample is selected from the cards. A computer program can also easily generate a random sample of any size.

The probability of selection in a true simple random sample is equal for each element. If a sample of 500 is selected from a population of 17,000 (i.e., a sampling frame of 17,000), then the probability of selection for each element is 500/17,000, or .03. Every element has an equal chance of being selected, just like the odds in a toss of a coin (1/2) or a roll of a die (1/6). Thus, simple random sampling is an "equal probability of selection method," or EPSEM.

Systematic Random Sampling

Systematic random sampling is a variant of simple random sampling. The first element is selected randomly from a list or from sequential files, and then every nth element is selected. This is a convenient method for drawing a random sample when the population elements are arranged sequentially. It is particularly efficient when the elements are not actually printed (i.e., there is no sampling frame) but instead are represented by folders in filing cabinets.

Systematic random sampling requires three steps:

1. The total number of cases in the population is divided by the number of cases required for the sample. This division yields the **sampling interval,** the number of cases from one sampled case to another. If 50 cases are to be selected out of 1,000, the sampling interval is 20; every 20th case is selected.

2. A number from 1 to 20 (or whatever the sampling interval is) is selected randomly. This number identifies the first case to be sampled, counting from the first case on the list or in the files.

3. After the first case is selected, every nth case is selected for the sample, where n is the sampling interval. If the sampling interval is not a whole number, the size of the sampling interval is varied systematically to yield the proper number of cases for the sample. For example, if the sampling interval is 30.5, the sampling interval alternates between 30 and 31.

In almost all sampling situations, systematic random sampling yields what is essentially a simple random sample. The exception is a situation in which the sequence of elements is affected by **periodicity**—that is, the sequence varies in some regular, periodic pattern. For example, the houses in a new development with the same number of houses on each block (e.g., eight) may be listed by block, starting with the house in the northwest corner of each block and continuing clockwise. If the sampling interval is 8, the same as the periodic pattern, all the cases selected will be in the same position (see Exhibit 5.3). But in reality, periodicity and the sampling interval are rarely the same, so this usually isn't a problem.

Exhibit 5.3 The Effect of Periodicity on Systematic Random Sampling

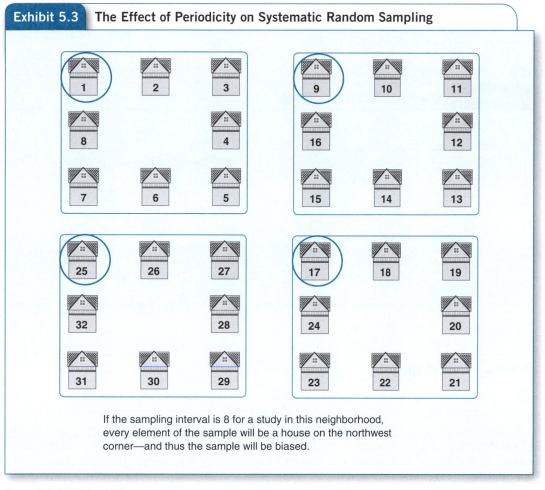

If the sampling interval is 8 for a study in this neighborhood, every element of the sample will be a house on the northwest corner—and thus the sample will be biased.

Source: Schutt (2009, p. 163).

Cluster Sampling

Cluster sampling is useful when a sampling frame—a definite list—of elements is not available, as often is the case for large populations spread out across a wide geographic area or among many different organizations. We don't have a good list of all the Catholics in America, all the businesspeople in Arizona, or all the waiters in New York. A **cluster** is a naturally occurring, mixed aggregate of elements of the population, with each element (person, for instance) appearing in one, and only one, cluster. Schools could serve as clusters for sampling students, blocks could serve as clusters for sampling city residents, counties could serve as clusters for sampling the general population, and restaurants could serve as clusters for sampling waiters.

Cluster sampling is, at least, a two-stage procedure. First, the researcher draws a random sample of clusters. (A list of clusters should be much easier to obtain than a list of all the individuals in each cluster in the population.) Next, the researcher draws a random sample of elements within each selected cluster. Because only a fraction of the total clusters is involved, obtaining the sampling frame at this stage should be much easier.

Cluster samples often involve multiple stages, with clusters within clusters. A national study of middle school students, for example, might involve first sampling states, then geographic units (cities, towns, counties)

within those states, then schools within those units, and, finally, students within each selected school (see Exhibit 5.4). In multistage cluster sampling, the clusters at the first stage of sampling are termed the *primary sampling units* (Levy & Lemeshow, 1999, p. 228).

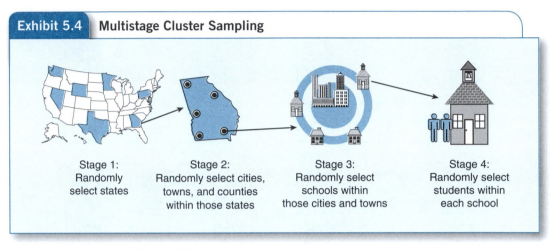

| Exhibit 5.4 | Multistage Cluster Sampling |

Stage 1: Randomly select states

Stage 2: Randomly select cities, towns, and counties within those states

Stage 3: Randomly select schools within those cities and towns

Stage 4: Randomly select students within each school

Source: Chambliss and Schutt (2010, p. 119).

Multistage Cluster Sampling

How many clusters and how many individuals within clusters should be selected? As a general rule, the more clusters you select, with the fewest individuals in each, the more representative your sampling will be. Unfortunately, this strategy also maximizes the time needed and cost for the sample. Remember, too, that the more internally homogeneous the clusters, the fewer cases needed per cluster. Homogeneity within a cluster is good. So if you set out to draw a cluster sample, be sure to consider how similar individuals are within the clusters, as well as, given the time and resources available, how many clusters you can afford to include.

Cluster sampling is a very popular method among survey researchers, but it has one general drawback: Sampling error is greater in a cluster sample than in a simple random sample because there are two steps involving random selection rather than just one. This sampling error increases as the number of clusters decreases, and it decreases as the homogeneity of cases per cluster increases. This is another way of restating the points above: It's better to include as many clusters as possible in a sample, and it's more likely that a cluster sample will be representative of the population if cases are relatively similar within clusters.

Stratified Random Sampling

Suppose you want to survey personnel in the Eastville school system to determine their attitude toward a proposed change in the length of the school day. Simple random sampling would produce large numbers of teachers—the most numerous employees—but very few, if any, principals or higher administrators. But you want administrators in your sample. **Stratified random sampling** ensures that various groups will be included.

First, all elements in the population (i.e., in the sampling frame) are distinguished according to their value on some relevant characteristic (administrator, teacher, instructional aide, custodian, etc.). That characteristic determines the sampling strata. Next, elements are sampled randomly from within these strata: so many administrators, so many teachers, and so on. Of course, using this method requires more information prior to sampling than is the case with simple random sampling. Each element must belong to one and only one stratum.

For "proportionate to size" sampling, the size of each stratum in the population must be known. This method efficiently draws an appropriate representation of elements across strata. Imagine that you plan to draw a sample of 500 students from the Eastville school system, which is ethnically diverse and has 10,000 students. The student population is 15% Black, 10% Hispanic, 5% Asian, and 70% White. If you drew a simple random sample, you might end up with somewhat disproportionate numbers of each group. But if you created sampling strata based on race and ethnicity, you could randomly select cases from each stratum: 75 Blacks (15% of the sample), 50 Hispanics (10%), 25 Asians (5%), and 350 Whites (70%). By using **proportionate stratified sampling,** you would eliminate any possibility of sampling error in the sample's distribution of ethnicity. Each stratum would be represented exactly in proportion to its size in the population from which the sample was drawn (see Exhibit 5.5).

In **disproportionate stratified sampling,** the proportion of each stratum that is included in the sample is intentionally varied from what it is in the population. In the case of the sample stratified by ethnicity, you

---

Exhibit 5.5 **Stratified Random Sampling**

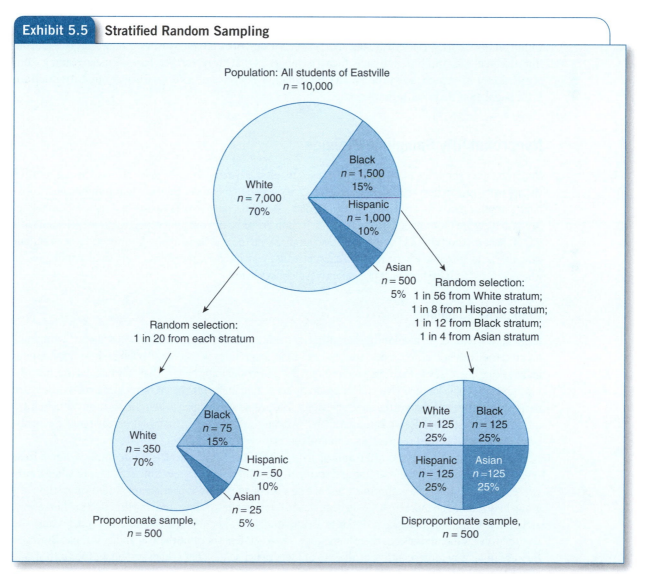

Source: Chambliss and Schutt (2010, p. 120).

might select equal numbers of cases from each racial or ethnic group: 125 Blacks (25% of the sample), 125 Hispanics (25%), 125 Asians (25%), and 125 Whites (25%). In this type of sample, the probability of selection of every case is known but unequal between strata. You know what the proportions are in the population, and so you can easily adjust your combined sample statistics to reflect these true proportions. For instance, if you want to combine the ethnic groups and estimate the average reading test score of the total population, you would have to "weight" each case in the sample. The weight is a number you multiply by the value of each case based on the stratum it is in. For example, you would multiply the scores of all Blacks in the sample by 0.6 (75/125), the scores of all Hispanics by 0.4 (50/125), and so on. Weighting in this way reduces the influence of the oversampled strata and increases the influence of the undersampled strata to what they would have been if pure probability sampling had been used.

Researchers sometimes include one element of *dis*proportionate random sampling in their otherwise proportionate random sampling strategy. Why would anyone select a sample that is so unrepresentative in the first place? The most common reason is to ensure that cases from smaller strata are included in the sample in sufficient numbers to allow separate statistical estimates and to facilitate comparisons between strata. Remember that one of the determinants of sample quality is sample size. The same is true for subgroups within samples. If a key concern in a research project is to describe and compare the reading scores of students from different racial and ethnic groups, then it is important that the researchers base the mean reading score of each group on enough cases to be a valid representation. If few members of a particular minority group are in the population, they need to be oversampled.

Nonprobability Sampling Methods

Nonprobability sampling methods are often used in qualitative research; they also are used in quantitative studies when researchers are unable to use probability selection methods. There are four common nonprobability sampling methods: availability sampling, quota sampling, purposive sampling, and snowball sampling. Because these methods do not use a random selection procedure, we cannot expect a sample selected with any of these methods to yield a representative sample. Nonetheless, these methods are useful when random sampling is not possible, when a research question calls for an intensive investigation of a small population, or when a researcher is performing a preliminary, exploratory study.

Availability Sampling

Elements are selected for **availability sampling** (sometimes called "haphazard" or "convenience" sampling) because they're available or easy to find. For example, sometimes people stand outside stores in shopping malls asking passersby to answer a few questions about their shopping habits. That may make sense, but asking the same people for their views on the economy doesn't. In important respects, regular mall shoppers are not representative members of the total population. The people who happen to be available in any situation are unlikely to be just like those who are unavailable. We can't be at all certain that what we learn can be generalized with any confidence to a larger population of concern.

An availability sample is often appropriate in educational research—for example, when a field researcher is exploring a new setting and trying to get some sense of prevailing attitudes or when a survey researcher conducts a preliminary test of a new set of questions. A participant observation study of a group may require no more sophisticated approach. A teacher-researcher studying the effects of homework assignments on sixth graders may decide to use the students in her own sixth-grade classroom because she sees them every day and assigns them homework. These students became the availability sample. However, they are in no way representative of all sixth graders in her school, her school system, or the sixth-grade population nationally.

Availability sampling often masquerades as a more rigorous form of research. Popular magazines periodically survey their readers by printing a questionnaire for readers to fill out and mail in. A follow-up article then appears in the magazine under a title such as "What You Think About Intimacy in Marriage?" If the magazine's circulation is large, a large sample can be achieved in this way. The problem is that usually only a tiny fraction of readers return the questionnaire, and these respondents are probably unlike other readers who did not have the interest or time to participate. So the survey is based on an availability sample. Even though the follow-up article may be interesting, we have no basis for thinking that the results describe the readership as a whole—much less the population at large.

Do you see now why availability sampling differs so much from random sampling methods, which require that "nothing but chance" affect the actual selection of cases? What makes availability sampling "haphazard" is precisely that a great many things other than chance can affect the selection of cases, ranging from the prejudices of the research staff to the work schedules of potential respondents. To truly leave the selection of cases up to chance, we have to design the selection process very carefully so that other factors are not influential. There's nothing "haphazard" about selecting cases randomly.

Quota Sampling

Quota sampling is intended to overcome the most obvious flaw of availability sampling—that the sample will just consist of whoever or whatever is available, without any concern for its similarity to the population of interest. In this approach, quotas are set to ensure that the sample represents certain characteristics in proportion to their prevalence in the population.

Suppose that you wish to sample adult residents of Eastville in a study of support for a tax increase to improve its schools. You know from the town's annual report what the proportions of town residents are in terms of gender, race, age, and number of children. You think that each of these characteristics might influence support for new school taxes, so you want to be sure that the sample includes men, women, Whites, Blacks, Hispanics, Asians, older people, younger people, big families, small families, and childless families in proportion to their numbers in the town population.

This is where quotas come in. Let's say that 48% of the town's adult residents are men and 52% are women and that 60% are employed, 5% are unemployed, and 35% are out of the labor force. These percentages and the percentages corresponding to the other characteristics become the quotas for the sample. If you plan to include a total of 500 residents in your sample, 240 must be men (48% of 500), 260 must be women, 300 must be employed, and so on. You may even set more refined quotas, such as certain numbers of employed women, employed men, unemployed men, and so on. With the quota list in hand, you (or your research staff) can now go out into the community looking for the right number of people in each quota category.

The problem is that even when we know that a quota sample is representative of the particular characteristics for which quotas have been set, we have no way of knowing if the sample is representative in terms of any other characteristics. In Exhibit 5.6, for example, quotas have been set for gender only. Under the circumstances, it's no surprise that the sample is representative of the population only in terms of gender, not in terms of race.

Of course, you must know the characteristics of the entire population to set the right quotas. In most cases, researchers know what the population looks like in terms of no more than a few of the characteristics relevant to their concerns—and in some cases, they have no such information on the entire population. Exhibit 5.7 summarizes the differences between quota sampling and stratified random sampling. The key difference, of course, is quota sampling's lack of random selection.

If you're now feeling skeptical of quota sampling, you've gotten the drift of our remarks. Nonetheless, in situations where you can't draw a random sample, it may be better to establish quotas than to have no parameters at all.

Exhibit 5.6 | **Quota Sampling**

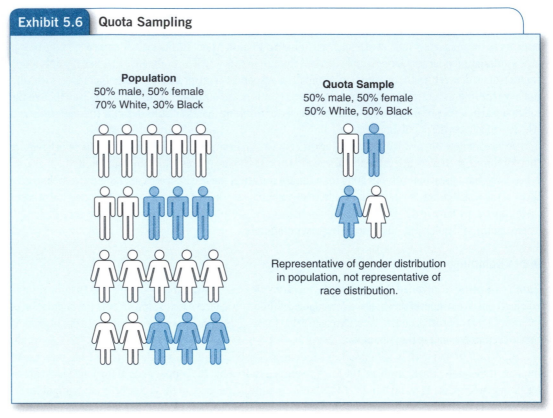

Source: Schutt (2009, p. 172).

Exhibit 5.7 | **Comparison of Stratified and Quota Sampling Methods**

Feature	Stratified	Quota
Unbiased (random) selection of cases	Yes	No
Sampling frame required	Yes	No
Ensures representation of key strata	Yes	Yes

Source: Schutt (2009, p. 173).

Purposive Sampling

In **purposive sampling,** each sample element is selected for a purpose, usually because of the unique position of the sample elements. Purposive sampling may involve studying the entire population of some limited group (middle school principals) or a subset of a population (high school guidance counselors who deal with ninth graders). Or a purposive sample may be a "key informant survey," which targets individuals who are particularly knowledgeable about the issues under investigation.

Herbert Rubin and Irene Rubin (1995) suggest three guidelines for selecting informants when designing any purposive sampling strategy. Informants should be:

- "Knowledgeable about the cultural arena or situation or experience being studied."

- "Willing to talk."

- "Represent[ative of] the range of points of view." (p. 66)

In addition, Rubin and Rubin (1995) suggest continuing to select interviewees until you can pass two tests:

- Completeness. "What you hear provides an overall sense of the meaning of a concept, theme, or process." (p. 72)

- Saturation. "You gain confidence that you are learning little that is new from subsequent interview[s]." (p. 73)

Adhering to these guidelines will help to ensure that a purposive sample adequately represents the setting or issues studied.

Of course, purposive sampling does not produce a sample that represents some larger population, but it can be exactly what is needed in a case study of a school, community, or some other clearly defined and relatively limited group. In an intensive case study of a large high school, a purposive sample of school leaders might be complemented with a probability sample of all school staff and students.

Snowball Sampling

Snowball sampling is useful for hard-to-reach or hard-to-identify populations for which there is no sampling frame, but the members of which are somewhat interconnected (at least some members of the population know each other). It can be used to sample members of such groups as closeted gay educators, informal organizational leaders, and students who have suffered from bullying. It also may be used for charting the relationships among members of some group (a sociometric study), exploring the population of interest prior to developing a formal sampling plan, and developing what becomes a census of informal leaders of small organizations or communities. However, researchers using snowball sampling normally cannot be confident that their sample represents the total population of interest, so generalizations must be tentative.

Yvonne Spicer (2004) used both purposive and snowball sampling to study a population that was hard to identify and had members who were known to each other: African American female K–12 public school principals in Massachusetts. Her review of previous research led her to conclude that

much of the research literature on educational leadership is dominated by the experience of men and White women. When African American women are discussed . . . , this tends to be in the context of White women and minorities as a whole. (p. 77)

Spicer (2004) initially assumed that local school districts, the state department of education, or the state principals' organization would have a list of African American women principals. This proved not to be the case, a circumstance that suggested to her that, as the literature predicted, these women leaders were institutionally invisible. To locate her target population, Spicer created a purposive sample "based on the recommendations of nominators from professional organizations, colleagues, and district data" (p. 77). Once she had contacted subjects identified by the nominators, Spicer used snowball sampling to increase her list, asking the recommended principals to put her in contact with others who met her criteria. Eventually she located 65 such women across the entire state (Spicer, 2004, p. 77).

Spicer's target population had a strong reason for assisting her in locating as many respondents as possible: They felt invisible as a group and wanted to help her get the word out that they existed and were succeeding in their leadership roles. Such an enthusiastic response is not always the case. Snowball sampling can sometimes be problematic because the initial contacts may shape the entire sample and foreclose access to some members of the population of interest. More systematic versions of snowball sampling can reduce the potential for bias. When the sampling is repeated through several waves, with new respondents bringing in more peers, the composition of the sample converges on a more representative mix of characteristics than would occur with uncontrolled snowball sampling. Exhibit 5.8 shows how the sample spreads out through successive recruitment waves to an increasingly diverse pool (Heckathorn, 1997, p. 178).

Exhibit 5.8   **Respondent-Driven Sampling**

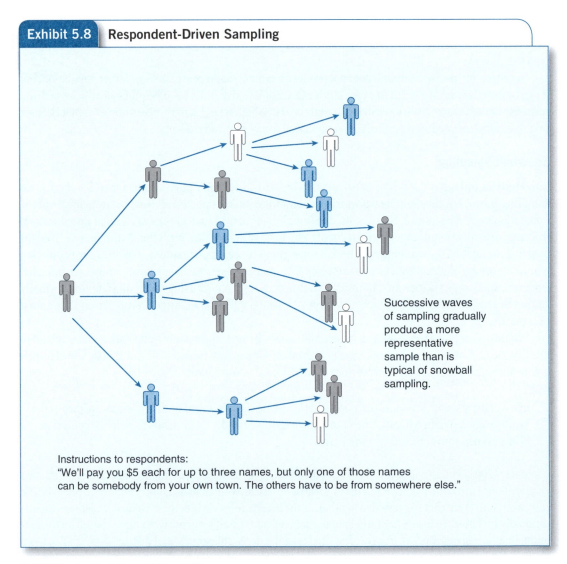

Successive waves of sampling gradually produce a more representative sample than is typical of snowball sampling.

Instructions to respondents:
"We'll pay you $5 each for up to three names, but only one of those names can be somebody from your own town. The others have to be from somewhere else."

Source: Based on Heckathorn (1997, p. 178).

Lessons About Sample Quality

Some lessons are implicit in our evaluations of the samples in this chapter. You should keep these lessons in mind when you read articles that use sampling, as well as when conducting your own research:

- We can't evaluate the quality of a sample if we don't know what population it is supposed to represent. If the population is unspecified because the researchers were never clear about the population they were trying to sample, then we can safely conclude that the sample itself is no good.

- We can't evaluate the quality of a sample if we don't know how cases in the sample were selected from the population. If the method was specified, we then need to know whether cases were selected in a systematic fashion and on the basis of chance. In any case, we know that a haphazard method of sampling (as in person-on-the-street interviews) undermines generalizability.

- Sample quality is determined by the sample actually obtained, not just by the sampling method itself. If many of the people selected for our sample are nonrespondents or people (or other entities) who do not participate in the study even though they have been selected for the sample, the quality of our sample is undermined—even if we chose the sample in the best possible way.

- We need to be aware that even researchers who obtain very good samples may talk about the implications of their findings for some group that is larger than, or just different from, the population they actually sampled. For example, findings from a representative sample of students in one university often are discussed as if they tell us about university students in general. And maybe they do; we just don't know for sure.

Generalizability in Qualitative Research

Qualitative research often focuses on populations that are hard to locate or very limited in size. In consequence, nonprobability sampling methods such as availability sampling and snowball are often used. Janet Ward Schofield (2002) suggests ways of increasing the generalizability of the samples obtained in such situations:

Studying the Typical. Choosing sites on the basis of their fit with a typical situation is far preferable to choosing on the basis of convenience. (p. 181)

Performing Multisite Studies. A finding emerging repeatedly in the study of numerous sites would appear to be more likely to be a good working hypothesis about some as yet unstudied site than a finding emerging from just one or two sites. . . . Generally speaking, a finding emerging from the study of several very heterogeneous sites would be more . . . likely to be useful in understanding various other sites than one emerging from the study of several very similar sites. (p. 184)

The effort of some qualitative researchers to understand the particulars of a situation in depth, as an important object of inquiry in itself, also leads some to question the value of generalizability as most researchers understand it. In the words of researcher Norman Denzin,

The interpretivist rejects generalization as a goal and never aims to draw randomly selected samples of human experience. . . . Every instance of social interaction . . . represents a slice from the life world that is the proper subject matter for interpretive inquiry. (cited in Schofield, 2002, p. 173)

Sampling Distributions

Sampling distribution: A hypothetical distribution of a statistic (e.g., proportion, mean) across an infinite number of random samples that could be drawn from a population.

A well-designed probability sample is one that is likely to be representative of the population from which it was selected. But as you've seen, random samples are subject to sampling error due just to chance. To deal with that problem, educational researchers take into account the properties of a sampling distribution, a hypothetical distribution of a statistic across an infinite number of random samples that could be drawn from a population. Any single random sample can be thought of as just one of an infinite number of random samples that, in theory, could have been selected from the population. If we had the finances of Bill Gates, had all the time in the world, and were able to draw an infinite number of samples, and we calculated the same type of statistic for each of these samples, we would then have a sampling distribution. Understanding sampling distributions is the foundation for understanding how statisticians can estimate sampling error.

What does a sampling distribution look like? Because a sampling distribution is based on some statistic calculated for different samples, we need to choose a statistic. Let's focus on the arithmetic average, or mean. We will explain the calculation of the mean in Chapter 13, but you may already be familiar with it: You add up the values of all the cases and divide by the total number of cases. Let's say you draw a random sample of 500 families and find that their average (mean) family income is $58,239. Imagine that you then draw another random sample. That sample's mean family income might be $60,302. Imagine marking these two means on graph paper and then drawing more random samples and marking their means on the graph. The resulting graph would be a sampling distribution of the mean.

Estimating Sampling Error

Inferential statistics: A mathematical tool for estimating how likely it is that a statistical result based on data from a random sample is representative of the population from which the sample is assumed to have been selected.

Random sampling error (chance sampling error): Differences between the population and the sample that are due only to chance factors (random error), not to systematic sampling error. Random sampling error may or may not result in an unrepresentative sample. The magnitude of sampling error due to chance factors can be estimated statistically.

We don't actually observe sampling distributions in real research. It would take too much time and money. Instead, researchers just draw the best sample they can. (Now you understand why it is important to have a sample that is representative of the population.) A sampling distribution usually remains a hypothetical or theoretical distribution. We can use the properties of sampling distributions, however, to calculate the amount of sampling error that was likely with the actual random sample used in a study. The tool for calculating sampling error is called **inferential statistics.**

Sampling distributions for many statistics, including the mean, have a "normal" shape. A graph of a normal distribution looks like a bell, with one "hump" in the middle, centered on the population mean, and a number of cases tapering off on both sides of the mean. Note that a normal distribution is symmetrical: If you fold it in half at its center (at the population mean), the two halves will match perfectly. This shape is produced by **random sampling error**—variation due purely to chance. The value of the statistic varies from sample to sample because of chance, so higher and lower values are equally likely.

Exhibit 5.9 shows what the sampling distribution of family incomes would look like if it formed a perfectly normal distribution—this would occur if, rather than 50 random samples, we had selected thousands of random samples.

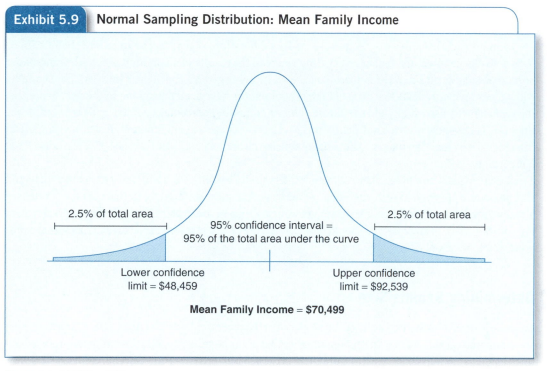

| Exhibit 5.9 | Normal Sampling Distribution: Mean Family Income |

2.5% of total area

2.5% of total area

95% confidence interval =
95% of the total area under the curve

Lower confidence
limit = $48,459

Upper confidence
limit = $92,539

Mean Family Income = $70,499

Source: Schutt (2009, p. 179).

As we have stated earlier, in research, our goal is to generalize what we observe in our sample to the population of interest. In statistical terminology, a sample statistic is an estimate of the population parameter we want to estimate. The properties of a sampling distribution facilitate this process of statistical inference. In the sampling distribution, the most frequent value of the **sample statistic**—the statistic (such as the mean) computed from sample data—is identical to the **population parameter**—the statistic computed for the entire population. In other words, we can have a lot of confidence that the value at the peak of the bell curve represents the norm for the entire population.

In a normal distribution, a predictable proportion of cases falls within certain ranges under the curve. Inferential statistics takes advantage of this feature and allow us to estimate how likely it is that, given a particular sample, the true population value will be within some range of the statistic. For example, a statistician might conclude from a sample of 30 families that *we can be 95% confident that the true mean family income in the total population is between $48,459 and $92,539.* The interval from $48,459 to $92,539 would then be called the "95% confidence interval for the mean." The lower ($48,459) and upper ($92,539) bounds of this interval are termed the *confidence limits.* Exhibit 5.9 marks such confidence limits, indicating the range that encompasses 95% of the area under the normal curve; 95% of all sample means would fall within this range.

Although all normal distributions have these same basic features, they differ in the extent to which they cluster around the mean. A sampling distribution is more compact when it is based on larger samples. Stated another way, we can be more confident in estimates based on larger random samples because we know that a larger sample creates a more compact sampling distribution. This should make intuitive sense. If you want to estimate the average family income of residents of New York City and you select a sample of only 30 families, the mean you estimate from this sample of 30 is less likely to reflect New York City residents' family income than a sample of, say, 3,000.

In most social science disciplines, including education, researchers typically rely on 95% or 99% confidence intervals. In fact, every time you read the results of an opinion poll in the newspaper or hear about one on a news broadcast, you are really being given a confidence interval. For example, when a newspaper reports that 30% of high school seniors have used marijuana in the past 6 months, the reporter will also usually add the phrase "plus or minus four percentage points." This is a confidence interval. These conventional confidence limits reflect the conservatism inherent in classical statistical inference: Don't make an inferential statement unless you are very confident (at least 95% confident) that it is correct.

We will explain how to calculate confidence intervals in Chapter 13. You will find it easier to understand this procedure after you have learned some of the basic statistics we introduce in that chapter. If you have already completed a statistics course, you might want to turn now to Chapter 13's confidence interval section for a quick review. In any case, you should now have a sense of how researchers make inferences from a random sample of a population.

Determining Sample Size

You have learned that more confidence can be placed in the generalizability of statistics from larger samples, so you may be eager to work with random samples that are as large as possible. Unfortunately, researchers often cannot afford to sample a very large number of cases. Therefore, they try to determine during the design phase of their study how large a sample they must have to achieve their purposes. They have to consider the degree of confidence desired, the homogeneity of the population, the complexity of the analysis they plan, and the expected strength of the relationships they will measure.

- The less sampling error desired, the larger the sample size must be.

- Samples of more homogeneous populations can be smaller than samples of more diverse populations. Stratified sampling uses prior information on the population to create more homogeneous population strata from which the sample can be selected, so stratified samples can be smaller than simple random samples.

- If the only analysis planned for a survey sample is to describe the population in terms of a few variables, a smaller sample is required than if a more complex analysis involving sample subgroups is planned. If much of the analysis will focus on estimating the characteristics of subgroups within the sample, it is the size of the subgroups that must be considered, not the size of the total sample (Levy & Lemeshow, 1999, p. 74).

- When the researchers will be testing hypotheses and expect to find very strong relationships among the variables, they will need a smaller sample to detect these relationships than if they expect weaker relationships.

Researchers can make more precise estimates of the sample size required through a method called "statistical power analysis" (Hedges & Rhoads, 2010). Statistical power analysis requires a good advance estimate of the strength of the hypothesized relationship in the population. In addition, the math is complicated, so it helps to have some background in mathematics or to be able to consult a statistician. For these reasons, many researchers do not conduct formal power analyses when deciding how many cases to sample.

Conclusions

The question that began this chapter—"How can we take a valid sample in an educational setting?"—was not linked to a particular research study. Rather, it addressed the overall issue of how we can make valid generalizations in educational research. Generalizing from smaller samples to larger populations is important because frequently we lack both the time and the money to undertake surveys involving thousands or tens of thousands of people.

Fortunately, sampling is a powerful tool for educational research. Probability sampling methods allow a researcher to use the laws of chance, or probability, to draw samples from which population parameters can be estimated with a high degree of confidence. A sample of just 1,000 or 1,500 individuals can be used to estimate reliably the characteristics of the population of a nation comprising millions of individuals.

But researchers do not come by representative samples easily. Well-designed samples require careful planning, some advance knowledge about the population to be sampled, and adherence to systematic selection procedures—all so that the selection procedures are not biased. And even after the sample data are collected, the researcher's ability to generalize from the sample findings to the population is not completely certain. The best that he or she can do is to perform additional calculations that state the degree of confidence that can be placed in the sample statistic.

The alternatives to random, or probability-based, sampling methods are almost always much less palatable for quantitative studies, even though they typically are much cheaper. Without a method of selecting cases likely to represent the population in which the researcher is interested, research findings will have to be carefully qualified. Qualitative researchers whose goal is to understand a small group or setting in depth may necessarily have to use unrepresentative samples, but they must keep in mind that the generalizability of their findings will not be known. Additional procedures for sampling in qualitative studies will be introduced in Chapter 8.

Educational researchers often seek to generalize their conclusions from the population that they studied to some larger target population. The validity of generalizations of this type is necessarily uncertain, because having a representative sample of a particular population does not at all ensure that what we find will hold true in other populations. Nonetheless, as you will see in Chapter 13, the cumulation of findings from studies based on local or otherwise unrepresentative populations can provide important information about broader populations.

Key Terms

Availability sampling   102
Census   96
Cluster   99
Cluster sampling   99
Disproportionate stratified
    sampling   101
Element   92
Enumeration units   92
Inferential statistics   108
Nonprobability sampling method   96
Nonrespondent   97
Periodicity   98

Population   91
Population parameter   109
Probability of selection   96
Probability sampling method   96
Proportionate stratified sampling   101
Purposive sampling   104
Quota sampling   103
Random number table   98
Random sampling   96
Random sampling error   108
Representative sample   95
Sample   92

Sample statistic   109
Sampling error   94
Sampling frame   92
Sampling interval   98
Sampling unit   92
Simple random sampling   98
Snowball sampling   105
Stratified random sampling   100
Systematic bias   96
Systematic random sampling   98
Target population   94

Highlights

- Sampling theory focuses on the generalizability of descriptive findings to the population from which the sample was drawn. It also considers whether statements can be generalized from one population to another.

- Sampling is unnecessary when the elements that would be sampled are identical, but the complexity of the educational world makes it difficult to argue very often that different elements are identical. Conducting a complete census of a population also eliminates the need for sampling, but the resources required for a complete census of a large population are usually prohibitive.

- Nonresponse undermines sample quality: It is the obtained sample, not the desired sample, that determines sample quality.

- Probability sampling methods rely on a random selection procedure to ensure no systematic bias in the selection of elements. In a probability sample, the odds of selecting elements are known, and the method of selection is carefully controlled.

- A sampling frame (a list of elements in the population) is required in most probability sampling methods. The adequacy of the sampling frame is an important determinant of sample quality.

- Simple random sampling and systematic random sampling are equivalent probability sampling methods in most situations.

- Stratified random sampling uses prior information about a population to make sampling more efficient. Stratified sampling may be either proportionate or disproportionate.

- Cluster sampling is less efficient than simple random sampling but is useful when a sampling frame is unavailable. It is also useful for large populations spread out across a wide area or among many organizations.

- Nonprobability sampling methods can be useful when random sampling is not possible, when a research question does not concern a larger population, and when a preliminary exploratory study is appropriate. However, the representativeness of nonprobability samples cannot be determined.

- The likely degree of error in an estimate of a population characteristic based on a probability sample decreases when the size of the sample and the homogeneity of the population from which the sample was selected increase. Sampling error is not affected by the proportion of the population that is sampled, except when that proportion is large.

Student Study Site

To assist in completing the web exercises, please access the study site at www.sagepub.com/check, where you will find the web exercise with accompanying links. You'll find other useful study materials such as self-quizzes and e-flashcards for each chapter, along with a group of carefully selected articles from research journals that illustrate the major concepts and techniques.

Discussion Questions

1. When, if ever, is it reasonable to assume that a sample is not needed because "everyone is the same"—that is, the population is homogeneous?
2. What increases sampling error in probability-based sampling designs? Stratified rather than simple random sampling? Disproportionate (rather than proportionate) stratified random sampling? Stratified rather than cluster random sampling? Why do researchers select disproportionate (rather than proportionate) stratified samples?

Practice Exercises

1. Select a random sample using the table of random numbers in Appendix D. Compute a statistic based on your sample, and compare it to the corresponding figure for the entire population. Here's how to proceed:

a. First, select a very small population for which you have a reasonably complete sampling frame. One possibility would be the list of asking prices for houses advertised in your local paper. Another would be the listing of some characteristic of states in a U.S. Census Bureau publication, such as average income or population size.

b. The next step is to create your sampling frame, a numbered list of all the elements in the population. If you are using a complete listing of all elements, as from a U.S. Census Bureau publication, the sampling frame is the same as the list. Just number the elements (states). If your population is composed of housing ads in the local paper, your sampling frame will be those ads that contain a housing price. Identify these ads, and then number them sequentially, starting with 1.

c. Decide on a method of picking numbers out of the random number table in Appendix D, such as taking every number in each row, row by row (or you may move down or diagonally across the columns). Use only the first (or last) digit in each number if you need to select 1 to 9 cases or only the first (or last) two digits if you want fewer than 100 cases.

d. Pick a starting location in the random number table. It's important to pick a starting point in an unbiased way, perhaps by closing your eyes and then pointing to some part of the page.

e. Record the numbers you encounter as you move from the starting location in the direction you decided on in advance, until you have recorded as many random numbers as the number of cases you need in the sample. If you are selecting states, 10 might be a good number. Ignore numbers that are too large (or small) for the range of numbers used to identify the elements in the population. Discard duplicate numbers.

f. Calculate the average value in your sample for some variable that was measured—for example, population size in a sample of states or housing price for the housing ads. Calculate the average by adding up the values of all the elements in the sample and dividing by the number of elements in the sample.

g. Go back to the sampling frame and calculate this same average for all the elements in the list. How close is the sample average to the population average?

h. Estimate the range of sample averages that would be likely to include 90% of the possible samples.

2. From professional journals, select four articles that describe research using a sample drawn from some population. Identify the type of sample used in each study, and note any strong and weak points in how the sample was actually drawn. Did the researchers have a problem due to nonresponse? Considering the sample, how confident are you in the validity of generalizations about the population based on the sample?

Web Exercises

1. What can you learn about sampling on the Web? Conduct a search on "sampling" and "population" and select a few of these sites. List a few new points that you learn about sampling.

2. Check out the "people" section of the U.S. Census Bureau website: www.census.gov. Based on some of the data you find there, write a brief summary of some aspect of the current characteristics of the American school-age population.

Developing a Research Proposal

Consider the possibilities for sampling.

1. Propose a sampling design that would be appropriate if you were to survey students on your campus only or in the school in which you work. Define the population, identify the sampling frame(s), and specify the elements and any other units at different stages. Indicate the exact procedure for selecting people to be included in the sample.

2. Propose a different sampling design for conducting your survey in a larger population, such as your city, state, or the entire nation.

PART II
Research Design and Data Collection

CHAPTER 6

Causation and
Research Design

Research Question: *How Do Educational Strategies Affect Educational Outcomes?*

Chapter Contents

I dentifying causes—figuring out why things happen—is the goal of much educational research. Unfortunately, valid explanations of the causes of educational phenomena do not come easily. The importance of early childhood learning is widely accepted. But which school strategies are best for young children, especially the disadvantaged? A connection between poverty and delinquency is well established, and both are linked to low achievement in school. But how exactly does poverty cause delinquency and low achievement, and what can schools do about it? Can early childhood programs such as Head Start have positive effects years later, helping their former students to avoid delinquency and get better grades? Causal questions such as these have stimulated much research.

In this chapter, our goal is to use studies on these and other, related questions to illustrate the ways educational researchers explore questions about causation through careful use of appropriate research methods.

We give special attention to key distinctions in research design that are related to our ability to come to causal conclusions: the criteria for causal explanations, reliance on a cross-sectional or longitudinal design, a focus on individual or group units of analysis, and the use of an experimental or nonexperimental design.

By the end of the chapter, you should have a good grasp of the different meanings of causation and be able to ask the right questions to determine whether causal inferences are likely to be valid, as well as a fuller understanding of research design. You may also have a better idea about the causes of success for early childhood students.

▣ Causal Explanation

A cause is an explanation of some characteristic, attitude, or behavior of groups, individuals, other entities (families, organizations), or events. For example, Jeremy Finn and Charles Achilles (1990) conducted a state-wide experiment to determine whether smaller class sizes led to long-term improved academic performance in the early grades. They concluded that it did, particularly for minority students. In Tennessee's Student Teacher Achievement Ratio experiment (Project STAR) involving 11,600 kindergarten through third-grade students in 80 elementary schools, they identified a causal effect of smaller class size on improved school performance. Although the original experiment took place more than 20 years ago, it is still the only large-scale, randomized trial study ever undertaken on class size effects. For this reason, many later researchers have used the Tennessee STAR experiment data to explore further causal connections about class size and learning (Schanzenbach, 2006).

More specifically, a causal effect is said to occur if variation in the hypothesized independent variable is followed by variation in the dependent variable, when all other things are equal (**ceteris paribus**). For instance, we know that for the most part, children who participate in early childhood education programs do better in school than children who do not participate in such programs, but this in itself does not establish that early childhood programs improve school performance. It could be that the parents who enroll their children in early childhood education programs also provided their children with more books and educational games before they started early childhood education. Maybe that is the real explanation for their better school performance. Or maybe neighborhoods that have more early childhood programs also have better schools. We just don't know. What we need to figure out is whether children who participate in early childhood programs do better after they enter school than other children, ceteris paribus—when all other things are equal.

We admit that you can legitimately argue that "all" other things can't literally be equal: We can't compare the same people at the same time in the same circumstances except for the variation in the independent variable (King et al., 1994). However, you will see that we can design research to create conditions that are very comparable so that we can isolate the impact of the independent variable on the dependent variable.

▣ Criteria for Causal Explanations

Five criteria should be considered in trying to establish a causal relationship. The first three criteria are generally considered requirements for identifying a causal effect: (1) empirical association, (2) appropriate time order, and (3) nonspuriousness. You must establish these three to claim a causal relationship. Evidence that meets the other two criteria—(4) identifying a causal mechanism and (5) specifying the context in which the effect occurs—can considerably strengthen causal explanations.

Research designs that allow us to establish these criteria require careful planning, implementation, and analysis. Many times, researchers have to leave one or more of the criteria unmet and are left with some important doubts about the validity of their causal conclusions, or they may even avoid making any causal assertions.

Association

The first criterion for establishing a causal effect is an empirical (or observed) **association** (sometimes called a *correlation*) between the independent and dependent variables. The variables must vary together such that when one goes up (or down), the other goes up (or down) at the same time. Here are some examples: The longer you stay in school, the more money you will make in life. When income goes up, so does overall health. In the Tennessee STAR Program experiment (Finn & Achilles, 1990; Schanzenbach, 2006), when class size went down, academic performance went up. In all of these cases, a change in an independent variable correlates, or is associated with, a change in a dependent variable. If there is no association, there cannot be a causal relationship. For instance, empirically there seems to be no correlation between the use of the death penalty and a reduction in the rate of serious crime. That may seem unlikely to some people, but empirically it is the case. If there is no correlation, there cannot be a causal relationship.

Time Order

Association is a necessary criterion for establishing a causal effect, but it is not sufficient. We must also ensure that the variation in the dependent variable occurred after the variation in the independent variable—the effect must come after its presumed cause. This is the criterion of **time order,** or the temporal priority of the independent variable. Motivational speakers sometimes say that to achieve success (the dependent variable), you really need to believe in yourself (the independent variable). And it is true that many very successful people seem remarkably confident—there is an association. But it may well be that their confidence is the result of their success, not its cause. Until you know which came first, you can't establish a causal connection.

Nonspuriousness

The third criterion for establishing a causal effect is **nonspuriousness.** *Spurious* means false or not genuine. We say that a relationship between two variables is **spurious** when it is due to changes in a third variable. Have you heard the old adage "Correlation does not prove causation"? It is meant to remind us that an association between two variables might be caused by something other than an effect of the presumed independent variable on the dependent variable. If we measure children's shoe sizes and their academic knowledge, for example, we will find a positive association. However, the association results from the fact that older children have larger feet as well as more academic knowledge. A third variable (age) is affecting both shoe size and knowledge so that they correlate, but one doesn't cause the other. Shoe size does not cause knowledge, or vice versa. The association between the two is, we say, spurious.

If you think this point is obvious, consider an education example. Do schools with more resources produce better students? Before you answer the question, consider the fact that parents with more education and higher income tend to live in neighborhoods that spend more on their schools. These parents also are more likely to have books in the home and provide other advantages for their children (see Exhibit 6.1). Do the parents cause variation in both school resources and student performance? If so, there would be an association between school resources and student performance that was at least partially spurious.

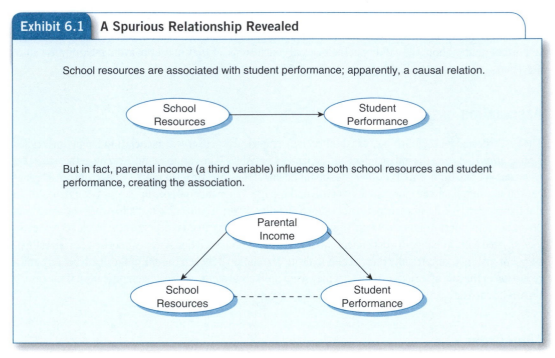

Source: Chambliss and Schutt (2010, p. 134).

Mechanism

A causal **mechanism** is the process that creates the connection between the variation in an independent variable and the variation in the dependent variable it is hypothesized to cause (Cook & Campbell, 1979, p. 35; Marini & Singer, 1988). Many researchers argue that no causal explanation is adequate until a causal mechanism is identified (Costner, 1989).

For instance, there seems to be an empirical association at the individual level between poverty and delinquency: Children who live in impoverished homes seem more likely to be involved in petty crime. But why? Researchers, including Agnew, Matthews, Bucher, Welcher, and Keyes (2008) and Sampson and Laub (1994), have found that children who grew up with such structural disadvantages as family poverty and geographic mobility were more likely to become juvenile delinquents. Their analysis indicates that multiple economic problems and structural disadvantages lead to less parent-child attachment, less maternal supervision, and more erratic or harsh discipline. In this way, figuring out some aspects of the process by which the independent variable influenced the variation in the dependent variable—the causal mechanism—can increase confidence in our conclusion that a causal effect was at work (Costner, 1989).

Context

No cause has its effect apart from some larger **context** involving other variables. When, for whom, and in what conditions does this effect occur? A cause is really one among a set of interrelated factors required for the effect (Hage & Meeker, 1988; Papineau, 1978). Do the causal processes in which we are interested vary across families? Among school systems? Over time? For different types of students and teachers? Identification of the context in which a causal relationship occurs is not itself a criterion for a valid causal relationship, but it can help us to understand the causal relationship.

Awareness of contextual differences helps us to make sense of the discrepant findings from local studies. Always remember that the particular cause on which we focus in a given research design may be only one among a set of interrelated factors required for the effect; when we take context into account, we specify these other factors (Hage & Meeker, 1988; Papineau, 1978).

🗐 Types of Research Designs

Researchers usually start with a question, although some begin with a theory or a strategy. If you're very systematic, the *question* is related to the *theory,* and an appropriate *strategy* is chosen for the research. All of these, you will notice, are critical defining issues for the researcher. If your research question is trivial (How many shoes are in my closet?), or your theory sloppy (More shoes reflect better fashion sense.), or your strategy inappropriate (I'll look at lots of shoes and see what I learn.), the project is doomed from the start.

But let's say you've settled these first three elements of a sound research study. Now we must begin a more technical phase of the research: the design of the study. From this point on, we will be introducing a number of terms and definitions that may seem strange or difficult. In every case, though, these terms will help you clarify your thinking. Like precisely the right word in an essay, these technical terms help, or even require, researchers to be absolutely clear about what they are thinking— and to be precise in describing their work to other people.

An overall research strategy can be implemented through several different types of research design. One important distinction between research designs is whether data are collected at one point in time—a **cross-sectional research design**—or at two or more points in time—a **longitudinal research design.** Another important distinction is between research designs that focus on individuals— the individual unit of analysis—and those that focus on groups, or aggregates of individuals—the group unit of analysis.

> **Cross-sectional research design:** A study in which data are collected at only one point in time.
>
> **Longitudinal research design:** A study in which data are collected that can be ordered in time; also defined as research in which data are collected at two or more points in time.
>
> **Individual unit of analysis:** A unit of analysis in which individuals are the source of data and the focus of conclusions.
>
> **Group unit of analysis:** A unit of analysis in which groups are the source of data and the focus of the conclusions.

Cross-Sectional Designs

In a cross-sectional design, all of the data are collected at one point in time. In effect, you take a "cross section"—a slice that cuts across the entire population under study—and use that to see all the different parts, or sections, of that population. Much of the research you have encountered so far in this text—the studies of maternal employment in Chapter 1 and of the academic effects of poverty in Chapter 4—has been cross-sectional. Although each of these studies took some time to carry out, they measured the actions, attitudes, and characteristics of respondents at only one time.

But cross-sectional studies, because they use data collected at only one time, suffer from a serious weakness: They don't take into account the time order of effects. For instance, you may see statistics showing that a certain high school has a very good college sending rate for seniors. You might conclude, then, that seniors' academic success is because of what transpired over time—that is, what they learned while in the school. But in fact, it may be that the school's policies resulted in less academically successful students leaving the school before reaching their senior year, through disciplinary expulsion, being "counseled out," or other reasons. A cross-sectional study of seniors doesn't distinguish if they are succeeding because of the instructional quality of the school or because, for whatever reason, those students least likely to graduate have already left the school before senior year begins. With a cross-sectional study, we can't be sure which explanation is correct, and that's a big weakness. To study change over time, we need a longitudinal design.

Longitudinal Designs

In longitudinal research, data are collected that can be ordered in time. By measuring the value of cases on an independent variable and a dependent variable at different times, the researcher can determine whether change in the independent variable precedes change in the dependent variable. In a cross-sectional study, when the data are collected all at one time, you can't really show if the hypothesized cause occurs first; in longitudinal studies, though, you can see if a cause occurs and then, later in time, the effect occurs. So if possible to do, longitudinal research is always preferable.

But collecting data two or more times takes time and work. Often researchers simply cannot, or are unwilling to, delay completion of a study for even 1 year to collect follow-up data. But think of the many research questions that really should involve a much longer follow-up period: What is the impact of elementary grade education on high school graduation? How effective is a high school parenting program in improving parenting skills when the students become adults? Under what conditions do traumatic experiences in early childhood result in a special-needs diagnosis in elementary school? It is safe to say that we will not be able to answer many important research questions because there was not enough time for a sufficiently long follow-up period. Nonetheless, the value of longitudinal data is so great that every effort should be made to develop longitudinal research designs of appropriate length when they are required for the research question.

In education, one technique for performing longitudinal studies is to tap into the immense amount of data routinely collected by governmental units such as public school systems and state and federal departments of education. This was the strategy Kathleen J. Skinner (2009) used to study charter schools in Boston, basing her research on longitudinal data from the Massachusetts Department of Education. She was interested in a variation of the question raised in the previous section: How should we view the success of charter schools that claim high rates of academic success for their graduating seniors? She found that although students were initially accepted to charter schools through a lottery system, once they enrolled, there was "significant student attrition resulting from the use of 'pushout' strategies based on student academic and/or behavioral performance" (Skinner, 2009, p. 1). Skinner tracked the number of students enrolled in each Boston charter school year by year to determine what percentage of entering students actually reached Grade 12. Exhibit 6.2 shows the figures from 2004–2009 for students who entered a charter school that claimed a 99% college acceptance rate for its graduates (Skinner, 2009, p. 30).

The final column in Exhibit 6.2 uses a metric called "promoting power" (Balfanz & Legters, 2004), which is simply the number of students in Grade 12 in a given year divided by the number of students who were in Grade 9 four years earlier. For example, for the senior class of 2009, promoting power is computed as 34/72 or 47%—of students who entered in 2005, only 47% made it to senior year. Taking the "promoting power" variable into account, Skinner's longitudinal study reveals a much lower success rate than the 99% graduation figure based on cross-sectional studies of the 12th graders.

Whether you plan to collect the data yourself or use an already existing data source, the following discussion of the three major types of longitudinal designs will give you a sense of the possibilities. (The three types are illustrated in Exhibit 6.3.)

Trend study (repeated cross-sectional design): A type of longitudinal study in which data are collected at two or more points in time from different samples of the same population.

Trend Studies

Studies that use a **repeated cross-sectional design,** also known as **trend studies,** are conducted as follows:

1. A sample is drawn from a population at Time 1, and data are collected from the sample.

2. As time passes, some people leave the population and others enter it.

3. At Time 2, a different sample is drawn from this population.

Exhibit 6.2 **Example Charter School, Student Attrition 2000-2009**

Graduating Class	Entry Year	Grade				Promoting Power (%)
		9	10	11	12	
2004	2000	78	54	32	27	35
2005	2001	65	50	38	28	43
2006	2002	79	56	24	18	23
2007	2003	49	38	25	20	41
2008	2004	96	72	54	46	48
2009	2005	72	61	46	34	47
Average, 2004–2009		73	55	36.5	29	40

Source: Adapted from Skinner (2009, p. 31). Statistics from Massachusetts Department of Elementary and Secondary Education.

Exhibit 6.3 **Three Types of Research Design**

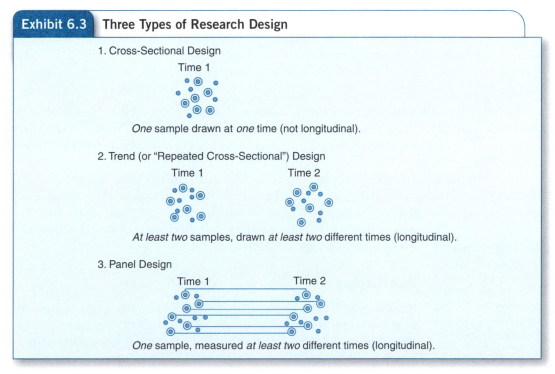

1. Cross-Sectional Design

Time 1

One sample drawn at *one* time (not longitudinal).

2. Trend (or "Repeated Cross-Sectional") Design

Time 1   Time 2

At least two samples, drawn *at least two* different times (longitudinal).

3. Panel Design

Time 1   Time 2

One sample, measured *at least two* different times (longitudinal).

Source: Chambliss and Schutt (2010, p. 33).

The Gallup polls, begun in the 1930s, are a well-known example of trend studies. One Gallup poll, for instance, asks people what they think is the best way to improve kindergarten through 12th-grade education in the United States. Exhibit 6.4 shows how a 1,010-person sample of American adults answered this question in 2004 and again 5 years later in 2009. The top four items remained the same from 2004 to 2009, but their order and percentage ranking changed slightly.

| Exhibit 6.4 | Best Way to Improve Education 2004 and 2009: The Gallup Organization |

Best Way to Improve Kindergarten Through 12th-Grade Education	Mentioning (%)	
	2004	2009
Quality teachers	15	17
Smaller class size	11	6
Basic curriculum	10	10
Improve funding	7	6
More parental involvement	6	5
Better teacher pay	6	6
Better discipline in schools	5	—
Hire more teachers	5	—
Teach about real life	—	5

Source: Gallup education poll, accessed at http://www.gallup.com/poll/1612/education.aspx

Each time the Gallup organization samples, it asks a different, though roughly demographically equivalent, group of people the same question; it isn't talking to the same people every time. Then it uses the results of a series of these questions to analyze change in Americans' opinions about education. This is a trend study.

These features make the trend study (repeated cross-sectional) design appropriate when the goal is to determine whether a population has changed over time. Has racial tolerance increased among Americans in the past 20 years? Are employers more likely to pay maternity benefits today than they were in the 1950s? These questions concern changes in the population as a whole, not changes in individuals.

Fixed-sample panel design (panel study): A type of longitudinal study in which data are collected from the same individuals—the panel—at two or more points in time. In another type of panel design, panel members who leave are replaced with new members.

Panel Designs

When we need to know whether individuals in the population have changed, we must turn to a panel design. Panel designs allow us to identify changes in individuals, groups, or whatever we are studying. This is the process for conducting **fixed-sample panel studies:**

1. A sample (called a panel) is drawn from a population at Time 1, and data are collected from the sample.

2. As time passes, some panel members become unavailable for follow-up, and the population changes.

3. At Time 2, data are collected from the same people as at Time 1 (the panel) — except for those people who cannot be located.

Because a panel design follows the same individuals, it is better than a repeated cross-sectional design for testing causal hypotheses. For example, Eliana Garces, Duncan Thomas, and Janet Currie (2002) used a panel design to study the long-term effects of the federal Head Start program. The panel, sponsored by the National Science Foundation, was a representative sample of U.S. families participating in Head Start; data were collected from the same families and their descendents 34 times between 1968 and 2005 (National Science Foundation, 2005). The researchers found that White Head Start students, in comparison to siblings who were not in the program, were "significantly more likely to complete high school, attend college, and possibly have higher earnings in their early twenties" (Garces et al., 2002, p. 999). They also found positive social and academic benefits for African American program participants (p. 999).

A panel design allows us to determine how individuals change, as well as how the population as a whole has changed; this is a great advantage. However, panel designs are difficult to implement successfully and often are not even attempted because of two major difficulties:

Expense and attrition. It can be difficult and expensive to keep track of individuals over a long period, and inevitably the proportion of panel members who can be located for follow-up will decline over time. Panel studies often lose more than one quarter of their members through attrition (D. C. Miller, 1991, p. 70).

Subject fatigue. Panel members may grow weary of repeated interviews and drop out of the study, or they may become so used to answering the standard questions in the survey that they start giving stock answers rather than actually thinking about their current feelings or actions. This is called the problem of **subject fatigue**.

Because panel studies are so useful, researchers have developed increasingly effective techniques for keeping track of individuals and overcoming subject fatigue. But when resources do not permit use of these techniques to maintain an adequate panel, repeated cross-sectional designs usually can be employed at a cost that is not a great deal higher than that of a one-time-only cross-sectional study. The payoff in explanatory power should be well worth the cost.

Cohort Designs

Trend and panel studies can track both the results of an event (such as the Vietnam War) and the progress of a specific historical generation (e.g., people born in 1985). In this case, the historically specific group of people being studied is known as a **cohort,** and this cohort makes up the basic population for your trend or panel study. Such a study has a **cohort design** (also called an **event-based design**). If you were doing a trend study, the cohort would be the population from which you drew your different samples. If you were doing a panel study, the cohort provides the population from which the panel itself is drawn. Examples include the following:

- *Birth cohorts*—those who share a common period of birth (those born in the 1940s, 1950s, 1960s, etc.)

- *Seniority cohorts*—those who have worked at the same place for about 5 years, about 10 years, and so on

- *School cohorts*—freshmen, sophomores, juniors, seniors

Cohort: Individuals or groups with a common starting point. Examples include individuals who began kindergarten in 1997, the college class of 2009, people who graduated from high school in the 1980s, and teachers who began teaching in 2005. Cohorts can form the initial population for either trend or panel studies.

Cohort design (event-based design): A type of longitudinal study in which data are collected at two or more points in time from individuals in a cohort.

We can see the value of event-based research in a comparison of two studies that estimated the impact of public and private schooling on high school students' achievement test scores. In an initial cross-sectional (not longitudinal) study, James Coleman, Thomas Hoffer, and Sally Kilgore (1982) compared standardized achievement test scores of high school sophomores and seniors in public, Catholic, and other private schools. They found that test scores were higher in the private high schools (both Catholic and other) than in the public high schools.

But was this difference a causal effect of private schooling? Perhaps the parents of higher-performing children were choosing to send them to private schools rather than to public ones.

So James Coleman and Thomas Hoffer (1987) went back to the high schools and studied the test scores of the former sophomores 2 years later, when they were seniors; in other words, the researchers used an event-based panel (longitudinal) design. This time they found that the verbal and math achievement test scores of the Catholic school students had increased more over the 2 years than the scores of the public school students had. Irrespective of students' initial achievement test scores, the Catholic schools seemed to "do more" for their students than did the public schools. The researchers' causal conclusion rested on much stronger ground because they used a cohort design.

Units and Levels of Analysis

Individual and Group Units of Analysis

As a student of educational research, you probably understand by now that groups don't act or think like individuals do. Groups and individuals are different units of analysis. **Units of analysis** are the things that you are studying, whose behavior you want to understand. Often, these are individual people, but they can also be, for instance, classrooms, schools, school systems, or the educational population of whole states. All of these could be units of analysis for your research.

Research on compulsory high-stakes testing, for instance, often uses the individual student as the unit of analysis. The researcher may collect survey data on individual test scores, then analyze the data, and then report on, say, how many individuals passed and how many failed.

Alternatively, units of analysis may instead be groups of some sort, such as grade levels, schools, or school systems. A researcher may analyze testing data published in the newspaper or on the website of the state department of education and find out what percentage of fifth graders passed in each elementary school in town or what percentage of all students in town passed from all grade levels. The researcher can then analyze the relationship between how long students have been in the school system and what happens to their scores. Does the percentage of students reaching competence go up or down the longer they are in the school system? Are math scores stronger than language, or vice versa? Because the data describe the city or town's school system, cities or towns are the units of analysis. In this example, either groups or individuals can be the units of analysis because data are collected from individuals (individual test scores), but taken together, the individual test scores create a profile of achievement in the town.

We also have to know what the units of analysis are to interpret statistics appropriately. Measures of association tend to be stronger for group-level than for individual-level data because measurement errors at the individual level tend to cancel out at the group level (Bridges & Weis, 1989, pp. 29–31).

The Ecological Fallacy and Reductionism

Researchers should make sure that their causal conclusions reflect the units of analysis in their study. Conclusions about processes at the individual level should be based on individual-level data; conclusions about group-level processes should be based on data collected about groups. In most cases, when this rule is violated, we can be misled about the existence of an association between two variables.

A researcher who draws conclusions about individual-level processes from group-level data could be making what is termed an **ecological fallacy** (see Exhibit 6.5). The conclusions may or may not be correct, but we must recognize that group-level data do not necessarily reflect solely individual-level processes. For example, a researcher may examine school records and find that the higher the percentage of male students at the high school, the higher the participation in school-sponsored sports activities. But the researcher would commit an ecological fallacy if she then concluded that boys are more interested in engaging in sports than girls are. This conclusion is about an individual-level causal process (the relationship between individual students and sports participation), even though the data describe groups (schools). It could actually be that prospective female athletes find there are fewer opportunities (not as many teams, lack of coaches) and poorer conditions (no locker rooms or shower facilities, lack of equal access to the gym or playing fields) and so do not participate. This is exactly the scenario that faced girls interested in athletics prior to federal Title IX legislation. Exploding participation in school sports by girls in the wake of Title IX proved that the problem was in the organization of schools, not in the interest of the girls.

Don't be too quick to reject all conclusions about individual processes based on group-level data; just keep in mind the possibility of an ecological fallacy. If we don't have individual-level data, we can't be sure that patterns at the group level will hold at the individual level.

On the other hand, when data about individuals are used to make inferences about group-level processes, a problem occurs that can be thought of as the mirror image of the ecological fallacy: the **reductionist fallacy,** also known as *reductionism,* or the *individualist fallacy* (see Exhibit 6.5). For example, Robert J. Sampson and William Julius Wilson (1995, pp. 37–38; Wilson, 1987, p. 58) note that we can be misled into concluding from individual-level data that race has a causal effect on violence because there is an association at the individual level between race and the likelihood of arrest for violent crime. However, community-level data reveal that a much higher percentage of poor Blacks live in high-poverty areas, as compared to poor

Exhibit 6.5	Errors in Causal Conclusions

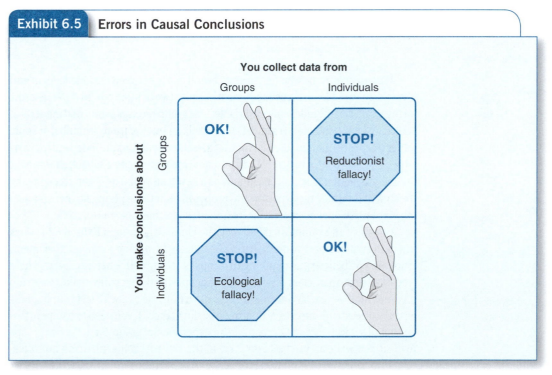

Source: Schutt (2009, p. 193).

Whites. The concentration of African Americans in poverty areas, not the race or other characteristics of the individuals in these areas, may be the cause of higher rates of violence. Explaining violence in this case requires community-level data.

The fact that errors in causal reasoning can be made should not deter you from conducting research with aggregate data or make you unduly critical of researchers who make inferences about individuals on the basis of aggregate data. The solution is to know what the units of analysis and **units of observation** were in a study and to take these into account in weighing the credibility of the researcher's conclusions. The goal is not to reject out of hand conclusions that refer to a level of analysis different from what was actually studied. Instead, the goal is to consider the likelihood that an ecological fallacy or a reductionist fallacy has been made when estimating the causal validity of the conclusions.

▣ True Experimental Designs

Experimental research provides the most powerful design for testing causal hypotheses because it allows us to establish confidently the first three criteria for causality—association, time order, and nonspuriousness. True experiments have at least three features that help us meet these criteria:

1. Two comparison groups (in the simplest case, an experimental group and a control group), which establishes association

2. Variation in the independent variable before assessment of change in the dependent variable, which establishes time order

3. Random assignment to the two (or more) comparison groups, which establishes nonspuriousness

> **True experiment:** Experiment in which subjects are assigned randomly to an experimental group that receives a treatment or other manipulation of the independent variable and a comparison group that does not receive the treatment or receives some other manipulation. Outcomes are measured in a posttest.

> **Experimental group:** In an experiment, the group of subjects that receives the treatment or experimental manipulation.

> **Comparison group:** In an experiment, groups that have been exposed to different treatments, or values of the independent variable (e.g., a control group and an experimental group).

> **Control group:** A comparison group that receives no treatment.

We can determine whether an association exists between the independent and dependent variables in a true experiment because two or more groups differ in terms of their value on the independent variable. One group receives some **treatment** (also called an "experimental treatment"), which is an intervention, stimulus, or some other purposely manipulated factor that affects the value of the independent variable. In a drug trial, a treatment can be a new medication. In a school, a treatment might be a new instructional technique or a new textbook. The group receiving the treatment is termed the experimental group. In a simple experiment, there is a second group that does not receive the treatment; it is termed the control group.

Consider an example in detail (see the simple diagram in Exhibit 6.6). Does drinking coffee improve one's writing of an essay? Imagine a simple experiment. Suppose you believe that drinking two cups of strong coffee before class will help you in writing an in-class essay. But other people think that coffee makes them too nervous and "wired" and so doesn't help in writing the essay. To test your hypothesis ("Coffee drinking causes improved performance"), you need to compare two groups of subjects, a control group and an experimental group. First, the two groups will sit and write an in-class essay. Then, the control group will drink no coffee, while the experimental group will drink two cups of strong coffee. Next, both groups will sit and write another in-class essay. At the end, all of the essays will be graded, and you will see whether the experimental group improved more than the control group. Thus, you may establish _association_.

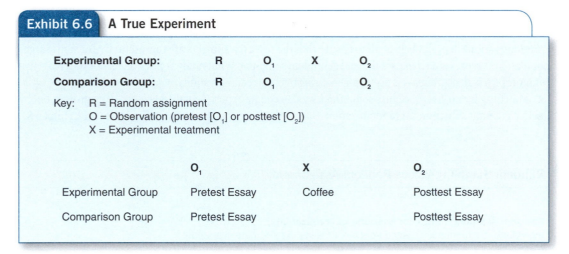

Exhibit 6.6	A True Experiment

Experimental Group: R O_1 X O_2

Comparison Group: R O_1 O_2

Key: R = Random assignment
O = Observation (pretest [O_1] or posttest [O_2])
X = Experimental treatment

	O_1	X	O_2
Experimental Group	Pretest Essay	Coffee	Posttest Essay
Comparison Group	Pretest Essay		Posttest Essay

Source: Chambliss and Schutt (2010, p. 136).

If you only conduct a survey and find that people who drink coffee score higher on tests, you can't be sure about the time order of effects. Perhaps people who write better have more time on their hands and so are more likely to go to coffeehouses and drink coffee and relax. By controlling who gets the coffee and when, we can establish *time order*.

All true experiments have a posttest—that is, a measurement of the outcome in both groups after the experimental group has received the treatment. In our example, you grade the papers. Many true experiments also have pretests, which measure the dependent variable before the experimental intervention. A pretest is the same as a posttest, just administered at a different time. Strictly speaking, though, a true experiment does not require a pretest. When researchers use random assignment, the groups' initial scores on the dependent variable and on all other variables are very likely to be similar. Any difference in outcome between the experimental and comparison groups is therefore likely to be due to the intervention (or to other processes occurring during the experiment), and the likelihood of a difference just on the basis of chance can be calculated.

Finally, it is crucial that the two groups be more or less equal at the beginning of the study. If you let students choose which group to be in, the more ambitious students may pick the coffee group, hoping to stay awake and do better on the paper. Or people who simply don't like the taste of coffee may choose the noncoffee group. Either way, your two groups won't be equivalent at the beginning of the study, so any difference in their writing may be the result of that initial difference (a source of spuriousness), not the drinking of coffee.

So you randomly sort the students into the two different groups. You can do this by flipping a coin for each student, by pulling names out of a hat, or by using a random number table or a computer program that generates random numbers. In any case, the subjects themselves should not be free to choose, nor should you (the experimenter) be free to put them into whatever group you want. (If you did that, you might unconsciously put the better students into the coffee group, hoping to get the results you're looking for.) Thus, we can achieve nonspuriousness with an experimental design.

The Tennessee STAR class size project, a true experiment, used randomization to reduce the risk of spuriousness. Students and teachers were randomly assigned to one of three types of classes: small class, regular-size class, or regular-size class with a teacher's aide (A. Krueger & Whitmore, 2001; Schanzenbach, 2006). As a result, the different groups were likely to be equivalent in all respects at the outset of the experiment. In general, the greater the number of cases assigned randomly to the groups, the more likely that the groups will be equivalent in all respects. The STAR experiment involved more than 11,000 students, and because students were randomly assigned, student characteristics such as free lunch status and amount of parental involvement were, on average, the same across class types (A. Krueger & Whitmore, 2001; Schanzenbach, 2006).

Note that the random assignment of subjects to experimental and comparison groups is not the same as random sampling of individuals from some larger population (see Exhibit 6.7). In fact, **random assignment** (randomization) does not help at all to ensure that the research subjects are representative of some larger population—representativeness is the goal of random sampling. What random assignment does—create two (or more) equivalent groups—is useful for ensuring internal (causal) validity, not generalizability.

Matching is another procedure sometimes used to equate experimental and comparison groups, but by itself, it is a poor substitute for randomization. One method is to match pairs of individuals (see Exhibit 6.8).

| Exhibit 6.7 | Random Sampling Versus Random Assignment |

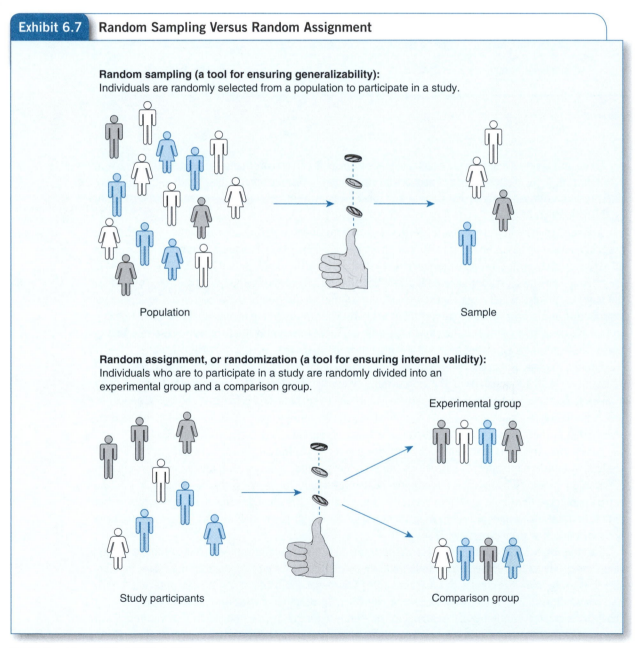

Random sampling (a tool for ensuring generalizability):
Individuals are randomly selected from a population to participate in a study.

Population

Sample

Random assignment, or randomization (a tool for ensuring internal validity):
Individuals who are to participate in a study are randomly divided into an experimental group and a comparison group.

Experimental group

Study participants

Comparison group

Source: Chambliss and Schutt (2010, p. 138).

Exhibit 6.8	Experimental Design Combining Matching and Random Assignment

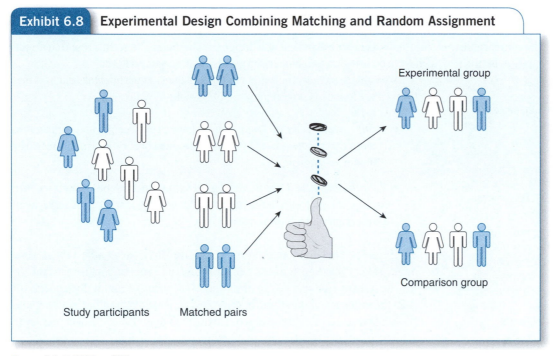

Source: Schutt (2009, p. 228).

...ntifying important characteristics that might affect the study, and then you match pairs of ...identical characteristics. In a study of middle school teachers, you might match ...on, and years of teaching experience and then assign each member of a pair to the ...oups. This method eliminates the possibility of differences due to chance in the gen-...ience composition of the groups. The basic problem is that, as a practical matter, indi-...on only a few characteristics, and so unmatched differences between the experimental ...s may still influence outcomes. However, when matching is combined with randomiza-...possibility of differences due to chance. A second problem with matching occurs when ...atched pair drops out of the study, unbalancing the groups. In this case, researchers will often exclu... ...ndings of the individual who remained in the study.

Quasi-Experimental Designs

Despite its advantages for establishing causation, testing a hypothesis with a true experimental design is often not feasible. A true experiment may be too costly or take too long to carry out, it may not be ethical to randomly assign subjects to the different conditions, or it may be too late to do so. For these reasons, researchers may use "quasi-experimental" designs that retain several components of experimental design but do not include randomization.

In quasi-experimental designs, a comparison group is predetermined to be comparable to the treatment group in critical ways, such as being eligible for the same services or being in the same school cohort

(Rossi & Freeman, 1989, p. 313). These research designs are *quasi*-experimental because subjects are not randomly assigned to the comparison and experimental groups. As a result, we cannot be as confident in the comparability of the groups as in true experimental designs. Nonetheless, to term a research design quasi-experimental, we have to be sure that the comparison groups meet specific criteria.

We will discuss here the two major types of quasi-experimental designs (other types can be found in Cook & Campbell, 1979; Mohr, 1992):

> **Quasi-experimental design:** A research design in which there is a comparison group that is comparable to the experimental group in critical ways but subjects are not randomly assigned to the comparison and experimental groups.
>
> **Nonequivalent control group design:** A quasi-experimental design in which there are experimental and comparison groups that are designated before the treatment occurs but are not created by random assignment.
>
> **Before-and-after design:** A quasi-experimental design consisting of several before-and-after comparisons involving the same variables but different groups.

- *Nonequivalent control group designs* have experimental and comparison groups that are designated before the treatment occurs but are not created by random assignment.

- *Before-and-after designs* have a pretest and posttest but no comparison group. In other words, the subjects exposed to the treatment serve, at an earlier time, as their own control group.

If quasi-experimental designs are longitudinal, they can establish time order. Where these designs are weaker than true experiments is in establishing the nonspuriousness of an observed association—that it does not result from the influence of some third, uncontrolled variable. On the other hand, because these quasi-experiments do not require the high degree of control necessary to achieve random assignment, quasi-experimental designs can be conducted using more natural procedures in more natural settings, so we may be able to achieve a more complete understanding of causal context. In identifying the mechanism of a causal effect, quasi-experiments are neither better nor worse than experiments.

Nonequivalent Control Group Designs

In this type of quasi-experimental design, a comparison group is selected so as to be as comparable as possible to the treatment group. Two selection methods can be used:

1. *Individual matching*—Individual cases in the treatment group are matched with similar individuals in the comparison group. This can sometimes create a comparison group that is very similar to the experimental group, such as when Head Start participants were matched with their siblings to estimate the effect of participation in Head Start (Garces et al., 2002). However, in many studies, it may not be possible to match on the most important variables.

2. *Aggregate matching*—In most situations when random assignment is not possible, the second method of matching makes more sense: identifying a comparison group that matches the treatment group in the aggregate rather than trying to match individual cases. This means finding a comparison group that has similar distributions on key variables: the same average age, the same percentage female, and so on. For this design to be considered quasi-experimental, however, it is important that individuals themselves have *not* chosen to be in the treatment group or the control group.

Before-and-After Designs

The common feature of before-and-after designs is the absence of a comparison group: All cases are exposed to the experimental treatment. The basis for comparison is instead provided by the pretreatment measures in the experimental group. These designs are thus useful for studies of interventions that are experienced by virtually every case in some population, such as a whole-school reform program or introduction of a new mathematics curriculum affecting all the mathematics classes in a school.

The simplest type of before-and-after design is the fixed-sample panel design. As you learned earlier, in a panel design, the same individuals are studied over time; the research may entail one pretest and one posttest. However, this simple type of before-and-after design does not qualify as a quasi-experimental design because comparing subjects to themselves at just one earlier point in time does not provide an adequate comparison group. Many influences other than the experimental treatment may affect a subject following the pretest—for instance, basic life experiences for a young subject.

Time-Series Designs

A time-series design typically involves only one group for which multiple observations of data have been gathered both prior to and after the intervention. Although many methodologists distinguish between repeated-measures panel designs, which include several pretest and posttest observations, and time-series designs, which include many (preferably 30 or more) such observations in both pretest and posttest periods, we do not make this distinction here.

A common design is the *interrupted time-series design,* in which three or more observations are taken before and after the intervention. It looks like this:

$$\text{Experimental Group } O_1\, O_2\, O_3 \,\text{X}\, O_4\, O_5\, O_6$$

As with other designs, there are variations on this basic design, including time-series designs with comparison or control groups and time-series designs in which multiple observations are also gathered during the course of the intervention.

One advantage of a time-series design is that there is only one group, so a second group need not be created. This is very useful when, for instance, one wishes to study a single classroom over the course of a marking period or a year. A second advantage is that, depending on the question, both the pretest and posttest observations need not occur prospectively; rather, the impacts of the programmatic or policy changes can be based on data already collected. For instance, if X in the diagram above referred to adoption of a new teaching strategy for the second marking period, then O_1, O_2, and O_3 could be grades for tests already taken in the first marking period.

A time-series design is based on the idea that, by taking repeated measures prior to an intervention or programmatic change, you have the opportunity to identify a pattern. A pattern may show a trend reflecting an ongoing increase or decline or it may simply stay flat. Having identified the preintervention pattern, the question is whether an intervention or program altered the nature of the pattern to what is considered a more favorable state.

What can we say about causality when using a time-series design? The before-and-after comparison enables you to determine whether an *association* exists between the intervention and the dependent variable. You can determine whether the change in the dependent variable occurred after the intervention, so *time order* is not a problem. However, there is no control group, so we cannot rule out the influence of extraneous factors as the actual cause of the change we observed; *spuriousness* may be a problem. Some other event may have occurred during the study that resulted in a change in posttest scores. What you *can* determine is that a trend caused by other factors did not cause the change in the dependent variable from before to after the exposure to the independent variable. Overall, the longitudinal nature of before-and-after designs can help to identify causal mechanisms, while the loosening of randomization requirements makes it easier to conduct studies in natural settings, where we learn about the influence of contextual factors.

▣ Threats to Validity in Experimental Designs

Experimental designs, like any research design, must be evaluated for their ability to yield valid conclusions. Remember, there are three kinds of validity: internal (causal) validity, external validity (generalizability), and measurement. True experiments are good at producing internal validity, but they fare less well in achieving external validity (generalizability). Quasi-experiments may provide more generalizable results than true experiments but are more prone to problems of internal invalidity. Measurement validity is a central concern for both kinds of research, but even a true experimental design offers no special advantages or disadvantages in measurement.

In general, nonexperimental designs, such as those used in survey research and field research, offer less certainty of internal validity, a greater likelihood of generalizability, and no particular advantage or disadvantage in terms of measurement validity. In this section, we focus on the ways in which experiments help (or don't help) to resolve potential problems of internal validity and generalizability.

Threats to Internal Causal Validity

The following sections discuss threats to validity (also referred to as "sources of invalidity") that occur frequently in social science research, including educational research (see Exhibit 6.9). These "threats" exemplify five major types of problems that arise in research design.

Noncomparable Groups

The problem of noncomparable groups occurs when the experimental group and the control group are not really comparable—that is, when something interferes with the two groups being essentially the same at the beginning (or end) of a study.

- *Selection bias*—Occurs when the subjects in your groups are initially different. If the ambitious students decide to be in the "coffee" group, you'll think their performance was helped by coffee—but it could have been their ambition.

Everyday examples of selection bias are everywhere. Harvard graduates are very successful people, but Harvard *admits* students who are likely to be successful anyway. Maybe Harvard itself had no effect on them. A few years ago, a psychotherapist named Mary Pipher wrote a best seller called *Reviving Ophelia* (1994) in which she described the difficult lives of—as she saw it—typical adolescent girls. Pipher painted a stark picture of depression, rampant eating disorders, low self-esteem, academic failure, suicidal thoughts, and even suicide itself. Where did she get this picture? From girls who selected themselves to be her patients—that is, from adolescent girls who were in deep despair or at least were unhappy enough to seek help. If Pipher had talked with a comparison sample of girls who hadn't sought help, perhaps the story would not have been so bleak.

- *Mortality*—Even when random assignment works as planned, the groups can become different over time because of mortality, or differential attrition; this can also be called "deselection." That is, the groups become different because subjects are more likely to drop out of one of the groups for various reasons. At some colleges, satisfaction surveys show that seniors are more likely to rate their colleges positively than are freshmen. But remember that the freshmen who really hated the place may have transferred out, so their ratings aren't included with senior ratings. In effect, the lowest scores are removed; that's a mortality problem.

Exhibit 6.9	Threats to Internal Validity

Problem	Example	Type
Selection	Girls who choose to see a therapist are not representative of population.	Noncomparable Groups
Mortality	Students who most dislike college drop out, so aren't surveyed.	Noncomparable Groups
Instrument Decay	Interviewer tires, losing interest in later interviews, so poor answers result.	Noncomparable Groups
Testing	If someone has taken the SAT before, they are familiar with the format, so do better.	Endogenous Change
Maturation	Everyone gets older in high school; it's not the school's doing.	Endogenous Change
Regression	The lowest-ranking students on IQ must improve their rank; they can't do worse.	Endogenous Change
History	The O. J. Simpson trial affects members of diversity workshops.	History
Contamination	"John Henry" effect; people in study compete with one another.	Contamination
Experimenter Expectation	Researchers unconsciously help their subjects, distorting results.	Treatment Misidentification
Placebo Effect	Fake pills in medical studies produce improved health.	Treatment Misidentification
Hawthorne Effect	Workers enjoy being subjects and work harder.	Treatment Misidentification

Source: Chambliss and Schutt (2010, p. 145).

Note that whenever subjects are not assigned randomly to treatment and comparison groups, the threat of selection bias or mortality is very great. Even if the comparison group matches the treatment group on important variables, there is no guarantee that the groups were similar initially in terms of either the dependent variable or some other characteristic. However, a pretest helps the researchers to determine and control for selection bias.

- *Instrument decay*—Measurement instruments of all sorts wear out, producing different results for cases studied later in the research. An ordinary spring-operated bathroom scale, for instance, may become "soggy" after some years, showing slightly heavier weights than would be correct. Or a college teacher—a kind of instrument for measuring student performance—gets tired after reading too many papers one weekend and starts giving everyone a B. Research interviewers can get tired or bored, too, leading perhaps to shorter or less thoughtful answers from subjects. In all these cases, the measurement instrument has "decayed" or worn out and so would result in a pretest to posttest change that is not due to the experimental treatment itself.

Endogenous Change

The next three problems, subsumed under the label *endogenous change*, occur when natural developments in the subjects, independent of the experimental treatment itself, account for some or all of the observed change between pretest and posttest.

- *Testing*—Taking the pretest can itself influence posttest scores. As the Kaplan SAT prep courses attest, there is some benefit just to getting used to the test format. Having taken the test beforehand can be an advantage. Subjects may learn something or may be sensitized to an issue by the pretest and, as a result, respond differently the next time they are asked the same questions on the posttest.

- *Maturation*—Changes in outcome scores during experiments that involve a lengthy treatment period may be due to maturation. Subjects may age, gain experience, or grow in knowledge—all as part of a natural maturational experience—and thus respond differently on the posttest than on the pretest. In many high school yearbooks, seniors are quoted as saying, for instance, "I started at West Geneva High School as a boy and leave as a man. WGHS made me grow up." Well, he probably would have grown up anyway, high school or not. WGHS wasn't the cause.

- *Regression*—Subjects who are chosen for a study because they received very low scores on a test may show improvement in the posttest, on average, simply because some of the low scorers on the pretest were having a bad day. Whenever subjects are selected for study because of extreme scores (either very high or very low), the next time you take their scores, they will likely "regress," or move toward the average. For instance, suppose you give an IQ test to third graders and then pull the bottom 20% of the class out for special attention. The next time that group (the 20%) takes the test, they'll almost certainly do better—and not just because of testing practice. In effect, they *can't* do worse—they were at the bottom already. On average, they must do better. A first-time novelist writes a wonderful book and gains worldwide acclaim and a host of prizes. The next book is not so good, and critics say, "The praise went to her head." But it may not have; she *couldn't* have done better. Whenever you pick people for being on an extreme end of a scale, odds are that next time, they'll be more average. This is called the *regression effect*.

> **Regression effect:** A source of causal invalidity that occurs when subjects who are chosen for a study because of their extreme scores on the dependent variable become less extreme on the posttest due to natural cyclical or episodic change in the variable.

Testing, maturation, and regression effects are generally not a problem in experiments that have a control group because they would affect the experimental group and the comparison group equally. However, these effects could explain any change over time in most before-and-after designs because these designs do not have a comparison group. Repeated measures, panel studies, and time-series designs are better in this regard because they allow the researcher to trace the pattern of change or stability in the dependent variable up to and after the treatment. Ongoing effects of maturation and regression can thus be identified and taken into account.

History

History, or external events during the experiment (things that happen outside the experiment), could change subjects' outcome scores. Examples are newsworthy events that concern the focus of an experiment and major disasters to which subjects are exposed. If you were running a series of diversity workshops for some insurance company employees while the notorious 1995 O. J. Simpson murder trial was taking place, for instance, participants' thoughts on race relations at the end of the workshops may say less about your training course than about O. J. Simpson or about their own relationship with the judicial system. This problem is often referred to as a history effect—history during the experiment, that is. It is a particular concern in before-and-after designs.

Causal conclusions can be invalid in some true experiments because of the influence of external events. For example, in an experiment in which subjects go to a special location for the treatment, something at that location unrelated to the treatment could influence these subjects. External events are a major concern in studies that compare the effects of programs in different cities or states (Hunt, 1985, pp. 276–277).

Contamination

Contamination occurs in an experiment when the comparison and treatment groups somehow affect each other. When comparison group members know they are being compared, they may increase their efforts just to be more competitive. This has been termed compensatory rivalry, or the John Henry effect, named after the "steel-driving man" of the folk song, who raced against a steam drill in driving railroad spikes and killed himself in the process. Knowing that they are being denied some advantage, comparison group subjects may as a result increase their efforts to compensate. On the other hand, comparison group members may become demoralized if they feel that they have been left out of some valuable treatment, performing worse than expected as a result. Both compensatory rivalry and demoralization thus distort the impact of the experimental treatment.

Treatment Misidentification

Sometimes the subjects experience a "treatment" that wasn't intended by the researcher. The following are three possible sources of treatment misidentification:

1. *Expectancies of experiment staff*—Change among experimental subjects may be due to the positive expectancies of experiment staff who are delivering the treatment rather than to the treatment itself. Even well-trained staff may convey their enthusiasm for an experimental program to the subjects in subtle ways. This is a special concern in evaluation research, when program staff and researchers may be biased in favor of the program for which they work and are eager to believe that their work is helping clients. Such positive staff expectations thus create a self-fulfilling prophecy.

2. *Placebo effect*—In medicine, a *placebo* is a chemically inert substance (a sugar pill, for instance) that looks like a drug but actually has no direct physical effect. Research shows that such a pill can actually produce positive health effects in two thirds of patients suffering from relatively mild medical problems (Goleman, 1993, p. C3). In other words, if you wish that a pill will help, it often actually does. In social science research, such placebo effects occur when subjects think their behavior should improve through an experimental treatment and then it does—not from the treatment, but from their own belief. Researchers might then misidentify the treatment as having produced the effect.

3. *Hawthorne effect*—Members of the treatment group may change in terms of the dependent variable because their participation in the study makes them feel special. This problem could occur when treatment group members compare their situation to that of members of the control group who are not receiving the treatment, in which case it would be a type of contamination effect. But experimental group members could feel special simply because they are in the experiment. This is termed a *Hawthorne effect* after a classic worker productivity experiment conducted at the Hawthorne electric plant outside Chicago in the 1920s. No matter what conditions the researchers changed to improve or diminish productivity (for instance, increasing or decreasing the lighting in the plant), the workers seemed to work harder simply because they were part of a special experiment. Oddly enough, some later scholars suggested that in the original Hawthorne studies, there was actually a selection bias, not a true Hawthorne effect—but the term has stuck (see Bramel & Friend, 1981). Hawthorne effects are also a concern in evaluation research, particularly when program clients know that the research findings may affect the chances for further program funding.

Process analysis is a technique for avoiding treatment misidentification (Hunt, 1985, pp. 272–274). Periodic measures are taken throughout an experiment to assess whether the treatment is being delivered as planned. Process analysis is often a special focus in evaluation research because of the possibility of improper implementation of the experimental program. For example, many school reform initiatives attempt to replicate their model program design in widely diverse school contexts. If we want to evaluate the impact of the innovation, we need to monitor whether the adopting school is implementing the model, which can be regarded as a "treatment," fully and correctly.

Generalizability

The need for generalizable findings can be thought of as the Achilles heel of true experimental design. The design components that are essential for a true experiment and that minimize the threats to causal validity make it more difficult to achieve sample generalizability—being able to apply the findings to some clearly defined larger population—and cross-population generalizability—generalizing across subgroups and to other populations and settings.

Subjects who can be recruited for a laboratory experiment, randomly assigned to a group, and kept under carefully controlled conditions for the duration of the study may not be representative of any large population of interest to educational researchers. Can they be expected to react to the experimental treatment in the same way as members of the larger population? The generalizability of the treatment and of the setting for the experiment also must be considered (Cook & Campbell, 1979, pp. 73–74). The more artificial the experimental arrangements, the greater the problem (D. T. Campbell & Stanley, 1966, pp. 20–21).

Cross-Population Generalizability

Researchers often are interested in determining whether treatment effects identified in an experiment hold true across different populations, times, or settings. When random selection is not feasible, the researchers may be able to increase the cross-population generalizability of their findings by selecting several different experimental sites that offer marked contrasts on key variables (Cook & Campbell, 1979, pp. 76–77).

Within a single experiment, researchers also may be concerned with whether the relationship between the treatment and the outcome variable holds true for certain subgroups. This demonstration of "external validity" is important evidence about the conditions that are required for the independent variable(s) to have an effect. School- and student-based research studies may not involve participants that are diverse in terms of income level and cultural/ethnic background, making it even more important for researchers to examine the relationship between the independent and dependent variable for all subgroups, not just one or two.

Finding that effects are consistent across subgroups does not establish that the relationship also holds true for these subgroups in the larger population, but it does provide supportive evidence. We have already seen examples of how the existence of treatment effects in particular subgroups of experimental subjects can help us predict the cross-population generalizability of the findings.

There is always an implicit trade-off in experimental design between maximizing causal validity and generalizability. The more that assignment to treatments is randomized and all experimental conditions are controlled, the less likely it is that the research subjects and setting will be representative of the larger population. However, although we need to be skeptical about the generalizability of the results of a single experimental test of a hypothesis, the body of findings accumulated from many experimental tests with different people in different settings can provide a very solid basis for generalization (D. T. Campbell & Russo, 1999, p. 143).

Interaction of Testing and Treatment

A variant on the problem of external validity occurs when the experimental treatment has an effect only when particular conditions created by the experiment occur. One such problem occurs when the treatment has an effect only if subjects have had the pretest. The pretest sensitizes the subjects to some issue so that when they are exposed to the treatment, they react in a way they would not have reacted if they had not taken the pretest. In other words, testing and treatment interact to produce the outcome. For example, answering questions in a pretest about racial prejudice may sensitize subjects so that when they are exposed to the experimental treatment, seeing a film about prejudice, their attitudes are different from what they would have been. In this situation, the treatment truly had an effect, but it would not have had an effect if it were repeated without the sensitizing pretest. This possibility can be evaluated by using the Solomon Four-Group Design to compare groups with and without a pretest (see Exhibit 6.10). If testing and treatment do interact, the difference in outcome scores between the experimental and comparison groups will be different for subjects who took the pretest and those who did not.

Exhibit 6.10	Solomon Four-Group Design Testing the Interaction of Pretesting and Treatment			
Experimental group:	R	O_1	X	O_2
Comparison group:	R	O_1		O_2
Experimental group:	R		X	O_2
Comparison group:	R			O_2

Key: R = Random assignment
O = Observation (pretest or posttest)
X = Experimental treatment

Source: Chambliss and Schutt (2010, p. 154).

As you can see, no single procedure establishes the external validity of experimental results. Ultimately, we must base our evaluation of external validity on the success of replications taking place at different times and places and using different forms of the treatment.

Limitations of True Experimental Designs

The distinguishing features of true experiments—experimental and comparison groups, pretests (which are not always used) and posttests, and randomization—do not help researchers identify the mechanisms by which treatments have their effects. In fact, this question of causal mechanisms often is not addressed in experimental research. The hypothesis test itself does not require any analysis of mechanism, and if the experiment was conducted under carefully controlled conditions during a limited span of time, the causal effect (if any) may seem to be quite direct. But attention to causal mechanisms can augment experimental findings. Evaluation researchers often focus attention on the mechanisms by which an educational program has its effect (Mohr, 1992, p. 25–27; Scriven, 1972). The goal is to measure the intermediate steps that lead to the change that is the program's primary focus.

True experimental designs also do not guarantee that the researcher has been able to maintain control over the conditions to which subjects are exposed after they are assigned to the experimental and comparison groups. If these conditions begin to differ, the variation between the experimental and comparison groups will not be what was intended. Such unintended variation is often not much of a problem in laboratory experiments, where the researcher has almost complete control over the conditions. But control over conditions can become a very big concern for field experiments, experimental studies that are conducted in the field, in real-world settings.

Nonexperiments

All of the other research designs we study are, of course, "nonexperimental." One of these designs, the ex post facto control group design, is often called quasi-experimental, but that's really not correct. Other designs are covered in other chapters under the headings of "cross-sectional" and "longitudinal" designs. Here, we'll briefly contrast these nonexperimental designs with experimental and quasi-experimental designs.

Ex Post Facto Control Group Designs

The ex post facto control group design is similar to the nonequivalent control group design and is often confused with it, but it does not meet as well the criteria for quasi-experimental designs. This design has experimental and comparison groups that are not created by random assignment, but unlike nonequivalent control group designs, individuals may decide themselves whether to enter the "treatment" or "control" group. As a result, in *ex post facto* (after the fact) designs, the people who join the treatment group may differ because of what attracted them to the group initially, not because of their experience in the group. However, in some studies, we may conclude that the treatment and control groups are so similar at the outset that causal effects can be tested (Rossi & Freeman, 1989, pp. 343–344).

One-Shot Case Studies and Longitudinal Designs

Cross-sectional designs, termed *one-shot case studies* in the experimental design literature, are easily able to establish whether an association exists between two variables, but we cannot be anywhere near as confident in their conclusions about appropriate time order or nonspuriousness as with true experiments or even quasi-experiments. Longitudinal designs improve greatly our ability to test the time order of effects, but they are unable to rule out all extraneous influences.

Christopher Brown (2009) used a one-shot case study design to explore ways in which the child-centered approach used in prekindergarten programs is being incorporated into the accountability-centered environment found in elementary schools. Brown hypothesized that, as more public school systems began to offer prekindergarten programs, there would be a disconnect between their approach and the academic accountability expected in grades after kindergarten. His case study examined implementation of an assessment tool designed to "align the academic achievement expectations of the prekindergarten with those in the corresponding elementary schools" (p. 202). At first, the tool did not work. It was modified to give a more accurate picture of skills students were meant to acquire in kindergarten. The difficulties in aligning the two ways of looking at children and instruction showed how complex it is to merge a child-centered orientation with test and standards-centered approaches and that the process requires effort and compromise on both sides.

Summary: Causality in Nonexperiments

How well do nonexperimental designs allow us to meet the criteria for causality identified earlier in this chapter?

Association: Nonexperiments can provide clear evidence of association between the independent and dependent variables.

Time order: For the most part, cross-sectional designs cannot establish time order. Longitudinal designs, even when nonexperimental, do allow identification of time order.

Nonspuriousness: Nonexperimental designs only weakly address the need to ensure nonspurious relationships because it is unlikely that we will be able to control for all potential **extraneous variables** that may confound the relationship between the independent and dependent variables.

Mechanism: Nonexperimental designs have no particular advantages or disadvantages for establishing causal mechanisms, although qualitative research designs facilitate investigations about causal process.

Context: Because they make it easy to survey large numbers of widely dispersed persons or organizations, one-shot cross-sectional studies facilitate investigation of **contextual effects.**

▣ Conclusions

In this chapter, you have studied the five criteria used to evaluate the extent to which particular research designs may achieve causally valid findings. You have learned how our ability to meet these criteria is shaped by research design features such as units of analysis, use of a cross-sectional or longitudinal design, and use of randomization to deal with the problem of spuriousness. You have also seen why the distinction between experimental and nonexperimental designs has so many consequences for how, and how well, we are able to meet criteria for causation.

We began this chapter by posing the general question, "How do educational strategies affect educational outcomes?" Throughout the chapter, you have seen a variety of research approaches to this question. What conclusions were reached by some of these studies? The Tennessee STAR study (Finn & Achilles, 1990; Schanzenbach, 2006) was a unique, large-scale, randomized trial of the effects of reducing class size in Grades K–3. It reached the conclusion that, other things being equal, smaller classes meant more learning, especially for disadvantaged students. A longitudinal panel study (Garces et al., 2002) concluded that the Head Start program has positive academic and social effects lasting into adolescence and early adulthood. A one-shot case study (C. P. Brown, 2009) showed that a "mismatch" in educational approaches (child centered vs. accountability centered) can create transition problems between kindergarten and elementary grades unless educators from both grade levels work together to integrate their approaches.

We also looked at researchers (Agnew et al., 2008; Sampson & Laub, 1994; Sampson & Wilson, 1995) who used a variety of methods to explore the relationship between poverty, delinquency, and low school achievement and concluded that poverty alone does not necessarily result in delinquency and low achievement. Rather, economic factors increase the likelihood of familial and social breakdowns that, in some cases but not others, lead to negative outcomes. A longitudinal study based on years of public data (Skinner, 2009) looked at charter schools in the city of Boston and found evidence that "push-out" strategies in some charter schools caused low achievers and problem students to leave the school before senior year, creating the impression that a higher percentage of students was graduating than was actually the case.

We should reemphasize that the results of any particular study are part of an always changing body of empirical knowledge about educational reality. Thus, our understandings of causal relationships are always partial. Researchers always wonder whether they have omitted some relevant variables from their controls, whether their experimental results would differ if the experiment were conducted in another setting, or whether they have overlooked a critical historical event. But by using consistent definitions of terms and maintaining clear standards for establishing the validity of research results—and by expecting the same of others who do research—educational researchers can contribute to a growing body of knowledge that can reliably guide educational policy and understanding.

When you read the results of an educational study, you should now be able to evaluate critically the validity of the study's findings. If you plan to engage in educational research, you should now be able to plan an approach that will lead to valid findings. And with a good understanding of three dimensions of validity (measurement validity, generalizability, and causal validity) under your belt, and with sensitivity also to the goal of "authenticity," you are ready to focus on the major methods of data collection used by educational researchers.

Key Terms

Association   119
Ceteris paribus   118
Cohort   125
Cohort design   125
Context   120
Contextual effect   141
Cross-sectional research design   121
Ecological fallacy   127
Event-based design
   (cohort study)   125

Extraneous variable   141
Fixed-sample panel design
   (panel study)   124
Longitudinal research
   design   121
Mechanism   120
Nonspuriousness   119
Random assignment   130
Reductionist fallacy
   (reductionism)   127

Repeated cross-sectional design
   (trend study)   122
Spurious relationship   119
Subject fatigue   125
Time order   119
Treatment   128
Trend study   122
Units of analysis   126
Units of observation   128

Highlights

- Three criteria are generally viewed as necessary for identifying a causal relationship: association between the variables, proper time order, and nonspuriousness of the association. In addition, the basis for concluding that a causal relationship exists is strengthened by identification of a causal mechanism and the context for the relationship.

- Association between two variables is in itself insufficient evidence of a causal relationship. This point is commonly made with the expression "Correlation does not prove causation."

- Experiments use random assignment to make comparison groups as similar as possible at the outset of an experiment to reduce the risk of spurious effects due to extraneous variables.

- Nonexperimental designs use statistical controls to reduce the risk of spuriousness. A variable is controlled when it is held constant so that the association between the independent and dependent variables can be assessed without being influenced by the control variable.

- Ethical and practical constraints often preclude the use of experimental designs.

- Longitudinal designs are usually preferable to cross-sectional designs for establishing the time order of effects. Longitudinal designs vary in terms of whether the same people are measured at different times, how the population of interests is defined, and how frequently follow-up measurements are taken. Fixed-sample panel designs provide the strongest test for the time order of effects, but they can be difficult to carry out successfully because of their expense as well as subject attrition and fatigue.

- We do not fully understand the variables in a study until we know what units of analysis they refer to.

- Invalid conclusions about causality may occur when relationships between variables measured at the group level are assumed to apply at the individual level (the ecological fallacy) and when

relationships between variables measured at the level of individuals are assumed to apply at the group level (the reductionist fallacy). Nonetheless, many research questions point to relationships at multiple levels and so may profitably be investigated at multiple units of analysis.

Student Study Site

To assist in completing the web exercises, please access the study site at www.sagepub.com/check, where you will find the web exercise with accompanying links. You'll find other useful study materials such as self-quizzes and e-flashcards for each chapter, along with a group of carefully selected articles from research journals that illustrate the major concepts and techniques.

Discussion Questions

1. Review articles in several newspapers, copying down all causal assertions. These might range from assertions that the stock market declined because of uncertainty in the Middle East to explanations about why a murder was committed or why test scores are declining in U.S. schools. Inspect the articles carefully, noting all evidence used to support the causal assertions. Which criteria for establishing causality are met? What other potentially important influences on the reported outcome have been overlooked?

2. Select several research articles in professional journals that assert, or imply, that they have identified a causal relationship between two or more variables. Are all of the criteria for establishing the existence of a causal relationship met? Find a study in which subjects were assigned randomly to experimental and comparison groups to reduce the risk of spurious influences on the supposedly causal relationship. How convinced are you by the study?

Practice Exercises

1. Search the *American Educational Research Journal* (*AERJ*) or another similar source for several articles on studies using any type of longitudinal design. You will be searching for article titles that use words such as *longitudinal, panel, trend,* or *over time.* How successful were the researchers in carrying out the design? What steps did the researchers who used a panel design take to minimize panel attrition? How convinced are you by those using repeated cross-sectional designs that they have identified a process of change in individuals? Did any researchers use

retrospective questions? How did they defend the validity of these measures?

2. Propose a hypothesis involving variables that could be measured with individuals as the units of analysis. How might this hypothesis be restated so as to involve groups as the units of analysis? Would you expect the hypothesis to be supported at both levels? Why or why not? Repeat the exercise, this time starting with a different hypothesis involving groups as the units of analysis and then restating it so as to involve individuals as the units of analysis.

Web Exercises

1. Try out the process of randomization. Go to the website http://www.randomizer.org. Now type numbers into the randomizer with two groups and 20 individuals per group. Repeat the process for four groups and 10 individuals per

group. Plot the numbers corresponding to each individual in each group. Does the distribution of numbers within each group truly seem to be random?

2. Go to the website of the U.S. Department of Education (http://www.ed.gov) and type *user friendly guide* into the search box. Click on the first item in the list that comes up, which should bring you to the publication *Identifying and Implementing Educational Practices Supported by Rigorous Evidence: A User Friendly Guide*. Open the pdf and read sections I, II, and III, which deal with randomized control trials, quasi-experimental designs, and comparison group studies. Do you agree with the designations "strong" and "possible" levels of effectiveness?

3. Read section IV of the "User Friendly Guide," concerning classroom implementation. As an educator, how helpful do you think this section is in giving you guidance for your own work?

Developing a Research Proposal

How will you try to establish the causal effects you hypothesize?

1. Identify at least one hypothesis involving what you expect is a causal relationship.

2. Identify key variables that should be controlled in your survey design to increase your ability to avoid arriving at a spurious conclusion about the hypothesized causal effect. Draw on relevant research literature and social theory to identify these variables.

3. Add a longitudinal component to your research design. Explain why you decided to use this particular longitudinal design.

4. Review the criteria for establishing a causal effect and discuss your ability to satisfy each one. Include in your discussion some consideration of how well your design will avoid each of the threats to experimental validity.

CHAPTER 7

Evaluation Research

Research Question: *How Can We Know How Well a New Curriculum Initiative Is Working?*

Chapter Contents

- **What Is Evaluation Research?**
- **What Can an Evaluation Study Focus On?**
- **How Can the Program Be Described? Creating a Program Logic Model**
- **What Are the Alternatives in Evaluation Design?**
- **Ethical Issues in Evaluation Research**

S uppose you are a sixth-grade teacher involved in your school's new, computer-based, integrated curriculum project. The project has these key elements:

- classrooms are organized into computer learning stations for small groups of students to work both individually and collaboratively, exploring hands-on tasks, writing tasks, and other work;

- in 1- to 3-week units on a topic, students rotate through all the stations;

- stations are intended to present material in a variety of ways, encourage teamwork, and equalize access to computers for all students;

- teams of four teachers covering the major subject areas (language arts, mathematics, science, social studies) work together to foster interdisciplinary learning (Cooksy, Gill, & Kelly, 2001, pp. 121–122).

Now suppose you were chosen as the teacher representative on a team working with an outside consultant to evaluate the program. The team's task is to find out if, and to what extent, the program is achieving its ambitious goals. How would you approach this task? How could you and your team plan and carry out such an evaluation?

As pressure for accountability becomes a fact of life in schools and teachers take on greater leadership roles, this kind of situation is becoming more common. In this chapter, you will read about an evaluation of a program like the one described above. You will also read about a variety of other educational and social program evaluations as we introduce the evaluation research process, illustrate different types of evaluation research, highlight alternative approaches, and review ethical concerns. You should finish the chapter with a much better understanding of how the methods of educational research can help to improve schools and society.

▣ What Is Evaluation Research?

Evaluation research is educational research that is conducted to investigate educational programs (e.g., federal and state initiatives, school-based professional development programs, new curricula, and new methods for teaching and discipline). For each project, an evaluation researcher must select a research design and method of data collection that are useful for answering the particular research questions posed and appropriate for the particular program investigated. When you review or plan evaluation research, you have to think about the research process as a whole and how different parts of that process can best be combined.

Exhibit 7.1 illustrates the process of evaluation research as a simple systems model. First, students, teachers, or some other persons or units—cases—enter the program as **inputs.** Students may begin a new school program, teachers may participate in professional development workshops, or school counselors may try out a new intervention technique. Resources and staff required by a program are also program inputs.

Next some service or treatment is provided to the cases. This may be attendance in a class, a new textbook, a new teaching technique, or a cash incentive for teachers to get further training. The process of service delivery—the **program process**—may be simple or complicated, short or long, but it is designed to have some impact on the cases as inputs are consumed and outputs are produced.

Program **outputs** are the direct product of the program's service delivery process. They could include students taking a statewide test, teachers trained, parental involvement with the school, or number of absences. The program outputs may be desirable in themselves, but they primarily serve to indicate that the program is operating.

Program **outcomes** indicate the impact of the program on the cases that have been processed. Outcomes can range from improved test scores or more highly qualified teachers to fewer unexcused absences and more

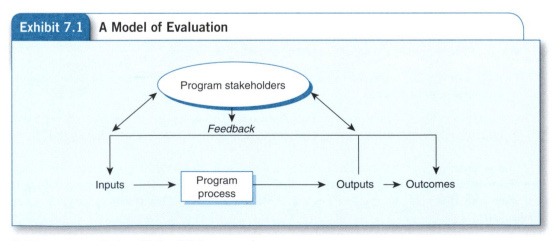

Exhibit 7.1 **A Model of Evaluation**

Source: Adapted from Martin and Kettner (1996).

parental involvement. Any educational program is likely to have multiple outcomes, some intended and some unintended, some positive and others that are viewed as negative.

Through a **feedback** process, variation in both outputs and outcomes can influence the inputs to the program. If not enough students are being served, recruitment of new students may increase. If too many low reading scores are measured, a new reading program may be limited or terminated. If a school-based program does not appear to lead to improved outcomes, parents may send their children elsewhere.

Evaluation research itself is just a systematic approach to feedback: It strengthens the feedback loop through credible analyses of program operations and outcomes. Evaluation research also broadens this loop to include connections to parties outside of the program itself. A funding agency or political authority may mandate the research, outside experts may be brought in to conduct the research, and the evaluation research findings may be released to the public, or at least funders, in a formal report.

The evaluation process as a whole, and feedback in particular, can be understood only in relation to the interests and perspective of program stakeholders. **Stakeholders** are those individuals and groups who have some basis of concern with the program. They might be students, educators, parents, funders, or the public. The board of a school or agency, the parents or spouses of clients, the foundations that award program grants, the auditors who monitor program spending, the members of Congress—each is a potential stakeholder, and each has an interest in the outcome of any program evaluation. Who the program stakeholders are and what role they play in the program evaluation can have tremendous consequences for the research.

Unlike explanatory or exploratory research, evaluation research is not designed to test the implications of an educational theory. For evaluation research, the particular program and its impact are paramount. How the program works also matters—not to advance a theory but to improve the program. Stakeholders of all sorts—not an abstract "scientific community"—have a legitimate role in setting the research agenda and may well intervene, even when they aren't supposed to. But overall, there is no sharp boundary between traditional educational research and evaluation research. In their attempt to explain how and why the program has an impact, as well as whether the program is needed, evaluation researchers often bring educational theories into their projects, but for immediately practical aims.

What Can an Evaluation Study Focus On?

Evaluation projects can focus on several questions. The questions asked will determine what research methods are used. Common evaluation questions for school-level programs are as follows:

- Can the program be evaluated?
- What is the level of need for the program?
- How does the program operate?
- What is the program's impact?
- How efficient is the program?

Evaluability Assessment

Some type of evaluation is always possible, but to identify the effects of a particular program may not be possible within the available time and resources. So researchers may conduct an **evaluability assessment** to learn this in advance, rather than expend time and effort on a fruitless project.

Why might an education program not be evaluable?

- Administrators only want to have their superior performance confirmed and do not really care whether the program is having its intended effects. This is a very common problem.

- Teachers are so alienated from the administration that they don't trust any attempt sponsored by administrators to check on their performance.

- Program personnel are just "helping people" or "putting in time" without any clear sense of what the program is trying to achieve.

- The program is not clearly distinct from other services delivered from the school system and so can't be evaluated by itself (Patton, 2002, p. 164).

Because they are preliminary studies to "check things out," evaluability assessments often rely on qualitative methods. Program managers and key staff may be interviewed in depth, or program sponsors may be asked about the importance they attach to different goals.

Needs Assessment

A **needs assessment** attempts to determine what needs exist in a population with systematic, credible evidence. Need may be assessed by social or educational indicators such as the poverty rate or test scores, by interviews of local experts such as school board members or experienced teachers, by surveys of populations potentially in need, or by focus groups with members of the school or the community (Rossi & Freeman, 1989).

The design of a needs assessment commissioned by the Massachusetts Department of Education in 2004 reveals the importance of taking a multidimensional approach. The project was designed to improve the collection and use of education data, which are highly important for judging the success of individual schools. The needs assessment called for the following:

- Interviews/focus groups/survey with local educators—superintendents, district data staff, teachers, and data users at the local level

- Interviews with state-level data people—staff at the Department of Education and other relevant state agencies/offices

- Models from other jurisdictions—a literature review and interviews to identify other data systems that may be useful models for Massachusetts (Massachusetts Department of Education, 2004)

In needs assessment, it is a good idea to use multiple indicators. Often there is no absolute definition of *need*. A good evaluation researcher will do his or her best to capture different perspectives on need and then to help others make sense of the results.

Process Evaluation

What actually happens in an educational program? Research to answer this question—to investigate the process of how services are actually delivered—is called process analysis or **process evaluation.** In a national program such as Head Start, for instance, with a large number of sites each with its own local conditions, student results can vary widely even though the program's goals (cognitive development, socialization, school success) are the same for every site. To identify the extent of this variation, evaluation researchers keep track of variables such as the goals and practices of preschool education, child care, home visiting programs, and level of program participation (Barnett, 1995).

As the Head Start example shows, process evaluation is particularly important when highly complex programs are evaluated. Many programs comprise multiple elements and are delivered over an extended period of time, often by different providers in different areas. Due to this complexity, it is quite possible that the program as delivered is not the same for all program recipients or consistent with the formal program design. Process evaluation also can be used to identify the specific aspects of the service delivery process that have an impact. This, in turn, will help to explain why the program has an effect and which conditions are required for these effects.

Formative evaluation occurs when the evaluation findings are used to help shape and refine the program (Rossi & Freeman, 1989), for instance, by being incorporated into the initial development of the service program. Evaluation may then lead to changes in recruitment procedures, program delivery, or measurement tools (Patton, 2002, p. 220).

Process evaluation can employ a wide range of indicators. Program coverage can be monitored through program records, student participant surveys, and analysis of program utilizers versus dropouts and ineligibles. Service delivery can be monitored through service records completed by program staff, a management information system maintained by program administrators, or reports by program recipients (Rossi & Freeman, 1989).

Qualitative methods are often a key component of process evaluation studies because they can be used to elucidate and understand internal program dynamics—even those that were not anticipated (Patton, 2002, p. 159; Posavac & Carey, 1997). Qualitative researchers may develop detailed descriptions of how program participants engage with each other, how the program experience varies for different people, and how the program changes and evolves over time.

Summative Evaluation (Impact Evaluation)

The core questions of evaluation research are as follows: Did the program work? Did it have the intended result? This kind of research is variously called **summative evaluation, impact analysis,** or **impact evaluation.** Formally speaking, impact analysis compares what happened after a program was implemented with what would have happened had there been no program at all.

> **Impact evaluation (or analysis):** Analysis of the extent to which a treatment or other service has an effect. Also known as summative evaluation.

Think of the program—such as a new strategy for teaching reading or a new approach to counseling adolescents—as an independent variable and the result it seeks as a dependent variable.

As in other areas of research, an experimental design is the preferred method for maximizing internal validity—that is, for making sure your causal claims about program impact are justified. Cases are assigned randomly to one or more experimental treatment groups and to a control group so that there is no systematic difference between the groups at the outset. The goal is to achieve a fair, unbiased test of the program itself, so that the judgment about the program's impact is not influenced by differences between the types of people who are in the different groups. It can be a difficult goal to achieve because a frequent practice in educational programs is to let people decide for themselves whether they want to enter a program and also to establish eligibility criteria that ensure that people who enter the program are different from those who do not (Boruch, 1997). In either case, a selection bias is introduced.

Of course, program impact may also be evaluated with quasi-experimental designs or survey or field research methods, without a randomized experimental design. But if current participants who are already in a program are compared to nonparticipants, it is unlikely that the treatment group will be comparable to the control group. Participants will probably be a selected group, different at the outset from nonparticipants. As a result, causal conclusions about program impact will be on much shakier ground.

Impact analysis is an important undertaking that fully deserves the attention it has been given in government program funding requirements. However, you should realize that more rigorous evaluation designs are less likely to conclude that a program has the desired effect; as the standard of proof goes up, success is harder to demonstrate.

Efficiency Analysis

Finally, a program may be evaluated for how efficiently it provides its benefits; typically, financial measures are used. Are the program's benefits sufficient to offset its costs? Are the taxpayers getting their money's worth? The answer is provided by **cost-benefit analysis.** How much does it cost to achieve a given effect? This answer is provided by **cost-effectiveness analysis.** Program funders routinely require one or both of these types of **efficiency analysis.**

A cost-benefit analysis must identify the specific program costs and the procedures for estimating the economic value of specific program benefits. This type of analysis also requires that the analyst identify whose perspective will be used to determine what can be considered a benefit rather than a cost. Students and parents will have a different perspective on these issues than do taxpayers or program staff.

Publicly funded early childhood education programs are one area in which a number of long-term, cost-benefit analyses have been conducted. A series of studies of the Perry Preschool Project in Chicago, which followed students from preschool into middle age, concluded that the project generated $258,888 in benefits and $15,166 in costs per preschool participant, which represents a benefit-cost ratio of roughly 17 to 1 (R. Lynch, 2005, p. 3). Exhibit 7.2 shows a sample of items that were regarded as costs and benefits in the study. A series of cost-benefit studies of publicly funded preschool programs (Masse & Barnett, 2002; Oden, Schweinhart, & Weikart, 2000; A. J. Reynolds, Temple, Robertson, & Mann, 2001) have come to the same conclusion: As a taxpayer investment, they represent tremendous value—a lot of "bang for the buck."

A cost-effectiveness analysis focuses attention directly on the program's outcomes rather than on the economic value of those outcomes. In a cost-effectiveness analysis, the specific costs of the program are compared to the program's outcomes, such as the number of teachers trained, the extent of improvement in reading scores, or the degree of decline in the dropout rate. For example, one result might be an estimate of how much it cost the program for each teacher trained to use a new instructional technique.

> **Efficiency analysis:** A type of evaluation research that compares program costs to program effects. It can be either a cost-benefit analysis or a cost-effectiveness analysis.
>
> **Cost-benefit analysis:** A type of evaluation research that compares program costs to the economic value of program benefits.
>
> **Cost-effectiveness analysis:** A type of evaluation research that compares program costs to actual program outcomes.

Exhibit 7.2   Cost-Benefit Analysis of the Perry Preschool Project

Costs ($15,166 per participant annually)	Benefits (approx. $258,888 per participant)
• Program staff • Program nonstaff expenses (supplies, educational materials, transportation, etc.)	• Reduced crime costs • Reduced subsequent public school costs (fewer students in special education, fewer students repeating grade, less truancy, etc.) • Reduced welfare spending • Higher earnings • More taxes paid because of higher earnings

Source: Adapted from R. Lynch (2005, p. 3).

In addition to measuring services and their associated costs, a cost-benefit analysis must be able to make some type of estimation of how clients benefited from the program. Normally, this will involve a comparison of some indicators of client status before and after clients received program services or between clients who received program services and a comparable group who did not.

▣ How Can the Program Be Described? Creating a Program Logic Model

How can an evaluation researcher bring all the aspects of a program together, summarizing it in an easy-to-understand fashion? One common method is to create a chart or diagram of the program that shows how all the pieces relate to each other. This type of diagram is called a logic model.

There is no single logic model design; the categories you choose to include often depend on the purpose for the logic model. One common type of logic model describes a theory and its link to change. This is called a *theory approach model,* and most of the attention is on how and why a program works. Alternatively, you might choose to develop an *outcome approach model,* where the focus is on connecting resources and activities to expected changes, or an *activity approach model,* where the focus is on describing what the program actually does (W. K. Kellogg Foundation, 2004).

Exhibit 7.3 presents a logic model developed by Cooksy et al. (2001) to evaluate Project TEAMS, a middle school curriculum initiative. Project TEAMS promoted an integrated approach to active learning strategies, computer use, and interdisciplinary teaching in the regular classroom (p. 121). It was implemented at three middle schools over several years, and the evaluators used the logic model as an integrative framework to focus data collection and to organize and interpret the resulting data (p. 119).

Cooksy et al. (2001) organized their analysis into four broad categories: Program Development, Program Activities, Initial Outcomes, and Intermediate Outcomes. Interpreting Exhibit 7.3 in terms of the process model presented in Exhibit 7.1, items in the Program Development column could be considered Inputs, Program Activities would represent the Program Process, items under Initial Outcomes would be Outputs, and the Intermediate Outcomes column would represent Outcomes.

Reading from the left, the first column in Exhibit 7.3 divides "Staff Activities" into three areas—Program Development (plan the program, secure funding, develop curriculum manual and teacher training plan), Project Management (program staff train and support teachers, involve parents), and School Administration (school staff support and monitor program activities).

Arrows indicate the flow of activity from the planning stage to the implementation stage, as well as from the two types of staff activity (program staff and school staff) to the next column, Participant Activities, which include teachers' activities (the bulk of the program) and parents' activities.

The next column, Initial Outcomes, shows program effects on teachers, students, and parents (e.g., "decreased isolation" and "working productively in groups") that can be measured immediately or in a relatively short time after the program starts. The final column lists longer term outcomes that the program staff hope will result from the program's activities, such as having other schools request the model and students graduating from high school.

As you can see, a logic model succinctly summarizes a great deal of information about the program and communicates "the relationship of program resources and operations to outcomes in a simple picture" (Cooksy et al., 2001, p. 121). After completing the logic model, the evaluator and often stakeholders should have a better understanding about the logic underlying the program.

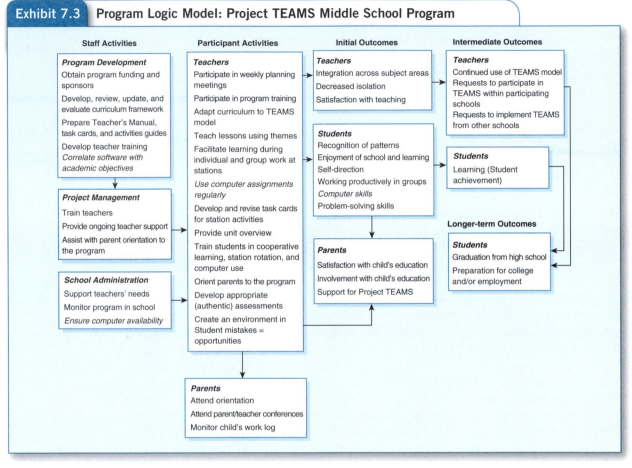

Exhibit 7.3 **Program Logic Model: Project TEAMS Middle School Program**

Source: Cooksy, Gill, and Kelly (2001).

What Are the Alternatives in Evaluation Design?

Evaluation research tries to learn if, and how, real-world programs produce results. There are several important alternative approaches to designing research to achieve this goal:

- *Black box or program theory*—How does the program get results?
- *Researcher or stakeholder orientation*—Whose goals matter most?
- *Quantitative or qualitative methods*—Which methods provide the best answers?
- *Simple or complex outcomes*—How complicated should the findings be?

Black Box or Program Theory

Most evaluation research tries to determine whether a program has the intended effect. If the effect occurred, the program "worked"; if the effect didn't occur, then, some would say, the program should be abandoned or redesigned. In this approach, the process by which a program produces outcomes is often treated as a "**black box**" in which the "inside" of the program is unknown. The focus of such research is whether cases have changed as a result of their exposure to the program between the time they entered as inputs and when they exited as outputs (Chen, 1990). The assumption is that program evaluation requires only the test of a simple input/output model, such as that shown in Exhibit 7.1. There may be no attempt to "open the black box" of the program process.

But there are good reasons to open the black box and investigate how the process works (or doesn't work). Consider recent research on welfare-to-work programs and their effects on adolescents' school performance. The Manpower Demonstration Research Corporation reviewed findings from research on these programs in Florida, Minnesota, and Canada (T. Lewin, 2001a). In each location, adolescents with parents in a welfare-to-work program were compared to a control group of teenagers whose parents were on welfare but were *not* enrolled in welfare-to-work. In all three locations, teenagers in the welfare-to-work program families actually did *worse* in school than those in the control group.

But why did requiring welfare mothers to get jobs hurt their children's schoolwork? Unfortunately, because the researchers had not investigated the program process—had not "opened the black box"—we can't know for sure. Martha Zaslow, an author of the resulting research report, speculated,

> Parents in the programs might have less time and energy to monitor their adolescents' behavior once they were employed. . . . Under the stress of working, they might adopt harsher parenting styles . . . the adolescents' assuming more responsibilities at home when parents got jobs was creating too great a burden. (T. Lewin, 2001b, p. A16)

Unfortunately, as Ms. Zaslow admitted, "We don't know exactly what's causing these effects, so it's really hard to say, at this point, what will be the long-term effects on these kids" (in T. Lewin, 2001b, p. A16).

If an investigation of the program process had been conducted, though, a **program theory** could have been developed. A program theory describes what has been learned about how the program has its effect. When a researcher has sufficient knowledge before the investigation begins, outlining a program theory can help to guide the investigation of the program process in the most productive directions. This is termed a *theory-driven evaluation*. The evaluation of Project TEAMS described earlier used a program theory approach, which the evaluators chose because "program theory guides an evaluation by identifying key program elements and articulating how these elements are expected to relate to each other" (Cooksy et al., 2001, p. 119).

> **Program theory:** A descriptive or prescriptive model of how a program operates and produces effects.

A program theory specifies how the program is expected to operate and identifies which program elements are operational (Chen, 1990, p. 32). In addition, a program theory specifies how a program is to produce its effects and so improves understanding of the relationship between the independent variable (the program) and the dependent variable (the outcome or outcomes). A program theory can also decrease the risk of failure when the program is transported to other settings because it will help to identify the conditions required for the program to have its intended effect.

Researcher or Stakeholder Orientation

What outcomes should a program strive to achieve? Whom should it serve? Most education research assumes that the researcher decides. In program evaluation, however, the research question is often set by the program sponsors or a government agency. When the evaluator is an outside consultant, a common situation for school-based programs, the client—a school administrator or a grant officer—decides what questions will be studied. Research findings are reported to these authorities, who most often also specify the outcomes to be investigated. The primary evaluator of evaluation research, then, is the funding agency, not the professional research community. Evaluation research is research for a client, and its results may directly affect the services or instructional techniques that program users receive. In this case, the person who pays the piper calls the tune.

Should the evaluation researcher insist on designing the project and specifying its goals? Or should he or she accept the suggestions and goals of the funding agency? What role should program staff and clients play? What responsibility does the evaluation researcher have to politicians and taxpayers when evaluating government-funded programs?

Various evaluation researchers have answered these questions through different approaches, the most common being *stakeholder, social science,* and *integrative* (Chen, 1990, pp. 66–68). **Stakeholder approaches** (also termed *responsive evaluation*) encourage researchers to be responsive to program stakeholders. Issues for study are to be based on the views of people involved with the program, and reports are to be made to program participants (Shadish, Cook, & Leviton, 1991, pp. 275–276). The program theory is developed by the researcher to clarify and develop the key stakeholders' theory of the program (Shadish et al., 1991, pp. 254–255). In evaluation research termed *action research* or *participatory research* (see Chapter 14), program participants are engaged with the researchers as co-researchers and help to design, conduct, and report the research.

Educational research approaches, in contrast, emphasize the importance of researcher expertise and maintenance of some autonomy to develop the most trustworthy, unbiased program evaluation. It is assumed that "evaluators cannot passively accept the values and views of the other stakeholders" (Chen, 1990, p. 78). Instead, the researcher derives a program theory from information on how the program operates and from current educational theory and knowledge, not from the views of stakeholders.

Of course, there are disadvantages to both stakeholder and educational research approaches to program evaluation. If stakeholders are ignored, researchers may find that participants are uncooperative and that their reports are unused. On the other hand, if educational research procedures are neglected, standards of evidence will be compromised, conclusions about program effects will likely be invalid, and results are unlikely to be generalizable to other settings. These equally undesirable possibilities have led to several attempts to develop more integrated approaches to evaluation research.

Integrative approaches attempt to cover issues of concern to both stakeholders and evaluators and to include stakeholders in the group from which guidance is routinely sought (Chen & Rossi, 1987, pp. 101–102). The emphasis given to either stakeholder or researcher concern is expected to vary with the specific project circumstances. Integrated approaches seek to balance responsiveness to stakeholders with objectivity and scientific validity. Evaluators negotiate regularly with key stakeholders during the planning of the research; preliminary findings are reported back to decision makers so they can make improvements in the program before it is formally evaluated. When the final evaluation is conducted, the research team may operate more autonomously, minimizing intrusions from program stakeholders. Evaluators and clients thus work together.

Quantitative or Qualitative Methods

Quantitative and qualitative approaches to evaluation each have their own strengths and appropriate uses. Quantitative research, with its clear percentages and numerical scores, allows quick comparisons over time and categories and thus is typically used in attempts to identify the effects of an educational program. Did students' test scores increase? Did the dropout rate go down? Did substance abuse decline? Quantified results can also prevent distraction by the powerful anecdote, forcing you to see what happens in most cases, not just in the dramatic cases.

Qualitative methods, on the other hand, can add depth, detail, and nuance; they can clarify the meaning of survey responses (see Chapter 8) and reveal more complex emotions and judgments people may have (Patton, 2002). Perhaps the greatest contribution qualitative methods can make is in investigating program process—finding out what is "inside the black box." Quantitative measures, such as staff contact hours and students' time-on-task, can track items such as service delivery, but finding out how clients experience the program is best accomplished by directly observing program activities and interviewing staff and clients intensively.

Qualitative methods also can uncover how different individuals react to the treatment. For example, a quantitative evaluation of student reactions to an adult basic skills program for new immigrants relied heavily on the students' initial statements of their goals. However, qualitative interviews revealed that most new immigrants lacked sufficient experience in the United States to set meaningful goals; their initial goal statements simply reflected their eagerness to agree with their counselors' suggestions (Patton, 2002, pp. 177–181). In general, the more complex the program, the more value that qualitative methods can add to the evaluation process.

Simple or Complex Outcomes

Few programs have only one outcome. Colleges provide not only academic education, for instance, but also— importantly—an amazingly efficient marketplace for potential spouses and lifetime friends. Some outcomes are direct and intended; others happen only over time, are uncertain, and may well not be desired. A decision to focus exclusively on a single outcome—probably the officially intended one—can easily cause a researcher to ignore even more important results.

Most evaluation researchers attempt to measure multiple outcomes (L. B. Mohr, 1992). The Project TEAMS researchers we read about earlier, for example, used both quantitative and qualitative data collection techniques to measure three levels of outcomes—"initial," "intermediate," and "longer term"—on three different groups of people: teachers, students, and parents. When researchers measure multiple outcomes, the result usually is a much more realistic, and richer, understanding of program impact.

In a sense, all of these choices (black box or program theory, researcher or stakeholder interests, etc.) hinge on what your real goals are in doing the project and how able you will be to achieve those goals. Not every agency really wants to know if its programs work, especially if the answer is no. Dealing with such issues, and the choices they require, is part of what makes evaluation research both scientifically and politically fascinating.

Ethical Issues in Evaluation Research

Evaluation research can affect people's lives. New teaching techniques, better test preparation strategies, expanded curricular options, treatment for substance abuse, training programs—each is a potentially important benefit—and an evaluation research project can make them more available and effective or make them disappear. This direct impact on program staff and leadership, as well as students who are receiving services and, potentially, their families, heightens the attention that evaluation researchers have to give to human subjects concerns. Their findings matter, so there are always serious ethical and political concerns for the evaluation researcher (Boruch, 1997, p. 13; Dentler, 2002, p.166).

There are many specific ethical challenges in evaluation research:

- How can confidentiality be preserved when the data are owned by a school system or a government agency or are subject to discovery in a legal proceeding?

- Who decides what level of burden an evaluation project may tolerably impose upon participants?

- Can a research decision legitimately be shaped by political considerations?

- Must findings be shared with all stakeholders or only with policy makers?

- Will a randomized experiment yield more defensible evidence than the alternatives?

- Will the results actually be used?

The Health Research Extension Act of 1985 (Public Law 99–158) mandated that the Department of Health and Human Services require all research organizations receiving federal funds to have an institutional review board (IRB) to assess all research for adherence to ethical practice guidelines. We have already reviewed the federally mandated criteria in Chapter 3 (Boruch, 1997, pp. 29–33):

- Are risks minimized?

- Are risks reasonable in relation to benefits?

- Is the selection of individuals equitable? (Randomization implies this.)

- Is informed consent given?

- Are the data monitored?

- Are privacy and confidentiality assured?

Evaluation researchers must consider whether it will be possible to meet each of these criteria long before they even design a study. Subject confidentiality is particularly thorny because researchers, in general, are not usually exempted from providing evidence sought in legal proceedings. When it appears that it will be difficult to meet the ethical standards in an evaluation project, at least from the perspective of some of the relevant stakeholders, modifications should be considered in the study design. It is also important to realize that it is costly to society and potentially harmful to participants to maintain ineffective programs. In the long run, it may be more ethical to conduct an evaluation study than to let the status quo remain in place.

Conclusions

We opened this chapter with the question, "How can we know how well a new curriculum initiative is working?" Cooksy et al. (2001) undertook such an evaluation, using a program logic model to build an integrated diagram of the program components and employing multiple data collection methods to measure multiple outcomes for a variety of stakeholders. They concluded that a small, positive effect was shown in two of the three schools participating but that factors in addition to Project TEAMS had a significant effect on student outcomes (Cooksy et al., 2001, pp. 124–127).

Hopes for evaluation research are high: Schools and society benefit from the development of programs that work well, that accomplish their goals, and that serve students and educators who genuinely need them. At least that is the hope. Unfortunately, there are many obstacles to realizing this hope (Posavac & Carey, 1997):

- Because educational programs and the people who use them are complex, evaluation research designs can easily miss important outcomes or aspects of the program process.

- Because the many program stakeholders all have an interest in particular results from the evaluation, researchers can be subject to an unusual level of cross-pressures and demands.

- Because the need to include program stakeholders in research decisions may undermine adherence to scientific standards, research designs can be weakened.

- Because some program administrators want to believe their programs really work well, researchers may be pressured to avoid null findings or, if they are not responsive, find their research report ignored. Plenty of well-done evaluation research studies wind up in a recycling bin or hidden away in a file cabinet.

- Because the primary audiences for evaluation research reports are program administrators, politicians, or members of the public, evaluation findings may need to be overly simplified, distorting the findings.

The rewards of evaluation research are often worth the risks, however. Evaluation research can provide educational scientists with rare opportunities to study complex learning processes, with real consequences, and to contribute to the public good. Although they may face unusual constraints on their research designs, most evaluation projects can result in high-quality analysis and publications in reputable scholarly journals. In many respects, evaluation research is an idea whose time has come. We may never achieve Donald Campbell's (Campbell & Russo, 1999) vision of an "experimenting society," in which research is consistently used to evaluate new programs and to suggest constructive changes, but we are close enough to continue trying.

Key Terms

Black box   152
Cost-benefit analysis   150
Cost-effectiveness analysis   150
Efficiency analysis   150
Evaluability assessment   147
Feedback   147
Formative evaluation   149

Impact evaluation
    (or analysis)   149
Inputs   146
Integrative approach   154
Needs assessment   148
Outcomes   146
Outputs   146

Process evaluation   148
Program process   146
Program theory   153
Stakeholder approach   154
Stakeholders   147
Summative evaluation   149

Highlights

- Evaluation research in education is conducted for a distinctive purpose: to investigate educational programs.

- The evaluation process can be modeled as a feedback system, with inputs entering the program, which generates outputs and then outcomes, which feed back to program stakeholders and affect program inputs.

- The evaluation process as a whole, and the feedback process in particular, can be understood only in relation to the interests and perspectives of program stakeholders.

- The process by which a program has an effect on outcomes is often treated as a "black box," but there is good reason to open the black box and investigate the process by which the program operates and produces, or fails to produce, an effect.

- A program theory may be developed before or after an investigation of the program process is completed. It may be either descriptive or prescriptive.

- Evaluation research is done for a client, and its results may directly affect the services and treatments that program users receive. Evaluation researchers differ in the extent to which they attempt to orient their evaluations to program stakeholders.

- Qualitative methods are useful in describing the process of program delivery.

- Multiple outcomes are often necessary to understand program effects.

- There are five primary types of program evaluation: needs assessment, evaluability assessment, process evaluation (including formative evaluation), impact evaluation (also termed *summative evaluation*), and efficiency (cost-benefit) analysis.

- Evaluation research raises complex ethical issues because it may involve withholding desired educational benefits.

Student Study Site

To assist in completing the web exercises, please access the study site at www.sagepub.com/check, where you will find the web exercise with accompanying links. You'll find other useful study materials such as self-quizzes and e-flashcards for each chapter, along with a group of carefully selected articles from research journals that illustrate the major concepts and techniques.

Discussion Questions

1. Would you prefer that evaluation researchers use a stakeholder or an educational research approach? Compare and contrast these perspectives and list at least three arguments for the one you favor.

2. Think about a school- or agency-based program that you are familiar with. Diagram the program using the simple process model shown in Exhibit 7.1 in this chapter. Now develop some categories for using a logic model to describe the program. Which one seems more useful to you?

Practice Exercises

1. Read and summarize an evaluation research report published in the journal *Evaluation and Program Planning*. Be sure to identify the type of evaluation research that is described. Discuss the strengths and weaknesses of the design.

2. Select one of the evaluation research studies described in this chapter, read the original report (book or article) about it, and review its adherence to the ethical guidelines for evaluation research. Which guidelines do you feel are most important? Which are most difficult to adhere to?

Web Exercises

1. Describe the resources available for evaluation researchers at one of the following three websites: http://www.wmich.edu/evalctr, http://www.campbellcollaboration.org/, and http://www.nwrac.org/whole-school/index.html.

2. Go to the website of the Center for Applied Research and Educational Improvement (http://www.cehd.umn.edu/carei/) and read one of the "top requested" current or archived reports. What kind of evaluation design was used? What was the focus of the evaluation? What ethical concerns do you see in the study?

Developing a Research Proposal

1. Develop a simple logic model for an educational program you are familiar with.

2. Who are the stakeholders in your program? How will you relate to them before, during, and after the evaluation?

3. Design a program evaluation to test the efficacy of your program model, using an impact approach or one of the other approaches mentioned in this chapter.

CHAPTER 8

Survey Research

Research Question: *How Can We Get a National Picture of K–12 Math and Science Teaching?*

Chapter Contents

S cience and mathematics education have assumed growing importance in an age of ubiquitous computers and constant technological innovation. The performance of U.S. students on math and science tests has been criticized in comparison to other countries (Hanushek, Peterson, & Woessmann, 2010; Provasnik, Gonzales, & Miller, 2009), and there has been a push for improvement in math and science teaching. But what does math and science instruction in U.S. schools actually look like? What materials are used? What methods are common? To answer this question, the National Science Foundation commissioned the 2000 National Survey of Science and Mathematics Education ("2000 National Survey"). The survey gathered data on teacher background and experience, curriculum and instruction, and the availability and use of instructional resources (Weiss, Banilower, McMahon, & Smith, 2001).

In this chapter, we use the 2000 National Survey and other examples to illustrate key features of survey research. You will learn about the challenges of designing a survey, some basic rules of question construction, and the ways in which surveys can be administered. This is followed by issues of survey design related to diverse school populations and a discussion of ethical issues surrounding surveys. By the chapter's end, you should be well on your way to becoming an informed consumer of survey reports and a knowledgeable developer of survey designs.

Why Is Survey Research So Popular?

Survey research involves the collection of information from a sample of individuals through their responses to questions. The National Science Foundation turned to survey research for the 2000 National Survey because it is an efficient method for systematically collecting data from a broad spectrum of individuals and educational settings. As you probably have observed, a great many researchers choose this method of data collection. In fact, surveys have become such a vital part of our social fabric that we cannot assess much of what we read in the newspaper or see on TV without having some understanding of survey research.

Survey research owes its continuing popularity to its versatility, efficiency, and generalizability. First and foremost is the *versatility* of survey methods. Researchers have used survey methods to investigate areas of education as diverse as school desegregation, academic achievement, teaching practice, and leadership. Although a survey is not the ideal method for learning about every educational process, a well-designed survey can enhance our understanding of just about any educational issue. The 2000 National Survey covered a range of topics about math and science teaching, and there is hardly any other topic of interest to educators that has not been studied at some time with survey methods.

Surveys are efficient in that many variables can be measured without substantially increasing the time or cost. Survey data can be collected from many people at relatively low cost and, depending on the survey design, relatively quickly.

Survey methods lend themselves to probability sampling from large populations. Thus, survey research is very appealing when *sample generalizability* is a central research goal. In fact, survey research is often the only means available for developing a representative picture of the attitudes and characteristics of a large population. To gather a representative national picture of math and science instruction, the 2000 National Survey sampled 5,765 science and mathematics teachers across the United States (Weiss et al., 2001).

Survey responses from these teachers produced a unique, national data set covering "science and mathematics course offerings and enrollments; teacher qualifications; textbook usage; instructional techniques; and use of science and mathematics facilities and equipment" (Weiss et al., 2001, p. 2). A mixture of methods was used, including interviews and questionnaires of teachers, program directors, and principals as well as on-site observations in both math and science classrooms. The data collected allowed Horizon Research, the firm that carried out the survey, to investigate topics such as the impact of professional development on math and science teaching (Rosenberg, Heck, & Banilower, 2005), the extent to which recommended reforms have actually been implemented (Smith, Banilower, McMahon, & Weiss, 2002), leadership issues, and the change process at the school level (Weiss et al., 2001). As a result, we know much more about how academic preparation and professional development influence math and science instruction, what teaching techniques and textbooks are being used, and how much progress has been made toward reform.

Want to Know More? You can access reports and survey instruments of the 2000 National Survey of Science and Mathematics at http://2000survey.horizon-research.com/.

Surveys also are the method of choice when cross-population generalizability is a key concern because they allow a range of educational contexts and subgroups to be sampled. The consistency of relationships can then be examined across the various subgroups. The 2000 National Survey sampled urban, suburban, and rural teachers K–12 and across subdisciplines such as earth science, chemistry, biology, and physics (Weiss et al., 2001).

Errors in Survey Research

It might be said that surveys are too easy to conduct. Organizations and individuals often decide that a survey will help to solve some important problem because it seems so easy to prepare a form with some questions and send it out. But without careful attention to sampling, measurement, and overall survey design, the effort is likely to be a flop. Such flops are too common for comfort, and the responsible survey researcher must take the time to design surveys properly and to convince sponsoring organizations that this time is worth the effort (Turner & Martin, 1984, p. 68).

For a survey to succeed, it must minimize the risk of two types of error: poor measurement of cases that are surveyed (*errors of observation*) and omission of cases that should be surveyed (*errors of nonobservation*) (Groves, 1989). Potential problems that can lead to errors of observation stem from the way questions are written, the characteristics of the respondents who answer the questions, the way questions are presented in questionnaires, and the interviewers used to ask the questions. The potential measurement errors that survey researchers confront in designing questions and questionnaires are summarized in Exhibit 8.1; we discuss each of these sources of error throughout the chapter.

There are three sources of errors of nonobservation:

- Coverage of the population can be inadequate due to a poor sampling frame.

- The process of random sampling can result in sampling error—differences between the characteristics of the sample members and the population that arise due to chance.

- Nonresponse can distort the sample when individuals refuse to respond or cannot be contacted. Nonresponse to specific questions can distort the generalizability of the responses to those questions.

We considered the importance of a good sampling frame and the procedures for estimating and reducing sampling error in Chapter 5; we only add a few more points here. We focus more attention in this chapter on procedures for reducing nonresponse in surveys, an increasing concern.

The next two sections focus on principles, including question writing, for developing a well-designed survey. Presenting clear and interesting questions in a well-organized questionnaire will help to reduce measurement error by encouraging respondents to answer questions carefully and to take seriously the request to participate in the survey.

Questionnaire Design

Survey questions are answered as part of a **questionnaire** (or **interview schedule,** as it is sometimes called in interview-based studies). The context created by the questionnaire has a major impact on how individual questions are interpreted and answered. As a result, survey researchers must carefully design the questionnaire as well as individual questions. There is no precise formula for a well-designed questionnaire. Nonetheless, some key principles should guide the design of any questionnaire, and some systematic procedures should be considered for refining it.

Questionnaire: A survey instrument containing the questions in a self-administered survey.

Interview schedule: A survey instrument containing the questions asked by the interviewer in an in-person or phone survey.

Exhibit 8.1 | **Measurement Errors Associated With Surveys**

Question Wording: Does the question have a consistent meaning to respondents? Problems can occur with

- *Lengthy wording* Words are unnecessarily long and complicated.
- *Length of question* Question is unnecessarily long.
- *Lack of specificity* Question does not specify the desired information.
- *Lack of frame of reference* Question does not specify what reference comparisons should be made to.
- *Vague language* Words and phrases can have different meanings to respondents.
- *Double negatives* Question uses two or more negative phrases.
- *Double barreled* Question actually asks two or more questions.
- *Using jargon and initials* Phrasing uses professional or academic discipline-specific terms.
- *Leading questions* Question uses phrasing meant to bias the response.
- *Cultural differences in meaning* Phrases or words have different meanings to different population subgroups.

Respondent Characteristics: Characteristics of respondents may produce inaccurate answers. These include

- *Memory recall* Problems remembering events or details about events.
- *Telescoping* Remembering events as happening more recently than when they really occurred.
- *Agreement or acquiescence bias* Tendency for respondents to "agree."
- *Social desirability* Tendency to want to appear in a positive light and therefore providing the desirable response.
- *Floaters* Respondents who choose a substantive answer when they really do not know.
- *Fence-sitters* People who see themselves as being neutral so as not to give the wrong answer.
- *Sensitive questions* Questions deemed too personal.

Presentation of Questions: The structure of questions and the survey instrument may produce errors including

- *Open-ended questions* Response categories are not provided, left to respondent to provide.
- *Closed-ended questions* Possible response categories are provided.
- *Agree-disagree* Tendency to agree when only two choices are offered.
- *Question order* The context or order of questions can affect subsequent responses as respondents try to remain consistent.
- *Response set* Giving the same response to a series of questions.
- *Filter questions* Questions used to determine if other questions are relevant.

Interviewer: The use of an interviewer may produce error.

- Mismatch of interviewer-interviewee demographic characteristics.
- Unconscious judgmental actions to responses.

Source: Engel and Schutt (2010, p. 179).

Maintain Consistent Focus

A survey should be guided by a clear conception of the research problem under investigation and the population to be sampled. Throughout the process of questionnaire design, the research objective should be the primary basis for making decisions about what to include and exclude and what to emphasize or treat in a cursory fashion. The questionnaire should be viewed as an integrated whole, in which each section and every question serve a clear purpose related to the study's objective and each section complements other sections.

Build on Existing Instruments

Surveys often include irrelevant questions and fail to include questions that, the researchers realize later, are crucial. One way to ensure that possibly relevant questions are asked is to use questions suggested by prior research, theory, experience, or experts (including participants) who are knowledgeable about the setting under investigation.

If another researcher already has designed a set of questions to measure a key concept, and evidence from previous surveys indicates that this measure is reliable and valid, then, by all means, use that instrument. Resources such as the *Handbook of Research Design and Social Measurement* (Miller & Salkind, 2002) can give you many ideas about existing instruments; your literature review at the start of a research project should be an even better source.

But there is a trade-off here. Questions used previously may not concern quite the right concept or may not be appropriate in some ways to your population. So even though using a previously designed and well-regarded instrument may reassure other researchers, it may not really be appropriate for your own specific survey. A good rule of thumb is to use a previously designed instrument if it measures the concept of concern to you and if you have no clear reason for thinking it is inappropriate with your survey population.

Refine and Test Questions

The only good question is a pretested question. Before you rely on a question in your research, you need evidence that your respondents will understand what it means. So try it out on a few people.

One important form of pretesting is discussing the questionnaire with colleagues. You can also review prior research in which your key questions have been used. Forming a panel of experts to review the questions can also help. For a student research project, "experts" might include a practitioner who works in a setting like the one to be surveyed, a methodologist, and a person experienced in questionnaire design. Another increasingly popular form of pretesting comes from guided discussions among potential respondents. Such "focus groups" let you check for consistent understanding of terms and to identify the range of events or experiences about which people will be asked to report. By listening to and observing the focus group discussions, researchers can validate their assumptions about what level of vocabulary is appropriate and what people are going to be reporting (Nassar-McMillan & Borders, 2002).

Professional survey researchers also use a technique for improving questions called the **cognitive interview** (Dillman, 2007). Although the specifics vary, the basic approach is to ask people, ideally individuals who reflect the proposed survey population, to "think aloud" as they answer questions. The researcher asks a test question, then probes with follow-up questions about how the respondent understood the question, how confusing it was, and so forth. This method can identify many problems with proposed questions.

Conducting a pilot study is the final stage of questionnaire preparation. Complete the questionnaire yourself and then revise it. Next, try it out on some colleagues or other friends, and revise it again. For the actual pretest, draw a small sample of individuals from the population you are studying, or one very similar to it, and try out the survey procedures with them, including mailings if you plan to mail your questionnaire and actual interviews if you plan to conduct in-person interviews.

Which pretesting method is best? Each has unique advantages and disadvantages. Simple pretesting is the least reliable but may be the easiest to undertake. Focus groups or cognitive interviews are better for understanding the bases of problems with particular questions. Review of questions by an expert panel identifies the greatest number of problems with questions (Presser & Blair, 1994).

Order the Questions

The sequence of questions on a survey matters. As a first step, the individual questions should be sorted into broad thematic categories, which then become separate sections in the questionnaire. For example, the 2000

National Survey Mathematics Questionnaire contained five sections: Teacher Opinions, Teacher Background, Your Mathematics Teaching in a Particular Class, Your Most Recent Mathematics Lesson in This Class, and Demographic Information. Both the sections and the questions within the sections must be organized in a logical order that would make sense in a conversation.

The first question deserves special attention, particularly if the questionnaire is to be self-administered. This question signals to the respondent what the survey is about, whether it will be interesting, and how easy it will be to complete ("Overall, would you say that your current teaching situation is excellent, good, fair, or poor?"). The first question should be connected to the primary purpose of the survey; it should be interesting, it should be easy, and it should apply to everyone in the sample (Dillman, 2007). Don't try to jump right into sensitive issues ("In general, what level of discipline problems do you have in your classes?"); respondents have to "warm up" before they will be ready for such questions.

Question order can lead to **context effects** when one or more questions influence how subsequent questions are interpreted (Schober, 1999). Prior questions can influence how questions are comprehended, what beliefs shape responses, and whether comparative judgments are made (Tourangeau, 1999). The potential for context effects is greatest when two or more questions concern the same issue or closely related issues. Often, respondents will try to be consistent with their responses, even if they really do not mean the response.

Whichever type of information a question is designed to obtain, be sure it is asked of only the respondents who may have that information. If you include a question about job satisfaction in a survey of the general population, first ask respondents whether they have a job. These **filter questions** create **skip patterns.** For example, respondents who answer no to one question are directed to skip ahead to another question, but respondents who answer yes go on to the **contingent question.** Skip patterns should be indicated clearly with arrows or other marks in the questionnaire, as demonstrated in Exhibit 8.2.

Some questions may be presented in a "matrix" format. Matrix questions are a series of questions that concern a common theme and that have the same response choices. The questions are written so that a common initial phrase applies to each one (see Exhibit 8.4). This format shortens the questionnaire by reducing the number of words that must be used for each question. It also emphasizes the common theme among the questions and so invites answering each question in relation to other questions in the matrix. It is very important to provide an explicit instruction to "Check one response on each line" in a matrix question because some respondents will think that they have completed the entire matrix after they have responded to just a few of the specific questions.

Exhibit 8.2 **Filter Questions and Skip Patterns**

3. Are you currently employed in a teaching position?

   a. _____ Yes
   b. _____ No ⟶ GO TO QUESTION 10

4. What type of educational institution is your current employer?

   a. _____ Public school
   b. _____ Private, nonprofit school
   c. _____ For-profit school
   d. _____ Other (specify)

Make the Questionnaire Attractive

An attractive questionnaire—neat, clear, clean, and spacious—is more likely to be completed and less likely to confuse either the respondent or, in an interview, the interviewer.

An attractive questionnaire does not look cramped; plenty of "white space"—more between questions than within question components—makes the questionnaire appear easy to complete. Response choices are listed vertically and are distinguished clearly and consistently, perhaps by formatting them in all capital letters and keeping them in the middle of the page. Skip patterns are indicated with arrows or other graphics. Some distinctive type of formatting should also be used to identify instructions. Printing a multipage questionnaire in booklet form usually results in the most attractive and simple-to-use questionnaire (Dillman, 2000, pp. 80–86).

Exhibit 8.3 contains portions of a telephone interview questionnaire that illustrates these features, making it easy for the interviewer to use.

Exhibit 8.3 | **Sample Interview Guide**

Hi, my name is _____. I am calling on behalf of (I am a student at) Hamilton College in New York. We are conducting a national opinion poll of high school students.

SCREENER: Is there a sophomore, junior, or senior in high school in your household with whom I may speak?

  1. Yes   2. No/not sure/refuse **(End)**

(If student not on phone, ask:) Could he or she come to the phone?

(When student is on the phone) Hi, my name is _____. I am calling on behalf of (I am a student at) Hamilton College in New York. We are conducting a national opinion poll of high school students about gun control. Your answers will be completely anonymous. Would you be willing to participate in the poll?

  1. Yes   2. No/not sure/refuse **(End)**

1. (SKOLYR) What year are you in school?
    1. Sophomore
    2. Junior
    3. Senior
    4. Not sure/refuse **(do not read) (End)**

Now some questions about your school:

2. (SKOL) Is it a public, Catholic, or private school?
    1. Public   2. Catholic   3. Private   4. Not sure **(do not read)**

Source: Chambliss and Schutt (2010, p. 172). Copyright © 2000 Dennis Gilbert. Reprinted with permission.

🔲 Writing Questions

Questions are the centerpiece of survey research. Because the way they are worded can have a great effect on the way they are answered, selecting good questions is the single most important concern for survey researchers.

Write Clear Questions

All hope for achieving measurement validity is lost unless the questions in a survey are clear and convey the intended meaning to respondents. You may be thinking that you ask people questions all the time and have no trouble understanding the answers you receive, but you may also remember misunderstanding or being confused by some questions. Consider just a few of the differences between everyday conversations and standardized surveys:

- Survey questions must be asked of many people, not just one person.

- The same survey question must be used with each person, not tailored to the specifics of a given conversation.

- Survey questions must be understood in the same way by people who differ in many ways.

- You will not be able to rephrase a survey question if someone doesn't understand it because that would result in a different question for that person.

- Survey respondents don't know you and so can't be expected to share the nuances of expression that help you and your friends and family to communicate.

Question writing for a particular survey might begin with a brainstorming session or a review of previous surveys. Then, whatever questions are being considered must be systematically evaluated and refined. Every question that is considered for inclusion must be reviewed carefully for its clarity and ability to convey the intended meaning. Questions that were clear and meaningful to one population may not be so to another. Nor can you simply assume that a question used in a previously published study was carefully evaluated. Adherence to a few basic principles will go a long way toward developing clear and meaningful questions.

Avoid Confusing Phrasing

In most cases, a simple direct approach to asking a question minimizes confusion. Use shorter rather than longer words: *brave* rather than *courageous; job concerns* rather than *work-related employment issues* (Dillman, 2000). Use shorter sentences when you can. A lengthy question often forces respondents to "work hard," that is, to have to read and reread the entire question. Lengthy questions can go unanswered or can be given only a cursory reading without much thought.

Avoid Vagueness

Questions should not be abbreviated in a way that results in confusion. The simple statement

Residential location _____

does not provide sufficient focus; rather, it is a general question when a specific kind of answer is desired. There are many reasonable answers to this question, such as Silver Lake (a neighborhood), Los Angeles (a city), or Forbes Avenue (a street). Asking, "In what neighborhood of Los Angeles do you live?" provides specificity so that respondents understand that the intent of the question is about their neighborhood.

It is particularly important to avoid vague language; there are words whose meaning may differ from respondent to respondent. The question

Do you usually or occasionally attend our school's monthly professional development workshops?

will not provide useful information, for the meaning of *usually* or *occasionally* can differ for each respondent. A better alternative is to define the two terms such as *usually (6 to 12 times a year)* and *occasionally (2 to 5 times a year)*. A second option is to ask respondents how many times they attended professional development sessions in the past year; the researcher can then classify the responses into categories.

Provide a Frame of Reference

Questions often require a frame of reference that provides specificity about how respondents should answer the question. The question

Overall, the performance of this principal is

_____Excellent

_____Good

_____Average

_____Poor

lacks a frame of reference. In this case, the researcher does not know the basis of comparison the respondent is using. Some respondents may compare the principal to other principals, whereas some respondents may use a personal "absolute scale" about a principal's performance. To avoid this kind of confusion, the basis of comparison should be specifically stated in the question: "Compared with other principals you are familiar with, the performance of this principal is...."

Avoid Negative Words and Double Negatives

Try answering, "Do you disagree that mathematics teachers should not be required to be observed by their supervisor if they have a master's degree?" Respondents have a hard time figuring out which response matches their sentiments because the statement is written as a **double negative.** Such errors can easily be avoided with minor wording changes: "Should mathematics teachers with a master's degree still be observed by their supervisor?" To be safe, it's best just to avoid using negative words such as *don't* and *not* in questions.

Avoid Double-Barreled Questions

Double-barreled questions produce uninterpretable results because they actually ask two questions but allow only one answer. For example, the question "Do you support increased spending on schools and social services?" is really asking two questions—one about support for schools and one about support for social services. It is perfectly reasonable for someone to support increased spending on schools but not on social services. A similar problem can also show up in response categories.

Minimize the Risk of Bias

Specific words in survey questions should not trigger biases, unless that is the researcher's conscious intent. Such questions are referred to as leading questions because they lead the respondent to a particular answer. Biased or loaded words and phrases tend to produce misleading answers. Some polls ask obviously loaded questions, such as "Isn't it time for Americans to stand up for morality and stop the shameless degradation of the airwaves?" Especially when describing abstract ideas (e.g., "freedom" "justice," "fairness"), your choice of words dramatically affect how respondents answer. Take the difference between "welfare" and "assistance for the poor." On average, surveys have found that public support for "more assistance for the poor" is about 39 points higher than for "welfare" (Smith, 1987). Most people favor helping the poor; most people oppose welfare. So the terminology a survey uses to describe public assistance can bias survey results quite heavily.

Responses can also be biased when response alternatives do not reflect the full range of possible sentiment on an issue. When people pick a response choice, they seem to be influenced by where they are placing themselves relative to the other response choices. A similar bias occurs when some but not all possible responses are included in the question. "What do you like about your community, such as the parks and the schools?" focuses respondents on those categories, and other answers may be ignored. It is best left to the respondent to answer the question without such response cues.

Closed-Ended and Open-Ended Questions

Questions can be designed with or without explicit response choices. When explicit response categories are offered, we call it a **closed-ended question.** For example, the following question asked in a survey of special-needs schools is closed-ended because the desired response categories are provided:

What type of special-needs services does your school offer?

_____Residential

_____Nonresidential

_____Both

Most surveys of a large number of people contain primarily closed-ended questions, which are easy to process with computers and analyze with statistics. Providing response choices in the survey reduces ambiguity, and respondents are more likely to answer the question the researcher really wants them to answer. However, closed-ended questions can obscure what people really think unless the choices are designed carefully to match the range of possible responses to the question.

Most important, closed-ended response choices should be mutually exclusive and exhaustive so that every respondent can find one and only one choice that applies to him or her (unless the question is of the "Check all that apply" format). To make response choices exhaustive, researchers may need to offer at least one option with room for ambiguity. For example, school superintendents were asked how they dealt with bullying in their school system. The list of choices included five different possible responses but concluded with the category "Other (Please specify_____)" because researchers were not sure they had all the possible responses on the list. If respondents do not find a response option that corresponds to their answer to the question, they may skip the question entirely or choose a response option that does not indicate what they are really thinking.

Open-ended questions are questions without explicit response choices so that the respondents provide their own answers in their own words. This type of question is usually used when there is little knowledge about a particular topic, and you want to learn as much as possible without limiting the responses. For example, if you are interested in learning the responses that school superintendents have developed on their own to bullying, you might ask,

How has your school system responded to the increase in attention to K–12 bullying issues?

The information obtained from a question such as this could be used as response categories for closed-ended questions in future surveys.

Although open-ended questions provide a wealth of information, they also require careful consideration. Administering, analyzing, and summarizing open-ended questions can be time-consuming and difficult. Some respondents do not like to write a lot and may find open-ended questions taxing. Interviewing is not necessarily the solution. The amount of information provided by a respondent may depend on the respondent's personality—some respondents may provide short or cursory answers; others may provide extensive answers with a great deal of relevant (and irrelevant) information.

Closed-Ended Questions and Response Categories

When writing response categories for closed-ended questions, several guidelines may help improve the questions. We have already mentioned that it is important to ensure that the responses are mutually exclusive and exhaustive. We offer these additional suggestions to consider when designing questions.

Allow for Disagreement

People often tend to "agree" with a statement just to avoid seeming disagreeable. You can take several steps to reduce the likelihood of agreement bias. As a general rule, you should present both sides of attitude scales in the question itself (Dillman, 2000, pp. 61–62): "In general, do you believe that *teaching strategies* or *student effort* are more to blame for poor mathematics performance in the United States?" The response choices themselves should be phrased to make each one seem as socially approved, as "agreeable," as the others. You should also consider replacing a range of response alternatives that focus on the word *agree* with others. For example, "To what extent do you support or oppose the new science curriculum reform?" (response choices range from "strongly support" to "strongly oppose") is probably a better approach than the question "To what extent do you agree or disagree with the statement: 'The new science curriculum reform is worthy of support'?" (response choices range from "strongly agree" to "strongly disagree").

Social Desirability

Social desirability is the tendency for individuals to respond in ways that make them appear in the best light to the interviewer. When an illegal or socially disapproved behavior or attitude is the focus, we have to be concerned that some respondents will be reluctant to agree that they have ever done or thought such a thing. In this situation, the goal is to write a question and response choices that make agreement seem more acceptable. For example, it would probably be better to ask, "Have you ever been suspended for a violation of school rules?" rather than "Have you ever been identified as a troublemaker by your principal?" Asking about a variety of behaviors or attitudes that range from socially acceptable to socially unacceptable will also soften the impact of agreeing with those that are socially unacceptable.

Minimize Fence-Sitting and Floating

Two related problems in question writing also stem from people's desire to choose an acceptable answer. There are fence-sitters who see themselves as being neutral and whose responses may skew the results if you force them to choose between opposites. Adding an explicit neutral response option is appropriate when you want to find out who is a fence-sitter. But adding a neutral response may provide an easy escape for respondents who do not want to reveal their true feelings.

Floaters are respondents who choose a substantive answer when they really do not know. Because there are so many floaters in the typical survey sample, the decision to include an explicit "Don't know" option for a question is important. Unfortunately, the inclusion of an explicit "Don't know" response choice leads some people who do have a preference to take the easy way out and choose "Don't know."

Use Likert-Type Response Categories

Likert-type responses generally ask respondents to indicate the extent to which they agree or disagree with statements. The response categories list choices for respondents to select their level of agreement with a statement from *strongly agree* to *strongly disagree*. The questions in Exhibit 8.4 have Likert-type response categories.

| Exhibit 8.4 | Matrix Questions Using Likert-Type Responses |

15. In general, how well do you feel that (Please circle one response for each question)	Strongly Agree				Strongly Disagree
a. Education classes prepared me for my teaching position.	1	2	3	4	5
b. Internships, observations, and student teaching prepared me for my teaching position.	1	2	3	4	5
c. Education classes prepared me for gaining my teaching license.	1	2	3	4	5

Matrix Questions

Some question formats lend themselves to a matrix format. Matrix questions are actually a series of questions that concern a common theme and that have the same response choices. The questions are written so that a common initial phrase applies to each one (see Exhibit 8.4). This format shortens the questionnaire by reducing the number of words that must be used for each question. It also emphasizes the common theme among the questions and so invites answering each question in relation to other questions in the matrix. It is important to provide an explicit instruction to "Circle one response on each line" in a matrix question since some respondents will think that they have completed the entire matrix after they have responded to just a few of the specific questions.

▣ Survey Design Alternatives

Surveys can be administered in at least five different ways: mailed, group administered, by phone, in person, and electronically (Exhibit 8.5 summarizes the typical features of each). Each approach differs from the others in one or more important features:

Manner of administration. Mailed, group, and electronic surveys are completed by the respondents themselves. During phone and in-person interviews, however, the researcher or a staff person asks the questions and records the respondent's answers.

Questionnaire structure. Most mailed, group, phone, and electronic surveys are highly structured, fixing in advance the content and order of questions and response choices. Some of these types of surveys, particularly

Exhibit 8.5	Typical Features of the Five Survey Designs

Design	Manner of Administration	Setting	Questionnaire Structure	Cost
Mailed survey	Self	Individual	Mostly structured	Low
Group survey	Self	Group	Mostly structured	Very low
Phone survey	Professional	Individual	Structured	Moderate
In-person interview	Professional	Individual	Structured or unstructured	High
Web survey	Self	Individual	Mostly structured	Very low

mailed surveys, may include some open-ended questions (respondents write in their answers rather than checking off one of several response choices). In-person interviews are often highly structured, but they may include many questions without fixed response choices. Moreover, some interviews may proceed from an interview guide rather than a fixed set of questions. In these relatively unstructured interviews, the interviewer covers the same topics with respondents but varies questions according to the respondent's answers to previous questions.

Setting. Mailed surveys, electronic questionnaires, and phone interviews are intended for completion by only one respondent. The same is usually true of in-person interviews, although sometimes researchers interview several family members at once. On the other hand, a variant of the standard survey is a questionnaire distributed simultaneously to a group of respondents, who complete the survey while the researcher (or assistant) waits.

Cost. As mentioned earlier, in-person interviews are the most expensive type of survey. Phone interviews are much less expensive, but surveying by mail is cheaper yet. Electronic surveys are now the least expensive method because there are no interviewer costs, no mailing costs, and, for many designs, almost no costs for data entry. Of course, extra staff time and expertise are required to prepare an electronic questionnaire.

Because of their different features, the five designs vary in the types of error to which they are most prone and the situations in which they are most appropriate. The rest of this section focuses on each format's unique advantages and disadvantages.

Mailed Surveys

A **mailed survey** is conducted by mailing a questionnaire to respondents, who then administer the survey themselves. The central concern in a mailed survey is maximizing the response rate. Even an attractive questionnaire full of clear questions requires additional efforts to maximize the response rate. A response rate of 70% or higher is desirable; lower response rates call into question the representativeness of the sample.

Sending follow-up mailings to nonrespondents is the single most important requirement for obtaining an adequate response rate. The follow-up mailings explicitly encourage initial nonrespondents to return a completed questionnaire; implicitly, they convey the importance of the effort. Dillman (2000) has demonstrated the effectiveness of a mailing process that includes the following:

1. A few days before mailing the questionnaire, send a brief letter that notifies sample members of the importance of the survey.

2. Include a personalized cover letter (see Exhibit 8.6) and a self-addressed, stamped return envelope with the questionnaire.

3. Send a friendly reminder postcard to all sample members 2 weeks after the initial mailing. The postcard is written to thank respondents and remind nonrespondents. Include a phone number for those people who may not have received the questionnaire or may have lost it.

4. Send a replacement questionnaire with a new cover letter only to nonrespondents 2 to 4 weeks after the initial questionnaire mailing and again after 6 to 8 weeks.

The **cover letter** is critical to the success of a mailed survey (Exhibit 8.6 is an example of a cover letter to principals from the 2000 Mathematics and Science Survey). This statement to respondents sets the tone for the questionnaire. A carefully prepared cover letter should increase the response rate and result in more honest and complete answers to the survey questions; a poorly prepared cover letter can have the reverse effects.

Exhibit 8.6	**Cover Letter to Principals for the 2000 Mathematics and Science Survey**

Dear Principal,

The purpose of this letter is to let you know that your school has been selected for the 2000 National Survey of Science and Mathematics Education and to request your cooperation in this effort. A total of 1,800 public and private schools and 9,000 K–12 teachers throughout the United States will be involved in the 2000 Survey. The survey, initiated by the National Science Foundation, is the fourth in a series of national surveys of science and mathematics education (the others were in 1977, 1985, and 1993). The enclosed *Fact Sheet* provides more information about the study.

The 2000 Survey will help determine how well prepared schools and teachers are for effective science and mathematics education, what would help them do a better job, and how federal resources can best be used to improve science and mathematics education. The survey is being conducted by Horizon Research, Inc., under the direction of Dr. Iris R. Weiss. Data collection is the responsibility of Westat, in Rockville, Maryland.

To help compensate participants for their time, the study has arranged to give each school a voucher to be used in purchasing science and mathematics education materials, including NCTM's Curriculum and Evaluation Standards, Project 2061's Science for All Americans, and NRC's *National Science Education Standards,* as well as calculators and other materials for classroom use. The amount of the voucher will depend on response rates, with each participating school receiving $50, plus $15 for each responding teacher. In addition, each school will receive a copy of the results of the survey.

[a few paragraphs describing an enclosed booklet have been omitted.]

Your cooperation is greatly appreciated. Please return the completed booklet for your school within the next 10 days so that we can begin the teacher selection process. If you have any questions about any of the items in the booklet or the study in general, please call us toll-free at 1-800-937-8288. Ask for the Science and Mathematics Survey specialist.

Thank you for your cooperation.

Sincerely,

Diane Ward

Data Collection Coordinator

Source: Horizon Research Incorporated and Westat.

The cover letter or introductory statement should be personalized to the respondent and signed by the researcher. The contents of the letter should establish the credibility of the research, catch the interest of the respondent, and note ethical obligations, such as confidentiality and voluntary participation. The letter should include a phone number to call if the respondent has any questions.

There are other strategies to increase the response rate (Fowler, 1988; Mangione, 1995; Miller & Salkind, 2002). The individual questions should be clear and understandable to all the respondents. There should be only a few open-ended questions because respondents are likely to be put off by the idea of having to write out answers. Having a credible sponsor known to respondents may increase the response rate. Enclosing a token incentive such as a coupon or ticket worth $1, $2, or $5 may help. (To encourage principals to participate, Exhibit 8.6 outlines several incentives that will go to participating schools, including a $15 payment for each teacher who responds.) Write an identifying number on the questionnaire so you can determine who non-respondents are. This is essential for follow-up efforts. Of course, the identification must be explained in the cover letter. Finally, include a stamped, self-addressed envelope with the questionnaire.

Group-Administered Surveys

A **group-administered survey** is completed by individual respondents assembled together. It is a common approach in classroom- or school-based surveys. The response rate is not usually a major concern in surveys that are distributed and collected in a group setting because most group members will participate. The real difficulty with this method is that it is seldom feasible because it requires what might be called a captive audience. With the exception of students, employees, members of the armed forces, and some institutionalized populations, most populations cannot be sampled in such a setting.

A special concern with group-administered surveys is the possibility that respondents will feel coerced to participate and as a result will be less likely to answer questions honestly. Also, because administering a survey in this way requires approval of the settings' administrators, respondents may infer that the researcher is not at all independent of the sponsor. No complete solution to this problem exists, but it helps to make an introductory statement emphasizing the researcher's independence and giving participants a chance to ask questions about the survey. The sponsor should also understand the need to keep a low profile and to allow the researcher both control over the data and autonomy in report writing.

A standard introductory statement should be read to the group that expresses appreciation for their participation, describes the steps of the survey, and emphasizes (in classroom surveys) that the survey is not the same as a test. A cover letter like that used in a mailed survey also should be distributed with the questionnaires. To emphasize confidentiality, respondents should be given an envelope in which to seal their questionnaire after it is completed.

Telephone Surveys

In a **phone survey**, interviewers question respondents over the phone and then record their answers. Phone interviewing is a popular method of conducting surveys in the United States because almost all families have phones. But two problems often threaten the validity of a phone survey: not reaching the proper sampling units (or "coverage error") and not getting enough complete responses to make the results generalizable.

Reaching Sample Units

Most telephone surveys use random digit dialing to contact a random sampling of households. A machine calls random phone numbers within the designated exchanges, regardless of whether the numbers are published. When the machine reaches an inappropriate household (such as a business in a survey that is directed to the general population), the phone number is simply replaced with another. When the households are contacted, the interviewers must ask a series of questions at the start of the survey to ensure that they are speaking to the appropriate member of the household.

But the tremendous recent (since 2000) popularity of cellular, or mobile, telephones has made accurate coverage of random samples almost impossible (Tourangeau, 2004, pp. 781–792): (1) Cell phones are typically not listed in telephone directories, so they can't be included in prepared calling lists; (2) laws generally forbid the use of automated (RDD) dialers to contact cell phones; (3) close to 20% of the U.S. population now has only a cell phone (no landline) and therefore can't be reached by either RDD or many directory lists; and (4) among 18- to 24-year-olds, some 30% have cell phones only, and cell phone–only households are also more common among non-English speakers.

The net effect, then, of widespread cell phone usage is to underrepresent young people and some minority groups from most large telephone surveys, obviously damaging the results.

Maximizing Response to Phone Surveys

Even if an appropriate (for sampling) number is dialed, responses may not be completed.

First, because people often are not home, multiple callbacks will be needed for many sample members. The number of callbacks needed to reach respondents by telephone has increased greatly in the past 20 years. With increasing numbers of single-person households, dual-earner families, and out-of-home activities, survey research organizations have had to increase the usual number of phone contact attempts from just 4–8 to 20—a lot of attempts to reach just one person. Caller ID and call waiting allow potential respondents to avoid answering calls from strangers, including researchers. The growth of telemarketing has accustomed people to refuse calls from unknown individuals and organizations or to use their answering machines to screen calls (Dillman, 2000, pp. 8, 28). And since a huge number of cell phone users are minors, and so legally not available for surveys, calls made to them are all wasted efforts for researchers.

Such problems mean that careful training and direction of interviewers are essential in phone surveys. The instructions shown in Exhibit 8.7 were developed to clarify procedures for asking and coding a series of questions in the phone interviews conducted for a survey regarding youth and guns.

Phone surveying is the method of choice for relatively short surveys of the general population. Response rates in phone surveys traditionally have tended to be very high—often above 80%—because few individuals would hang up on a polite caller or refuse to answer questions (at least within the first 30 minutes or so). But the problems we have noted, especially those connected with cell phone usage, make this method of surveying populations increasingly difficult.

In-Person Interviews

What is unique to the **in-person interview,** compared to the other survey designs, is the face-to-face social interaction between interviewer and respondent. In-person interviewing has several advantages: Responses rates are higher than with any other survey design; questionnaires can be much longer than with mailed or phone surveys; the questionnaire can be complex, with both open-ended and closed-ended questions and frequent branching patterns; the order in which questions are read and answered can be controlled by the interviewer; the physical and social circumstances of the interview can be monitored; and respondents' interpretations of questions can be probed and clarified. The interviewer, therefore, is well placed to gain a full understanding of what the respondent really wants to say.

But researchers must be alert to some special hazards due to the presence of an interviewer. Ideally, every respondent should have the same interview experience—asked the same questions in the same way by the same type of person, who reacts similarly to the answers. Careful training and supervision are essential

Exhibit 8.7	Sample Interviewer Instructions

Sample Interviewer Instructions, Youth and Guns Survey, 2000

22. (CONSTIT) To your knowledge, does the U.S. Constitution guarantee citizens the right to own firearms?

    1. Yes   2. No (**skip to 24**)   3. Not sure (**do not read**)

23. (CONLAW) Do you believe that laws regulating the sale and use of handguns violate the constitutional rights of gun owners?

    1. Yes   2. No   3. Not sure (**do not read**)

24. (PETITION) In some localities, high school students have joined campaigns to change the gun laws, and sometimes they have been successful. Earlier you said that you thought that the current gun control laws were (**if Q11 = 1, insert "not strict enough"; if Q11 = 2, insert "too strict"**). Suppose a friend who thinks like you do about this asked you to sign a petition calling for (**if Q11 = 1, insert "stronger gun control laws"; if Q11 = 2, insert "less restrictive gun control laws"**). On a scale from 1 to 5, with 1 being very unlikely and 5 being very likely, how likely is it that you would sign the petition?

    1. (Very unlikely)
    2.
    3.
    4.
    5. (Very likely)
    6. Not sure (**do not read**)

Source: Chambliss and Schutt (2010, p. 177). Copyright © 2000 Dennis Gilbert. Reprinted by permission.

because small differences in intonation or emphasis on particular words can alter respondents' interpretations of questions meaning (Groves, 1989, pp. 404–406; Peterson, 2000, p. 24).

Balancing Rapport and Control

Adherence to some basic guidelines for interacting with respondents can help interviewers to maintain an appropriate balance between personalization and standardization:

- Project a professional image in the interview: that of someone who is sympathetic to the respondent but nonetheless has a job to do.

- Establish rapport at the outset by explaining what the interview is about and how it will work and by reading the consent form. Ask the respondent if he or she has any questions or concerns, and respond to these honestly and fully. Emphasize that everything the respondent says is confidential.

- During the interview, ask questions from a distance that is close but not intimate. Stay focused on the respondent and make sure that your posture conveys interest. Maintain eye contact, respond with appropriate facial expressions, and speak in a conversational tone of voice.

- Be sure to maintain a consistent approach; deliver each question as written and in the same tone of voice. Listen empathetically, but avoid self-expression or loaded reactions.

- Repeat questions if the respondent is confused. Use nondirective probes—such as "Can you tell me more about that?"—for open-ended questions.

As with phone interviewing, computers can be used to increase control of the in-person interview. In a computer-assisted personal interviewing (CAPI) project, interviewers carry a laptop computer that is programmed to display the interview questions and to process the responses that the interviewer types in, as well as to check that these responses fall within allowed ranges. Interviewers seem to like CAPI, and the data obtained are comparable in quality to data obtained in a noncomputerized interview (Shepherd, Hill, Bristor, & Montalvan, 1996). A CAPI approach also makes it easier for the researcher to develop skip patterns and experiment with different types of questions for different respondents without increasing the risk of interviewer mistakes (Couper et al., 1998).

Web-Based Surveys

The widespread use of personal computers and the growth of the Internet have created new possibilities for survey research. Electronic surveys can be prepared in two ways (Dillman, 2000, pp. 352–354). E-mail surveys can be sent as messages to respondents' e-mail addresses. Respondents then mark their answers in the message and send them back to the researcher. This approach is easy for researchers to develop and for respondents to use. However, it is cumbersome for surveys that are more than four or five pages in length. By contrast, Web surveys are stored on a server that is controlled by the researcher; respondents are then asked to visit the website (often by just clicking an e-mailed link) and respond to the questionnaire by checking answers. Web surveys require more programming by the researcher, but a well-designed Web survey can tailor its questions to a given respondent and thus seem shorter, more interesting, and more attractive. The U. S. Department of Education wished to use its website (ED.gov) to gather information about who uses the site, how often they use it, and for what purposes. The ED.gov survey combined several types of questions—multiple choice, Likert scale, and open-ended—to gain a picture of respondents and their needs. Exhibit 8.8 shows examples of the types of questions asked on the survey and the choices respondents were given. Question 1 is multiple choice, Question 2 is open-ended, Question 3 combines yes/no and multiple choice, Question 4 uses a Likert scale, and Question 5 is multiple choice with brief explanations of the choices.

Web surveys are becoming a popular form of electronic survey in part because they are so flexible and inexpensive. The questionnaire's design can feature many graphic and typographic elements. Respondents can view definitions of words or instructions for answering questions by clicking on linked terms. Lengthy sets of response choices can be presented with pull-down menus. Pictures and audio segments can be added when they are useful. Because answers are recorded directly in the researcher's database, data entry errors are almost eliminated and results can be reported quickly.

The most important drawback to either electronic survey approach is the large number of U.S. households—about 30% in 2009—that are not yet connected to the Internet (U.S. Census Bureau, 2011, p. 724). Households without Internet access differ systematically from those with access, tending to be older, poorer, and more likely to be in rural areas than those that are connected (Tourangeau, 2004, pp. 792–793). But there's another, almost opposite, problem with Web surveys: Because they are so easy and cheap to set up, you can find hundreds of Web surveys on a wide range of topics and for many different purposes. Among Internet users, almost anyone can participate in many of these Web surveys. But the large numbers of respondents that this uncontrolled method can generate should not cause you to forget the importance of a representative sample. Uncontrolled Web surveys are guaranteed to produce, instead, a very biased sample (Dillman, 2000, p. 355).

When the population to be surveyed has a high rate of Internet use, however, the Web makes possible fast and effective surveys (Dillman, 2000, pp. 354–355). A skilled Web programmer can generate a survey layout with many attractive features that make it more likely that respondents will give their answers—and have a

---

Exhibit 8.8 | **U.S. Department of Education Web Survey**

1. How often do you visit ED.gov?

   Daily ___
   Weekly ___
   Monthly ___
   Less than once a month ___

2. Why are you visiting ED.gov today—what task did you hope to accomplish?

3. Were you successful in completing your task?

   ___ Yes, easily.
   ___ Yes, but it took some effort.
   ___ Only part of it.
   ___ No.
   ___ I was just browsing.

4. How satisfied are you with the usefulness of information on ED.gov: (1 being very dissatisfied, 5 being very satisfied)

1	2	3	4	5
___	___	___	___	___

5. Which of the following technologies do you use anywhere on the Internet (select all that apply):

   ___ Blogs (a forum for exchanging information).
   ___ Wikis (online resource where users add and edit content)
   ___ RSS (automatic alerts to product updates)
   ___ Podcasting (downloaded audio content)
   ___ Videocasting (downloaded video content from sources such as YouTube)

Source: Adapted from U. S. Department of Education Web Survey OMB #1800-0011.

---

clear understanding of the question (Smyth, Dillman, Christian, & Stern, 2004, pp. 4–5). Under proper conditions, electronic surveys are an excellent tool.

Mixed-Mode Surveys

Survey researchers increasingly are combining different survey designs. Mixed-mode surveys allow the strengths of one survey design to compensate for the weaknesses of another and can maximize the likelihood of securing data from different types of respondents (Dillman, 2007; Selm & Jankowski, 2006). For example, a survey may be sent electronically to sample members who have e-mail addresses and mailed to those who do not. Phone reminders may be used to encourage responses to Web or paper surveys.

Nonrespondents in a mailed survey may be interviewed in person or over the phone. An interviewer may use a self-administered questionnaire to present sensitive questions to a respondent.

Mixing survey designs like this makes it possible that respondents will give different answers to different questions because of the mode in which they are asked, rather than because they actually have different opinions. When responses differ by survey mode, there is often no way to know which responses are more accurate (Peterson, 2000, p. 24). However, use of the same question structures, response choices, and skip instructions across modes substantially reduces the likelihood of mode effects, as does using a small number of response choices for each question (Dillman & Christian, 2005).

A Comparison of Survey Designs

Which survey design should be used when? Group-administered surveys are similar, in most respects, to mailed surveys, except that they require the unusual circumstance of having access to the sample in a group setting. We therefore do not need to consider this survey design by itself; what applies to mail surveys applies to group-administered survey designs, with the exception of sampling issues. Thus, we can focus our comparison on the four survey designs that involve the use of a questionnaires with individuals sampled from a larger population: mail surveys, phone surveys, in-person surveys, and electronic surveys. Exhibit 8.9 summarizes the strong and weak points of each design.

The most important consideration is the likely response rate each method will generate. Because of the low response rates of *mailed surveys,* they are the weakest from a sampling standpoint. However, researchers with limited time, money, and staff (including most student researchers) may still prefer a mailed survey. Mailed surveys can be useful in asking sensitive questions because respondents won't be embarrassed by answering in front of an interviewer.

Contracting with an established survey research organization for a *phone survey* is often the best alternative to a mailed survey. The persistent follow-up attempts that are necessary to secure an adequate response rate are much easier over the phone than in person. However, the declining rate of response to phone interview calls is reducing the advantages of this method.

In-person surveys can be long and complex, and the interviewer can easily monitor the conditions (the room, noise, and other distractions). Although interviewers may themselves distort results, either by changing the wording of the questions or failing to record answers properly, this problem can be lessened by careful training and monitoring of interviewers and by audio-recording the answers.

The advantages and disadvantages of *electronic surveys* depend on the populations to be surveyed. Too many people lack Internet connections for general use of Internet surveying. But when the entire sample has access and ability (e.g., college students, school principals), Web-based surveys can be very effective.

So overall, in-person interviews are the strongest design and generally preferable when sufficient resources and a trained interview staff are available; telephone surveys have many of the advantages of in-person interviews at much less cost, but response rates are an increasing problem. Decisions about the best survey design must take into account the particular study's features and goals.

Combining Methods

Conducting qualitative interviews can often enhance a research design that uses primarily quantitative measurement techniques. Qualitative data can provide information about the quality of standardized case records and quantitative survey measures, as well as offer some insight into the meaning of particular fixed responses.

Exhibit 8.9	Advantages and Disadvantages of the Four Survey Designs

Characteristics of Design	Mail Survey	Phone Survey	In-Person Survey	Web Survey
Representative sample				
Opportunity for inclusion is known				
For completely listed populations	High	High	High	Medium
For incompletely listed populations	Medium	Medium	High	Low
Selection within sampling units is controlled (e.g., specific family members must respond)	Medium	High	High	Low
Respondents are likely to be located				
If samples are heterogeneous	Medium	High	High	Low
If samples are homogeneous and specialized	High	High	High	High
Questionnaire construction and question design				
Allowable length of questionnaire	Medium	Medium	High	Medium
Ability to include				
Complex questions	Medium	Low	High	High
Open questions	Low	High	High	Medium
Screening questions	Low	High	High	High
Tedious, boring questions	Low	High	High	Low
Ability to control question sequence	Low	High	High	High
Ability to ensure questionnaire completion	Medium	High	High	Low
Distortion of answers				
Odds of avoiding social desirability bias	High	Medium	Low	High
Odds of avoiding interviewer distortion	High	Medium	Low	High
Odds of avoiding contamination by others	Medium	High	Medium	Medium
Administrative goals				
Odds of meeting personnel requirements	High	High	Low	Medium
Odds of implementing quickly	Low	High	Low	High
Odds of keeping costs low	High	Medium	Low	High

Source: Adapted from Dillman (2007, p. 200). Copyright © 2007 John Wiley and Sons, Inc.

Adding Qualitative Data

The 2000 National Survey used a variety of data collection instruments given to several types of participants to assemble a comprehensive and representative picture of math and science instruction in the United States. Quantitative data were collected by questionnaires from nationally representative, K–12 samples of program heads, teachers, and presidential awardees in mathematics and science. These data were complemented by qualitative measures such as classroom observations and interviews with the same groups.

The combination of qualitative and quantitative data gave a much more comprehensive picture of K–12 math and science instruction than could have been developed by using either method alone. Survey designers increasingly look to combine methods to gain a more complete answer to the questions their survey seeks to answer.

Survey Research Design in a Diverse Society

Diversity and the impact of differences in shared belief systems must be considered in designing questions, constructing questionnaires, and choosing a data collection method. This is especially true when surveys are aimed at students, parents, and community members—groups that are increasingly diverse in language, cultural identification, and religion. When developing individual questions, you need to be careful about your choice of language; when constructing the questionnaire, you need to ensure that the format provides the same meaning for all respondents; when deciding on a data collection method, particularly interviewing, you may find that responses to questions are affected by interviewer-respondent characteristics.

To ensure valid data, all survey respondents should attach the same meaning to a question. Therefore, you should make certain, for example, through pretesting with members of all the groups to be surveyed, that the question has the same meaning across different population subgroups. Although it is important that the wording be appropriate for different groups, it is also necessary to show that the concept being examined is equivalent across groups—that questions adequately reflect group values, traditions, and beliefs (Huer & Saenz, 2003; Tillman, 2004). For example, the wording of a question about *family* and the available response categories would need to account for cultural differences in both the boundaries used to establish membership in a family and the expectations and obligations of family members (Luna et al., 1996).

English is not the first language of some respondents, and many would prefer to use their native language as they do in their daily lives (Marin & Marin, 1991). Translating questions creates an additional challenge to ensure that the questions have the same meaning in all languages in which the survey or interview is conducted.

Another challenge arises when there are regional or national differences in a spoken language. Marin and Marin (1991) offer these suggestions to deal with regional variations for Hispanics, but in many ways, these suggestions are generalizable when a particular language is used in many different countries:

1. Use all appropriate variations of a word in a self-administered questionnaire.

2. Target vocabulary variations to each subgroup. When there are subgroups, alter the wording to conform to the vocabulary of that subgroup.

3. Avoid colloquialisms. Colloquialisms may differ from place to place and add to the confusion of a word's meaning.

4. Use alternate questions. (pp. 85–86)

Ethical Issues in Survey Research

Survey research designs usually pose fewer ethical dilemmas than do experimental or field research designs. Potential respondents to a survey can easily decline to participate, and a cover letter or introductory statement that identifies the sponsors of, and motivations for, the survey gives them the information required to make this decision. Little is concealed from the respondents, and the methods of data collection are quite obvious. Only in group-administered survey designs might the respondents (such as students or employees) be, in effect, a captive audience, and so these designs require special attention to ensure that participation is truly voluntary. (Those who do not wish to participate may be told they can just hand in a blank form.)

Confidentiality is most often the primary focus of ethical concern in survey research. Many surveys include some essential questions that might prove damaging to the subjects if their answers were disclosed. When a survey of teachers asks, "Do you think the administration, especially your principal, is doing a good job?" or when student course evaluations ask, "On a scale of 1 to 5, how fair would you say the professor is?" respondents may well hesitate; if the principal or professor saw the results, teachers or students could be hurt.

To prevent any disclosure of such information, it is critical to preserve subject confidentiality. Only research personnel should have access to information that could be used to link respondents to their responses, and even that access should be limited to what is necessary for specific research purposes. Only numbers should be used to identify respondents on their questionnaires, and the researcher should keep the names that correspond to these numbers in a safe, private location, unavailable to staff and others who might otherwise come across them. Follow-up mailings or contact attempts that require linking the ID numbers with names and addresses should be carried out by the researcher or trustworthy assistants under close supervision. If an electronic survey is used, encryption technology should be used to make information provided over the Internet secure from unauthorized people. Usually confidentiality can be protected readily; the key is to be aware of the issue. Don't allow principals or supervisors to collect teachers' surveys or teachers to pick up course evaluations. Be aware of your respondents' concerns and be even a little more careful than you need to be.

Few surveys can provide true anonymity, where no identifying information is ever recorded to link respondents with their responses. The main problem with anonymous surveys is that they preclude follow-up attempts to encourage participation by initial nonrespondents, and they prevent panel designs, which measure change through repeated surveys of the same individuals. In-person surveys rarely can be anonymous because an interviewer must, in almost all cases, know the name and address of the interviewee. However, phone surveys that are meant only to sample opinion at one point in time, as in political polls, can safely be completely anonymous. When no future follow-up is desired, group-administered surveys also can be anonymous. To provide anonymity in a mail survey, the researcher should omit identifying codes from the questionnaire but could include a self-addressed, stamped postcard so the respondent can notify the researcher that the questionnaire has been returned without creating any linkage to the questionnaire itself (Mangione, 1995, p. 69).

▣ Conclusions

We began this chapter with the research question, "How can we get a national picture of K–12 math and science teaching?" The National Science Foundation set out to answer this question with its comprehensive "2000 National Survey of Science and Mathematics Education," which questioned a representative sample of schools in the United States from the elementary grades through high school. Because of its comprehensive nature, the 2000 survey was able to draw conclusions across a wide range of grade levels and subject areas. In elementary science classes, for instance, the survey found "low frequency of technology use," which it attributed to teachers not being "comfortable with their knowledge of how to integrate computers with instruction" (Fulp, 2002, p. 15). At the high school level, mathematics teachers reported "placing heavy emphasis on mathematics concepts and reasoning," but observations found that their actual classes were dominated by worksheets, problem solving, homework review, and "practicing routine computation" (Whittington, 2002, p. 24).

The 2000 survey was able to reach significant conclusions such as these because survey research is an exceptionally efficient and productive method for investigating a wide array of educational research questions. In addition to the potential benefits for education, considerations of time and expense frequently make a survey the preferred data collection method. One or more of the five survey designs reviewed in this chapter (including mixed mode) can be applied to almost any research question. It is no wonder that surveys have become a popular research method in education and that they frequently inform discussion and planning about important educational questions. As use of the Internet increases, survey research should become even more efficient and popular.

The relative ease of conducting at least some types of survey research leads many people to imagine that no particular training or systematic procedures are required. Nothing could be further from the truth. But as a result of this widespread misconception, you will encounter a great many nearly worthless survey results. You must be prepared to examine carefully the procedures used in any survey before accepting its findings as credible. And if you decide to conduct a survey, you must be prepared to invest the time and effort required by proper procedures.

Key Terms

Anonymity   181
Behavior coding   183
Closed-ended question   168
Cognitive interview   163
Confidentiality   181
Context effects   164
Contingent question   164
Cover letter   172
Double-barreled question   167
Double negative   167

Electronic survey   176
E-mail survey   176
Fence-sitters   169
Filter question   164
Floaters   169
Group-administered survey   173
In-person interview   174
Interpretive questions   183
Interview schedule   161

Mailed survey   171
Mixed-mode survey   177
Open-ended question   168
Phone survey   173
Questionnaire   161
Skip pattern   164
Survey research   160
Web survey   176

Highlights

- Surveys are a popular form of educational research because of their versatility, efficiency, and generalizability.

- Survey designs must minimize the risk of errors of observation (measurement error) and errors of nonobservation (errors due to inadequate coverage, sampling error, and nonresponse). The likelihood of both types of error varies with the survey goals.

- Social exchange theory asserts that behavior is motivated by the return expected to the individual for the behavior. Survey designs must maximize the social rewards, minimize the costs of participating, and establish trust that the rewards will outweigh the costs.

- A survey questionnaire or interview schedule should be designed as an integrated whole, with each question and section serving some clear purpose and complementing the others.

- Questions must be worded carefully to avoid confusing respondents, encouraging a less-than-honest response, or triggering biases. Inclusion of "Don't know" choices and neutral responses may help, but the presence of such options also affects the distribution of answers. Open-ended questions can be used to determine the meaning that respondents attach to their answers. Answers to any survey questions may be affected by the questions that precede them in a questionnaire or interview schedule.

- Questions can be tested and improved through review by experts, focus group discussions, cognitive interviews, **behavior coding,** and pilot testing. Every questionnaire and interview schedule should be pretested on a small sample that is like the sample to be surveyed.

- **Interpretive questions** should be used in questionnaires to help clarify the meaning of responses to critical questions.

- The cover letter for a mailed questionnaire should be credible, personalized, interesting, and responsible.

- Response rates in mailed surveys are typically well below 70% unless multiple mailings are made to nonrespondents and the questionnaire and cover letter are attractive, interesting, and carefully planned. Response rates for group-administered surveys are usually much higher.

- Phone interviews using random digit dialing allow fast turnaround and efficient sampling. Multiple callbacks are often required, and the rate of nonresponse to phone interviews is rising. Phone interviews should be limited in length to about 30 to 45 minutes.

- In-person interviews have several advantages over other types of surveys: They allow longer and more complex interview schedules, monitoring of the conditions when the questions are answered, probing for respondents' understanding of the questions, and high response rates. However, the interviewer must balance the need to establish rapport with the respondent with the importance of maintaining control over the delivery of the interview questions.

- Electronic surveys may be e-mailed or posted on the Web. Interactive voice response systems using the telephone are another option. At this time, use of the Internet is not sufficiently widespread to allow e-mail or Web surveys of the general population, but these approaches can be fast and efficient for populations with high rates of computer use.

- Mixed-mode surveys allow the strengths of one survey design to compensate for the weaknesses of another. However, questions and procedures must be designed carefully, using "unimode design" principles, to reduce the possibility that responses to the same question will vary as a result of the mode of delivery.

- In deciding which survey design to use, researchers must take into account the unique features and goals of the study. In general, in-person interviews are the strongest, but most expensive, survey design.

- Most survey research poses few ethical problems because respondents are able to decline to participate—an option that should be stated clearly in the cover letter of the introductory statement. Special care must be taken when questionnaires are administered in group settings (to "captive audiences") and when sensitive personal questions are to be asked; subject confidentiality should always be preserved.

Student Study Site

To assist in completing the web exercises, please access the study site at www.sagepub.com/check, where you will find the web exercise with accompanying links. You'll find other useful study materials such as self-quizzes and e-flashcards for each chapter, along with a group of carefully selected articles from research journals that illustrate the major concepts and techniques.

Discussion Questions

1. Think of at least three experiences you have had with surveys—taking them, giving them, or reading about the results. Be sure to include Internet surveys. What observations can you make about positive and negative effects of surveys, based on the experiences you cite?

2. Each of the following questions was used in a survey that one of the authors received at some time in the past. Evaluate each question and its response choices using the guidelines for question writing presented in this chapter. What errors do you find? Try to rewrite each question to avoid such errors and improve question wording.

   a. The first question in an Info World (computer publication) "product evaluation survey":

      How interested are you in PostScript Level 2 printers?

      _____Very _____Somewhat _____Not at all

   b. From the Greenpeace "National Marine Mammal Survey":

      Do you support Greenpeace's nonviolent, direct action to intercept whaling ships, tuna fleets and other commercial fishermen in order to stop their wanton destruction of thousands of magnificent marine mammals?

      _____Yes _____No _____Undecided

   c. Of the students you have observed while teaching college courses, please indicate the percentage who significantly improve their performance in the following areas.

      Reading_____%

      Organization_____%

      Abstraction_____%

Practice Exercises

1. One of the authors received in his university mailbox some years ago a two-page questionnaire that began with the following "cover letter" at the top of the first page:

   Faculty Questionnaire

   This survey seeks information on faculty perception of the learning process and student performance in their undergraduate careers. Surveys have been distributed in universities in the Northeast, through random deposit in mailboxes of selected departments. This survey is being conducted by graduate students affiliated with the School of Education and the Sociology Department. We greatly appreciate your time and effort in helping us with our study.

   Critique this cover letter, and then draft a more persuasive one.

2. Go to http://2000survey.horizon-research.com/, the site for the 2000 Science and Mathematics Survey. At the top of the page, click on Instruments. Open one of the survey questionnaires and read through it. Identify examples of at least three survey techniques described in this chapter (e.g., closed-ended questions, matrix questions). Analyze the appearance of the survey—do you find it attractive and easy to follow? Are the instructions clear? How long do you think it would have taken you to fill out this survey?

Web Exercises

1. Go to the Research Triangle Institute site at http://www.rti.org. Click on "Tools and Methods," then "Surveys," and then "Survey Design and Development." Read about their methods for computer-assisted interviewing (under "Survey Methods") and their cognitive laboratory methods for refining questions (under "Usability Testing"). What does this add to our treatment of these topics in this chapter?

2. Go to The Question Bank at http://qb.soc.surrey.ac.uk/docs/home.htm. Go to the "Surveys" link and then click on one of the listed surveys or survey sections that interests you. Review 10 questions used in the survey, and critique them in terms of the principles for question writing that you have learned. Do you find any question features that might be attributed to the use of British English?

Developing a Research Proposal

1. Write 10 questions for a one-page questionnaire that concerns your proposed research question. Your questions should operationalize at least three of the variables on which you have focused, including at least one independent and one dependent variable (you may have multiple questions to measure some variables). Make all but one of your questions closed-ended. If you completed the "Developing a Research Proposal" exercises in Chapter 4, you can select your questions from the ones you developed for those exercises.

2. Conduct a preliminary pretest of the questionnaire by conducting cognitive interviews with two students or other persons like those to whom the survey is directed. Follow up the closed-ended questions with open-ended probes that ask the students what they meant by each response or what came to mind when they were asked each question. Take account of the feedback you receive when you revise your questions.

3. Polish up the organization and layout of the questionnaire, following the guidelines in this chapter. Prepare a rationale for the order of questions in your questionnaire. Write a cover letter directed to the appropriate population that contains appropriate statements about research ethics (human subjects' issues).

CHAPTER 9

Qualitative Methods

Observing, Participating, Listening

Research Question: *How Do Communities and Families Affect Children's Literacy Development?*

Chapter Contents

- **Fundamentals of Qualitative Methods**
- **History of Qualitative Research**
- **Participant Observation**
- **Intensive Interviewing**

- **Focus Groups**
- **Combining Qualitative and Quantitative Methods**
- **Ethical Issues in Qualitative Research**

I was taking a college class during the fall semester and [a colleague] comes into the classroom and [asks] . . . "Did anybody see the news? Did they say that there was a cold front coming in?" And someone in the class said, "Yes, it is supposed to be cold tomorrow." "Oh, no!" she says, "*Mañana* [Tomorrow], all the kids are going to smell horrible: like *brasas* [hot coals/embers]!" . . . when she said that, I looked at her and I told her: "You know what? When I was little, I smelled like *brasas*, too. . . . I couldn't take a bath in the morning inside my house. I would take a bath at night. And the only thing that my parents had to warm us with was *brasas*, . . . And I think as a teacher and a counselor, if that is how you feel, then maybe you should look for another profession." And she was like, "Oh no, I didn't mean it like that!" And I said, . . . "if you haven't been there, you'll never know how to deal with migrants or how to develop a relationship with those kids." (López, Scribner, & Mahitivanichcha, 2001, p. 263)

This story was told by a district-level school administrator involved in an outreach program to parents of Mexican migrant students. It was recorded as part of a group interview format that included, from each school, a building administrator, a school counselor or social worker, a parent or community outreach worker, and sometimes a parent or teacher (López et al., 2001, p. 259).

Throughout the chapter, you will learn that some of our greatest insights into educational processes can result from what appear to be very ordinary activities: observing, participating, listening, and talking.

But you will also learn that qualitative research is much more than doing what comes naturally. Qualitative researchers must observe keenly, take notes systematically, question respondents strategically, and invest more of their whole selves than often occurs with experiments or surveys. Moreover, if we are to have any confidence in the value of a qualitative study's conclusions, each element of its design must be reviewed as carefully as we would review the elements of an experiment or survey.

We begin with an overview of the major features of qualitative research. The next section discusses participant observation research, which is the most distinctive qualitative method. We then discuss intensive interviewing—a type of interviewing that qualifies as qualitative rather than quantitative research—and focus groups, an increasingly popular qualitative method. The last section covers ethical issues that are of concern in any type of qualitative research project.

🔲 Fundamentals of Qualitative Methods

Qualitative methods refer to several distinctive research activities: **participant observation, intensive (depth) interviewing,** and **focus groups.**

Although these three qualitative designs differ in many respects, they share several features that distinguish them from experimental and survey research designs (Denzin & Lincoln, 2005; Maxwell, 1996; Wolcott, 1995):

Participant observation: A qualitative method for gathering data that involves developing a sustained relationship with people while they go about their normal activities.

Intensive (depth) interviewing: A qualitative method that involves open-ended, relatively unstructured questioning in which the interviewer seeks in-depth information on the interviewee's feelings, experiences, and perceptions (Lofland, Snow, Anderson, & Lofland, 2005).

Focus groups: A qualitative method that involves unstructured group interviews in which the focus group leader activity encourages discussion among participants on the topics of interest.

- Qualitative researchers typically begin with *an exploratory research question* about what people think and how they act, and why, in some educational setting.

- The designs focus on *previously unstudied processes and unanticipated phenomena* because previously unstudied attitudes and actions can't adequately be understood with a structured set of questions or within a highly controlled experiment. López and his colleagues (2001) undertook their study because of "a paucity of literature that addresses effective parent involvement practices that are particular to the specific needs of migrant families" (p. 258).

- They have an *orientation to the social context,* to the interconnections between social and educational phenomena rather than to their discrete features.

- They *focus on human subjectivity,* on the meanings that participants attach to educational events and that people give to their lives.

- They have a *sensitivity to the subjective role of the researcher.* The researcher considers himself or herself as necessarily part of the educational process or situation being studied and, therefore, keeps track of his or her own actions in, and reactions to, that educational situation.

With its focus on particular actors and situations and the processes that connect them, qualitative research tends to identify causes as particular events embedded within an unfolding, interconnected action sequence (Maxwell, 1996, pp. 20–21). The language of variables and hypotheses appears only rarely in the qualitative literature.

Qualitative researchers often use reflexive research designs, in which the design develops as the research progresses:

> Each component of the design may need to be reconsidered or modified in response to new developments or to changes in some other component. . . . The activities of collecting and analyzing data, developing and modifying theory, elaborating or refocusing the research questions, and identifying and eliminating validity threats are usually all going on more or less simultaneously, each influencing all of the others. (Maxwell, 1996, pp. 2–3)

William Miller and Benjamin Crabtree (1999a) capture the entire process of qualitative research in a simple diagram (Exhibit 9.1). In this diagram, qualitative research begins with the qualitative researcher reflecting on the setting and her relation

> **Qualitative methods:** Designed to capture educational reality as participants experience it rather than in categories predetermined by the researcher. These methods typically involve exploratory research questions, inductive reasoning, an orientation to the social context of educational activities, and a focus on human subjectivity and the meanings attached by participants to events and to their lives.

Exhibit 9.1   Qualitative Research Process

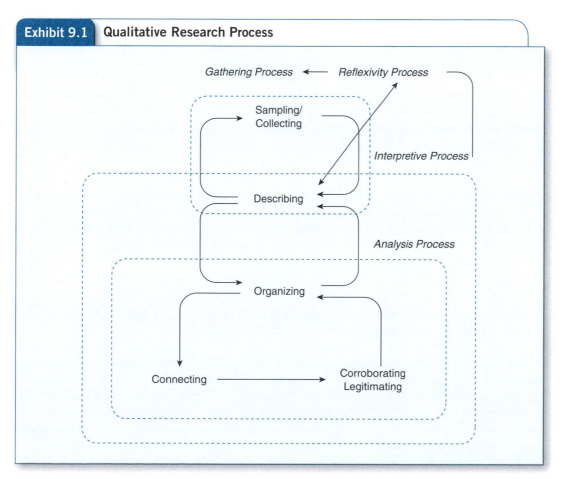

Source: W. L. Miller and Crabtree (1999a, p. 16).

to it and interpretations of it. The researcher then describes the goals and means for the research. This description is followed by *sampling* and *collecting* data, *describing* the data, and *organizing* those data. Thus, the *gathering process* and the *analysis process* proceed together, with repeated description and analysis of data as they are collected. As the data are organized, *connections* are identified between different data segments, and efforts are made to *corroborate* the credibility of these connections. This *interpretive process* begins to emerge in a written account that represents what has been done and how the data have been interpreted. Each of these steps in the research process informs the others and is repeated throughout the research process.

The Case Study Approach

Case study: A setting or group that the analyst treats as an integrated unit that must be studied holistically and in its particularity.

Qualitative researchers often use a technique called the "case study." **Case study** is not so much a single method as it is a way of thinking about what a qualitative research project can focus on: an organization, community, classroom, school or school system, a family, or even an individual that must be understood in its entirety. The idea is that the educational world functions as an integrated whole, and so the focus in quantitative research on variables and hypotheses involves "slicing and dicing" that whole in a way that obscures how it actually functions. Educational researcher Robert Stake (1995) presents the logic of the case study approach:

> Case study is the study of the particularity and complexity of a single case, coming to understand its activity within important circumstances. . . . The qualitative researcher emphasizes episodes of nuance, the sequentiality of happenings in context, the wholeness of the individual. (pp. xi–xii)

Central to much qualitative case study research is the goal of creating a **thick description** of the setting studied—a description that provides a sense of what it is like to experience that setting from the standpoint of the natural actors in that setting (Geertz, 1973). Stake's (1995) description of "a case within a case," a student in a school he studied, illustrates how a thick description gives a feel of the place and persons within it.

> At 8:30 A.M. on Thursday morning. Adam shows up at the cafeteria door. Breakfast is being served but Adam doesn't go in. The woman giving out meal chits has her hands on him, seems to be sparring with him, verbally. And then he disappears. Adam is one of five siblings, all arrive at school in the morning with less than usual parent attention. Short, with a beautifully sculpted head. . . . Adam is a person of notice.
>
> At 8:55 he climbs the stairs to the third floor with other upper graders, turning to block the girls behind them and thus a string of others. Adam manages to keep the girls off balance until Ms Crain . . . spots him and gets traffic moving again. Mr. Garson . . . notices Adam, has a few quiet words with him before a paternal shove toward the room. (p. 150)

The technique of "thick description" is part of a research tradition called *ethnography,* which was first used by anthropologists to study other cultures and then began to be used by educational researchers to study our own school and community cultures. The connection is that "ethnographers study cultures. Building on the premise that classroom interactions do not take place in a vacuum, ethnographic . . . researchers look at classroom interactions as well as the culture-laden contexts in which these interactions occur" (Rex, Steadman, & Graciano, 2006, p. 744).

We will now look at some excerpts from a classic educational ethnography, Shirley Brice Heath's (1983) *Ways With Words.* Heath undertook a long-term, participant/observer case study exploring the effects of community and family on one specific area of learning: children's family and school literacy development in two small, rural Carolina communities, one Black, one White.

Case Study Example

Trackton and Roadville

In the years between 1969 and 1978, I lived, worked, and played with the children and their families and friends in Roadville and Trackton. My entry into these specific communities came through a naturally occurring chain of events. In each case, I knew an old-time resident of the community, and my relationship with that individual opened the community to me. I had grown up in a rural Piedmont area in a neighboring state, so the customs of both communities were very familiar to me though many years had passed since I had been a daily part of such cultural ways. (Heath, 1983, p. 5)

As this excerpt indicates, Heath's research involved becoming a participant in the social/educational setting that was the object of her study. Note how long Heath spent gathering data: more than 9 years. Case studies often involve more than a year of data collection, but 9 years is an extraordinary length of time.

Heath's (1983, p. 11) general research focus was on social and familial influences on literacy. She sought to explore ways in which differences in children's literacy development were rooted in differences in family structure, roles in the community, the community's concept of childhood, and religious activities.

But Heath had an interventionist goal as well as an exploratory goal, and she organized her book to reflect this:

In Part I of the book, the reader moves with me, the ethnographer, as unobtrusively as possible in the worlds of Trackton and Roadville children. In Part II, . . . my role as an ethnographer is intrusive, as I work with teachers to enable them to become participant observers in their own domains and to use the knowledge from the ethnographies of Trackton and Roadville to inform their motivations, practices, and programs of teaching. (Heath, 1983, pp. 12–13)

For Heath, the interventionist part reflected an ethical decision: She chose not to be an objective, detached observer for the duration of the project. She gathered data as accurately and unobtrusively as possible but then felt an obligation to actively share what she had learned with those who could directly make a difference in the lives of children.

To summarize, Heath's research began with an exploratory question and then continued inductively as she developed general concepts to make sense of specific observations. Although Heath, an educated White woman, was something of an outsider in Trackton and Roadville, she also had something approaching insider status due to her earlier experience growing up in a similar setting and to her strategy of entering each community with the support of a trusted informant. Her insights about what she observed emerged in part because her semi-insider status enabled her to share many participants' experiences and perspectives. Her in-depth descriptions and ability to connect sequences of events enabled her to construct plausible explanations about what seemed to be a typical group. She thus successfully used field research to explore human experiences in depth, carefully analyzing the community and educational contexts in which they occur.

🔲 Participant Observation

Many educational researchers, like Heath (1983), carry out their studies through participant observation, termed *fieldwork* in anthropology. Natural educational processes are studied as they happen (in "the field" rather than in the laboratory). Participant observation is the seminal qualitative research method—a means for seeing the world as the research subjects see it, in its totality, and for understanding subjects' interpretations of that world (Wolcott, 1995, p. 66). By observing people and interacting with them in the course of their normal activities, participant observers seek to avoid the artificiality of experimental designs and the unnatural structured questioning of survey research (Koegel, 1987, p. 8). This method encourages consideration of the context in which social interaction occurs, of the complex and interconnected nature of social relations, and of the sequencing of events (Bogdewic, 1999, p. 49).

The term *participant observer* actually refers to several different specific roles that a qualitative researcher can adopt (see Exhibit 9.2). As a **covert observer,** a researcher observes others without participating in social interaction and does not identify herself as a researcher.

This role is often adopted for studies in public places where there is nothing unusual about someone sitting and observing others. However, in many settings, a qualitative researcher will function as a **complete observer,** who does not participate in group activities and is publicly defined as a researcher. These two relatively passive roles contrast with the roles of covert and overt participation. A qualitative researcher is a complete or **covert participant** when she acts just like other group members and does not disclose her research role. If she publicly acknowledges being a researcher but nonetheless participates in group activities, she can be termed an *overt participant* or true **participant observer.**

Choosing a Role

The first concern of every participant observer is to decide what balance to strike between observing and participating and whether to reveal his or her role as a researcher. These decisions must take into account the specifics of the social situation being studied, the researcher's own background and personality, the larger educational/political context, and ethical concerns. The balance between participating and observing also changes during most projects, often many times. And the researcher's ability to maintain either a covert or an overt role will many times be challenged.

Covert Observation

In both observational roles, researchers try to see things as they happen, without actively participating in these events. Although there is no fixed formula to guide the observational process, observers try to identify the *who, what, when, where, why,* and *how* of activities in the setting. Their observations will usually become more focused over time, as the observer develops a sense of the important categories of people and activities and gradually develops a theory that accounts for what is observed. (Bogdewic, 1999, pp. 54–56)

In settings involving many people, in which observing while standing or sitting does not attract attention, covert observation is possible and is unlikely to have much effect on social processes. You may not even want to call this "covert" observation because your activities as an observer may be no different than those of others who are simply "people watching" to pass the time. However, when you take notes, when you systematically check out the different areas of a public space or different people in a crowd, and when you arrive and leave at

Exhibit 9.2	The Participation Observation Continuum

Source: Adapted from Marshall and Rossman (1999, pp. 75–76).

particular times to do your observing, you are acting differently in important respects from others in the setting. Moreover, when you write up what you have observed and, possibly, publish it, you have taken something unique from the people in that setting. If you adopt the role of covert observer, you should always remember to evaluate how your actions in the setting and your purposes for being there may affect the actions of others and your own interpretations.

Overt Observation

When a researcher announces her role as a research observer, her presence is much more likely to alter the situation being observed. This is the problem of **reactive effects.** It is not "natural" in most educational situations for someone to be present who will record her or his observations for research and publication purposes, and so individuals may alter their behavior. The overt, or complete, observer is even more likely to have an impact when the setting involves few people or if observing is unlike the usual activities in the setting. Observable differences between the observer and those being observed also increase the likelihood of reactive effects. For example, some children treated Barrie Thorne (1993, pp. 16–17) as a teacher when she was observing them in a school playground and asked her to resolve disputes. No matter how much she tried to remain aloof, she still appeared to children as an adult authority figure and so experienced pressure to participate (Thorne, 1993, p. 20).

Overt Participation (Participant Observer)

Most **field researchers** adopt a role that involves some active participation in the setting. Usually they inform at least some group members of their research interests, but then they participate in enough group activities to develop rapport with members and to gain a direct sense of what group members experience. This is not an easy balancing act.

> The key to participant observation as a fieldwork strategy is to take seriously the challenge it poses to participate more, and to play the role of the aloof observer less. Do not think of yourself as someone who needs to wear a white lab coat and carry a clipboard to learn about how humans go about their everyday lives. (Wolcott, 1995, p. 100)

Participating while overtly observing has two clear ethical advantages as well. Because group members know the researcher's real role in the group, they can choose to keep some information or attitudes hidden. By the same token, the researcher can decline to participate in unethical or dangerous activities without fear of exposing his or her identity.

Most field researchers who opt for disclosure get the feeling that, after they have become known and at least somewhat trusted figures in the group, their presence does not have any palpable effect on members' actions. The major influences on individual actions and attitudes are past experiences, personality, group structure, and so on, so the argument goes, and these continue to exert their influence even when an outside observer is present. As a result, it is argued, the participant observer can be ethical about identity disclosure and still observe the educational world.

Experienced participant observers try to lessen the potential for problems due to identity disclosure by evaluating both their effect on others in the setting and the effect of others on them as observers. They do this by writing about these effects throughout the time they are in the field and while they analyze their data. They also are sure, while in the field, to preserve some physical space and regular time when they can concentrate on their research and schedule occasional meetings with other researchers to review the fieldwork. Participant observers modify their role as circumstances seem to require, perhaps not always disclosing their research role at casual social gatherings or group outings but being sure to inform new members of it.

Covert Participation

To lessen the potential for reactive effects and to gain entry to otherwise inaccessible settings, some field researchers adopt the role of covert participant, keeping their research secret and trying their best to act like other participants in a social setting or group. Although the role of covert participant lessens some of the reactive effects encountered by the complete observer, covert participants confront other problems:

Covert participants cannot take notes openly or use any obvious recording devices. They must write up notes based solely on memory and must do so at times when it is natural for them to be away from group members.

Covert participants cannot ask questions that will arouse suspicion. Thus, they often have trouble clarifying the meaning of other participants' attitudes or actions.

The role of covert participant is difficult to play successfully. Covert participants will not know how regular participants would act in every situation in which the researchers find themselves. Regular participants have entered the situation from different social backgrounds and with different goals than the researcher, so the researcher's spontaneous reactions to every event are unlikely to be consistent with those of the regular participants (Mitchell, 1993). Suspicion that researchers are not "one of us" may then have reactive effects, obviating the value of complete participation (Erikson, 1967).

Ethical issues have been at the forefront of debate over the strategy of covert participation. Kai Erikson (1967) argues that covert participation is, by its very nature, unethical and should not be allowed except in public settings. Covert researchers cannot anticipate the unintended consequences of their actions for research subjects, Erikson points out. If others suspect the researcher's identity or if the researcher contributes to, or impedes, group action, there may be adverse consequences. If the researcher maintains the confidentiality of others, keeps commitments to others, and does not directly lie to others, some degree of deception may be justified in exchange for the knowledge gained (Punch, 1994, p. 90).

Entering the Field

Entering the field—the setting under investigation—is a critical stage in a participant observation project because it can shape many subsequent experiences. Some background work is necessary before entering the field—at least enough to develop a clear understanding of what the research questions are likely to be and to review one's personal stance toward the people and problems likely to be encountered. With participant observation, researchers must also learn in advance how participants dress and what their typical activities are, so as to avoid being caught completely unprepared. Finding a participant who can make introductions is often critical (Rossman & Rallis, 1998, pp. 102–103), and formal permission may be needed in an organizational setting (Bogdewic, 1999, pp. 51–53).

To observe classrooms and other school-related activities such as meetings and discussions, researchers often need to engage in a formal entry process in which they seek permission from teachers, school principals, and others. Many school systems have a system-wide permission process regarding educational research in their buildings that must be carefully observed by prospective researchers.

In short, field researchers must be very sensitive to the impression they make and the ties they establish when entering the field. This stage lays the groundwork for collecting data from people who have different perspectives and for developing relationships that the researcher can use to surmount any problems in data collection. The researcher should be ready with a rationale for her participation and some sense of the potential benefits to participants. Discussion about these issues with key participants or gatekeepers should be honest and should identify what the participants can expect from the research, without necessarily going into detail about the researcher's hypotheses or research questions (Rossman & Rallis, 1998, pp. 51–53, 105–108). Exhibit 9.3 outlines several steps that can be usefully reviewed by both experienced and inexperienced researchers entering the field on a new project.

Developing and Maintaining Relationships

Researchers must be careful to manage their relationships in the research setting so they can continue to observe and interview throughout the long period typical of participant observation (Maxwell, 1996, p. 66).

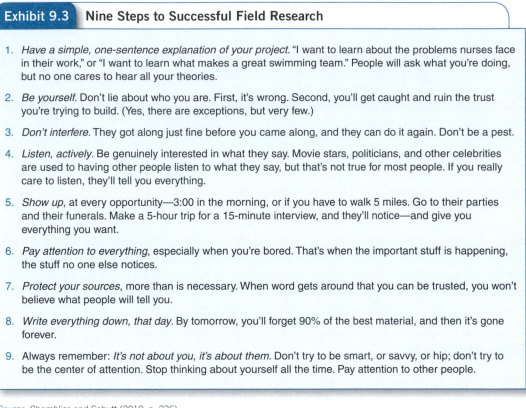

Exhibit 9.3 **Nine Steps to Successful Field Research**

1. *Have a simple, one-sentence explanation of your project.* "I want to learn about the problems nurses face in their work," or "I want to learn what makes a great swimming team." People will ask what you're doing, but no one cares to hear all your theories.

2. *Be yourself.* Don't lie about who you are. First, it's wrong. Second, you'll get caught and ruin the trust you're trying to build. (Yes, there are exceptions, but very few.)

3. *Don't interfere.* They got along just fine before you came along, and they can do it again. Don't be a pest.

4. *Listen, actively.* Be genuinely interested in what they say. Movie stars, politicians, and other celebrities are used to having other people listen to what they say, but that's not true for most people. If you really care to listen, they'll tell you everything.

5. *Show up*, at every opportunity—3:00 in the morning, or if you have to walk 5 miles. Go to their parties and their funerals. Make a 5-hour trip for a 15-minute interview, and they'll notice—and give you everything you want.

6. *Pay attention to everything*, especially when you're bored. That's when the important stuff is happening, the stuff no one else notices.

7. *Protect your sources*, more than is necessary. When word gets around that you can be trusted, you won't believe what people will tell you.

8. *Write everything down, that day.* By tomorrow, you'll forget 90% of the best material, and then it's gone forever.

9. Always remember: *It's not about you, it's about them.* Don't try to be smart, or savvy, or hip; don't try to be the center of attention. Stop thinking about yourself all the time. Pay attention to other people.

Source: Chambliss and Schutt (2010, p. 236).

Every action the researcher takes can develop or undermine this relationship. Interaction early in the research process is particularly sensitive because participants don't know the researcher and the researcher doesn't know the routines. Thorne (1993) felt she had gained access to kids' more private world "when kids violated rules in my presence, like swearing or openly blowing bubble gum where these acts were forbidden, or swapping stories about recent acts of shoplifting" (pp. 18–19).

Experienced participant observers have developed some sound advice for others seeking to maintain relationships in the field (Bogdewic, 1999, pp. 53–54; Rossman & Rallis, 1998, pp. 105–108; Whyte, 1955, pp. 300–306; Wolcott, 1995, pp. 91–95):

- Develop a plausible (and honest) explanation for yourself and your study.

- Maintain the support of key individuals in groups or organizations under study.

- Be unobtrusive and unassuming. Don't "show off" your expertise.

- Don't be too aggressive in questioning others (e.g., don't violate implicit norms that preclude discussion of illegal activity with outsiders). Being a researcher requires that you not simultaneously try to be the guardian of law and order. Instead, be a reflective listener.

- Ask very sensitive questions only of informants with whom your relationship is good.

- Be self-revealing, but only up to a point. Let participants learn about you as a person, but without making too much of yourself.

- Don't fake your social similarity with your subjects. Taking a friendly interest in them should be an adequate basis for developing trust.

- Be prepared for special difficulties and tensions if multiple groups are involved. It is hard to avoid taking sides or being used in situations of intergroup conflict.

Sampling People and Events

Sampling decisions in qualitative research are guided by the need to study intensively the people, places, or phenomena of interest. In fact, most qualitative researchers limit their focus to just one or a few sites or programs, so that they can focus all their attention on the social dynamics of those settings. This focus on a limited number of cases does not mean that sampling is unimportant. The researcher must be reasonably confident that she can gain access and that the site can provide relevant information. The sample must be appropriate and adequate for the study, even if it is not representative. The qualitative researcher may select a "critical case" that is unusually rich in information pertaining to the research question, a "typical case" precisely because it is judged to be typical, and/or a "deviant case" that provides a useful contrast (Kuzel, 1999). Studying more than one case or setting almost always strengthens the causal conclusions and makes the findings more generalizable (King et al., 1994).

You already learned in Chapter 5 about some of the nonprobability sampling methods that are used in field research. For instance, purposive sampling can be used to identify opinion leaders and representatives of different roles. With snowball sampling, field researchers learn from participants about who represents different subgroups in a setting. Quota sampling also may be employed to ensure the representation of particular categories of participants.

Using some type of intentional sampling strategy within a particular setting can allow tests of some hypotheses that would otherwise have to wait until comparative data can be collected from several settings (King et al., 1994). Within a research site, plans can be made to sample different settings, people, events, and artifacts to obtain different types of information (for an example, see Exhibit 9.4). A method called theoretical sampling (see Exhibit 9.5) is a systematic approach to sampling in participant observation studies (Glaser & Strauss, 1967). When field researchers discover in an investigation that particular processes seem to be important, inferring that certain comparisons should be made or that similar instances should be checked, the researchers then choose new settings or individuals that permit these comparisons or checks (Ragin, 1994, pp. 98–101).

Taking Notes

Written notes are the primary means of recording participant observation data (Emerson, Fretz, & Shaw, 1995). Of course, "written" no longer means handwritten; many field researchers jot down partial notes while observing and then retreat to their computer to write up more complete notes on a daily basis. The computerized text can then be inspected and organized after it is printed out, or it can be marked up and organized for analysis using one of several computer programs designed especially for the task.

Many qualitative researchers use new technologies for data collection and analysis. We can now take notes on netbooks and tablet computers and record interviews, focus groups, and observations on a variety of devices. These include dedicated audio and video recorders that create files that transfer straight to a computer, as well as cell phones with audio and video capability, iPods, BlackBerries, flip cams, point-and-shoot cameras, and other devices. Improved speech recognition software may soon make it possible to audio record an interview and have it automatically transcribed into a word-processing program. In general, the new

Exhibit 9.4 **Sampling Plan for a Participant Observation Project in Schools**

Information Source[a]	Type of Information to Be Obtained				
	Collegiality	Goals and Community	Action Expectations	Knowledge Orientation	Base
Settings					
Public places (halls, main offices)					
Teachers' lounge	X	X		X	X
Classrooms		X	X	X	X
Meeting rooms	X		X	X	
Gymnasium or locker room		X			
Events					
Faculty meetings	X		X		X
Lunch hour	X				X
Teaching		X	X	X	X
People					
Principal		X	X	X	X
Teachers	X	X	X	X	X
Students		X	X	X	
Artifacts					
Newspapers		X	X		X
Decorations		X			

Source: Marshall and Rossman (1995, pp. 77–76).

a. Selected examples in each category.

technologies are smaller, cheaper, less obtrusive, and easier to use than earlier equipment, so qualitative researchers need to keep abreast of technological developments. However, remember that no matter what means are used, the researcher is still the single most important tool in the research process.

It is almost always a mistake to try to take comprehensive notes while engaged in the field—the process of writing extensively is just too disruptive. The usual procedure is to jot down brief notes about highlights of the observation period. These brief notes (called **jottings**) can then serve as memory joggers when writing the actual **field notes** at a later session. It will also help to maintain a daily log in which each day's

Exhibit 9.5 Theoretical Sampling

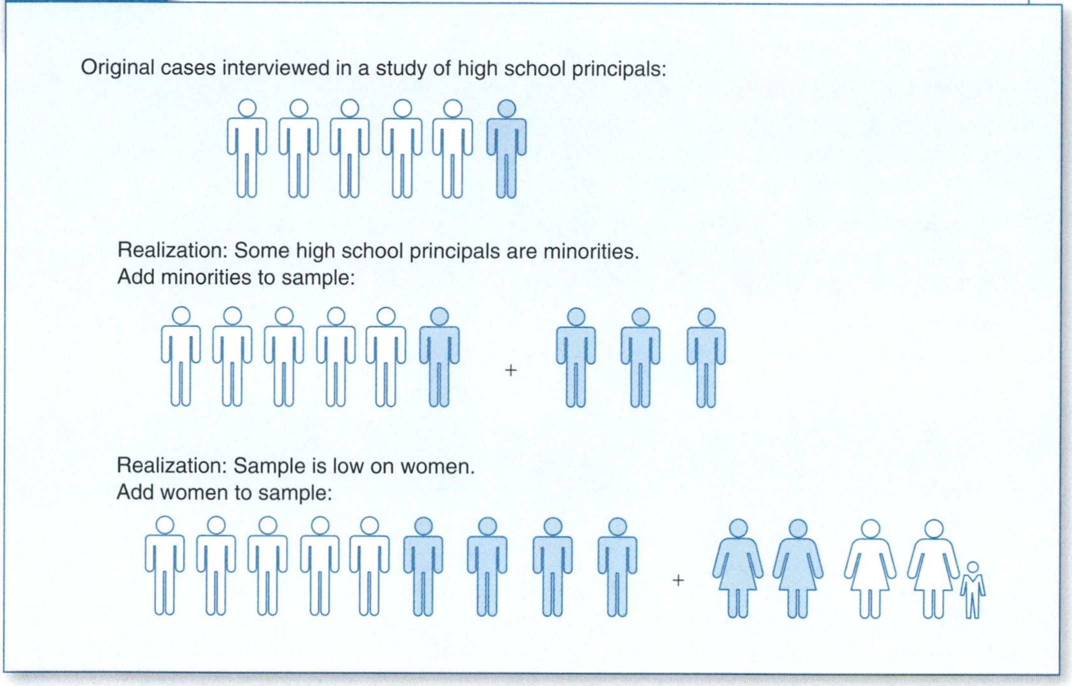

Original cases interviewed in a study of high school principals:

Realization: Some high school principals are minorities.
Add minorities to sample:

Realization: Sample is low on women.
Add women to sample:

Source: Schutt (2009).

activities are recorded (Bogdewic, 1999, pp. 58–67). With the aid of the jottings and some practice, researchers usually remember a great deal of what happened—as long as the comprehensive field notes are written immediately afterward, or at least within the next 24 hours, and before they have been discussed with anyone else.

The following excerpt sheds light on the note-taking processes that Thorne (1993) used while in the field:

> I went through the school days with a small spiral notebook in hand, jotting descriptions that I later expanded into field notes. When I was at the margins of a scene, I took notes on the spot. When I was more fully involved, sitting and talking with kids at a cafeteria table or playing a game of jump rope, I held observation in my memory and recorded them later. (p. 17)

Natasha Mack, Cynthia Woodsong, Kathleen M. MacQueen, Greg Guest, and Emily Namey (2005) offer the following tips for novice researchers conducting observations for the first time.

Usually, writing up notes takes much longer—at least three times longer—than the observing did. Field notes must be as complete, detailed, and true as possible to what was observed and heard. Direct quotes should be distinguished clearly from paraphrased quotes, and both should be set off from the researcher's observation and reflections. Pauses and interruptions should be indicated. The surrounding context should receive as much attention as possible, and a map of the setting always should be included, with indications of where individuals were at different times.

Careful note taking yields a big payoff. On page after page, field notes will suggest new concepts, causal connections, and theoretical propositions. Social processes and settings can be described in rich detail, with

> ### Tips for Taking Field Notes
>
> **Begin each notebook entry** with the date, time, place, and type of data collection event.
>
> **Leave space** on the page for expanding your notes, or plan to expand them on a separate page.
>
> **Take notes strategically.** It is usually practical to make only brief notes during data collection. Direct quotes can be especially hard to write down accurately. Rather than try to document every detail or quote, write down key words and phrases that will trigger your memory when you expand notes.
>
> **Use shorthand.** Because you will expand and type your notes soon after you write them, it does not matter if you are the only person who can understand your shorthand system. Use abbreviations and acronyms to quickly note what is happening and being said.
>
> **Cover a range of observations.** In addition to documenting events and informal conversations, note people's body language, moods, or attitudes; the general environment; interactions among participants; ambiance; and other information that could be relevant.
>
> *Source:* Adapted from Mack et al. (2005, p. 24). Reprinted by permission of Family Health International: The Science of Improving Lives.

ample illustrations. Complete field notes must provide even more than a record of what was observed or heard. Notes also should include descriptions of the methodology: where researchers were standing or sitting while they observed, how they chose people for conversation or observation, what counts of people or events they made and why. Sprinkled throughout the notes also should be a record of the researchers' feelings and thoughts while observing: when they were disgusted by some statement or act, when they felt threatened or intimidated, why their attention shifted from one group to another, and what ethical concerns arose. Notes like these provide a foundation for later review of the likelihood of bias or of inattention to some salient features of the situation.

Notes may, in some situations, be supplemented by still pictures, videotapes, and printed material circulated or posted in the research setting. Such visual material can bring an entirely differently qualitative dimension into the analysis and call attention to some features of the social situation and actors within it that were missed in the notes (Grady, 1996). Commentary on this material can be integrated with the written notes (Bogdewic, 1999, pp. 67–68).

Managing the Personal Dimensions

Our overview of participant observation would not be complete without considering its personal dimensions. Because field researchers become a part of the situation they are studying, they cannot help but be affected on a personal, emotional level. At the same time, those being studied react to researchers, not just as researchers but as personal acquaintances—often as friends, sometimes as personal rivals. Managing and learning from this personal side of field research is an important part of any project.

The impact of personal issues varies with the depth of researchers' involvement in the setting. The more involved researchers are in multiple aspects of the ongoing social situation, the more important personal issues become and the greater the risk of "going native."

The correspondence between researchers' social attributes—age, sex, race, and so on—and those of their subjects also shapes personal relationships. Thorne (1993) wondered whether "my moments of remembering, the times when I felt like a ten-year-old girl, [were] a source of distortion or insight?" She concluded they were both: "Memory, like observing, is a way of knowing and can be a rich resource," but "When my own responses . . . were driven by emotions like envy or aversion, they clearly obscured my ability to grasp the full social situation" (p. 26). Deborah Ceglowski (2002) found that

> the feelings well up in my throat when Brian [a child in the Head Start program she studied] asks me to hold his hand. It's the gut reaction to hearing Ruth [a staff member] tell about Brian's expression when they pull into his yard and his mother isn't there. It is the caring connection of sitting next to Steven [another child] and hearing him say, "I miss my mom." (p. 15)

There is no formula for successfully managing the personal dimension of field research. It is much more art than science and flows more from the researcher's own personality and natural approach to other people than from formal training. But novice field researchers often neglect to consider how they will manage personal relationships when they plan and carry out their projects. Then, suddenly, they find themselves doing something they don't believe they should, just to stay in the good graces of research subjects, or juggling the emotions resulting from conflict within the group.

If you plan a field research project, follow these guidelines (Whyte, 1955, pp. 300–317):

- Take the time to consider how you want to relate to your potential subjects as people.

- Speculate about what personal problems might arise and how you will respond to them.

- Keep in touch with other researchers and personal friends outside the research setting.

- Maintain standards of conduct that make you comfortable as a person and that respect the integrity of your subjects.

When you evaluate participant observers' reports, pay attention to how they defined their role in the setting and dealt with personal problems. Don't place too much confidence in such research unless the report provides this information. The primary strengths of participant observation—learning about the educational world from participants' perspectives, as they experience it, and minimizing the distortion of these perspectives by the methods used to measure them—should not blind us to its primary weaknesses—the lack of consistency in the data collected, particularly when different observers are used, and the many opportunities for direct influence of the researcher's perspective on what is observed. Whenever we consider using the method of participant observation, we also must realize that the need to focus so much attention on each setting studied will severely restrict the possible number of settings or people we can study.

Intensive Interviewing

Intensive or depth interviewing is a qualitative method of finding out about people's experiences, thoughts, and feelings. Although intensive interviewing can be an important element in a participant observation study, it is often used by itself (Wolcott, 1995, pp. 102–105). It shares with other qualitative research methods a commitment to learning about people in depth and on their own terms, as well as in the context of their situation.

Unlike the more structured interviewing that may be used in survey research (discussed in Chapter 8), intensive or depth interviewing relies on open-ended questions. Rather than asking standard questions in a fixed order, intensive interviewers may allow the specific content and order of questions to vary from one interviewee to another. Rather than presenting fixed responses that presume awareness of the range of answers that respondents might give or that intensive interviewers expect respondents might give, intensive interviewers expect respondents to answer questions in their own words.

What distinguishes intensive interviewing from less structured forms of questioning is consistency and thoroughness. The goal is to develop a comprehensive picture of the interviewee's background, attitudes, and actions, in his or her own terms; to "listen to people as they describe how they understand the worlds in which they live and work" (Rubin & Rubin, 1995, p. 3).

Intensive interview studies do not reveal as directly as does participant observation the social context in which action is taken and opinions are formed. Nonetheless, intensive depth interviewers seek to take context into account. Jack D. Douglas (1985) made the point succinctly in *Creative Interviewing*:

> *Creative interviewing is purposefully situated interviewing.* Rather than denying or failing to see the situation of the interview as a determinant of what goes on in the questioning and answering processes, creative interviewing embraces the immediate, concrete situation; tries to understand how it is affecting what is communicated; and, by understanding these effects, changes the interviewer's communication processes to increase the discovery of the truth about human beings. (p. 22)

So, like participant observation studies, intensive interviewing engages researchers more actively with subjects than standard survey research does. The researchers must listen to lengthy explanations, ask follow-up questions tailored to the preceding answers, and seek to learn about interrelated belief systems or personal approaches to things rather than measure a limited set of variables. As a result, intensive interviews are often much longer than standardized interviews, sometimes as long as 15 hours, conducted in several different sessions. The intensive interview becomes more like a conversation between partners than an interview between a researcher and a subject (S. R. Kaufman, 1986, pp. 22–23). Some call it "a conversation with a purpose" (Rossman & Rallis, 1998, p. 126).

Intensive interviewers actively try to probe understandings and engage interviewees in a dialogue about what they mean by their comments. To prepare for this active interviewing, the interviewer should learn in advance about the setting to be studied. Preliminary discussion with **key informants,** inspection of written documents, and even a review of your own feelings about the setting can all help (W. L. Miller & Crabtree, 1999b, pp. 94–96).

The intensive interview follows a preplanned outline of topics. It may begin with a few simple questions that gather background information while building rapport. These are often followed by a few general **"grand tour" questions** that are meant to elicit lengthy narratives (W. L. Miller & Crabtree, 1999b, pp. 96–99). Some projects may use relatively structured interviews, particularly when the focus is on developing knowledge about prior events or some narrowly defined topic. But more exploratory projects, particularly those aiming to learn about interviewees' interpretations of the world, may let each interview flow in a unique direction in response to the interviewee's experiences and interests (Kvale, 1996, pp. 3–5; Rubin & Rubin, 1995, p. 6; Wolcott, 1995, pp. 113–114). In either case, qualitative interviewers must adapt nimbly throughout the interview, paying attention to nonverbal cues, expressions with symbolic value, and the ebb and flow of the interviewee's feelings and interests. "You have to be free to follow your data where they lead" (Rubin & Rubin, 1995, p. 64).

Random selection is rarely used to select respondents for intensive interviews, but the selection method still must be considered carefully. If interviewees are selected in a haphazard manner, as by speaking just to those who happen to be available at the time that the researcher is on site, the interviews are likely to be of less value than when a more purposive selection strategy is used. Researchers should try to select interviewees who are knowledgeable about the subject of the interview, who are open to talking, and who represent the range of perspectives (Rubin & Rubin, 1995, pp. 65–92). Selection of new interviewees should continue, if possible, at least until the **saturation point** is reached, the point when new interviews seem to yield little additional information (see Exhibit 9.6). As new issues are uncovered, additional interviewees may be selected to represent different opinions about these issues.

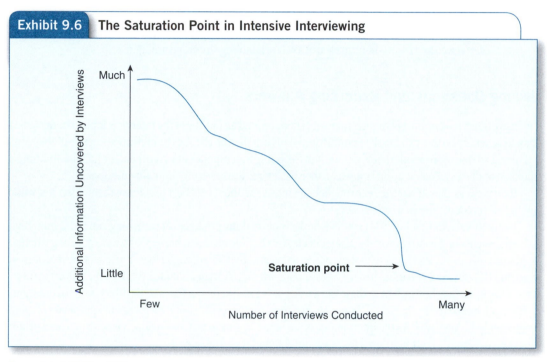

| Exhibit 9.6 | The Saturation Point in Intensive Interviewing |

Source: Schutt (2009, p. 342).

Establishing and Maintaining a Partnership

Because intensive interviewing does not engage researchers as participants in subjects' daily affairs, the problems of entering the field are much reduced. However, the logistics of arranging long periods for personal interviews can still be pretty complicated. It also is important to establish rapport with subjects by considering in advance how they will react to the interview arrangements and by developing an approach that does not violate their standards for social behavior. Interviewees should be treated with respect, as knowledgeable partners whose time is valued (in other words, avoid coming late for appointments). A commitment to confidentiality should be stated and honored (Rubin & Rubin, 1995).

But the intensive interviewer's relationship with the interviewee is not an equal partnership because the researcher seeks to gain certain types of information and strategizes throughout to maintain an appropriate relationship (Kvale, 1996, p. 6). In the first few minutes of the interview, the goal is to show interest in the interviewee and to explain clearly what the purpose of the interview is (Kvale, 1996, p. 128). During the interview, the interviewer should maintain an appropriate distance from the interviewee, one that doesn't violate cultural norms; the interviewer should maintain eye contact and not engage in districting behavior. An appropriate pace is also important; pause to allow the interviewee to reflect, elaborate, and generally not feel rushed (Gordon, 1992). When an interview covers emotional or otherwise stressful topics, the interviewer should give the interviewee an opportunity to unwind at the interview's end (Rubin & Rubin, 1995, p. 138).

More generally, intensive interviewers must be sensitive to the broader social context of their interaction with the interviewee and to the implications of their relationship for the way they ask questions and interpret answers. Tom Wengraf (2001) cautions new intensive interviewers to take account of their unconscious orientations to others based on prior experience:

Your [prior] experience of being interviewed may lead you to behave and "come across" in your interviewing . . . like a policeman, or a parent, a teacher or academic, or any "authority" by whom you have been interviewed and from whom you learnt a way of handling stress and ambiguity. (p. 18)

Asking Questions and Recording Answers

Intensive interviewers must plan their main questions around an outline of the interview topic. The questions should generally be short and to the point. More details can then be elicited through nondirective probes (e.g., "Can you tell me more about that?" or "uh-huh," echoing the respondent's comment, or just maintaining a moment of silence). Follow-up questions can then be tailored to answers to the main questions.

Interviewers should strategize throughout an interview about how best to achieve their objectives while taking into account interviewees' answers.

James R. Valadez (2008, p. 834) studied the decision-making processes of rural Mexican immigrant high school students in Washington state. The students were high academic achievers who were deciding whether to attend college. Mr. Patrick, a school counselor, suggested that Valadez interview Enrique, who had been in the United States for 7 years and had a 3.2 grade point average (Valadez, 2008, p. 841). In the following interview excerpt, notice the way James, the interviewer, keeps Enrique on track by asking direct, focused questions ("Have you talked to Mr. Patrick?" "Have you registered for the SAT?") but then gives Enrique plenty of room to answer in his own way. As the interview goes on, James begins to mirror Enrique's less formal level of language ("you know," "stuff like that") to increase his rapport with Enrique.

Enrique: I would like to go to college . . . maybe art . . . definitely college . . . I have a problem with it sometimes . . . like I feel I'm not going to be ready.

James: Have you talked to Mr. Patrick?

Enrique: Yeah . . . I got information from him. He gave me forms for the SAT, financial aid.

James: Have you registered for the SAT?

Enrique: No . . . I know I need the SAT. I need a lot of things. I've been thinking about it, but I'm not sure. Not that I'm not sure; it's just a lot, you know. Sometimes I don't know . . . I need to register, yeah, take the test.

James: Has Mr. Patrick helped you, you know, about college, financial aid, stuff like that?

Enrique: I talked to him. He's really the only one. He tells me things, like I said, he gave me the forms and talked to me about them . . . I have a lot to think about, and he really doesn't give me the things I need to get ahead.

James: Like what; what do you mean?

Enrique: Well, he tells me what to do and I appreciate it and everything, and really, he's pretty cool . . . but I need to know more. He tries to tell me what I need to know. . . . I want to know how I am going to get into these schools? My parents tell me, how do we pay? I don't know what to say. I tell them there is financial aid and they want to know more. . . . I can't tell them because I don't know everything about it.

James: You're sure you're going?

Enrique: Yeah, I want to go . . . I don't know sometimes about what to do. (Valadez, 2008, pp. 842–843)

Becoming a good intensive interviewer means learning how to "get out of the way" as much as possible in this process. Becoming an informed critic of intensive interview studies means, in part, learning to consider how the social interaction between the interviewer and interviewee may have shaped in subtle ways what the interviewee said.

Voice recorders commonly are used to record intensive and focus group interviews. Most researchers who have voice-recorded interviews (including the authors) feel that they do not inhibit most interviewees and, in fact, are routinely ignored. The occasional respondent is very concerned with his or her public image and may therefore speak "for the recorder," but such individuals are unlikely to speak frankly in any research interview. In any case, constant note taking during an interview prevents adequate displays of interest and appreciation by the interviewer and hinders the degree of concentration that results in the best interviews. If a voice recorder cannot be used, it is best to record only brief notes during the interview and then to write up detailed notes soon after the interview ends.

◫ Focus Groups

Focus groups are groups of unrelated individuals that are formed by a researcher and then led in group discussion of a topic for 1 to 2 hours. The researcher asks specific questions and guides the discussion to ensure that group members address these questions, but the resulting information is qualitative and relatively unstructured. Focus groups do not involve representative samples; instead, a few individuals are recruited who have the time to participate, have some knowledge pertinent to the focus group topic, and share key characteristics with the target population.

Focus groups generate qualitative data using open-ended questions posed by the researcher (or group leader). Thus, a focused discussion mimics the natural process of forming and expressing opinions—and may give some sense of validity. The researcher, or group moderator, uses an interview guide, but the dynamics of group discussion often require changes in the order and manner in which different topics are addressed (J. B. Brown, 1999, p. 120). No formal procedure exists for determining the generalizability of focus group answers, but the careful researcher should conduct at least several focus groups on the same topic and check for consistency in the findings. Some focus group experts advise conducting enough focus groups to reach the point of "saturation," when an additional focus group adds little new information to that which already has been generated (J. B. Brown, 1999, p. 118).

Most focus groups involve 7 to 10 people, a number that facilitates discussion by all in attendance. Participants usually do not know one another, although some studies in organized settings may include friends or coworkers. Opinions differ on the value of using homogeneous versus heterogeneous participants. Homogeneous groups may be more convivial and willing to share feelings, but heterogeneous groups may stimulate more ideas (J. B. Brown, 1999, pp. 115–117). Focus group leaders must begin the discussion by creating the expectation that all will participate and that the researcher will not favor any particular perspective or participant.

Richard Krueger (1988) provides a good example of a situation in which focus groups were used effectively:

[A] university recently launched a $100 million fund drive. The key aspect of the drive was a film depicting science and research efforts. The film was shown in over two dozen focus groups of alumni, with surprising results to University officials. Alumni simply did not like the film and instead were more attracted to supporting undergraduate humanistic education. (pp. 33–37)

Focus group methods share with other field research techniques an emphasis on discovering unanticipated findings and exploring hidden meanings. Check (2002) wanted to investigate what effect the rapid turnover of school principals in urban areas had on the aspirations of senior teachers, especially minority women, to become principals themselves. He gathered a focus group of diverse senior female teachers from schools, in San Francisco and Oakland, where no principal had lasted more than 3 years, and some had left in the same year they were hired. An excerpt from their discussion on principal turnover should give you a feel for how a focus group proceeds (all names are pseudonyms). Ana revealed that she had applied to be principal at her school the year before and been selected, but

I withdrew myself, because seeing all the principals that we've had and seeing how large our school is—well, more than 500 students K–5. The women principals that we've had, one divorced while in administration. I'm married still, two kids, young kids. And the other one was divorced and her kids were already adults. So basically the school became their family, right? And I still have my young family and I didn't want to have them orphaned. That was a real big issue for me. I felt I would have had to choose, one way or the other, my school or my family.

Betsy: I completely agree with that, because I've thought very seriously about being a principal, but my kids are eleven and twelve, and I just keep making the decision to be with them. . . .

Carmen: But I also want to say something about this . . . they're going to yank a good principal from our school. . . . If they don't, it will be a miracle. And these principals, the most intelligent, the most caring, the most compassionate and politically savvy people, they don't want to live like that . . . if a principal is really good in one community then the district has got to grab that person because there's such scarcity of people that are effective and they stick them into a new place. And so the stress level, it never changes unless they choose not to do that job anymore. (Check, 2002, pp. 173–174)

The women in the focus group build on each other's comments in a way that would not have been possible in a survey or a one-on-one interview situation. Because of their spontaneous nature, focus groups can be an indispensable aid for developing hypotheses and survey questions, for investigating the meaning of survey results, and for quickly assessing the range of opinion about an issue. Because it is not possible to conduct focus groups with large, representative samples, it is always important to consider how recruitment procedures have shaped the generalizability of focus group findings. The issue of impact of interviewer style and questioning on intensive interview findings, which was discussed in the previous section, also must be considered when evaluating the results of focus groups (see Exhibit 9.7).

Exhibit 9.7 | Keys to Running Focus Groups

- A great moderator—Is neutral and genuinely respects the participants and is a great listener who can draw people out.
- Main questions—These ask what you really want to know, can be answered by participants, are clear and understandable to the participants, and provide useful answers.
- Participants—Are homogeneous by relevant category for comparisons, with no power differentials within the group.
- Sampling—Is purposeful, representing the entire range of responses, and is random within the pools meeting criteria. Ideally, participants in any group should be strangers to each other. Use reminders to attend with incentives.
- Recording—Audio recording, with an assistant taking notes, is best.
- Analysis—Compare answers of different groups to different questions (groups on differently colored paper, sorted by question, etc.).
- Reporting—You are speaking for the participants. Lead with the big insights and answer the questions that were asked of the study. Interesting quotations get attention!
- When in doubt—Ask the potential participants about food, setting, issues, moderator, etc.

Basically, good focus groups get honest answers, on important topics, from people who know.

Source: R. A. Krueger and Casey (2000).

🔲 Combining Qualitative and Quantitative Methods

You learned earlier that Heath (1983) studied home and school language learning in two racially segregated small communities she called Trackton (Black) and Roadville (White). Her observation of "playsongs" illustrates both the value of multiple methods and the technique of recording observations in a form from which quantitative data can be obtained. Heath was particularly concerned with understanding the way playsongs created a public performance role for young girls. Playsongs included "jump-rope songs, hand-clap songs, as well as 'made up' playsongs which accompany a wide variety of activities, such as just sitting around, play-dancing, washing dishes, and pretending to be cheerleaders" (Heath, 1983, p. 99).

The results of Heath's (1983) observations are presented in Exhibit 9.8, which combines quantitative analysis with observation.

Heath's (1983) analysis of data led her to conclude that

the most frequently used (songs) at home are those for which an integral audience co-performer is a young child: imitating nonsense word play, learning to count and name body parts, and talking about immediate and important realities, such as family members and food. . . . At school, on the other hand, characters known to all girls, black and white, form the basis of the majority of the play-songs. (pp. 100–101)

Heath's combining of qualitative and quantitative methods gives us much greater confidence in the measurement of the range and frequency of song topics among girls, an important element in language learning.

Conducting qualitative interviews can often enhance the value of a research design that uses primarily quantitative measurement techniques (you will learn more about so-called mixed-method research

| **Exhibit 9.8** | **Types of Playsongs Recorded in Trackton and at Schools** | | | |

	Trackton		Schools	
Types	*n*	%	*n*	%
Nonsense word plays	62	28.2	5	2.1
Numbers	43	19.5	26	11.0
Body parts	38	17.3	11	4.6
Mamma and daily life	35	15.9	64	27.0
Food	16	7.2	12	5.1
Set characters	14	6.4	96	40.5
Animals	12	5.5	23	9.7
Total	220		237	

Source: Heath (1983, p. 100). Reprinted with permission of Cambridge University Press.

designs in Chapter 11). Qualitative data can provide information about the quality of standardized case records and quantitative survey measures, as well as offer some insight into the meaning of particular fixed responses.

Ethical Issues in Qualitative Research

No matter how hard the qualitative researcher strives to study the educational world naturally, leaving no traces, the very act of research itself imposes something "unnatural" on the situation, so the qualitative researcher may have an impact that has ethical implications. Five ethical issues should be given particular attention:

Voluntary participation. Ensuring that subjects are participating in a study voluntarily is not often a problem with intensive interviewing and focus group research but often is a point of contention in participant observation studies. Few researchers or institutional review boards are willing to condone covert participation because it offers no way to ensure that participation by the subjects is voluntary. Even when the researcher's role is more open, interpreting the standard of voluntary participation still can be difficult. Practically, much field research would be impossible if the participant observer were required to request permission of everyone having some contact, no matter how minimal, with a group or setting being observed. And should the requirement of voluntary participation apply equally to every member of an organization being observed? What if the manager consents, the workers are ambivalent, and the union says no? Requiring everyone's consent would limit participant observation research to settings without serious conflicts of interest.

Subject well-being. Every field researcher should consider carefully before beginning a project how to avoid harm to subjects. It is not possible to avoid every theoretical possibility of harm or to be sure that any project will cause no adverse consequences whatsoever to any individual. Direct harm to the reputations or feelings of particular individuals is what researchers must carefully avoid. They can do so, in part, by maintaining the confidentiality of research subjects. They also must avoid adversely affecting the course of events while engaged in a setting. These problems are rare in intensive interviewing and focus groups, but even there, researchers should try to identify negative feelings and help distressed subjects cope with their feelings through debriefing or referrals for professional help.

Identity disclosure. We already have considered the problems of identity disclosure, particularly in the case of covert participation. Current ethical standards require informed consent of research subjects, and most would argue that this standard cannot be met in any meaningful way if researchers do not disclose fully their identity. But how much disclosure about the study is necessary, and how hard should researchers try to make sure that their research purposes are understood? Less-educated subjects may not readily comprehend what a researcher is or be able to weigh the possible consequences of the research for themselves. Internet-based research can violate the principles of voluntary participation and identity disclosure when researchers participate in discussions and record and analyze text but do not identify themselves as researchers (Jesnadum, 2000). Must researchers always inform everyone of their identity as researchers? Should researchers inform subjects if the study's interests and foci change while it is in progress? Can a balance be struck between the disclosure of critical facts and a coherent research strategy?

Confidentiality. Field researchers normally use fictitious names for the characters in their reports, but doing so does not always guarantee confidentiality to their research subjects. Individuals in the setting studied may be able to identify those whose actions are described and thus may become privy to some knowledge about their colleagues or neighbors that had formerly been kept from them. Therefore, researchers should make every effort to expunge possible identifying material from published information and to alter unimportant aspects of a description when necessary to prevent identity disclosure. In any case, no field research project should begin if some participants clearly will suffer serious harm by being identified in project publications.

Appropriate boundaries. This is an ethical issue that cuts across several of the others, including identity disclosure, subject well-being, and voluntary participation. You are probably familiar with this issue in the context of guidelines for professional practice. Guidance counselors and school psychologists are cautioned to maintain appropriate boundaries with clients; teachers, administrators, and coaches must maintain appropriate boundaries with students. This is a special issue in qualitative research because it often involves lessening the boundary between the "researcher" and the research "subject." Qualitative researchers may seek to build rapport with those they plan to interview by expressing an interest in their concerns and conveying empathy for their situation. Is this just "faking friendship" for the purpose of the research? Jean Duncombe and Julie Jessop (2002) posed the dilemma clearly in a book chapter titled "'Doing Rapport' and the Ethics of 'Faking Friendship.'"

> With deeper rapport, interviewees become more likely to explore their more intimate experiences and emotions. Yet they also become more likely to discover and disclose experiences and feelings which, upon reflection, they would have preferred to keep private from others, . . . or not to acknowledge even to themselves. (p. 112)

These ethical issues cannot be evaluated independently. The final decision to proceed must be made after weighing relative benefits and risks to participants. Few qualitative research projects will be barred by consideration of these ethical issues, however, except for those involving covert participation. The more important concern for researchers is to identify the ethically troublesome aspects of their proposed research and resolve them before the project begins and to act on new ethical issues as they come up during the project.

🖼 **Conclusions**

We opened this chapter with the question, "How do communities and families affect children's literacy development?" First we showed techniques used by qualitative researchers to gather information about families and students. These included an example of a focus group on Mexican migrant students that combined parents, community members, and educators, as well as a "thick description" of Adam, a single student of interest in a larger school study. We then looked at Heath's (1983) *Ways With Words*, which combined these techniques with others to answer the full question posed. This long-term ethnographic case study involved participant observation of families, communities, students, teachers, and schools and included both research and intervention. *Ways With Words* (1983) demonstrated that before they even entered formal schooling, the children of Trackton and Roadville had acquired a wide range of literacy-related practices and attitudes, including ideas about how questions should properly be asked and answered, the role of games and playsongs, and the proper relationship between adults and children around listening and speaking and that these learnings were based in family and community culture and thus differed between the groups.

The kinds of things Heath (1983) learned using qualitative methods never could have been learned in a laboratory or a controlled setting. Qualitative research allows the careful investigator to obtain a richer and more intimate view of the educational world than is possible with more structured methods. It is not hard to understand why so many qualitative studies have become classics in the educational research literature. And the emphases in qualitative research on inductive reasoning and incremental understanding help to stimulate and inform other research approaches. Exploratory research to chart the dimensions of previously unstudied educational settings and intensive investigations of the subjective meanings that motivate individual action are particularly well served by the techniques of participant observation, intensive interviewing, and focus groups.

The very characteristics that make qualitative research techniques so appealing restrict their use to a limited set of research problems. It is not possible to draw representative samples for study using participant observation, and, for this reason, the generalizability of any particular field study's results cannot really be known. Only the cumulation of findings from numerous qualitative studies permits confident generalization, but here again, the time and effort required to collect and analyze the data make it unlikely that many field research studies will be replicated.

Even if qualitative researchers made more of an effort to replicate key studies, their notion of developing and grounding explanations inductively in the observations made in a particular setting would hamper comparison of findings. Measurement reliability is thereby hindered, as are systematic tests for the validity of key indicators and formal tests for causal connections.

In the final analysis, qualitative research involves a mode of thinking and investigating different from that used in experimental and survey research. Qualitative research is inductive and idiographic, whereas experiments and surveys tend to be conducted in a deductive, quantitative, and nomothetic framework. Both approaches can help educational researchers learn about the educational world; the proficient researcher must be ready to use either. Qualitative data are often supplemented with counts of characteristics or activities. And as you have already seen, quantitative data are often enriched with written comments and observations, and focus groups have become a common tool of survey researchers seeking to develop their questionnaires. Thus, the distinction between qualitative and quantitative research techniques is not always clear-cut, and combining methods is often a good idea.

Key Terms

Case study   190
Complete observer   192
Covert observer   192
Covert participant   192
Field notes   198
Field researcher   194
Focus groups   188
Grand tour question   202
Intensive (depth) interviewing   188
Jottings   198
Key informant   202
Participant observation   188
Participant observer   192
Reactive effect   194
Saturation point   203
Systematic observation   211
Thick description   190

Highlights

- Qualitative methods are most useful in exploring new issues, investigating hard-to-study groups, and determining the meaning people give to their lives and actions. In addition, most educational research projects can be improved, in some respects, by taking advantage of qualitative techniques.

- Qualitative researchers tend to develop ideas inductively, try to understand the educational context and sequential nature of attitudes and actions, and explore the subjective meanings that participants attach to events. They rely primarily on participant observation, intensive interviewing, and, in recent years, focus groups.

- Participant observers may adopt one of several roles for a particular research project. Each role represents a different balance between observing and participating. Many field researchers prefer a moderate role, participating as well as observing in a group but acknowledging publicly the researcher role. Such a role avoids the ethical issues posed by covert participation while still allowing the insights into the social world derived from participating directly in it. The role that the participant observer chooses should be based on an evaluation of the problems likely to arise from reactive effects and the ethical dilemmas of covert participation.

- Systematic observation techniques quantify the observational process to allow more systematic comparison between cases and greater generalizability.

- Field researchers must develop strategies for entering the field, developing and maintaining relations in the field, sampling, and recording and analyzing data. Selection of sites or other units to study may reflect an emphasis on typical cases, deviant cases, and/or critical cases that can provide more information than others. Sampling techniques commonly used within sites or in selecting interviewees in field research include theoretical sampling, purposive sampling, snowball sampling, quota sampling, and, in special circumstances, random selection with the experience sampling method.

- Recording and analyzing notes is a crucial step in field research. Jottings are used as brief reminders about events in the field, while daily logs are useful to chronicle the researcher's activities. Detailed field notes should be recorded and analyzed daily. Analysis of the notes can guide refinement of methods used in the field and of the concepts, indicators, and models developed to explain what has been observed.

- Intensive interviews involve open-ended questions and follow-up probes, with specific question content and order varying from one interview to another. Intensive interviews can supplement participant observation data.

- Focus groups combine elements of participant observation and intensive interviewing. They can increase the validity of attitude measurement by revealing what people say when they present their opinions in a group context instead of in the artificial one-on-one interview setting.

- Five ethical issues that should be given particular attention in field research concern voluntary participation, subject well-being, identity disclosure, confidentiality, and appropriate boundaries. Qualitative research conducted online, with discussion groups or e-mail traffic, raises special concerns about voluntary participation and identity disclosure.

- Adding qualitative elements to structured survey projects and experimental designs can enrich understanding of educational processes.

Student Study Site

To assist in completing the web exercises, please access the study site at www.sagepub.com/check, where you will find the web exercise with accompanying links. You'll find other useful study materials such as self-quizzes and e-flashcards for each chapter, along with a group of carefully selected articles from research journals that illustrate the major concepts and techniques.

Discussion Questions

1. Define and describe participant observation, intensive interviewing, and focus groups. What features do these research designs share? How are they different?

2. Discuss the relative merits of complete observation, participant observation, and covert participation. What are the ethical considerations inherent in each?

Practice Exercises

1. Conduct a brief observational study in a public location on campus where students congregate. A cafeteria, a building lobby, or a lounge would be ideal. You can sit and observe, taking occasional notes unobtrusively, without violating any expectations of privacy. Observe for 30 minutes. Write up field notes, being sure to include a description of the setting and a commentary on your own behavior and your reactions to what you observed.

2. Develop an interview guide that focuses on a research question addressed in one of the studies in this book. Using this guide, conduct an intensive interview with one person who is involved with the topic in some way. Take only brief notes during the interview, and then write up as complete a record of the interview as you can immediately afterward. Turn in an evaluation of your performance as an interviewer and note taker, together with your notes.

Web Exercises

1. Spend some time exploring the site of the Digital Ethnography Project at Kansas State University (http://medi atedcultures.net/). This is an award-winning project in ethnography at the higher education level that uses cutting-edge media tools to explore the contemporary world and welcomes student input. What are some of the techniques the project uses? Can you see ways you could use similar techniques in your own work in education?

2. Go to the website at http://www.content-analysis.de. From the main menu, choose Software. When the Software menu comes up, choose Qualitative Software. Read the brief descriptions of the available programs, then choose one that looks interesting to you. Most of the software packages will have a website with a trial software package that you can download. Choose and download one of the packages and work your way through it, noting its strengths and weaknesses.

Developing a Research Proposal

Add a qualitative component to your proposed study. You can choose to do this with a participant observation project or intensive interviewing. Pick the method that seems most likely to help answer the research question for the overall survey project.

1. For a participant observation component, propose an observational plan that would complement the overall survey project. Present in your proposal the following information about your plan: (a) Choose a site and justify its selection in terms of its likely value for the research, (b) choose a role along the participation-observation continuum and justify your choice, (c) describe access procedures and note any likely problems, (d) discuss how you will develop and maintain relations in the site, (e) review any sampling issues, and

(f) present an overview of the way in which you will analyze the data you collect.

2. For an intensive interview component, propose a focus for the intensive interviews that you believe will add the most to findings from the survey project. Present in your proposal the following information about your plan: (a) Present and justify a method for selecting individuals to interview, (b) write out three introductory biographical questions and five "grand tour" questions for your interview schedule, (c) list at least six different probes you will use, (d) present and justify at least two follow-up questions for one of your grand tour questions, and (e) explain what you expect this intensive interview component to add to your overall survey project.

CHAPTER 10

Single-Subject Design

Research Question: *How Can We Validly Study an Individual Student?*

Chapter Contents

- **Foundations of Single-Subject Design**
- **Measuring Targets of Intervention**
- **Types of Single-Subject Designs**
- **Analyzing Single-Subject Designs**
- **Ethical Issues in Single-Subject Design**

Many teachers and counselors work with students identified as having attention deficit hyperactivity disorder (ADHD) or autism spectrum disorders, which are being diagnosed earlier and in increasing numbers of children (Wazana, Bresnahan, & Kline, 2007). How can they find out whether their instructional and behavioral strategies are succeeding? Consider the case of 6-year-old Scott, reported by researchers Kara Hume and Sam Odom (2007).

Scott was diagnosed with autism at the age of 2. At age 6, he entered a kindergarten for students with disabilities. He was nonverbal and his behavior included frequent spinning, hand-flapping, climbing, and chewing. He had tantrums several times a day and took the powerful antipsychotic medicine Risperdal. He hit other students and fell to the floor. Scott was able to match colors and shapes, put the numbers 1 to 5 in order, and hold a book right-side up and turn the pages. He was not yet reading or writing. He was just beginning to dress himself and go to the toilet on his own (Hume & Odom, 2007, pp. 1168–1169).

What could Scott's teachers do to help him develop, and how would they know whether it was working? They instituted a curricular intervention called an individual work system (IWS) designed to increase his independent functioning (IWS was defined as "a visually organized space where children practice or perform work previously mastered under the direct supervision of an adult," Hume & Odom, 2007, p. 1170). Using a single-subject design, Hume and Odom (2007, p. 1173) were able to show that the IWS was effective in making Scott more independent both in his school work and in his play, and he was able to sustain these gains when they did a follow-up visit 1 month later.

As Scott's case shows, the use of single-subject research and evaluation designs is increasing in schools, particularly among special needs teachers, counselors, school psychologists, and reading specialists

(Best & Howard, 2005; Macy & Bricker, 2007). These fields are moving toward "evidence-based practice," and single-subject research provides a tool to validly measure and document interventions with single students (Eschenauer & Chen-Hayes, 2005; Horner et al., 2005; Schottelkorb & Ray, 2009).

This is important because providing appropriate support for students with learning difficulties is a challenge many teachers and counselors face daily. As practitioners, we often think we "know" when an approach is working. Yet, when we use our own subjective conclusions, we are prone to human error—to seeing what we want to see. In this chapter, you will learn how single-subject designs are being used to test the effectiveness of particular interventions, as Scott's teachers did, as well as to monitor student progress.

Single-subject research designs (sometimes referred to as single-case or single-system designs) focus on a single participant as opposed to a group of participants. In some cases, the "single participant" can be a single classroom or single school, as opposed to a group of classrooms or group of schools. These designs are useful for measuring educational interventions at all levels and in many situations. In particular, the process of assessment—establishing intervention goals, providing the intervention, and evaluating progress—parallels the structure of single-subject design, which depends on identifying the focus of the intervention, taking pre-intervention measurements, providing the intervention, taking additional measurements, and making decisions about the efficacy of the intervention. Because of these parallels, single-subject designs can be used not just for research but also to evaluate practice and to improve outcomes by monitoring the progress of a single student or single class.

In this chapter, we begin by taking you through the foundations, or basic features, of single-subject designs. Next we describe ways to measure changes in the student or case that is the target of the intervention. We then describe different designs and connect them to their uses for teaching, student evaluation, and research and briefly outline methods for interpreting the findings. We end the chapter with a discussion of ethical issues in single-subject design.

▣ Foundations of Single-Subject Design

The underlying principle of a single-subject design is that if an intervention with a student, teacher, classroom, or school is effective, it should be possible to see a change in status from the period prior to the intervention to the period during and after the intervention. At a minimum, single-subject designs include the following:

1. Repeated measurement to identify the subject's status

2. A baseline phase or the time period prior to the start of the intervention

3. A treatment phase or the time period during the intervention

Furthermore, the baseline and treatment phase measurements are usually displayed using graphs.

Hume and Odom (2007) used a "withdrawal of treatment" design, in which the independent variable (the treatment, in this case the work system) was introduced, then withdrawn, then reintroduced while researchers looked for corresponding changes in the dependent variable (independent performance in work and play). Throughout the period of the study, key contextual factors (the teacher, classroom surroundings, length of class periods) were held constant. The careful implementation of this design allowed the researchers to conclude that Scott's independent behavior improved when the work system was introduced, decreased when the teachers stopped using the work system, and increased when they began using it again (Hume & Odom, 2007, p. 1173).

Repeated Measurement

Single-subject designs require the repeated measurement of a dependent variable or, in other words, the target problem or focus of the intervention. The target is measured at regular time intervals such as hours, days, weeks, or months, prior to the intervention and during the intervention. The preferred method is to take measures of the target problem prior to implementing the intervention (e.g., during the assessment process) and then continue during the course of the intervention. This may mean withholding the intervention until repeated measures can be taken.

There are times when it is not possible to delay the intervention, either because there is a crisis or because to delay intervention would not be ethically appropriate. Yet you may still be able to construct a set of preintervention measures using data already collected or asking about past experiences. Student records may have information from which a baseline can be produced.

When using student, teacher, or classroom records, you are limited to the information that is available, and even that information may be missing. Another option is to ask research subjects about past behavior, such as how many times they completed a homework assignment during the past 2 weeks. Similarly, if permission is granted, significant members of the subject's network—parents, friends, past teachers—could be asked questions about the subject's behaviors. Trying to construct measures by asking students or family members assumes that the information is both remembered and reported accurately. Generally, behaviors and events are easier to recall than moods or feelings. Even the recall of behaviors or events becomes more difficult with the passage of time and probably should be limited to the past month.

There are other times when using retrospective data is feasible. Schools collect quite a bit of data, and these data can be used to obtain repeated measurements. For example, if a school principal is trying to find an outreach method that would increase the number of involved parents, previous end-of-year reports from the school could be used to find out what methods had already been tried.

Baseline Phase

The **baseline phase** (signified by an **A**) represents the period in which the intervention to be evaluated is not offered to the subject. During the baseline phase, repeated measurements of the dependent variable are taken or reconstructed. These measures reflect the status of the student (or classroom or school) on the dependent variable prior to the implementation of the intervention. In Scott's case, dependent variables measured included whether Scott was *on or off task*, how much *teacher prompting* was needed, how many tasks reached *task completion*, and the *number of play materials utilized* (Hume & Odom, 2007, p. 1174).

The baseline phase measurements provide two aspects of control analogous to a control group in a group design. First, in a group design, we expect the treatment group to have different scores than the control group after the intervention. In a single-subject design, the subject serves as the control, as the repeated baseline measurements establish the pattern of scores that we expect the intervention to change. Without the intervention, researchers assume that the baseline pattern of scores would continue its course. Second, in a control group design, random assignment controls for threats to internal validity. In a single-subject design, the repeated baseline measurements allow the researcher to discount some of the threats to the internal validity of the design.

Patterns

In the baseline phase, measurements are taken until a pattern emerges. You have found a pattern when you can predict with some certainty the next score. Predicting the next score requires a minimum of three observations in the baseline stage. When there are only two measures, the next data point could be higher or lower, or it could stay the same (see Exhibit 10.1a). With three measures, your certainty about the nature of the problem increases. But even three measures might not be enough, depending on the pattern that is emerging. Is the pattern in Exhibit 10.1b predictable? You probably should take at least two more baseline measures, but three or four additional measures may be necessary before you see a pattern emerge. As a rule, the more data points you have, the more certain you will be about the pattern; it takes at least three consecutive measures that fall in some pattern for you to have confidence in the shape of the baseline pattern.

The three common types of patterns are a stable line, a trend line, and a cycle. A **stable line** (see Exhibit 10.2a) is a relatively flat line, with little variability in the scores so that the scores fall in a narrow band. This kind of line is desirable because changes can easily be detected, and it is likely that there are few problems of testing or instrumentation in the data. A wider band or range of scores (see Exhibit 10.2b) is more difficult to interpret than a stable line with little variation.

A **trend** occurs when scores are either increasing or decreasing during the baseline phase. When there is a linear trend (see Exhibit 10.2c), the scores tend to increase (or decrease) at a more or less constant rate over time. A trend may also be curvilinear (see Exhibit 10.2d) so that the rate of change is accelerating over time, rather than increasing or decreasing at a constant rate.

> **Stable line:** A stable line is a line that is relatively flat with little variability in the scores so that the scores fall in a narrow band.

> **Trend:** An ascending or descending line.

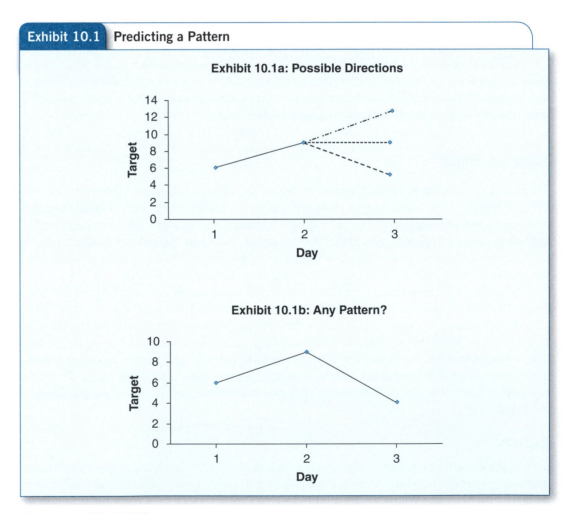

Exhibit 10.1 **Predicting a Pattern**

Exhibit 10.1a: Possible Directions

Exhibit 10.1b: Any Pattern?

Source: Engel and Schutt (2005).

A **cycle** (see Exhibit 10.2e) is a pattern in which there are increases and decreases in scores depending on the time of year (month or week) when the measures are taken. For example, student absences due to sickness may be cyclical, with more absences occurring in the traditional winter "cold and flu" season.

> **Cycle:** A pattern reflecting ups and downs depending on time of measurement.

Finally, there are situations in which no pattern is evident (see Exhibit 10.2f). In such cases, it is important to consider the reasons for the variability in scores. Is it due to the lack of reliability of the measurement process? If so, then an alternative measure might be sought. On the other hand, the measure may be good but the information may not be reported consistently. Also, the variability in scores may be due to some changing circumstance in the life of the student.

Internal Validity

Findings of causality depend on the internal validity of the research design. When repeated measurements are taken during the baseline phase, some threats to internal validity are controlled. However, the most significant threat to internal validity is history. Repeated measurement in a baseline will not control for an extraneous event (history) that occurs between the last baseline measurement and the first intervention measurement. The longer the time period between the two measurement points, the greater the possibility that an event might influence the subject's scores. At the end of the study or intervention, the teacher or researcher should check with participants to determine whether some outside event may have influenced the results.

> **History:** A source of causal invalidity that occurs when something other than the treatment or intervention influences outcome scores; also called an effect of *external events*.

Treatment Phase

The **treatment phase** (signified by a **B**) represents the time period during which the intervention is implemented. During the treatment phase, repeated measurements of the same dependent variable using the same measures are obtained. Ultimately, the patterns and magnitude of the data points will be compared to the data points in the baseline phase to determine whether a change has occurred. The length of the treatment phase should be as long as the baseline phase (Tripodi, 1994).

Graphing

The phases of a single-subject design are virtually always summarized on a graph. Graphing the data facilitates monitoring and evaluating the impact of the intervention. The *y*-axis is used to represent the scores of the dependent variable, while the *x*-axis represents a unit of time, such as an hour, a day, a week, or a month. Although you may make your graph by hand, both statistical software and spreadsheet software offer the tools to present data in graphs. For example, Dixon et al. (2009) provide simple, step-by-step instructions for using Microsoft Excel to create graphs for different types of single-subject designs.

Measuring Targets of Intervention

Three questions to answer about measurement are (a) what should be measured, (b) how should it (the target of the intervention) be measured, and (c) who will do the measuring. With each decision, there are important issues to consider.

Exhibit 10.2   **Different Baseline Patterns**

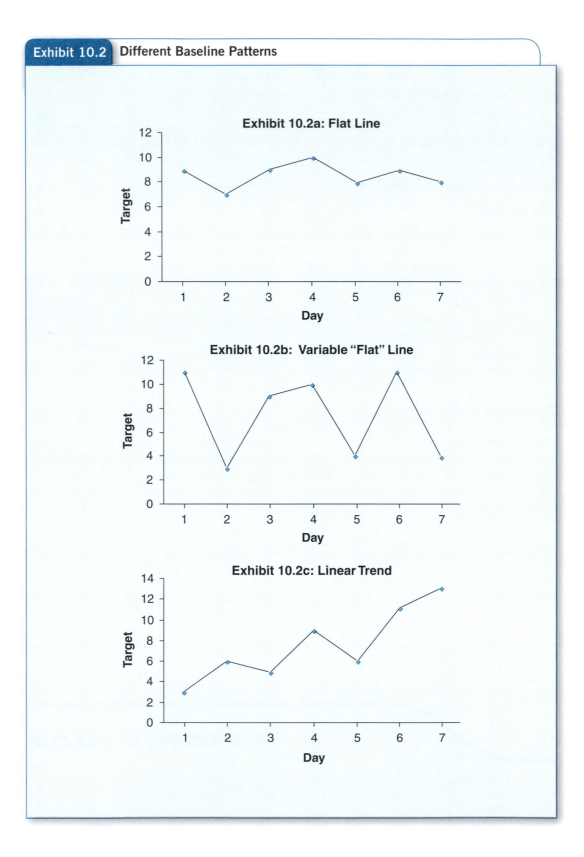

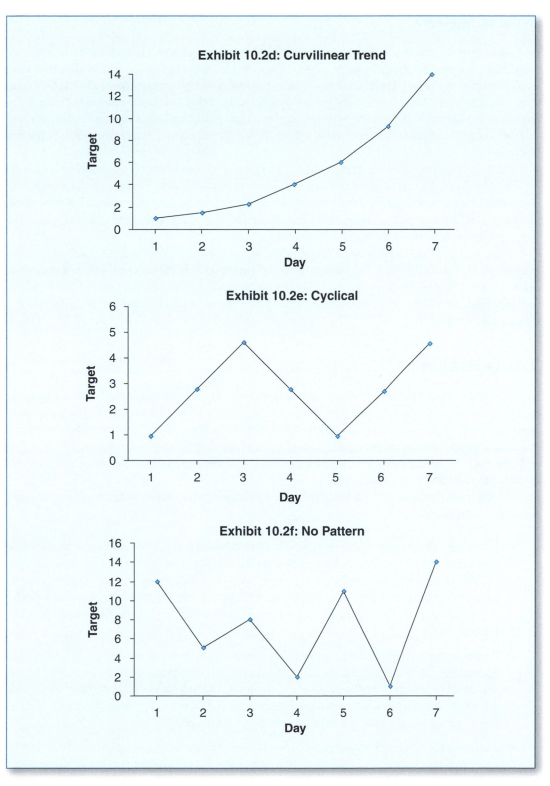

What to Measure

The dependent variable in a single-subject design is the concern or issue that is the focus of the intervention. Education practitioners using single-subject design methods to evaluate practice or monitor their work typically arrive at the target problem through their interaction with students, colleagues, or school communities. Students may start with some general problem or need that, through the process of assessment and discussion, becomes narrowed to a specific set of treatment goals. Similarly, a school administrator may identify the general needs of a school community and, through discussion and meetings, identify specific outcomes.

The target may focus on one problem or several. For example, with an adolescent who is having behavioral problems in school, you may decide to measure the frequency of the behavioral problems. Or you may hypothesize that the adolescent's behavioral problems are caused by poor family communication and low self-esteem. Therefore, you would measure family communication and self-esteem in addition to school behavior. The target problems can be measured simultaneously or sequentially.

Single-subject design is applicable to other systems, such as schools and communities. A school principal may decide to evaluate the efficacy of different methods to improve discipline or examine the extent to which a community-based program, say an after-school sports program, produces changes in students' in-school behavior. The choice of the target then becomes a question of determining the information that is important to the school or community.

How to Measure

Once the target or outcome of the intervention has been identified, you must determine how you will operationalize the outcome. For example, if you are evaluating the impact of positive parenting techniques on altering a child's behavior, you would identify jointly with the parents and the behavior such as tantrums. You would then guide the parents to distinguish a tantrum from other behaviors or verbal expressions. This engagement is particularly important because there may be gender and ethnic differences in how a general problem may manifest itself (Nelson, 1994).

Measures of behaviors, status, or functioning are often characterized in four ways: frequency, duration, interval, and magnitude.

- Frequency refers to counting the number of times a behavior occurs or the number of times people experience different feelings within a particular time period. On the basis of the above example, you could ask the parents to count the number of tantrums their child had each week. Frequency counts are useful for measuring targets that happen regularly, but counting can be burdensome if the behavior occurs too often. On the other hand, if the behavior happens only periodically, the counts will not be meaningful.

- Duration refers to the length of time an event or some symptom lasts and usually is measured for each occurrence of the event or symptom. Rather than counting the number of tantrums in a week, the parents could be asked to time the length of each tantrum. The parents would need a clear operational definition that specifies what constitutes the beginning and the end of a tantrum. A measure of duration requires fewer episodes than do frequency counts of the target.

- The interval, or the length of time between events, may be measured. Using a measure of interval, the parents in our example would calculate the length of time between tantrums. This kind of measure may not be appropriate for events or symptoms that happen frequently unless the intent of the intervention is to delay their onset.

- Finally, the magnitude or intensity of a particular behavior or psychological state can be measured. A scale might be developed by which the parents rate or score the intensity of the tantrum—how loud the screaming is, whether there is rolling around on the floor or hitting, and the like. Often, magnitude or intensity measures are applied to psychological symptoms or attitudes such as measures of depressive symptoms, quality of peer interactions, or self-esteem.

Standardized instruments and rapid assessment tools cover a wide range of student academic performance, as well as psychological dimensions, family functioning, individual functioning, and the like. Another option is to collect data based on clinical observations. Observations are particularly useful when the target problem involves a behavior. A third option is to develop measures within the school such as a goal attainment scale. Combinations of these measures are typically used by teachers and counselors to create and monitor educational plans for students with identified special needs. Regardless of how the data are collected, the measures should be reliable and valid. In particular, the reliability and validity of the instruments should have been tested on subjects of the same age, gender, and ethnicity as the subject who is the focus of the single-subject design.

Who Should Measure

It is important to consider who will gather the data and to understand the potential consequence of each choice. Participants or students can be asked to keep logs and to record information in the logs. Participants can complete instruments at specified time points, either through self-administration or by an interview. Or the educational researcher may choose to observe the participant's behavior.

A particular problem in gathering data is reactivity; that is, you want measures that do not influence the responses that people provide. The very process of measurement might change a subject's behavior. If you ask a subject to keep a log and to record each time a behavior occurs, the act of keeping the log may reduce the behavior. Observing a father interacting with his children might change the way the father behaves with the children. Teachers, knowing that supervisors are looking for certain activities, may increase the number of those activities. It is important to recognize that there might be reactivity and to choose methods that limit reactivity.

There are other considerations about the choice of measurement. Repeatedly taking measures can be cumbersome, inconvenient, and difficult. Repeated measurement may be too time-consuming for the subject or the researcher, and continuous measurements may reduce the incentive of the subject to participate in the research or treatment.

Finally, the choice of measurement must be sensitive enough to detect changes. If the measuring device is too global, it may be impossible to detect incremental or small changes, particularly in such target problems as psychological status, feelings, emotions, and attitudes. In addition, whatever is measured must occur frequently enough or on a regular basis so that repeated measurements can be taken.

🔲 Types of Single-Subject Designs

We need to distinguish three uses of single-subject design: as a research tool, as a method to assess instructional or behavioral outcomes, and as a tool to monitor student progress. There are more constraints when using a single-subject design for research than when using it for practice evaluation; monitoring student progress has even fewer constraints.

Research

The goal of a research experiment is to test the efficacy of an intervention on a particular target and, therefore, to enhance educational knowledge about what works. The example of Scott with which we began the chapter is taken from a research experiment designed to test the efficacy of the IWS approach. Scott's case was one of three cases studied simultaneously involving an IWS-based intervention (Hume & Odom, 2007). In single-subject research experiments, the intervention has already been specified, as has the target problem(s) that will be evaluated. The measures should be reliable and valid indicators of the target problem(s). Typically, the baseline should include at least three data points, and measurement should continue until there is a pattern. The baseline measures should also be collected during the course of the experiment. To establish causality, the design should control for all internal validity threats, including history.

Evaluating Practice

The focus of practice evaluation is to describe the effectiveness of the program or particular intervention. Increasing knowledge about a particular treatment approach may be a goal, but that is secondary to the overall purpose of evaluation. Practice or program evaluation is conducted to provide feedback about the program to program staff and school administrators so that demonstrating a causal relationship is less important. The specific target and the appropriate intervention emerge from the interaction of the teacher or counselor with the student, rather than being established before the interaction. As in a research study, the measures should be reliable and valid indicators of the target problem. Ideally, the baseline should include at least three measures and be characterized by a stable pattern, but this may not be possible so that only one or two measures are available. The baseline measures may be produced through the recollection of the student, significant others, or student records.

Monitoring

The purpose of monitoring is to systematically keep track of a student's progress. Monitoring using a single-subject design provides ongoing feedback that may be more objective than just relying on the practitioner's impressions. Monitoring helps to determine whether the intervention should continue without change or should be modified. As with practice evaluation, the target problem and intervention are not specified in advance; rather, they emerge through the practitioner-student interaction. Ideally, the measures are reliable and valid indicators. There may not be any baseline, or the baseline may be limited to a single assessment. When the techniques are used to monitor a student's progress, threats to internal validity are not a concern.

Keep these distinctions in mind as you read about the various designs. Some designs can be used for both research and practice evaluation, while others are more suited to monitoring.

Basic Design (A-B)

The *A-B design* is the basic single-subject design and is often used for all three purposes: research, evaluation, and monitoring. There is a baseline phase with repeated measurements and an intervention phase continuing the same measures. Take, for example, two parents who are having behavior problems, at school and at home, with their adolescent daughter. Meeting with their child's school psychologist or guidance counselor, they report that over the past month, the child has been squabbling constantly with her brother and being rude and sarcastic with her parents. The practitioner suggests that they use a point system, with points being accrued for poor behavior. Once a certain number of points are attained, the child will begin to lose certain privileges. To test the intervention, the parents are instructed to count and record every 3 days over a 15-day period the number of instances of sibling arguments begun by the child and the number of rude and sarcastic comments. The intervention begins on the 16th day, with the parents explaining how the child might get negative points and face the consequences of accumulating points. The results of the intervention are displayed in Exhibit 10.3.

As you can see, there is a very significant improvement. The question is whether the improvement is due to the intervention alone. The parents thought so, but in a debriefing with the counselor, it appeared that other factors might have been involved. For example, each day during the first week, the child asked her parents if they were proud of her behavior. The parents lavished praise on the child. The threat associated with the negative consequences may have been confounded by the positive reinforcement provided by the parents. It also turned out that about the same time the intervention began, the child stopped hanging out with two peers who had begun to tease her. So the changes could be attributable to the child's removing herself from a negative peer group.

The example points to the limits of the A-B design as a tool for research. The design cannot rule out other extraneous events, so it is impossible to conclude that the treatment *caused* the change. The A-B design does provide evidence of an association between the intervention and the change, and given that some threats to internal validity are controlled, it is analogous to a quasi-experimental design. The researcher-practitioner may have more confidence that history did not affect the findings if, after debriefing the subjects, there appear to be no influential external events.

Exhibit 10.3 **A-B Design of Behavior**

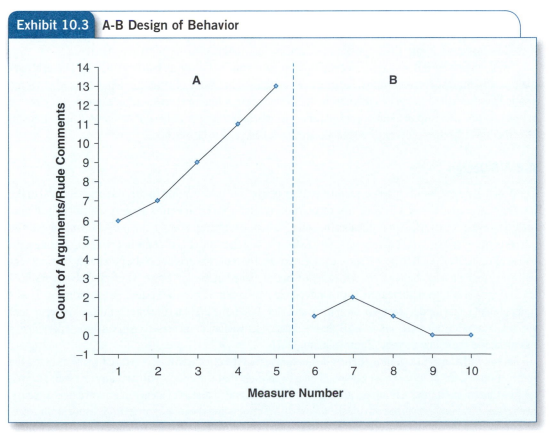

Source: Engel and Schutt (2005).

Withdrawal Designs

There are two withdrawal designs: the *A-B-A design* and the *A-B-A-B design*. By withdrawal, we mean that the intervention is concluded (A-B-A design) or is stopped for some period of time before the intervention is begun again (A-B-A-B design). The premise is that if the intervention is effective, the target should be improved only during the course of intervention, and the target scores should worsen when the intervention is removed. If this assumption is correct, then the impact of an extraneous event (history) between the baseline and intervention phase would not explain the change.

This premise, however, is problematic for educational research. Ideally, the point of the intervention is to reduce or eliminate the target problem—excessive tardiness, fighting in school, intermittent completion of homework—without the need for ongoing intervention. We would like the impact of the intervention to be felt long after the student has stopped the intervention itself. Practice theories in counseling, school psychology, and special needs, such as behavioral or cognitive behavioral treatment, are based on the idea that the therapeutic effects will persist. This concern, referred to as the **carryover effect,** may inhibit the use of these designs for research. To be used for research, the implementation of each withdrawal design may necessitate limiting the length of the intervention and ending it prematurely. If the designs are being used for evaluation, it is unnecessary to prematurely withdraw the intervention; rather, the second baseline provides important follow-up information.

A-B-A Design

The A-B-A design builds on the A-B design by integrating a posttreatment follow-up that would typically include repeated measures. This design answers the question left unanswered by the A-B design: Does the effect of the intervention persist beyond the period in which treatment is provided? Depending on the length of the follow-up period, it may also be possible to learn how long the effect of the intervention persists.

The follow-up period should include multiple measures until a follow-up pattern emerges. This arrangement is built into the research study. For practice evaluation, the practicality of this depends on whether the relationship with the student extends beyond the period of the actual intervention. For example, the effect of an intervention designed to reduce problem behaviors in school might be amenable to repeated measurement after the end of the intervention, given that the student is likely still to be in school.

A-B-A-B Design

The A-B-A-B design builds in a second intervention phase. The intervention in this phase is identical to the intervention used in the first B phase. The second intervention phase makes this design useful for educational practice research. The design replicates the intervention. For example, if during the follow-up phase, the effects of the intervention begin to reverse (see Exhibit 10.4a), then the effects of the intervention can be established by doing it again. If there is a second improvement, the replication reduces the possibility that an event or history explains the change. This was exactly what happened in the Scott case. The first B phase, in which the IWS was introduced, increased Scott's independent behavior. When the system was withdrawn, Scott's independent behavior decreased in both work and play. When the system (the intervention or independent variable) was reintroduced (the second B phase), independent behavior increased again and was still evident a month later at the follow-up visit (Hume & Odom, 2007).

Just as with the A-B-A design, there is no guarantee that the effects will be reversed by withdrawing the intervention. If the practice theory holds, then it is unlikely that the effects will actually be reversed. So it may be that this first intervention period has to be short and ended just as evidence of improvement appears. Even if the effect is not reversed during the follow-up, reintroducing the intervention may demonstrate a second period of additional improvement, as displayed in Exhibit 10.4b. This pattern suggests that the changes between the no-treatment and treatment phases are due to the intervention and not the result of history.

Exhibit 10.4 A-B-A-B Designs

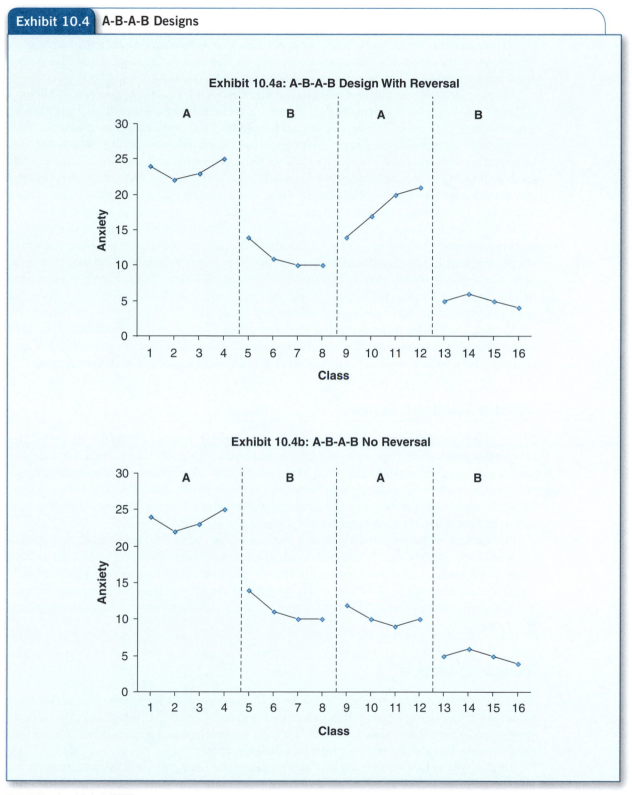

Exhibit 10.4a: A-B-A-B Design With Reversal

Exhibit 10.4b: A-B-A-B No Reversal

Source: Engel and Schutt (2005).

Multiple Baseline Designs

In the three previous designs, the individual baseline scores serve as the control for the impact of the intervention. An alternative is to add additional subjects, target problems, or settings to the study. This method provides researchers with a feasible method of controlling for the effects of history.

The basic format of a **concurrent multiple baseline design** is to implement a series of A-B designs (although A-B-A or A-B-A-B designs could also be used) at the same time for at least three cases (students, target problems, or settings). Therefore, the data will be collected at the same time. The unique feature of this design is that the length of the baseline phase is staggered (see Exhibit 10.5) to control for external events (i.e., history) across the three cases. The baseline phase for the second case extends until the intervention data points for the first case become more or less stable. Similarly, the intervention for the third case does not begin until the data points in the intervention phase for the second case become stable. The second and third cases act as a control for external events in the first case, and the third case acts as a control for the second case.

Multiple baseline design offers great flexibility for evaluating interventions and monitoring progress. It can be implemented with three (or more) subjects, with each subject receiving the same intervention but at a different starting point to address the same target. Or it can be implemented with one subject, with the same intervention applied to different, but related, problems and behaviors. Finally, it can be applied to test the effects of an intervention applied to one subject, dealing with one behavior, such as arriving on time, but sequentially applied to different settings such as home, school, and work.

Multiple baseline designs are also useful as a research tool. They introduce two replications, so that if consistent results are found, the likelihood that some external event is causing the change is reduced. If some extraneous event might affect all three cases, the effect of the event may be picked up by the control cases.

Multiple Treatment Designs

In a multiple treatment design, the nature of the intervention changes over time, and each change represents a new phase of the design. One type of change that might occur is the *intensity* of the intervention. For example, a counselor might be working with a family that is having communication problems. The actual amount of contact the counselor has with the family may change over time, starting with counseling sessions twice a week, followed by a period of weekly sessions, and concluding with monthly interactions. In this case, the amount of contact declines over time. Changing intensity designs are characterized by $A-B_1-B_2-B_3$.

Another type of changing intensity design is when, during the course of the intervention, you add additional tasks to be accomplished. For example, a high school student whose school performance has declined may need to rebuild good academic habits step by step. The intervention goal is returning to a previously held high level of academic success. The B_1 may involve doing at least 45 minutes of homework every week night, the B_2 may add methods for improved class participation, and the B_3 adds a component on volunteering for extra credit work.

Monitoring Designs

When monitoring a student's progress, the A-B design is recommended for the baseline information it provides. But there are times when establishing a baseline is not possible, other than to have a single point based on an initial assessment. Nonetheless, to ascertain whether a student is making progress, a form of monitoring should be done. Therefore, a practitioner might use a B or a B-A design.

The *B design* (see Exhibit 10.6a) only has an intervention phase. During the course of the intervention, you take repeated measurements. This design can be used to determine if the student is making progress in the

Exhibit 10.5 Multiple Baseline Design

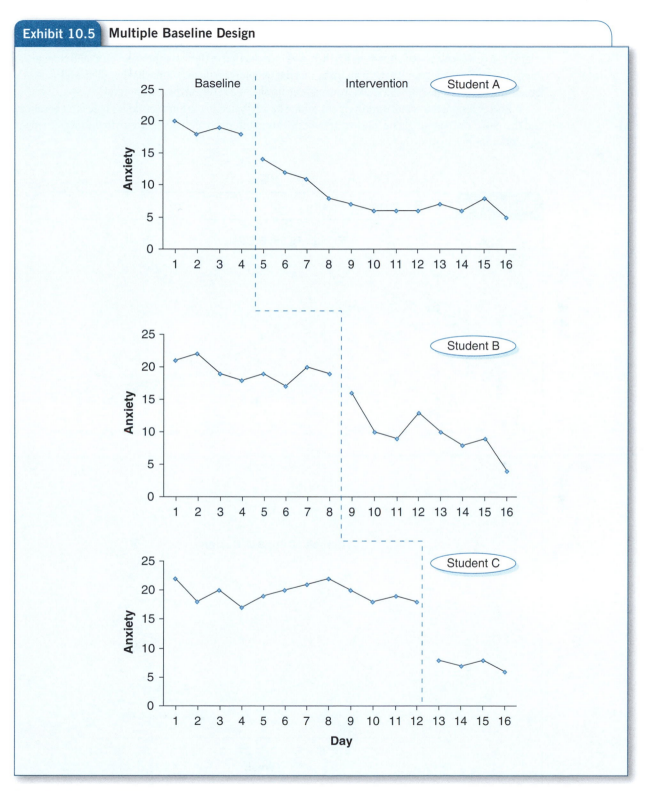

Source: Engel and Schutt (2005).

desired direction. If the student is not making progress, you may decide to change the type of intervention or the intensity of the intervention. For example, if you were working with a student with symptoms of anxiety related to a certain class, but after 4 weeks, there was no reduction in these symptoms, you would change the intensity or type of intervention. Or it might be that the symptoms reduced somewhat but then leveled off at a level still above a cutoff score; as a result, you might again alter the nature of the intervention.

With a B design, the actual improvement cannot be attributed to the intervention. There is no baseline, and therefore, changes might be due to different threats to internal validity, reactivity to the measurement process, or the reactivity to the situation.

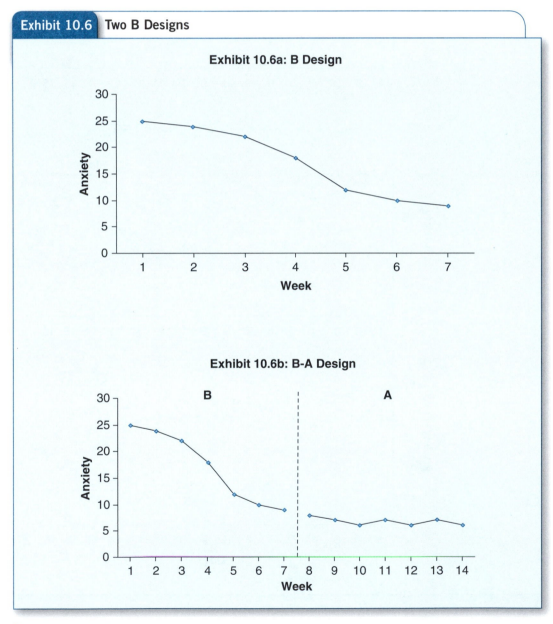

Exhibit 10.6   **Two B Designs**

Exhibit 10.6a: B Design

Exhibit 10.6b: B-A Design

Source: Engel and Schutt (2005).

If a period of follow-up measurements can be introduced, then a *B-A design* might be used (see Exhibit 10.6b). The intervention period is followed by a period of no intervention for the specific problem. Although it is harder to get repeated measurements after the intervention has concluded, if treatment about other problems continues, then follow-up measures are possible. Having reduced anxiety symptoms to an acceptable level, the teacher, counselor, or school psychologist may address academic support network building with the student. Measurement of the anxiety symptoms still might continue.

Analyzing Single-Subject Designs

How might we analyze data from a single-subject design? One way is to visually examine the graphed data. A second option is to use a statistical technique such as the two–standard deviation band, chi-square analysis, or time series to analyze the data (Barlow, Nock, & Hersen, 2009; Bloom, Fischer, & Orme, 2009). In this chapter, we concentrate on visual analysis.

Regardless of whether you use visual inspection or one of these statistical approaches, the overriding issue is the practical (or clinical) significance of the findings. Has the intervention made a meaningful difference in the well-being of the subject? Although practical significance at times is subjective, you might apply several principles to reduce the uncertainty. These include the following:

- *Setting criteria.* One simple method is to establish with the student or school community the criteria for success. If the intervention reaches that point, then the change is meaningful.

- *Cutoff scores.* A second method, particularly useful for psychological symptoms, is whether the intervention has reduced the problem to a level below a clinical cutoff score. For example, if you were a school psychologist using a scale to measure levels of depression, you would determine if the depressive symptom scores fall below the cutoff score for depression for that particular scale.

- *Costs and benefits.* A third way to view practical significance is to weigh the costs and benefits to produce the change. Do efforts to increase regular attendance among at-risk students in a school result in sufficient change to be worth the cost and effort to produce the improvement in attendance?

Visual Analysis

Visual analysis is the process of looking at a graph of the data points to determine whether the intervention has altered the subject's preintervention pattern of scores. Three concepts that help guide visual inspection are level, trend, and variability.

Level

Level refers to the amount or magnitude of the target variable. Has the amount of the target variable changed from the baseline to the intervention phase? Changes in level are typically used when the observations fall along relatively stable lines. A simple method to describe changes in level is to inspect the actual data points (see Exhibit 10.7a). It appears that the actual amount of the target variable—anxiety—has decreased.

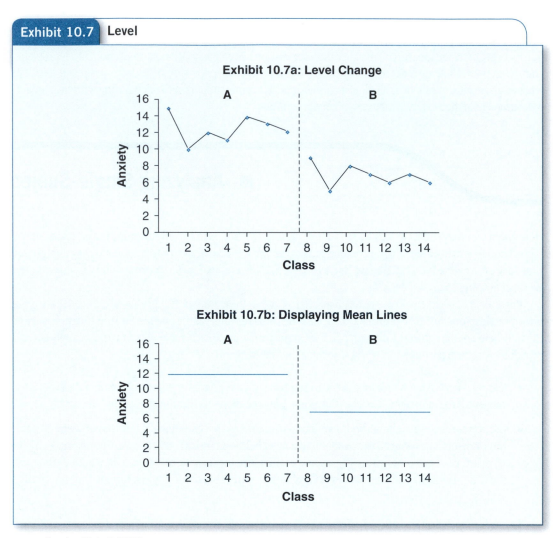

Exhibit 10.7 Level

Exhibit 10.7a: Level Change

Exhibit 10.7b: Displaying Mean Lines

Source: Engel and Schutt (2005).

Trend

As you have seen, a trend refers to the direction in the pattern of the data points and can be increasing, decreasing, cyclical, or curvilinear. When the data points reflect trend lines rather than stable lines, there are two different questions depending on the nature of the lines. The first question is this: Has the intervention altered the direction of the trend? If the baseline trend line is ascending, is the treatment trend line descending? When the direction does not change, you may be interested in whether the rate of increase or decrease in the trend has changed. You might ask the second question: Does the treatment alter the slope of the line?

Trends can also be represented by summary lines. Different methods may be used to represent the best line to describe the trend, as displayed in Exhibit 10.8. William Nugent (2000) has suggested a simple approach to represent the trend in a phase, an approach that does not require a computer. When the trend is linear (as opposed to curvilinear), draw a straight line connecting the first and last data points in the baseline phase with an arrow at the end to summarize the direction. A similar line would then be drawn for the points in the

Exhibit 10.8 Displaying Trend Lines

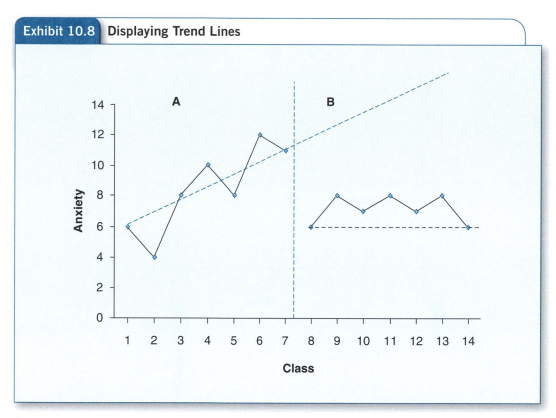

intervention phase. These two lines could then be compared. In the case of an outlier, Nugent recommends that the line be drawn either from the second point to the last point, if the first point is the outlier, or from the first point to the second to last point if the last point is the outlier. The same methods can be used to summarize nonlinear trends except that two lines are drawn in the baseline phase, one representing the segment of the first point to the lowest (or highest) point and the second line from the lowest (or highest point) to the last data point.

Exhibit 10.8 illustrates the use of Nugent's method. A line was drawn through the first and last time points in the baseline; this line was extended into the intervention phase. A similar line was drawn through the first and last time points in the intervention phase. A comparison of the lines suggests that the level of anxiety was no longer increasing but had stabilized at a much lower score.

Variability

By **variability,** we mean how different the scores are in the baseline and intervention phases. Widely divergent scores in the baseline make the assessment of the intervention more difficult, as do widely different scores in the intervention phase. One way to summarize variability with a visual analysis is to draw range lines, as done in Exhibit 10.9. Whether the intervention had an effect depends on what goal was established. As you can see, the only change has been a reduction in the spread of the points. But this does not mean that the intervention has not been effective, as it depends on the goal of the intervention. There are some conditions and concerns for which the lack of stability is the problem, and so creating stability may represent a positive change.

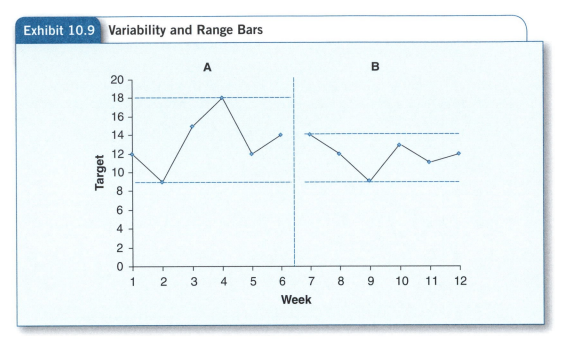

Exhibit 10.9 Variability and Range Bars

Source: Engel and Schutt (2005).

Regardless of whether you use visual analysis or a statistical approach, the overriding issue is the *practical significance* of the findings. Has the intervention made a meaningful difference in the well-being of the subject? Although practical significance is at times subjective, you might apply several principles to reduce the uncertainty. One method is to establish with the student, the family, or the community the criterion for success. If the intervention achieves the predetermined criterion, the change is meaningful. In the case of 6-year-old Scott described earlier, the analysis showed a measurable increase in independent functioning, both in school work and in play. This was a change of great practical significance for Scott, his parents, and his teachers (Hume & Odom, 2007). Practical significance may also be achieved if the intervention reduces the scores to a level below a predetermined cutoff score, thereby indicating the absence of a condition.

Ethical Issues in Single-Subject Design

Like any form of research, single-subject designs require the informed consent of the participant. The structure of single-subject designs for research involves particular conditions that must be discussed with potential participants. All aspects of the research, such as the purpose, measurement, confidentiality, and data collection, are a part of the information needed for informed consent. In particular, the need for repeated baseline measurements and the possibility of premature withdrawal of treatment are unique to single-subject design research.

Participants must understand that the onset of the intervention is likely to be delayed until either a baseline pattern emerges or some assigned time period elapses. Until this condition is met, a needed intervention may be withheld. Furthermore, the length of the baseline also depends on the type of design. In a multiple baseline design, the delay in the intervention may be substantial. The implications of this delay must be discussed as part of obtaining informed consent.

When a withdrawal or reversal design is used, there are additional considerations. The structure of such designs means that the intervention may be withdrawn just as the research subject is beginning to improve. The risks associated with prematurely ending treatment may be hard to predict. If there is a carryover effect, the subject's condition may not worsen, but it is possible that the subject's condition or status may indeed worsen. Given this possibility, the use of an A-B-A-B design as opposed to the A-B-A design is preferable for the purpose of research.

Because interventions measured by single-subject designs focus on individual students with difficult issues and frequently involve their families, special attention must be paid to issues of diversity. Researchers and practitioners must understand that the way problems are identified and defined may depend on student characteristics, such as gender, ethnicity, religion, sexual orientation, and class. Ideas of what constitutes family and what the proper social roles are for family members versus school personnel may be heavily influenced by cultural or religious norms. Measures must be acceptable and applicable (reliable and valid) to different population subgroups. Similarly, issues regarding informed consent are relevant for all population subgroups (Martin & Knox, 2000).

Single-subject design may be a useful method for engaging members of diverse groups who have been underrepresented in research and in particular experimental group designs or clinical research trials. Because it is often practice based, it may be easier to mitigate distrust of the researcher. Because it focuses on the individual, as opposed to the group, single-subject designs can more easily incorporate cultural factors and test for cultural variation (Arbin & Cormier, 2005).

Conclusions

We began this chapter with the question, "How can we validly study an individual student?" illustrated by the case of Scott, a kindergartner diagnosed with autism. A single-subject research design measured whether, and to what extent, the individual work system used by Scott's teachers improved his independent behaviors. At the same time, the study added to our research knowledge about a significant educational issue: teaching autistic children.

As the Scott example shows, single-subject designs are useful for doing research, evaluating practice, and monitoring student progress. Historically, these designs have been underused by school-based practitioners and educational researchers. They have been called "the best kept secret in counseling" because they are both "scientifically credible" and "clinically relevant" (Lundervold & Bellwood, 2000, p. 92). Recently, they have been getting more attention, particularly in clinically based disciplines such as special needs, counseling, and remedial reading, which are emphasizing evidence-based practice. For practitioners, the success or failure of different interventions can be evaluated with distinct subjects and under differing conditions. Furthermore, single-subject designs may be useful to understanding the process of change and how change occurs with particular students. Applying these techniques to your own practice can be beneficial to your students. As Rosen (2003) warns, "Uncertainty regarding the effectiveness of any intervention for attaining any outcome pervades all practice situations, regardless of the extent and quality of empirical support" (p. 203). If you monitor what you do, you will add to your own practice experience, which will enhance your future work with students.

Key Terms

Highlights

- Single-subject designs are tools for researchers and practitioners to evaluate the impact of an intervention on a single system such as a student, classroom, or school.

- Single-subject designs have three essential components: the taking of repeated measurements, a baseline phase (A), and a treatment phase (B).

- Repeated measurements control for many potential threats to internal validity. The period between the last baseline measure and the first treatment measure is susceptible to the effect of history.

- The baseline phase typically continues, if practical, until there is a predictable pattern. To establish a pattern requires at least three measurements. The pattern may include a stable line, an increasing or decreasing trend line, or a cycle of ups and downs dependent on time of measurement.

- Researchers often measure behaviors, status, or level of functioning. These measures are typically characterized by frequency (counts), duration (length of time), interval (time between events), or magnitude (intensity).

- Reactivity to the process of measurement may affect the outcomes, and efforts to limit reactivity are important.

- Data analysis typically involves visually inspecting graphs of the measurements. A researcher may look for changes in level (magnitude), rate or directional changes in the trend line, or reductions in variability. The most important criterion is whether the treatment has made a practical (or clinical) difference in the subject's well-being.

- Generalizability from single-subject designs requires direct replication, systematic replication, and clinical replication.

Student Study Site

To assist in completing the web exercises, please access the study site at www.sagepub.com/check, where you will find the web exercise with accompanying links. You'll find other useful study materials such as self-quizzes and e-flashcards for each chapter, along with a group of carefully selected articles from research journals that illustrate the major concepts and techniques.

Discussion Questions

1. Single-subject designs lack the inclusion of additional subjects serving as controls to demonstrate internal validity. How do the measurements during the baseline phase provide another form of control?

2. Single-subject research seeks to confirm an intervention's effectiveness by observing scores when students or clients no longer receive the intervention. Yet, the carryover effect may necessitate using a withdrawal design—ending a treatment prematurely—to do this successfully. Debate the merits of the withdrawal design in educational research. What are the advantages and disadvantages? Do the benefits outweigh the risks or vice versa?

Practice Exercises

1. Stress is a common occurrence in many students' lives. Measure the frequency, duration, interval, and magnitude of school-related stress in your life in 1 week. Take care to provide a clear operational definition of stress and construct a meaningful scale to rate magnitude. Did you notice any issues of reactivity? Which measurement processes did you find most feasible? Finally, do you believe that your operational definition was sufficient to capture your target problem and to detect changes?

2. Patterns detected in the baseline phase of single-subject designs also emerge in the larger population. Obtain a copy of a national newspaper (e.g., *New York Times, USA Today*) and locate stories describing contemporary issues that can be described as having the pattern of a stable line, a trend, and a cycle. Is information provided about the number of observations made? If so, does this number seem sufficient to warrant the conclusion about what type of pattern it is?

Web Exercises

1. Visit the Northwest Regional Education Laboratory's website and read Close Up #9, Schoolwide and Classroom Discipline (go to http://www.nwrel.org; in the search box, type "SIRS," then click on "The School Improvement Research Series," then go to Series V). Select three of the techniques that educators use to minimize disruption in educational settings and then suggest a single-subject design that could be used to evaluate the effectiveness of each technique. Bear in mind the nature of the misbehavior and the treatment. Which of the designs seems most appropriate? How would you go about conducting your research? Think about things such as operationalizing the target behavior, determining how it will be measured (frequency, duration, magnitude, etc.), deciding on the length of the baseline and treatment periods, and accounting for threats to internal validity.

2. Search ERIC for articles describing single-subject designs. Try to identify the type of design used. Read three of the articles. How well did the designs satisfy the need for internal validity?

Developing a Research Proposal

If you are planning to use a single-subject design:

1. What specific design will you use? How long will the study last? How will the data be collected? How often?

2. Discuss the extent to which each source of internal validity is a problem in the study.

3. Discuss the extent to which reactivity is a problem. How will you minimize the effects of reactivity?

4. How generalizable would you expect the study's findings to be? What can be done to improve generalizability?

5. Develop appropriate procedures for the protection of human subjects in your study. Include in these procedures a consent form.

CHAPTER 11

Mixing and Comparing Methods and Studies

Research Question: *How Can Schools Help Students With Special Needs?*

Chapter Contents

- **Mixed Methods**
- **Comparing Research Designs**
- **Performing Meta-Analyses**

Are preschool children with disabilities accepted by their classmates? Samuel Odom and his colleagues (Odom, Zercher, Marquart, Sandall, & Brown, 2006) realized that no single method would reveal both the extent of acceptance of children with disabilities and the subtleties of interaction among preschool children, so they adopted a "mixed-methods" approach to answering this research question. Using quantitative analysis of data collected in an 800-school national survey, they determined how prevalent teachers felt acceptance was. Using qualitative analysis of observed interactions between individual preschoolers in specific classrooms, they described inclusive and exclusive patterns of group interaction. Their overall conclusions were then based on a combination of quantitative and qualitative methods, that is, on "mixed methods":

Socially accepted children tended to have disabilities that were less likely to affect social problem solving and emotional regulation, whereas children who were socially rejected had disabilities that were more likely to affect such skills and developmental capacities. (Odom et al., 2006, p. 807)

Samuel Odom's decision was not unique. An increasing number of educational researchers are turning to mixed methods to answer more sophisticated research questions and to capture the same setting with different methodological lenses (see Exhibit 11.1). We focus in this chapter on these mixed-methods approaches. We first introduce the logic of mixed methods and different ways of combining methods, illustrating our points with several mixed-methods projects: In addition to Odom et al.'s (2006) study, we examine an analysis of reporting accuracy in the juvenile justice system and an investigation of teachers' reliability in reporting suspected child abuse. We then review the strengths and limitations of the methods we have discussed; this review will help you choose the most appropriate research design for a particular investigation and decide when a combination of methods—"mixed methods"—is most useful. Finally, we introduce the method of meta-analysis, which allows systematic evaluation of findings from numerous published studies that have all used similar quantitative methods. We will look briefly at two meta-analyses, one involving the use of music therapy to treat autistic children, the other asking whether spending more on schools improves student achievement.

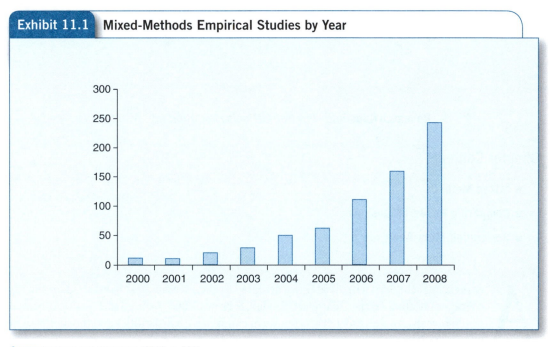

| Exhibit 11.1 | Mixed-Methods Empirical Studies by Year |

Source: Ivankova and Kawamura (2010, p. 591).

▣ Mixed Methods

Why mix quantitative and qualitative methods? You learned in Chapter 2 that research involves both deductive processes—testing ideas against observations—and inductive processes—developing ideas from observations. You have also learned that quantitative methods are used most often in deductively oriented research and that qualitative methods are often used in inductively oriented research. So a common reason for mixing both quantitative and qualitative methods in one research project is to take advantage of the unique strengths of each methodological approach when engaged in different stages of the research process (Tashakkori & Teddlie, 2010). What educational practices do children with disabilities experience as exclusionary? A qualitative investigation might explore children's experiences to answer this question. This investigation might be followed by a quantitative investigation of the effects of each of these exclusionary practices.

Another reason for mixing methods is to add unique insights about educational process that cannot easily be obtained from the primary method used in an investigation. Why did a new teaching strategy increase test scores? A qualitative investigation of the process of teacher-student interaction may provide the answer. Do the student perceptions of teachers' caring identified in a qualitative investigation influence the amount that students learn? A quantitative test of the effect of perceptions may lead to an answer. Examining the same educational process from both quantitative and qualitative vantage points may also be used to identify apparent contradictions that could then lead to new research questions (Onwuegbuzie & Combs, 2010, p. 411).

Educational researcher John W. Creswell (2010) has helped to popularize a simple notational system for distinguishing different ways of mixing quantitative and qualitative methods. This system distinguishes the priority given to one method over the other and the sequence in which they are used in a research project. For example,

- QUAL + QUAN: equal importance of the two approaches and their concurrent use;

- QUAL quan: → sequenced use, with qualitative methods given priority;

- QUAN(qual): qualitative methods embedded within a primarily quantitative project.

Should methods be mixed in one or more of these ways? That's a decision you will have to make for yourself. Methodological purists believe that only qualitative or quantitative methods provide adequate tools for investigating the educational world, while methodological pragmatists believe that different methods should be used to answer the questions to which they are most suited (Onwuegbuzie & Combs, 2010, pp. 412–413). Methodological pluralists believe the educational world is composed of multiple realities that cannot be understood without multiple methods: a subjective reality reflected in individual experiences; an intersubjective reality reflected in social structures, languages, and social institutions; and an objective reality comprising material things and physical processes (B. Johnson & Gray, 2010, p. 72). Qualitative methods may be best suited to investigate subjective reality, while quantitative methods may be most appropriate for investigating objective reality; an investigation of intersubjective reality may require some of both methods.

In addition to these philosophical questions, you should also consider some practical questions before you decide to mix methods in an investigation or review other investigations using mixed methods. Is a mixed-methods approach consistent with your own goals and prior experiences? Are you well trained to mix methods (of course you are, if you have studied methods with *Research Methods in Education!*)? Do your research questions allow for unanticipated results? Are your different research questions congruent and do they convey a need for integration (Plano Clark & Badiee, 2010, pp. 284–299)?

Rather than being planned in advance, steps to combine research designs may emerge naturally as a project is developed: An experiment conducted in the field can be supplemented with qualitative observations about delivery of the experimental treatment; some intensive open-ended questions can follow closed-ended survey questions; field research may use quantitative counts of phenomena or random samples of events;

comparative historical studies may add survey research results to an inspection of historical documents or compilation of national statistics.

Several examples will convey the possibilities for mixed-methods designs.

Case Study

Effective Provision of Preschool Education

England's Effective Provision of Preschool Education Study illustrates a mixed-methods study in which quantitative and qualitative methods were both important, in a sequenced QUAN→QUAL design. Sylva, Melhuishi, Sammons, Siraj-Blatchford, and Taggart (2008) first used quantitative methods to identify different influences on children's cognitive and social/behavioral outcomes. They then used these data to distinguish preschool centers that were more and less effective in producing positive outcomes. Field staff visited each of the preschool centers and developed rich descriptions of educational processes. This in turn allowed careful comparisons of the processes that seemed to explain the differential rates of effectiveness between centers.

Case Study

Peer Response to Preschool Children With Disabilities

Quantifying observational data is a key element in some mixed-methods designs.

Odom et al. (2006) transformed on-site behavioral observations in the classroom into quantitative data with the Code for Active Student Participation and Engagement–Revised (CASPER-II). CASPER-II "is a momentary time sampling procedure in which children's behavior and characteristics of the classroom ecology are recorded every 30 seconds. Six 30-minute sessions were collected for each child." (Odom et al., 2006, p. 808). Observation leaders received 3 days of training in CASPER-II, then went back and trained observer teams at their sites. The researchers tracked each focal child's social and negative behaviors toward peers, as well as their peers' behaviors toward them. Social behavior included "talking, greeting, sharing, touching, calling a name to another child," while negative behavior included "hitting, pushing, kicking, biting, negative remarks, crying" (p. 808). The coding scheme allowed observations to be recorded as numerical ratings, and standard statistical tests were used to compare observation and coding results both within and across sites (p. 808). The CASPER-II coding data provided one element of a carefully constructed mixed-methods design that combined quantitative and qualitative data collection and analysis. Exhibit 11.2 shows the design used by the Odom team, indicating clearly, in the right-hand column ("Purpose"), where each quantitative and qualitative element fit into the overall scheme.

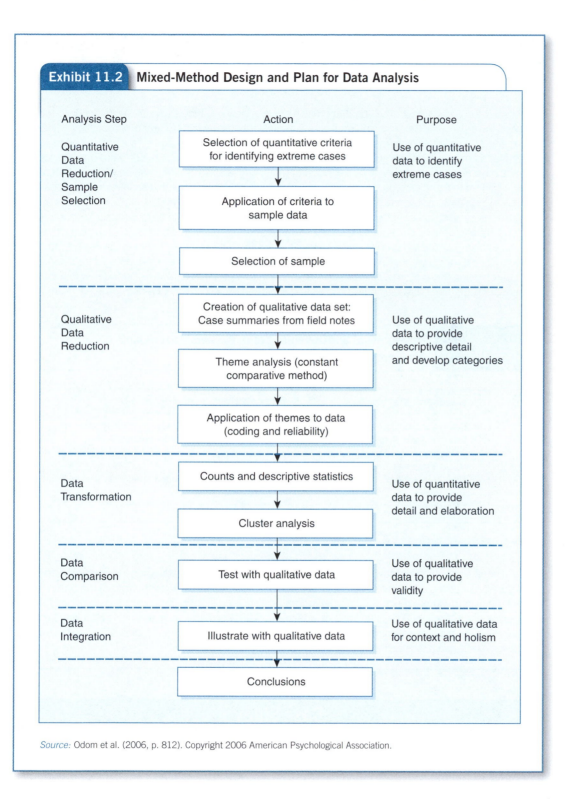

Exhibit 11.2 Mixed-Method Design and Plan for Data Analysis

Analysis Step	Action	Purpose
Quantitative Data Reduction/ Sample Selection	Selection of quantitative criteria for identifying extreme cases → Application of criteria to sample data → Selection of sample	Use of quantitative data to identify extreme cases
Qualitative Data Reduction	Creation of qualitative data set: Case summaries from field notes → Theme analysis (constant comparative method) → Application of themes to data (coding and reliability)	Use of qualitative data to provide descriptive detail and develop categories
Data Transformation	Counts and descriptive statistics → Cluster analysis	Use of quantitative data to provide detail and elaboration
Data Comparison	Test with qualitative data	Use of qualitative data to provide validity
Data Integration	Illustrate with qualitative data → Conclusions	Use of qualitative data for context and holism

Source: Odom et al. (2006, p. 812). Copyright 2006 American Psychological Association.

Case Study

Juvenile Justice

Research on official records can be strengthened by interviewing officials who create the records or by observing them while they record information. A participant observation study of how probation officers screened cases in two New York juvenile court intake units shows how important such information can be (Needleman, 1981). As indicated in Exhibit 11.3, Carolyn Needleman (1981) found that the concepts most researchers believe they are measuring with official records differ markedly from the meaning attached to these records by probation officers. Researchers assume that sending a juvenile case to court indicates a more severe disposition than retaining a case in the intake unit, but probation officers often diverted cases from court because they thought the court would be too lenient. Researchers assume that probation officers evaluate juveniles as individuals, but in these settings, probation officers often based their decisions on juveniles' current social situation (whether they were living in a stable home, for example), without learning anything about the individual juvenile. Perhaps most troubling for research using case records, Needleman (1981) found that probation officers decided how to handle cases first and then created an official record that appeared to justify their decisions.

Exhibit 11.3	**Researchers' and Juvenile Court Workers' Discrepant Assumptions**

Researchers' Assumptions	Intake Workers' Assumptions
• Being sent to court is a harsher sanction than diversion from court • Screening involves judgments about individual juveniles • Official records accurately capture case facts	• Being sent to court often results in more lenient and less effective treatment • Screening centers on the juvenile's social situation • Records are manipulated to achieve the desired outcome

Source: Needleman (1981, pp. 248–256).

This example highlights the value of using multiple methods, particularly when the primary method of data collection is analysis of records. When officials both make decisions and record the bases for their decisions without much supervision, records may diverge considerably from the decisions they are supposed to reflect. More generally, Needleman's (1981) research indicates how important it is to learn how people make sense of their judgments and actions when we want to describe their circumstances and explain their behavior (see Chapter 8).

Case Study

Obedience to Authority

Even the results of laboratory experiments can be enriched by incorporating some field research techniques. For example, consider Stanley Milgram's (1965) classic study of obedience to authority, which you saw in Chapter 3. Volunteers were recruited for what they were told was a study of the learning process. The experimenter told the volunteers they were to play the role of "teacher" and to administer an electric shock to a "student" in the next room when the student failed a memory test. Although the shocks were phony (and the "students" were actors), the volunteers were told the intensity of the shocks increased beyond a lethal level. Many subjects obeyed the authority in the study (the experimenter), even when their obedience involved administering potentially lethal shocks to another person. But did the experimental subjects actually believe that they were harming someone? Observational data suggest they did: "Persons were observed to sweat, tremble, stutter, bite their lips, and groan as they found themselves increasingly implicated in the experimental conflict" (Milgram, 1965, p. 66). And verbatim transcripts of the sessions also clarified what participants were thinking as they disobeyed or complied with the experimenter's instructions:

150 volts delivered.	You want me to keep going?
165 volts delivered.	That guy is hollering in there. There's a lot of them here. He's liable to have a heart condition. You want me to go on?
180 volts delivered.	He can't stand it! I'm not going to kill that man in there! You hear him hollering? He's hollering. He can't stand it. . . . I mean who is going to take responsibility if anything happens to that gentleman?
[The experimenter accepts responsibility.]	All right.
195 volts delivered.	You see he's hollering. Hear that. Gee, I don't know. *[The experimenter says: "The experiment requires that you go on."]* I know it does, sir, but I mean—uhh—he don't know what he's in for. He's up to 195 volts. . . . (Milgram, 1965, p. 67)

In each of these instances, qualitative data resulted in an understanding that was better than that based solely on quantitative data. In Needleman's (1981) study involving official records and the officials who create such records, qualitative methods called into question common assumptions about the validity of measures and causal conclusions. Milgram's use of qualitative data serves to increase confidence in his conclusions.

Intermethod and Intramethod: Two Types of Mixing

In **intermethod mixing,** researchers use two or more methods, such as questionnaires and observations, either at the same time or sequentially (B. Johnson & Turner, 2003). **Intramethod mixing,** on the other hand, signifies the mixing of qualitative and quantitative components within a single method, such as a questionnaire or observation. Exhibit 11.4 shows an Intramethod Data Collection Matrix for a project that uses five types of methods: Questionnaires, Interviews, Focus Groups, Observations, and Secondary Data. Each method can be used one of three ways: qualitatively, quantitatively, or mixed, along a continuum numbered from 1 (purely qualitative) to 15 (purely quantitative). Examples of intramethod mixing would be using both open-ended and closed-ended items on a single questionnaire or using a closed-ended questionnaire, followed by an open-ended questionnaire at a later time in the same study.

Exhibit 11.4 **Data Collection Matrix**

Methods of Data Collection	Research Approach Continuum		
	Pure Qualitative	Mixed	Pure Quantitative
1. Questionnaires	1	2	3
2. Interviews	4	5	6
3. Focus groups	7	8	9
4. Observations	10	11	12
5. Secondary data (e.g., personal and official documents, physical data, archived research data)	13	14	15

Source: Adapted from B. Johnson and Turner (2003, p. 298).

Conducting Factorial Surveys

Factorial surveys combine those features of true experiments that maximize causal validity with the features of surveys that maximize generalizability. In the simplest type of factorial survey, randomly selected subsets of survey respondents are asked different questions. These different questions represent, in effect, different experimental treatments; the goal is to determine the impact of these questions on answers to other questions. In another type of factorial survey, respondents are asked for their likely responses to one or more vignettes about hypothetical situations. The content of these vignettes is varied randomly among survey respondents so as to create "treatment groups" that differ in terms of particular variables reflected in the vignettes.

Case Study

Teachers as Reporters of Child Abuse

Public school teachers have a legal and professional obligation to report instances of child abuse and neglect, but the literature on child abuse shows evidence of both overreporting and underreporting (Besharov, 1993). Richard O'Toole, Stephen W. Webster, Anita W. O'Toole, and Betsy Lucal (1999) used a factorial survey method to study abuse and neglect, using probability sampling (see Chapter 4) to select 480 public and nonpublic school teachers in the state of Ohio.

The authors hypothesized that teachers' ability to recognize and report child abuse would vary based on three factors: "characteristics of the event" (e.g., type and seriousness of abuse, characteristics of the perpetrator and victim such as age, race, gender), "teacher's professional characteristics" (e.g., amount of previous contact with abuse or with a particular child, teaching experience, evaluation of Child Protective Services [CPS] and police), and "organizational characteristics" of the school setting (e.g., public/private/religious, large or small school, rural/urban/suburban) (O'Toole et al., 1999, p. 1087).

To test these hypotheses, the authors created a set of vignettes of abuse events incorporating known or suspected variables affecting the three factors. These vignettes created a range of variation in the independent variables in the study. The vignettes involved descriptions of an act between a perpetrator and a child, and variations included physical, sexual, and emotional abuse at four different levels of seriousness that started with acts that could be seen as marginal or nonabusive (O'Toole et al., 1999, p. 1088).

Here are two examples (O'Toole et al., 1999, p. 1089):

1. The mother hit her 12-year-old son in the face using the fist. Mother is White, works as a dishwasher, and is known to be belligerent. Child appears to be difficult to communicate with.

2. The father ignores his 4-year-old daughter most of the time, seldom talking with or listening to the child. Father is Black, works as a pharmacist, and is known to be cooperative. Child appears to be below-average mentally.

The dependent variables were recognition and reporting of child abuse. Recognition was measured on a scale that went from 0 ("not child abuse") to 9 ("child abuse"); reporting was measured on a similar scale, ranging from 0 ("unlikely to report") to 9 ("likely to report") (O'Toole et al., 1999, p. 1089). Every teacher was first presented with four "base vignettes" to assess their rating tendency. They were then asked to judge 24 vignettes, which were randomized so that no particular types of teachers were more likely to rate particular types of events (O'Toole et al., 1999, pp. 1089–1090).

The authors found that slightly more than half the variance in both recognition and reporting could be attributed solely to the characteristics of each case and that teacher and school variables added only a little more to the explanation of the teacher's responses (O'Toole et al., 1999, p. 1083). Their overall conclusion was that

> Teachers' responses to child abuse are relatively unbiased by either the extraneous characteristics of the perpetrator or victim, the responding teacher, or the school setting. The findings do not appear to support the problem of "overreporting." There is evidence for "underreporting," particularly in less serious cases involving physical and emotional abuse. (O'Toole et al., 1999, p. 1083)

There is still an important limitation to the generalizability of factorial surveys: They only indicate what respondents *say* they would do in situations that have been described to them. If these individuals had to make decisions in comparable real-life situations, we cannot be sure that they would act in accord with their stated intentions. So factorial surveys do not completely resolve the problems caused by the difficulty of conducting true experiments with representative samples. Nonetheless, by combining some of the advantages of experimental and survey designs, factorial surveys can provide stronger tests of causal relations than surveys and more generalizable findings than experiments.

回 Comparing Research Designs

You have now seen the value of mixing methods. Next we will review the central features of single-method designs—experiments, surveys, qualitative methods, and historical/comparative methods—to help you select the most appropriate method for a particular investigation and to decide when it is most important to combine two or more methods.

Comparing subjects randomly assigned to a treatment and to a comparison group, asking standard questions of the members of a random sample, observing while participating in a natural educational setting, recording published statistics on national characteristics, and reading historical documents involve markedly different decisions about measurement, causality, and generalizability. As you can see in Exhibit 11.5, none of these methods is superior to the others in all respects, and each varies in its suitability to different research questions and goals. Choosing among them for a particular investigation requires consideration of the research problem, opportunities and resources, prior research, philosophical commitments, and research goals.

Exhibit 11.5	Comparison of Research Methods				
Design	**Measurement Validity**	**Generalizability**	**Type of Causal Assertions**	**Causal Validity**
Experiments	+	–	Nomothetic	+
Surveys	+	+	Nomothetic	–/+[a]
Participant observation	–/+[b]	–	Idiographic	–
Historical/ comparative[c]	–	–/+	Idiographic or nomothethic	–

a. Surveys are a weaker design for identifying causal effects than true experiments, but use of statistical controls can strengthen causal arguments.

b. Reliability is low compared to surveys, and systematic evaluation of measurement validity is often not possible. However, direct observations may lead to great confidence in the validity of measures.

c. All conclusions about this type of design vary with the specific approach used.

Experimental designs are strongest for testing nomothetic causal hypotheses and are most appropriate for studies of treatment effects (see Chapter 6). Research questions that are believed to involve basic learning-related psychological or cognitive processes, such as abstract thinking or learning language, are most appealing for laboratory studies because the problem of generalizability is reduced. Random assignment reduces the possibility of preexisting differences between treatment and comparison groups to small, specifiable, chance levels, so many of the variables that might create a spurious association are controlled. But despite this clear advantage, an experimental design requires a degree of control that cannot always be achieved outside of the laboratory. It can be difficult to ensure in real-world settings that a treatment is delivered in the way that was intended and that was possible in the laboratory. As a result, when treatments are transferred from the laboratory to the real world, other influences may intrude, and so what appears to be a treatment effect may be something else altogether. Experiments happen "in a particular context (time and place) and constitute a social world" (M. L. Smith, 2006, p. 467).

Laboratory experiments permit much more control over conditions but at the cost of less generalizable findings. People must volunteer for most laboratory experiments, and so there is a good possibility that experimental subjects differ from those who do not volunteer. Ethical and practical constraints limit the types of treatments that can be studied experimentally (you can't assign social class or race experimentally). The problem of generalizability in an experiment using volunteers lessens when the object of investigation is an orientation, behavior, or educational process that is relatively invariant among people, but it is difficult to know which orientations, behaviors, or processes are so invariant. If a search of the research literature on the topic identifies many prior experimental studies, the results of these experiments will suggest the extent of variability in experimental effects and point to the unanswered questions about these effects. Experiments that are conducted "in the field," or in real-world settings such as classrooms, can overcome some of the limitations of laboratory experiments, but they require careful monitoring of the treatment process. Unfortunately, field experiments also often require more open access to students and instructional settings, as well as more financial resources than can often be obtained.

Both surveys and experiments typically use standardized, quantitative measures of attitudes, behaviors, or educational processes. Closed-ended questions are most common and are well suited for the reliable measurement of variables that have been studied in the past and whose meanings are well understood. Of course, surveys often include measures of many more variables than are included in an experiment, but this quality is not inherent in either design. Phone surveys may be quite short, and some experiments can involve very lengthy sets of measures (see Chapter 7). The level of funding for a survey will often determine which type of survey is conducted and thus how long the questionnaire is.

Many educational surveys rely on random sampling for their selection of cases from some larger population, and it is this feature that makes them preferable for descriptive research that seeks to develop generalizable findings (see Chapter 4). However, survey questionnaires can only measure what respondents are willing to report verbally; they may not be adequate for studying behaviors or attitudes that are regarded as socially unacceptable. Surveys are also often used to test hypothesized causal relationships. When variables that might create spurious relations are included in the survey, they can be controlled statistically in the analysis and thus eliminated as rival causal influences.

Qualitative methods presume an intensive measurement approach in which indicators of concepts are drawn from direct observation or in-depth commentary (see Chapter 8). This approach is most appropriate when it is not clear what meaning people attach to a concept or what sense they might make of particular questions about it. Qualitative methods are also admirably suited to the exploration of new or poorly understood educational settings or problems, when it is not even clear what concepts would help to understand the situation. They may also be used instead of survey methods when the population of interest is not easily identifiable or seeks to remain hidden. For these reasons, qualitative methods tend to be preferred when exploratory research questions are posed or when new groups are investigated. But, of course, intensive measurement necessarily makes the study of large numbers of cases or situations difficult, resulting in the limitation of many field research efforts to small numbers of people or unique educational settings. The individual field researcher may not require many financial resources, but the amount of time required for many field research projects serves as a barrier to prospective researchers.

Qualitative methods are suited to the elucidation of causal mechanisms. In addition, qualitative methods can be used to identify the multiple successive events that might have led to some outcome, thus identifying idiographic causal processes.

Historical and comparative methods range from cross-national quantitative surveys to qualitative comparisons of schooling practices and educational policy. For example, U.S. newspapers regularly feature state-to-state test score comparisons and comparisons of U.S. students to foreign students in subjects such as geography, math, and science. The suitability of such methods for exploration, description, explanation, and evaluation varies in relation to the particular method used, but they are essential for research on historical processes and national differences. If the same methods are used to study multiple eras or nations rather than just one nation at one time, the results are likely to be enhanced generalizability and causal validity.

Despite their different advantages and disadvantages, none of these methods of data collection provides a foolproof means for achieving measurement validity, causal validity, or generalizability. Each will have some liabilities in a specific research application and may benefit from combination with one or more other methods

(Sechrest & Sidani, 1995). Many educational researchers would agree with Mary Lee Smith (2006) that this is particularly true for complex, field-based studies and evaluations:

> Any methodology has inherent deficiencies and fails to capture the chaos, complexity, and contextuality of applied fields such as education, particularly in light of issues of culture, politics, values, and ideology. If lowering class size raises achievement on the average, what happens in smaller classes to set that effect into motion? . . . Can teachers learn to teach to high academic standards, cognitively complex curriculum, and alternative assessment? If so, what resources are necessary to facilitate their learning? . . . None of these questions can be satisfactorily asked and answered with single research approaches. (p. 458)

For these reasons, educational researchers often consider mixed methods for investigations planned in actual classroom or other teaching settings. Mixed methods may also be appropriate in laboratory experiments to investigate treatment effects, in structured surveys to explore the meaning attached to words, and in participant observation studies to facilitate comparisons between settings.

Performing Meta-Analyses

We also can gain insights into the impact of educational context and the consequences of particular methodologies with meta-analysis. A **meta-analysis** is a quantitative method for identifying patterns in findings across multiple studies of the same research question (Cooper & Hedges, 1994). Unlike a traditional literature review, which describes previous research studies verbally, meta-analyses treat previous studies as cases whose features are measured as variables and are then analyzed statistically. Whereas a macro-level analysis shows how educational processes vary across educational contexts, meta-analysis shows how evidence about educational processes varies across research studies. If the methods used in these studies varied, then meta-analysis can describe how this variation affected study findings. If educational contexts varied across the studies, then meta-analysis will indicate how educational context affected study findings.

Meta-analysis can be used when a number of studies have attempted to answer the same research question with some quantitative method, most often experiments. Once a research problem is formulated about the findings of such research, then the literature must be searched systematically to identify the entire population of relevant studies. Typically, multiple bibliographic databases are used; some researchers also search for relevant dissertations and conference papers. Once the studies are identified, their findings, methods, and other features are coded (e.g., sample size, location of sample, strength of the association between the independent and dependent variables). Statistics are then calculated to identify the average effect of the independent variable on the dependent variable, as well as the effect of methodological and other features of the studies (Cooper & Hedges, 1994).

Eligibility criteria must be specified carefully to determine which studies to include and which to omit as too different. Mark Lipsey and David Wilson (2001, pp. 16–21) suggested that eligibility criteria include the following:

- *Distinguishing features:* This includes the specific intervention tested and perhaps the groups compared.

- *Research respondents:* The pertinent characteristics of the research respondents (subject sample) who provided study data must be similar to those of the population about which the generalization is sought.

- *Key variables:* These must be sufficient to allow tests of the hypotheses of concern and control for likely additional influences.

- *Research methods:* Apples and oranges cannot be directly compared, but some trade-off must be made between including the range of studies about a research question and excluding those that are so different in their methods as to not yield comparable data.

- *Cultural and linguistic range:* If the study population is going to be limited to English-language publications or limited in some other way, this must be acknowledged, and the size of the population of relevant studies in other languages should be estimated.

- *Timeframe:* Social processes relevant to the research question may have changed for reasons such as historical events or the advent of new technologies, so temporal boundaries around the study population must be considered.

- *Publication type:* Will the analysis focus only on published reports in professional journals, or will it include dissertations and/or unpublished reports?

Statistics are then calculated to identify the average effect of the independent variable on the dependent variable, as well as the effect of methodological and other features of the studies (Cooper & Hedges, 1994). The effect size statistic is the key to capturing the association between the independent and dependent variables across multiple studies. The effect size statistic is a standardized measure of association—often the difference between the mean of the experimental group and the mean of the control group on the dependent variable, adjusted for the average variability in the two groups (Lipsey & Wilson, 2001).

The meta-analytic approach to synthesizing research results can result in much more generalizable findings than those obtained with just one study. Methodological weaknesses in the studies included in the meta-analysis are still a problem, however; it is only when other studies without particular methodological weaknesses are included that we can estimate effects with some confidence. In addition, before we can place any confidence in the results of a meta-analysis, we must be confident that all (or almost all) relevant studies were included and that the information we need to analyze was included in all (or most) of the studies (Matt & Cook, 1994).

Two Examples of Meta-Analysis

Case Study

Music Therapy for Children With Autism Spectrum Disorders

We began the previous chapter with a study of effective instructional techniques for autistic students, an area that presents a significant research challenge. Because of the rapid rise in diagnoses of autism and autism spectrum disorders since the mid-1990s (Newschaffer et al., 2007), educators and parents have a keen interest in what research has to say about best methods for teaching this population. Music therapy presents one possible avenue of treatment. Jennifer Whipple (2004, p. 90) performed a meta-analysis analyzing 12 dependent variables from nine quantitative studies that compared music to no-music conditions in the treatment of autistic children and adolescents. Whipple analyzed the type of dependent variables measured, their theoretical approach, the number and age of subjects in the study, the way music was used, and whether the study had been published or not (p. 90). She found that "all music intervention, regardless of purpose or implementation, has been effective for children and adolescents with autism" (pp. 90–91). The fact that all the available studies on this difficult-to-study topic reached the same, positive conclusion strongly suggests (but does not conclusively prove) that music therapy works for autistic students. Such a clear-cut outcome, where all the evidence points in the same direction, is relatively rare in a meta-analysis.

Case Study

Spending on Schools and Student Achievement

Many studies have tested the hypothesis that supplying more financial resources to schools will raise student achievement, but findings have often been contradictory or inconclusive. Rob Greenwald, Larry V. Hedges, and Richard D. Laine (1996) were able to find 60 studies that tested this hypothesis. They used an approach adapted from economics called "education production function," which looks at school performance (test scores, graduation rates) as a function of inputs (students, financial support). The studies represented a variety of resource types and achievement measures and "aggregated data at the level of school districts or smaller units and either controlled for socioeconomic characteristics or were longitudinal in design" (p. 361). The authors made sure their "universe" of 60 studies (articles and books) was comprehensive by considering four types of possible sources for inclusion: (1) studies covered in a respected recent meta-analysis by a colleague; (2) "electronic databases in economics, education, and psychology" (EconLit, ERIC, PsycLIT); (3) literature reviews; and (4) "citations in sources identified by the first three methods" (pp. 362–363). Of the 60 studies originally considered, only 31 met the criteria for inclusion in the final meta-analysis. Studies were eliminated if they had not been published in a refereed book or journal, did not study schools in the United States, looked at units larger than a single school district, or did not meet certain statistical or measurement qualifications.

The 31 studies included were then subjected to statistical procedures aimed at determining two things: how statistically significant were their conclusions and how strong were the relations they showed between inputs and outputs. To determine the first point, the authors used "combined significance tests," which "provide a means of combining statistical significance values (p-values) from studies which test the same conceptual hypothesis" with differing "designs or measurement methods" (p. 365). To gauge how strong the relationship was between inputs and outputs, the authors used "effect magnitude analysis" to standardize the strength of effects statistically. The significance of relationships between inputs and outputs was tracked across a large number of inputs, including school size, per pupil expenditure, teacher ability, education, experience, salary, and pupil ratio. The results showed unequivocally that overall "greater resource inputs are related to higher achievement" (p. 369). Effects varied with the studies' substantive features and their methods, however. The authors caution that although the overall direction of their findings is clear—"money is positively related to student achievement"—they do not argue that "money is everything. How we spend the money and the incentives we create for both children and teachers are equally important" (p. 385).

Meta-analyses such as the Whipple (2004) and the Greenwald et al. (1996) studies make us aware of how hazardous it is to base understanding of educational and social processes on single studies that are limited in time, location, and measurement. Although one study may not support the hypothesis that we deduced from what seemed to be a compelling theory, this is not a sufficient basis for discarding the theory itself or even for assuming that the hypothesis is no longer worthy of consideration in future research. You can see that a meta-analysis combining the results of many studies may identify conditions when the hypothesis is supported and others when it is not.

Of course, we need to have our wits about us when we read reports of meta-analytic studies. It is not a good idea to assume that a meta-analysis is the definitive word on a research question just because it cumulates the results of multiple studies. Fink (2005, pp. 215–237) suggests evaluating meta-analytic studies in terms of the following seven criteria:

- *Clear statement of the analytic objectives.* The study's methods cannot be evaluated without knowledge of the objectives they were intended to achieve. Meta-analyses are most appropriate for summarizing research conducted to identify the effect of some type of treatment or some other readily identifiable individual characteristic.

- *Explicit inclusion and exclusion criteria.* On what basis were research reports included in the analysis? Were high-quality studies distinguished from low-quality studies? If low-quality studies were included, were they analyzed separately, so that effects could be identified separately for only the population of high-quality studies?

- *Satisfactory search strategies.* Both electronic and written reference sources should be searched. Was some method used to find studies that were conducted but not published? It may be necessary to write directly to researchers in the field and to consult lists of papers presented at conferences.

- *A standardized protocol for screening the literature.* Screening involves rating the quality of the study and its relevance to the research question. This screening should be carried out with a simple rating form.

- *A standardized protocol for collecting data.* It is best to have two reviewers use a standard form for coding the characteristics of the reported research. The level of agreement between these reviewers should be assessed.

- *Complete explanation of the method of combining results.* Some checks should be conducted to determine where variable study features influenced the size of the treatment effect.

- *Report of results, conclusions, and limitations.* This seems obvious, but it's easy for a researcher to skirt over study limitations or some aspects of the findings.

🔲 Conclusions

We began this chapter by asking what mixed-methods research has to tell us about the question, "How can schools help students with special needs?" Odom et al. (2006) used both quantitative and qualitative techniques to study how well an 800-school national sample of preschool students with disabilities were accepted by peers. The researchers concluded that "socially accepted children tended to have disabilities that were less likely to affect social problem solving and emotional regulation" (Odom et al., 2006, p. 807). In another special-needs study, Whipple (2004) performed a meta-analysis of studies analyzing use of music therapy for children with autism spectrum disorders. She found that all of the examples she studied, whatever the context, showed that music therapy was effective.

Odom et al. (2006), Whipple (2004), and other mixed-methods examples from this chapter demonstrate that a research design is an integrated whole. Designing research means deciding how to measure empirical phenomena, how to identify causal connections, and how to generalize findings—not as separate decisions, but in tandem, with each decision having implications for the others. Choice of a method of data collection should be guided in part by the aspect of validity that is of most concern, but each aspect of validity must be considered in attempting to answer every research question. Experiments may be the preferred method when causal validity is a paramount concern and surveys the natural choice if generalizability is critical. But generalizability must still be a concern when assessing the results of an experiment, and causal validity is a key concern in most educational surveys. Field research, such as classroom observation, has unique value for measuring educational processes as they happen, but the causal validity and generalizability of field research results are often open to question. A researcher should always consider whether data of another type should be collected in what is basically a single-method study and whether additional research using different methods is needed before the research question can be answered with sufficient confidence. A basic question the researcher must ask is, "Will a mixed-methods approach give a better picture of the research target than a single-method approach?" If the answer is yes, then the researcher must consider which combination of methods will offer the best mix of validity, generalizability, and rich, accurate data on the target research question.

The ability to apply diverse techniques to address different aspects of a complex research question is one mark of a sophisticated educational researcher. Awareness that one study's findings must be understood in the context of a larger body of research is another. And the ability to speculate on how the use of different methods might have altered a study's findings is a prerequisite for informed criticism of educational research. As educational research methods and substantive findings continue to grow in number, these insights should stimulate more ambitious efforts to combine research methods and integrate many studies' findings.

But the potential for integrating methods and combining findings does not decrease the importance of single studies using just one method of data collection. The findings from well-designed studies in carefully researched settings are the necessary foundation for broader, more integrative methods. There is little point in combining methods that are poorly implemented or in merging studies that produced invalid results. Whatever the research question asked, the researcher should consider the full range of methodological possibilities, make an informed and feasible choice, and then carefully carry out that strategy.

Finally, realistic assessment of the weaknesses as well as the strengths of each method of data collection should help you to remember that humility is a virtue in research. Advancement of knowledge and clear answers to specific research questions are attainable with the tools you now have in your methodological toolbox. Perfection, however, is not a realistic goal. No matter what research method we use, our mental concepts cannot reflect exactly what we measured, our notions of causation cannot reveal a tangible causal force, and our generalizations always extend beyond the cases that were actually studied. This is not cause for disillusionment, but it should keep us from being excessively confident in our own interpretations or unreasonably resistant to change. Final answers to every research question we pose cannot be achieved; what we seek are new, ever more sophisticated questions for research and additional propositions for educational theory.

Key Terms

Factorial survey   244

Intermethod mixing   243

Intramethod mixing   243

Meta-analysis   248

Highlights

- The three dimensions of validity (measurement, causality, and generalizability) must be considered as an integrated whole when evaluating and planning research projects. Decisions about each dimension have implications for the others.

- Research on most topics can be improved by using mixed methods.

- Factorial surveys combine features of experimental design with survey research methods. Variation of hypothetical vignettes or particular questions across randomly assigned survey subgroups can strengthen the validity of conclusions about causal processes if these processes can be modeled with vignettes or questions.

- Researchers can test statistically for patterns across multiple studies with meta-analysis. This technique can be used only in areas of research in which there have been many prior studies using comparable methods.

- Understanding of many educational processes can be enriched by taking into account related biological and physical processes.

Student Study Site

To assist in completing the web exercises, please access the study site at www.sagepub.com/check, where you will find the web exercise with accompanying links. You'll find other useful study materials such as self-quizzes and e-flashcards for each chapter, along with a group of carefully selected articles from research journals that illustrate the major concepts and techniques.

Discussion Questions

1. Think of a possible school- or classroom-based research question. Now think of at least two methods, one quantitative and one qualitative, that could be combined in a research design to explore this question.

2. Do you find the idea of a meta-analysis (or "study of studies") convincing? Give at least two reasons why conclusions reached from analyzing a group of studies may be more convincing than conclusions reached by individual studies.

Practice Exercises

1. Some research projects use an "inverted pyramid" data collection strategy, with broad, quantitative measures gathered from a large population on top, narrowing to more intensive qualitative measures (focus groups, individual interviews) with a smaller subset of the population at the bottom. Think of a school-based research project with either teachers or students and design such an inverted pyramid, showing what measures and what sample size and research subjects you would use at each level of the design.

2. Think of at least three areas of education where you believe much research has been done—for example, teaching reading to elementary grade students. Where are you likely to find such studies? What sources would you use to see if a meta-analysis had been done in these areas in the past 5 to 8 years? Choose two of these topic areas and try to find a recent meta-analysis. You may wish to start by looking in ERIC and JSTOR. Almost all meta-analyses have the word *meta-analysis* in the article title.

Web Exercises

1. Find the website for the online *Journal of Mixed-Methods Research* (http://mmr.sagepub.com/). On the home page, click the button Current Issue. When the table of contents for the current issue comes up, click on the abstracts for three of the articles, and for each article write down two or more methods that the authors used to conduct their research. Did any methods occur more than once? Were there any methods you had not heard of before?

2. Go to the home page of the *Journal of Mixed-Methods Research*. At the button for Article Statistics, click on "Most Read." When the most-read article titles come up, read the abstracts for the top five articles. What themes or main points do you see running through these articles? Based on the top-five abstracts, write a paragraph or two describing the most important issues currently being discussed or investigated by mixed-method researchers.

Developing a Research Proposal

Now is the time to mix your methods.

1. Add a component involving a second method to your research proposal. If you already developed alternative approaches in answer to the exercises in earlier chapters, just write a justification for these additions that points out the potential benefits.

2. Consider the possible influences of educational context factors on the variables pertinent to your research question. Write a rationale for including a test for contextual influences in your proposed research.

3. Describe a method for studying the contextual influences in Question 2.

CHAPTER 12

Teacher Research and Action Research

Chapter Contents

- **Teacher Research: Three Case Studies**
- **Teacher Research: A Self-Planning Outline for Your Own Project**
- **Action Research and How It Differs From Teacher Research**
- **Validity and Ethical Issues in Teacher Research and Action Research**

Howard Banford had a question. Banford, a California teacher who used the writing workshop method in his second-grade classroom, wanted active participation by all of his students. Every student needed to take a turn in the author's chair; everyone had to respond to other students' writing. But Maricar—a shy Philippine American student—seemed silent, a loner. To better understand what was happening with Maricar in the writing workshop, Banford decided to conduct his own classroom-based research—to observe, record, and reflect on her participation in a systematic way. Banford's research question was, "What can a close look at Maricar teach me about 'improving writing workshop and student learning in general?'" (Banford, 1996, p. 5). One teacher, one classroom, one student, and a teacher's need to answer a question—this is a starting point for **teacher research.**

What kinds of questions do teacher researchers ask? What methods do they use? Teachers' questions are wide-ranging, and their methods are many and varied, depending on the situation. Typical questions might be the following:

- What happens when chemistry is taught in heterogeneous groups?

- What happens when students choose their own spelling words?

- How do first graders learn number facts?

- What is teaching and learning from the student's perspective? (Lieberman, 1994, p. vii)

Over time, some teacher researchers take things to another level. Building on their initial questions and investigations, they develop what Marilyn Cochran-Smith and Susan L. Lytle (2001) call an "inquiry stance" toward their own work, a stance that is "critical and transformative" and linked not just to high standards for all students but to "social justice," and "the individual and collective professional growth of teachers" (p. 46). Many teachers find an **inquiry stance** empowering because it "talks back to, and challenges, many of the assumptions that define teaching and research on teaching in the current era of acute educational accountability" (Cochran-Smith & Lytle, 2009, p. 44).

In this chapter, you will learn about the origins of teacher research and why it has become so popular. You will see multiple examples of teacher research and the methods that teacher researchers employ, and you will learn about several types of teacher research. You will also be given an outline for creating a teacher research project of your own. In the second part of the chapter, you will learn about **action research,** a cyclic, team-based method for creating school change that is closely related to teacher research. Finally, we will discuss issues of validity and ethics that arise when school-based practitioners conduct research in the classrooms and schools where they work.

▣ Teacher Research: Three Case Studies

Case 1: Maricar

Howard Banford undertook his project as part of a teacher research initiative sponsored by the National Writing Project (NWP). He conducted his research during the school year supported by a local teacher researcher group. In the summers preceding and following the data collection year, he attended a national institute for teacher researchers sponsored by the NWP, where he received technical and resource support in planning the project, conducting data analysis, and writing up the project.

Because of previous experience with quiet students, Banford began his project with the belief that the writing workshop worked for them, too. But he also realized that he had little understanding of *how* the writing workshop worked for these students, as opposed to louder, more gregarious students whose involvement was much easier to see. Banford (1996, p. 5) studied Maricar's participation in the writing workshop for an entire school year. He collected her writing from writing workshop sessions, audiotaped her writing response group, conducted several interviews with her, and kept his own teacher's journal in which he regularly wrote about what he was seeing in class and on the playground.

What he found was a style of participation and growth he had not anticipated. Central to Maricar's growth was a supportive family. Her kindergarten and first-grade teachers remembered her as a slow worker and unsure student. Both of her parents worked, and she and her 5-year-old sister were cared for by their grandmother, who spoke to them only in Tagalog, the native language of the Philippines. Her family placed a strong value on education, and Maricar had high aspirations for herself (Banford, 1996).

Maricar began the year as one of the slowest writers Banford (1996) had ever taught. Her stories were also short, and the classroom "buzz" during writing time bothered her concentration. But she was quietly persistent in her writing, and she was a keen listener, both to Banford's mini-lessons and to other student's stories. Once she learned the rules of the workshop format, she excelled at responding to the writing of others. By February, her stories had lengthened considerably. As the year went on, she overcame her fear of the author's chair, and she used the response groups to build social bridges to other girls in the class.

In summing up his findings, Banford (1996) concluded that the writing workshop succeeded for Maricar because it was "ordered, structured, and predictable" (p. 21) and so gave her a way to work at her own pace and to interact with other students in a safe environment. Initially thinking of Maricar as an immature writer, Banford (1996) found that studying her closely changed his views and that at the end of the project, he saw her as an above-average writer who took risks with topics and spelling, had "an extraordinary ability to stick with stories over a long period of time," and was "unusually responsive to both mini-lessons and her peers" (p. 23). His close, year-long study of one quiet student changed his view of what successful writers do and caused him to think more deeply about the "quiet side" of his classroom.

Teacher Researchers as Knowledge Makers

When he finished this project, Banford (1996) knew many things about Maricar and his teaching that he didn't know before. He knew, most of all, that the writing workshop worked for Maricar, and he knew some of the reasons *why* it worked for her: It provided "a safe haven for a shy student" (p. 20), it allowed her to work at her own pace, and it drew on one of her strongest assets as a learner—her ability to listen (p. 21). He didn't guess these things, or feel them, or believe them without evidence—he *knew* them. It is this "knowledge dimension" that teacher researchers often cite as its most powerful, transformative benefit.

Traditionally, university researchers have been seen as the knowledge makers, the "knowers," in education. Teachers (and administrators) were considered the "doers" (Check, 1997). For decades, the dominant shape of education research was this: The knowers studied the doers, and their conclusions and recommendations were used by policy makers to attempt to improve schools. One frequent criticism of this approach was that it created a gulf between theory and practice. University libraries were filled with educational research studies that few practitioners ever read.

Over the past 20 years or so, teacher research has become increasingly popular because it bridges the gulf between theory and practice, between research and implementation. It has been called "a radical departure from the traditional view of educational research as a specialist activity, the results of which teachers apply rather than create" (Elliott, 1981, p. 1). By providing an alternative to the traditional relationship of research to practice (university faculty = knowers, teachers = doers), it changes the power relationships between practitioners and researchers.

Roots of Teacher Research

Today's teacher research movement has a long intellectual heritage. John Dewey (1933) envisioned teachers as reflective professionals who build theory from practice. In the late 1950s, British researcher Lawrence Stenhouse, a teacher educator, argued that teachers were "highly competent professionals who should be in charge of their own practice" (Stenhouse, 1975, p. 144). He maintained that professional education meant that teachers were committed to systematic questioning of their own practice as a basis for development and to testing theory in practice (McNiff & Whitehead, 2006, p. 37).

In the 1980s, Donald Schon (1983), a professor of urban studies and education at MIT, investigated what he called "reflection-in-action" (p. viii), also called **reflective practice,** in the work of various professions, including teaching. Schon asked, "What is the kind of knowing in which competent practitioners engage? How is professional knowing like and unlike the kinds of knowledge presented in academic textbooks, scientific papers, and learned journals?" (p. viii). Schon pointed out that for professionals such as architects, lawyers, and teachers, real-world problems do not arise as "well-formed structures" but as

> messy, indeterminate situations. . . . A teacher of arithmetic, listening to a child's question, becomes aware of a kind of confusion and, at the same time, a kind of intuitive understanding, for which she has no readily available response. . . . The case is not "in the book." If she is to deal with it competently, she must do so by a kind of improvisation, inventing and testing in the situation strategies of her own devising. (Schon, 1987, pp. 4–5)

Conceptually, it is a very short step from a reflective practice that identifies a problem, then devises and tests solution strategies, to teacher research.

Types of Teacher Research

How does a teacher researcher go about "inventing and testing in the situation strategies of her own devising?" More generally, how do teachers construct useful knowledge about teaching and learning by systematically studying their own practice? In the Banford (1996) case, you have seen concrete examples of the kinds of questions asked and research techniques used by one teacher researcher. Exhibit 12.1 shows a more general analytic framework for teacher research forms proposed by Marilyn Cochran-Smith and Susan Lytle (1993). They identify two categories of teacher research, one empirical—involving data collection and interpretation, the other conceptual—involving "analysis of ideas" (p. 27). As Exhibit 12.1 makes clear, in the empirical category, they locate "Journals (teachers' accounts of classroom life over time)," "Oral Examinations (Teachers' oral examinations of classroom/school issues, contexts, texts, and experiences)," and "Classroom/School Studies (Teachers' explorations of practice-based issues using data based on observation, interview, and document collection)." In the conceptual category, they place "Essays" (Teachers' interpretations of the assumptions and characteristics of classroom and school life and/or research itself.)" (p. 27).

Our second case study demonstrates how Joseph Kelly, an elementary school teacher, used a number of the methods identified by Cochran-Smith and Lytle (1993) to become not just a "doer" but a "knower" in relation to his own teaching.

Case 2: Self-Reflection in a Science Class

Joseph Kelly, a fifth-grade science teacher, designed a teacher research project to help him understand how the use of portfolios in his classroom affected students' science learning. He framed the question, "What happens when students use self-reflection in science as a means of assessing growth?" (Hubbard & Power, 1999, p. 73).

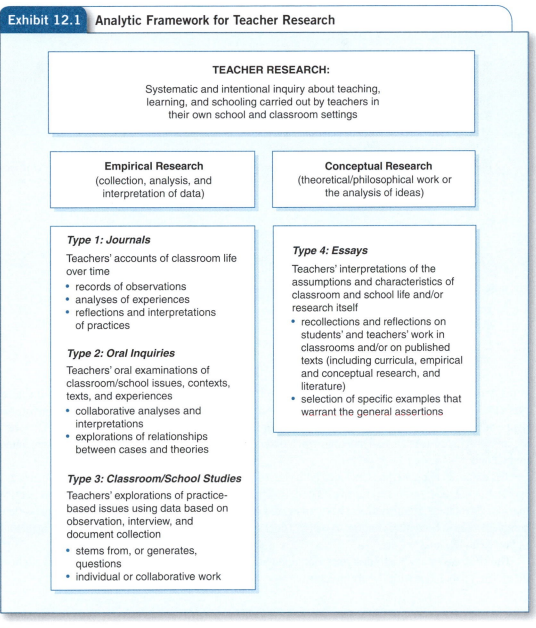

| Exhibit 12.1 | Analytic Framework for Teacher Research |

TEACHER RESEARCH:

Systematic and intentional inquiry about teaching, learning, and schooling carried out by teachers in their own school and classroom settings

Empirical Research
(collection, analysis, and interpretation of data)

Conceptual Research
(theoretical/philosophical work or the analysis of ideas)

Type 1: Journals

Teachers' accounts of classroom life over time

- records of observations
- analyses of experiences
- reflections and interpretations of practices

Type 2: Oral Inquiries

Teachers' oral examinations of classroom/school issues, contexts, texts, and experiences

- collaborative analyses and interpretations
- explorations of relationships between cases and theories

Type 3: Classroom/School Studies

Teachers' explorations of practice-based issues using data based on observation, interview, and document collection

- stems from, or generates, questions
- individual or collaborative work

Type 4: Essays

Teachers' interpretations of the assumptions and characteristics of classroom and school life and/or research itself

- recollections and reflections on students' and teachers' work in classrooms and/or on published texts (including curricula, empirical and conceptual research, and literature)
- selection of specific examples that warrant the general assertions

Source: Cochran-Smith and Lytle (1993, p. 27).

His data collection methods and calendar for the project looked like this (Hubbard & Power, 1999, pp. 73–74):

August

Letter to parents
Develop survey questions
Start teacher journal

September–January

    Notetaking
    Keep teacher journal
    Student folders
    Model self-reflection
    Survey records kept in teacher log
    Review student responses weekly
    Make and review one student videotape weekly
    Talk with co-teacher to share information
    Parent partner to make observations and meet weekly to discuss and see if there are any connections at home
    Look for patterns

February–April

    Analyze student growth in portfolios
    Continue all of the above

June

    Draw conclusions from portfolios
    Complete final survey
    Review entry and exit survey/compare differences
    Summary statement

As you can see, in this ambitious, year-long project, Kelly's research methods and instruments included a letter to parents, an entry/exit survey, his own reflective journal, note taking on classes, portfolios of student work, teaching his students how to write reflections and analyzing them, periodic videotapes, conversations with his co-teacher, and meetings with "parent partners" to assess the connection between home and school.

His data collection methods included both classroom activities that would have happened in any case (portfolios of student work) and activities undertaken specifically for the research project (his reflective journal, videotapes). His activities as a researcher did not conflict with or supplant his teaching role—they complemented it. Becoming a knower as well as a doer served as self-initiated professional development that improved his teaching practice.

Our third case study briefly describes a large, long-term teacher research initiative conducted by a school district in collaboration with a local university.

Case 3: A District-Wide Teacher Research Program

Cathy Caro-Bruce, Mary Klehr, Ken Zeichner, and Ana Maria Sierra-Piedrahita (2009) reported on a district-sponsored teacher research program in Madison, Wisconsin. From small beginnings in 1990, the program grew until it became available to all teachers in the Madison Metropolitan School District (MMSD), which in 2009 served 25,000 students in 47 schools K–12. The program, which has between 30 and 100 participants each year, involves a partnership with the school of education at the University of Wisconsin–Madison (Caro-Bruce et al., 2009, pp. 104–105).

Reflective practice is at the heart of the program. Essential to the program's success are a set of core principles that include voluntary participation, teachers being treated as knowledgeable professionals who control their own research questions and methods, research groups of 6 to 10 members who meet in a supportive environment, and the use of facilitators to provide a framework for the research process and technical assistance (Caro-Bruce et al., 2009, pp. 108–110).

With the aid of a facilitator, teachers focus on an area of their own pedagogy that they wish to investigate, then go through a process of refinement to develop a research question. With the aid of facilitators and fellow group members, they learn about a range of inquiry methods but ultimately have autonomy in choosing strategies that they think best fit their context. A key element is the use of triangulation—the use of multiple research methods and perspectives for data collection and analysis (you will see more about triangulation a little later in this chapter). When the project is completed, they write final reports that are shared with others and posted on the district's website (Caro-Bruce et al., 2009, pp. 108–112).

In research studies on the effects of the program, "many of the teachers . . . felt a greater sense of control over their work . . . they now looked at their teaching in a more analytic, focused manner, a habit they claimed to have internalized and applied beyond the research experience" (Caro-Bruce et al., 2009, p. 113).

▣ Teacher Research: A Self-Planning Outline for Creating Your Own Project

Many states now require or recommend that teacher preparation candidates take a course in teacher research as part of their initial or advanced training. Here is a general outline for a classroom-based teacher research project, developed by one of the authors for such a course at the graduate level. If you find yourself embarking on a teacher research project of your own, this outline can help you think through the steps needed to organize your efforts. This particular outline was for a one-semester course, but it can work just as well for a year-long project, with more time devoted to data collection and analysis. Although it can be used as a self-tutorial, it works best when you have another person—a mentor, a colleague, a friend, a professor—read what you've written and give you feedback at each stage, before going on to the next. Suggested length guidelines are given, but they are suggestions only. You should determine how much you want to do in each area and how long you wish to spend on it.

Self-Planning Outline

1. *Personal/School/Teaching Context (3–5 pp.)*

Begin by thinking, and writing reflectively in a journal, about yourself and your teaching context—the demographics of your school system/school/classroom; your colleagues and administration; your own background, training, and interests; and how you got to where you are right now as a teacher.

To accompany this reflection, make a diagram or map of your classroom indicating the location of your desk, where you sit/stand/move as you teach, student desks, what's on the walls, what floor your room is on, location of doors and windows, some idea of the dimensions of the room, what media are available or present (computers, TV, etc.), and any other items you think are pertinent (story area or rug, author's chair, time-out area, etc.). This will be the context and setting for your research.

(Continued)

(Continued)

2. *Research Purpose (1–2 pp.)*

Try to state as well as you can why you are undertaking a research project. Ask yourself: Why do I want to do this? What am I hoping to accomplish? What do I expect to learn through the project that I did not know before?

3. *Research Question (1 p.)*

What is your research question, and why is it important to you? Although it may be difficult to do so, you have to articulate your question at this point as clearly as you can. Your question will probably be broad and tentative at first but will be modified as you go along. Many teacher researchers find that their research question changes or transforms for weeks or even months before it achieves a final form. Do not let this bother you—it's a normal part of the process. Right now you just need a question that will help you get the project started. Use the case studies and conceptual diagrams from this chapter to give you ideas, and follow up by looking at some of the items on the resource list.

4. *Literature Review (3–5 pp.)*

You are probably aware that scholarly articles in education journals typically begin with an extensive review of the literature. You may not be aiming for publication in a scholarly journal, but you do need to familiarize yourself to a certain extent with what others have done in the area of your research question. You need to get some sense of the state of knowledge in the field and how previous work by others can help you shape your own inquiry.

A realistic goal is to identify three to five sources—books, journal articles, research reports—published within the past 5 years that deal with your subject in a way that makes sense to you. You should briefly summarize these and give a brief statement of what you have learned from them. These may include sources you have already read and are familiar with, or you may need to do a literature search.

5. *Data Collection and Data Analysis (Includes Timeline) (3–6 pp.)*

Describe how you plan to go about answering your question. What data will you gather? From whom will you gather data? When and in what sequence? Will you use interviews, a survey, classroom observation, a journal, etc.? How will your inquiry unfold in time?

The cases and exhibits in this chapter can give you a sense of the wide variety of research methods available to you. Other chapters in this book contain information on many of them. You will also need to consider ethical questions such as privacy and confidentiality, gathering data from minors, and potential harm to human subjects. Triangulation and reflexivity, which are described in detail a little later in this chapter, will be important considerations here.

6. *Reflections/Conclusions/Recommendations (2–5 pp.)*

You should plan, when your project is complete, to write a reflective report or essay about how you conducted your research and what you learned from it. You will need to ask yourself questions such as the following: What seemed significant about the data I collected and about the process? What conclusions, if any, did I reach about my own teaching, and what might be changed or improved? What did I learn about my students and my school? Do I plan to change anything as a result of this inquiry? Who else would be interested in hearing about what I've learned? How can I publicly share what I've done?

Resources for Teacher Researchers

The outline above is a skeleton that will help you get started. To help you go into greater depth, collections of teacher research and how-to manuals are readily available, with more being published every year. Here are several titles that many teachers have found particularly accessible and useful:

Banford, H., Berkman, M., Chin, C., Cziko, C., Fecho, B., Jumpp, D., et al. (1996). *Cityscapes: Eight views from the urban classroom.* Berkeley, CA: National Writing Project.

Cochran-Smith, M., & Lytle, S. L. (1993). *Inside/outside: Teacher research and knowledge.* New York: Teachers College Press.

Cochran-Smith, M., & Lytle, S. L. (2009). *Inquiry as stance: Practitioner research for the next generation.* New York: Teachers College Press.

Hubbard, R. S., & Power, B. M. (1999). *Living the questions: A guide for teacher researchers.* Portland, ME: Stenhouse.

Mohr, M., Rogers, C., Sanford, B., Nocerino, M., MacLean, M. S., & Clawson, S. (2004). *Teacher research for better schools.* New York: Teachers College Press/National Writing Project.

Teel, K. M., & Obidah, J. E. (Eds.). (2008). *Building racial and cultural competence in the classroom: Strategies from urban educators.* New York: Teachers College Press.

We will now turn to action research, also called **participatory action research,** another increasingly popular practitioner research method.

▣ Action Research and How It Differs From Teacher Research

Action research emerged in the 1940s from the work of anthropologist John Collier and social psychologist Kurt Lewin. Collier (1945) and Lewin (1946) were both interested, in different ways, in the intersection of social justice, research methods, and organizational change. Lewin outlined an approach to research that used successive cycles of planning, action, and fact finding about the result of the action. This circular or, more accurately, spiral process has become an essential, defining element of action research. Exhibit 12.2 shows a recent example of such a circle from Alice McIntyre's (2008, p. 6) work, showing action research as a **recursive process**—a process that loops back on itself—and "involves a spiral of adaptable steps" that include questioning a particular issue, reflecting upon and investigating the issue, developing an action plan, and implementing and progressively refining the plan.

Action research is now used in many countries and in fields such as public health, sociology, psychology, and some business settings. Its use in education is rapidly growing, both in the United States and internationally. Many educators and community workers find it to be highly compatible with the emancipatory theory and methods of the iconic Brazilian educator Paolo Friere (Friere, 1970, 1985; McIntyre, 2008, p. 3; Minkler, 2000).

Confusion can be caused by the fact that in education, the terms *action research, teacher research,* and *practitioner inquiry* (or *practitioner research*) are often used almost interchangeably. One recent how-to book, for example, carries the title *Action Research: Teachers as Researchers in the Classroom* (Mertler, 2009). Nolen and Vander Putten (2007) use *action research* to refer to "the entire body of research in which the practitioner is engaged in collecting data or information for the purpose of solving a practical problem in an authentic setting" (p. 406).

Exhibit 12.2 **The Recursive Process of Participatory Action Research**

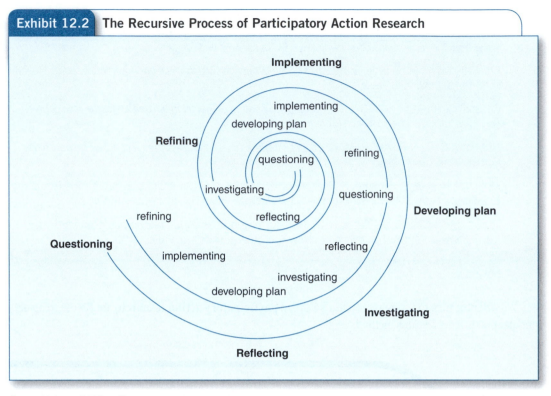

Source: McIntyre (2008, p. 7).

Strictly speaking, though, there are important differences between *action research* and *teacher research*. *Teacher research* is commonly used to describe all kinds of school- and classroom-based research conducted by practitioners. It has been defined as "inquiry that is *intentional, systematic, public, voluntary, ethical, and contextual*" (M. Mohr et al., 1994, p. 23). *Teacher research* as a general term embraces many methodologies and many situations.

In contrast, *action research* in its strict sense refers to research activities that use a cyclical, **action reflection model** to investigate and attempt to make change in an organization, for example, a whole school. The term *participatory action research* emphasizes, within this action reflection cycle, the involvement of those who, in other research methods, would be called research "subjects." In participatory action research, they are seen as co-researchers, participants in the conceptualization, implementation, and interpretation of the research project as it unfolds.

To simplify, all action research conducted by practitioners can properly be termed *teacher research,* but not all teacher research can properly be labeled *action research.* Here are three ways in which *teacher research* can differ from *action research:*

1. Teacher research is not necessarily cyclic in nature.

2. Teacher research allows for but does not necessarily require a team element—one teacher can conduct practitioner inquiry in his or her own classroom, for his or her own benefit.

3. Teacher research does not necessarily require a specific action or improvement as an outcome—it can produce a change in a teacher's perceptions, attitudes, or thinking that will eventually result in particular changes, but the immediate result of a practitioner inquiry project need not be a set of specific actions.

Using Action Research to Promote Whole-School Change

In educational action research, the school (rather than one student or classroom) is the organizational unit that is most often the target of the research. McLaughlin (2001) studied a 5-year school change initiative involving schools in 118 districts throughout California's Bay Area (San Francisco's metropolitan area). The initiative sought "to 'reculture' schools," to "change the way schools do business," replacing the existing school culture with one built on "evidence-based decision-making centered on a focused reform effort" (p. 79).

To accomplish this goal, the program used a modified action research model, "a school-based cycle of inquiry" that supported teams of teachers in each school as they pursued "learning and change" (p. 79). Exhibit 12.3 shows a diagram of the inquiry cycle used in the project. Notice the similarity to McIntyre's (2008) model (Exhibit 12.2), with the emphasis on stages in a cyclic process.

Exhibit 12.3	The Cycle of Inquiry

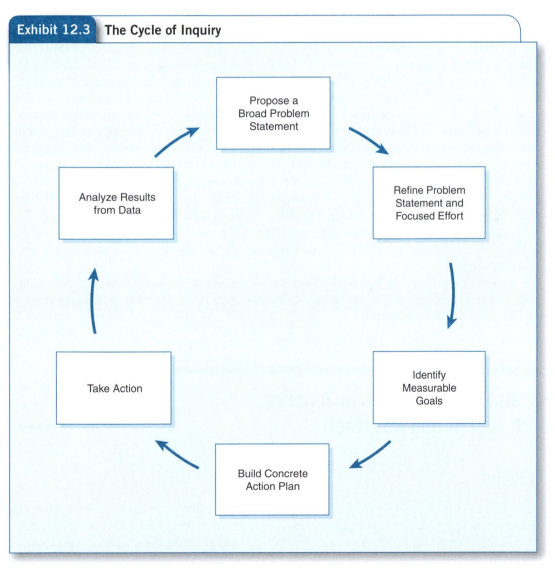

Source: Adapted from McLaughlin (2001, p. 80).

Case 4: Identity and Power in an Action Research Project

Sharon M. Ravitch, a university researcher, and Kathleen Wirth, a Philadelphia elementary school teacher, collaborated on an action research study (Ravitch & Worth, 2007) that illustrates many facets of the way action research is currently being used in education. Wirth, an experienced teacher and literacy leader, used both qualitative and quantitative methods to study a professional development program that she was conducting in her own school.

Wirth was particularly concerned that change efforts incorporate the perspectives of colleagues and not just become an attempt to impose her own or the district's pedagogical beliefs on them. At the same time, Wirth was taking a graduate research course with Ravitch, who acted as an outside voice and observer to Wirth's process. The result was (1) an extensive school-wide, change-oriented professional development program; (2) an ongoing, process-oriented study of that program conducted by Wirth; and (3) a meta-level look at the whole process conducted by Ravitch.

Wirth's greatest challenge, and one that confronts many teacher researchers involved in school change, was developing "a balance between being a colleague, school leader, friend, and researcher" (Ravitch & Worth, 2007, p. 78). She began by gathering information from teachers through a questionnaire and interviews and factored the results into her research design. Her project aimed for organizational change, and she found at first that many teachers were comfortable with the way things were, afraid of change, and uninterested in doing additional work (p. 79). Wirth soon realized that she was attempting to work collaboratively with fellow teachers in an existing school climate that supported a philosophy of "just close your door and teach" at the expense of collaboration and mutual support (p. 79). Overall, teacher resistance was a "major issue" (p. 79). Wirth had to begin by gaining the trust of her colleagues and incorporating their ideas into the research design. She incorporated a number of reflective steps to increase validity and build ownership among participants, including field notes, memos, "varied and overlapping data collection and analysis strategies so that triangulation was a central component," and "keeping collaboration and research logs that specifically related to my interaction with participants" (p. 86). Ultimately, Wirth had to share her power as a leader and researcher and become more of a facilitator and integrator of group ideas. Although this was not what she had originally envisioned, her research opened up opportunities for an active exchange of ideas, especially in "difficult and historically taboo topics like race, racism, social class, and equity" (p. 87).

As Wirth's case illustrates, both teacher researchers and action researchers explore their own settings, where they play multiple roles, so questions of validity require special consideration. In the next section, we will consider some of these questions.

Validity and Ethical Issues in Teacher Research and Action Research

Validity

As you have seen in the examples above, two important aspects of validity in teacher research are **triangulation** and reflexivity. Triangulation requires the use of multiple data sources. Reflexivity involves conscious, critical self-awareness by individuals and teams about their own preconceptions, biases, and assumptions both before the research begins and as it unfolds.

Multiple Data Sources

The use of multiple data sources is an important guarantor of validity in teacher research. Ferrance (2000, p. 17) suggests that school-based researchers consider a wide range of sources, including interviews, student portfolios, field notes, photographs, journals, audio and video recordings, test results, report cards, attendance records, and samples of student work and projects. Notice that Banford (1996), Kelly (Hubbard & Power, 1999), and Wirth (Ravitch & Wirth, 2007) all used multiple sources of data similar to those listed and also engaged in ongoing, written reflection before, during, and after data collection.

The important thing to understand is that no one data source can give you a whole and accurate picture of what is happening. Teacher researchers need multiple perspectives, represented by a range of data collection techniques, to illustrate different aspects of the same question or problem. As you have seen, this principle is called triangulation, usually implying that at least three sources or data collection techniques are brought to bear on the research question (Waters-Adams, 2006). In the Banford (1996), Kelly (Hubbard & Power, 1999), and Wirth (Ravitch & Worth, 2007) examples, more than three were used. Exhibit 12.4 shows an example of triangulation from a teacher research project in an elementary-grade science class.

In reference to Exhibit 12.4, Waters-Adams (2006) says,

In this case, [the question mark in the middle of the triangle in Exhibit 12.4] might be children's engagement during science sessions. Each method will give access to different aspects of the situation. There will still be areas not illuminated, but more is known than if only one method is used. Also, cross-referencing of data from different methods adds to the overall reliability of the research process. (http://www.edu.plymouth.ac.uk/RESINED/actionresearch/arhome.htm)

| Exhibit 12.4 | Triangulation in an Elementary-Grade Science Action Research Project |

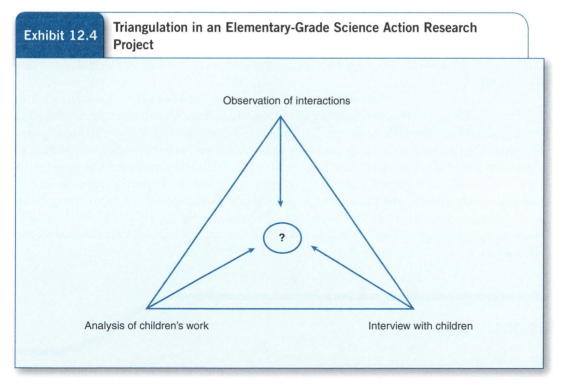

Reflexivity

A reflexive element, almost always expressed in written form, is an essential part of teacher research, including action research. Why? Teacher researchers are themselves actors in the context they explore. Action research is often done in teams where each member brings a different perspective. The success or failure of the interventions attempted must be evaluated by the researchers themselves. All of these elements contain potential threats to validity.

Teacher researchers use a number of techniques to try to gain separation from context and reflective clarity on their own perceptions and actions. In Case 2 above, Kelly (Hubbard & Power, 1999) kept a reflective journal throughout the project, talked with his teaching partner and parents to gain additional perspective, and even modeled self-reflection for his students. In Case 4, Wirth (Ravitch & Wirth, 2007) reported that "ongoing analysis of . . . field notes, research journals, memos, and collaborative logs helped me to address issues of validity in a structured way" (p. 86). In team research settings such as the one described in Case 3 (Caro-Bruce et al., 2009) in Madison, Wisconsin, reflective efforts by individuals are often complemented by group critical reflection and discussion to get over rough spots and to come to consensus on outcomes.

Ethical Considerations in Teacher Research

Teacher researchers must follow the same ethical practices as other educational researchers. As insiders, teacher researchers are typically part of the school setting and in charge of the classroom they are researching. This means that the entry process, an initial hurdle for outside researchers, will be fairly easy for the teacher researcher. However, there are other ethical pitfalls to be wary of. Their research subjects will probably be minors, so gaining informed consent will be a two-stage process involving both a consent form from the parent or guardian and an assent form from the student. This is required to collect, for example, student interviews and work samples for research purposes. Because teacher researchers have access to students' grades and other school records, they must be especially vigilant about confidentiality. Because they are in control of the classroom, they must guard against abuse of power relationships. If the project is funded through a college, university, or agency, the project proposal may need to go before an institutional review board for approval.

Research participants, whether students or colleagues, must be treated with fairness and respect. Both negative and positive data must be acknowledged and reported, and school and district policies that affect the research must be followed (M. Mohr et al., 2004, p. 144). While the project is under way, participants must be protected by rigorously maintaining anonymity and confidentiality in the data collection and analysis process but also by shielding them from controversy or negative fallout from the unfolding of the project itself. Wirth (Ravitch & Wirth, 2007) refers to such issues when she describes teachers' fears that she was "an instrument of the district," which produced a pronounced lack of trust, and her coming to understand the need to share power and authority if the project was to be successful. Finally, if you have ethical questions concerning your research or that of a colleague, seek dialogue, expert help, and resources to help you address the situation.

▣ Conclusions

We began this chapter by posing the question, "What methods do teachers use to research their own practice?" We have seen multiple answers to this question in the case studies. Banford (1996, p. 5) collected samples of Maricar's writing over the school year, audiotaped her writing response group, interviewed her, and kept his own teacher's journal. Kelly (Hubbard & Power, 1999) used a wide area of methods that included a teacher's journal, a classroom survey, and portfolios of student work. Caro-Bruce et al. (2009) reported on a district-wide teacher research program in which school-based groups assisted by outside facilitators developed a question, then learned about and considered a range of methods before deciding which ones were appropriate to their situation. Wirth (Ravitch & Worth, 2007) used an action research model to promote school change and had a university collaborator (Ravitch) who was closely involved. Because reflexivity plays such a large role in action research, Wirth collected data not just on the school and on teacher attitudes and practices but also on herself and her changing attitudes in the face of identity and power issues that arose during the research.

Teacher research, including action research, represents an exciting, fast-growing, and relatively new approach to educational inquiry. Teacher research helps to address some of the traditional failings of educational research in that it is change oriented, its results are immediately applicable, and it positions practitioners as knowledge creators as well as knowledge users. Teacher research also has limitations—reporting of results is usually confined to the local community, and many research questions are not possible to undertake within the parameters of teacher research.

Teacher researchers position themselves as epistemologically unique, in that as practitioners they have access to a type of knowledge that is grounded in a combination of practice and reflection. Teacher researchers identify the problem to be investigated, formulate the research question(s) to be asked, decide on the methods used to investigate those questions, gather the data, and interpret the results. They use a variety of methods, both qualitative and quantitative, to ensure triangulation, and reflection is central to their work. They abide by the same ethical codes and face the same ethical challenges as other researchers. They share their work publicly, although the sharing may be in a local context only. Because teacher researchers are located "on the ground," in the classrooms and schools where education actually takes place, they minimize the gulf between theory and practice.

Because they are teachers and not professional researchers, teacher researchers often seek resource help throughout the research process, typically from a university faculty member or other outside researcher. The context for many teacher research projects is a funded project (Banford's case), a graduate course (Wirth's case), or a district- or school-wide initiative (Madison, Wisconsin) that provides this support. Typically, such help is sought at critical stages of the project such as the literature review, deciding what methods are realistic to use, and interpretation of the data.

Paradoxically, the growth of teacher research has been both challenged and reinforced by accountability-based federal and state mandates (No Child Left Behind, state-level education reforms). Investigating their own practice, teacher researchers build a knowledge base that is independent of sweeping curricular mandates and narrow testing-based measurements of student achievement. At the same time, governmental reforms call for the use of "research-proven" methods in curriculum and instruction and "data-driven decision making" at the school level. Teachers and administrators with experience as school-based researchers are in an excellent position to respond to these mandates, both as evaluators of outside research and initiators of their own investigations, even if they disagree with them.

Cochran-Smith and Lytle (2009) assert that "the Practitioner Research movement is thriving worldwide and it is pushing back against constraints" (p. 7).We can expect that it will continue to grow because

research by teachers represents a distinctive way of knowing about teaching that will alter—not just add to—what we know in the field. (Cochran-Smith & Lytle, 1993, p. 85)

Key Terms

Action reflection model 264	Participatory action research 263	Teacher research 255
Action research 256	Reflective practice 258	Triangulation 266
Inquiry stance 256	Recursive process 263	

Highlights

- Teacher researchers use a wide variety of approaches and data collection methods.
- The idea of teachers as reflective practitioners has a long history.
- Teacher research minimizes the gap between research and practice.

- Teacher research offers a unique way of creating knowledge about teaching.
- Action research is a cyclic, recursive, team-based research method.
- Educational action research projects are often aimed at whole-school change.

Student Study Site

To assist in completing the web exercises, please access the study site at www.sagepub.com/check, where you will find the web exercise with accompanying links. You'll find other useful study materials such as self-quizzes and e-flashcards for each chapter, along with a group of carefully selected articles from research journals that illustrate the major concepts and techniques.

Discussion Questions

1. After reading this chapter, do you feel ready to do research in a classroom? If you were to try to follow the self-planning outline, what further reading would you need to do? What assistance would you need from an experienced researcher? Where could you find such assistance?

2. Do you know a teacher who has researched his or her own classroom or school? If you could talk to an experienced teacher researcher, what questions would you ask?

Practice Exercises

1. Locate and read the complete chapter or article for one of the cases used in this chapter. Write a response/reaction describing, each in a short paragraph, two things you learned from the article, two things that surprised you about the article, and your one strongest "take-home" point from the article.

2. Using the planning outline, think about your own classroom (or an imaginary classroom if you do not yet have a classroom of your own) and do Items 2 and 3 on the outline. As the final step, write a brief reflection on answering the following questions: Was it harder than you thought? Are you happy with your research question? What did you learn by answering the questions?

Web Exercises

1. Visit these three websites where teacher researchers report their work: Teacher and Action Research (http://gse.gmu.edu/research/tr), Networks: An On-line Journal for Teacher Research (http://journals.library.wisc.edu/index.php/networks), and Teachers Network (http://www.teachersnetwork.org/tnli/research). Find at least one article on

each site that interests you and read it. How do these write-ups differ from articles in peer-reviewed academic journals that you are familiar with? Did you find the articles useful? How valid do you think the results reported are? Did the authors report any changes in themselves as teachers as a result of doing the research? Are the findings generalizable at all? What does your analysis tell you about the goals and processes of teacher research in comparison to traditional educational research?

2. Through your library, search the table of contents for the last 3 years of issues of these two journals: *Action Research* and *Educational Action Research*. What differences do you see in the types of articles they publish? Find one article from each journal that you are interested in, and look at it. What types of research methods were used in the research reported? Who were the members of the research team (teachers, community members, etc.)? What steps were taken to address ethical concerns?

Developing a Research Proposal

Using Steps 1 to 5 of the Teacher Research Project outline, create a Teacher Research Proposal for investigating a question in your classroom or a classroom you have access to. Use the cases and examples in this chapter to help you with methods for data collection. Be sure to include measures for reflexivity and triangulation, and identify an audience to which you will report your results. Be sure to include issues such as the following: What ethical concerns will you have to address? How long will the proposed project take?

PART III
Analyzing and Reporting Data

CHAPTER 13

Quantitative Data Analysis

Research Question: *How Can We Analyze and Present Educational Statistics?*

Chapter Contents

- Why We Need Statistics
- Preparing Data for Analysis
- Displaying Univariate Distributions
- Summarizing Univariate Distributions

- Relationships (Associations) Among Variables
- Presenting Data Ethically: How Not to Lie With Statistics

"Show me the data," says your principal, superintendent, or school committee. Presented with a research conclusion, most people—not just decision makers—want evidence to support it. As a researcher, you need to figure out what the piles of data you have gathered all mean—what story do they tell? As an educator, you need a basic knowledge of statistics to be an informed and critical consumer of published research.

This chapter introduces several common statistics used in educational research and highlights the factors that must be considered in using and interpreting statistics. Such quantitative data analysis, using numbers to describe patterns in data, is the most elementary use of educational statistics. We start with a preliminary section outlining the process of preparing data for analysis. Next, we review statistical methods to describe the distribution of single variables and the relationships of two variables. We close by outlining some of the ethical issues involved in presenting data honestly.

> **Quantitative data analysis:**
> Statistical techniques used to describe and analyze variation in quantitative measures.

We use what is called secondary data analysis for many of our examples in this chapter. It is secondary because other researchers collected the data and we then obtained them for reanalysis. Many high-quality data sets are available for reanalysis from the government, individual researchers, and other research organizations. Secondary data used in this chapter come from the 2007–2008 Schools and Staffing Survey (SASS) of the National Center for Educational Statistics (NCES) and the General Social Survey (GSS). The SASS is a sample survey of teachers, principals, and school districts that the U.S. Department of Education has conducted periodically since 1987–1988. The GSS is a national probability survey of the adult American population.

Why We Need Statistics

A statistic, in ordinary language, is a numerical description of a population, usually based on a sample of that population. Some statistics are useful for describing the results of measuring single variables or of using multi-item scales. These statistics include frequency distributions, graphs, measures of central tendency and variation, and reliability tests. Other statistics are used primarily to describe the association among variables and to control for other variables and thus to enhance the causal validity of our conclusions. All of these statistics are termed **descriptive statistics** because they describe the distribution of and relationship among variables.

We will also look at some common inferential statistics, used by researchers to estimate the degree of confidence that can be placed in generalizations from a sample to the larger population from which the sample was selected. In other words, the researcher uses statistics to "infer" conclusions beyond what's immediately visible in the descriptive statistics. Inferential statistics are also used to determine the probability that data showing a relationship between two or more variables reflect a pattern in the real world, rather than just chance fluctuations in the measured variables.

Here's an example of the difference between descriptive and inferential statistics. Suppose a high school teacher/researcher wants to know what the 400-student sophomore class in her school thinks of the new policy banning cell phones. To find out, she surveys a representative sample of 25% of the 10th graders and receives responses from 100 students—almost all of those surveyed. Descriptive statistics will help her analyze the responses themselves. But she will need to use inferential statistics to estimate the level of confidence she can have in her descriptive statistics as valid reflections of the whole 400-student population, as well as to estimate the likelihood that any association she finds between variables is due to chance.

Although many colleges and universities offer statistics in a separate course, and for good reason (there's a *lot* to learn), we don't want you to think of this chapter as somehow on a different topic than the rest of this book. Data analysis is an integral component of research methods, and it's important that any proposal for quantitative research include a plan for the data analysis that will follow data collection. (As you will learn in Chapter 14, data analysis in qualitative projects often occurs in tandem with data collection, rather than after it.) You have to anticipate your data analysis needs if you expect your research design to yield the requisite data.

Preparing Data for Analysis

If you have conducted your own survey or experiment, the information that you have on assorted questionnaires, survey instruments, observational checklists, or interview transcripts needs to be prepared in a format suitable for data analysis. Generally, this involves a process of assigning a number to a particular response to a question, observation, or the like. Questionnaires or other data entry forms can be designed to facilitate this process. Note that in Exhibit 13.1, each question has its own unique numeric code, and each answer choice is numbered. In addition, in this survey, each individual survey form had its own barcode so that every answer on every survey became a separate, identifiable piece of computer data comprising (barcode number + question number + answer choice). Exhibit 13.1 is a professionally developed survey, but the principle of designing the data collection instruments with the analysis process in mind can be followed by anyone designing a research project.

We suggest following these steps to prepare your own data for analysis:

Assign a unique identifying number. A unique identifying number should be assigned to each form, questionnaire, survey, or transcript, and this identifier should appear on the form. You should include the identifier as a variable in the data. Having an identifier enables you to go back to the original form if you find data entry errors or decide to enter additional information. If you are collecting data from the same people at different points in time, the unique identifier helps you to link their responses.

Review the forms. As you review the instruments or questionnaires to record responses, you may encounter mistakes or unanticipated problems. You need to establish rules that you will follow when you encounter such mistakes. Here are some problems you may encounter:

- Responses that are not clearly indicated. You may find mistakes such as a circle crossing more than one category or an x or a check mark falling between two responses. This presents a dilemma since the respondent has given a response, but because of the ambiguity of what was circled or checked, you are not sure which response to consider correct. Some researchers do not record the information and treat it as missing, whereas others try to discern the intent of the respondent.

- Respondents misreading instructions. Sometimes respondents do not follow instructions about how to respond to a question. They might check responses when they are asked to rank different responses or they may circle multiple answers when they have been asked to choose the best answer.

- Incomplete questionnaires. Some respondents may decide not to complete the entire instrument or may end the interview before it is completed. You have to decide whether to include the responses you have obtained and treat the rest as missing or to consider the entire instrument as missing. There are no hard rules. Your decision may be influenced by your sample size and the number of questions that the respondent failed to answer.

- Unexpected responses. You may get responses that you had not anticipated. For example, you might ask age and get a response like 30½. Decide how you will treat such responses.

Code open-ended questions. Two types of open-ended questions are common in structured surveys: (a) when the entire question is left open-ended and (b) where you have *Other (specify)* _____ as one of your possible responses. You will have to develop categories for each type; it is easier to develop response categories for "other" because the responses are likely to be fewer in number, and the responses most likely to be common already appear in the questionnaire.

Create a codebook. A codebook contains the set of instructions used to link a number to a category for a particular variable. This is a record for you to know the values assigned to the response categories for each variable. You may define each variable as you build a data set in a statistical program, or you may create a paper version of your codebook. You should also use the codebook to keep track of any new variables you create as you analyze the data.

Exhibit 13.1	Excerpt From 2007–2008 NCES Survey Questionnaire for Public School Principals

12. *Continued –* **How much ACTUAL influence do you think each group or person has on decisions concerning the following activities?**

b. ESTABLISHING CURRICULUM AT THIS SCHOOL

Mark (X) one box on each line.

		No influence	Minor influence	Moderate influence	Major influence	Not applicable
(1)	State department of education or other state-level bodies (e.g., state board of education)	0050	1 ☐	2 ☐	3 ☐	4 ☐	5 ☐
(2)	Local school board	0051	1 ☐	2 ☐	3 ☐	4 ☐	5 ☐
(3)	School district staff	0052	1 ☐	2 ☐	3 ☐	4 ☐	5 ☐
(4)	Principal	0053	1 ☐	2 ☐	3 ☐	4 ☐	
(5)	Teachers	0054	1 ☐	2 ☐	3 ☐	4 ☐	
(6)	Curriculum specialists	0055	1 ☐	2 ☐	3 ☐	4 ☐	5 ☐
(7)	Parent association	0056	1 ☐	2 ☐	3 ☐	4 ☐	5 ☐

c. DETERMINING THE CONTENT OF IN-SERVICE PROFESSIONAL DEVELOPMENT PROGRAMS FOR TEACHERS OF THIS SCHOOL

Mark (X) one box on each line.

		No influence	Minor influence	Moderate influence	Major influence	Not applicable
(1)	State department of education or other state-level bodies (e.g., state board of education)	0057	1 ☐	2 ☐	3 ☐	4 ☐	5 ☐
(2)	Local school board	0058	1 ☐	2 ☐	3 ☐	4 ☐	5 ☐
(3)	School district staff	0059	1 ☐	2 ☐	3 ☐	4 ☐	5 ☐
(4)	Principal	0060	1 ☐	2 ☐	3 ☐	4 ☐	
(5)	Teachers	0061	1 ☐	2 ☐	3 ☐	4 ☐	
(6)	Curriculum specialists	0062	1 ☐	2 ☐	3 ☐	4 ☐	5 ☐
(7)	Parent association	0063	1 ☐	2 ☐	3 ☐	4 ☐	5 ☐
(8)	College and university partners	0064	1 ☐	2 ☐	3 ☐	4 ☐	5 ☐

FORM SASS-2A

7

Source: Principal Questionnaire, p. 7, 2007-08 Schools and Staffing Survey, National Center for Education Statistics/U.S. Dept. of Education and Institute of Education Sciences (http://nces.ed.gov/surveys/sass/pdf/0708/sass2a.pdf).

Enter the data. There are several common methods of data entry. One is to use optical scan sheets. These are the familiar sheets many of us have used to record responses to standardized tests or to complete class evaluations. Data are coded on the sheets, and then the sheets are read by an optical scanner. A second method is to directly enter the data by hand into a spreadsheet such as Excel or Lotus or into a statistical package such as SPSS, SAS, or Stata. If the data are entered into a statistics program, you have to "define" the data by identifying each variable and its characteristics. The procedures for doing so vary with the specific statistical or spreadsheet package. Exhibit 13.2 illustrates a variable definition file from SPSS. The information provided for each variable includes the variable name, labels for each variable and its values, values used to represent missing data, and the variable's level of measurement (Measure).

Exhibit 13.2 | Data Definition File From SPSS

*data.sav [DataSet1] - SPSS Data Editor

File   Edit   View   Data   Transform   Analyze   Graphs   Utilities   Add-ons   Window   Help

	Name	Type	Width	Decimals	Label	Values	Missing	Columns	Align	Measure
1	case	Numeric	8	0	Id Number	None	None	8	Right	Scale
2	gender	Numeric	8	0	Respondent's Gender	{1, female}...	9	8	Right	Nominal
3	ethnic	Numeric	8	0	Respondent's Ethnicity	{1, African American	9	8	Right	Nominal
4	q1t1	Numeric	8	0	Attitude 1 Time 1	{1, strongly agree}...	9	8	Right	Scale
5	q2t1	Numeric	8	0	Attitude 2 Time 1	{1, strongly agree}...	9	8	Right	Scale
6	q3t1	Numeric	8	0	Attitude 3 Time 1	{1, strongly agree}...	9	8	Right	Scale
7	q4t1	Numeric	8	2	Intensity Time 1	None	9.00	8	Right	Scale
8	q1t2	Numeric	8	0	Attitude 1 Time 2	{1, strongly agree}...	9	8	Right	Scale
9	q2t2	Numeric	8	0	Attitude 2 Time 2	{1, strongly agree}...	9	8	Right	Scale
10	q3t2	Numeric	8	0	Attitude 3 Time 2	{1, strongly agree}...	9	8	Right	Scale
11	q4t2	Numeric	8	2	Intensity Time 2	None	9.00	8	Right	Scale

Data View \ **Variable View** /

SPSS Processor is ready

Source: Engel and Schutt (2005).

Cleaning the data. Whatever data entry method is used, the data must be checked carefully for errors—a process called **data cleaning**. When using check coding, a second person recodes a sample of the forms and then the percentage of agreement on all the items on the forms is computed; if the percentage falls below a preestablished criterion for accuracy, then all forms should be recoded and reevaluated a second time. You should also examine the frequency distribution for every variable to see if there are cases with values that fall outside the range of allowable values for a given variable (we discuss frequency distribution in the next section). This helps you identify instances in which a respondent should have skipped a question but a response was actually coded. Any mistakes you find can be corrected by going back to the original questionnaire.

Displaying Univariate Distributions

The first step in data analysis is usually to describe the distribution of each variable of interest. How many teachers in the United States are members of each racial and ethnic group? What fraction of the U.S. population has graduated from high school, college, and graduate school? Graphs and frequency distributions are the two most popular formats for displaying the distribution of variables. Whatever

Central tendency: The most common value (for variables measured at the nominal level) or the value around which cases tend to center (for a quantitative variable).

Variability: The extent to which cases are spread out through the distribution or clustered in just one location.

Skewness: The extent to which cases are clustered more at one or the other end of the distribution of a quantitative variable rather than in a symmetric pattern around its center. Skew can be positive (a right skew), with the number of cases tapering off in the positive direction, or negative (a left skew), with the number of cases tapering off in the negative direction.

format is used, the primary concern of the analyst is to display accurately the distribution's shape—that is, to show how cases are distributed across the values of the variable.

Three features are important in describing the shape of the distribution: **central tendency, variability,** and **skewness** (lack of symmetry). All three features can be represented in a graph or in a frequency distribution.

We will now examine graphs and frequency distributions that illustrate the three features of shape. Several summary statistics used to measure specific aspects of central tendency and variability will be presented in a separate section.

Graphs

There are many types of graphs, but the most widely used in descriptive statistics are bar charts, histograms, and frequency polygons. Each has two axes, the vertical axis (the *y*-axis) and the horizontal axis (the *x*-axis), and labels or a numerical scale to identify the values of the variable on one axis.

A **bar chart** contains solid bars separated by spaces. It is a good tool for displaying the distribution of variables measured in discrete categories (e.g., nominal variables such as religion or race/ethnicity) because such categories don't blend into each other. The bar chart of race/ethnicity in Exhibit 13.3 indicates that more than 8 out of 10 of U.S. K–12 teachers were White

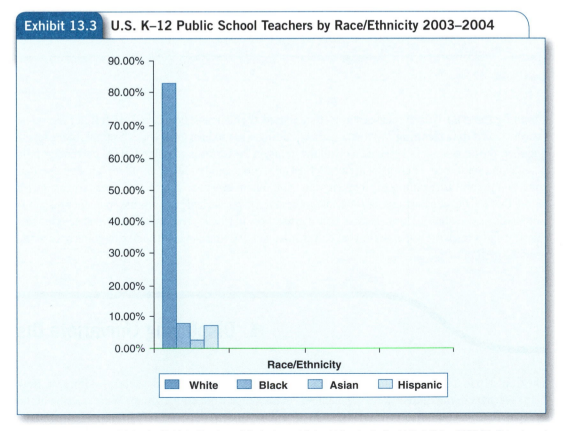

Exhibit 13.3 **U.S. K–12 Public School Teachers by Race/Ethnicity 2003–2004**

Race/Ethnicity

☐ White   ☐ Black   ☐ Asian   ☐ Hispanic

Source: Characteristics of Schools, Districts, Teachers, Principals, and School Libraries in the United States 2003-04. Schools and Staffing Study, Table 18 (http://nces.ed.gov/pubs2006/2006313.pdf).

in 2003–2004. Smaller percentages were Black, Asian, Hispanic, or mixed ethnicity. The most common value in the distribution is "White." All the values of the variable are represented by labels on the *x*-axis, and the percentage of cases within each of these racial/ethnic groups is represented by the height of the bar on the *y*-axis. (Bar charts can also be displayed with the labels on the *y*-axis and the frequencies or percents on the *x*-axis.) There is only a small amount of variability in the distribution since more than 80% of the respondents are White; the rest are mostly either Black or Hispanic. Because race/ethnicity is not a quantitative variable, the order in which the categories are presented is arbitrary, and the concept of skewness does not apply.

Histograms are used to display the distribution of quantitative variables that vary along a continuum that has no necessary gaps. The bars in a histogram represent the number of cases falling in the intervals into which that continuum is divided, and so the bars are shown as adjacent to each other. Exhibit 13.4 is a histogram of years of education of respondents from the 2006 GSS data. The distribution has a clump of cases centered at 12 years. The distribution is negatively or left-skewed because there are more cases just above the central point than below it (the "tail" of the distribution is to the left).

In a **frequency polygon,** a continuous line connects the points representing the number or percentage of cases with each value. The frequency polygon is an alternative to the histogram when the distribution of

Bar chart: A graphic for qualitative variables in which the variable's distribution is represented by solid bars separated by spaces.

Histogram: A graphic for continuous quantitative variables in which the variable's distribution is displayed with adjacent bars.

Frequency polygon: A graphic for quantitative variables in which a continuous line connects data points representing the variable's distribution.

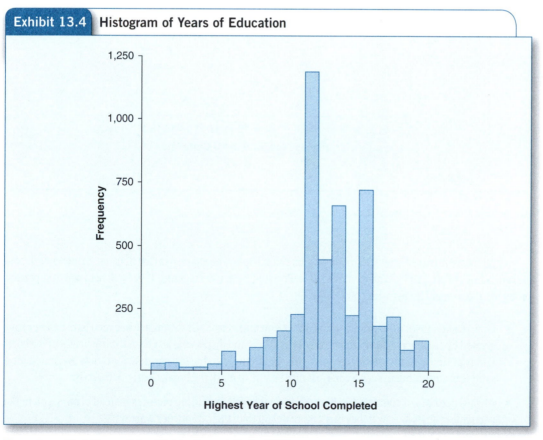

| Exhibit 13.4 | Histogram of Years of Education |

Source: General Social Survey, National Opinion Research Center (2006).

a quantitative variable must be displayed. It is easy to see in the frequency polygon of years of education in Exhibit 13.5 that the most common value is 12 years (high school completion) and that this value also seems to be the center of the distribution. There is moderate variability in the distribution, with many cases having more than 12 years of education and almost one third having completed at least 4 years of college (16 years). The distribution is highly skewed in the negative direction, with few respondents reporting less than 10 years of education.

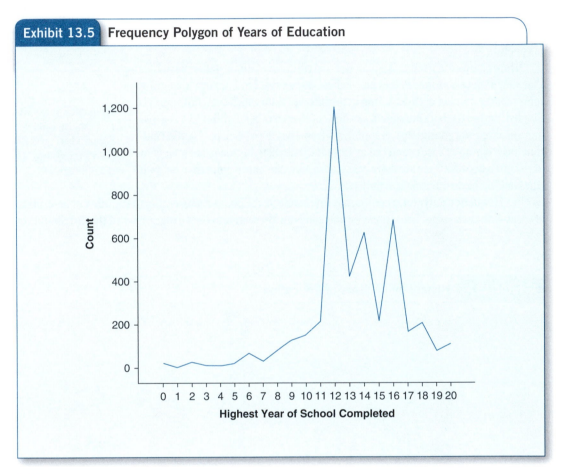

Exhibit 13.5 **Frequency Polygon of Years of Education**

Source: General Social Survey, National Opinion Research Center (2006).

If graphs are misused, they can distort rather than display the shape of a distribution. Adherence to several guidelines (Tufte, 1983; Wallgren, Wallgren, Persson, Jorner, & Haaland, 1996) will help you to spot such problems and to avoid them in your own work:

- Begin the graph of a quantitative variable at 0 on both axes. The difference between bars can be exaggerated by cutting off the bottom of the vertical axis and displaying less than the full height of the bars. It may at times be reasonable to violate this guideline, as when an age distribution is presented for a sample of adults, but in such a circumstance be sure to mark the break clearly on the axis.

- Always use bars of equal width. Bars of unequal width, including pictures instead of bars, can make particular values look as if they carry more weight than their frequency warrants.

- The two axes usually should be of approximately equal length. Either shortening or lengthening the vertical axis will obscure or accentuate the differences in the number of cases between values.

- Avoid "chart junk"—a lot of verbiage or excessive marks, lines, lots of cross-hatching, and the like. It can confuse the reader and obscure the shape of the distribution.

A variable's level of measurement is the most important determinant of the appropriateness of particular statistics. For example, we cannot talk about the skewness (lack of symmetry) of a qualitative variable (those measured at the nominal level). If the values of a variable cannot be ordered from lowest or highest—if the ordering of the values is arbitrary—we cannot say that the distribution is asymmetric because we could just reorder the values to make the distribution more (or less) symmetric. Most measures of central tendency and variability are also inappropriate for qualitative variables.

Frequency Distributions

The other way to present a univariate (one-variable) distribution is with a frequency distribution. A **frequency distribution** displays the number, **percentage** (the relative frequencies), or both of cases corresponding to each of a variable's values or group of values. The components of the frequency distribution should be clearly labeled, with a title, a stub (labels for the values of the variable), a caption (identifying whether the distribution includes frequencies, percentages, or both), and perhaps the number of missing cases. If percentages rather than frequencies are presented (sometimes both are included), the total number of cases in the distribution (the **base** N) should be indicated. In Exhibit 13.6, which shows responses from a behavior survey of 10th graders in South Carolina, $N = 1,272$. Remember that a percentage is simply a relative frequency. A percentage shows the frequency (f) of a given value relative to the total number of cases (N) times 100. The formula is $\% = f/N * 100$.

Exhibit 13.6 | **Frequency Distribution**

How much of a problem would it be if you went to court for drinking liquor under age?		
Value	**Frequency (f)**	**Percentage (%)**
No problem at all	14	1.1
Hardly any problem	53	4.2
A little problem	196	15.4
A big problem	421	33.1
A very big problem	588	46.2
Total	1,272	100.0%

Source: Bachman and Schutt (2008, p. 278).

When the distributions of variables with many values are to be presented, the values must first be grouped. Exhibit 13.7 shows a grouped frequency distribution from the same teen survey regarding the number of hours per week respondents spent studying. You can see why it is important to group the values, but we have to be sure that in doing so, we do not distort the distribution. Follow these two rules and you'll avoid problems:

| Exhibit 13.7 | Example of a Grouped Frequency Distribution From Hours Studied |

Value	Frequency (f)	Percentage (%)
0–7	881	69.26
8–15	317	24.92
16–23	42	3.30
24–31	18	1.42
32–39	2	0.16
40–47	5	0.39
48–55	1	0.08
56–63	2	0.16
64–71	2	0.16
72–79	1	0.08
80–87	1	0.08
Total	1,272	100.00

Source: Bachman and Schutt (2008, p. 282).

Note: Total may not equal 100.0% due to rounding error.

1. Categories should be logically defensible and preserve the shape of the distribution.

2. Categories should be mutually exclusive and exhaustive so that every case is classified in one and only one category.

Summarizing Univariate Distributions

Summary statistics describe particular features of a distribution and facilitate comparison among distributions. For example, if you wanted to report eighth-grade mathematics test scores by state, you would be well advised to present average test scores for each state; many people (including us) would find it difficult to make sense of a display containing 50 frequency distributions. A display of average test scores would also be preferable to multiple frequency distributions if you wanted merely to provide a general idea of test score differences among states.

Measures of Central Tendency

Central tendency is usually summarized with one of three statistics: the mode, the median, or the mean. For any particular application, one of these statistics may be preferable, but each has a role to play in data analysis.

To choose an appropriate measure of central tendency, the analyst must consider a variable's level of measurement, the skewness of a quantitative variable's distribution, and the purpose for which the statistic is used.

Mode

The **mode** is the most frequent value in a distribution. In a distribution representing race/ethnicity of American teachers, as we have seen, White is the most frequently occurring value—the largest single group. In the educational distribution in Exhibit 13.4, those with 12 years of education completed (high school graduation) are by far the largest group and, therefore, the mode. One silly, but easy, way to remember the definition of the *mode* is to think of apple pie "á la mode," which means pie with a big blob of vanilla ice cream on top. Just remember, the mode is where the big blob is—the largest collection of cases.

> **Mode:** The most frequent value in a distribution; also termed the *probability average.*

The mode is also sometimes termed the **probability average** because, being the most frequent value, it is the most probable. For example, if you were to pick a case at random from the distribution of hours studied (refer to Exhibit 13.7), the probability of the case being in the category 0–7 hours would be 881 out of 1,272, or 69.26%—the most probable value in the distribution.

The mode is used much less often than the other two measures of central tendency because it can so easily give a misleading impression of a distribution's central tendency. One problem with the mode occurs when a distribution is not **unimodal** but **bimodal.** A bimodal distribution has two categories with a roughly equal number of cases and more cases than the other categories. In this situation, there is no single mode.

> **Bimodal:** A distribution of a variable in which two nonadjacent categories have about the same number of cases and these categories have more cases than any others.
>
> **Unimodal:** A distribution of a variable in which only one value is the most frequent.

Nevertheless, there are occasions when the mode is very appropriate. The mode is the only measure of central tendency that can be used to characterize the central tendency of variables measured at the nominal level. In addition, because it is the most probable value, it can be used to answer questions such as which ethnic group is most common in a given school.

Median

The **median** is the position average: the point that divides the distribution in half (the 50th percentile). Think of the median of a highway—it divides the road exactly in two parts. To determine the median, we simply array a distribution's values in numerical order and find the value of the case that has an equal number of cases above and below it. If the median point falls between two cases (which happens if the distribution has an even number of cases), the median is defined as the average of the two middle values and is computed by adding the values of the two middle cases and dividing by 2. The median is not appropriate for variables that are measured at the nominal level; their values cannot be put in order, so there is no meaningful middle position.

> **Median:** The position average, or the point that divides a distribution in half (the 50th percentile).

The median in a frequency distribution is determined by identifying the value corresponding to a cumulative percentage of 50. Starting at the top of the years of education distribution in Exhibit 13.8, for example, and adding up the percentages, we find that we reach 44% in the 12 years category and then 72% in the 13–15 years category. The median is therefore 13–15, since that is the category containing the 50th percentile.

Mean

The **mean** is just the arithmetic average. (Many people, you'll notice, use the word *average* a bit more generally to mean any measure of "central tendency.") In calculating a mean, higher numbers pull it up, and lower numbers pull it down. Therefore, it takes into account the values of each case in a distribution—it is a weighted average.

> **Mean:** The arithmetic, or weighted, average, computed by adding up the value of all the cases and dividing by the total number of cases.

Exhibit 13.8	Years of Education Completed

Years of Education	Percentage
Less than 8	4.5%
8–11	12.8
12	26.7
13–15	28.0
16	15.2
17 or more	12.8
	100.0% (4,510)

Source: General Social Survey, National Opinion Research Center (2006).

(The median, by contrast, only depends on whether the numbers are higher or lower compared to the middle, not *how* high or low.)

The mean is computed by adding up the values of all the cases and dividing the result by the total number of cases, thereby taking into account the value of each case in the distribution:

$$\text{Mean} = \text{Sum of value of cases/Number of cases.}$$

In algebraic notation, the equation is $X = \Sigma X_i / N$. For example, to calculate the mean value of 8 cases, we add the values of all the cases (ΣX_i) and divide by the number of cases (N):

$$(28 + 117 + 42 + 10 + 77 + 51 + 64 + 55)/8 = 444/8 = 55.5.$$

Computing the mean obviously requires adding up the values of the cases. So it makes sense to compute a mean only if the values of the cases can be treated as actual quantities—that is, if they reflect an interval or ratio level of measurement—or if we assume that an ordinal measure can be treated as an interval (which is a fairly common practice). It makes no sense to calculate the mean of a qualitative (nominal) variable such as religion, for example. Imagine a group of four high school students in which there were 2 Protestants, 1 Catholic, and 1 Jew. To calculate the mean, you would need to solve the equation (Protestant + Protestant + Catholic + Jew)/4 = ?. Even if you decide that Protestant = 1, Catholic = 2, and Jew = 3 for data entry purposes, it still doesn't make sense to add these numbers because they don't represent quantities of religion. In general, certain statistics (such as the mean) can apply only to quantitative measures.

Median or Mean?

Because the mean is based on adding the value of all the cases, it will be pulled in the direction of exceptionally high (or low) values. In a positively skewed distribution, the value of the mean is larger than the median—more so the more extreme the skew. For instance, the presence of Microsoft owner Bill Gates—the world's richest person—pulls the mean wealth number up a bit in his neighborhood. A small number of extreme cases can have a disproportionate effect on the mean.

The disproportionate impact of skewness on the mean as compared to the median is illustrated in Exhibit 13.9. On the first balance beam, the cases (bags) are spread out equally, and the median and mean are in the same location. On the second balance beam, the median corresponds to the value of the middle case, but the mean is pulled a bit toward the value of the one case with an extremely high value. On the third beam, the mean is clearly pulled up toward an exceptionally high value.

Measures of Variation

Central tendency is only one aspect of the shape of a distribution—the most important aspect for many purposes but still just a piece of the total picture. The distribution, we have seen, also matters. A summary of distributions based only on their central tendency can be very incomplete, even misleading. It is important to know that the median household income in the United States is a bit over $50,000 a year, but if the variation in income isn't known—the fact that incomes range from zero up to hundreds of millions of dollars—we don't really know very much.

Exhibit 13.9	The Mean as a Balance Point

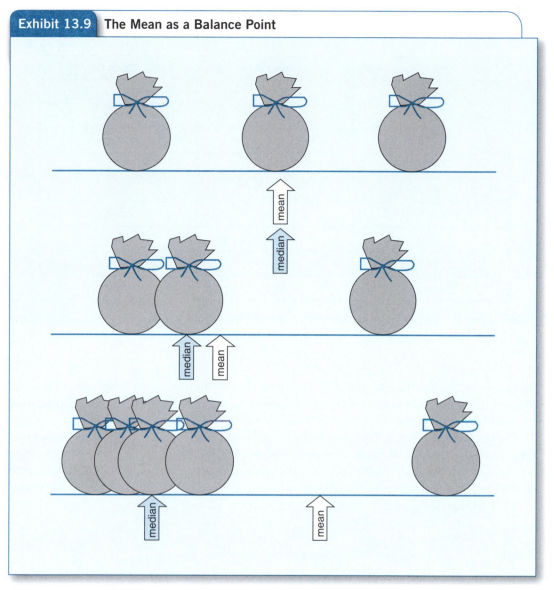

Source: Chambliss and Schutt (2010).

For example, a science teacher may have randomly divided her class of 27 students into three groups of 9 and instituted a portfolio grading system with extra credit options in which a superior student could achieve 115 points. Her three groups could have the same mean and median grades but still be very different in character due to the shape of the grade distributions. Exhibit 13.10 shows final grade distributions for the three groups, A, B, and C. If you calculate the mean and median grade for each group, you will find that all three are the same. In terms of grades, then, each group has the same central tendency. As you can see, however, there is something very different about these groups. Group A is a very heterogeneous group in which the grades are spread out from one end of the distribution to the other. Group B is characterized by students with very homogeneous grades; there are no real high or low achievers because each student is not far from the overall mean grade of 62. Group C is characterized by students with either very high or very low grades. The first four

Exhibit 13.10	Final Grades for Groups A, B, and C	
Group A	**Group B**	**Group C**
19.5	58.1	8.9
28.2	59.7	15.4
35.7	60.1	18.3
41.9	62.7	21.9
63.2	63.2	63.2
75.8	63.9	103.5
92.0	64.2	104.2
95.7	64.5	110.7
109.4	65.0	105.3

Source: Bachman and Schutt (2010).

students are much lower than the mean (62), whereas the last four students are much higher than the mean. Although they share identical measures of central tendency, these three groups have distributions of student grades that are very different.

The way to capture these differences is with statistical measures of variation. Four popular measures of variation are the range, the interquartile range, the variance, and the standard deviation (which is the single most popular measure of variability). To calculate each of these measures, the variable must be at the interval or ratio level. Statistical measures of variation are used infrequently with qualitative variables, so these measures will not be presented here.

Range

Range: The highest rounded value minus the lowest rounded value in a distribution, plus 1 (or the true upper limit in a distribution minus the true lower limit).

Outlier: An exceptionally high or low value in a distribution.

The **range** is the simplest measure of variation, calculated as the highest value in a distribution minus the lowest value, plus 1:

$$\text{Range} = \text{Highest value} - \text{Lowest value} + 1.$$

It often is important to report the range of a distribution—to identify the whole range of possible values that might be encountered. However, because the range can be altered drastically by just one exceptionally high or low value (termed an **outlier**), it does not do an adequate job of summarizing the extent of the variability in a distribution. For our three groups in Exhibit 13.10, the range in grades is 90.9 (109.4 – 19.5 + 1) for Group A, 7.9 (65.0 – 58.1 + 1) for Group B, and 97.4 (105.3 – 8.9 + 1) for Group C.

Interquartile Range

The **interquartile range** avoids the problem created by outliers by showing the range where most cases lie. **Quartiles** are distinguished by the points in a distribution that correspond to the first 25% of the cases, the first 50% of the cases, and the first 75% of the cases. You already know how to determine the second quartile, corresponding to the point in the distribution covering half of the cases—it is another name for the median. The interquartile range is the difference between the first quartile and the third quartile (plus 1).

> **Interquartile range:** The range in the distribution between the end of the first quartile and the beginning of the third quartile.
>
> **Quartiles:** The points in a distribution corresponding to the first 25% of the cases, the first 50% of the cases, and the first 75% of the cases.

Variance

If the mean is a good measure of central tendency, then it would seem that a good measure of variability would be the distance each score is away from the mean. Unfortunately, we cannot simply take the average distance of each score from the mean. One property of the mean is that it exactly balances the negative and positive distances of cases from it, so if we were to sum the difference between the mean of a distribution and each score in that distribution, the sum would always be zero. What we can do, though, is to square the deviation of each score from the mean (which makes each difference positive) and then add these squared deviations. This is the notion behind the variance as a measure of variability.

The **variance** is the average squared deviation of each case from the mean; you take each case's distance from the mean, square that number, and take the average of all such numbers. The equation to calculate the variance is

> **Variance:** A statistic that measures the variability of a distribution as the average squared deviation of each case from the mean.

$$\sigma^2 = \frac{\sum (X_i - \overline{X})^2}{N},$$

where X = mean, N = number of cases, Σ = sum over all cases, and X_i = value of case i on variable X.

In words, this formula says to take each score and subtract the mean, then square the difference, then sum all these differences, then divide this sum by N or the total number of scores.

We will calculate the variance for the grades in Group A in Exhibit 13.10.

We can now determine that the variance is

$$\Sigma^2 = \frac{8,517.44}{9} = 946.38.$$

The variance of these data, then, is 946.38. The variance is used in many other statistics, although it is more conventional to measure variability with the closely related standard deviation than with the variance.

Standard Deviation

The **standard deviation** is simply the square root of the variance. It is the square root of the average squared deviation of each case from the mean:

$$\sigma = \sqrt{\frac{\sum (X_i - \overline{X})^2}{N}},$$

where X = mean, N = number of cases, Σ = sum over all cases, X_i = value of case i on variable X, and $\sqrt{}$ = square root.

The standard deviation has mathematical properties that make it the preferred measure of variability in many cases, particularly when a variable is normally distributed. A **normal distribution** is a distribution that results from chance variation around a mean. A graph of a normal distribution looks like a bell, with one "hump" in the middle, centered around the population mean, and the number of cases tapering off on both sides of the mean (see Exhibit 13.11). A normal distribution is symmetric: If you were to fold the distribution in half at its center (at the population mean), the two halves would match perfectly. If a

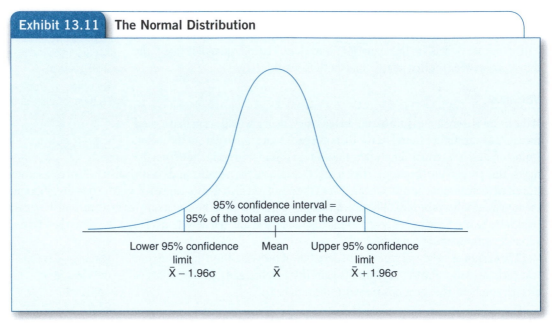

Exhibit 13.11   The Normal Distribution

95% confidence interval =
95% of the total area under the curve

Lower 95% confidence
limit
$\bar{X} - 1.96\sigma$

Mean

$\bar{X}$

Upper 95% confidence
limit
$\bar{X} + 1.96\sigma$

Source: Chambliss and Schutt (2010).

variable is normally distributed, 68% of the cases (almost two thirds) will lie between ±1 standard deviation from the distribution's mean, and 95% of the cases will lie between 1.96 standard deviations above and below the mean.

This correspondence of the standard deviation to the normal distribution enables us to infer how confident we can be that the mean of a population sampled randomly is within a certain range of the sample mean. This is the logic behind calculating confidence limits around the mean. Confidence limits indicate how confident we can be, given our particular random sample, that the value of some statistic in the population falls within a particular range. Now that you know how to compute the standard deviation, it is just a short additional step to compute the confidence limits around a mean. There are just four more steps:

1. Calculate the standard error. This is the estimated value of the standard deviation of the sampling distribution from which your sample was selected. $SE = \sigma \sqrt{(n-1)}$.

2. Decide on the degree of confidence that you wish to have that the population parameter falls within the confidence interval you compute. It is conventional to calculate the 95%, 99%, or the 99.9% confidence limits around the mean. Most often, the 95% confidence limits are used, so we will just show the calculation for this estimate.

3. Multiply the value of the SE × 1.96. This is because 95% of the area under the normal curve falls within ±1.96 standard deviation units of the mean.

4. Add and subtract the number in (3) from the sample mean. The resulting numbers are the upper and lower confidence limits.

So the standard deviation, in a single number, tells you quickly about how wide the variation is of any set of cases or the range in which most cases will fall in a normal distribution. It's very useful.

🔲 Relationships (Associations) Among Variables

Univariate distributions are useful, but they don't tell us how variables relate to each other—whether years of education is related to income level, for instance, or whether grade level is related to teachers' job satisfaction. To establish a causal effect, your first task is to determine whether there is an association between the independent and dependent variables (see Chapter 6). In research reports and journal articles, educational researchers usually summarize the strength of association between variables with a statistic called a **measure of association.** In this chapter, we will only consider one measure of association, the correlation coefficient. Inferential statistics are used to decide how likely it is that an association found in a sample exists in the larger population from which the sample was drawn. These inferential statistics also enable us to determine how likely it is that an association is due to chance. We will first review the logic of these inferential tests.

When the analyst feels reasonably confident (at least 95% confident, or $p < .05$) that an association was not due to chance, it is said that the association is statistically significant. **Statistical significance** basically means the relationship is not likely to be due to chance. Convention (and the desire to avoid concluding that an association exists in the population when it doesn't) dictates that the criterion for statistical significance be a probability of less than 5%. Statistical significance, though, doesn't equal substantive significance. That is, while we conclude that the relationship is likely to exist in the population, not just appearing by chance, it may still not matter very much.

Note that we have emphasized that the analyst "feels reasonably confident" that the association is "not likely to be due to chance" when there is a statistically significant relationship. There is still a degree of doubt since statistical testing is based on probability, which means that whatever we conclude, it is possible we could be wrong. When we draw a sample from a population, we have no guarantee that the sample is truly representative; rather, we are confident it is representative within some degree of error. Because the conclusion made from statistical testing is based on probability, it is possible to make the wrong conclusion (see Exhibit 13.12). For example, we can test the relationship between the number of hours studied and student scores on examinations. One hypothesis, the *null hypothesis*, is that there is no relationship in the population, whereas the alternative hypothesis, the *research hypothesis*, suggests that there is a relationship.

Exhibit 13.12 **Type I and Type II Errors**

In the Sample	In the Population	
	The groups differ	**The groups do not differ**
The groups differ by a statistically significant amount, so the researcher *rejects the null hypothesis*	*The researcher's decision is* **CORRECT**	*The researcher has made a* **Type I Error (α)**
The groups do not differ by a statistically significant amount, so the researcher *fails to reject the null hypothesis*	*The researcher has made a* **Type II Error (β)**	*The researcher's decision is* **CORRECT**

Source: Engel and Schutt (2010).

With our sample of students, we find a statistically significant relationship, and so we are 95% sure that a relationship exists in the population. Yet note: There still remains a 5% possibility that we have reached the wrong conclusion. We have to consider the possibility that we have concluded that there is a relationship based on our one sample, but in fact there is no relationship between the two variables in the population we sampled. This type of error, called Type I error, threatens our ability to conclude that there is an association. Type I error (symbolized by *alpha*) is the *p* (probability) value that we can obtain with statistical software.

Type I and Type II Error

Type I error is influenced by the strength of the relationship between an independent variable and a dependent variable. The greater the effect or impact of the intervention, the more likely the effect will be significant. Weaker relationships are less likely to provide statistically significant results.

Type I error is also influenced by sample size. A small sample is less likely to produce a statistically significant result for a relationship of any given strength. However, larger sample sizes are likely to find statistically significant relationships even when the strength of the relationship is weak. You may remember from Chapter 5 that sampling error decreases as sample size increases. For this same reason, an association is less likely to appear on the basis of chance in a larger sample than in a smaller sample. In a table with more than 1,000 cases, the odds of a chance association are often low indeed. Even rather weak associations can be statistically significant with a large random sample, which means that the analyst must be careful not to assume that just because a statistically significant association exists, it is therefore important. In other words, in a large sample, an association may be statistically significant but still too weak to be substantively significant.

Type I error is not the only wrong conclusion that we can make. Let us return to the test of the relationship between the number of hours studied and examination scores. In our sample, we find that there is not a statistically significant relationship and conclude that the number of hours studied is unrelated to the examination scores. But we have to consider the possibility that we have concluded that there is no relationship based on our one sample when in fact there is a relationship between the two variables in the population we sampled (see Exhibit 13.12). This is referred to as Type II error and is symbolized by *beta*.

Type I and Type II errors are particularly important because finding an association between two variables is a necessary condition to establish causality. The problem that researchers encounter is that the risk of making Type I and Type II errors cannot be completely eliminated. When a researcher chooses an alpha level of .05, it means that the researcher is willing to accept a 5% chance of concluding that there is a relationship in a particular sample when there is no relationship in the population. The researcher could reduce Type I error by making it more difficult to find a statistically significant relationship: Setting an alpha level of .01, for example, would mean that the researcher is willing to accept only a 1% chance of finding that there is a relationship when there is none in the population. By doing this, the likelihood of Type I error is reduced.

By minimizing Type I error, however, the researcher has increased the probability of Type II error. By making it less likely that we will falsely conclude that there is a relationship in the population, we have made it more likely that we will falsely conclude from sample data that there is no relationship in the population when there really is.

Which type of error should be minimized? There is no easy answer. It depends on the level of risk associated with concluding there is a relationship when there is none (Type I error) or concluding there is no relationship when there is a relationship (Type II error). For example, you might need to assess the risk or consequence of using an intervention shown to be effective in a research study that is really not effective (Type I error) versus the consequence of not using an intervention found to be ineffective in a research study

(Type II error) when it really is effective. Statisticians normally focus on the risk of Type I error, to minimize the risk of concluding there is a relationship (that the favored hypothesis is supported) when in fact there is no relationship in the population.

Therefore, it is important to keep Type I and Type II error in mind as you weigh the evidence about the effectiveness of a particular intervention in the research articles you read or the research you conduct. What is the probability that these errors may explain the findings? Is the sample size so big that even trivial effects are statistically significant? It is through replication that researchers try to reduce doubts generated by the potential for Type I and Type II errors.

Choosing a Statistical Test

There are many different statistical methods to test hypotheses. It is common for a researcher to start the analysis of an independent and a dependent variable with a bivariate statistical test, which is a test that measures the variation or difference between two variables. In this chapter, we do not have the space to go into these methods, but several of the most commonly used are the **chi-square** test, the *t* test (briefly described below), and the analysis of variance, typically abbreviated as ANOVA.

A multivariate statistical test is used when the analyst tests simultaneously the relation of several independent variables with a dependent variable; these tests allow the analyst to evaluate the effect of an independent variable while controlling for the effects of other independent variables on the dependent variable. For example, we could test separately the relationship of ethnicity and high school graduation and gender and high school graduation using bivariate tests. But with a multivariate test, we could examine the relationship of ethnicity and high school graduation holding gender constant. It is not unusual to find that a statistically significant relationship found with a bivariate statistical test is no longer statistically significant when the effects of other variables are controlled in a multivariate statistical test.

Different statistical tests depend on the level of measurement of the variables. For example, the commonly used *t* test requires that the independent variable be dichotomous and the dependent variable be at least an interval measure. To conduct a bivariate regression analysis, both the independent and dependent variable must be at least interval measures. The level of measurement of independent and dependent variables also influences the choice of multivariate tests.

The *t* test is a common statistical test often used to compare average outcomes on one variable between two groups. A simple *t* test (there are many varieties) can tell you how likely it is that the two groups differ on that variable. It could be used to test whether there is a mean difference in eighth-grade mathematics test scores between boys and girls or how likely it is that the mean attitude toward new programs differs between high school teachers in small charter schools and in large, comprehensive schools.

Discussing the full range of inferential statistical tests is beyond the focus of this book, and some of you may have already had a class in statistics. To read many statistical reports and to conduct more sophisticated analyses of educational data, you have to extend your statistical knowledge.

Regression Analysis

Many statistical reports and articles published in educational research journals use statistical techniques called **regression analysis** and **correlational analysis** to describe the association between two or more quantitative variables. The terms actually refer to different aspects of the same technique.

We'll give you only an overview here of this approach. Take a look at Exhibit 13.13. It's a plot, termed a *scatterplot,* of the relationship in a statistical sample of the U.S. population between years of education and occupational prestige (a score that ranges from 0 to 100, reflecting the prestige accorded to the respondent's occupation). You can see that we didn't collapse the values of either of these variables into categories. Instead,

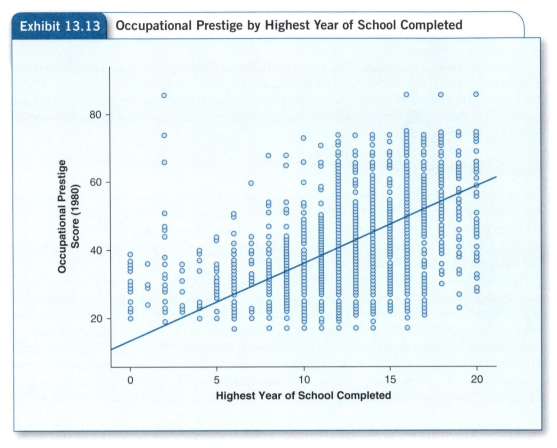

Exhibit 13.13 **Occupational Prestige by Highest Year of School Completed**

Source: National Opinion Research Center (2010).

the scatterplot shows the location of each case in the data in terms of years of education (the horizontal axis) and occupational prestige level (the vertical axis).

You can see that the data points in the scatterplot tend to run from the lower left to the upper right of the chart, indicating a positive relationship: The more the years of education, the higher the occupational prestige. The line drawn through the points is the regression line. The regression line summarizes this positive relationship between years of education, which is the independent variable (often simply termed X in regression analysis), and occupational prestige, the dependent variable (often simply termed Y in regression analysis). This regression line is the "best-fitting" straight line for this relationship—it is the line that lies closest to all the points in the chart, according to certain criteria.

How well does the regression line fit the points? In other words, how close does the regression line come to the points? (Actually, it's the average of the square of the vertical distances, on the y-axis, between the points and the regression line that is used as the criterion.) The **correlation coefficient,** also called "Pearson's r," or just "r," gives an answer to that question. The value of r for this relationship is .56, which indicates a moderately strong positive linear relationship (if it were a negative relationship, r would have a negative sign). The value of r is 0 when there is absolutely no linear relationship between the two variables, and it is 1 when the points representing all the cases lie exactly on the regression line (which would mean that the regression line describes the relationship perfectly). The correlation coefficient is a summary statistic that tells us about the strength of the association between the two variables. Values of r close to

0 indicate that the relationship is weak; values of r close to +1 or –1 indicate the relationship is strong—in between there is a lot of room for judgment.

You can also use correlation coefficients and regression analysis to study simultaneously the association between three or more variables. For example, you could test to see whether several other variables in addition to education are associated with occupational prestige scores.

You will need to learn more about when correlation coefficients and regression analysis are appropriate (e.g., both variables have to be quantitative, and the relationship has to be linear [not curvilinear]). But that's for another time and place. To learn more about correlation coefficients and regression analysis, you'll have to take a statistics course. For now, this short introduction will enable you to make sense of more of the statistical analyses you find in research articles.

Presenting Data Ethically: How Not to Lie With Statistics

Using statistics ethically means first and foremost being honest and open. Findings should be reported honestly, and the researcher should be open about the thinking that guided the decision to use particular statistics. Although this section has a mildly humorous title (after Darrell Huff's 1954 little classic, *How to Lie With Statistics*), make no mistake about the intent: It is possible to distort educational reality with statistics, and it is unethical to do so knowingly, even when the error is due more to carelessness than deceptive intent.

There are a few basic rules to keep in mind:

- Inspect the shape of any distribution for which you report summary statistics to ensure that the statistics do not mislead your readers because of an unusual degree of skewness.

- When you create graphs, be sure to consider how the axes you choose may change the distribution's apparent shape; don't deceive your readers. You have already seen that it is possible to distort the shape of a distribution by manipulating the scale of axes, clustering categories inappropriately, and the like.

- Whenever you need to group data in a frequency distribution or graph, inspect the ungrouped distribution and then use a grouping procedure that does not distort the distribution's basic shape.

- Hypotheses formulated in advance of data collection must be tested as they were originally stated. When evaluating associations between variables, it becomes very tempting to search around in the data until something interesting emerges. Researchers sometimes call this a "fishing expedition." Although it's not wrong to examine data for unanticipated relationships, inevitably some relationships between variables will appear just on the basis of chance association alone. Exploratory analyses must be labeled in research reports as such.

- Be honest about the limitations of using survey data to test causal hypotheses. Finding that a hypothesized relationship is not altered by controlling for some other variables does not establish that the relationship is causal. There is always a possibility that some other variable that we did not think to control, or that was not even measured in the survey, has produced a spurious relationship between the independent and dependent variables in our hypothesis (Lieberson, 1985). We have to think about the possibilities and be cautious in our causal conclusions.

▣ Conclusions

With some simple statistics (means, standard deviations, *t* tests, and the like), a researcher can describe educational phenomena, identify relationships among them, explore the reasons for these relationships (especially through multivariate statistics), and test hypotheses about them. Statistics—carefully constructed numbers that describe an entire population of data—are remarkably helpful in giving a simple summation of complex situations. Statistics provide a useful tool for understanding the educational world, a tool that we can use both to test our ideas and to generate new ones.

Unfortunately, to the uninitiated, the use of statistics can seem to end debate right there—one can't argue with the numbers. But you now know better. Numbers are worthless if the methods used to generate the data are not valid, and numbers can be misleading if they are not used appropriately, taking into account the type of data to which they are applied. For example, in a small elementary school with many new teachers but several 30-year veterans, the mean experience level will be fairly high—but grossly misleading. And even assuming valid methods and proper use of statistics, there's one more critical step, because the numbers do not speak for themselves. Ultimately, how we interpret and report statistics determines their usefulness.

Key Terms

Bar chart   280
Base number (*N*)   283
Bimodal   285
Central tendency   280
Chi-square   293
Correlation coefficient   294
Correlational analysis   293
Data cleaning   279
Descriptive statistics   276
Frequency distribution   283

Frequency polygon   281
Histogram   281
Interquartile range   288
Mean   285
Measure of association   291
Median   285
Mode   285
Normal distribution   289
Outlier   288
Percentage   283

Probability average   285
Quartile   288
Range   288
Regression analysis   293
Skewness   280
Standard deviation   289
Statistical significance   291
Unimodal   285
Variability   280
Variance   289

Highlights

- Data entry options include direct collection of data through a computer, use of scannable data entry forms, and use of data entry software. All data should be cleaned during the data entry process.

- Use of secondary data can save considerable time and resources but may limit data analysis possibilities.

- Bar charts, histograms, and frequency polygons are useful for describing the shape of distributions. Care must be taken with graphic displays to avoid distorting a distribution's apparent shape.

- Frequency distributions display variation in a form that can be easily inspected and described. Values should be grouped in frequency distributions in a way that does not alter the shape of the distribution. Following several guidelines can reduce the risk of problems.

- Summary statistics often are used to describe the central tendency and variability of distributions. The appropriateness of the mode, mean, and median varies with a variable's level of measurement, the distribution's shape, and the purpose of the summary.

- The variance and standard deviation summarize variability around the mean. The interquartile range is usually preferable to the range to indicate the interval spanned by cases, due to the effect of outliers on the range. The degree of skewness of a distribution is usually described in words rather than with a summary statistic.

- Some of the data in many reports can be displayed more efficiently by using combined and compressed statistical displays.

- Honesty and openness are the key ethical principles that should guide data summaries.

- Inferential statistics are used with sample-based data to estimate the confidence that can be placed in a statistical estimate of a population parameter. Estimates of the probability that an association between variables may have occurred on the basis of chance are also based on inferential statistics.

- Regression analysis is a statistical method for characterizing the relationship between two quantitative variables with a linear equation and for summarizing the extent to which the linear equation represents that relationship. Correlation coefficients summarize the fit of the relationship to the regression line.

Student Study Site

To assist in completing the web exercises, please access the study site at www.sagepub.com/check, where you will find the web exercise with accompanying links. You'll find other useful study materials such as self-quizzes and e-flashcards for each chapter, along with a group of carefully selected articles from research journals that illustrate the major concepts and techniques.

Discussion Questions

1. Become a media critic. For the next week, scan a newspaper or some magazines for statistics. How many articles can you find that use frequency distributions, graphs, and the summary statistics introduced in this chapter? Are these statistics used appropriately and interpreted correctly? Would any other statistics have been preferable or useful in addition to those presented?

2. When should we control just to be honest? Should educational researchers be expected to investigate alternative explanations for their findings? Should they be expected to check to see if the associations they find occur for different subgroups in their samples? Justify your answer.

Practice Exercises

1. Examine a quantitative study from an education journal. Does the author provide you with summary statistics? With information about the association among variables? What statistics does the researcher use? Do the statistics he or she uses support the researcher's hypothesis?

2. Exhibit 13.14 (next page) is a three-variable table created with survey data from 355 employees hired during the previous year at a large telecommunications company. Employees were asked if the presence of on-site child care at the company's offices was important in their decision to join the company.

Reading the table:

   a. Does gender affect attitudes?
   b. Does marital status affect attitudes?
   c. Which of the preceding two variables matters more?
   d. Does being married affect men's attitudes more than women's?

| Exhibit 13.14 | Is Child Care Important? By Gender and Marital Status | | | |

	MEN		WOMEN	
	Single	Married	Single	Married
Not important	54%	48%	33%	12%
Somewhat important	24%	30%	45%	31%
Very important	22%	22%	22%	57%
	100%	100%	100%	100%
$n =$	(125)	(218)	(51)	(161)

Source: Chambliss and Schutt (2010).

Web Exercises

1. Go to the website of the National Center for Education Statistics (http://www.nces.ed.gov). From the drop-down menu, choose Data Tools, select Build Custom Tables and Datasets, then click on National Assessment for Educational Progress (NAEP) Data Explorer. Follow the instructions and build a data report in an area of the NAEP that interests you. What did you learn from building this report? What did you find out that surprised you?

2. Go to the website of the National Center for Education Statistics (http://www.nces.ed.gov). From the drop-down menu, choose Data Tools, select Build Custom Tables and Datasets, then click on Powerstats, then on Quickstats. Follow the instructions and create a simple table using at least three variables. Add to or replace some of the variables in both columns and rows to see what effect that has on the table.

Developing a Research Proposal

1. Develop a plan to prepare your data for analysis. How will you ensure the quality of the data?

2. Describe how you would analyze and present your data. What descriptive or inferential procedures would you use?

CHAPTER 14

Qualitative Data Analysis

Research Question: *How Does Conflict Develop in Schools?*

Chapter Contents

- **Features of Qualitative Data Analysis**
- **Techniques of Qualitative Data Analysis**
- **Alternatives in Qualitative Data Analysis**

- **Visual Data Analysis**
- **Computer-Assisted Qualitative Data Analysis**
- **Ethics in Qualitative Data Analysis**

> *I was at lunch standing in line and he [another male student] came up to my face and started saying stuff and then he pushed me. I said … I'm cool with you, I'm your friend and then he push me again and calling me names. I told him to stop pushing me and then he push me hard and said something about my mom. And then he hit me, and I hit him back. After he fell I started kicking him.*
>
> —Morrill, Yalda, Adelman, Musheno,
> and Bejarano (2000, p. 521)

This statement was made by a real student writing an in-class essay about conflicts in which he had participated. It was written for a team of researchers who were studying conflicts in high schools in order to better understand their origins and to inform prevention policies. In this chapter, you will see several studies of various kinds of school conflict, including bullying. You will also see studies that use qualitative analytic methods to research topics such as curriculum innovation, literacy development, and the maturation of special-needs students.

In qualitative data analysis, the raw data to be analyzed are text—words—rather than numbers. In the high school conflict study quoted above, there were initially no variables or hypotheses. The use of text, not numbers, and the (initial) absence of variables are just two of the ways in which qualitative analysis differs from quantitative.

In this chapter, we present and illustrate the features that most qualitative analyses share. There is no one correct way to analyze textual data. To quote Michael Quinn Patton (2002),

> Qualitative analysis transforms data into findings. No formula exists for that transformation. Guidance, yes. But no recipe. Direction can and will be offered, but the final destination remains unique for each inquirer, known only when—and if—arrived at. (p. 432)

We first discuss different types of qualitative analysis and then describe computer programs for qualitative data analysis. These increasingly popular programs are blurring the traditional distinctions between quantitative and qualitative approaches to textual analysis.

回 Features of Qualitative Data Analysis

Qualitative data analysis:
Techniques used to search and code textual, aural, and pictorial data and to explore relationships among the resulting categories.

The focus on text—on qualitative data rather than on numbers—is the most important feature of qualitative data analysis. The "text" that qualitative researchers analyze is most often transcripts of interviews or notes from participant observation sessions, but text can also refer to pictures or other images that the researcher examines.

What can one learn from a "text"? There are two kinds of answers to this question. Some researchers view textual analysis as a way to understand what participants "really" thought, felt, or did in some situation or at some point in time. The text becomes a way to get "behind the numbers" that are recorded in a quantitative analysis to see the richness of real educational experience. In this approach, interviews or field studies can, for instance, illuminate what survey respondents really meant by their answers.

Other qualitative researchers have adopted a "hermeneutic" perspective on texts—viewing interpretations as never totally true or false. The text has many possible interpretations (Patton, 2002, p. 114). The meaning of a text, then, is negotiated among a community of interpreters, and to the extent that some agreement is reached about meaning at a particular time and place, that meaning can only be based on consensual community validation. From the hermeneutic perspective, a researcher is constructing a "reality" with his or her interpretations of a text provided by the subjects of research; other researchers, with different backgrounds, could come to markedly different conclusions.

Emic focus: Representing a setting with the participants' terms.

Etic focus: Representing a setting with the researcher's terms.

Qualitative and quantitative data analyses differ, then, in the priority given to the views of the subjects of the research versus those of the researcher. Qualitative data analysts seek to capture the setting or people who produced this text on their own terms rather than in terms of predefined (by researchers) measures and hypotheses. What this means is that qualitative data analysis tends to be inductive—the analyst identifies important categories in the data, as well as patterns and relationships, through a process of discovery. There are often no predefined measures or hypotheses. Anthropologists term this an **emic focus,** which means representing the setting in terms of the participants, rather than an **etic focus,** in which the setting and its participants are represented in terms that the researcher brings to the study.

Good qualitative data analyses also are distinguished by their focus on the interrelated aspects of the setting or group, or person, under investigation—the case—rather than breaking the whole up into separate parts. The whole is always understood to be greater than the sum of its parts, and so the social context of events, thoughts, and actions becomes essential for interpretation. Within this framework, it doesn't really make sense to focus on two variables out of an interacting set of influences and test the relationship between just those two.

Qualitative data analysis is an iterative and reflexive process that begins as data are being collected rather than after data collection has ceased (Stake, 1995). Next to her field notes or interview transcripts, the qualitative analyst jots down ideas about the meaning of the text and how it might relate to other issues. This process of reading through the data and interpreting them continues throughout the project. When it appears that additional concepts need to be investigated or new relationships explored, the analyst adjusts the data collection itself. This process is termed **progressive focusing** (Parlett & Hamilton, 1976).

> **Progressive focusing:** The process by which a qualitative analyst interacts with the data and gradually refines his or her focus.

Elijah Anderson (2003) describes the progressive focusing process used in one of his field-based, qualitative studies:

> Throughout the study, I also wrote conceptual memos to myself to help sort out my findings. Usually no more than a page long, they represented theoretical insights that emerged from my engagement with the data in my field notes. As I gained tenable hypotheses and propositions, I began to listen and observe selectively, focusing on those events that I thought might bring me alive to my research interests and concerns. This method of dealing with the information I was receiving amounted to a kind of a dialogue with the data, sifting out ideas, weighing new notions against the reality with which I was faced there on the streets and back at my desk. (pp. 235–236)

Following a few guidelines will help when a researcher starts analyzing qualitative data (W. L. Miller & Crabtree, 1999b, pp. 142–143):

- Know yourself, your biases, and preconceptions.

- Know your question.

- Seek creative abundance. Consult others and keep looking for alternative interpretations.

- Be flexible.

- Exhaust the data. Try to account for all the data in the texts, then publicly acknowledge the unexplained and remember the next principle.

- Celebrate anomalies. They are the windows to insight.

- Get critical feedback. The solo analyst is a great danger to self and others.

- Be explicit. Share the details with yourself, your team members, and your audiences.

Qualitative Data Analysis as an Art

If you miss the certainty of predefined measures and deductively derived hypotheses, you are beginning to understand the difference between quantitative and qualitative data analysis. Qualitative data analysis is even described by some as involving as much "art" as science—as a "dance." In the words of William Miller and Benjamin Crabtree (1999b),

> Interpretation is a complex and dynamic craft, with as much creative artistry as technical exactitude, and it requires an abundance of patient plodding, fortitude, and discipline. There are many changing rhythms; multiple steps; moments of jubilation, revelation, and exasperation. . . . The dance of interpretation is a dance for two, but those two are often multiple and frequently changing, and there is always an audience, even if it is not always visible. Two dancers are the interpreters and the texts. (pp. 138–139)

The "dance" of qualitative data analysis is represented in Exhibit 14.1, which captures the alternation between immersion in the text to identify meanings and editing the text to create categories and codes. The process involves three different modes of reading the text:

1. When the researcher reads the text *literally* (L, in Exhibit 14.1), she is focused on its literal content and form, so the text "leads" the dance.

2. When the researcher reads the text *reflexively* (R), she focuses on how her own orientation shapes her interpretations and focus. Now, the researcher leads the dance.

3. When the researcher reads the text *interpretively* (I), she tries to construct her own interpretation of what the text means.

In this artful way, analyzing text involves both inductive and deductive processes. The researcher generates concepts and linkages between them based on reading the text; he or she also checks the text to see whether his or her concepts and interpretations are reflected in it.

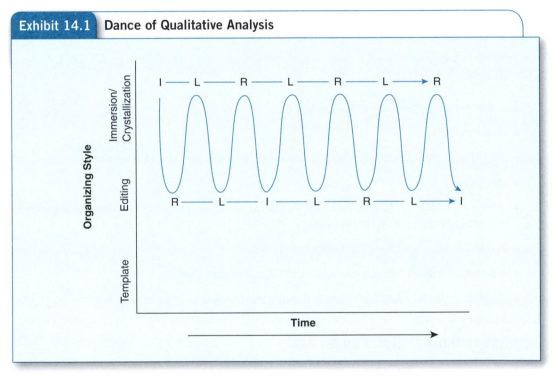

| Exhibit 14.1 | Dance of Qualitative Analysis |

Source: W. L. Miller and Crabtree (1999b, p. 139). Based on Addison (1999).

Qualitative Compared With Quantitative Data Analysis

With these points in mind, let's review the differences in the logic behind qualitative versus quantitative analysis (Denzin & Lincoln, 2000, pp. 8–10; Patton, 2002, pp. 13–14).

- A focus on meanings rather than on quantifiable phenomena
- Collection of many data on a few cases rather than few data on many cases

- Study in depth and detail, without predetermined categories or directions, rather than emphasis on analyses and categories determined in advance

- Conception of the researcher as an "instrument," rather than as the designer of objective instruments to measure particular variables

- Sensitivity to context rather than seeking universal generalizations

- Attention to the impact of the researcher's and others' values on the course of the analysis rather than presuming the possibility of value-free inquiry

- A goal of rich descriptions of the world rather than measurement of specific variables

Of course, even the most qualitative textual data can be transposed to quantitative data through a process of categorization and counting. Some qualitative analysts also share with quantitative researchers a goal of describing better the world as it "really" is, but as we have already noted, others have adopted a postmodern "hermeneutic" goal of trying to understand how different people see and make sense of the world, without believing that there is one uniquely correct description.

▣ Techniques of Qualitative Data Analysis

Most approaches to qualitative data analysis use five steps:

1. Documentation of the data and the process of data collection

2. Organization/categorization of the data into concepts

3. Examining relationships to show how one concept may influence another

4. Authenticating conclusions by evaluating alternative explanations, disconfirming evidence, and searching for negative cases

5. Reflexivity

The analysis of qualitative research notes begins in the field, at the time of observation, interviewing, or both, as the researcher identifies problems and concepts that appear likely to help in understanding the situation. Simply reading the notes or transcripts is an important step in the analytic process. Researchers should make frequent notes in the margins to identify important statements and to propose ways of coding the data: "teacher/student conflict," perhaps, or "small-group teaching strategy."

An interim stage may consist of listing the concepts reflected in the notes and diagramming the relationships among concepts (Maxwell, 1996, pp. 78–81). This process continues throughout the project and should assist in refining concepts during the report-writing phase, long after data collection has ceased. Let's examine each of the stages of qualitative research in more detail.

Documentation

The data for a qualitative study most often are notes jotted down in the field or during an interview or text transcribed from audio or video recordings. "The basic data are these observations and conversations, the actual words of people reproduced to the best of my ability from the field notes" (Diamond, 1992, p. 7). What to do with all this material? Many novice researchers have become overwhelmed by the quantity of information collected, and as a result, their research projects have ground to a halt. A 1-hour interview can generate 20 to 25 pages of single-spaced text (Kvale, 1996, p. 169).

Analysis is less daunting, however, if the researcher maintains a disciplined transcription schedule.

> Usually, I wrote these notes immediately after spending time in the setting or the next day. Through the exercise of writing up my field notes, with attention to "who" the speakers and actors were, I became aware of the nature of certain social relationships and their positional arrangements within the peer group. (Anderson, 2003, p. 235)

You can see Anderson's analysis already emerging from this simple process of taking notes.

The first formal analytical step is documentation. The various contacts, interviews, written documents, and whatever it is that preserves a record of what happened all need to be saved and catalogued in some fashion. Documentation is critical to qualitative research for several reasons: It is essential for keeping track of what will be a rapidly growing volume of notes, audio or video recordings, and documents; it provides a way of developing an outline for the analytic process; and it encourages ongoing conceptualizing and strategizing about the text.

Conceptualization, Coding, and Categorizing

Identifying and refining important concepts is a key part of the iterative process of qualitative research. Sometimes, conceptualizing begins with a simple observation that is interpreted directly, "pulled apart," and then put back together more meaningfully. Robert Stake (1995) provides an example, from an observation of a student named Adam, a student who habitually created conflicts with other children:

> When Adam ran a pushbroom into the feet of the children nearby, I jumped to conclusions about his interactions with other children: aggressive, teasing, arresting. Of course, just a few minutes earlier I had seen him block the children climbing the steps in a similar moment of smiling bombast. So I was aggregating, and testing my unrealized hypotheses about what kind of kid he was, not postponing my interpreting. . . . My disposition was to keep my eyes on him. (p. 74)

The focus in this conceptualization "on the fly" is to provide a detailed description of what was observed and a sense of why it was important.

More often, analytic insights are tested against new observations, the initial statement of problems and concepts is refined, the researcher then collects more data and interacts with the data again, and the process continues. In this way, the researcher progressively refines his concept as he gains experience in the setting, often over a long period of time.

Matrix: A chart used to condense qualitative data into simple categories and provide a multidimensional summary that will facilitate subsequent, more intensive analysis.

A well-designed chart, or **matrix,** can facilitate the coding and categorization process. Exhibit 14.2 shows an example of a coding form designed by Miles and Huberman (1994, pp. 93–95) to represent the extent to which teachers and teachers' aides ("users") and administrators at a school gave evidence of various supporting conditions that indicate preparedness for a new reading program. The matrix condenses data into simple categories, reflects further analysis of the data to identify "degree" of support, and provides a multidimensional summary that will facilitate subsequent, more intensive analysis. Direct quotes still impart some of the flavor of the original text.

Exhibit 14.2	Example of Checklist Matrix

Presence of Supporting Conditions		
Conditions	**For Users**	**For Administrators**
Commitment	Strong—"wanted to make it work."	• *Weak* at building level • Prime movers in central office committed; others not.
Understanding	*"Basic"* ("felt I could do it, but I just wasn't sure how.") for teacher.	*Absent* at building level and among staff.
	Absent for aide ("didn't understand how we were going to get all this.")	• *Basic* for 2 prime movers ("got all the help we needed from developer.") • *Absent* for other central office staff.
Materials	*Inadequate:* ordered late, puzzling ("different from anything I ever used"), discarded.	NA
Front-end training	*"Sketchy"* for teacher ("it all happened so quickly"); no demo class.	Prime movers in central office had training at developer site; none for others.
	None for aide ("totally unprepared. I had to learn along with the children.")	
Skills	*Weak-adequate* for teacher. "None" for aide.	One prime mover (Robeson) skilled in substance; others unskilled.
Ongoing inservice	*None,* except for monthly committee meeting; no substitute funds.	*None*
Planning coordination time	*None:* both users on other tasks during day; tab tightly scheduled, no free time.	*None*
Provisions for debugging	*None* systematized; spontaneous work done by users during summer.	*None*
School admin. support	Adequate	NA
Central admin. support	*Very strong* on part of prime movers.	Building admin. only acting on basis office commitment.
Relevant prior experience	*Strong* and useful in both cases; had done individualized instruction, worked with low achievers. But aide no diagnostic experience	*Present* and useful in central office, esp. Robeson (specialist).

Source: Miles and Huberman (1994, p. 95).

Note: NA = not applicable.

Examining Relationships and Displaying Data

Examining relationships is the centerpiece of the analytic process because it allows the researcher to move from simple description of the people and settings to explanations of why things happened as they did with those people in that setting. The process of examining relationships can be captured in a matrix that shows how different concepts are connected or perhaps what causes are linked with what effects.

Exhibit 14.3 displays a matrix used to relate stakeholders' stake in a new program with the researcher's estimate of stakeholder attitudes toward the program. Each cell of the matrix was to be filled in with a summary of an illustrative case study. In other matrix analyses, quotes might be included in the cells to represent the opinions of these different stakeholders, or the number of cases of each type might appear in the cells. The possibilities are almost endless. Keeping this approach in mind will generate many fruitful ideas for structuring a qualitative data analysis.

Exhibit 14.3   **Coding Form for Relationships: Stakeholders' Stakes**

How high are the stakes for various primary stakeholders?	Estimate of Various Stakeholders' Inclination Toward the Program		
	Favorable	**Neutral or Unknown**	**Antagonistic**
High			
Moderate			
Low			

Source: Patton (2002, p. 472).

Note: Construct illustrative case studies for each cell based on fieldwork.

The simple relationships that are identified with a matrix such as that shown in Exhibit 14.3 can be examined and then extended to create a more complex causal model. Such a model represents the multiple relationships among the constructs identified in a qualitative analysis as important for explaining some outcome. A great deal of analysis must precede the construction of such a model, with careful attention to identification of important variables and the evidence that suggests connections between them. Exhibit 14.4 provides an example of these connections from a study of the implementation of a school program.

Authenticating Conclusions

No set standards exist for evaluating the validity or "authenticity" of conclusions in a qualitative study, but the need to consider carefully the evidence and methods on which conclusions are based is just as great as with other types of research. Individual items of information can be assessed in terms of at least three criteria (Becker, 1958, pp. 654–656):

- *How credible was the informant?* Were statements made by someone with whom the researcher had a relationship of trust or by someone the researcher had just met? Did the informant have reason to lie? If the statements do not seem to be trustworthy as indicators of actual events, can they at least be used to help understand the informant's perspective?

- *Were statements made in response to the researcher's questions, or were they spontaneous?* Spontaneous statements are more likely to indicate what would have been said had the researcher not been present.

- *How does the presence or absence of the researcher or the researcher's informant influence the actions and statements of other group members?* Reactivity to being observed can never be ruled out as a possible explanation for some directly observed social phenomenon. However, if the researcher carefully compares what the informant says goes on when the researcher is not present, what the researcher observes directly, and what other group members say about their normal practices, the extent of reactivity can be assessed to some extent.

Exhibit 14.4 **Example of a Causal Network Model**

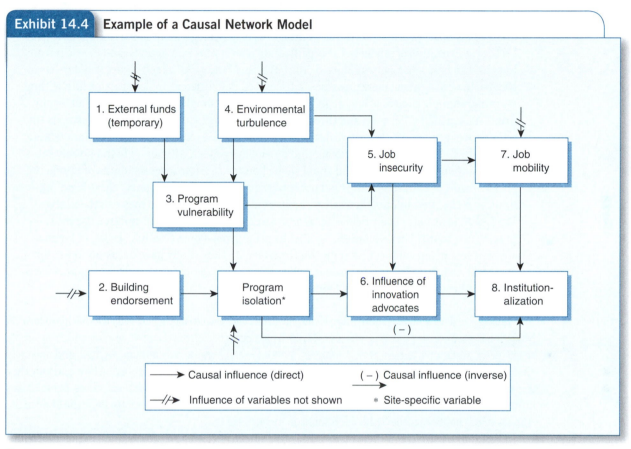

Source: Miles and Huberman (1994, p. 159).

A qualitative researcher's conclusions should also be judged by his or her ability to explain credibly some aspect of educational life. Explanations should capture group members' **tacit knowledge** of the educational processes that were observed, not just their verbal statements about these processes. Tacit knowledge— "the largely unarticulated, contextual understanding that is often manifested in nods, silences, humor, and naughty nuances"—is reflected in participants' actions as well as their words and in what they fail to state but nonetheless feel deeply and even take for granted (Altheide & Johnson, 1994, pp. 492–493). Comparing conclusions from a qualitative research project to those obtained by other researchers conducting similar projects can also increase confidence in their authenticity.

Reflexivity

Confidence in the conclusions from a field research study is also strengthened by an honest and informative account about how the researcher interacted with subjects in the field, what problems he or she encountered, and how these problems were or were not resolved. Such a "natural history" of the development of the evidence enables others to evaluate the findings. Such an account is important first and foremost because of the evolving and variable nature of field research: To an important extent, the researcher "makes up" the method in the context of a particular investigation rather than applying standard procedures that are specified before the investigation begins.

Barrie Thorne (1993) provides a good example of this final element of the analysis:

> Many of my observations concern the workings of gender categories in social life. For example, I trace the evocation of gender in the organization of everyday interactions, and the shift from boys and girls as loose aggregations to "the boys" and "the girls" as self-aware, gender-based groups. In writing about these processes, I discovered that different angles of vision lurk within seemingly simple choices of language. How, for example, should one describe a group of children? A phrase like "six girls and three boys were chasing by the tires" already assumes the relevance of gender. An alternative description of the same event—"nine fourth-graders were chasing by the tires"—emphasizes age and downplays gender. Although I found no tidy solutions, I have tried to be thoughtful about such choices. . . . After several months of observing at Oceanside, I realized that my field notes were peppered with the words "child" and "children," but that the children themselves rarely used the term. "What do they call themselves?" I badgered in an entry in my field notes. The answer, it turned out, is that children use the same practices as adults. They refer to one another by using given names ("Sally", "Jack") or language specific to a given context ("that guy on first base"). They rarely have occasion to use age-generic terms. But when pressed to locate themselves in an age-based way, my informants used "kids" rather than "children." (pp. 8–9)

Qualitative data analysts, more often than quantitative researchers, display real sensitivity to how an educational situation or process is interpreted from a particular background and set of values and not simply based on the situation itself (Altheide & Johnson, 1994). Researchers are only human, after all, and must rely on their own senses and process all information through their own minds. By reporting how and why they think they did what they did, they can help others determine whether, or how, the researchers' perspectives influenced their conclusions. "There should be clear 'tracks' indicating the attempt [to show the hand of the ethnographer] has been made" (Altheide & Johnson, 1994, p. 493).

In Chapter 9, you were introduced to Shirley Brice Heath's (1983) classic study of language development in two small towns in the Carolinas, one Black (Trackton) and one White (Roadville). Heath's study illustrates the type of "tracks" that a qualitative researcher makes as well as how she can describe those tracks:

> I am white, but while I was growing up, my family's nearest neighbors were black families; the black church was across the road from my house, and the three black school teachers in our area lived just down the road. In our area, both white and black children lived too far from the nearest school to walk, so we took buses to our respective schools, but in the afternoons and the summers, we joined each other for ballgames, bike-riding, and trips to the creek to look for "crawfish." In the summers, we all worked for local tobacco farmers, black and white. These shared experiences and unconscious habits of interaction eased my transition into both Trackton and Roadville. . . . I spent many hours cooking, chopping wood, gardening, sewing, and minding children by the rules of the communities. . . . Often I was able to write in a field notebook while minding children, tending food, or watching television with families; otherwise, I wrote field notes as soon as possible afterwards when I left the community on an errand or to go to school. (pp. 5–9)

Heath's analysis of qualitative data resulted, in part, not just from the setting itself but from the way in which she "played her role" as a researcher and participant.

▣ Alternatives in Qualitative Data Analysis

The qualitative data analyst can choose from many interesting alternative approaches. Of course, the research question under investigation should shape the selection of an analytic approach, but the researcher's preferences will also inevitably play a role as well. The alternative approaches we present here (ethnography, ethnomethodology, conversation analysis, narrative analysis, grounded theory, and visual data analysis) will give you a good sense of the possibilities (Patton, 2002).

Ethnography

Ethnography is the study of a culture or cultures that a group of people share (Van Maanen, 1995, p. 4). As a method, it usually is meant to refer to the process of participant observation by a single investigator who immerses himself or herself in the group for a long period of time (often one or more years). Ethnographic research can also be called "naturalistic" because it seeks to describe and understand the natural social world as it really is, in all its richness and detail. Anthropological field research has traditionally been ethnographic, and much educational fieldwork shares these same characteristics. For example, *Anthropology and Education Quarterly* focuses on ethnographic studies of education in its social and cultural contexts. The analytic process of classic ethnography relies on the trustworthiness and accuracy of the researcher's **"thick" description** and thus on the thoroughness and insight of the researcher to "tell us like it is" in the setting, as he or she experienced it.

Ways With Words, Heath's (1983) award-winning "ethnography of communication" in Trackton and Roadville, attempts to create "a full description of the primary face-to-face interactions of children from community cultures" other than the mainstream one, including "ways of living, eating, sleeping, worshiping, using space, and filling time" with the central question being, "For each of these groups, what were the effects of the preschool home and community environment on the learning of those language structures and uses which were needed in classrooms and job settings?" (pp. 3–4).

As part of her ethnography of the two communities, Heath documented children's nonsense rhymes, songs, and verbal games, as well as conversations between children and adults. In Trackton,

> children are not seen as information-givers or question-answerers. This is especially true of questions for which adults already have an answer. Since adults do not consider children appropriate conversational partners to the exclusion of other people who are around, they do not construct questions especially for children, . . . The questions they ask preschool children are of five types. (p. 103)

The five types of questions are shown in Exhibit 14.5.

Heath contrasts this Trackton style of questioning to the use of questions by the culturally mainstream group she calls "the townspeople." Adult townspeople used questions to children, for instance, "as reminders: ('Where do those blocks belong?') and [the adult] expected children to respond with appropriate behavior (removing the blocks to the place where they were usually kept). . . . Many questions were reminders of polite behavior: 'What do you say?' (used to remind the child to say 'thank you,' 'excuse me,' and the like)" (p. 253).

Exhibit 14.5	Types of Questions Asked of Preschool Children in Trackton (listed in approximate order of frequency)		

| Type | Response Called For | Examples | |
		Question	Response
Analogy	Nonspecific comparison of one item, event, or person with another	What's that like? (referring to a flat tire on a neighbor's car)	Doug's car, never fixed
Story starter	Question that asks for explanation of events leading to first questioner's question	Did you see Maggie's dog yesterday?	What happened to Maggie's dog?
Accusation	Either nonverbal response and a lowered head or a story creative enough to take the questioner's attention away from the original infraction	What's that all over your face?	You know about that big mud puddle?
A-1 (Answerer has information)	Specific information known to addressee but not to questioner	What do you want?	Some juice
Q-1 (Questioner has information)	Specific piece of information known to both questioner and addressee	What's your name, huh?	Peanuts

Source: Heath (1983, pp. 104). Reprinted with permission of Cambridge University Press.

Heath uses these observations to develop key analytic ideas, for example, that the pattern of language development found in Trackton and, by implication, in other nonmainstream communities is completely absent from the research literature and from theories of childhood language development based on that literature:

The sequence of habits Trackton children develop in learning language, telling stories, making metaphors, and seeing patterns across items and events do not fit the developmental patterns of either linguistic or cognitive growth reported in the research literature on mainstream children. (Heath, 1983, p. 343)

This rich ethnographic tradition is being abandoned by some qualitative data analysts, however. Many have become skeptical of the ability of researchers to perceive the educational world in a way that is not distorted by their own subjective biases or to receive impressions from the actors in that educational world that are not altered by the fact of being studied (Van Maanen, 2002). As a result, both specific techniques and alternative approaches to qualitative data analysis have proliferated. The next sections introduce several of these alternative approaches.

Ethnomethodology and Conversation Analysis (CA)

Ethnomethodology focuses on the way that participants construct the world in which they live—how they "create reality"—rather than on describing the educational world itself. In fact, ethnomethodologists do not necessarily believe that we can find an objective reality; instead, it is the ways that participants come to create and sustain a sense of "reality" that is the focus of study. In the words of Jaber F. Gubrium and James A. Holstein (1997), in ethnomethodology, as compared to the naturalistic orientation of ethnography,

The focus shifts from the scenic features of everyday life onto the ways through which the world comes to be experienced as real, concrete, factual, and "out there." An interest in members' methods of constituting their world supersedes the naturalistic project of describing members' worlds as they know them. (p. 41)

> **Ethnomethodology:** A qualitative research method focused on the way that participants in a social setting create and sustain a sense of reality.

Unlike the ethnographic analyst, who seeks to describe the social or educational world as the participants see it, the ethnomethodological analyst seeks to maintain some distance from that world. The ethnomethodologist focuses on how reality is *constructed,* not on what it *is.* Ethnomethodology is not used as much in education research as it is in sociology, but it has given rise to a related method, conversation analysis, that is frequently used in education.

Conversation analysis (often abbreviated as CA) is a specific qualitative method for analyzing ordinary conversation. It focuses on the sequence and details of conversational interaction rather than on the "stories" that people are telling. Like ethnomethodology, from which it developed, conversation analysis focuses on how reality is constructed, rather than on what it "is."

Three premises guide conversation analysis (Gubrium & Holstein, 2000, p. 492):

1. Interaction is sequentially organized, and talk can be analyzed in terms of the process of social interaction rather than in terms of motives or social status.

2. Talk, as a process of social interaction, is contextually oriented—it is both shaped by interaction and creates the social context of that interaction.

3. These processes are involved in all social interaction, so no interactive details are irrelevant to understanding it.

Consider these premises as you read the following dialogue between British researcher Ann Phoenix (2004, p. 235) and a boy she called "Thomas" in her study of notions of masculinity, bullying, and academic performance among 11- to 14-year-old boys in 12 London schools.

Thomas: It's your attitude, but some people are bullied for no reason whatsoever just because other people are jealous of them.

Q. How do they get bullied?

Thomas: There's a boy in our year called James, and he's really clever and he's basically got no friends, and that's really sad because . . . he gets top marks in every test and everyone hates him. I mean, I like him. . . .

Phoenix (2004) notes that here,

Thomas dealt with the dilemma that arose from attempting to present himself as both a boy and sympathetic to school achievement. He . . . distanced himself from . . . being one of those who bullies a boy just because they are jealous of his academic attainments . . . constructed for himself the position of being kind and morally responsible. (p. 235)

Note that Thomas was a boy talking to a woman. Do you imagine that his talk would have been different if his conversation had been with other boys?

Bethan Benwell and Elizabeth Stokoe (2006, pp. 61–62) used a conversation between three friends to illustrate key concepts in conversation analysis. The text is prepared for analysis by numbering the lines, identifying the speakers, and inserting ∧ symbols to indicate the inflection and decimal numbers to indicate elapsed time.

104 **Marie**: ^Has ^ anyone-(0.2) has anyone got any really non:

105 sweaty stuff.

106 **Dawn**: Dave has, but you'll smell like a ma:n,

107 (0.9)

108 **Kate**: Eh [^huh heh]

109 **Marie**: [Right has] anyone got any^fe:minine non sweaty stuff.

The gap at line 107, despite being less than a second long, is nevertheless quite a long time in conversation and indicates an interactional glitch or trouble. As Kate starts to laugh, Marie reformulates her request from '^has anyone got any really non:sweaty stuff,' to 'right has anyone got any, ^feminine non sweaty stuff.' . . . the word 'really' is replaced by 'feminine,' and is produced with a hearable increase in pitch and emphasis. This replacement, together with the addition of 'right,' displays her understanding of the problem with her previous question . . . for these speakers, smelling like a 'man' (when one is a 'woman') is treated as a trouble source, a laughable thing and something that needs attending to and fixing.

Narrative Analysis

> **Narrative analysis:** A form of qualitative analysis in which the analyst focuses on how respondents impose order on the flow of experience in their lives and so make sense of events and actions in which they have participated.

Narrative methods use interviews and sometimes documents or observations to "follow participants down *their* trails" (Reissman, 2008, p. 24). **Narrative analysis** focuses on "the story itself" and seeks to preserve the integrity of personal biographies or a series of events that cannot adequately be understood in terms of their discrete elements (Reissman, 2002, p. 218). It seeks to discover the "big picture" about experiences and events as the participants understand them. The coding for a narrative analysis is typically of the narratives as a whole, rather than of the different elements within them. The coding strategy revolves around reading the stories and classifying them into general patterns.

For example, Calvin Morrill and his colleagues (2000, p. 534) read through 254 conflict narratives written by the ninth graders they studied and found four different types of stories:

1. *Action tales,* in which the author represents himself or herself and others as acting within the parameters of taken-for-granted assumptions about what is expected for particular roles among peers.

2. *Expressive tales,* in which the author focuses on strong, negative emotional responses to someone who has wronged him or her.

3. *Moral tales,* in which the author recounts explicit norms that shaped his or her behavior in the story and influenced the behavior of others.

4. *Rational tales,* in which the author represents him- or herself as a rational decision maker navigating through the events of the story.

Morrill et al. (2000, pp. 534–535) also classified the stories along four stylistic dimensions: plot structure (such as whether the story unfolds sequentially), dramatic tension (how the central conflict is represented), dramatic resolution (how the central conflict is resolved), and predominant outcomes (how the story ends). Coding reliability was checked through a discussion by the two primary coders, who found that their classifications agreed for a large percentage of the stories.

The excerpt that begins this chapter exemplifies what Morrill et al. (2000) termed an "action tale." Such tales

> unfold in matter-of-fact tones kindled by dramatic tensions that begin with a disruption of the quotidian order of everyday routines. A shove, a bump, a look . . . triggers a response. . . . Authors of action tales typically organize their plots as linear streams of events as they move briskly through the story's scenes. . . . This story's dramatic tension finally resolves through physical fighting, but . . . only after an attempted conciliation. (p. 536)

You can contrast that "action tale" with the following narrative, which Morrill et al. (2000) classify as a "moral tale," in which the students "explicitly tell about their moral reasoning, often referring to how normative commitments shape their decision making":

> I . . . got into a fight because I wasn't allowed into the basketball game. I was being harassed by the captains that wouldn't pick me and also many of the players. The same type of things had happened almost every day where they called me bad words so I decided to teach the ring leader a lesson. I've never been in a fight before but I realized that sometimes you have to make a stand against the people that constantly hurt you, especially emotionally. I hit him in the face a couple of times and I got respect I finally deserved. (pp. 545–546)

Morrill et al. (2000, p. 553) summarize their classification of the youth narratives in a simple table that highlights the frequency of each type of narrative and the characteristics associated with each of them (Exhibit 14.6). How does such an analysis contribute to our understanding of youth violence? Morrill et al. first emphasize that their narratives "suggest that consciousness of conflict among youths—like that among adults—is not a singular entity, but comprises a rich and diverse range of perspectives" (p. 551).

Theorizing inductively, Morrill et al. (2000, pp. 553–554) then attempt to explain why action tales were much more common than the more adult-oriented normative, rational, or emotionally expressive tales. One

Exhibit 14.6   Summary Comparison of Youth Narratives*

Representation of	Action Tales (*N* = 144)	Moral Tales (*N* = 51)	Expressive Tales (*N* = 35)	Rational Tales (*N* = 24)
Bases of everyday conflict	Disruption of everyday routines and expectations	Normative violation	Emotional provocation	Goal obstruction
Decision making	Intuitive	Principled stand	Sensual	Calculative choice
Conflict handling	Confrontational	Ritualistic	Cathartic	Deliberative
Physical violence**	In 44% (*N* = 67)	In 27% (*N* = 16)	In 49% (*N* = 20)	In 29% (*N* = 7)
Adults in youth conflict control	Invisible or background	Sources of rules	Agents of repression	Institutions of social control

Source: Morrill et al. (2000, p. 551).

*Total *N* = 254.

**Percentages based on the number of stories in each category.

possibility is Gilligan's (1988) theory of moral development, which suggests that younger students are likely to limit themselves to the simpler action tales that "concentrate on taken-for-granted assumptions of their peer and wider cultures, rather than on more self consciously reflective interpretation and evaluation" (Morrill et al., 2000, p. 554). More generally, Morrill et al. argue, "We can begin to think of the building blocks of cultures as different narrative styles in which various aspects of reality are accentuated, constituted, or challenged, just as others are deemphasized or silenced" (p. 556).

In this way, the narrative analysis by Morrill et al. (2000) allowed an understanding of youth conflict to emerge from the youths' own stories while also informing our understanding of broader social theories and processes.

Grounded Theory

Grounded theory: Systematic theory developed inductively, based on observations that are summarized into conceptual categories, reevaluated in the research setting, and gradually refined and linked to other conceptual categories.

Theory development occurs continually in qualitative data analysis (Coffey & Atkinson, 1996, p. 23). The goal of many qualitative researchers is to create **grounded theory**—that is, to build inductively a systematic theory that is "grounded" in, or based on, the observations. The observations are summarized into conceptual categories, which are tested directly in the research setting with more observations. Over time, as the conceptual categories are refined and linked, a theory evolves (Glaser & Strauss, 1967; Huberman & Miles, 1994, p. 436).

As observation, interviewing, and reflection continue, researchers refine their definitions of problems and concepts and select indicators. They can then check the frequency and distribution of phenomena: How many teachers made a particular type of comment? How often did faculty discussion lead to arguments? Social system models may then be developed, which specify the relationships among different phenomena. These models are modified as researchers gain experience in the setting. For the final analysis, the researchers check their models carefully against their notes and make a concerted attempt to discover negative evidence that might suggest that the model is incorrect. Exhibit 14.7 shows a graphic illustration of this process created by Naresh R. Pandit (1996).

Visual Data Analysis

For about 150 years, people have been creating a record of the world with photography. This creates the possibility of "observing" educational reality through photographs and films and of interpreting the resulting images as a "text." It is no surprise that visual educational research has been developed as a method both to learn how others "see" the world and to create images of it for further study. As in the analysis of written text, however, the visual educational researcher must be sensitive to the way in which a photograph or film "constructs" the reality that it depicts.

Visual methodology is becoming an increasingly important aspect of qualitative analyses of educational settings and the people in them. But whether you examine or also produce pictures for such analyses, remember Darren Newbury's (2005) reminder that "images cannot be simply taken of the world, but have to be made within it" (p. 1).

Photovoice: A method in which research participants take pictures of their everyday surroundings with cameras distributed by the researcher and then meet in a group with the researcher to discuss the pictures' meanings.

Photovoice is a method of using photography to engage research participants in explaining how they have made sense of their educational and social worlds. Rather than using images from other sources, the researcher directing a photovoice project distributes cameras to research participants and invites them to take pictures of their surroundings or everyday activities. The participants then meet with the researcher to present their pictures and discuss their meaning. In this way, the researchers learn more about the participants' worlds as they see it and react to it. The photovoice method also engages participants as part of the research team themselves, thus enriching the researcher's interpretations.

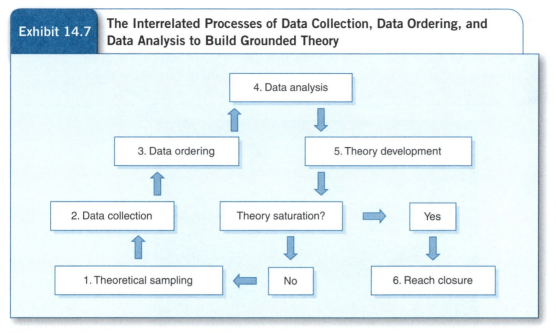

| Exhibit 14.7 | **The Interrelated Processes of Data Collection, Data Ordering, and Data Analysis to Build Grounded Theory** |

Source: Pandit (1996, http://www.nova.edu/ssss/QR/QR2-4/pandit.html). Reprinted by permission of the author.

Note: Start at the lower left and follow the arrows clockwise until you reach "Theory saturation?" If all possible theories have been extracted from the data, the answer is "Yes" and the process moves to "Reach closure." If the answer is "No," the process begins again until "Theoretical sampling" is reached.

Photovoice can be particularly significant for populations who might be underrepresented in research methods that rely solely on words, such as second-language learners or students with cognitive impairments. Maria Paiewonsky (2005) used photovoice to help students with "significant intellectual disabilities" to participate in planning for their own transition from high school to independent living. According to Paiewonsky,

> Without their involvement, other members of their planning team, who may not know them well, make decisions for students, generally based on educational reports and assessments. To address this issue, the use and function of photovoice, an educational tool designed to assist individuals to direct actions and resources that will have an impact on their lives (Wang, 1994) was explored with five students identified with significant intellectual disabilities. Given digital cameras, students were asked to photograph how they envisioned their futures and then present their work to invited guests, including members of an interagency team. . . . Using the photovoice process, the students indicated that outside of formal education and transition meetings, they were discussing their plans informally with their parents, and other trusted family members, teachers and friends. Recommendations were made to explore further how photovoice can be used with students with significant intellectual disabilities to bridge the formal and informal discussions concerning their transition from school. (p. iii)

Photovoice combines words and still photography to empower research participants to record their own points of view. Exhibits 14.8a and b show two examples of the photos students took and the captions they created telling why the photo was important to them.

The field of video analysis is growing rapidly as new tools, such as smaller cameras and computer-based software such as QuickTime and the video editing software iMovie, become cheap and readily available. Trica Kress and Kelly Silva (2009) used two techniques, **discourse analysis (DA)** and video-microanalysis, to investigate

Exhibit 14.8a	"Room Where Graduation Party Will Be Held," Taken by Kim. Kim: "I took this picture because I want my family to come to my graduation party. People will worry about me. I want people to know that I think about what will happen after graduation and people worrying about me. I want help thinking about what to do after graduation so my family doesn't have to worry much."

Source: Paiewonsky (2005, p. 142). Used by permission.

Exhibit 14.8b	"Bankbook," Taken by Rick. Rick: "This is a picture of my bankbook and it makes me think about saving money to buy a car. And a class ring. I took this picture because I get more money from work. Making more money makes me feel great. After graduation I need to go to work to make more money. I want people to learn that I want to work. Maybe the people who see this can help me find a job. I need help."

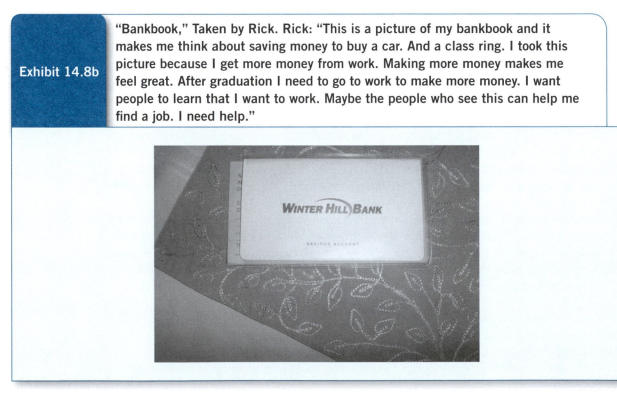

Source: Paiewonsky (2005, p. 289). Used by permission.

a professional development session for teachers about technology in the classroom. DA is concerned with spoken and written language use in social contexts, particularly interaction or dialogue among speakers, and it treats video data as "text" to be read and interpreted. Video-microanalysis looks at extremely small snippets of video data and interprets not just spoken language but gestures, body movements, and facial expressions.

Here Silva, a classroom teacher, describes some of the technical aspects of the study she undertook in collaboration with Kress, a professor in her graduate program:

> In order to understand and assess how the group functioned, I videotaped the group's interactions and used discourse analysis and video-microanalysis to look for patterns in what participants said and did. I began the analysis by isolating vignettes using iMovie. I transcribed the dialogue and inserted it into two different tables created in MS Word. The first showed who was speaking, at what time, and when they overlapped. I used QuickTime to slow down the video to 1/30 of a second to identify rhythmic body movements (e.g. head nods, eye gazes), which are indications of intense positive emotional energy and mutual engagement referred to by Collins (2004) as "entrainment." (Kress & Silva, 2009, p. 2845)

If you are interested in learning more about research techniques using video, you may want to look at some recent issues of *Visual Studies,* a leading journal in the field, and to download *Guidelines for Video Research in Education: Recommendations From an Expert Panel* (2007), available at the website of the University of Chicago's Data Research and Development Center, drdc.uchicago.edu/what/video-research-guidelines.pdf.

🔲 Computer-Assisted Qualitative Data Analysis

The analysis process can be enhanced in various ways by using a computer. Programs designed for qualitative data can speed up the analysis process, making it easier for researchers to experiment with different codes, test different hypotheses about relationships, and facilitate diagrams of emerging theories and preparation of research reports (Coffey & Atkinson, 1996; Richards & Richards, 1994). The steps involved in **computer-assisted qualitative data analysis** parallel those used traditionally to analyze such text as notes, documents, or interview transcripts: preparation, coding, analysis, and reporting. We use three of the most popular programs to illustrate these steps: HyperRESEARCH, QSR NVivo, and ATLAS.ti. (Each of these programs maintains a website that will allow you to download a free trial program for evaluation purposes.)

Text preparation begins with typing or scanning text in a word processor or, with NVivo, directly into the program's rich text editor. NVivo will create or import a rich text file. HyperRESEARCH requires that your text be saved as a text file (as "ASCII" in most word processors) before you transfer it into the analysis program. HyperRESEARCH expects your text data to be stored in separate files corresponding to each unique case, such as an interview with one subject. These programs now allow multiple types of files, including pictures and videos as well as text. Exhibit 14.9 displays the different file types and how they are connected in the organization of a project (a "hermeneutic unit") with ATLAS.ti.

Coding the text involves categorizing particular text segments. This is the foundation of much qualitative analysis. Each program allows you to assign a code to any segment of text (in NVivo, you drag through the characters to select them; in HyperRESEARCH, you click on the first and last words to select text). You can make up codes as you go through a document and also assign codes that you have already developed to text segments. Exhibit 14.10 shows the screens that appear in the two programs at the coding stage, when a particular text segment is being labeled. You can also have the programs "autocode" text by identifying a word or phrase that should always receive

| Exhibit 14.9 | File Types and Unit Structure in ATLAS.ti |

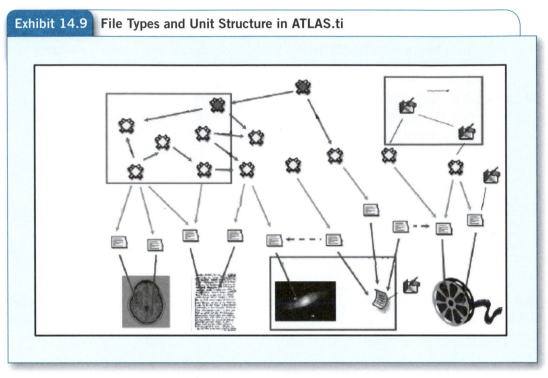

the same code or, in NVivo, by coding each section identified by the style of the rich text document—for example, each question or speaker (of course, you should check carefully the results of autocoding). Both programs also let you examine the coded text "in context"—embedded in its place in the original document.

In qualitative data analysis, coding is not a one-time-only or one-code-only procedure. Each program allows you to be inductive and holistic in your coding. You can revise codes as you go along, assign multiple codes to text segments, and link your own comments ("memos") to text segments. You can work "live" with the coded text to alter coding or create new, more subtle categories. You can also place hyperlinks to other documents in the project or any multimedia files outside it.

Analysis focuses on reviewing cases or text segments with similar codes and examining relationships among different codes. You may decide to combine codes into larger concepts. You may specify additional codes to capture more fully the variation among cases. You can test hypotheses about relationships among codes and develop more free-form models (see Exhibit 14.11). You can specify combinations of codes that identify cases that you want to examine.

Reports from each program can include text to illustrate the cases, codes, and relationships that you specify. You can also generate counts of code frequencies and then import these counts into a statistical program for quantitative analysis. However, the many types of analyses and reports that can be developed with qualitative analysis software do not lessen the need for a careful evaluation of the quality of the data on which conclusions are based.

In reality, using a qualitative data analysis computer program is not always as straightforward as it appears. Scott Decker and Barrik Van Winkle (1996) describe the difficulty they faced in using a computer program to identify instances of the concept of "drug sales":

The software we used is essentially a text retrieval package.... One of the dilemmas faced in the use of such software is whether to employ a coding scheme within the interviews or simply to leave

Exhibit 14.10a HyperRESEARCH Coding Stage

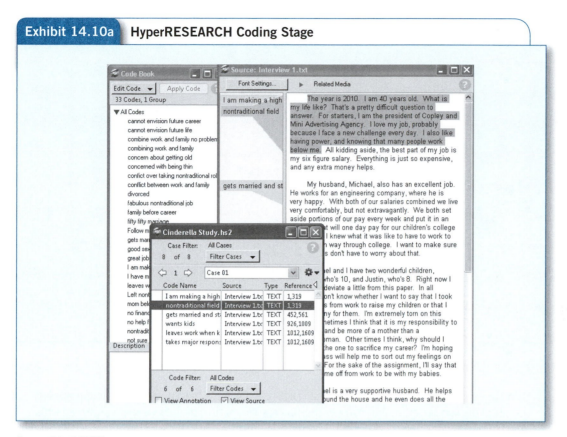

Source: Schutt (2012).

Exhibit 14.10b NVivo Coding Stage

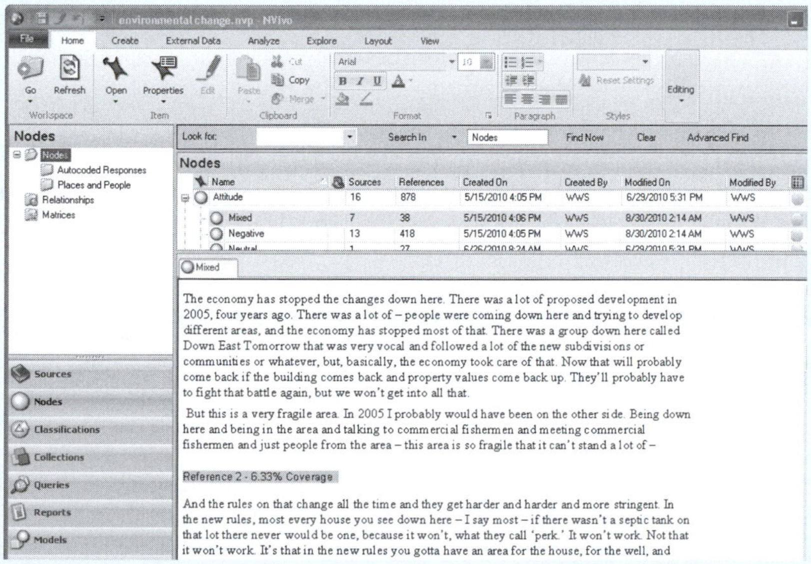

Source: Schutt (2012).

| Exhibit 14.11 | A Free-Form Model in NVivo |

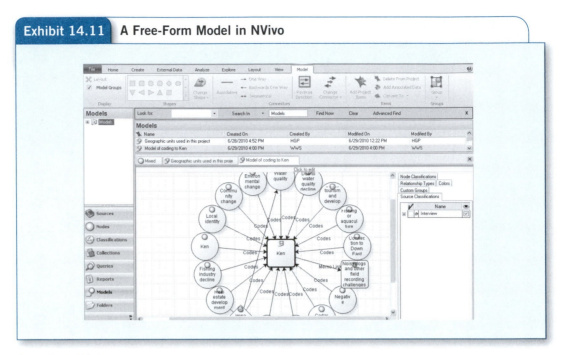

Source: Schutt (2012).

them as unmarked text. We chose the first alternative, embedding conceptual tags at the appropriate points in the text. An example illustrates this process. One of the activities we were concerned with was drug sales. Our first chore (after a thorough reading of all the transcripts) was to use the software to "isolate" all of the transcript sections dealing with drug sales. One way to do this would be to search the transcripts for every instance in which the word "drugs" was used. However, such a strategy would have the disadvantages of providing information of too general a character while often missing important statements about drugs. Searching on the word "drugs" would have produced a file including every time the word was used, whether it was in reference to drug sales, drug use, or drug availability, clearly more information than we were interested in. However, such a search would have failed to find all of the slang used to refer to drugs ("boy" for heroin, "Casper" for crack cocaine) as well as the more common descriptions of drugs, especially rock or crack cocaine. (pp. 53–54)

Decker and Van Winkle solved this problem by parenthetically inserting conceptual tags in the text whenever talk of drug sales was found. This process allowed them to examine all of the statements made by gang members about a single concept (drug sales). As you can imagine, however, this still left the researchers with many pages of transcripts to analyze.

⊡ Ethics in Qualitative Data Analysis

The qualitative data analyst is never far from ethical issues and dilemmas. Throughout the analytic process, the analyst must consider how the findings will be used and how participants in the setting will react. Miles and Huberman (1994, pp. 293–295) suggest several specific questions that are of particular importance during the process of data analysis:

Privacy, confidentiality, and anonymity. "In what ways will the study intrude, come closer to people than they want? How will information be guarded? How identifiable are the individuals and organizations studied?" We have considered this issue already in the context of qualitative data collection, but it also must be a concern during the process of analysis. It can be difficult to present a rich description in a case study while at the same time not identifying the setting. It can be easy for participants in the study to identify each other in a qualitative description, even if outsiders cannot. Qualitative researchers should negotiate with participants early in the study the approach that will be taken to protect privacy and to maintain confidentiality. Selected participants should also be asked to review reports or other products before their public release in order to gauge the extent to which they feel privacy has been appropriately preserved.

Intervention and advocacy. "What do I do when I see harmful, illegal, or wrongful behavior on the part of others during a study? Should I speak for anyone's interests besides my own? If so, whose interests do I advocate?" Maintaining what is called "guilty knowledge" may force the researcher to suppress some parts of the analysis so as not to disclose the wrongful behavior, but presenting "what really happened" in a report may prevent ongoing access and violate understandings with participants. In school-based studies, particular care must be taken to protect the identity of the school and of individual participants, because others in the community may find them easy to identify.

Research integrity and quality. "Is my study being conducted carefully, thoughtfully, and correctly in terms of some reasonable set of standards?" Real analyses have real consequences, so you owe it to yourself and those you study to adhere strictly to the analysis methods that you believe will produce authentic, valid conclusions.

Ownership of data and conclusions. "Who owns my field notes and analyses: I, my organization, my funders? And once my reports are written, who controls their diffusion?" Of course, these concerns arise in any educational research project, but the intimate involvement of the qualitative researcher with participants in the setting studied makes conflicts of interest between different stakeholders much more difficult to resolve. Working through the issues as they arise is essential.

Use and misuse of results. "Do I have an obligation to help my findings be used appropriately? What if they are used harmfully or wrongly?" It is prudent to develop understandings early in the project with all major stakeholders that specify what actions will be taken in order to encourage appropriate use of project results and to respond to what is considered misuse of these results.

🖩 Conclusions

We began this chapter by asking, "How does conflict develop in schools?" Throughout the chapter, you saw research examples using various qualitative analytic techniques to explore this question. Morrill et al. (2000) solicited written conflict narratives from ninth graders, then used textual analysis to identify four narrative types, which they labeled Action Tales, Moral Tales, Expressive Tales, and Rational Tales. Robert Stake (1995) focused on a single child, Adam, who seemed to create conflicts with other students throughout the school day. Ann Phoenix (2004) used interviews with 11- to 14-year-old boys in 12 schools to study the relationship of masculinity, bullying, and academic performance. In addition, you saw a variety of qualitative approaches to other educational questions, including a checklist matrix that helped to track the impact of a new reading program (Miles & Huberman, 1994), a classic 10-year ethnographic study to explore differences in the language development of young children between two racially different communities (Heath, 1983), and the photovoice technique to investigate the passage of special-needs students out of high school and into the adult world (Paiewonsky, 2005).

The variety of approaches to qualitative data analysis makes it difficult to provide a consistent set of criteria for interpreting their quality. Norman Denzin's (2002, pp. 362–363) "interpretive criteria" are a good place to start. Denzin suggests that at the conclusion of their analyses, qualitative data analysts ask the following questions about the materials they have produced. Reviewing several of them will serve as a fitting summary for your understanding of the qualitative analysis process.

- *Do they illuminate the phenomenon as lived experience?* In other words, do the materials bring the setting alive in terms of the people in that setting?

- *Are they based on thickly contextualized materials?* We should expect thick descriptions that encompass the social setting studied.

- *Are they historically and relationally grounded?* There must be a sense of the passage of time between events and the presence of relationships between social actors.

- *Are they processual and interactional?* The researcher must have described the research process and his or her interactions within the setting.

- *Do they engulf what is known about the phenomenon?* This includes situating the analysis in the context of prior research and also acknowledging the researcher's own orientation upon first starting the investigation.

When an analysis of qualitative data is judged as successful in terms of these criteria, we can conclude that the goal of "authenticity" has been achieved.

As a research methodologist, you should be ready to use qualitative techniques, evaluate research findings in terms of these criteria, and mix and match specific analytic methods as required by the research problem to be investigated and the setting in which it is to be studied.

Key Terms

Computer-assisted qualitative data analysis   317
Discourse analysis (DA)   315
Emic focus   300
Ethnography   309

Etic focus   300
Grounded theory   314
Matrix   304
Narrative analysis   312
Photovoice   314

Progressive focusing   301
Tacit knowledge   307
"Thick" description   309

Highlights

- Qualitative data analysts are guided by an emic focus of representing persons in the setting on their own terms rather than by an etic focus on the researcher's terms.

- Case studies use thick description and other qualitative techniques to provide a holistic picture of a setting or group.

- Ethnographers attempt to understand the culture of a group.

- Narrative analysis attempts to understand a life or a series of events as they unfolded, in a meaningful progression.
- Grounded theory connotes a general explanation that develops in interaction with the data and is continually tested and refined as data collection continues.

- Special computer software can be used for the analysis of qualitative, textual, and visual data. Users can record their notes, categorize observations, specify links between categories, and count occurrences.

Student Study Site

To assist in completing the web exercises, please access the study site at www.sagepub.com/check, where you will find the web exercise with accompanying links. You'll find other useful study materials such as self-quizzes and e-flashcards for each chapter, along with a group of carefully selected articles from research journals that illustrate the major concepts and techniques.

Discussion Questions

1. List the primary components of qualitative data analysis strategies. Compare and contrast each of these components with those relevant to quantitative data analysis. What are the similarities and differences? What differences do these make?

2. Does qualitative data analysis result in trustworthy results? Why would anyone question its use? What would you reply to the doubters?

3. Which analytic alternative do you prefer? Why?

Practice Exercises

1. Read the complete text of one of the qualitative studies presented in this chapter and evaluate its conclusions for authenticity, using the criteria in this chapter.

2. Go forth and take pictures. Conduct a "photovoice" project with your classmates and write up your own review of the group's discussion of your pictures.

Web Exercises

1. The *Qualitative Report* is an online journal about qualitative research. Inspect the table of contents for a recent issue at http://www.nova.edu/ssss/QR/index.html. Read one of the articles and write a brief article review.

2. Be a qualitative explorer! Go to the list of qualitative research websites and see what you can find that enriches your understanding of qualitative research (http:/www.qualitativeresearch .uga.edu/QualPage/). Be careful to avoid textual data overload.

Developing a Research Proposal

Which qualitative data analysis alternative is most appropriate for the qualitative data you proposed to collect for your project?

Using the approach, develop a strategy for using the techniques of qualitative data analysis to analyze your textual data.

CHAPTER 15

Proposing and Reporting Research

Research Question: *Does Social Investment in Preschool Pay Economic Dividends?*

Chapter Contents

- **Educational Research Proposals Part II**
- **Reporting Research**
- **Ethics, Politics, and Research Reports**

There can be positive returns for California society from investing in a one-year high-quality universal preschool program. . . . Every dollar invested by the public sector beyond current spending will generate $2.62 in returns. . . . Other potential benefits include lower intangible losses from crime and child abuse and neglect averted, reduced reliance on public welfare programs, improved labor market outcomes for parents of preschoolers, improved health and well-being of preschool participants, and the intergenerational transmission of favorable benefits.

Karoly and Bigelow (2005, p. 1)

Y ou learned in Chapter 2 that research is a circular process, so it is appropriate that we end this book where we began. The quotation above is from the Executive Summary of a research report measuring, in dollars and cents, the potential impact of universal preschool programs for the state of California. The research was undertaken by Lynn A. Karoly and James H. Bigelow (2005) for the RAND Corporation, and later in the chapter, you will see how the entire report was organized. Part of reporting research results is identifying areas for further research. It is the time when, so to speak, "the rubber meets the road"—when we have to make our research make sense to others. We have to answer questions such as, To whom will our research be addressed? How should we present our results to them? Will we seek to influence how our research report is used?

The primary goals of this chapter are to guide you in preparing research proposals, writing worthwhile reports of your own, and communicating with the public about research. This chapter also gives particular attention to the writing process itself and points out how that process can differ when writing up qualitative versus quantitative research. We will conclude by considering some of the ethical issues unique to the reporting process, with special attention to the problem of plagiarism.

Educational Research Proposals, Part II

We discussed the basics of educational research proposals in Chapter 2, including these six elements of any good proposal (Locke et al., 2000):

1. An introductory statement of the research problem

2. A literature review

3. A methodological plan

4. A budget

5. An ethics statement

6. A statement of limitations

The variety of research designs and techniques, as well as the ethical challenges you have learned about throughout the book, will help you to fill in the details about these elements in any proposal. If you have completed the proposal development exercises at the end of some of the chapters, you will already have drafted some of these elements. All that is left now is to consider the proposal preparation process as a whole.

When you develop a complete research proposal, it helps to ask yourself the series of questions posed in Exhibit 15.1. It is easy to omit important details and to avoid being self-critical while rushing to put a proposal together. The items in Exhibit 15.1 can serve as a map for using preceding chapters in this book to develop your proposal, as well as a checklist of decisions that must be made throughout any research project. The questions are organized in five sections, each concluding with a checkpoint at which you should consider whether to proceed with the research as initially planned, to modify the plans, or to stop the proposal or project altogether. The sequential ordering of these questions obscures a bit the way in which they should be answered: not as single questions, one at a time, but as a unit—first as five separate stages, and then as a whole.

As you develop your proposal, you will find yourself revising your answers to earlier questions on the basis of your answers to later questions, simply because you realize there is some room for improvement in your initial approach. Think of the process of revision as an essential part of proposal writing. The goal is to write a proposal that is complete and persuasive and leads to a favorable review, not to write one quickly. No proposal is ready for review until it has been revised and edited, critiqued by knowledgeable others, and revised again—and again. If you submit a proposal as part of your class requirements, you shouldn't be surprised if your professor finds some areas that could be improved. Don't take that too personally; the grant proposals that professors (and others) submit for funding are usually reviewed by a committee of experts who will provide many critical comments and will often ask for substantial revisions before accepting the proposal for funding—if they accept it at all. As you revise the proposal, the time you spend reviewing *Research Methods in Education* in order to remind yourself of issues to be addressed and alternative approaches to be considered will be time well spent.

Reporting Research

The goal of research is not just to discover something but also to communicate that discovery to a larger audience: other educators, government officials, teachers, the general public—perhaps several of these audiences. Whatever the study's particular outcome, if the intended audience for the research comprehends the results and learns from them, the research can be judged a success. If the intended audience does not learn about the study's results, the research should be judged a failure—no matter how expensive or time-consuming the research or how sophisticated the design.

Forms Reporting Can Take

There are now so many types of educational research going on at so many levels that research reporting can take many forms. In particular, certain research situations and certain types of research typically require reporting out in forms other than the traditional journal article or applied research report. These include teacher research, which may be of interest primarily to the community of a single school or school system, and action research, whose principal goal is to create change in an organization. Research that uses visual analysis, to be fully representative, often needs to be reported in a medium that will allow video and sound to be part of the reporting.

If you are a school-based practitioner—a teacher, a counselor, an administrator—conducting a study in your own school, you may want to think about prospective audiences for your research in terms of progressively wider **circles of interest** (Exhibit 15.2). As the circles get bigger, the method of reporting called for begins to change. You should begin thinking about strategies for reporting your research by asking yourself some questions. Starting with the people closest to you and working outward, who is likely to be interested in what you did, how you did it, and what you found out? Who do you want to reach, to inform and influence, with the story of your research?

The initial audience for a school-based research project is likely to include, at a minimum, other teachers in the school who have heard about the project and want to know what the researcher(s) found out, the principal of the school, the students in the classes involved in the project, and the parents of those students. Likely formats for this type of reporting, which we have labeled *Internal/Local,* might include a few-page summary of the project concentrating on the research question, why it was important, the data collected, the conclusions reached, and any recommendations for change. This might be accompanied by a short talk or a PowerPoint presentation at a faculty meeting, school or district in-service day, parent council meeting, or school committee meeting. For many projects, this is all the reporting that will be required. This level of reporting reaches the audience of greatest interest to the researcher—the school and its immediate community.

If the project has received financial support from an outside entity or is part of the activities of a larger grant project or educational network such as the National Writing Project, the Coalition of Essential

Exhibit 15.1 Decisions in Research

PROBLEM FORMULATION (Chapters 1–2)

1. Developing a research question

2. Assessing researchability of the problem

3. Consulting prior research

4. Relating to social theory

5. Choosing an approach: Deductive? Inductive? Descriptive?

6. Reviewing research guidelines

> Checkpoint 1
>
> Alternatives: • Continue as planned.
> • Modify the plan.
> • STOP. Abandon the plan.

RESEARCH VALIDITY (Chapters 4–6)

7. Establishing measurement validity:

   - How are concepts defined?
   - Choose a measurement strategy.
   - Assess available measures or develop new measures.
   - What evidence of reliability and validity is available or can be collected?
   - Are the measures appropriate for use with the study population?

8. Establishing generalizability:

   - Was a representative sample used?
   - Are the findings applicable to particular subgroups?
   - Does the population sampled correspond to the population of interest?

9. Establishing causality:

   - What is the possibility of experimental or statistical controls?
   - How to assess the causal mechanism?
   - Consider the causal process

10. Data required: Longitudinal or cross-sectional?

11. Units of analysis: Individuals, families, groups, organizations, or communities?

12. What are the major possible sources of causal invalidity?

> Checkpoint 2
>
> Alternatives: • Continue as planned.
> • Modify the plan.
> • STOP. Abandon the plan.

RESEARCH DESIGN (Chapters 6–12)

13. Choosing a research design and procedures:

    Experimental?   Single-subject?   Survey?   Participant observation?   Multiple methods?

14. Specifying the research plan: Type of surveys, observations, etc.

15. Secondary analysis? Availability of suitable data sets?

16. Causal approach: Idiographic or nomothetic?

17. Assessing ethical concerns

> Checkpoint 3
>
> Alternatives: • Continue as planned.
> • Modify the plan.
> • STOP. Abandon the plan.

DATA ANALYSIS (Chapters 13 & 14)

18. Choosing a statistical approach:

- Statistics and graphs for describing data
- Identifying relationships between variables
- Deciding about statistical controls
- Testing for interaction effects
- Evaluating inferences from sample data to the population

> Checkpoint 4
>
> Alternatives: • Continue as planned.
> • Modify the plan.
> • STOP. Abandon the plan.

REVIEWING, PROPOSING, REPORTING RESEARCH (Chapters 2, 3 & 15)

19. Clarifying research goals

20. Identifying the intended audience

21. Searching the literature and the Web

22. Organizing the text

23. Reviewing ethical and practical constraints

> Checkpoint 5
>
> Alternatives: • Continue as planned.
> • Modify the plan.
> • STOP. Abandon the plan.

Source: Engel and Schutt (2010).

Schools, or a state or national educational initiative, then more detailed reporting will be required. For this *External* reporting, at a minimum, there will be a thorough, written report (not just a summary) to the funder or sponsor of the research, and possibly further publication, either electronically on a website or in print, in a volume that collects the results of all the projects that are part of the initiative. If the intended audience for the report is wider than the staff of the organization that funded the program—if it is to be printed or posted for the general public—this may be considered a form of the applied research report as described later in this chapter.

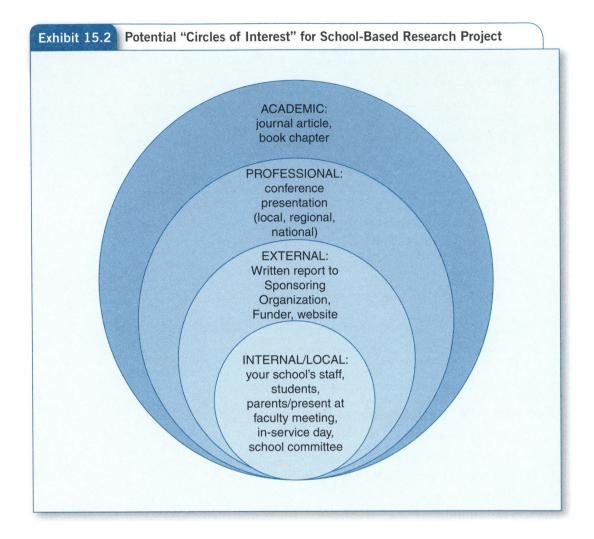

Exhibit 15.2 Potential "Circles of Interest" for School-Based Research Project

If the researcher wishes, or a sponsoring agency encourages, the next circle may be a *Professional* presentation at a local, regional, or national conference. Typically, this will involve submitting a brief proposal to whoever is sponsoring the conference and having your proposal read and accepted by the conference organizers. A conference presentation can take many forms. The researcher may give a talk describing the project or participate in a roundtable, a "poster session," or some other format. A PowerPoint may be involved, and in any event, either a brief, printed summary of the project or an entire paper reporting the project in detail will be required, depending on the conference.

Finally, the largest circle, demanding the most complete form of reporting, is the academic journal article or book chapter. This will involve a competitive selection process and rewriting and revisions overseen by a journal or book editor. A detailed explanation of this format is given later in this chapter.

The reporting for many projects remains at the local/internal level, and that is quite appropriate. But some projects migrate through several levels, changing their reporting format as they do so. Howard Banford's (1996) study of Maricar, which you encountered in Chapter 12, eventually reached audiences at all four levels. It was reported out locally, was part of a much larger national project, got reported at several conferences, and ultimately became a book chapter.

Writing the Report

Whatever form the reporting takes, we often hear "It is impossible to know where to begin," or "I have a hard time getting started." We have said it ourselves, more than once, when we must begin to write a research report or article. Our suggestion? "Begin where you are most comfortable but begin early!" You do not have to start at the beginning, with the introduction; you can start in the methods section if you prefer, or at whatever point you feel most confident or clearest in your mind. Proceed in whatever order seems easiest. The main point is to start somewhere and then keep writing. Get as much down on paper as you can, in whatever order you can, leaving gaps or questions to be filled in later. Then begin revising. It is easier to rewrite than to write the first draft, and you will certainly need multiple drafts to get your report the way you want it. The art of writing is really in the rewriting!

At the end of the day, a successful research report or article (or research proposal) must be well organized and clearly written. Getting to such a product may be difficult, but it *is* possible! Consider the following principles formulated by experienced writers (Booth, Colomb, & Williams, 1995, pp. 150–151):

- Respect the complexity of the task and don't expect to write a polished draft in a linear fashion. Your thinking will develop as you write, causing you to reorganize and rewrite.

- Leave enough time for dead ends, restarts, revisions, and so on, and accept the fact that you will discard much of what you write.

- Write as fast as you comfortably can. Don't worry about spelling, grammar, and so on until you are polishing things up.

- Ask anyone whom you trust for reactions to what you have written.

- Write as you go along, so you have notes and report segments drafted even before you focus on writing the report.

It is important to outline a report before writing it, but neither the report's organization nor the first draft should be considered fixed. As you write, you will get new ideas about how to organize the report. Try them out. As you review the first draft, you will see many ways to improve your writing. Focus particularly on how to shorten and clarify your statements. Make sure each paragraph concerns only one topic. Remember the golden rule of good writing: Writing is revising!

Many people find it helpful to use what is called **reverse outlining:** After you have written a first complete draft, outline it on a paragraph-by-paragraph basis, ignoring the actual section headings you used. See if the paper you wrote actually fits the outline you planned.

If you began with a research proposal, you have a head start. Your proposal already has many of the components you will need for the final report. Reorganize and edit your proposal on your computer and ask the opinions of friends, teachers, and some of those to whom your research report will be directed before turning in the final product (maybe even your professor). And most important, leave yourself enough time so that you can revise, several times if possible, before turning in the final draft.

Journal Articles

Writing for academic journals is perhaps the toughest form of writing because articles are submitted to several experts in your field for careful review—anonymously, with most journals—prior to acceptance for publication (or, more commonly, rejection). This process is called *peer review.* Perhaps it wouldn't be such an arduous process if so many academic journals did not have exceedingly high rejection rates and turnaround times of several months or more for reviews. Even the articles that the reviewers judge initially to be the best are most often given a "revise and resubmit" decision after the first review and then are evaluated all over again after the revised version is resubmitted.

But there are some important benefits of journal article procedures. First and foremost is the identification of areas in need of improvement, as the eyes of the author(s) are replaced by those of previously uninvolved subject matter experts and methodologists. A good journal editor makes sure that he or she has a list of many different types of experts available for reviewing the types of articles the journal is likely to receive. There is parallel benefit for the author(s): It is always beneficial to review criticisms of your own work by people who know the field well. It can be a difficult and time-consuming process, but the entire field moves forward as researchers continually critique and suggest improvements in each others' research reports. Many worthwhile articles "find a home" in a journal only after they have been rejected by one or more journals and revised multiple times. Since you must submit articles to only one journal at a time, it can literally be years from the completion of the research until the results appear in a journal article.

While there are slight variations in style across journals, there are typically seven standard sections within a journal article after the title page:

1. *Abstract.* The abstract is a concise summary of the research report that describes the research problem, the sample, the method, findings, discussion, and conclusion.

2. *Introduction.* The body of a paper should open with an introduction that presents the specific problem under study, highlights why such a study is important, and describes the research strategy. A good introduction answers *what, why,* and *how* in a few paragraphs.

3. *Literature Review.* Discuss the literature relevant to the topic, including what is known about the particular topic and what has been left unanswered. At the end of this section, you are ready to conceptually define your variables and formally state your hypotheses.

4. *Method.* Describe in detail how the study was carried out. This description enables the reader to evaluate the appropriateness of your methods and the reliability and validity of your results. It enables other researchers to replicate your study. In this section, you typically include subsections that describe the research design, the sample, the independent and dependent variables (measures), data collection procedures, and statistical or other analytic procedures.

5. *Findings.* Summarize the results of the statistical or qualitative analyses performed on the data. The findings section in quantitative research investigations will include tables and/or figures to which the summary refers, while in qualitative research investigations, the findings section will often include illustrative quotes or observations. Of course, in mixed-methods investigations, the findings section will often include both types of data displays.

6. *Discussion and Conclusions.* Evaluate and interpret the findings, taking into account the purpose of the study. The findings may be discussed in light of the current state of knowledge as reflected in the literature review and the utility of the findings for educational practice, policy, or theory. Address the limitations of the study, the generalizability of the findings, and directions for future research. Some journals require general conclusions in a separate section.

7. *References.* All citations in the manuscript must appear in the reference list, and all references must be cited in the text. References must always be formatted in the specific style required by the journal; unfortunately, different journals often require different formats.

Applied Research Reports

Applied research reports are written for a different audience than the educational researchers and students who read academic journals. Typically, an applied report is written with a wide audience of potential users in mind and to serve multiple purposes. Often, both the audience and the purpose are established by the agency or other organization that funded the research project on which the report is based. Sometimes, the researcher may use the report to provide a broad descriptive overview of study findings that will be presented more succinctly in a subsequent journal article. In either case, an applied report typically provides much more information about a research project than does a journal article and more complete descriptive statistics than those useful for the specific hypothesis tests that are likely to be the primary focus of a journal article. Writing an applied research report also allows much more rapid dissemination of the study findings than does publication in a peer-reviewed journal.

Exhibit 15.3 outlines the sections in one applied research report. This particular report described the projected economic impact if the state of California were to institute statewide, universal, publicly funded preschool education. The research project described in the report was funded by the David and Lucile Packard Foundation and conducted by the RAND Corporation, a nonprofit, independent research company. The study focused on two questions:

- What are the expected direct costs and benefits for the public sector and society as a whole of implementing a high-quality universal preschool program in California?

- What are the other potential indirect economic and noneconomic benefits for California that may be associated with such a program? (Karoly & Bigelow, 2005, p. iii)

As is evident from the outline in Exhibit 15.3, much of the report, including the two appendices, analyzes preschool education as a statewide policy issue and outlines the methodology used to construct a cost-benefit analysis to generate the economic data needed to answer the two focal questions.

One of the major differences between an applied research report and a journal article is that a journal article must focus on a particular research question, whereas an applied report is likely to have the broader purpose of describing a wide range of study findings and attempting to meet the needs of diverse audiences that have divergent purposes in mind for the research. But a research report that simply describes "findings" without some larger purpose in mind is unlikely to be effective in reaching any audience. Anticipating the needs of the intended audience(s) and identifying the ways in which the report can be useful to them will result in a product that is less likely to be ignored.

Another good example of applied research reporting comes from The Robert Wood Johnson Foundation, which presented an online research report in order to make widely available the findings from an investigation about the impact of welfare reform, particularly on children (Sunderland, 2005). This topic is of interest to educators and policy makers because of the current "achievement gap" in test scores and its relationship to race, ethnicity, and social class. Researcher P. Lindsay Chase-Lansdale and colleagues (2003) examined the impact of the 1996 federal act requiring changes in welfare requirements, the Personal Responsibility and Work Opportunity Reconciliation Act (PRWORA) of 1996.

The Robert Wood Johnson Foundation's online report (Sunderland, 2005) provides a good example of a basic principle that should always be kept in mind by researchers writing for a nonacademic audience: The findings and conclusions should be engaging and clear. This holds true whether the audience is a school principal or superintendent, a school committee, the town council, the local parent group, or, as in this case, national policy makers and the general public.

Exhibit 15.3 Sections in an Applied Report

Karoly, Lynn A. and James H. Bigelow. 2005. *The Economics of Investing in Universal Preschool Education in California*. Santa Monica, CA: The RAND Corporation.

Summary

Previous research has shown that well-designed pre-kindergarten programs for disadvantaged children can generate measurable educational and social benefits that exceed program costs, creating net social gains that extend beyond formal schooling. There is a growing constituency for public-sector investment in this area, particularly in California, the nation's most populous state. This report focuses on discovering the "direct costs and benefits for the public sector and society as a whole of implementing a high-quality universal preschool program in California" as well as "potential indirect economic and noneconomic benefits" of such a program. This report estimates that in California such a program would return $2.62 for every dollar invested, and that due to data limitations, this estimate may actually be understated. (pp. xiii–xiv)

Introduction

The Status of Preschool Education in the United States

A Universal Preschool Education Program in California

The Benefits of Preschool Education

Methods for Program Evaluation

Effectiveness of Preschool Education for Disadvantaged Children

Effectiveness of Preschool Education for Advantaged Children

Potential Impacts of a Universal Preschool Program in California

A Benefit-Cost Analysis of Universal Preschool Education in California

Overview of Benefit-Cost Analysis for Preschool Education

Valuing the Benefits of a Universal Preschool Program in California

Costs of a Universal Preschool Program in California

Benefit-Cost Analysis Results Under Alternative Assumptions

Indirect Economic and Non-Economic Benefits of Preschool Education

Labor Force Benefits

Macroeconomic Benefits of Education Investments

Consequences for Economic and Social Inequality

Conclusions

Preschool as Economic Development

Key Choices for States Funding Preschool Programs

Extending the Investment in Public Education

Appendix

A. Methodology and Sources for Benefit-Cost Analysis

B. Benefit-Cost Estimates for a Targeted Preschool Program

Source: Karoly and Bigelow (2005).

Overall, the nonacademic research report should outline key findings in an executive summary, emphasize the importance of the research in the introduction, use formatting and graphing to draw attention to particular findings in the body of the text, and tailor recommendations to the specific constituency or policy context most relevant to the research. It should also include a clear, orderly presentation of these five elements: *Purpose of the Research, Research Design, Conclusions, Limitations,* and *Recommendations.*

We present aspects of the online report below, arranged under these headings.

Purpose of the Research

The project's three-city (Boston, Chicago, San Antonio) research design sought to test the alternative arguments of reform proponents and opponents about the consequences of the reforms for families and children:

> Proponents of welfare reform argued that . . . moving mothers from welfare to work would benefit children because it would increase their families' income, model disciplined work behavior, and better structure their family routines. Opponents of PRWORA countered that . . . the reforms [would] reduce the time mothers and children spend together, . . . increase parental stress and decrease responsive parenting, and . . . move children into low-quality childcare of unsupervised settings while their parents worked. (Chase-Lansdale et al., 2002, p. 1548)

Research Design

The online report describes the three different components of the research design and refers leaders to sources for details about each (Sunderland, 2005, p. 4):

- A longitudinal survey of adults and children [2,402 families] designed to provide information on the health, cognitive, behavioral and emotional development of the children and on their primary caregivers' work-related behavior, welfare experiences, health, well-being, family lives and use of social services.

- An "embedded" developmental study of a subsample of children [630 families] to improve the breadth and depth of the child evaluations.

- Ethnographic studies of [256] low-income families in each city to describe how changes in welfare policy affected their daily lives and influenced neighborhood resources over time.

Conclusions

The researchers concluded the following:

- This study suggests that mothers' welfare and employment transitions during this unprecedented era of welfare reform are not associated with negative outcomes for preschoolers or young adolescents. A few positive associations were tenuously indicated for adolescents. . . . The well-being of preschoolers appeared to be unrelated to their mothers' leaving welfare or entering employment, at least as indexed in measures of cognitive achievement and behavior problems. (Sunderland, 2005, p. 6)

The online report also summarized findings about the characteristics of children at the start of the study (Sunderland, 2005, p. 7):

- Within a sample of 1,885 low-income children and their families, preschoolers and adolescents show patterns of cognitive achievement and problem behavior that should be of concern to policy-makers. The preschoolers and adolescents in [the] sample are more developmentally at risk compared to middle-class children in national samples. In addition, adolescents whose mothers were on welfare in 1999 have lower levels of cognitive achievement and higher levels of behavioral and emotional problems than do adolescents whose mothers had left welfare or whose mothers had never been on welfare. For preschoolers, mothers' current or recent welfare participation is linked with poor cognitive achievement; preschoolers of recent welfare leavers have the most elevated levels of problem behavior. Preschoolers and adolescents in sanctioned families also show problematic cognitive and behavioral outcomes (sanctioning is the withholding of all or part of a family's TANF benefits for noncompliance with work requirements or other rules). Mothers' marital, educational, mental and physical health status, as well as their parenting practices, seems to account for most of the welfare group differences.

Limitations

Because so few families in the sample had reached their time limits, investigators could not tell if families that leave the welfare system after reaching their time limits would show patterns similar to those that leave after sanctions.

Recommendations

In a policy brief on this project, the researchers recommended the following (Chase-Lansdale, Coley, Lohman, & Pittman, 2002, p. 6):

- The intense focus on welfare reform in our country should not impede a general concern and plan of action for all children in poverty, whether on welfare or not. In order to lessen developmental risks and improve the developmental trajectories of these children, numerous avenues should be pursued for the provision of supportive mental health and educational services.

- State and federal governments should explore options for identifying and reaching out to the most disadvantaged and high-risk families involved in the welfare system—families experiencing welfare sanctions. Sanctioned families have a number of characteristics that serve as markers of concern for the healthy development of children and youth.... Possible policy options include assistance to bring families into compliance with rules before they are sanctioned, closer monitoring of sanctioned families and the provision of additional supports, such as mental health services, academic enrichment, after-school programs and other family support services.

Here is one final word on organization. What can be termed the **front matter** and the **back matter** of an applied report also are important. Applied reports usually begin with an executive summary: a summary list of the study's main findings, often in bullet fashion. Appendixes, the back matter, may present tables containing supporting data that were not discussed in the body of the report. Applied research reports also often append a copy of the research instrument(s).

Ethics, Politics, and Research Reports

It is at the time of reporting research results that the researcher's ethical duty to be honest becomes paramount. Here are some guidelines:

- *Provide an honest accounting of how the research was carried out and where the initial research design had to be changed.* Readers do not have to know about every change you made in your plans and each new idea you had, but they should be informed about major changes in hypotheses or research design.

- *Maintain a full record of the research project so that questions can be answered if they arise.* Many details will have to be omitted from all but the most comprehensive reports, but these omissions should not make it impossible to track down answers to specific questions about research procedures that may arise in the course of data analysis or presentation.

- Avoid "lying with statistics" or using graphs to mislead.

- *Acknowledge the sponsors of the research.* This is important, in part, so that others can consider whether this sponsorship may have tempted you to bias your results in some way.

- *Thank staff who made major contributions.* This is an ethical as well as a political necessity. Let's maintain our social relations!

- Be sure that the order of authorship for coauthored reports is discussed in advance and reflects agreed-upon principles. Be sensitive to coauthors' needs and concerns.

Ethical research reporting should not mean ineffective reporting. You need to tell a coherent story in the report and avoid losing track of the story in a thicket of minuscule details. You do not need to report every twist and turn in the conceptualization of the research problem or the conduct of the research. But be suspicious of reports that don't seem to admit to the possibility of any room for improvement. Educational research is an ongoing enterprise in which one research report makes its most valuable contribution by laying the groundwork for another, more sophisticated, research project. Highlight important findings in the research report, but also use the research report to point out what are likely to be the most productive directions for future researchers.

Communicating With the Public

Even following appropriate guidelines like these, however, will not prevent controversy and conflict over research on sensitive issues. Does this mean that ethical researchers should avoid political controversy by side-stepping media outlets for their work? Many educational researchers argue that the media offer one of the best ways to communicate the practical application of educational knowledge and that when we avoid these opportunities, important educational insights and research findings never reach policy makers and the general public.

The American Educational Research Association (AERA) in recent years has taken an active role both in research ethics and in media communication. The AERA publishes a code of guiding ethical standards that covers seven areas: Responsibilities to the Field; Research Populations; Educational Institutions and the Public; Intellectual Ownership; Editing, Reviewing and Appraising Research; Sponsors, Policymakers, and Other Users of Research; and Students and Student Researchers. These standards are available online at no cost at the AERA website (aera.net) or directly at this URL: http://www.aera.net/uploadedFiles/About_AERA/Ethical_Standards/EthicalStandards.pdf.

The AERA also reaches out to the policy community and general public in a publication series called *Research Points*. These are research summaries explicitly intended to bring basic research information on important topics to legislators and policy leaders in Washington, D.C. and the 50 states. Report topics have included *Ensuring Early Literacy Success* (Foorman, 2009), *Time to Learn* (Berliner, 2007) (a look at research on the effects of increased instructional time), and *Science Education that Makes Sense* (Linn, 2007). These reports can be accessed and downloaded at no charge on the AERA website and can serve as a guide for your own ventures into this area.

Policy researcher William Julius Wilson (1998, p. 438) urges the following principles for engaging the public through the media:

1. Focus on issues of national concern, issues that are high on the public agenda.

2. Develop creative and thoughtful arguments that are clearly presented and devoid of technical language.

3. Present the big picture whereby the arguments are organized and presented so that the readers can see how the various parts are interrelated.

Ultimately, each researcher must make a decision about the most appropriate and important outlets for his or her work. You are the best judge of your own needs and context. For you, "the media" may be a school or parent newsletter, a local newspaper, or a blog post. It could also mean a formal presentation to faculty colleagues, an administrator, a parents group, or the local school committee or a report to a funding source. You may wish to address local or regional rather than national concerns. Whatever the context, be sure your points are clear and that you relate the various parts of the report to each other.

Plagiarism

It may seem depressing to end a book on research methods with a section on plagiarism, but it would be irresponsible to avoid the topic. Of course, you may have a course syllabus detailing instructor or university policies about plagiarism and specifying the penalties for violating that policy, so we're not simply going to repeat that kind of warning. You probably realize that the practice of selling term papers is revoltingly widespread (a search of "term papers" on Google returned 3,140,000 websites on August 24, 2010), so we're not going to just repeat that academic dishonesty is widespread. Instead, we will use this section to review the concept of plagiarism and to show how that problem connects to the larger issue of the integrity of educational research. When you understand the dimensions of the problem and the way it affects research, you should be better able to detect plagiarism in other work and avoid it in your own.

You learned in Chapter 3 that maintaining professional integrity—honesty and openness in research procedures and results—is the foundation for ethical research practice. When it comes to research publications and reports, being honest and open means avoiding plagiarism—that is, presenting as one's own the ideas or words of another person or persons for academic evaluation without proper acknowledgment (Hard, Conway, & Moran, 2006, p. 1059).

An increasing body of research suggests that plagiarism is a growing problem on college campuses. Jason Stephen and others (Stephen, Young, & Calabrese, 2007, p. 243) found in a Web-based survey of self-selected students at two universities that one quarter acknowledged having plagiarized a few sentences (24.7%) or a complete paper (.3%) in coursework within the past year (many others admitted to other forms of academic dishonesty, such as copying homework). Hard et al. (2006) conducted an anonymous survey in selected classes in one university, with almost all students participating, and found much higher plagiarism rates: 60.6% reported that they had copied "sentences, phrases, paragraphs, tables, figures or data directly or in slightly modified form from a book, article, or other academic source without using quotation marks or giving proper acknowledgment to the original author or source" (p. 1069), and 39.4% reported that they had "copied information from Internet Web sites and submitted it as [their] work."

So the plagiarism problem is not just about purchasing term papers—although that is really about as bad as it gets (Broskoske, 2005, p. 1); plagiarism is also about what you do with the information you obtain from a literature review or inspection of research reports. And rest assured that this is not only about student papers; it also is about the work of established scholars and researchers who publish reports that you want to rely on for accurate information. Several noted historians have been accused of plagiarizing passages that they used in popular books; some have admitted to not checking the work of their research assistants, to not keeping track of their sources, or to being unable to retrieve the data they claimed they had analyzed. Some social scientists have had to retract findings that were revealed to have been based on poorly analyzed data. Whether the cause is cutting corners to meet deadlines or consciously fudging facts, the effect is to undermine the trustworthiness of research.

Now that you are completing this course in research methods, it's time to think about how to do your part to reduce the prevalence of plagiarism. Of course, the first step is to maintain careful procedures for documenting the sources that you rely on for your own research and papers, but you should also think about how best to reduce temptations among others. After all, what people believe about what others do is a strong influence on their own behavior (Hard et al., 2006, p. 1058).

Reviewing the definition of plagiarism is an important first step. These definitions and procedures reflect a collective effort to help social scientists, including educational researchers, maintain standards. Awareness is the first step (American Sociological Association [ASA], 1999, p. 19). Lack of awareness and misunderstanding of an ethical standard are not, in themselves, adequate defenses against a charge of unethical conduct.

The ASA's (1999) Code of Ethics includes an explicit prohibition of plagiarism that applies equally well to education research:

14. Plagiarism

    (a) In publications, presentations, teaching, practice, and service, sociologists explicitly identify, credit, and reference the author when they take data or material verbatim from another person's written work, whether it is published, unpublished, or electronically available.

    (b) In their publications, presentations, teaching, practice, and service, sociologists provide acknowledgment of and reference to the use of others' work, even if the work is not quoted verbatim or paraphrased, and they do not present others' work as their own whether it is published, unpublished, or electronically available. (p. 16)

The next step toward combating the problem and temptation of plagiarism is to keep focused on the goal of educational research methods: investigating the educational world. If researchers are motivated by a desire to learn about educational processes, to understand how teaching and learning happen, and to discover which strategies, programs, and policies work best, they will be as concerned with the integrity of their research methods as are those, like yourself, who read and use the results of their research. Throughout *Research Methods in Education,* you have been learning how to use research processes and practices that yield valid findings and trustworthy conclusions. Failing to report honestly and openly on the methods used or sources consulted derails progress toward that goal.

It works the same as with cheating in school. When students are motivated only by the desire to "ace" their tests and receive better grades than others, they are more likely to plagiarize and use other illicit means to achieve that goal. Students who seek first to improve their understanding of the subject matter and to engage in the process of learning are less likely to plagiarize sources or cheat on exams (Kohn, 2008, pp. 6–7). They are also building the foundation for becoming successful educational researchers who help others understand our world.

Conclusions

In this chapter, we considered several ways of reporting research. We introduced the concept of circles of interest as a way to think about what level and what type of reporting is appropriate for a given project: Internal/Local, External, Professional, or Academic. For some projects, one of these levels is all that is required. Other projects migrate through several levels and are consequently reported out in several different ways depending on the audience and purpose.

As one example, we looked at an applied research report that estimated the impact, in economic terms, of a 1-year, universal preschool program in California (Karoly & Bigelow, 2005). Using cost-benefit analysis, the researchers found that every dollar invested in high-quality, 1-year preschool programs would yield $2.62 in economic benefits, as well as additional social benefits. We also looked at excerpts from a project on welfare-to-work programs that was reported out in both an academic journal (Chase-Lansdale et al., 2002) and as a policy report for the general public (Sunderland, 2005).

From these examples, you can see that a well-written research article or report (to be just a bit melodramatic) requires blood, sweat, and tears—and more time than you will, at first, anticipate. But the process of writing one will help you to write the next. And the issues you consider, if you approach your writing critically, will be sure to improve your subsequent research projects and sharpen your evaluations of other investigators' research projects.

Good critical skills are essential when evaluating research reports, whether your own or those produced by others. There are *always* weak points in any research, even published research. It is an indication of strength, not weakness, to recognize areas where one's own research needs to be, or could have been, improved. And it is really not just a question of sharpening your knives and going for the jugular. You need to be able to weigh the strengths and weaknesses of particular research results and to evaluate a study in terms of its contribution to understanding the social world—not in terms of whether it gives a definitive answer for all time.

But this is not to say that anything goes. Much research lacks one or more of the three legs of validity—measurement validity, causal validity, or generalizability—and contributes more confusion than understanding about the educational world. Top journals generally maintain very high standards, partly because they have good critics in the review process and distinguished editors who make the final acceptance decisions. But some daily newspapers do a poor job of screening, and research reporting standards in many popular magazines, TV shows, Internet sites, and books are often abysmally poor. Keep your standards high and your view critical when reading research reports, but not so high or so critical that you turn away from studies that make tangible contributions to understanding the educational world—even if they don't provide definitive answers. And don't be so intimidated by the need to maintain high standards that you shrink from taking advantage of opportunities to conduct research yourself.

Of course, educational research methods are no more useful than the commitment of researchers to their proper application. Research methods, like all knowledge, can be used poorly or well, for good purposes or bad, when appropriate or not. A claim that a belief is based on educational research in itself provides no extra credibility. As you have learned throughout this book, we must first learn which methods were used, how they were applied, and whether interpretations square with the evidence. To investigate the educational world, we must keep in mind the lessons of research methods.

Key Terms

Highlights

- Research reports should be evaluated systematically, using the review guide in Appendix A and also taking account of the interrelations among the design elements.

- Proposal writing should be a time for clarifying the research problem, reviewing the literature, and thinking ahead about the report that will be required. Trade-offs between different design elements should be considered and the potential for mixing methods evaluated.

- Research reporting can take many different forms. The appropriate format will change depending on the audience and purpose of the reporting.

- School-based researchers can define "circles of interest" to help them strategize about appropriate forms for reporting their work.

- Different types of reports typically post different problems. Authors of student papers must be guided in part by the expectations of their professor. Thesis writers have to meet the requirements of different committee members but can benefit greatly from the areas of expertise represented on a typical thesis committee. Applied researchers are constrained by the expectations of the research sponsor; an advisory committee from the applied setting can help to avoid problems. Journal articles must pass a peer review by other educational researchers and often are much improved in the process.

- Research reports should include an introductory statement of the research problem, a literature review, a methodology section, a findings section with pertinent data displays, and a conclusions section that identifies any weaknesses in the research design and points out implications for future research and theorizing. This basic report format should be modified according to the needs of a particular audience.

- All reports should be revised several times and critiqued by others before being presented in final form.

- The central ethical concern in research reporting is to be honest. This honesty should include providing a truthful accounting of how the research was carried out, maintaining a full record about the project, using appropriate statistics and graphs, acknowledging the research sponsors, and being sensitive to the perspectives of coauthors.

- Plagiarism is a grievous violation of scholarly ethics. All direct quotes or paraphrased material from another author's work must be appropriately cited.

- Credit must be given where credit is due. The contributions of persons and organizations to a research project must be acknowledged in research reports.

- Social scientists are obligated to evaluate the credibility of information obtained from any source before using it in their research reports. Special attention should be given to the credibility of information acquired through the Internet.

Student Study Site

To assist in completing the web exercises, please access the study site at www.sagepub.com/check, where you will find the web exercise with accompanying links. You'll find other useful study materials such as self-quizzes and e-flashcards for each chapter, along with a group of carefully selected articles from research journals that illustrate the major concepts and techniques.

Discussion Questions

1. A good place to start developing your critical skills would be with one of the articles in this chapter. Try reading one and fill in the answers to the article review questions that we did not cover (see Chapter 2). What lessons on research design do you draw from our critique, and from your own?

2. If someone conducted a research project in your school, what would you want to know about it? How would they create a presentation or report that would answer your questions?

Practice Exercises

1. Contact a local educator or administrator and arrange for an interview. Ask the interviewee about his or her experience with applied research reports and conclusions about the value of educational research and the best techniques for reporting to practitioners.

2. Interview a student who has written an independent paper or thesis based on collecting original data. Ask the interviewee to describe his or her experiences while writing the thesis. Discuss the decisions the student made in designing the research, and ask about the stages of research design, data collection and analysis, and report writing that proved to be difficult.

Web Exercises

1. Go to the web address given in the chapter and read the AERA code of guiding ethical standards, paying special attention to the sections on Reviewing and Appraising Research and Students and Student Researchers. Summarize the most important "take-away" points in each section.

2. Using the Web, find five different examples of educational research projects that have been completed. Briefly describe each. How does each differ in its approach to reporting the research results? Who do you think the author(s) of each are "reporting" to (i.e., who is the "audience")? How do you think the predicted audience has helped to shape the author's approach to reporting the results? Be sure to note the websites at which you located each of your five examples.

Developing a Research Proposal

Now it's time to bring all the elements of your proposal together.

1. Organize the proposal material you wrote for previous chapters in a logical order. Select what you feel is the strongest research method (Chapters 7–13) as your primary method.

2. Add a multiple method component to your research design with one of the other methods sections you prepared in Chapters 7 to 13.

3. Rewrite the entire proposal, adding an introduction. Also add sections that outline a budget, and state the limitations of your study.

4. Review the proposal with the "decision checklist" (see Exhibit 15.1). Answer each question, and justify your decision at each checkpoint.

Appendixes

Appendix A

Questions to Ask About a Research Article

1. What is the basic research question, or problem? Try to state it in just one sentence.

2. Is the purpose of the study explanatory, evaluative, exploratory, or descriptive? Did the study have more than one purpose? (Chapter 1)

3. Was a theoretical framework presented? What was it? Did it seem appropriate for the research question addressed? Can you think of a different theoretical perspective that might have been used? What philosophy guides the research? Is this philosophy appropriate to the research question? (Chapters 1, 2)

4. What prior literature was reviewed? Was it relevant to the research problem? To the theoretical framework? Does the literature review appear to be adequate? Are you aware of (or can you locate) any important studies that have been omitted? (Chapter 2)

5. How well did the study live up to the guidelines for science? Do you need additional information in any areas to evaluate the study? To replicate it? (Chapters 1, 2)

6. Did the study seem consistent with current ethical standards? Were any trade-offs made between different ethical guidelines? Was an appropriate balance struck between adherence to ethical standards and use of the most rigorous scientific practices? (Chapter 3)

7. Were any hypotheses stated? Were these hypotheses justified adequately in terms of the theoretical framework? In terms of prior research? (Chapter 2)

8. What were the independent and dependent variables in the hypothesis or hypotheses? Did these variables reflect the theoretical concepts as intended? What direction of association was hypothesized? Were any other variables identified as potentially important? (Chapter 2)

9. What were the major concepts in the research? How, and how clearly, were they defined? Were some concepts treated as unidimensional that you think might best be thought of as multidimensional? (Chapter 4)

10. Did the instruments used, the measures of the variables, seem valid and reliable? How did the authors attempt to establish this? Could any more have been done in the study to establish measurement validity? (Chapter 4)

11. Was a sample or the entire population of elements used in the study? What type of sample was selected? Was a probability sampling method used? Did the authors think the sample was generally representative of the population from which it was drawn? Do you? How would you evaluate the likely generalizability of the findings to other populations? (Chapter 5)

12. Was the response rate or participation rate reported? Does it appear likely that those who did not respond or participate were markedly different from those who did participate? Why or why not? Did the author(s) adequately discuss this issue? (Chapters 5, 8)

13. What were the units of analysis? Were they appropriate for the research question? If some groups were the units of analysis, were any statements made at any point that are open to the ecological fallacy? If individuals were the units of analysis, were any statements made at any point that suggest reductionist reasoning? (Chapter 6)

14. Was the study design cross-sectional or longitudinal, or did it use both types of data? If the design was longitudinal, what type of longitudinal design was it? Could the longitudinal design have been improved in any way, such as by collecting panel data rather than trend data or by decreasing the dropout rate in a panel design? If cross-sectional data were used, could the research question have been addressed more effectively with longitudinal data? (Chapter 6)

15. Were any causal assertions made or implied in the hypotheses or in subsequent discussions? What approach was used to demonstrate the existence of causal effects? Were all five issues in establishing causal relationships addressed? What, if any, variables were controlled in the analysis to reduce the risk of spurious relationships? Should any other variables have been measured and controlled? How satisfied are you with the internal validity of the conclusions? (Chapter 6)

16. Was an experimental survey, participant observation, historical comparative, or some other research design used? How well was this design suited to the research question posed and the specific hypotheses tested, if any? Why do you suppose the author(s) chose this particular design? How was the design modified in response to research constraints? How was it modified in order to take advantage of research opportunities? (Chapters 7–13)

17. Was this an evaluation research project? If so, which type of evaluation was it? Which design alternatives did it use? (Chapter 7)

18. Was any attention given to social context and subjective meanings? If so, what did this add? If not, would it have improved the study? Explain. (Chapter 1)

19. Summarize the findings. How clearly were statistical and/or qualitative data presented and discussed? Were the results substantively important? (Chapters 11, 13, 14)

20. Did the author(s) adequately represent the findings in the discussion and/or conclusions sections? Were conclusions well grounded in the findings? Are any other interpretations possible? (Chapter 15)

21. Compare the study to others addressing the same research question. Did the study yield additional insights? In what ways was the study design more or less adequate than the design of previous research? (Chapter 15)

22. What additional research questions and hypotheses are suggested by the study's results? What light did the study shed on the theoretical framework used? On social policy questions? (Chapters 2, 15)

Appendix B

How to Read a Research Article

The discussions of research articles throughout the text may provide all the guidance you need to read and critique research on your own. But reading about an article in bits and pieces in order to learn about particular methodologies is not quite the same as reading an article in its entirety in order to learn what the researcher found out. The goal of this appendix is to walk you through an entire research article, answering the review questions introduced in Appendix A. Of course, this is only one article and our "walk" will take different turns than would a review of other articles, but after this review, you should feel more confident when reading other research articles on your own.

We will use for this example an article by South and Spitze (1994) on housework in marital and nonmarital households, reprinted on pages 352 to 372 of this appendix. It focuses on a topic related to everyone's life experiences as well as to important questions in social theory. Moreover, it is a solid piece of research published in a top journal, the American Sociological Association's *American Sociological Review.*

I have reproduced below each of the article review questions from Appendix A, followed by my answers to them. After each question, I indicate the chapter where the question was discussed, and after each answer, I cite the article page or pages that I am referring to. You can also follow my review by reading through the article itself and noting my comments.

1. What is the basic research question, or problem? Try to state it in just one sentence. (Chapter 2)

   - The clearest statement of the research question—actually three questions—is that "we seek to determine how men and women in these [six] different situations [defined by marital status and living arrangement] compare in the amounts of time they spend doing housework, whether these differences can be attributed to differences in other social and economic characteristics, and which household tasks account for these differences" (p. 353). Prior to this point, the authors focus on this research question, distinguishing it from the more general issue of how housework is distributed within marriages and explaining why it is an important research question.

2. Is the purpose of the study explanatory, evaluative, exploratory, or descriptive? Did the study have more than one purpose? (Chapter 1)

   - The problem statement indicates that the study will have both descriptive and explanatory purposes: It will "determine how men and women . . . compare" and then try to explain the differences in housework between them. The literature review that begins on page 353 also makes it clear that the primary purpose of the research was explanatory, since the authors review previous explanations for gender differences in housework and propose a new perspective (pp. 353–358).

3. Was a theoretical framework presented? What was it? Did it seem appropriate for the research question addressed? Can you think of a different theoretical perspective that might have been used? (Chapters 1, 2)

   - The "gender perspective" is used as a framework for the research (p. 354). This perspective seems very appropriate to the research question addressed because it highlights the importance of examining differences between married and other households. The authors themselves discuss three other theoretical perspectives on the division of household labor that might have been used as a theoretical framework but identify weaknesses in each of them (pp. 353–354).

4. What prior literature was reviewed? Was it relevant to the research problem? To the theoretical framework? Does the literature review appear to be adequate? Are you aware of (or can you locate) any important studies that have been omitted? (Chapter 2)

   - Literature is reviewed from the article's first page until the "Data and Methods" section (pp. 352–358). It all seems relevant to the particular problem as well as to the general theoretical framework. In the first few paragraphs, several general studies are mentioned to help clarify the importance of the research problem (pp. 352–353). In the "Models of Household labor" section, alternative theoretical perspectives used in other studies are reviewed, and the strength of the support for them is noted (pp. 353–355). After identifying the theoretical perspective they will use, the authors then introduce findings from particular studies that are most relevant to their focus on how housework varies with marital status (pp. 355–358). I leave it to you to find out whether any important studies were omitted.

5. How well did the study live up to the guidelines for science? Do you need additional information in any areas to evaluate the study? To replicate it? (Chapters 1, 2)

   - It would be best to return to this question after reading the whole article. The study clearly involves a test of ideas against empirical reality as much as that reality could be measured; it was carried out systematically and disclosed, as far as we can tell, fully. Since the authors used an available data set, others can easily obtain the complete documentation for the study and try to replicate the authors' findings. The authors explicitly note and challenge assumptions made in other theories of the division of housework (p. 354), although they do not clarify their own assumptions as such. Two of their assumptions are that the appropriation of another's work is likely to occur "perhaps only" in heterosexual couple households (p. 354) and that "a woman cannot display love for or subordination to a man through housework when no man is present" (p. 354). The authors also assume that respondents' reports of the hours they have spent on various tasks are reasonably valid (p. 359). These seem to be reasonable assumptions, but a moment's reflection should convince you that they are, after all, unproved assumptions that could be challenged. This is not in itself a criticism of the research, since some assumptions must be made in any study. The authors specified the meaning of key terms, as required in scientific research. They also searched for regularities in their data, thus living up to another guide-line. A skeptical stance toward current knowledge is apparent in the literature review and in the authors' claim that they have found only "suggestive evidence" for their theoretical perspective (p. 369). They aim clearly to build social theory and encourage others to build on their findings, "to further specify the conditions" (p. 369). The study thus seems to exemplify adherence to basic scientific guidelines and to be very replicable.

6. Did the study seem consistent with current ethical standards? Were any trade-offs made between different ethical guidelines? Was an appropriate balance struck between adherence to ethical standards and use of the most rigorous scientific practices? (Chapter 3)

   - The authors use survey data collected by others and so encounter no ethical problems in their treatment of human subjects. The reporting seems honest and open. Although the research should help inform social policy, the authors' explicit focus is on how their research can inform social theory. This is quite appropriate for research reported in a scientific journal, so there are no particular ethical problems raised about the uses to which the research is put. The original survey used by the authors does not appear at all likely to have violated any ethical guidelines concerning the treatment of human subjects, although it would be necessary to inspect the original research report to evaluate this.

7. Were any hypotheses stated? Were these hypotheses justified adequately in terms of the theoretical framework? In terms of prior research? (Chapter 2)

   - Five primary hypotheses are stated, although they are labeled as "several important contrasts" that are sug-gested by the "doing gender" approach, rather than as hypotheses. For example, the first hypothesis is that "women in married-couple households [are expected] to spend more time doing housework than women in any other living situation" (p. 355). A more general point is made about variation in housework across household types before these specific hypotheses are introduced. Several more specific hypotheses are then introduced about variations among specific types of households (pp. 355–356). Some questions about patterns of housework in households that have not previously been studied are presented more as speculations than as definite hypotheses (pp. 357–358). Three additional hypotheses are presented concerning the expected effects of the control variables (p. 358).

8. What were the independent and dependent variables in the hypothesis or hypotheses? Did these variables reflect the theoretical concepts as intended? What direction of association was hypothesized? Were any other variables identified as potentially important? (Chapter 2)

   • The independent variable in the first hypothesis is marital status (married vs. other); the dependent variable is time spent doing housework. The hypothesis states that more time will be spent by married women than by other women, and it is stated that this expectation is "net of other differences among the household types" (p. 355). Can you identify the variables in the other hypotheses (the second and fourth hypotheses about men just restate the preceding hypotheses for women)? Another variable, gender differences in time spent on housework, is discussed throughout the article, but it is not in itself measured; rather, it is estimated by comparing the aggregate distribution of hours for men and women.

9. What were the major concepts in the research? How, and how clearly, were they defined? Were some concepts treated as unidimensional that you think might best be thought of as multidimensional? (Chapter 4)

   • The key concept in the research is that of "doing gender"; it is discussed at length and defined in a way that becomes reasonably clear when it is said that "housework 'produces' gender through the everyday enactment of dominance, submission, and other behaviors symbolically linked to gender" (p. 354). The central concept of housework is introduced explicitly as "a major component of most people's lives" (p. 355), but it is not defined conceptually—presumably because it refers to a widely understood phenomenon. A conceptual definition would have helped to justify the particular operationalization used and the decision to exclude childcare from what is termed housework (p. 359). (A good, practical reason for this exclusion is given in footnote 2.) The concept of housework is treated as multidimensional by distinguishing what are termed "male-typed," "female-typed," and "gender-neutral" tasks (p. 367). Another key concept is that of marital status, which the authors define primarily by identifying its different categories (pp. 355–358).

10. Did the instruments used, the measures of the variables, seem valid and reliable? How did the authors attempt to establish this? Could any more have been done in the study to establish measurement validity? (Chapter 4)

    • The measurement of the dependent variable was straightforward but required respondents to estimate the number of hours per week they spent on various tasks. The authors report that some other researchers have used a presumably more accurate method—time diaries—to estimate time spent on household tasks and that the results they obtain are very similar to those of the recall method used in their study. This increases confidence in the measurement approach used, although it does not in itself establish the validity or reliability of the self-report data. Measures of marital status and other variables involved relatively straightforward questions and do not raise particular concerns about validity. The researchers carefully explain in footnotes how they handled missing data.

11. Was a sample or the entire population of elements used in the study? What type of sample was selected? Was a probability sampling method used? Did the authors think the sample was generally representative of the population from which it was drawn? Do you? How would you evaluate the likely generalizability of the findings to other populations? (Chapter 5)

    • The sample was a random (probability) sample of families and households. A disproportionate stratified sampling technique was used to ensure the representation of adequate numbers of single-parent families, cohabitors, and other smaller groups that are of theoretical interest (pp. 358–359). The sample is weighted in the analysis to compensate for the disproportionate sampling method and is said to be representative of the U.S. population. The large size of the sample ($N = 11,016$ after cases with missing values were excluded) indicates that the confidence limits around sample statistics will be very small. Do you think the findings could be generalized to other countries with different cultural values about gender roles and housework?

12. Was the response rate or participation rate reported? Does it appear likely that those who did not respond or participate were markedly different from those who did participate? Why or why not? Did the author(s) adequately discuss this issue? (Chapter 7)

- The response rate was not mentioned—a major omission, although it could be found in the original research report. The authors omitted 2,001 respondents from the obtained sample due to missing data and adjusted values of variables having missing data for some other cases. In order to check the consequences of these adjustments, the authors conducted detailed analyses of the consequences of various adjustment procedures. They report that the procedures they used did not affect their conclusions (pp. 358–359). This seems reasonable.

13. What were the units of analysis? Were they appropriate for the research question? If some groups were the units of analysis, were any statements made at any point that are open to the ecological fallacy? If individuals were the units of analysis, were any statements made at any point that suggest reductionist reasoning? (Chapter 6)

- The survey sampled adults, although it was termed a survey of families and households, and it is data on individuals (and the households in which they live) that are analyzed. You can imagine this same study being conducted with households forming the units of analysis and the dependent variable being the percentage of total time in the family spent on housework, rather than the hours spent by individuals on housework. The conclusions generally are appropriate to the use of individuals as the units of analysis, but there is some danger in reductionist misinterpretation of some of the interpretations, such as that "men and women must be 'doing gender' when they live together" (p. 359). Conclusions like this would be on firmer ground if they were based on household-level data that revealed whether one person's approach to housework did, in fact, vary in relation to that of his or her partner.

14. Was the study design cross-sectional or longitudinal, or did it use both types of data? If the design was longitudinal, what type of longitudinal design was it? Could the longitudinal design have been improved in any way, such as by collecting panel data rather than trend data or by decreasing the dropout rate in a panel design? If cross-sectional data were used, could the research question have been addressed more effectively with longitudinal data? (Chapter 6)

- The survey was cross-sectional. The research question certainly could have been addressed more effectively with longitudinal data that followed people over their adult lives since many of the authors' interpretations reflect their interest in how individuals' past experiences with housework shape their approach when they enter a new marital status (pp. 359–360).

15. Were any causal assertions made or implied in the hypotheses or in subsequent discussions? What approach was used to demonstrate the existence of causal effects? Were all five issues in establishing causal relationships addressed? What, if any, variables were controlled in the analysis to reduce the risk of spurious relationships? Should any other variables have been measured and controlled? How satisfied are you with the internal validity of the conclusions? (Chapter 6)

- The explanatory hypotheses indicate that the authors were concerned with causality. Mention is made of a possible causal mechanism when it is pointed out that "doing gender"—the presumed causal influence—may operate at both unconscious and conscious levels (p. 354). In order to reduce the risk of spuriousness in the presumed causal relationship (between marital status and housework time), variables such as age, education, earnings, and the presence of children are controlled (p. 360). There are, of course, other variables that might have created a spurious relationship, but at least several of the most likely contenders have been controlled. For example, the use of cross-sectional data leaves us wondering whether some of the differences attributed to marital status might really be due to generational differences—the never-married group is likely to be younger and the widowed group older; controlling for age gives us more confidence that this is not the case. On the other hand, the lack of longitudinal data means that we do not know whether the differences in housework might have preceded marital status: Perhaps women who got married also did more housework even before they were married than women who remained single.

16. Was an experimental survey, participant observation, content analysis, or some other research design used? How well was this design suited to the research question posed and the specific hypotheses tested, if any? Why

do you suppose the author(s) chose this particular design? How was the design modified in response to research constraints? How was it modified in order to take advantage of research opportunities? (Chapters 7–13)

- Survey research was the method of choice and probably was used for this article because the data set was already available for analysis. Survey research seems appropriate for the research questions posed, but the limitation of the survey to one point in time was a major constraint (p. 358).

17. Was this an evaluation research project? If so, which type of evaluation was it? Which design alternatives did it use? (Chapter 11)

- This study did not use an evaluation research design. The issues on which it focuses might profitably be studied in some program evaluations.

18. Was any attention given to social context and subjective meanings? If so, what did this add? If not, would it have improved the study? Explain. (Chapter 1)

- In a sense, the independent variable in this study is social context: The combinations of marital status and living arrangements distinguish different social contexts in which gender roles are defined. However, no attention is given to the potential importance of larger social contexts, such as neighborhood, region, or nation. It is also possible to imagine future research that tests the influence of biological factors on the household division of labor.

19. Summarize the findings. How clearly were statistical and/or qualitative data presented and discussed? Were the results substantively important? (Chapters 11, 13, 14)

- Statistical data are presented clearly using descriptive statistics (multiple regression analysis, a multivariate statistical technique) and graphs that highlight the most central findings. In fact, the data displays are exemplary because they effectively convey findings to a wide audience and also subject the hypotheses to rigorous statistical tests. No qualitative data are presented. The findings seem substantively important since they identify large differences in the household roles of men and women and in how these roles vary in different types of household (pp. 361–368).

20. Did the author(s) adequately represent the findings in the discussion and/or conclusions sections? Were conclusions well grounded in the findings? Are any other interpretations possible? (Chapter 15)

- The findings are well represented in the discussion and conclusions section (pp. 368–370). The authors point out in their literature review that a constant pattern of gender differences in housework across household types would "cast doubt on the validity of the gender perspective" (p. 355), and the findings clearly rule this out. However, the conclusions give little consideration to the ways in which the specific findings might be interpreted as consistent or inconsistent with reasonable predictions from each of the three other theoretical perspectives reviewed. You might want to consider what other interpretations of the findings might be possible. Remember that other interpretations always are possible for particular findings—it is a question of the weight of the evidence, the persuasiveness of the theory used, and the consistency of the findings with other research.

21. Compare the study to others addressing the same research question. Did the study yield additional insights? In what ways was the study design more or less adequate than the design of previous research? (Chapter 15)

- The study investigated an aspect of the question of gender differences in housework that had not previously received much attention (variation in gender differences across different types of households). This helped the authors to gain additional insights into gender and housework, although the use of cross-sectional data and a retrospective self-report measure of housework made their research in some ways less adequate than others.

22. What additional research questions and hypotheses are suggested by the study's results? What light did the study shed on the theoretical framework used? On social policy questions? (Chapters 2, 15)

- The article suggests additional questions for study about "the conditions under which [the dynamics of doing gender] operate" and how equity theory might be used to explain the division of labor in households (p. 369). The authors make a reasonable case for the value of their "gender perspective." Social policy questions are not addressed directly, but the article would be of great value to others concerned with social policy.

HOUSEWORK IN MARITAL AND NONMARITAL HOUSEHOLDS*

SCOTT J. SOUTH   GLENNA SPITZE
State University of New York at Albany   *State University of New York at Albany*

Although much recent research has explored the division of household labor between husbands and wives, few studies have examined housework patterns across marital statuses. This paper uses data from the National Survey of Families and Households to analyze differences in time spent on housework by men and women in six different living situations: never married and living with parents, never married and living independently, cohabiting, married, divorced, and widowed. In all situations, women spend more time than men doing housework, but the gender gap is widest among married persons. The time women spend doing housework is higher among cohabitants than among the never-married, is highest in marriage, and is lower among divorcees and widows. Men's housework time is very similar across both never-married living situations, in cohabitation, and in marriage. However, divorced and widowed men do substantially more housework than does any other group of men, and they are especially more likely than their married counterparts to spend more time cooking and cleaning. In addition to gender and marital status, housework time is affected significantly by several indicators of workload (e.g., number of children, home ownership) and time devoted to nonhousehold activities (e.g., paid employment, school enrollment)—most of these variables have greater effects on women's housework time than on men's. An adult son living at home increases women's housework, whereas an adult daughter at home reduces housework for women and men. These housework patterns are generally consistent with an emerging perspective that view's housework as a symbolic enactment of gender relations. We discuss the implications of these findings for perceptions of marital equity.

Until 20 years ago, social science research on housework was largely nonexistent (Glazer-Malbin 1976; Huber and Spitze 1983), but since then, research on the topic has exploded. Patterns of housework and how housework is experienced by participants have been documented in both qualitative (e.g., Hochschild with Machung 1989; Oakley 1974) and quantitative studies (e.g., Berk 1985; Blair and Lichter 1991; Coverman and Sheley 1986; Goldscheider and Waite 1991; Rexroat and Shehan 1987; Ross 1987; Shelton 1990; Spitze 1986; Walker and Woods 1976). The vast majority of these studies have focused on married couples, but a few have examined cohabiting couples as well (e.g., Blumstein and Schwartz 1983; Shelton and John 1993; Stafford, Backman, and Dibona 1977). The rationale for focusing on couples is typically a research interest in equity (Benin and Agostinelli 1988; Blair and Johnson 1992; Ferree 1990; Peterson and Maynard 1981; Thompson 1991) and in how changes in women's employment and gender roles have changed, or failed to change, household production functions.

Very few studies have examined housework as performed in noncouple households composed of never-married, separated or divorced, or widowed persons (e.g., Grief 1985; Sanik and Mauldin 1986). Such studies are important for two reasons. First, people are spending increasing amounts of time in such households at various points in their lives due to postponed marriages, higher divorce rates, and a preference among adults in all age categories (including the later years) for independent living. For example, the proportion of households that includes married couples decreased from 76.3 percent to 60.9 percent between 1940 and 1980 (Sweet and Bumpass 1987), and the number of years adult women spend married has decreased by about seven years during the past several decades (Watkins, Menken, and Bon-

*Direct all correspondence to Scott J. South or Glenna Spitze, Department of Sociology, State University of New York at Albany, Albany, NY 12222. The authors contributed equally to this research and are listed alphabetically. We acknowledge with gratitude the helpful comments of several anonymous *ASR* reviewers.

gaarts 1987). It is important to learn how housework is experienced by this substantial segment of the population to understand the household production function in general and because performance of housework is related to decisions about paid work and leisure time for people in these categories.

Second, the housework experiences of single, divorced, and widowed persons go with them if they move into marriage or cohabitation—these experiences are part of the context in which they negotiate how to accomplish tasks jointly with a partner. People may use those prior experiences or assumptions about what they *would* do if the marriage or cohabiting relationship dissolved to set an alternative standard when assessing an equitable division of household labor, rather than simply comparing their own investment in housework to their partner's. Thus, by understanding factors affecting housework contributions by men and women not living in couple relationships, we can better understand what happens when they do form those relationships.

Our broadest objective in this paper is to analyze how time spent doing housework by men and women varies by marital status and to interpret this analysis in relation to the "gender perspective" on household labor. Focusing on six situations defined by marital status and living arrangement, we seek to determine how men and women in these different situations compare in the amounts of time they spend doing housework, whether these differences can be attributed to differences in other social and economic characteristics, and which household tasks account for these differences. We are particularly interested in those persons who are living independently and who are not married or cohabiting, since previous research has focused heavily on married persons and, to a lesser extent, on cohabiting couples (Shelton and John 1993; Stafford et al. 1977) and children still living at home (Benin and Edwards 1990; Berk 1985; Blair 1991; Goldscheider and Waite 1991; Hilton and Haldeman 1991).

MODELS OF HOUSEHOLD LABOR

Beginning with Blood and Wolfe's (1960) classic study, sociologists have attempted to explain the division of household labor between husbands and wives and to determine whether the division is changing over time. The *re-source-power perspective* originating in that work focuses on the economic and social contexts in which husbands and wives bring their individual resources (such as unequal earnings) to bear in bargaining over who will do which household chores. This resource-power theory has since been modified and elaborated upon in several ways, focusing on determining which resources are important and the conditions under which they are useful for bargaining. Rodman's (1967) theory of resources in cultural context and Blumberg and Coleman's (1989) theory of gender stratification (as applied to housework) suggest that there are limits on how effectively resources can be used, especially by women. Several observers suggest that wives' resources may be "discounted" by male dominance at the societal level (Aytac and Teachman 1992; Blumberg and Coleman 1989; Ferree 1991b; Gillespie 1971).

Two other perspectives are used frequently in the study of household labor. One focuses on *socialization and gender role attitudes*, suggesting that husbands and wives perform household labor in differing amounts depending upon what they have learned and have come to believe about appropriate behavior for men and women (see Goldscheider and Waite 1991). An alternative perspective, the *time availability hypothesis*, suggests that husbands and wives perform housework in amounts relative to the time left over after paid work time is substracted. A variation on this, the demand response capability hypothesis (Coverman 1985), is somewhat broader and includes factors that increase the total amount of work to be done and spouses' availability to do it. The focus on time allocation as a rational process is akin to the economic perspective, most closely associated with Becker (1981; see also critique in Berk 1985). However, sociologists and economists differ in their views on this perspective: Economists assume that time allocation to housework and paid work is jointly determined and based on the relative efficiency of husbands and wives in both arenas; sociologists assume that decisions about paid work are causally prior (Godwin 1991; Spitze 1986).

The above three perspectives (power-resources, socialization-gender roles, and time availability) have guided much of the sociological research on household labor over the past 20 years (see reviews of these theories and their variations in Ferree 1991a; Godwin 1991; Shelton 1992; Spitze 1988). However, they have produced mixed results, and, as several reviewers have pointed out, much more variance is explained by gender per se than by any of the other factors in these models (Ferree 1991a; Thompson and Walker 1991). Moreover, studies show that women who earn more than their husbands often do a disproportionate share of the housework, perhaps in an attempt to prevent those earnings from threatening the husband's self-esteem (Thompson and Walker 1991). While both husbands' and wives' time in paid employment does affect the time they spend doing housework (Goldscheider and Waite 1991), it is argued that the basic distribution of household labor calls for an explanation of its gendered, asymmetrical nature (Thompson and Walker 1991).

A new direction in the explanation of household labor originates in West and Zimmerman's (1987) concept of "doing gender." They argue that gender can be understood as "a routine accomplishment embedded in everyday interaction" (1987:125). Berk (1985) applied their perspective to the division of household labor, observing that the current situation among husbands and wives is neither inherently rational (as the New Home Economics had argued; see Becker 1981) nor fair. Thus, Berk concludes that more than goods and services are "produced" through household labor. She describes the marital household as a "gender factory" where, in addition to accomplishing tasks, housework "produces" gender through the everyday enactment of dominance, submission, and other behaviors symbolically linked to gender (Berk 1985; see also Hartmann 1981; Shelton and John 1993).

Ferree (1991a) elaborates on the "gender perspective" and its application to household labor and argues that it challenges three assumptions of resource theory. First, as Berk pointed out in her critique of economic analyses of housework, housework is not allocated in the most efficient manner. Second, gender is more influential than individual resources in determining the division of household labor. And third, housework is not necessarily defined as "bad" and to be avoided. On the contrary, in addition to expressing subordination, housework can also express love and care, particularly for women (Ferree 1991a). Relatedly, DeVault (1989) describes in detail how the activities surrounding the planning and prepara-

tion of meals are viewed not only as labor but also as an expression of love. In support of the general argument that housework has important symbolic meanings, Ferree (1991a) points out that "housework-like chores are imposed in other institutions to instill discipline" (p. 113), such as KP in the army.

The process of "doing gender" is not assumed to operate at a conscious level; on the contrary, Berk (1985) points out that it goes on "without much notice being taken" (p. 207). Ferree (1991a) finds it "striking how little explicit conflict there is over housework in many families" (p. 113). Hochschild's (with Machung 1989) pathbreaking study shows how gender ideologies are enacted through the performance of housework and may operate in a contradictory manner at conscious and unconscious levels. She discovers through in-depth case studies that people's ideas about gender are often "fractured and incoherent" (p. 190) and that contradictions abound between what people say they believe, what they seem to feel, and how these beliefs and feelings are reflected in their household behavior.

This developing "doing gender" approach suggests several important contrasts between couple households (especially those of married couples) and other household types. Indeed, one could argue that *only* by examining a range of household types, including those *not* formed by couples, can one determine the usefulness of this explanation for the behavior of married or cohabiting persons. If gender is being "produced," one would expect this process to be more important in heterosexual couple households than in other household types—there would be less need or opportunity for either men or women to display dominance and subordination or other gender-linked behaviors when they are not involved in conjugal relations. Berk (1985) argues that "in households where the appropriation of *another's* work is possible, in practice the expression of work and the expression of gender become inseparable" (p. 204). Of course, we recognize that gender role socialization is likely to produce gender differentials, even among unmarried persons. However, this *appropriation* seems likely to occur mainly, or perhaps only, in heterosexual couple households, particularly when the couples are married. Berk observes a sharp contrast in the housework patterns of married couples versus same-sex roommate arrangements, the latter seeming "so uncomplicated" to respondents (1985:204).

If heterosexual couples indeed produce gender through performing housework, we would expect women in married-couple households to spend more time doing housework than women in any other living situation; we would expect men's time spent doing housework to be lower in married-couple households than in other household types. These expectations are net of other differences between the household types, such as the presence of children, that affect housework. We would expect women to display submission to and/or love for their husbands or male partners by performing a disproportionate share of the housework, whereas men would display their gender/dominance by avoiding housework that they might perform in other household settings—in particular female-typed housework that constitutes the vast majority of weekly housework time in households. Because a woman cannot display love for or subordination to a man through housework when no man is present, this avenue for displaying gender does not exist in one-adult households. Thus, we would predict smaller gender differences in noncouple than couple household settings once other relevant factors are controlled.

An alternative empirical outcome—one that would cast doubt on the validity of the gender perspective—would be a pattern across household type involving a more or less constant gender difference. We know that there is a gender gap in time spent doing housework between married men and women and between teenage boys and girls. We do not know, however, whether that gap is constant across other situations. If, for example, gender differences in childhood training produce standards or skill levels that vary with gender, one might argue that men and women would carry these attitudes or behaviors with them as they move among different household situations.

HOUSEWORK AND MARITAL STATUS

Housework is a major component of most people's lives, just as is paid work. It is first experienced in childhood as "chores" and continues into retirement. Yet, while housework is performed prior to marriage and after its dissolution, most studies of household labor focus exclusively on husbands and wives. This tends

to create the false impression that housework occurs only within marital households.

Our analysis of housework is based on a categorization by marital status. We focus on men and women who have *never married*, or are currently *married, divorced*, or *widowed*. However, because a key aspect of our theoretical argument focuses on gender relations in heterosexual households, we add a "cohabiting" category, which includes persons who are currently cohabiting whether or not they have ever been married, divorced, or widowed. Further, the situation of never-married persons (who are not cohabiting) varies greatly depending upon whether they are *living independently* or *living in a parental household*; thus we divide never-married persons into two groups based on living situation. In the sections below, we review studies of housework performed by persons in each of these six categories.

Never-Married Persons Living in Their Parents' Homes

The performance of household chores is one of many gender-differentiated socialization experiences gained in families of origin. A number of studies have examined housework performed by boys and girls up to the age of 18 who are living with their parents. These studies have focused on three kinds of questions: how parents define the meaning of housework (White and Brinkerhoff 1981a), how children's contributions relate to or substitute for mothers' or fathers' work (Berk 1985; Goldscheider and Waite 1991), and how housework varies by the gender of the child, mother's employment, and number of parents in the household (e.g., Benin and Edwards 1990; Blair 1991; Hilton and Haldeman 1991).

Housework done by boys and by girls mirrors that of adults, with girls doing stereotypical "female" chores and spending more time doing housework than boys (Benin and Edwards 1990; Berk 1985; Blair 1991; Goldscheider and Waite 1991; Hilton and Haldeman 1991; Timmer, Eccles, and O'Brien 1985; White and Brinkerhoff 1981b). Patterns by gender and age suggest that, under certain conditions, children (particularly older girls) actually assist their parents. Gender differences increase with age, so that in the teenage years girls are spending about twice as much time per week as boys doing housework (Timmer et al.

1985), and the gender-stereotyping of tasks is at a peak. This pattern holds even in single-father families, where one might expect less traditional gender-typed behavior (Grief 1985). Adolescent girls' housework time has been shown to substitute for that of their mothers, while boys' housework time does not (Bergen 1991; Goldscheider and Waite 1991). Differences between single-parent and two-parent families also suggest more actual reliance on girls' work: Boys in single-parent households do less housework than do boys in two-parent households, while girls in single-parent households do more (Hilton and Haldeman 1991). Similar differences have been found between single- and dual-earner two-parent families. Again, girls do more when parents' time is constrained (dual earners) while boys do less, suggesting that parents actually rely on girls to substitute for their mothers' time doing housework (Benin and Edwards 1990).

One would expect parallel differences in the behavior of young adult men and women who still live with their parents. To our knowledge, only three studies have examined housework performed by adult children living in parental households. Ward, Logan, and Spitze (1992) find that adult children living with parents perform only a small proportion of total household tasks when compared to their parents, and parents whose adult children do not live at home actually perform fewer household tasks per month than do parents whose adult children live with them. There are also major differences between adult sons and adult daughters in the amount of housework they do, with daughters performing more tasks than sons when they live in a parent's home. This holds for all parent age groups, particularly those under 65. These gender differences are consistent with results on adult children's share of household tasks reported by Goldscheider and Waite (1991). Hartung and Moore (1992) report qualitative findings that are consistent with the conclusion that adult children, especially sons, contribute little to household chores and typically add to their mothers' burdens.

Never-Married Persons Living Independently

We know of no empirical research that focuses specifically on never-married persons living independently, so we will speculate briefly about factors affecting them. One likely consequence of experiences with housework in the parental home is that girls acquire the skills required for independent living, including shopping, cooking, cleaning, and laundry. To the extent that they have already been doing significant amounts of housework at home, girls' transitions to independent living may not create a major change in the amount or types of housework they perform. The skills boys are more likely to learn in the parental home (e.g., yard work) may be less useful, particularly if their first independent living experience is in an apartment. They may reach adulthood enjoying housework less than women, feeling less competent at household tasks, holding lower standards of performance, embracing gender-stereotyped attitudes about appropriateness of tasks, and preferring to pay for substitutes (e.g., laundry, meals eaten out). On the other hand, single men living independently (and not cohabiting) are forced, to a certain extent, to do their own housework (Goldscheider and Waite 1991), because their living situations are unlikely to provide household services. Thus, the time spent by single men doing housework should increase when they move out of parental households.

Cohabiters

Cohabiting couples share some characteristics of both married and single persons (Shelton and John 1993; Stafford et al. 1977). As Rindfuss and VandenHeuvel (1992) point out, most discussions have used married persons as the comparison group, viewing cohabitation as an alternative kind of marriage or engagement. The division of household labor between cohabiters may be closer to that of married persons, but in other areas such as fertility plans, employment, school enrollment, and home ownership, cohabiters more closely resemble single persons (Rindfuss and VandenHeuvel 1992). Thus, we would expect cohabiters to fall at an intermediate position, between never-married living independently and married persons, in the allocation of time to housework.

A few empirical studies have examined housework by heterosexual cohabiting couples. One early study (Stafford et al. 1977) uses a relative contribution measure of housework and finds cohabiting couples to be fairly "traditional" in their division of household labor. A more recent study using an absolute measure of time expenditure in housework (Shelton and John 1993) sheds more light on the comparison between cohabiting and married couples. Adjusted means of time spent doing housework for cohabiting men are not significantly different from those for married men, but cohabiting women do less housework than do married women. These results are consistent with Blumstein and Schwartz's (1983) comparisons of married and cohabiting men and women. Blair and Lichter (1991) find no significant differences between married and cohabiting men's housework time, but find less task segregation by gender among cohabitants. As is true of comparisons on other dimensions (Rindfuss and VandenHeuvel 1992), studies of housework among cohabiting couples have used married persons as the comparison group, and there have been few comparisons of housework patterns in cohabiting relationships to patterns in other marital statuses.

Married Persons

Marriage often entails a number of changes that increase housework, including parenthood and home ownership, but it also might increase housework for less tangible reasons. Marriage and parenthood entail responsibility for the well-being of others, which is likely to be reflected in higher standards of cleanliness and nutrition, and thus require that more time be devoted to housework. However, the net result of this increase in total work is different for men and for women, and this gender division of household labor has been the subject of much research and theorizing in recent years. Averages tend to range widely depending on the definitions of housework used, but women generally report performing over 70 percent of total housework, even if they are employed (Bergen 1991; Ferree 1991a). One recent study reported married women (including nonemployed) doing 40 hours of housework per week and men 19 hours (Shelton and John 1993), and countless studies have documented that wives' employment has little effect on married men's housework load (see reviews in Spitze 1988; Thompson and Walker 1991). Clearly, wives are responsible for the vast bulk of household chores and for maintaining standards of cleanliness and health in the family. Married men have been described as doing less

housework than they create (Hartmann 1981). Further, when they do contribute to household chores, men are more likely to take on those jobs which are more pleasant, leaving women with those than can be described as "unrelenting, repetitive, and routine" (Thompson and Walker 1991:86). Thus, past empirical results for married persons are consistent with the gender perspective, but comparative analyses that include persons in other marital statuses are needed.

Divorced Persons

To our knowledge there have been no studies of the time divorced persons spend doing housework except those studies focusing on children's housework. Divorced persons (who are not cohabiting) have had the prior experience of living with a heterosexual partner. Women may experience a decrease in housework hours if in fact their partner was creating more housework than he was doing. Men's experience, on the other hand, may be similar to that of moving out of the parental household, that is, of having to do some household tasks for themselves that were previously performed by others. Those who never lived independently before may have to do some of these chores for the first time. Gove and Shin (1989) point out that both divorced and widowed men have more difficulty carrying out their daily household routines than do their female counterparts, who are more likely to experience economic strains.

Widowed Persons

In empirical studies, housework has been identified as an important source of strain for widowed men. Widowed men reduce the time they spend doing housework as the years since widowhood pass, and they are more likely than widows to have help doing it as time goes on (Umberson, Wortman, and Kessler 1992). Of course, today's widows and widowers came of age when the gendered division of labor in households was much more segregated than it is today and when living independently before or between marriages was much less common. While we expect widowed men today to have entered widowhood with relatively little experience in certain kinds of household chores, this may not be true in the future.

Widowed women may share some characteristics with divorced women; they may actually feel some relief from the strain of doing the bulk of household tasks for two (Umberson et al. 1992). Like widowed men, however, current cohorts of widowed women may have little experience in certain kinds of chores, in this case traditionally male chores such as yard work, car care, or financial management.

Other Factors Influencing Time Doing Housework

Men and women in different marital statuses are likely to differ on a variety of factors that can influence the performance of housework, such as their health, employment status, presence of children and other adults, and home ownership. We would expect the performance of housework to vary by marital status both because of these factors and because of the ways in which the marital status itself (or experience in a previous status) influences housework behavior. Here, we describe a model of time spent in housework that can be applied to persons in all marital situations. This model will then guide us in choosing control variables for the analysis of housework.

A person is expected to spend more time in housework as the *total amount to be done* increases. (Berk [1985] calls this the total "pie" in her study of married couple households.) We would expect the amount of housework to increase as the number of children increases, particularly when children are young, but to some extent for older children as well (Bergen 1991; Berk 1985; Ishii-Kuntz and Coltrane 1992; Rexroat and Shehan 1987). The amount of work will also increase with the addition of adults to the household, although of course they may perform housework as well. Work may also increase with the size of house and the responsibilities that go with home ownership, car ownership, and presence of a yard (Bergen 1991; Berk 1985).[1]

---

[1] While owning appliances would be expected to decrease time spent doing housework, it has had much less clear-cut effects than expected, both over time and in cross-sectional studies (Gershuny and Robinson 1988).

Note that the total housework to be done is to some extent a subjective concept. Two households with the same composition and type of home may accomplish different amounts of housework for several reasons. The standards held by the adults in the household will vary (Berk 1985) and may even vary systematically along dimensions such as education and age. Also, some households purchase more services than others, due to available income (Bergen 1991) and time constraints.

A second factor influencing the amount of housework a person does is the number of *other people* there are in the household with whom to share the work. Other people are most helpful if they are adults, and women are likely to contribute more than men. Teenagers and even grade-school-age children may be helpful, and their contribution may also vary by gender. The way that household labor is divided, and thus the amount performed by a particular man or woman, may also relate to gender-role attitudes that may vary with education, age, race, and other factors.

Third, persons with more *time and energy* will do more housework. Available time would be limited by hours spent in paid work, school enrollment status, health and disability status, and age (Coltrane and Ishii-Kuntz 1992; Ishii-Kuntz and Coltrane 1992; Rexroat and Shehan 1987). Concurrent roles, in addition to that of homemaker, detract from the time available to be devoted to housework.

DATA AND METHODS

Data for this study are drawn from the National Survey of Families and Households (NSFH), a national probability sample of 13,017 adults interviewed between March of 1987 and May of 1988 (Sweet, Bumpass, and Call 1988). The NSFH includes a wide variety of questions on sociodemographic background, household composition, labor force behavior, and marital and cohabitation experiences, as well as items describing respondents' allocation of time to household tasks. The NSFH oversamples single-parent families and cohabiters (as well as minorities and recently married persons), thus facilitating comparisons of household labor among persons in different—and relatively rare—household situations. Sample weights are used throughout the analysis to achieve the proper representation of respondents in the U.S. population.

The dependent variable, hours devoted to housework in the typical week, is derived from a series of questions asking respondents how many hours household members spend on various tasks. Respondents were provided with a chart and instructed: "Write in the approximate number of hours per week that you, your spouse/partner, or others in the household normally spend doing the following things." Nine household tasks include "preparing meals," "washing dishes and cleaning up after meals," "cleaning house," "outdoor and other household maintenance tasks (lawn and yard work, household repair, painting, etc.)," "shopping for groceries and other household goods," "washing, ironing, mending," "paying bills and keeping financial records," "automobile maintenance and repair," and "driving other household members to work, school, or other activities." This analysis uses only the number of hours that the respondents report *themselves* as spending on these tasks. To construct the dependent variable, we sum the number of hours spent on each of the nine tasks.[2]

We make two adjustments to this dependent variable. First, because a few respondents reported spending inordinate numbers of hours on specific tasks, we recode values above the 95th percentile for each task to the value at that percentile. This adjustment reduces skewness in the individual items and therefore in the summed variable as well. Second, so we can include respondents who omit one or two of the nine questionnaire items, we impute values for the household tasks for these respondents.[3] In-

dividuals who failed to respond to more than two of the questions are excluded from the analysis. Omitting these respondents and excluding cases with missing values on the independent variables leaves 11,016 respondents available for analysis.

Given our focus on differences in housework between unmarried and married persons, it is essential that the dependent variable records the absolute number of hours devoted to housework rather than the proportional distribution of hours (or tasks) performed by various household members (e.g., Waite and Goldscheider 1992; Spitze 1986). Of course, estimates of time spent on household tasks made by respondents (as recorded in the NSFH) are likely to be less accurate than estimates from time diaries (for a review of validity studies dealing with time use, see Gershuny and Robinson 1988). Yet, estimates of the relative contribution of wives and husbands to household labor are generally comparable across different reporting methods (Warner 1986). Moreover, the effects of respondent characteristics on the time spent on housework shown here are quite similar to the effects observed in time diary studies. The size of the NSFH (approximately five times larger than the typical time-use survey), its oversampling of atypical marital statuses, and its breadth of coverage of respondent characteristics adequately compensate for the lack of time-diary data.

The key explanatory variable combines respondents' marital status' with aspects of their

---

[2] The research literature on housework is inconsistent regarding the inclusion of time spent in childcare. Many data sets commonly used to analyze household labor do not include childcare in their measure (e.g., Bergen 1991; Rexroat and Shehan 1987) or, as is the case here, childcare time is not included as a separate task (Coltrane and Ishii-Kuntz 1992), in part because respondents have difficulty separating time spent in childcare from leisure and from time spent in other tasks. Thus, we are not able to include childcare in our measure. This probably creates a downward bias in estimates of household labor time.

[3] The NSFH assigns four different codes to the household task items for respondents who did not give a numerical reply: some unspecified amount of time spent; inapplicable; don't know; and no answer. Our imputation procedure substitutes a value of 0 for

those who did not answer this question (but answered at least seven of the nine items) or who said the task was inapplicable. In the former case, skipping the item most likely indicates that the respondent spent no time on that task; in the latter case, the respondent most likely could not logically spend time on that task (e.g., persons without cars could not spend any time maintaining them). For respondents who indicated spending some unspecified amount of time on a task and for those who indicated they didn't know, our imputation procedure substitutes the mean value for that task. In both of these instances, respondents presumably spent at least some time on that task. Our explorations of alternative ways of handling missing data, including omitting respondents who failed to answer one or more of the questions, treating all non-numerical responses as 0, and substituting all non-numerical responses with the mean, showed quite clearly that our substantive conclusions are unaffected by the method used to handle missing data.

living arrangements. (For stylistic convenience, we refer to this variable simply as marital status.) We distinguish six mutually exclusive statuses: never married and living in the parental household, never married (not cohabiting) and living independently, cohabiting, currently married, divorced or separated (not cohabiting), and widowed (not cohabiting). Because we are interested in the impact of a spouse or partner on respondents' time doing housework, cohabiters include divorced, separated, and widowed cohabiters as well as never-married cohabiters.

The other explanatory variables measure respondents' demographic background, socioeconomic standing, household composition, concurrent roles, and disability status. As suggested above, several of these factors may help explain any differences that we observe in housework time by marital status and gender. *Age* is measured in years. Because housework demands are likely to peak during the middle adult years and to moderate at older ages, we also include *age squared* as an independent variable. *Education* is measured by years of school completed. *Household earnings* refers to the wage, salary, and self-employment income of all members of the household.[4] *Home ownership* is a dummy variable scored 1 for respondents who own their own home and 0 for those who do not.

Several variables reflect the presence in the household of persons who may create or perform housework. *Children* in the household are divided into the number of children younger than 5 years old, the number age 5 through 11, and the number age 12 through 18. Among the latter group, girls might be expected to create less (or perform more) housework than boys (Goldscheider and Waite 1991), and thus we include separate counts of male and female teenagers. We use several dummy variables to indicate the presence in the household of an *adult male* or *adult female* other than the respondent's spouse or cohabiting partner. Adult females are expected to reduce respondent's time devoted to housework, while adult males are expected to increase it. We further distinguish between adult household members who are the children of the respondent and those who are not.

Respondents who invest their time in activities outside the home are anticipated to devote less time to domestic labor. Employment status is measured by the usual number of *hours worked per week* in the labor force. And, whether the respondent is currently *attending school* is indicated by a dummy variable scored 1 for currently enrolled respondents and 0 for those not attending school.

Finally, *disability status* is measured by the response to the question, do you "have a physical or mental condition that limits your ability to do day-to-day household tasks?" Individuals reporting such a condition are scored 1 on this dummy variable; unimpaired respondents are scored 0.[5]

Our primary analytic strategy is to estimate OLS regression equations that examine the impact of gender, marital status, and the other explanatory variables on the time spent doing housework. Of particular importance for our theoretical model is whether marital status differences in housework time vary by gender—that is, do gender and marital status interact in affecting time spent doing housework? The "gender perspective" implies that marital status differences in housework will be more pronounced for women than for men and that the gender differences in housework will be greatest for married persons. The regression models are also used to determine the extent to which marital status differences in time doing

---

[4] So as not to lose an inordinate number of cases to missing data, we substituted the mean for missing values on household earnings, and we included a dummy variable for these respondents in the regression models (coefficients not shown). One potential difficulty with this procedure is that all respondents who were not the householder or the spouse of the householder receive the mean value, because respondents were not asked the earnings of other household members. Equations estimated only with repondents who are householders revealed effects almost identical to those reported in the text, although never-married respondents living in the parental household are necessarily excluded from these equations. Given that households with adult children include more adults than other households, the household earnings of these latter respondents are likely to be higher than average, but any bias in the effect of earnings is apt to be slight. With one exception (see footnote 5), the amount of missing data on the other explanatory variables is small.

[5] To retain the 5 percent of respondents who did not reply to the question on disability status, the regression equations also include a dummy variable for these respondents (coefficients not shown).

Table 1. Descriptive Statistics for Hours Spent in Housework per Week and for Explanatory Variables, by Gender: U.S. Men and Women, 1987 to 1988

Variable	Women		Men	
	Mean	Standard Deviation	Mean	Standard Deviation
Housework hours per week	32.62	18.18	18.14	12.88
Marital Status[a]				
Never married/living in parental home	.06	.23	.11	.32
Never married/living independently	.10	.30	.11	.32
Cohabiting	.04	.19	.04	.20
Married	.57	.50	.63	.48
Divorced/separated	.12	.33	.08	.26
Widowed	.12	.33	.03	.17
Number of children ages 0 to 4	.26	.59	.22	.55
Number of children ages 5 to 11	.33	.70	.29	.66
Number of girls ages 12 to 18	.16	.44	.15	.43
Number of boys ages 12 to 18	.17	.45	.15	.43
Adult male child present (0 = no; 1 = yes)	.10	.29	.07	.25
Adult male nonchild present (0 = no; 1 = yes)	.09	.29	.18	.38
Adult female child present (0 = no; 1 = yes)	.08	.27	.05	.22
Adult female nonchild present (0 = no; 1 = yes)	.14	.35	.17	.38
Home ownership (0 = no; 1 = yes)	.59	.49	.58	.49
Household earnings (in $1,000s)	28.72	37.69	31.64	36.51
Education 12.45	2.93	12.94	3.32	
Age	44.30	17.99	42.24	17.07
Age squared (/100)	22.86	17.81	20.75	16.38
Hours employed per week	18.43	20.01	31.81	22.55
School enrollment (0 = no; 1 = yes)	.06	.24	.07	.26
Disabled (0 = no; 1 = yes)	.06	.24	.05	.22
Number of cases	6,764		4,252	

[a]May not add to 1.00 because of rounding.

housework can be explained by other respondent characteristics and to assess whether the gender-specific impact of the explanatory variables holds for the general population (including unmarried people) in ways previously shown for married persons.

RESULTS

Table 1 presents descriptive statistics for all variables in the analysis. Immediately apparent is the sharp but unsurprising difference between men and women in the amount of time spent doing housework. In this sample, women report spending almost 33 hours per week on

household tasks, while men report spending slightly more than 18 hours. Both figures are roughly comparable to the findings of prior studies, although of course those studies did not include unmarried persons.

Gender differences in current marital status are relatively slight. Men are somewhat more likely than women to have never married, reflecting longstanding differences in age at marriage. And, among the never married, men are more likely than women to reside in the parental household. Women are more likely than men to be currently divorced or widowed, a probable consequence of their lower remarriage rates following divorce and men's higher mortality. Four percent of both sexes are co-habiters.

Differences between women and men on the other explanatory variables are also generally small. The sole exception is the number of hours worked outside the home, with women averaging approximately 18 hours per week and men 32 hours.

The regression analysis of time spent on housework is shown in Table 2. In our initial equations (not shown here), we pooled the male and female respondents and regressed housework hours on the explanatory variables, including dummy variables for gender and marital status. We then added to this equation product terms representing the interaction of gender and marital status. As predicted by the theoretical model, allowing marital status and gender to interact in their effects on housework significantly increases the variance explained ($F = 67.06$; $p < .001$). And specifically, the difference in housework hours between married women and married men is significantly larger than the housework hours differences between women and men in each of the other marital statuses. Product terms representing the interaction of gender with the other explanatory variables also revealed that several of the effects varied significantly by gender; thus, we estimate and present the equations separately for women and for men.[6]

The first equation in Table 2 is based only on the women respondents and regresses weekly housework hours on dummy variables representing five of the six marital statuses, with married respondents serving as the reference category. Persons in all five marital statuses work significantly fewer hours around the house than do the married respondents; at the extreme, married women spend over 17 hours more per week on housework than do never-married women who reside in the parental household. As anticipated, the amount of time spent on housework by women who are never

married and living independently, cohabiting, divorced (including separated), or widowed falls between that of women who have not married (and remain in the parental home) and those who have married.

The third column of Table 2 presents the parallel equation for men. As reflected in the constant term, married men report spending almost 18 hours per week in housework, compared to almost 37 hours for their female counterparts (the constant term in column 1). More importantly, marital status differences in housework hours among men are relatively small compared to the analogous differences among women. Married men do significantly more housework than never-married men who still live with their parents and significantly less than divorced and widowed men, but most of these differences are modest. Moreover, the pattern of time spent doing housework across marital statuses differs substantially between men and women; it is greatest for men during widowhood and greatest for women during marriage.

Equation 2 in Table 2 re-estimates marital status differences in housework hours for men and women, controlling for the other explanatory variables. As shown in column 2, differences among women in these additional variables account for some, though by no means all, of the marital status differences in housework. Controlling for these variables reduces the differences between married women and other women by between 17 percent (for widows) and 66 percent (for cohabiters). Further, the difference between married women and cohabiting women is no longer statistically significant once these variables are controlled. Thus, among women a moderate proportion of the marital status differences in time spent doing housework is attributable to compositional differences. Particularly important in accounting for these marital status differences in housework hours are the number of hours the respondent works outside the home and the presence of children in the household; both variables vary significantly by marital status and are at least moderately related to time spent doing housework. We discuss these and the other effects of the explanatory variables in detail below.

For men, in contrast, controlling for the other explanatory variables does somewhat less to explain marital status differences in house-

---

[6] The distribution of some of the factors that explain variation in housework hours differs by age group. For example, enrollment in school and the presence of children in the household are most prevalent for younger respondents, while disability and widowhood are more common among the aged. Yet, the correlation matrices showed little evidence of multicollinearity, and disaggregating the equations by age revealed patterns and determinants quite similar to those for the sample as a whole.

Table 2. OLS Coefficients for Regression of Hours Spent in Housework per Week on Marital Status and Other Explanatory Variables, by Gender: U.S. Men and Women, 1987 to 1988

Independent Variable	Women		Men	
	(1)	(2)	(1)	(2)
Marital Status				
Never married/living in parental home	−17.41***†	−9.73***	−2.90***†	−.52†
	(.93)	(1.34)	(.63)	(1.18)
Never married/living independently	−11.62***†	−6.45***	1.09†	1.43†
	(.74)	(.84)	(.63)	(.80)
Cohabitating	−5.54***	−1.86†	1.34*	1.73†
	(1.14)	(1.14)	(.98)	(1.03)
Married	Reference		Reference	
Divorced/separated	−5.30***	−3.68***	3.73***†	4.58***†
	(.66)	(.68)	(.75)	(.80)
Widowed	−9.08***	−7.51***	5.66***†	6.97***
	(.67)	(.77)	(1.16)	(1.21)
Number of children ages 0 to 4	—	3.63***†	—	.67†
		(.38)		(.39)
Number of children ages 5 to 11	—	3.77***	—	.85***†
		(.31)		(.32)
Number of girls ages 12 to 18	—	1.62***†	—	−.64†
		(.46)		(.46)
Number of boys ages 12 to 18	—	1.88**	—	.74
		(.47)		(.47)
Adult male child parent (0 = no; 1 = yes)	—	1.79*	—	.91
		(.74)		(.82)
Adult male nonchild present (0 = no; 1 = yes)	—	−.10	—	−.37
		(.97)		(.72)
Adult female child present (0 = no; 1 = yes)	—	−2.46**	—	−2.93**
		(.80)		(.92)
Adult female nonchild present (0 = no; 1 = yes)	—	−1.18	—	−1.40
		(.85)		(.84)
Home ownership (0 = no; 1 = yes)	—	2.24**	—	−1.22*
		(.52)		(.52)
Household earnings (in $1,000s)	—	−.03***†	—	−.02***†
		(.01)		(.01)
Education	—	−.44***	—	.14*†
		(.08)		(.06)
Age	—	.40***†	—	.05†
		(.08)		(.08)
Age squared (/100)	—	−.44***†	—	−.15†
		(.08)		(.08)
Hours employed per week	—	−.17***	—	−.08***
		(.01)		(.01)
School enrollment (0 = no; 1 = yes)	—	−4.07**	—	−2.48**
		(.91)		(.82)
Disabled (0 = no; 1 = yes)	—	−5.34**	—	−2.96**
		(.86)		(.94)
Constant	36.67**	34.26**	17.83**	19.87**
	(.28)	(2.07)	(.25)	(2.08)
Root mean squared error	17.39	16.37	12.76	12.57
R^2	.08	.19	.02	.05
Number of cases	6,764	6,764	4,252	4,252

*$p < .05$ **$p < .01$ (two-tailed tests)

Note: Numbers in parentheses are standard errors. Equations in columns 2 and 4 include dummy variables for missing values on household earnings and disabled.

†Difference in coefficients for women and men is statistically significant at $p < .05$.

work. Although the difference between never-married men living in the parental home and married men becomes statistically nonsignificant when these variables are controlled, the absolute size of the decline (about 2.5 hours per week) is small. More important, with these controls the initially larger differences between married men and both divorced and widowed men actually increase.

Most of the explanatory variables have significant effects on time spent doing housework for either the men *or* the women, and many have significant effects for both sexes. Several variables have stronger effects among one sex than the other. The presence of children in the household creates more housework, especially for women, with pre-teenagers creating slightly more work than older children. The impact of children on housework hours tends to be significantly stronger for women than for men, a finding also found in studies limited to married couples (Bergen 1991; Rexroat and Shehan 1987). The presence in the household of the respondent's adult children also significantly affects housework hours, but the direction of the effect depends on both the sex of the adult children and the respondent. For female respondents, the presence of an adult male child increases housework hours, while for both female and male respondents the presence of an adult female child significantly reduces time allocated to housework. These findings are consistent with the view that men create housework, while women perform work men would otherwise do themselves (Hartmann 1981). Adults who are *not* children of the respondent do not add or subtract significantly, on average, from the respondent's housework time. This may be because the household is a heterogeneous group, including some roommates, siblings and other relatives, and elderly parents. Some household members may be helpful and others may be a burden, and their effects may cancel out.[7]

As expected, home ownership significantly increases housework time, and it appears to do so about equally for men and women. This may

be due to larger amounts of living space to be cleaned and to the increase in yard work and maintenance and repair chores among homeowners. Total household earnings reduce housework significantly more for women than for men, suggesting that purchased household services substitute more for women's than for men's domestic labor.[8] Among women, education is inversely associated with housework, while for men the association is positive and significant. Educated women and men tend to hold egalitarian attitudes, which may lead to greater symmetry in their housework patterns (Huber and Spitze 1983). The hypothesized curvilinear (bell-shaped) association between age and housework emerges for women, but not for men.

As indicated by the significant effects of employment and school enrollment on time spent doing housework, investing time in nonhousehold activities significantly reduces household labor. The impact of hours employed is significantly greater for women than for men, a finding consistent with prior research (Gershuny and Robinson 1988; Rexroat and Shehan 1987). This suggests that women have less discretionary time than men, so that increased expenditures of time outside the home must necessarily divert time away from housework.[9]

---

[7] While it is possible to separate persons in heterogeneous households into a number of categories and attempt to sort out those who tend to help and those who create more work, the small number of respondents with *any* other adult present suggests that this would not be a useful refinement to the analysis.

[8] The gender difference in the effect of household earnings on housework is complicated by the fact that, for couple households, wife's (or female cohabiting partner's) hours employed per week is controlled for in the women's equation, but not in the men's equation. If hours employed are deleted from both equations, the gender difference in the effect of household earnings becomes statistically nonsignificant. Hence, this difference, which is barely significant to begin with, should be interpreted cautiously.

[9] From the perspective of the New Home Economics, the amount of time allocated to housework and to paid labor are frequently considered to be jointly determined, and thus the inclusion of employment hours as a predictor of housework has been questioned (Godwin 1991). We believe that for most persons, and particularly persons in nonmarital households, decisions regarding the allocation of time to the paid labor force are made prior to decisions about housework time (especially given that our measure of housework excludes childcare), and thus that the treatment of paid employment as an explanatory variable is justified. In any event, omitting respondent's hours employed per week from the equations does not

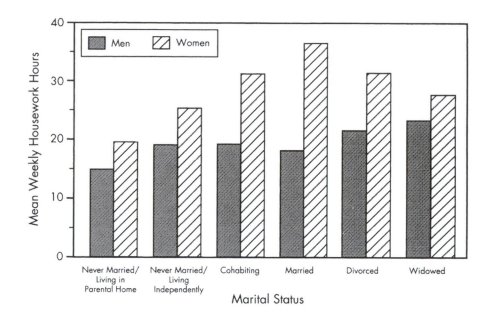

Figure 1. Mean Hours Spent Doing Housework Each Week, by Gender and Marital Status

Because the combined effects of gender and marital status are moderately complex, we present Figure 1 to help clarify the nature of their interaction. This figure graphs the (unadjusted) mean housework hours for men and women along the most common temporal sequence of marital statuses. In all marital statuses, women spend more hours than men on housework. The gender gap among never-married men and women living in the parental home is about 4 hours. Both never-married women and men who live independently do more housework than their counterparts who remain at home, but because the increase is slightly greater for women than for men (almost a 6-hour increase for women versus 4 hours for men), the gender difference in housework in this group grows to a little over 6 hours. Presumably, both men and women who live independently perform household tasks that previously had been done for them by their parents when the respondents resided in the parental homes.

The gender difference in housework hours widens dramatically as one moves to the couple households—cohabiters and married persons. Cohabiting women do more housework than never-married women (regardless of the latter's living arrangements), while cohabiting men work about the same hours around the house as never-married men living independently. The result of these discrepant trajectories is that the gender difference among cohabiters increases to approximately 12 hours per week. The gender gap in housework hours reaches its zenith among married women and men, at approximately 19 hours per week. This disparity is primarily a consequence of married women doing substantially more housework than never-married and cohabiting women, although these differences diminish with controls, as shown in Table 2. Rather than simply maintaining a behavioral pattern established prior to forming a conjugal union, married and, to a lesser extent, cohabiting women appear to increase substantially the time they devote to housework. In contrast, the amount of housework done by married men is fairly similar to that done by never-married and cohabiting men. Hence, as the "gender perspective" would suggest, it is in marital and cohabiting

appreciably alter the effects of marital status and gender that are the crux of our analysis, nor does the omission modify the impact of the other explanatory variables.

Table 3. Mean Hours Spent per Week in Various Household Tasks, by Marital Status and Gender: U.S. Men and Women, 1987 to 1988

Household Task[b]	Marital Status[a]					
	Never Married/ Living in Parental Home	Never Married/ Living Inde- pendently	Cohabiting	Married	Divorced	Widowed
Women						
Preparing meals	3.64	6.74	7.99	10.14	8.15	7.96
Washing dishes	3.92	4.38	5.51	6.11	5.14	4.73
Cleaning house	3.95	5.16	7.10	8.31	6.68	5.68
Washing/ironing	2.45	2.63	3.44	4.16	3.37	2.50
Outdoor maintenance	1.39	1.24	1.34	2.06	1.94	2.26
Shopping	1.72	2.28	2.69	2.86	2.67	2.40[ns]
Paying bills	.81[ns]	1.53	1.66	1.52	1.70	1.48[ns]
Car maintenance	.48	.42	.28	.16	.40	.20
Driving	.90[ns]	.65	1.10[ns]	1.34	1.30	.38[ns]
Total housework hours	19.26	25.04	31.12	36.67	31.37	27.59
Number of cases	383	649	248	3,838	829	817
Men						
Preparing meals	2.23	5.06	3.71	2.69	5.50	6.48
Washing dishes	1.92	2.77	2.63	2.15	3.24	3.87
Cleaning house	2.20	2.97	2.60	2.03	3.54	3.38
Washing/ironing	1.30	1.92	1.16	.70	1.75	1.67
Outdoor maintenance	3.56	1.56	3.18	4.94	2.60	3.38
Shopping	.83	1.92	1.73	1.58	1.93	2.14[ns]
Paying bills	.90[ns]	1.38	1.35	1.32	1.45	1.65[ns]
Car maintenance	1.23	.92	1.51	1.37	.99	.52
Driving	.75[ns]	.42	1.28[ns]	1.04	.57	.41[ns]
Total housework hours	14.93	18.92	19.16	17.83	21.56	23.49
Number of cases	477	476	181	2,668	323	127

[a]All associations between marital status and time spent on household tasks are significant at the $p < .05$ level.

[b]Within marital status and task type, all gender differences are significant at the $p < .05$ level with the following exceptions (marked ns): for never married in parental home—paying bills and driving; for cohabitors—driving; for widows—shopping, paying bills, and driving.

unions that gender differences in housework are most evident.

Among the formerly married, hours spent on housework by men and women begin to converge. Relative to their married counterparts, women who are divorced or widowed do less housework, while divorced or widowed men do more, with or without controlling for other variables. For women, this difference is perhaps best explained by a reduction in the total amount of housework required brought about by the absence of a husband in the household. For men, divorce and widowhood means doing household tasks previously done by a wife.

In general, then, patterns of time spent in housework across different marital statuses appear at least broadly consistent with the emerging "gender perspective." While there is a gender gap in housework in all marital statuses, this disparity varies dramatically and, as predicted, is widest for men and women in couple households (i.e., married or cohabiting relationships). However, to determine the extent to which these totals reflect behavior that becomes more gender-differentiated in couple households, we examine marital status differences in the completion of particular household tasks.

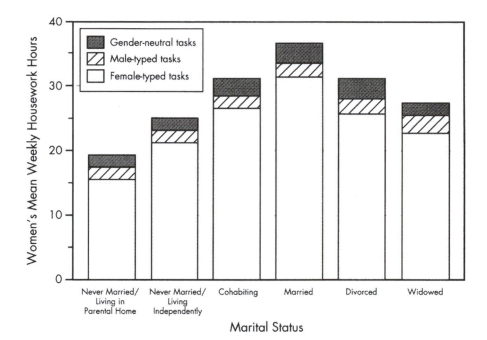

Figure 2. Mean Hours Spent by Women Doing Housework each Week, by Sex Type of Task and Marital Status

Accordingly, Table 3 presents the mean hours spent per week in each of the individual nine household tasks, disaggregated by gender and marital status. Figures 2 and 3 summarize the information in Table 3, graphing for women and men the (unadjusted) amounts of time spent in "female-typed" tasks (preparing meals, washing dishes, cleaning house, washing and ironing, and shopping), "male-typed" tasks (outdoor chores and automobile maintenance), and "gender-neutral" tasks (paying bills and driving other household members).[10] Among women, the marital status differences in *total* housework hours shown in Figure 1 are replicated for the female-typed tasks, which constitute in each marital status category the vast bulk of housework hours (see Figure 2). Of the female-typed tasks, the largest differences are in the number of hours spent prepar-

ing meals and cleaning house, although all five tasks consume more time for married women than for any of the other groups (Table 3). Because in each marital status the amount of time allocated to male-typed tasks is small, *differences* by marital status in these tasks are also slight. Married women do less car maintenance than do other women, but, with the exception of widows, spend slightly more time on outdoor maintenance. For women, then, marital status differences in total housework hours are largely a consequence of differences in hours spent on female-typed tasks.

Among men, however, marital status differences in gender-specific tasks do not always reflect those for housework as a whole. For example, as shown in Figure 3, although the difference in *total* housework hours between never-married men living independently and married men is small (about 1 hour), the difference is composed of several counterbalancing components. Never-married men living independently spend over 5 hours more per week than married men on female-typed tasks, but offset most of this difference by spending less time on male-typed tasks. Similarly, never-married men living independently spend al-

[10] This categorization is consistent with other analyses, including those by Ferree (1991b) and Aytac and Teachman (1992). Shelton (1992) shows shopping to be somewhat intermediate between female- and neutral-typed tasks, and others (e.g., Presser 1993) have treated it as a gender-neutral task.

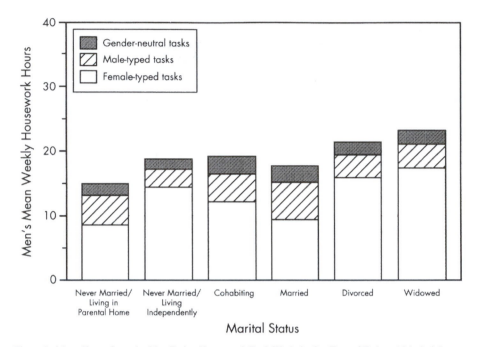

Figure 3. Mean Hours Spent by Men Doing Housework Each Week, by Sex Type of Task and Marital Status

most 3 hours per week more than cohabiting men in female-typed chores, but cohabiting men more than compensate for this difference by spending more time doing male-typed and gender-neutral tasks. Hence, to the extent that cohabiting men differ from never-married men living independently, they do so not by greater participation in female-typed chores, but by increasing their time doing stereotypically male tasks (e.g., automobile maintenance and outdoor chores) and gender-neutral tasks (e.g., driving other household members). On a smaller scale, the difference between cohabiting men and married men in total housework (about 1.3 hours per week) masks an important difference: Cohabiting men spend over 2.5 more hours per week than do married men on traditionally female chores, but married men make up over half of this difference by spending more time on outdoor maintenance. Like never-married men living independently, cohabiting men do more female-typed tasks than do married men, although they do not work on outdoor maintenance tasks to the same degree as their married counterparts.

The difference in total housework hours between married men and divorced men and be-

tween married men and widowed men is also composed of counterbalancing chores. Divorced and widowed men spend 6 to 8 hours more per week than married men on female-typed tasks, but the greater time expenditures by married men on outdoor and automobile maintenance partially offset this difference. In general, the distribution of housework hours by the sex-type of task appears consistent with the gender perspective: Married and cohabiting men spend less time on female-typed tasks and more time on male-typed tasks than do men in most other marital statuses.

DISCUSSION AND CONCLUSION

Doing housework is a significant part of many people's lives, yet few studies have explored housework patterns and determinants across household types. Indeed, because much prior research has been motivated by concerns about marital equity, the erroneous impression may exist that housework is performed only by members of married-couple families. Clearly, this is not the case.

Our results suggest that even never-married men, who might be expected to eschew housework, spend almost half as much time working around the home as they do in the paid labor force. Given prior studies suggesting little contribution by adult sons who live at home (Hartung and Moore 1992; Ward et al. 1992), the amount of housework reported being done by never-married men living in parental homes may seem surprisingly high — approximately 2 hours per day. However, the largest single component of this time (approximately one-quarter of it) is spent on outdoor maintenance, and outdoor and automobile maintenance together constitute one-third of the total time spent. Further, it is likely that much of the time spent in other chores, such as cooking, cleaning, or laundry, is directed more toward self-maintenance than to the well-being of the entire household (Hartung and Moore 1992). Thus, given this context, the amount of housework reported by never-married men living in the parental home appears reasonable.

The performance of housework by men is substantially similar across marital statuses. Differences in total housework hours among never-married, cohabiting, and married men are rather small and are partly attributable to differences in other social and economic characteristics. The most noteworthy differences among men in housework hours involve the appreciable differences between divorced and widowed men and the men in other marital statuses. The number of hours married women spend doing housework approaches a typical full-time work week and is termed the "second shift" by Hochschild (1989). But women in other living situations that do not include a male partner also spend 20 to 30 hours a week doing household chores. The gender gap in housework hours is highest in marriage, but is evident in other marital statuses as well. Although social and economic differences among women in various marital situations (especially the presence of children and hours spent in paid work) account for approximately half of these differences in housework hours, marital status differences in housework among women are generally greater than the corresponding differences among men.

From these patterns and from our detailed analysis of individual household tasks, we have concluded that there is suggestive evidence for the "gender perspective." Housework that women perform for and in the presence of men displays gender more so than the same work

performed with no man present. We find that the gender gap in housework time is greatest in married couple households relative to other households, and that much of this difference *cannot* be explained by the fact that marriage often brings children and reduced hours of paid work for women. Thus, we conclude that men and women must be "doing gender" when they live together. Moreover, relative to their unmarried counterparts, married men spend very little time in the traditionally female tasks of cooking and cleaning.

Of course, there are also significant gender gaps among persons in nonmarital households, implying that the dynamics of doing gender are not entirely absent in other household situations. However, we view our analysis and the patterns displayed in couple and noncouple households to be suggestive evidence that these dynamics operate differentially across household types. Perhaps our analysis and tentative interpretation will encourage those theorists working in the new gender perspective to further specify the conditions under which these processes operate so that future empirical tests can be more precise.

Analysis across household type and marital status may also have implications for the application of equity theory to the allocation of household labor. While most analyses of equity in household labor have used a comparison between husbands and wives as the implicit or explicit base for judging fairness, several recent discussions have raised the possibility that other standards may be used as well. Thompson (1991) discusses the issue of comparison referents and points out that husbands may compare themselves with *other husbands* and wives with *other wives*, while both Ferree (1990) and Kollock, Blumstein, and Schwartz (1988) present empirical comparisons between the predictive value of intracouple and intragender standards. To our knowledge, however, the idea that spouses may compare themselves to *their own past or projected experiences in another marital status*, or even to others who are not currently married, has not been discussed in the empirical literature on housework equity, although fear of divorce was certainly a potent factor in the ideological and behavioral choices of Hochschild's (1989) female respondents. Although this is necessarily speculative, we suggest that married men might use their experience prior to marriage as a reference point for both negotiating and evaluating their own contribution to household labor within marriage. People are spending increasing amounts of time in nonmarital statuses, particularly never-married, cohabiting, and divorced. During their lives, they often go through transitions which include a sequence from being never married to cohabiting to married to divorced or widowed. By examining the time men and women spend doing housework in each of these living situations we may be better able to understand what occurs when people negotiate how housework will be divided within marriage.

SCOTT J. SOUTH is Associate Professor of Sociology at the State University of New York at Albany. His recent research focuses on the social demography of American families, with particular emphasis given to contextual influences on patterns of family formation and dissolution. He is Co-Editor (with Stewart E. Tolnay) of The Changing American Family: Sociological and Demographic Perspectives (Westview Press, 1992).

GLENNA SPITZE is Professor of Sociology and Women's Studies at the State University of New York at Albany. In addition to her research on household labor, she is working on a book with John R. Logan based on their research on family structure and intergenerational relations.

REFERENCES

Aytac, Isik A. and Jay D. Teachman. 1992. "Occupational Sex Segregation, Marital Power, and Household Division of Labor." Paper presented at the meetings of the American Sociological Association, 20–24 Aug., Pittsburgh, PA.

Becker, Gary. 1981. A Treatise on the Family. Chicago, IL: University of Chicago.

Benin, Mary H. and Joan Agostinelli. 1988. "Husbands' and Wives' Satisfaction with the Division of Labor." Journal of Marriage and the Family 50:349–61.

Benin, Mary Holland and Debra A. Edwards. 1990. "Adolescents' Chores: The Difference Between Dual and Single-Earner Families." Journal of Marriage and the Family 52:361–73.

Bergen, Elizabeth. 1991. "The Economic Context of Labor Allocation." Journal of Family Issues 12:140–57.

Berk, Sarah Fenstermaker. 1985. The Gender Factory. New York: Plenum.

Blair, Sampson Lee. 1991. "The Sex-Typing of Children's Household Labor: Parental Influence on Daughters' and Sons' Housework." Paper presented at the meeting of the American Sociological Association, 23–27 Aug., Cincinnati, OH.

Blair, Sampson Lee and Michael P. Johnson. 1992. "Wives' Perceptions of the Fairness of the Division of Household Labor: The Intersection of Housework and Ideology." Journal of Marriage and the Family 54:570–81.

Blair, Sampson Lee and Daniel T. Lichter. 1991. "Measuring the Division of Household Labor: Gender Segregation Among American Couples." Journal of Family Issues 12:91–113.

Blood, Robert O. and Donald M. Wolfe. 1960. Husbands and Wives. New York: Free Press.

Blumberg, Rae Lesser and Marion Tolbert Coleman. 1989. "A Theoretical Look at the Gender Balance of Power in the American Couple." Journal of Family Issues 10:255–50.

Blumstein, Philip and Pepper Schwartz. 1983. American Couples. New York: William Morrow.

Coltrane, Scott and Masako Ishii-Kuntz. 1992. "Men's Housework: A Life-Course Perspective." Journal of Marriage and the Family 54:43–57.

Coverman, Shelley. 1985. "Explaining Husbands' Participation in Domestic Labor." Sociological Quarterly 26:81–97.

Coverman, Shelley and Joseph F. Sheley. 1986. "Changes in Men's Housework and Child-Care Time, 1965–1975." Journal of Marriage and the Family 48:413–22.

DeVault, Marjorie L. 1991. Feeding the Family: The Social Organization of Caring as Gendered Work. Chicago, IL: University of Chicago.

Ferree, Myra Marx. 1990. "Gender and Grievances in the Division of Household Labor: How Husbands and Wives Perceive Fairness." Paper presented at the meeting of the American Sociological Association, 11–15 Aug., Washington, DC.

———. 1991a. "Feminism and Family Research." Pp. 103–21 in Contemporary Families, edited by A. Booth. Minneapolis, MN: National Council on Family Relations.

———. 1991b. "The Gender Division of Labor in Two-Earner Marriages: Dimensions of Variability and Change." Journal of Family Issues 12:158–80.

Gershuny, Jonathan and John P. Robinson. 1988. "Historical Changes in the Household Division of Labor." Demography 25:537–52.

Gillespie, Dair L. 1971. "Who Has the Power: The Marital Struggle." Journal of Marriage and the Family 33:445–58.

Glazer-Malbin, Nona. 1976. "Housework." Signs 1:905–22.

Godwin, Deborah D. 1991. "Spouses' Time Allocation to Household Work: A Review and Critique." Lifestyles: Family and Economic Issues 12:253–94.

Goldscheider, Frances K. and Linda J. Waite. 1991. New Families, No Families? The Transformation of the American Home. Berkeley, CA: University of California.

Gove, Walter R. and Hee-Choon Shin. 1989. "The Psychological Well-Being of Divorced and Widowed Men and Women: An Empirical Analysis." *Journal of Family Issues* 10:122–44.

Grief, Geoffrey L. 1985. "Children and Housework in the Single Father Family." *Family Relations* 34:353–57.

Hartmann, Heidi I. 1981. "The Family as the Locus of Gender, Class, and Political Struggle: The Example of Housework." *Signs* 6:366–94.

Hartung, Beth and Helen A. Moore, 1992. "The Return of the 'Second Shift': Adult Children Who Return Home." Paper presented at the meeting of the American Sociological Association, 20–24 Aug., Pittsburgh, PA.

Hilton, Jeanne M. and Virginia A. Haldeman. 1991. "Gender Differences in the Performance of Household Tasks by Adults and Children in Single-Parent and Two-Parent, Two-Earner Families." *Journal of Family Issues* 12:114–30.

Hochschild, Arlie with Anne Machung. 1989. *The Second Shift: Working Parents and the Revolution at Home*. New York: Viking.

Huber, Joan and Glenna Spitze. 1983. *Sex Stratification: Children, Housework, and Jobs*. New York: Academic Press.

Ishii-Kuntz, Masako and Scott Coltrane. 1992. "Remarriage, Stepparenting, and Household Labor." *Journal of Family Issues* 13:215–33.

Kollock, Peter, Philip Blumstein, and Pepper Schwartz. 1988. "The Judgment of Equity in Intimate Relationships." Paper presented at the meeting of the American Sociological Association, 24–28 Aug., Atlanta, GA.

Oakley, Ann. 1974. *The Sociology of Housework*. New York: Pantheon.

Peterson, Larry R. and Judy L. Maynard. 1981. "Income, Equity, and Wives' Housekeeping Role Expectations." *Pacific Sociological Review* 24: 87–105.

Presser, Harriet B. 1993. "Gender, Work Schedules, and the Division of Family Labor." Paper presented at the meeting of the Population Association of American, 1–3 April, Cincinnati, OH.

Rexroat, Cynthia and Constance Shehan. 1987. "The Family Life Cycle and Spouses' Time in Housework." *Journal of Marriage and the Family* 49:737–50.

Rindfuss, Ronald R. and Audrey VandenHeuvel. 1992. "Cohabitation: A Precursor to Marriage or an Alternative to Being Single?" Pp. 118–42 in *The Changing American Family: Sociological and Demographic Perspectives*, edited by S. J. South and S. E. Tolnay. Boulder, CO: Westview Press.

Rodman, Hyman, 1967. "Marital Power in France, Greece, Yugoslavia, and the United States: A Cross-National Discussion." *Journal of Marriage and the Family* 29:320–24.

Ross, Catherine E. 1987. "The Division of Labor at Home." *Social Forces* 65:816–33.

Sanik, Margaret Mietus and Teresa Mauldin. 1986.

"Single Versus Two-Parent Families: A Comparison of Mothers' Time." *Family Relations* 35:53–56.

Shelton, Beth Anne. 1990. "The Distribution of Household Tasks: Does Wife's Employment Status Make a Difference?" *Journal of Family Issues* 11:115–35.

———. 1992. *Women, Men and Time*. New York: Greenwood Press.

Shelton, Beth Anne and Daphne John. 1993. "Does Marital Status Make a Difference? Housework Among Married and Cohabiting Men and Women." *Journal of Family Issues* 14:401–20.

Spitze, Glenna. 1986. "The Division of Task Responsibility in U.S. Households: Longitudinal Adjustments to Change." *Social Forces* 64:689–701.

———. 1988. "Women's Employment and Family Relations: A Review." *Journal of Marriage and the Family* 50:595–618.

Stafford, Rebecca, Elaine Backman, and Pamela Dibona. 1977. "The Division of Labor Among Cohabiting and Married Couples." *Journal of Marriage and the Family* 39:43–57.

Sweet, James, Larry Bumpass, and Vaughn Call. 1988. "The Design and Content of the National Survey of Families and Households." (Working Paper NSFH-1). Center for Demography and Ecology, University of Wisconsin, Madison, WI.

Sweet, James A. and Larry L. Bumpass. 1987. *American Families and Households*. New York: Russell Sage Foundation.

Thompson, Linda and Alexis J. Walker. 1991. "Gender in Families." Pp. 76–102 in *Contemporary Families*, edited by A. Booth. Minneapolis, MN: National Council on Family Relations.

Thompson, Linda. 1991. "Family Work: Women's Sense of Fairness." *Journal of Family Issues* 12: 181–96.

Timmer, Susan G., Jacquelynne Eccles, and Keith O'Brien. 1985. "How Children Use Time." Pp. 353–82 in *Time, Goods, and Well-Being*, edited by T. F. Juster and F. P. Stafford. Ann Arbor, MI: Institute for Social Research, University of Michigan.

Umberson, Debra, Camille B. Wortman, and Ronald C. Kessler. 1992. "Widowhood and Depression: Explaining Long-Term Gender Differences in Vulnerability." *Journal of Health and Social Behavior* 33:10–24.

Waite, Linda and Frances K. Goldscheider. 1992. "Work in the Home: The Productive Context of Family Relationships." Pp. 267–99 in *The Changing American Family: Sociological and Demographic Perspectives*, edited by S. J. South and S. E. Tolnay. Boulder, CO: Westview Press.

Walker, Kathryn E. and Margaret E. Woods. 1976. *Time Use: A Measure of Household Production of Goods and Services*. Washington, DC: American Home Economics Association.

Ward, Russell, John Logan, and Glenna Spitze. 1992. "The Influence of Parent and Child Needs on

Coresidence in Middle and Later Life." *Journal of Marriage and the Family* 54:209–21.

Warner, Rebecca A. 1986. "Alternative Strategies for Measuring Household Division of Labor: A Comparison." *Journal of Family Issues* 7:179–95.

Watkins, Susan Cotts, Jane A. Menken, and John Bongaarts. 1987. "Demographic Foundations of Family Change." *American Sociological Review* 52:346–58.

West, Candace and Don H. Zimmerman. 1981. "Doing Gender." *Gender and Society* 1:125–51.

White, Lynn K. and David B. Brinkerhoff. 1981a. "Children's Work in the Family: Its Significance and Meaning." *Journal of Marriage and the Family* 43:789–98.

———. 1981b. "The Sexual Division of Labor: Evidence from Childhood." *Social Forces* 60:170–81.

Appendix C

Finding Information

Elizabeth Schneider and Russell K. Schutt

How can you locate the published literature, including results of prior research, that you can use to develop your research question (Chapter 2), guide your selection of research methods (Chapters 4–13), and summarize in your literature review (Chapter 2)? The purpose of this appendix is to provide you with practical pointers for finding high-quality information in a timely and efficient manner. Our primary focus is on locating published research in the social science literature. We also provide guidelines for searching the Internet, both to find published literature and to locate other resources that are useful in research. For readers who want more in-depth information on searching the Internet, we highly recommend *The Extreme Searcher's Internet Handbook* (Hock, 2010).

🔲 Searching the Literature

The scholarly literature should be consulted at the beginning and end of an investigation. Even while an investigation is in progress, consultations with the literature may help to resolve methodological problems or facilitate supplementary explorations. As with any part of the research process, the method you use will affect the quality of your results. You should try to ensure that your search method includes each of the following steps.

Specify your research question. Your research question should be neither so broad that hundreds of articles are judged relevant nor so narrow that you miss important literature. "Is informal social control effective?" is probably too broad. "Does informal social control reduce rates of burglary in large cities?" is probably too narrow. "Is informal social control more effective in reducing crime rates than policing?" provides about the right level of specificity.

Identify appropriate bibliographic databases to search. The federal Education Resources Information Center (ERIC) (www.eric.ed.gov/) may meet many of your needs, but if you are studying a question about counseling, special needs, or mental health, you'll also want to include a search in the online Psychological Abstracts database, PsycINFO, or the version that also contains the full text of articles since 1985, PsycARTICLES. You might also find relevant literature in EconLit, which indexes the economic literature, and in ContempWomenIss, which indexes literature on contemporary women's issues. It will save you a lot of time in the long run if you ask a librarian to teach you the best techniques for retrieving the most relevant articles to answer your questions.

Choose a search technology. For most purposes, an online bibliographic database that references the published journal literature will be all you need. However, searches for unpopular topics or very recent literature may require that you also search websites or bibliographies of relevant books.

The search engine Google now offers anyone with Web access "Google Scholar" (which indexes and searches scholarly journals, books, and other sources) and "Google Print" (which digitizes and searches selections of text in books that are owned by selected research libraries). (The search engine and directory Yahoo has a similar venture focused only on older books that are no longer covered by copyright law [Hafner, 2005, p. C1].) You can also search for books related to your research question in your library's catalog and at Amazon.com—the large online retailer.

Create a tentative list of search terms. List the parts and subparts of your research question and any related issues that you think are important: "informal social control," "polishing," "influences on crime rates," and perhaps "community cohesion and crime." List the authors of relevant studies. Specify the most important journals that deal with your topic.

Narrow your search. The sheer number of references you find can be a problem. Depending on the database you are working with and the purposes of your search, you may want to limit your search to English-language publications, to journal articles rather than conference papers or dissertations (both of which are more difficult to acquire), and to materials published in recent years.

Refine your search. Learn as you go. If your search yields too many citations, try specifying the search terms more precisely. If you have not found much literature, try using more general terms. Whatever terms you search first, don't consider your search complete until you have tried several different approaches and have seen how many articles you find. A search for "domestic violence" in *Sociological Abstracts* on September 7, 2008, yielded 2,836 hits; by adding "effects" OR "influences" as required search terms, the number of hits dropped to 744.

Use Boolean search logic. It's often a good idea to narrow your search by requiring that abstracts contain combinations of words or phrases that include more of the specific details of your research question. Using the Boolean connector such as AND allows you to do this, while using the connector OR allows you to find abstracts containing different words that mean the same thing. Exhibit C.1 provides an example.

Exhibit C.1	Use of Boolean Connectors in a Literature Search

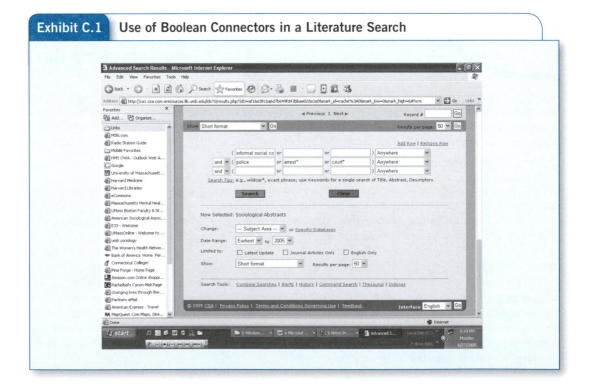

Use appropriate subject descriptors. Once you have found an article that you consider to be appropriate, take a look at the "descriptors" field in the citation (see Exhibit C.2). You can then redo your search after requiring that the articles be classified with some or all of these descriptor terms.

Exhibit C.2   **Checking Standard Subject Matter Descriptors**

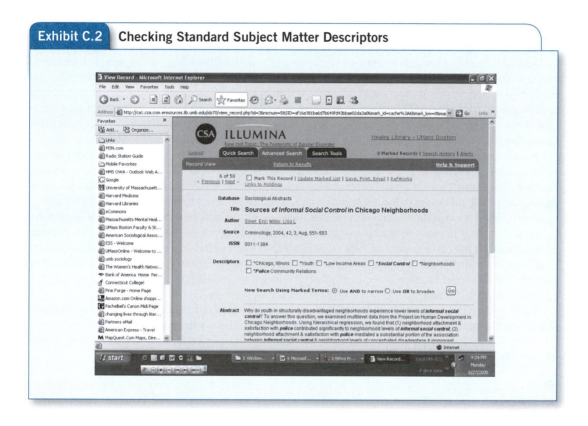

Check the results. Read the titles and abstracts you have found and identify the articles that appear to be most relevant. If possible, click on these article titles and generate a list of their references. See if you find more articles that are relevant to your research question but that you have missed so far. You will be surprised (I always am) at how many important articles your initial online search missed.

Locate the articles. Whatever database you use, the next step after finding your references is to obtain the articles themselves. You will probably find the full text of many articles available online, but this will be determined by what journals your library subscribes to. Older articles published before 1990 may not be online. Keep in mind that your library will not have anywhere near all the journals (and books) that you run across in your literature search, so you will have to add another step to your search: checking the "holdings" information.

If an article that appears to be important for your topic isn't available from your own library, either online or in print, don't give up yet. Here are some additional strategies for tracking it down:

- Find out if your college has reciprocal arrangements with other colleges that would allow you to use their materials.

- Find out if colleges in your area allow students from other colleges to use their collections and databases.

- Do not overlook your public library—you may be pleasantly surprised.

- Check to see if your library can get the desired resource for you from another library (through interlibrary loan).

- Check with a commercial vendor such as PubList (www.publist.com) to see if you can purchase the article.

Read the articles. You may be tempted to write up a "review" of the literature based on reading the abstracts or using only those articles available online, but you will be selling yourself short. Many crucial details about methods, findings, and theoretical implications will be found only in the body of the article, and many important articles will not be available online. To understand, critique, and really learn from previous research studies, you must read the important articles, no matter how you have to retrieve them.

Develop the literature review. If you have done your job well, you will now have more than enough literature as background for your own research, unless it is on a very obscure topic (see Exhibit C.3). At this point, your main concern is to construct a coherent framework in which to develop your research question, drawing as many lessons as you can from previous research. You may use the literature to identify a useful theory and hypotheses to be reexamined, to find inadequately studies-specific research questions, to explicate the disputes about your research question, to summarize the major findings of prior research, and to suggest appropriate methods of investigation. Refer to the literature review guidelines in Appendixes A and B as well as the examples in Chapter 2.

Be sure to take notes on each article you read, organizing your notes into standard sections: theory, methods, findings, and conclusions. In any case, write your review of the literature so that it contributes to your study in some concrete way; don't feel compelled to discuss an article just because you have read it. Be judicious. You are conducting only one study of one issue, and it will only obscure the value of your study if you try to relate it to every tangential point in related research.

Don't think of searching the literature as a one-time-only venture—something that you leave behind as you move on to your real research. You may encounter new questions or unanticipated problems as you conduct your research or as you burrow deeper into the literature. Searching the literature again to determine what others have found in response to these questions or what steps they have taken to resolve these problems can yield substantial improvements in your own research. There is so much literature on so many topics that it often is not possible to figure out in advance every subject you should search the literature for or what type of search will be most beneficial.

Another reason to make searching the literature an ongoing project is that the literature is always growing. During the course of one research study, whether it takes only one semester or several years, new findings will be published and relevant questions will be debated. Staying attuned to the literature and checking it at least when you are writing up your findings may save your study from being outdated.

Refer to a good book for even more specific guidance. Arlene Fink's (2005) *Conducting Research Literature Reviews: From the Internet to Paper* is an excellent guide.

Exhibit C.3 **A Search in *Sociological Abstracts* on Informal Control**

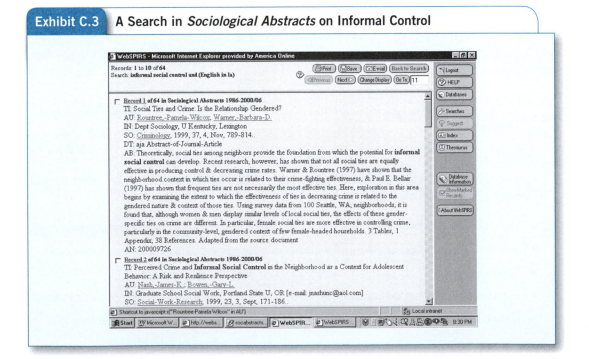

🔲 Searching the Web

The World Wide Web provides access to vast amounts of information of many different sorts (Ó Dochartaigh, 2002). You can search the holdings of other libraries and download the complete text of government reports, some conference papers, and newspaper articles. You can find policies of local governments, descriptions of individual social scientists and particular research projects, and postings of advocacy groups. It's also hard to avoid finding a lot of information in which you have no interest, such as commercial advertisements, third-grade homework assignments, or college course syllabi. In 1999, there were already about 800 million publicly available pages of information on the Web (Davis, 1999). Today there may be more than 15 billion pages on the Web (Novak, 2003).

After you are connected to the Web with a browser such as Microsoft Internet Explorer or Firefox, you can use three basic strategies for finding information: searching with a "search engine"—the most common approach; direct addressing—typing in the address, or URL, of a specific site; and browsing—reviewing online lists of websites. For some purposes, you will need to use only one strategy; for other purposes, you will want to use all three.

Search Engines

Search engines are powerful Internet tools—it is already impossible to imagine life without them. There are many search engines, and none of them will give you identical results when you use them to search the Web. Different search engines use different strategies to find websites and offer somewhat different search options for users. Due to the enormous size of the Web and its constantly changing content, it simply isn't possible to identify one search engine that will give you completely up-to-date and comprehensive results. You can find the latest information about search engines at http://searchenginewatch.com. Hock's (2010) *The Extreme Searcher's Internet Handbook* contains a wealth of information on specific search engines. Although there are many search engines, you may find the following to be particularly useful for general searching:

- Google (www.google.com) has become the leading search engine for many users in recent years. Its coverage is relatively comprehensive, and it does a good job of ranking search results by their relevancy (based on the terms in your search request). Google also allows you to focus your search just on images, discussions, or directories.

- All the Web is a more recent comprehensive search engine that also does a good job of relevancy ranking and allows searches restricted to images and so on. You can find it at www.alltheweb.com.

- Microsoft's search engine (http://search.msn.com) adds a unique feature: Editors review and pick the most popular sites. As a result, your search request may result in a "popular topics" list that can help you to focus your search. Ask (http://www.ask.com) is one of the newest search engines and has sections that link users to specialized directories.

Exhibit C.4 illustrates the first problem that you may encounter when searching the Web: the sheer quantity of resources that are available. It is a much bigger problem than when searching bibliographic databases. On the Web, less is usually more. Limit your inspection of websites to the first few pages that turn up in your list (they're ranked by relevance). See what those first pages contain and then try to narrow your search by including some additional terms. Putting quotation marks around a phrase that you want to search will also help to limit your search—searching for "informal social control" on Google (on June 9, 2008) produced 66,300 sites, compared with the roughly 3,420,000 sites retrieved when I omitted the quotes, so Google searched "informal" and "social" and "control."

If the number of results is still unmanageable with "phrase searching," you can try a title search: alltitle: "informal social control." This search will retrieve those pages that have that phrase in their title rather than just anywhere in the page. This practice usually results in a dramatically smaller yield of results (1,210 in this instance).You can also narrow your search by date or in other ways by using Google's "Advanced Search" feature. If you are looking for graphical information such as a graph or a chart, you can limit your search to those pages that contain an image. On Google, this just requires clicking on the "Images" link located above the search box.

Exhibit C.4   The Results of a Google Title Search

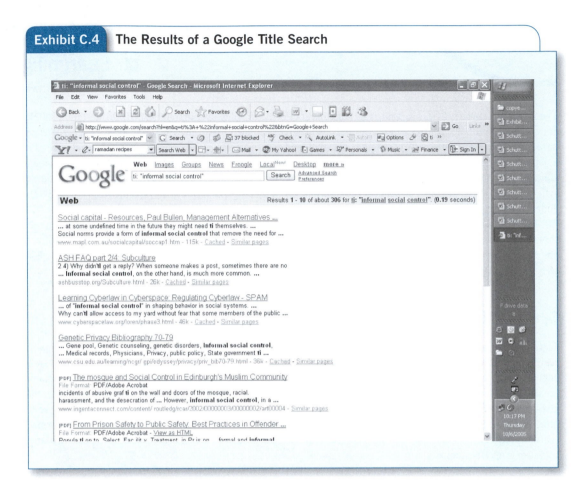

Remember the following warnings when you conduct searches on the Web:

- *Clarify your goals.* Before you begin the search, jot down the terms that you think you need to search for as well as a statement of what you want to accomplish with your search. This will help to ensure that you have a sense of what to look for and what to ignore.

- *Quality is not guaranteed.* Anyone can post almost anything, so the accuracy and adequacy of the information you find are always suspect. There's no journal editor or librarian to evaluate quality and relevance.

- *Anticipate change.* Websites that are not maintained by stable organizations can come and go very quickly. Any search will result in attempts to link to some URLs that no longer exist.

- *One size does not fit all.* Different search engines use different procedures for indexing websites. Some attempt to be all-inclusive, whereas others aim to be selective. As a result, you can get different results from different search engines (such as Google or Yahoo) even though you are searching for the same terms.

- *Be concerned about generalizability.* You might be tempted to characterize police department policies by summarizing the documents you find at police department websites. But how many police departments are there? How many have posted their policies on the Web? Are these policies representative of all police departments? To answer all these questions, you would have to conduct a research project just on the websites themselves.

- *Evaluate the sites.* There's a lot of stuff out there, so how do you know what's good? Some websites contain excellent advice and pointers on how to differentiate the good from the bad.

- *Avoid Web addiction.* Another danger of the enormous amount of information available on the Web is that one search will lead to another and to another and so on. There are always more possibilities to explore and one more interesting source to check. Establish boundaries of time and effort to avoid the risk of losing all sense of proportion.

- *Cite your sources.* Using text or images from Web sources without attribution is plagiarism. It is the same as copying someone else's work from a book or article and pretending that it is your own. Record the Web address (URL), the name of the information provider, and the date on which you obtain material from the site. Include this information in a footnote to the material that you use in a paper.

Direct Addressing

Knowing the exact address (uniform resource locator [URL]) of a useful website is the most efficient way to find a resource on the Web. The following sections highlight a few categories and examples that may prove helpful to you.

Professional Organizations

- American Educational Research Association (www.aera.net)
- American Psychological Association (www.apa.org)
- American School Counselor Association (www.schoolcounselor.org)

Government Sites

- National Center for Education Statistics (nces.ed.gov/)
- U.S. Department of Education (www.ed.gov)
- U.S. Bureau of the Census (www.census.gov)

Journals and Newspapers

- *American Educational Research Journal* (www.aera.net)
- *Educational Researcher* (www.aera.net)
- *Review of Educational Research* (www.aera.net)
- *Review of Research in Education* (www.aera.net)
- *The New York Times* (www.nytimes.com)

Bibliographic Formats for Citing Electronic Information

- Electronic reference formats suggested by the American Psychological Association (www.apastyle.org/elecref.html)
- Karla Tonella's Guide to Citation Style Guides contains more than a dozen links to online style guides (http://bailiwick.lib.uiowa.edu/journalism/cite.html)
- Style Sheets for Citing Resources (Print & Electronic) (www.lib.berkeley.edu/ TeachingLib/Guides/Internet/Style.html)

When you find websites that you expect you will return to often, you can save their addresses as "bookmarks" or "favorites" in your Web browser. However, since these can multiply very quickly, you should try to be selective.

▣ Browsing Subject Directories

Subject directories (also called guides, indexes, or clearinghouses) contain links to other Web resources that are organized by subject. They vary in quality and authoritativeness, but a good one can be invaluable to your research and can save you much time. The main advantage to using subject directories is that they contain links to resources that have been selected, evaluated, and organized by human beings and thus present a much more manageable number of resources. If the person managing the guide is an expert in the field of concern, or just a careful and methodological evaluator of Web resources, the guide can help you identify good sites that contain useful and trustworthy information, and you can avoid wading through thousands of "hits" and evaluating all the sites yourself.

There are general and specialized directories. The following are three examples of general directories:

- Yahoo! (www.yahoo.com) is often mistaken for a search engine, but it is actually a subject directory—and a monster one at that. It also functions as a portal or a gateway for a collection of resources that can be customized by the user. Unlike search engines, when you search Yahoo!, you are not searching across the Web but rather just within the Web pages that Yahoo! has cataloged. Yahoo! has a subject directory for the social sciences with more specific listings, including one for social work (http://dir.yahoo.com/social_science/social_work). Yahoo! also links to versions of its site in about 20 countries, which would be good to go to when conducting extensive research on one of those countries (http:world.yahoo.com).

- Open Directory (http://dmoz.org) is the largest Web directory with four million sites (Hock, 2010), and unlike Yahoo!, it is not a portal. In fact, other directories and search engines such as Yahoo! and Google use it. It has 16 top-level categories, including Social Sciences.

- Librarians' Index to the Internet (http://lii.org) is a small and highly selective Web directory produced by the Library of California.

The following are some examples of specialized subject directories:

- Educational Technology Clearinghouse (http://etc.usf.edu/ss/index.htm) links to social science resources.

- BUBL LINK (http://bubl.ac.uk) contains more than 12,000 links covering all academic areas.

- INFOMINE: Scholarly Internet Resource Collections (http://infomine.ucr.edu) is produced by librarians across several campuses of the University of California system, and it includes a subject directory for the social sciences.

- Intute (www.intute.ac.uk/socialsciences): social sciences Web resources selected by subject experts.

Many other Internet subject directories are maintained by academic departments, professional organizations, and individuals. It's often hard to determine whether a particular subject directory like this is up-to-date and reasonably comprehensive, but you can have some confidence in subject directories published by universities or government agencies. The *Internet Research Handbook* is an excellent source for more information on subject directories (Ó Dochartaigh, 2002).

In conclusion, use the appropriate tool for your searches. Do not use a search engine in place of searching literature that is indexed in tools such as *Sociological Abstracts*. Bookmark the key sites that you find in your area of interest. Become familiar with subject directories that cover your areas of interest, and look there before going to a search engine. And when you do use a search engine, take a moment to learn about how it works and what steps you should take to get the best results in the least amount of time.

Appendix D

Table of Random Numbers

Line/Col.	(1)	(2)	(3)	(4)	(5)	(6)	(7)	(8)	(9)	(10)	(11)	(12)	(13)	(14)
1	10480	15011	01536	02011	81647	91646	69179	14194	62590	36207	20969	99570	91291	90700
2	22368	46573	25595	85393	30995	89198	27982	53402	93965	34095	52666	19174	39615	99505
3	24130	48360	22527	97265	76393	64809	15179	24830	49340	32081	30680	19655	63348	58629
4	42167	93093	06243	61680	07856	16376	39440	53537	71341	57004	00849	74917	97758	16379
5	37570	39975	81837	16656	06121	91782	60468	81305	49684	60672	14110	06927	01263	54613
6	77921	06907	11008	42751	27756	53498	18602	70659	90655	15053	21916	81825	44394	42880
7	99562	72905	56420	69994	98872	31016	71194	18738	44013	48840	63213	21069	10634	12952
8	96301	91977	05463	07972	18876	20922	94595	56869	69014	60045	18425	84903	42508	32307
9	89579	14342	63661	10281	17453	18103	57740	84378	25331	12566	58678	44947	05585	56941
10	85475	36857	43342	53988	53060	59533	38867	62300	08158	17983	16439	11458	18593	64952
11	28918	69578	88231	33276	70997	79936	56865	05859	90106	31595	01547	85590	91610	78188
12	63553	40961	48235	03427	49626	69445	18663	72695	52180	20847	12234	90511	33703	90322
13	09429	93969	52636	92737	88974	33488	36320	17617	30015	08272	84115	27156	30613	74952
14	10365	61129	87529	85689	48237	52267	67689	93394	01511	26358	85104	20285	29975	89868
15	07119	97336	71048	08178	77233	13916	47564	81056	97735	85977	29372	74461	28551	90707
16	51085	12765	51821	51259	77452	16308	60756	92144	49442	53900	70960	63990	75601	40719
17	02368	21382	52404	60268	89368	19885	55322	44819	01188	65255	64835	44919	05944	55157
18	01011	54092	33362	94904	31273	04146	18594	29852	71585	85030	51132	01915	92747	64951
19	52162	53916	46369	58586	23216	14513	83149	98736	23495	64350	94738	17752	35156	35749
20	07056	97628	33787	09998	42698	06691	76988	13602	51851	46104	88916	19509	25625	58104
21	48663	91245	85828	14346	09172	30168	90229	04734	59193	22178	30421	61666	99904	32812

Line/Col.	(1)	(2)	(3)	(4)	(5)	(6)	(7)	(8)	(9)	(10)	(11)	(12)	(13)	(14)
22	54164	58492	22421	74103	47070	25306	76468	26384	58151	06646	21524	15227	96909	44592
23	32639	32363	05597	24200	13363	38005	94342	28728	35806	06912	17012	64161	18296	22851
24	29334	27001	87637	87308	58731	00256	45834	15398	46557	41135	10367	07684	36188	18510
25	02488	33062	28834	07351	19731	92420	60952	61280	50001	67658	32586	86679	50720	94953
26	81525	72295	04839	96423	24878	82651	66566	14778	76797	14780	13300	87074	79666	95725
27	29676	20591	68086	26432	46901	20849	89768	81536	86645	12659	92259	57102	80428	25280
28	00742	57392	39064	66432	84673	40027	32832	61362	98947	96067	64760	64584	96096	98253
29	05366	04213	25669	26422	44407	44048	37937	63904	45766	66134	75470	66520	34693	90449
30	91921	26418	64117	94305	26766	25940	39972	22209	71500	64568	91402	42416	07844	69618
31	00582	04711	87917	77341	42206	35126	74087	99547	81817	42607	43808	76655	62028	76630
32	00725	69884	62797	56170	86324	88072	76222	36086	84637	93161	76038	65855	77919	88006
33	69011	65797	95876	55293	18988	27354	26575	08625	40801	59920	29841	80150	12777	48501
34	25976	57948	29888	88604	67917	48708	18912	82271	65424	69774	33611	54262	85963	03547
35	09763	83473	73577	12908	30883	18317	28290	35797	05998	41688	34952	37888	38917	88050
36	91567	42595	27958	30134	04024	86385	29880	99730	55536	84855	29080	09250	79656	73211
37	17955	56349	90999	49127	20044	59931	06115	20542	18059	02008	73708	83317	36103	42791
38	46503	18584	18845	49618	02304	51038	20655	58727	28168	15475	56942	53389	20562	87338
39	92157	89634	94824	78171	84610	82834	09922	25417	44137	48413	25555	21246	35509	20468
40	14577	62765	35605	81263	39667	47358	56873	56307	61607	49518	89656	20103	77490	18062
41	98427	07523	33362	64270	01638	92477	66969	98420	04880	45585	46565	04102	46880	45709

(Continued)

(Continued)

Line/Col.	(1)	(2)	(3)	(4)	(5)	(6)	(7)	(8)	(9)	(10)	(11)	(12)	(13)	(14)
42	34914	63976	88720	82765	34476	17032	87589	40836	32427	70002	70663	88863	77775	69348
43	70060	28277	39475	46473	23219	53416	94970	25832	69975	94884	19661	72828	00102	66794
44	53976	54914	06990	67245	68350	82948	11398	42878	80287	88267	47363	46634	06541	97809
45	76072	29515	40980	07391	58745	25774	22987	80059	39911	96189	41151	14222	60697	59583
46	90725	52210	83974	29992	65831	38857	50490	83765	55657	14361	31720	57375	56228	41546
47	64364	67412	33339	31926	14883	24413	59744	92351	97473	89286	35931	04110	23726	51900
48	08962	00358	31662	25388	61642	34072	81249	35648	56891	69352	48373	45578	78547	81788
49	95012	68379	93526	70765	10593	04542	76463	54328	02349	17247	28865	14777	62730	92277
50	15664	10493	20492	38391	91132	21999	59516	81652	27195	48223	46751	22923	32261	85653
51	16408	81899	04153	53381	79401	21438	83035	92350	36693	31238	59649	91754	72772	02338
52	18629	81953	05520	91962	04739	13092	97662	24822	94730	06496	35090	04822	86772	98289
53	73115	35101	47498	87637	99016	71060	88824	71013	18735	20286	23153	72924	35165	43040
54	57491	16703	23167	49323	45021	33132	12544	41035	80780	45393	44812	12515	98931	91202
55	30405	83946	23792	14422	15059	45799	22716	19792	09983	74353	68668	30429	70735	25499
56	16631	35006	85900	98275	32388	52390	16815	69298	82732	38480	73817	32523	41961	44437
57	96773	20206	42559	78985	05300	22164	24369	54224	35083	19687	11052	91491	60383	19746
58	38935	64202	14349	82674	66523	44133	00697	35552	35970	19124	63318	29686	03387	59846
59	31624	76384	17403	53363	44167	64486	64758	75366	76554	31601	12614	33072	60332	92325
60	78919	19474	23632	27889	47914	02584	37680	20801	72152	39339	34806	08930	85001	87820
61	03931	33309	57047	74211	63445	17361	62825	39908	05607	91284	68833	25570	38818	46920
62	74426	33278	43972	10119	89917	15665	52872	73823	73144	88662	88970	74492	51805	99378

Line/Col.	(1)	(2)	(3)	(4)	(5)	(6)	(7)	(8)	(9)	(10)	(11)	(12)	(13)	(14)
63	09066	00903	20795	95452	92648	45454	09552	88815	16553	51125	79375	97596	16296	66092
64	42238	12426	87025	14267	20979	04508	64535	31355	86064	29472	47689	05974	52468	16834
65	16153	08002	26504	41744	81959	65642	74240	56302	00033	67107	77510	70625	28725	34191
66	21457	40742	29820	96783	29400	21840	15035	34537	33310	06116	95240	15957	16572	06004
67	21581	57802	02050	89728	17937	37621	47075	42080	97403	48626	68995	43805	33386	21597
68	55612	78095	83197	33732	05810	24813	86902	60397	16489	03264	88525	42786	05269	92532
69	44657	66999	99324	51281	84463	60563	79312	93454	68876	25471	93911	25650	12682	73572
70	91340	84979	46949	81973	37949	61023	43997	15263	80644	43942	89203	71795	99533	50501
71	91227	21199	31935	27022	84067	05462	35216	14486	29891	68607	41867	14951	91696	85065
72	50001	38140	66321	19924	72163	09538	12151	06878	91903	18749	34405	56087	82790	70925
73	65390	05224	72958	28609	81406	39147	25549	48542	42627	45233	57202	94617	23772	07896
74	27504	96131	83944	41575	10573	08619	64482	73923	36152	05184	94142	25299	84387	34925
75	37169	94851	39117	89632	00959	16487	65536	49071	39782	17095	02330	74301	00275	48280
76	11508	70225	51111	38351	19444	66499	71945	05422	13442	78675	84081	66938	93654	59894
77	37449	30362	06694	54690	04052	53115	62757	95348	78662	11163	81651	50245	34971	52924
78	46515	70331	85922	38329	57015	15765	97161	17869	45349	61796	66345	81073	49106	79860
79	30986	81223	42416	58353	21532	30502	32305	86482	05174	07901	54339	58861	74818	46942
80	63798	64995	46583	09765	44160	78128	83991	42865	92520	83531	80377	35909	81250	54238
81	82486	84846	99254	67632	43218	50076	21361	64816	51202	88124	41870	52689	51275	83556
82	21885	32906	92431	09060	64297	51674	64126	62570	26123	05155	59194	52799	28225	85762
83	60336	98782	07408	53458	13564	59089	26445	29789	85205	41001	12535	12133	14645	23541

(Continued)

(Continued)

Line/Col.	(1)	(2)	(3)	(4)	(5)	(6)	(7)	(8)	(9)	(10)	(11)	(12)	(13)	(14)
84	43937	46891	24010	25560	86355	33941	25786	54990	71899	15475	95434	98227	21824	19585
85	97656	63175	89303	16275	07100	92063	21942	18611	47348	20203	18534	03862	78095	50136
86	03299	01221	05418	38982	55758	92237	26759	86367	21216	98442	08303	56613	91511	75928
87	79626	06486	03574	17668	07785	76020	79924	25651	83325	88428	85076	72811	22717	50585
88	85636	68335	47539	03129	65651	11977	02510	26113	99447	68645	34327	15152	55230	93448
89	18039	14367	61337	06177	12143	46609	32989	74014	64708	00533	35398	58408	13261	47908
90	08362	15656	60627	36478	65648	16764	53412	09013	07832	41574	17639	82163	60859	75567
91	79556	29068	04142	16268	15387	12856	66227	38358	22478	73373	88732	09443	82558	05250
92	92608	82674	27072	32534	17075	27698	98204	63863	11951	34648	88022	56148	34925	57031
93	23982	25835	40055	67006	12293	02753	14827	22235	35071	99704	37543	11601	35503	85171
94	09915	96306	05908	97901	28395	14186	00821	80703	70426	75647	76310	88717	37890	40129
95	50937	33300	26695	62247	69927	76123	50842	43834	86654	70959	79725	93872	28117	19233
96	42488	78077	69882	61657	34136	79180	97526	43092	04098	73571	80799	76536	71255	64239
97	46764	86273	63003	93017	31204	36692	40202	35275	57306	55543	53203	18098	47625	88684
98	03237	45430	55417	63282	90816	17349	88298	90183	36600	78406	06216	95787	42579	90730
99	86591	81482	52667	61583	14972	90053	89534	76036	49199	43716	97548	04379	46370	28672
100	38534	01715	94964	87288	65680	43772	39560	12918	86537	62738	19636	51132	25739	56947

Glossary

Action-reflection model: Alternating phases (action/reflection on action) of an action research project repeated over time, represented by a spiral diagram where time moves from left to right.

Action research: Research approach in which systemic or organizational change is attempted by members of a group or organization using alternating phases of action and reflection on action. The research is conducted by members of the organization in their own setting to change their own environment.

Anonymity: Provided by research in which no identifying information is recorded that could be used to link respondents to their responses.

Association: A criterion for establishing a nomothetic causal relationship between two variables: Variation in one variable is related to variation in another variable.

Authenticity: When the understanding of an educational process or educational setting is one that reflects fairly the various perspectives of participants in that setting.

Availability sampling: Sampling in which elements are selected on the basis of convenience.

Back matter: The section of an applied research report that may include appendixes, tables, and the research instrument(s).

Bar chart: A graphic for qualitative variables in which the variable's distribution is displayed with solid bars separated by spaces.

Baseline phase (A):   The initial phase of a single-subject design, typically abbreviated by the letter A; it represents the period in which the intervention to be evaluated is not offered to the subject. During the baseline phase, repeated measurements of the dependent variable are taken or reconstructed.

Base number (*N*):   The total number of cases in a distribution.

Behavior coding: Observation in which the research categorizes, according to strict rules, the number of times certain behaviors occur.

Bimodal: A distribution that has two nonadjacent categories with about the same number of cases, and these categories have more cases than any others.

Black box: This type of evaluation occurs when an evaluation of program outcomes ignores and does not identify the process by which the program produced the effect.

Carryover effect: The impact of an intervention persists after the end of the treatment process.

Case study: A setting or group that the analyst treats as an integrated social unit that must be studied holistically and in its particularity.

Census: Research in which information is obtained through the responses that all available members of an entire population give to questions.

Central tendency: The most common value (for variables measured at the nominal level) or the value around which cases tend to center (for a quantitative variable).

Ceteris paribus: Latin phrase meaning "other things being equal."

Chi-square: An inferential statistic used to test hypotheses about relationships between two or more variables in across-tabulation.

Circles of interest: Progressively wider spheres of influence that a practitioner-researcher may seek to reach, starting from his or her own site and moving outward to more public settings such as conferences and publications.

Closed-ended questions: Survey questions designed with explicit response categories.

Cluster: A naturally occurring, mixed aggregate of elements of the population.

Cluster sampling: Sampling in which elements are selected in two or more stages, with the first stage being the random selection of naturally occurring clusters and the last stage being the random selection of elements within clusters.

Cognitive interview: A technique for evaluating questions in which researchers ask people test questions and then probe with follow-up questions to learn how they understood the question and what their answers mean.

Cohort: Individuals or groups with a common starting point. Examples include college class of 1997, people who graduated from high school in the 1980s, General Motors employees who started work between the years 1990 and 2000, and people who were born in the late 1940s or the 1950s (the baby boom generation).

Cohort design: Research project that uses a cohort or cohorts as subjects and units of analysis, rather than individuals.

Complete observer: A role in participant observation in which the researcher does not participate in group activities and is publicly defined as a researcher.

Computer-assisted qualitative data analysis: Uses special computer software to assist qualitative analyses through creating, applying, and refining categories; tracing linkages between concepts; and making comparisons between cases and events.

Conceptualization: The process of specifying what we mean by a term. In deductive research, conceptualization helps to translate portions of an abstract theory into specific variables that can be used in testable hypotheses. In inductive research, conceptualization is an important part of the process used to make sense of related observations.

Concurrent multiple baseline design: A series of A-B designs (although A-B-A or A-B-A-B designs could also be used) are implemented at the same time for at least three cases.

Confidentiality: Provided by research in which identifying information that could be used to link respondents to their responses is available only to designated research personnel for specific research needs.

Constant: A number that has a fixed value in a given situation; a characteristic or value that does not change.

Constructivism: Methodology based on questioning belief in an external reality. Emphasizes the importance of exploring the way in which different stakeholders in an educational setting construct their beliefs.

Construct validity: The type of validity that is established by showing that a measure is related to other measures as specified in a theory.

Content analysis (CA): A research method for systematically analyzing and making inferences from text.

Content validity: The type of validity that exists when the full range of a concept's meaning is covered by the measure.

Context: A focus of idiographic causal explanation; a particular outcome is understood as part of a larger set of interrelated circumstances.

Context effects: Occur in a survey when one or more questions influence how subsequent questions are interpreted.

Contingent question: A question that is asked of only a subset of survey respondents.

Convergent validity: The type of validity achieved when one measure of a concept is associated with different types of measures of the same concept.

Correlational analysis: A statistical technique that summarizes the strength of a relationship between two quantitative variables in terms of its adherence to a linear pattern.

Correlation coefficient: A summary statistic that varies from 0 to 1 or −1, with 0 indicating the absence of a linear relationship between two quantitative variables and 1 or −1 indicating that the relationship is completely described by the line representing the regression of the dependent variable on the independent variable.

Cost-benefit analysis: A type of evaluation research that compares program costs with the economic value of program benefits.

Cost-effectiveness analysis: A type of evaluation research that compares program costs with actual program outcomes.

Cover letter: The letter sent with a mailed questionnaire. It explains the survey's purpose and auspices and encourages the respondent to participate.

Covert observer: A role in participant observation in which the researcher does not participate in group activities and is not publicly defined as a researcher.

Covert participant: A role in field research in which the researcher does not reveal his or her identity as a researcher to those who are observed.

Criterion validity: The type of validity that is established by comparing the scores obtained on the measure being validated to those obtained with a more direct or already validated measure of the same phenomenon (the criterion).

Cross-sectional research design: A study in which data are collected at only one point in time.

Data cleaning: The process of checking data for errors after the data have been entered in a computer file.

Debriefing: A researcher's informing subjects after an experiment about the experiment's purposes and methods and evaluating subjects' personal reactions to the experiment.

Deductive research: The type of research in which a specific expectation is deduced from a general premise and is then tested.

Dependent variable: A variable that is hypothesized to vary depending on or under the influence of another variable.

Descriptive research: Research in which educational or social phenomena are defined and described.

Descriptive statistics: Statistics used to describe the distribution of and relationship among variables.

Discourse analysis (DA):   An umbrella term covering a group of research approaches used to analyze a wide variety of language or communication ("discourse"), including speech, conversation, writing, gestures, and signing.

Disproportionate stratified sampling: Sampling in which elements are selected from strata in different proportions from those that appear in the population.

Double-barreled question: A single survey question that actually asks two questions but allows only one answer.

Double negative: A question or statement that contains two negatives, which can muddy the meaning of the question.

Ecological fallacy: An error in reasoning in which incorrect conclusions about individual-level processes are drawn from group-level data.

Efficiency analysis: A type of evaluation research that compares program costs with program effects. It can be either a cost-benefit analysis or a cost-effectiveness analysis.

Electronic survey: A survey that is sent and answered by computer, either through e-mail or on the Web.

Elements: The individual members of the population whose characteristics are to be measured.

E-mail (electronic) survey: A survey that is sent and answered by computer, either through e-mail or on the Web.

Emic focus: Representing a setting with the participants' terms.

Empirical generalization: A statement that describes patterns found in data.

Enumeration units: Units that contain one or more elements and that are listed in a sampling frame.

Ethnography: The study of a culture or cultures that some group of people shares, using participant observation over an extended period of time.

Etic focus: Representing a setting with the researchers' terms.

Evaluability assessment: A type of evaluation research conducted to determine whether it is feasible to evaluate a program's effects within the available time and resources.

Evaluation research: Research that describes or identifies the impact of educational policies and programs.

Event-based design (cohort study): A type of longitudinal study in which data are collected at two or more points in time from individuals in a cohort.

Explanatory research: Seeks to identify causes and effects of social phenomena and to predict how one phenomenon will change or vary in response to variation in some other phenomenon.

Exploratory research: Seeks to find out how people get along in the setting under question, what meanings they give to their actions, and what issues concern them.

Extraneous variable: A variable that influences both the independent and dependent variables so as to create a spurious association between them that disappears when the extraneous variable is controlled.

Face validity: The type of validity that exists when an inspection of items used to measure a concept suggests that they are appropriate "on their face."

Factorial survey: A survey in which randomly selected subsets of respondents are asked different questions, or are asked to respond to different vignettes, in order to determine the causal effect of the variables represented by these differences.

Feedback: Information about service delivery system outputs, outcomes, or operations that is available to any program input.

Fence-sitters: Survey respondents who see themselves as being neutral on an issue and choose a middle (neutral) response that is offered.

Field notes: Notes that describe what has been observed, heard, or otherwise experienced in a participant observation study. These notes usually are written after the observational session.

Field researcher: A researcher who uses qualitative methods to conduct research in the field.

Filter question: A survey question used to identify a subset of respondents who then are asked other questions.

Fixed-sample panel design (panel study): A type of longitudinal study in which data are collected from the same individuals—the panel—at two or more points in time. In another type of panel design, panel members who leave are replaced with new members.

Floaters: Survey respondents who provide an opinion on a topic in response to a closed-ended question that does not include a "Don't know" option but who will choose "Don't know" if it is available.

Focus groups: A qualitative method that involves unstructured group interviews in which the focus group leader actively encourages discussion among participants on the topics of interest.

Formative evaluation: Process evaluation that is used to shape and refine program operations.

Frequency distribution: Numerical display showing the number of cases, and usually the percentage of cases (the relative frequencies), corresponding to each value or group of values of a variable.

Frequency polygon: A graphic for quantitative variables in which a continuous line connects data points representing the variable's distribution.

Front matter: The section of an applied research report that includes an executive summary, abstract, and table of contents.

Generalizability: Exists when a conclusion holds true for the population, group, setting, or event that we say it does, given the conditions that we specify.

Grand tour question: A broad question at the start of an interview that seeks to engage the respondent in the topic of interest.

Grounded theory: Systematic theory developed inductively, based on observations that are summarized into conceptual categories, reevaluated in the research setting, and gradually refined and linked to other conceptual categories.

Group-administered survey: A survey that is completed by individual respondents who are assembled in a group.

Histogram: A graphic for quantitative variables in which the variable's distribution is displayed with adjacent bars.

Hypothesis: A tentative statement about empirical reality, involving a relationship between two or more variables.

Idiosyncratic errors: Errors that affect a relatively small number of individuals in unique ways that are unlikely to be repeated in just the same way.

Illogical reasoning: When we prematurely jump to conclusions or argue on the basis of invalid assumptions.

Impact evaluation (or analysis): Analysis of the extent to which a treatment or other service has an effect. Also known as summative evaluation.

Inaccurate observation: An observation based on faulty perceptions of empirical reality.

Independent variable: A variable that is hypothesized to cause, or lead to, variation in another variable.

Index: The sum or average of responses to a set of questions about a concept.

Inductive research: The type of research in which general conclusions are drawn from specific data.

Inferential statistics: A mathematical tool for estimating how likely it is that a statistical result based on data from a random sample is representative of the population from which the sample is assumed to have been selected.

In-person interview: A survey in which an interviewer questions respondents face-to-face and records their answers.

Inputs: The resources, raw materials, clients, and staff that go into a program.

Inquiry stance: A habitual attitude or "stance" toward one's teaching or professional work characterized by a willingness to engage in ongoing critical inquiry of one's own purposes, context, pedagogy, assumptions, and beliefs.

Institutional review board (IRB): A group of organizational and community representatives required by federal law to review the ethical issues in all proposed research that is federally funded, involves human subjects, or has any potential for harm to subjects.

Integrative approach: An orientation to evaluation research that expects researchers to respond to the concerns of people involved with the program—stakeholders—as well as to the standards and goals of the social scientific community.

Interitem reliability: An approach that calculates reliability based on the correlation among multiple items used to measure a single concept. Also known as internal consistency.

Intermethod mixing: The use of two or more research methods (e.g., questionnaires and focus groups) within a single research design; also called *method triangulation*.

Interobserver reliability: When similar measurements are obtained by different observers rating the same persons, events, or places.

Interpretive questions: Questions included in a questionnaire or interview schedule to help explain answers to other important questions.

Interquartile range: The range in a distribution between the end of the first quartile and the beginning of the third quartile.

Interval level of measurement: A measurement of a variable in which the numbers indicating a variable's values represent fixed measurement units but have no absolute, or fixed, zero point.

Interview schedule: The survey instrument containing the questions asked by the interviewer in an in-person or phone survey.

Intramethod mixing: The use of both qualitative and quantitative elements, either concurrently or sequentially, within a single research method.

Jottings: Brief notes written in the field about highlights of an observation period.

Key informant: An insider who is willing and able to provide a field researcher with superior access and information, including answers to questions that arise in the course of the research.

Level of measurement: The mathematical precision with which the values of a variable can be expressed. The nominal level of measurement, which is qualitative, has no mathematical interpretation; the quantitative levels of measurement—ordinal, interval, and ratio—are progressively more precise mathematically.

Longitudinal research design: A study in which data are collected that can be ordered in time; also defined as research in which data are collected at two or more points in time.

Mailed survey: A survey involving a mailed questionnaire to be completed by the respondent.

Matrix: A form on which can be recorded systematically particular features of multiple cases or instances that a qualitative data analyst needs to examine.

Mean: The arithmetic, or weighted, average, computed by adding up the value of all the cases and dividing by the total number of cases.

Measure of association: A type of descriptive statistic that summarizes the strength of an association.

Measurement: The process of linking abstract concepts to empirical indicants.

Mechanism: A discernible process that creates a causal connection between two variables.

Median: The position average, or the point that divides a distribution in half (the 50th percentile).

Meta-analysis: The quantitative analysis of findings from multiple studies.

Mixed-mode survey: A survey that is conducted by more than one method, allowing the strengths of one survey design to compensate for the weaknesses of another and maximizing the likelihood of securing data from different types of respondents; for example, nonrespondents in a mailed survey may be interviewed in person or over the phone.

Mode: The most frequent value in a distribution; also termed the *probability average*.

Mutually exclusive: A variable's attributes (or values) are mutually exclusive when every case can be classified as having only one attribute (or value).

Narrative analysis: A form of qualitative analysis in which the analyst focuses on how respondents impose order on the flow of experience in their lives and thus make sense of events and actions in which they have participated.

Needs assessment: A type of evaluation research that attempts to determine the needs of some population that might be met with a social program.

Nominal level of measurement: Variables whose values have no mathematical interpretation; they vary in kind or quality but not in amount.

Nonprobability sampling method: Sampling method in which the probability of selection of population elements is unknown.

Nonrespondents: People or other entities who do not participate in a study although they are selected for the sample.

Nonspuriousness: A criterion for establishing a causal relation between two variables; when a relationship between two variables is not due to variation in a third variable.

Normal distribution: A symmetric, bell-shaped distribution that results from chance variation around a central value.

Open-ended question: A survey question to which the respondent replies in his or her own words, either by writing or by talking.

Operation: A procedure for identifying or indicating the value of cases on a variable.

Operationalization: The process of specifying the operations that will indicate the value of cases on a variable.

Ordinal level of measurement: A measurement of a variable in which the numbers indicating a variable's values specify only the order of the cases, permitting "greater than" and "less than" distinctions.

Outcomes: The impact of the program process on the cases processed.

Outlier: An exceptionally high or low value in a distribution.

Outputs: The services delivered or new products produced by the program process.

Participant observation: A qualitative method for gathering data that involves developing a sustained relationship with people while they go about their normal activities.

Participant observer: A researcher who gathers data through participating and observing in a setting where he or she develops a sustained relationship with people while they go about their normal activities. The term *participant observer* is often used to refer to a continuum of possible roles, from complete observation, in which the researcher does not participate along with others in group activities, to complete participation, in which the researcher participates without publicly acknowledging being an observer. Also termed *overt participant*.

Participatory action research (PAR):   A type of research in which the researcher involves some organizational members as active participants throughout the process of studying an organization; the goal is to make changes in the organization. Also termed *community-based participatory research*.

Percentages: Relative frequencies, computed by dividing the frequency of cases in a particular category by the total number of cases and then multiplying by 100.

Periodicity: A sequence of elements (in a list to be sampled) that varies in some regular, periodic pattern.

Phone survey: A survey in which interviewers question respondents over the phone and then record their answers.

Photovoice: A method in which research participants take pictures of their everyday surroundings with cameras the researcher distributes and then meet in a group with the researcher to discuss the pictures' meaning.

Population: The entire set of individuals or other entities to which study findings are to be generalized.

Population parameter: The value of a statistic, such as a mean, computed using the data for the entire population; a sample statistic is an estimate of a population parameter.

Positivism: The belief, shared by most scientists, that there is a reality that exists quite apart from our own perception of it, that it can be understood through observation, and that it follows general laws.

Postpositivism: A philosophical view that modifies the positivist premise of an external, objective reality by recognizing its complexity, the limitations of human observers, and therefore the impossibility of developing more than a partial understanding of reality.

Practical or clinical significance: When evaluating the impact of an intervention in a single-subject design, whether or not the intervention made a meaningful difference in the well-being of the subject.

Probability average: The most frequent value in a distribution.

Probability of selection: The likelihood that an element will be selected from the population for inclusion in the sample. In a census of all the elements of a population, the probability that any particular element will be selected is 1.0. If half the elements in the population are sampled on the basis of chance (say, by tossing a coin), the probability of selection for each element is one half, or .5. As the size of the sample as a proportion of the population decreases, so does the probability of selection.

Probability sampling method: A sampling method that relies on a random, or chance, selection method so that the probability of selection of population elements is known.

Process evaluation: Evaluation research that investigates the process of service delivery.

Program process: The complete treatment or service delivered by the program.

Program theory: A descriptive or prescriptive model of how a program operates and produces effects.

Progressive focusing: The process by which a qualitative analyst interacts with the data and gradually refines his or her focus.

Proportionate stratified sampling: Sampling method in which elements are selected from strata in exact proportion to their representation in the population.

Purposive sampling: A nonprobability sampling method in which elements are selected for a purpose, usually because of their unique position.

Qualitative methods: Methods such as participant observation, intensive interviewing, and focus groups that are designed to capture life as participants experience it rather than in categories predetermined by the researcher. These methods rely on written or spoken words or observations that do not have a direct numerical interpretation and typically involve exploratory research questions, inductive reasoning, an orientation to educational context and human subjectivity, and the meanings attached by participants to events and to their lives.

Quantitative methods: Methods such as surveys and experiments that record variation in educational activity in terms of categories that vary in amount. Data that are treated as quantitative are either numbers or attributes that can be ordered in terms of magnitude.

Quartiles: The points in a distribution corresponding to the first 25% of the cases, the first 50% of the cases, and the first 75% of the cases.

Questionnaire: The survey instrument containing the questions in a self-administered survey.

Quota sampling: A nonprobability sampling method in which elements are selected to ensure that the sample represents certain characteristics in proportion to their prevalence in the population.

Random assignment: A procedure by which each experimental subject is placed in a group randomly.

Random number table: A table containing lists of numbers that are ordered solely on the basis of chance; it is used for drawing a random sample.

Random sampling: A method of sampling that relies on a random, or chance, selection method so that every element of the sampling frame has a known probability of being selected.

Random sampling error (chance sampling error):   Differences between the population and the sample that are due only to chance factors (random error), not to systematic sampling error. Random sampling error may or may not result in an unrepresentative sample. The magnitude of sampling error due to chance factors can be estimated statistically.

Range: The true upper limit in a distribution minus the true lower limit (or the highest rounded value minus the lowest rounded value, plus one).

Ratio level of measurement: A measurement of a variable in which the numbers indicating a variable's values represent fixed measuring units and an absolute zero point.

Reactive effects: The changes in an individual or group behavior that are due to being observed or otherwise studied.

Recursive process: A process that repeatedly loops back on itself; often used to describe the action-reflection spiral in an action research project.

Reductionist fallacy (reductionism):   An error in reasoning that occurs when incorrect conclusions about group-level processes are based on individual-level data. Also known as individualist fallacy.

Reflective practice: A characteristic of high-level professional practice in which the practitioner regularly interrogates and reflects on his or her own daily practice in order to continually improve it; often a precursor to teacher research.

Regression analysis: A statistical technique for characterizing the pattern of a relationship between two quantitative variables in terms of a linear equation and for summarizing the strength of this relationship in terms of its deviation from that linear pattern.

Reliability: A measurement procedure yields consistent scores when the phenomenon being measured is not changing.

Repeated cross-sectional design (trend study):   A longitudinal study in which data are collected at two or more points in time from different samples of the same population.

Replication: Repetitions of a study using the same research methods to answer the same research question.

Representative sample: A sample that "looks like" the population from which it was selected in all respects that are potentially relevant to the study. The distribution of characteristics among the elements of a representative sample is the same as the distribution of those characteristics among the total population. In an unrepresentative sample, some characteristics are overrepresented or underrepresented.

Research circle: A diagram of the elements of the research process, including theories, hypotheses, data collection, and data analysis.

Resistance to change: The reluctance to change our ideas in light of new information.

Reverse outlining: Outlining the sections in an already written draft of a paper or report to improve its organization in the next draft.

Sample: A subset of a population that is used to study the population as a whole.

Sample statistic: The value of a statistic, such as a mean, computed from sample data.

Sampling error: Any difference between the characteristics of a sample and the characteristics of a population. The larger the sampling error, the less representative the sample.

Sampling frame: A list of all elements or other units containing the elements in a population.

Sampling interval: The number of cases from one sampled case to another in a systematic random sample.

Sampling units: Units listed at each stage of a multistage sampling design.

Saturation point: The point at which subject selection is ended in intensive interviewing, when new interviews seem to yield little additional information.

Science: A set of logical, systematic, documented methods for investigating nature and natural processes; the knowledge produced by these investigations.

Selective observation: Choosing to look only at things that are in line with our preferences or beliefs.

Simple random sampling: A method of sampling in which every sample element is selected only on the basis of chance, through a random process.

Skewness: The extent to which cases are clustered more at one or the other end of the distribution of a quantitative variable rather than in a symmetric pattern around its center. Skew can be positive (a right skew), with the number of cases tapering off in the positive direction, or negative (a left skew), with the number of cases tapering off in the negative direction.

Skip pattern: The unique combination of questions created in a survey by filter questions and contingent questions.

Snowball sampling: A method of sampling in which sample elements are selected as they are identified by successive informants or interviewees.

Split-halves reliability: Reliability achieved when responses to the same questions by two randomly selected halves of a sample are about the same.

Spurious relationship: A relationship between two variables that is due to variation in a third variable.

Stable line: A line in the baseline phase that is relatively flat, with little variability in the scores so that the scores fall in a narrow band.

Stakeholder approach: An orientation to evaluation research that expects researchers to be responsive primarily to the people involved with the program. Also termed *responsive evaluation.*

Stakeholders: Individuals and groups who have some basis of concern with the program.

Standard deviation: The square root of the average squared deviation of each case from the mean.

Statistical significance: The mathematical likelihood that an association is not due to chance, judged by a criterion set by the analyst.

Stratified random sampling: A method of sampling in which sample elements are selected separately from population strata that are identified in advance by the researcher.

Subject fatigue: Problems caused by panel members growing weary of repeated interviews and dropping out of a study or becoming so used to answering the standard questions in the survey that they start giving stock or thoughtless answers.

Summative evaluation: Type of evaluation that answers the questions "Did the program work?" and "Did it have the intended result?" Compares what happened as a result of the program with what would have happened had there been no program.

Survey research: Research in which information is obtained from a sample of individuals through their responses to questions about themselves or others.

Systematic bias: Overrepresentation or underrepresentation of some population characteristics in a sample due to the method used to select the sample. A sample shaped by systematic sampling error is a biased sample.

Systematic random sampling: A method of sampling in which sample elements are selected from a list or from sequential files, with every *n*th element being selected after the first element is selected randomly within the first interval.

Tacit knowledge: In field research, a credible sense of understanding social processes that reflects the researcher's awareness of participants' actions as well as their words and of what they fail to state, feel deeply, and take for granted.

Target population: A set of elements larger than or different from the population sampled and to which the researcher would like to generalize study findings.

Teacher research: Research in which the choice of the research topic, the formation of research questions, and the collection and analysis of data are all performed primarily by a teacher or practitioner, usually in his or her own classroom or school.

Test-retest reliability: A measurement showing that measures of a phenomenon at two points in time are highly correlated, if the phenomenon has not changed, or have changed only as much as the phenomenon itself.

Theory: A logically interrelated set of propositions about empirical reality.

Thick description: A rich description that conveys a sense of what it is like from the standpoint of the natural actors in that setting.

Time order: A criterion for establishing a causal relation between two variables. The variation in the presumed cause (the independent variable) must occur before the variation in the presumed effect (the dependent variable).

Treatment phase (B):   The intervention phase, usually signified by the letter B, of a single-subject design.

Trend: Repeated measurement scores that are either ascending or descending in magnitude. Identifying a trend requires at least three points of measurement.

Trend study: *See* Repeated cross-sectional design.

Triangulation: The use of multiple methods to study one research question. Also used to mean the use of two or more different measures of the same variable.

Unimodal: A distribution of a variable in which there is only one value that is the most frequent.

Units of analysis: The level of social life on which a research question is focused, such as individuals, groups, towns, or nations.

Units of observation: The cases about which measures actually are obtained in a sample.

Unobtrusive measure: A measurement based on physical traces or other data that are collected without the knowledge or participation of the individuals or groups that generated the data.

Validity: The state that exists when statements or conclusions about empirical reality are correct.

Variable: A characteristic or property that can vary (take on different values or attributes).

Variability: The extent to which cases are spread out through the distribution or clustered in just one location.

Variance: A statistic that measures the variability of a distribution as the average squared deviation of each case from the mean.

Visual analysis (VA):   In education and the social sciences, a research approach that uses various techniques to analyze the content of images and other visual material, including drawings, photographs, graphic art, and moving images.

Web survey: A survey that is accessed and responded to on the World Wide Web.

References

Addison, R. B. (1999). A grounded hermeneutic editing approach. In B. F. Crabtree & W. L. Miller (Eds.), *Doing qualitative research* (pp. 145–161). Thousand Oaks, CA: Sage.

Agnew, R., Matthews, S. K., Bucher, J., Welcher, A. N., & Keyes, C. (2008). Socioeconomic status, economic problems, and delinquency. *Youth & Society, 40*(2), 159–181.

Altheide, D. L., & Johnson, J. M. (1994). Criteria for assessing interpretive validity in qualitative research. In N. K. Denzin & Y. S. Lincoln (Eds.), *Handbook of qualitative research* (pp. 485–499). Thousand Oaks, CA: Sage.

American Educational Research Association, American Psychological Association, & the National Council on Measurement in Education. (1999). *Standards for educational and psychological testing.* Washington, DC: Author.

American Sociological Association. (1999). *Code of ethics and policies and procedures of the ASA committee on professional ethics.* Washington, DC: Author.

Anderson, E. (2003). Jelly's place: An ethnographic memoir. *Symbolic Interaction, 26,* 217–237.

Anderson, R. C., Hiebert, E. H., Scott, A., & Wilkinson, I. A. G. (1985). *Becoming a nation of readers: A report of the Commission on Reading.* Washington, DC: National Institutes of Education.

Arbin, A. O., & Cormier, E. (2005). Racial disparity in nursing research: Is single subject experimental design a solution? *Journal of Theory Construction & Testing, 9*(1), 11–13.

Arwood, T., & Panicker, S. (2007). Assessing risk in social and behavioral sciences. *Collaborative Institutional Training Initiative.* Retrieved June 5, 2008, from https://www.citiprogram.org/members/learners.

Auerbach, E. R. (1995). Deconstructing the discourse of strengths in family literacy. *Journal of Reading Behavior, 27,* 643–661.

Austin, M. C., & Morrison, C. (1963). *The first R: The Harvard report on reading in elementary schools.* New York: Macmillan.

Bachman, R., & Schutt, R. (2008). *Fundamentals of research in criminology and criminal justice.* Thousand Oaks, CA: Sage.

Bachman, R., & Schutt, R. (2010). *Fundamentals of research in criminology and criminal justice* (2nd ed.). Thousand Oaks, CA: Sage.

Baker, J. A. (1999). Teacher-student interaction in urban at-risk classrooms: Differential behavior, relationship quality, and student satisfaction with school. *Elementary School Journal, 100*(1), 57–70.

Balfanz, R., & Legters, N. (2004). *Locating the dropout crisis: Which high schools produce the nation's dropouts?* Baltimore: Center for Research on the Education of Students Placed At Risk (CRESPAR).

Banford, H. (1996). The blooming of Maricar. In H. Banford, M. Berkman, C. Chin, C. Cziko, B. Fecho, D. Jumpp, et al. (Eds.), *Cityscapes: Eight views from the urban classroom* (pp. 3–24). Berkeley: National Writing Project.

Barlow, D. H., Nock, M. K., & Hersen, M. (2009). *Single case experimental designs: Strategies for studying behavior change* (3rd ed.). Boston: Pearson Education.

Barnett, W. S. (1995). Long-term effects of early childhood programs on cognitive and school outcomes. *The Future of Children, 5*(3), 25–50.

Baumann, J. F., Hoffman, J. V., Duffy-Hester, A. M., & Ro, J. M. (2000). The first R yesterday and today: U.S. elementary reading instruction practices reported by teachers and administrators. *Reading Research Quarterly, 35*(3), 338–377.

Baumrind, D. (1964). Some thoughts on ethics of research: After reading Milgram's "Behavioral study of obedience." *American Psychologist, 19,* 421–423.

Baumrind, D. (1985). Research using intentional deception: Ethical issues revisited. *American Psychologist, 40,* 165–174.

Becker, H. S. (1958). Problems of inference and proof in participant observation. *American Sociological Review, 23,* 652–660.

Benwell, B., & Stokoe, E. (2006). *Discourse and identity.* Edinburgh, UK: Edinburgh University Press.

Besharov, D. (1993). Overrreporting and underreporting are twin problems. In R. J. Gelles & D. R. Loseke (Eds.), *Current controversies on family violence* (pp. 257–272). Newbury Park, CA: Sage.

Best, W., & Howard, D. (2005). "The W and M are mixing me up": Use of a visual code in verbal short term memory tasks. *Brain and Cognition, 58, 3,* 274–285.

Biesta, G. J. J., & Burbules, N. (2003). *Pragmatism and educational research.* Lanham, MD: Rowman & Littlefield.

Black, D. J. (1976). *The behavior of law.* New York: Academic Press.

Black, D. J. (Ed.). (1984). *Toward a general theory of social control.* Orlando, FL: Academic Press.

Bloom, M., Fischer, J., & Orme, J. (2009). *Evaluating practice: Guidelines for the accountable professional* (5th ed.). Boston: Allyn & Bacon.

Bogdewic, S. P. (1999). Participant observation. In B. F. Crabtree & W. L. Miller (Eds.), *Doing qualitative research* (2nd ed., pp. 47–70). Thousand Oaks, CA: Sage.

Booth, W. C., Colomb, G. G., & Williams, J. M. (1995). *The craft of research.* Chicago: University of Chicago Press.

Boruch, R. F. (1997). *Randomized experiments for planning and evaluation: A practical guide.* Thousand Oaks, CA: Sage.

Bramel, D., & Friend, R. (1981). Hawthorne, the myth of the docile worker, and class bias in psychology. *American Psychologist, 36*(8), 867–878.

Brewer, J., & Hunter, A. (1989). *Multimethod research: A synthesis of styles.* Newbury Park, CA: Sage.

Bridges, G. S., & Weis, J. G. (1989). Measuring violent behavior: Effects of study design on reported correlates of violence. In N. A. Weiner & M. E. Wolfgang (Eds.), *Violent crime, violent criminals* (pp. 14–34). Newbury Park, CA: Sage.

Brooks-Gunn, J., Han, W., & Waldfogel, J. (2002). Maternal employment and child cognitive outcomes in the first three years of life: The NICHD study of early child care. *Child Development, 73*(4), 1052–1072.

Broskoske, S. (2005). How to prevent paper recycling. *The Teaching Professor, 19,* 1, 4.

Brown, C. P. (2009). Pivoting a prekindergarten program off the child or the standard? A case study of integrating the practices of early childhood education into elementary school. *Elementary School Journal, 110*(2), 202–227.

Brown, J. B. (1999). The use of focus groups in clinical research. In B. F. Crabtree & W. L. Miller (Eds.), *Doing qualitative research* (2nd ed., pp. 109–124). Thousand Oaks, CA: Sage.

Brown, R., Pressley, M., Van Meter, P., & Schuder, T. (1996). A quasi-experimental validation of transactional strategies instruction with low-achieving second-grade readers. *Journal of Educational Psychology, 88*(1), 18–37.

Campbell, D. T., & Stanley, J. C. (1966). *Experimental and quasi-experimental designs for research.* Chicago: Rand McNally.

Campbell, D. T., & Russo, M. J. (1999). *Social experimentation.* Thousand Oaks, CA: Sage.

Carmines, E. G., & Zeller, R. A. (1979). *Reliability and validity assessment* (Quantitative Applications in the Social Sciences No. 17). Beverly Hills, CA: Sage.

Caro-Bruce, C., Klehr, M., Zeichner, K., & Sierra-Piedrahita, A. M. (2009). A school-district-based action research program in the United States. In S. Noffke & B. Somekh (Eds.), *Sage handbook of educational action research* (pp. 104–117). Thousand Oaks, CA: Sage.

Cava, A., Cushman, R., & Goodman, K. (2007). HIPAA and human subjects research. *Collaborative Institutional Training Initiative.* Retrieved June 5, 2008, from https://www.citiprogram.org/members/learners.

Cave, E., & Holm, S. (2003). Milgram and Tuskegee—Paradigm research projects in bioethics. *Health Care Analysis, 11,* 27–40.

Ceglowski, D. (2002). Research as relationship. In N. K. Denzin & Y. S. Lincoln (Eds.), *The qualitative inquiry reader* (pp. 5–27). Thousand Oaks, CA: Sage.

Center for Survey Research, University of Massachusetts at Boston. (1987, April). Methodology: Designing good survey questions. *Newsletter,* p. 3.

Chambliss, D. F., & Schutt, R. S. (2010). *Making sense of the social world: Methods of investigation* (3rd ed.). Thousand Oaks, CA: Pine Forge Press.

Chase-Lansdale, P. L., Coley, R. L., Lohman, B. J., & Pittman, L. D. (2002). *Welfare reform: What about the children?* (Policy brief 02-1). Baltimore: Johns Hopkins University. http://web.jhu.edu/bin/q/v/14_19382_Welfare_jan02.pdf

Chase-Lansdale, P., Moffitt, R., Lohman, B., Cherllin, A., Coley, R., Pittman, L., Roff, J., & Votruba-Drzal, E. (2003). Mothers' transitions from welfare to work and the well-being of preschoolers and adolescents. *Science, 299*, 1548–1552.

Check, J. W. (1997, May/June). Teacher research as powerful professional development. *The Harvard Education Letter,* p. 7.

Check, J. W. (2002). *Politics, language, and culture: A critical look at urban school reform.* Westport, CT: Praeger.

Chen, H. (1990). *Theory-driven evaluations.* Newbury Park, CA: Sage.

Chen, H., & Rossi, P. H. (1987). The theory-driven approach to validity. *Evaluation and Program Planning, 10,* 95–103.

Christakis, D. A., Zimmerman, F. J., DiGiuseppe, D. L., & McCarty, C. A. (2004). Early television exposure and subsequent attentional problems in children. *Pediatrics, 113*(4), 708–713.

Clandinin, D. J., Pushor, D., & Orr, A. M. (2007). Navigating sites for narrative inquiry. *Journal of Teacher Education, 58*(1), 21–35.

Cochran-Smith, M., & Lytle, S. L. (1993). *Inside/outside: Teacher research and knowledge.* New York: Teachers College Press.

Cochran-Smith, M., & Lytle, S. L. (2001). Beyond certainty: Taking an inquiry stance on practice. In A. Lieberman & L. Miller (Eds.), *Teachers caught in the action: Professional development that matters* (pp. 45–58). New York: Teachers College Press.

Cochran-Smith, M., & Lytle, S. L. (2009). *Inquiry as stance: Practitioner research for the next generation.* New York: Teachers College Press.

Coffey, A., & Atkinson, P. (1996). *Making sense of qualitative data: Complementary research strategies.* Thousand Oaks, CA: Sage.

Cohen, S., Mermelstein, R., Kamarck, T., & Hoberman, H. M. (1985). Measuring the functional components of social support. In I. G. Sarason & B. R. Sarason (Eds.), *Social support: Theory, research and applications* (pp. 73–94). The Hague, The Netherlands: Martinus Nijhoff.

Coleman, J. S., & Hoffer, T. (1987). *Public and private schools.* New York: Basic Books.

Coleman, J. S., Hoffer, T., & Kilgore, S. (1982). *High school achievement.* New York: Basic Books.

Collier, J. (1945). United States Indian administration as a laboratory of ethnic relations. *Social Research, 12,* 265–303.

Cook, T. D., & Campbell, D. T. (1979). *Quasi-experimentation: Design and analysis issues for field settings.* Chicago: Rand McNally.

Cooksy, L. J., Gill, P., & Kelly, P. A. (2001). The program logic model as an integrative framework for a multimethod evaluation. *Evaluation and Program Planning, 24*(2), 119–128.

Cooper, H., & Hedges, L. V. (1994). Research synthesis as a scientific enterprise. In H. Cooper & L. V. Hedges (Eds.), *The handbook of research synthesis* (pp. 3–14). New York: Russell Sage Foundation.

Core Institute. (1994). *Core Alcohol and Drug Survey: Long form.* Carbondale: FIPSE Core Analysis Grantee Group, Core Institute, Student Health Programs, Southern Illinois University.

Costner, H. L. (1989). The validity of conclusions in evaluation research: A further development of Chen and Rossi's theory-driven approach. *Evaluation and Program Planning, 12,* 345–353.

Couper, M. P., Baker, R. P., Bethlehem, J., Clark, C. Z. F., Martin, J., Nicholls, W. L., II, et al. (Eds.). (1998). *Computer-assisted survey information collection.* New York: John Wiley.

Creswell, J. W. (2010). Mapping the developing landscape of mixed methods research. In A. Tashakkori & C. Teddlie (Eds.), *Sage handbook of mixed methods in social & behavioral research* (2nd ed., pp. 45–68). Thousand Oaks, CA: Sage.

Davis, R. (1999, July 8). Study: Search engines can't keep up with expanding net. *The Boston Globe,* pp. C1, C3.

Dawes, R. (1995). How do you formulate a testable exciting hypothesis? In W. Pequegnat & E. Stover (Eds.), *How to write a successful research grant application: A guide for social and behavioral scientists* (pp. 93–96). New York: Plenum Press.

Decker, S. H., & Van Winkle, B. (1996). *Life in the gang: Family, friends, and violence.* Cambridge, UK: Cambridge University Press.

Dentler, R. A. (2002). *Practicing sociology: Selected fields.* Westport, CT: Praeger.

Denzin, N. K. (2002). The interpretive process. In A. M. Huberman & M. B. Miles (Eds.), *The qualitative researcher's companion* (pp. 349–368). Thousand Oaks, CA: Sage.

Denzin, N., & Lincoln, Y. S. (2000). Introduction: The discipline and practice of qualitative research. In N. K Denzin & Y. S. Lincoln (Eds.), *Handbook of qualitative research* (2nd ed., pp. 1–28). Thousand Oaks, CA: Sage.

Denzin, N. K., & Lincoln, Y. S. (2005). *The SAGE handbook of qualitative research.* Thousand Oaks, CA: Sage.

Dewey, J. (1933). *How we think.* Buffalo, NY: Prometheus Books.

Diamond, T. (1992). *Making gray gold: Narratives of nursing home care.* Chicago: University of Chicago Press.

Dillman, D. A. (2000). *Mail and Internet surveys: The tailored design method* (2nd ed.). New York: John Wiley.

Dillman, D. A. (2007). *Mail and internet surveys: The tailored design method* (2nd ed.). Update with new Internet, visual, and mixed-mode guide. Hoboken, NJ: John Wiley.

Dillman, D. A., & Christian, L. M. (2005). Survey mode as a source of instability in responses across surveys. *Field Methods, 17,* 30–52.

Dixon, M. R., Jackson, J. W., Small, S. L., Horner-King, M. J., Lik, N. M., Garcia, Y., et al. (2009). Creating single-subject design graphs in Microsoft Excel TM2007. *Journal of Applied Behavioral Analysis, 42*(2), 277–293.

Douglas, J. D. (1985). *Creative interviewing.* Beverly Hills, CA: Sage.

Duncombe, J., & Jessop, J. (2002). "Doing rapport" and the ethics of "faking friendship." In M. Mauthner, M. Birch, J. Jessop, & T. Miller (Eds.), *Ethics in qualitative research* (pp. 107–122). Thousand Oaks, CA: Sage.

Educational Resources Information Clearinghouse (ERIC). (2008). *Thesaurus descriptors entry: At risk students.* http://www.eric.ed.gov/

Elliott, J. (1981). Foreword. In J. Nixon (Ed.), *A teachers' guide to action research: Evaluation, enquiry, and development in the classroom.* London: Grant McIntyre.

Emerson, R. M. (Ed.). (1983). *Contemporary field research.* Prospect Heights, IL: Waveland.

Emerson, R. M., Fretz, R. I., & Shaw, L. L. (1995). *Writing ethnographic fieldnotes.* Chicago: University of Chicago Press.

Engel, R. J., & Schutt, R. (2005). *The practice of research in social work.* Thousand Oaks, CA: Sage.

Engel, R. J., & Schutt, R. (2010). *Fundamentals of social work research.* Thousand Oaks, CA: Sage.

Erikson, K. T. (1967). A comment on disguised observation in sociology. *Social Problems, 12,* 366–373.

Erwin, E., Alimaras, E., & Price, N. (1999). A qualitative study of social dynamics in an inclusive preschool. *Journal of Research in Childhood Education, 14*(1), 56–67.

Eschenauer, R., & Chen-Hayes, S. F. (2005). The transformative individual school counseling model: An accountability model for urban school counselors. *Professional School Counseling, 8*(3), 244–248.

Ferrance, E. (2000). *Action research.* Providence, RI: Northeast and Islands Regional Educational Laboratory at Brown University.

Fink, A. (2005). *Conducting research literature reviews: From the Internet to paper* (3rd ed.). Thousand Oaks, CA: Sage.

Finn, J. D. (2006). *The adult lives of at-risk students: The roles of attainment and engagement in high school* (NCES 2006-328). Washington, DC: National Center for Education Statistics.

Finn, J. D., & Achilles, C. M. (1990). Answers and questions about class size: A statewide experiment. *American Educational Research Journal, 27*(3), 557–577.

Fowler, F. J. (1988). *Survey research methods* (Rev. ed.). Newbury Park, CA: Sage.

Fowler, F. J. (1995). *Improving survey questions: Design and evaluation.* Thousand Oaks, CA: Sage.

Friere, P. (1970). *Pedagogy of the oppressed* (M. B. Ramos, Trans.). New York: Seabury Press.

Friere, P. (1985). *The politics of education: Culture, power, and liberation* (D. Macedo, Trans.). South Hadley, MA: Bergin and Garvey.

Fulp, S. L. (2002). The *2000 national survey of science and mathematics education: Status of elementary school science teaching.* Chapel Hill, NC: Horizon Research, Inc.

Garces, E., Thomas, D., & Currie, J. (2002). Longer term effects of Head Start. *American Economic Review, 92*(4), 999–1012.

Geertz, C. (1973). Thick description: Toward an interpretive theory of culture. In C. Geertz (Ed.), *The interpretation of cultures* (pp. 3–30). New York: Basic Books.

Gilligan, C. (1988). Adolescent development reconsidered. In C. Gilligan, J. V. Ward, & J. M. Taylor (Eds.), *Mapping the moral domain* (pp. vii–xxxix). Cambridge, MA: Harvard University Press.

Glaser, B. G., & Strauss, A. L. (1967). *The discovery of grounded theory: Strategies for qualitative research.* London: Weidenfeld and Nicholson.

Goleman, D. (1993, August 17). Placebo effect is shown to be twice as powerful as expected. *The New York Times,* p. C3.

Gordon, R. (1992). *Basic interviewing skills.* Itasca, IL: Peacock.

Grady, J. (1996). The scope of visual sociology. *Visual Sociology, 11,* 10–24.

Greenwald, R., Hedges, L. V., & Laine, R. D. (1996). The effect of school resources on student achievement. *Review of Educational Research, 66*(3), 361–396.

Groves, R. M. (1989). *Survey errors and survey costs.* New York: John Wiley.

Guba, E. G., & Lincoln, Y. S. (1989). *Fourth generation evaluation.* Newbury Park, CA: Sage.

Guba, E. G., & Lincoln, Y. S. (1994). Competing paradigms in qualitative research. In N. K. Denzin & Y. S. Lincoln (Eds.), *Handbook of qualitative research* (pp. 105–117). Thousand Oaks, CA: Sage.

Gubrium, J. F., & Holstein, J. A. (1997). *The new language of qualitative method.* New York: Oxford University Press.

Gubrium, J. F., & Holstein, J. A. (2000). *The self we live by: Narrative identity in a postmodern world.* New York: Oxford University Press.

Hafner, K. (2005, October 3). In challenge to Google, Yahoo will scan books. *The New York Times,* pp. C1, C4.

Hage, J., & Meeker, B. F. (1988). *Social causality.* Boston: Unwin Hyman.

Hanushek, E. A., Peterson, P., & Woessmann, L. (2010). *U.S. math performance in global perspective: How well does each state do at producing high-achieving students?* (PEPG Report No. 10–19). Cambridge, MA: Harvard Kennedy School. http://www.hks.harvard.edu/pepg

Hard, S. F., Conway, J. M., & Moran, A. C. (2006). Faculty and college student beliefs about the frequency of student academic misconduct. *Journal of Higher Education, 77,* 1058–1080.

Hart, C. (1998). *Doing a literature review: Releasing the social science research imagination.* London: Sage.

Hatch, A. J. (1993, April). *Ethical conflicts in a study of peer stigmatization in kindergarten.* Unpublished conference paper. ERIC document ED357 860, PS 021 383. http://eric.ed.gov/

Hawkins, D. N., Amato, P. R., & King, V. (2007). Nonresident father involvement and adolescent well-being: Father effects or child effects? *American Sociological Review, 72,* 990–1010.

Heath, S. B. (1983). *Ways with words.* Cambridge, UK: Cambridge University Press.

Heckathorn, D. D. (1997). Respondent-driven sampling: A new approach to the study of hidden populations. *Social Problems, 44,* 174–199.

Hedges, L. V., & Rhoads, C. (2010). *Statistical power analysis in education research* (Pub. No. NCSER 20103006). Washington, DC: Institute of Educational Statistics. http://ies.ed.gov/pubsearch

Hock, R. (2010). *The extreme searcher's internet handbook* (3rd ed.). Medford, NJ: Cyber Age Books.

Horner, R. H., Carr, E. G., Halle, J., McGee, G., Odom, S., & Wolery, M. (2005). The use of single-subject research to identify evidence-based practice in special education. *Exceptional Children, 71*(2), 165.

Howe, K. R. (1998). The interpretive turn and the new debate in education. *Educational Researcher, 27*(8), 13–21.

Hox, J. J. (2010). *Multilevel analysis: Techniques and applications* (2nd ed.). New York: Routledge.

Hubbard, R. S., & Power, B. M. (1999). *Living the questions: A guide for teacher researchers.* Portland, ME: Stenhouse.

Huberman, A. M., & Miles, M. B. (1994). Data management and analysis methods. In N. K. Denzin & Y. S. Lincoln (Eds.), *Handbook of qualitative research* (pp. 428–444). Thousand Oaks, CA: Sage.

Huer, M. B., & Saenz, T. I. (2003). Challenges and strategies for conducting survey and focus group research with culturally diverse groups. *American Journal of Speech-Language Pathology, 12,* 209–220.

Huff, D. (1954). *How to lie with statistics.* New York: W. W. Norton.

Hume, K., & Odom, S. (2007). Effects of an individual work system on the independent functioning of students with autism. *Journal of Autism and Developmental Disorders, 37,* 1166–1180.

Humphrey, N. (1992). *A history of the mind: Evolution and the birth of consciousness.* New York: Simon & Schuster.

Hunt, M. (1985). *Profiles of social research: The scientific study of human interactions.* New York: Russell Sage Foundation.

Huston, A. C., Wright, J. C., Rice, M. L., Kerkman, D., & St. Peters, M. (1990). The development of television viewing patterns in early childhood: A longitudinal investigation. *Developmental Psychology, 26*(3), 409–420.

Ivankova, N. V., & Kawamura, Y. (2010). Emerging trends in the utilization of integrated designs in the social, behavioral, and health sciences. In A. Tashakkori & C. Teddlie (Eds.), *Sage handbook of mixed methods in social & behavioral research* (2nd ed.). Thousand Oaks, CA: Sage.

Jesnadum, A. (2000). *Researchers fear privacy breaches with online research.* Retrieved September 15, 2000, from www.digitalmass.com/news/daily/09/15/researchers.html

Johnson, B., & Gray, R. (2010). A history of philosophical and theoretical issues for mixed methods research. In A. Tashakkori & C. Teddlie (Eds.), *Sage handbook of mixed methods in social & behavioral research* (2nd ed., pp. 69–94). Thousand Oaks, CA: Sage.

Johnson, B., & Turner, L. A. (2003). Data collection strategies in mixed-methods research. In A. Tashakkori & C. Teddlie (Eds.), *Handbook of mixed methods in social and behavioral research* (pp. 297–320). Thousand Oaks, CA: Sage.

Johnson, D. W., & Johnson, R. T. (1996). Conflict resolution and peer mediation programs in elementary and secondary schools: A review of the research. *Review of Educational Research, 66,* 459–506.

Jones, J. H. (1993). *Bad blood: The Tuskegee syphilis experiment.* New York: Free Press.

Karoly, L. A., & Bigelow, J. H. (2005). *The economics of investing in universal preschool education in California.* Santa Monica, CA: RAND Corporation.

Kaufman, P., Alt, M. N., & Chapman, C. (2001). *Dropout rates in the United States: 2000.* Washington, DC: National Center for Educational Statistics.

Kaufman, S. R. (1986). *The ageless self: Sources of meaning in late life.* Madison: University of Wisconsin Press.

King, G., Keohane, R. O., & Verba, S. (1994). *Scientific inference in qualitative research.* Princeton, NJ: Princeton University Press.

Koegel, P. (1987). *Ethnographic perspectives on homeless and homeless mentally ill women.* Washington, DC: National Academy Press,

Kohn, A. (2008). Who's cheating whom? *The Education Digest, 73,* 4–11.

Kominski, R., Jamieson, A., & Martinez, G. (2001). *At-risk conditions of U.S. school-age children* (Working Paper Series No. 52). Washington, DC: U. S. Bureau of the Census.

Kress, T., & Silva, K. (2009). Using digital video for professional development and leadership: Understanding and initiating teacher learning communities. In C. Maddux (Ed.), *Research highlights in information technology and teacher education.* Chesapeake, VA: Society for Information Technology and Teacher Education (SITE).

Krueger, A., & Whitmore, D. (2001). The effect of attending a small class in the early grades on college-test taking and middle school test results: Evidence from Project STAR. *Economic Journal, 111,* 1–28.

Krueger, R. A. (1988). *Focus groups: A practical guide for applied research.* Newbury Park, CA: Sage.

Krueger, R. A., & Casey, M. A. (2000). *Focus groups. A practical guide for applied research* (3rd ed.). Thousand Oaks, CA: Sage.

Kuhn, M. R., & Stahl, S. A. (2003). Fluency: A review of developmental and remedial practices. *Journal of Educational Psychology, 95*(1), 3–21.

Kuzel, A. J. (1999). Sampling in qualitative inquiry. In B. F. Crabtree & W. L. Miller (Eds.), *Doing qualitative research* (2nd ed., pp. 33–45). Thousand Oaks, CA: Sage.

Kvale, S. (1996). *Interviews: An introduction to qualitative research interviewing.* Thousand Oaks, CA: Sage.

Kvale, S. (2002). The social construction of validity. In N. K. Denzin & Y. S. Lincoln (Eds.), *The qualitative inquiry reader* (pp. 299–325). Thousand Oaks, CA: Sage.

Lagemann, E. C. (1997). Contested terrain: A history of education research in the United States, 1890–1990. *Educational Researcher, 26*(9), 5–17.

Lagemann, E. C. (2000). *An elusive science: The troubling history of education research.* Chicago: University of Chicago.

Levy, P. S., & Lemeshow, S. (1999). *Sampling of populations: Methods and applications* (3rd ed.). New York: John Wiley.

Lewin, K. (1946). Action research and minority problems. *Journal of Social Issues, 2*(4), 34–46.

Lewin, T. (2001a, November 16). Income education is found to lower risk of new arrest. *The New York Times,* p. A18.

Lewin, T. (2001b, July 31). Surprising result in welfare-to-work studies. *The New York Times,* p. A16.

Lieberman, A. (1994). Foreword. In M. M. Mohr, C. Rogers, B. Sanford, M. A. Nocerino, M. S. MacLean, & S. Clawson (Eds.), *Teacher research for better schools.* New York: Teachers College Press.

Lieberson, S. (1985). *Making it count: The improvement of social research and theory.* Berkeley: University of California Press.

Lipsey, M. W., & Wilson, D. B. (2001). *Practical meta-analysis.* Thousand Oaks, CA: Sage.

Litwin, M. S. (1995). *How to measure survey reliability and validity.* Thousand Oaks, CA: Sage.

Locke, L. F., Silverman, S. J., & Spirduso, W. W. (1998). *Reading and understanding research.* Thousand Oaks, CA: Sage.

Locke, L. F., Spirduso, W. W., & Silverman, S. J. (2000). *Proposals that work: A guide for planning dissertations and grant proposals* (4th ed.). Thousand Oaks, CA: Sage.

Lofland, J., Snow, D. A., Anderson, L., & Lofland, L. H. (2005). *Analyzing social settings: A guide to qualitative observation and analysis* (4th ed.). Belmont, CA: Wadsworth.

López, G. R., Scribner, J. D., & Mahitivanichcha, K. (2001). Redefining parental involvement: Lessons from high-performing migrant-impacted schools. *American Educational Research Journal, 38,* 253–288.

Luna, I., Torres de Ardon, E., Lim, Y. M., Cromwell, S. L., Phillips, L. R., & Russell, C. K. (1996). The relevance of familism in cross-cultural studies of family caregiving. *Western Journal of Nursing Research, 18*(3), 267–283.

Lundervold, D. A., & Belwood, M. F. (2000). The best kept secret in counseling: Single-case ($N = 1$) experimental designs. *Journal of Counseling & Development, 78*(1), 92–102.

Lynch, M., & Bogen, D. (1997). Sociology's asociological "core": An examination of textbook sociology in light of the sociology of scientific knowledge. *American Sociological Review, 62,* 481–493.

Lynch, R. (2005). *Early childhood investment yields big payoffs.* San Francisco: Wested.

MacDonald, G. J. (2005, September 4). Child behavioral problems hard lesson for pre-K parents. *Boston Globe,* p. A8.

Mack, N., Woodsong, C., MacQueen, K. M., Guest, G., & Namey, E. (2005). *Qualitative research methods: A data collector's field guide.* Research Triangle Park, NC: Family Health International.

Macy, M. G., & Bricker, D. D. (2007). Embedding individualized social goals into routine activities in inclusive early childhood classrooms. *Early Child Development and Care, 177*(2), 107–120.

Mangione, T. W. (1995). *Mail surveys: Improving the quality.* Thousand Oaks, CA: Sage.

Marin, G., & Marin, B. V. (1991). *Research with Hispanic populations.* Newbury Park, CA: Sage.

Marini, M. M., & Singer, B. (1988). Causality in the social sciences. In C. C. Clogg (Ed.), *Sociological methodology* (Vol. 18, pp. 347–409). Washington, DC: American Sociological Association.

Marshall, C., & Rossman, G. B. (1995). *Designing qualitative research* (2nd ed.). Thousand Oaks, CA: Sage.

Marshall, C., & Rossman, G. B. (1999). *Designing qualitative research* (3rd ed.). Thousand Oaks, CA: Sage.

Martin, J. I., & Knox, J. (2000). Methodological and ethical issues in research on lesbians and gay men. *Social Work Research, 24,* 51–59.

Martin, L. L., & Kettner, P. M. (1996). *Measuring the performance of human service programs.* Thousand Oaks, CA: Sage.

Massachusetts Department of Education. (2004). *The Department seeks input on education data needs.* http://www.doe.mass.edu/infoservices/news04/

Masse, L. N., & Barnett, W. S. (2002). *A benefit cost analysis of the Abecedarian early childhood intervention.* New Brunswick, NJ: NIEER.

Matt, G. E., & Cook, T. D. (1994). Threats to the validity of research syntheses. In H. Cooper & L. V. Hedges (Eds.), *The handbook of research synthesis* (pp. 503–520). New York: Russell Sage Foundation.

Maxwell, J. A. (1996). *Qualitative research design: An interactive approach.* Thousand Oaks, CA: Sage.

Mayrl, D., Moodie, B., Norman, J., Short, J., Staveteig, S., & Solari, C. (2004). A theory of relativity. *Contexts, 3,* 10.

McIntyre, A. (2008). *Participatory action research.* Thousand Oaks, CA: Sage.

McLaughlin, M. (with Zarrow, J.). (2001). Teachers engaged in evidence-based reform: Trajectories of teachers' inquiry, analysis, and action. In A. Lieberman & L. Miller (Eds.), *Teachers caught in the action: Professional development that matters* (pp. 79–101). New York: Teachers College Press.

McLellan, A. T., Luborsky, L., Cacciola, J., Griffith, J., Evans, F., Barr, H. L., et al. (1985). New data from the addiction severity index: Reliability and validity in three centers. *Journal of Nervous and Mental Disease, 173*(7), 412–423.

McNiff, J., & Whitehead, J. (2006). *All you need to know about action research.* Thousand Oaks, CA: Sage.

Mertler, C. A. (2009). *Action research: Teachers as researchers in the classroom.* Thousand Oaks, CA: Sage.

Miles, M. B., & Huberman, A. M. (1994). *Qualitative data analysis* (2nd ed.). Thousand Oaks, CA: Sage.

Milgram, S. (1963). Behavioral study of obedience. *Journal of Abnormal and Social Psychology, 67,* 371–378.

Milgram, S. (1964). Issues in the study of obedience: A reply to Baumrind. *American Psychologist, 19,* 848–852.

Milgram, S. (1965). Some conditions of obedience and disobedience to authority. *Human Relations, 18,* 57–76.

Milgram, S. (1974). *Obedience to authority: An experimental view.* New York: Harper & Row.

Miller, A. G. (1986). *The obedience experiments: A case study of controversy in social science.* New York: Praeger.

Miller, D. C. (1991). *Handbook of research design and social measurement* (5th ed.). Newbury Park, CA: Sage.

Miller, D. C., & Salkind, N. J. (2002). *Handbook of research design and social measurement* (6th ed.). Thousand Oaks, CA: Sage.

Miller, W. L., & Crabtree, B. F. (1999a). Clinical research: A multimethod typology and qualitative roadmap. In B. F. Crabtree & W. L. Miller (Eds.), *Doing qualitative research* (2nd ed., pp. 3–30). Thousand Oaks, CA: Sage.

Miller, W. L., & Crabtree, B. F. (1999b). The dance of interpretation. In B. F. Crabtree & W. L. Miller (Eds.), *Doing qualitative research* (2nd ed., pp. 127–143). Thousand Oaks, CA: Sage.

Mills, C. W. (1959). *The sociological imagination.* New York: Oxford University Press.

Minkler, M. (2000). Using participatory action research to build healthy communities. *Public Health Reports, 115*(2–3), 191–197.

Mitchell, R. G., Jr. (1993). *Secrecy and fieldwork.* Newbury Park, CA: Sage.

Mohr, L. B. (1992). *Impact analysis for program evaluation.* Newbury Park, CA: Sage.

Mohr, M., Rogers, C., Sanford, B., Nocerino, M., MacLean, M. S., & Clawson, S. (2004). *Teacher research for better schools.* New York: Teachers College/Berkeley: National Writing Project.

Moll, L. C., Amanti, C., Neff, D., & Gonzalez, N. (1992). Funds of knowledge for teaching: Using a qualitative approach to connect homes and classrooms. *Theory Into Practice, 31,* 132–141.

Montano, E. (2010). *"I think they feel like visitors," white educators and the METCO program: Perspectives of METCO and race.* Unpublished doctoral dissertation, University of Massachusetts, Boston.

Morrill, C., Yalda, C., Adelman, M., Musheno, M., & Bejarano, C. (2000). Telling tales in school: Youth culture and conflict narratives. *Law & Society Review, 34,* 521–565.

Muhr, T., & Friese, S. (2004). *User's manual for Atlas.ti 5.0* (2nd ed.). Berlin: Scientific Software Development.

Nassar-McMillan, S. C., & Borders, L. D. (2002). Use of focus groups in survey item development. *The Qualitative Report, 7,* 1. http://www.nova.edu/ssss/QR/QR7-1/nassar.html

National Center for Education Statistics. (2006). *Characteristics of schools, districts, teachers, principals, and school libraries in the United States 2003–2004.* Washington, DC: U.S. Department of Education, Institute of Education Sciences. http://nces.ed.gov/pubs2006/2006313.pdf

National Center for Education Statistics. (2009). *Schools and staffing survey, 2007–2008.* Washington, DC: U.S. Department of Education, Institute of Education Sciences.

National Commission for the Protection of Human Subjects of Biomedical and Behavioral Research. (1979). *The Belmont report: Ethical principles and guidelines for the protection of human subjects of research.* Washington, DC: U.S. Department of Health, Education, and Welfare.

National Institute of Child Health and Human Development, Early Child Care Research Network. (2002). Early child care and children's development prior to school entry: Results from the NICHD study of early child care. *American Educational Research Journal, 39*(1), 133–164.

National Institute on the Education of At-Risk Students. (2002). *Mission statement.* http://www.ed.gov/offices/OERI/At-Risk/index.html

National Opinion Research Center. (2006). *General Social Survey.* Chicago: Author.

National Opinion Research Center. (2010). *General Social Survey.* Chicago: Author.

National Poverty Center. (2009). *How many children live in poverty? Poverty in the United States frequently asked questions.* http://www.npc.umich.edu/poverty

National Science Foundation. (2005). *Panel study of income dynamics (PSID) competition.* Retrieved May 25, 2007, from http://nsf.gov/pubs/2005/nsf05541/nsf05541.htm

Needleman, C. (1981). Discrepant assumptions in empirical research: The case of juvenile court screening. *Social Problems, 28,* 247–262.

Nelson, J. C. (1994). Ethics, gender, and ethnicity in single-case research and evaluation. *Journal of Social Service Research, 18,* 139–152.

Newbury, D. (2005). Editorial: The challenge of visual studies. *Visual Studies, 20,* 1–3.

Newschaffer, C. J., Croen, L. A., Daniels, J., Giarelli, E., Grether, J. K., Levy, S. E., et al. (2007). The epidemiology of autism spectrum disorders. *Annual Review of Public Health, 28,* 235–258.

Nolen, A., & Vander Putten, J. (2007). Action research in education: Gaps in ethical principles and practice. *Educational Researcher, 36*(7), 401–407.

Nord, C. W., Lennon, J., Liu, B., Westat, & Chandler, K. (1999). *Home literacy activities and signs of children's emerging literacy, 1993 and 1999* (NCES 2000-026). Washington, DC: National Center for Education Statistics.

North Central Regional Educational Laboratory. (1996). *Critical issue: Providing effective schooling for students at risk.* http://www.ncrel.org/sdrs/areas/issues/students/atrisk/at600.htm

Novak, D. (2003). The evolution of Internet research: Shifting allegiances. *Online, 27,* 21.

Nugent, W. (2000). Single case design visual analysis procedure for use in practice evaluation. *Journal of Social Service Research, 27,* 39–75.

Oden, S., Schweinhart, L. J., & Weikart, D. P. (2000). *Into adulthood: A study of the effects of Head Start.* Ypsilanti, MI: High/Scope Press.

Ó Dochartaigh, N. (2002). *The Internet research handbook: A practical guide for students and researchers in the social sciences.* Thousand Oaks, CA: Sage.

Odom, S. L., Zercher, C., Li, S., Marquart, J. M., Sandall, S., & Brown, W. H. (2006). Social acceptance and rejection of preschool children with disabilities: A mixed-methods analysis. *Journal of Educational Psychology, 98*(4), 807–823.

Onwuegbuzie, A. J., & Combs, J. P. (2010). Emergent data analysis techniques in mixed methods research. In A. Tashakkori & C. Teddlie (Eds.), *Sage handbook of mixed methods in social & behavioral research* (2nd ed., pp. 397–430). Thousand Oaks, CA: Sage.

Orshansky, M. (1977). Memorandum for Daniel P. Moynihan. Subject: History of the poverty line. In M. Orshansky (Ed.), *The measure of poverty. Technical Paper I: Documentation of background information and rationale for current poverty matrix* (pp. 232–237). Washington, DC: U.S. Department of Health, Education, and Welfare.

O'Toole, R., Webster, S.W., O'Toole, A. W., & Lucal, B. (1999). Teachers' recognition and reporting of child abuse: A factorial survey. *Child Abuse & Neglect, 23*(11), 1083–1101.

Paiewonsky, M. (2005). *See what I mean: Using photovoice to plan for the future.* Unpublished doctoral dissertation, University of Massachusetts, Boston.

Pandit, N. R. (1996). The creation of theory: A recent application of the grounded theory method. *The Qualitative Report, 2.* http://www.nova.edu/ssss/QR/QR2-4/pandit.html.

Papineau, D. (1978). *For science in the social sciences.* London: Macmillan.

Paratore, J. R. (2002). Home and school together: Helping beginning readers succeed. In A. E. Farstrup & S. J. Samuels (Eds.), *What research has to say about reading instruction* (pp. 48–68). Newark, DE: International Reading Association.

Parlett, M., & Hamilton, D. (1976). Evaluation as illumination: A new approach to the study of innovative programmes. In G. Glass (Ed.), *Evaluation studies review annual* (Vol. 1, pp. 140–157). Beverly Hills, CA: Sage.

Patton, M. Q. (2002). *Qualitative research and evaluation methods* (3rd ed.). Thousand Oaks, CA: Sage.

Peters, K. M., & Blumberg, F. C. (2002). Cartoon violence: Is it as detrimental to preschoolers as we think? *Early Childhood Education Journal, 29*(3), 143–148.

Peterson, R. A. (2000). *Constructing effective questionnaires.* Thousand Oaks, CA: Sage.

Phoenix, A. (2004) Neoliberalism and masculinity: Racialisation and the contradictions of schooling for 11–14 year olds. *Youth & Society, 36*(2), 227–244.

Pipher, M. (1994). *Reviving Ophelia.* New York: Ballantine.

Plano Clark, V. L., & Badiee, M. (2010). Research questions in mixed methods research. In A. Tashakkori & C. Teddlie (Eds.), *Sage handbook of mixed methods in social & behavioral research* (2nd ed., pp. 275–304). Thousand Oaks, CA: Sage.

Posavac, E. J., & Carey, R. G. (1997). *Program evaluation: Methods and case studies* (5th ed.). Upper Saddle River, NJ: Prentice Hall.

Presley, C. A., Meilman, P. W., & Lyerla, R. (1994). Development of the core alcohol and drug survey: Initial findings and future directions. *Journal of American College Health, 42,* 248–255.

Presser, J., & Blair, J. (1994). Survey pretesting: Do different methods produce different results? In P. V. Marsden (Ed.), *Sociological methodology* (Vol. 24, pp. 73–104).). Washington, DC: American Sociological Association.

Provasnik, S., Gonzales, P., & Miller, D. (2009). *U.S. performance across international assessments of student achievement: Special supplement to The Condition of Education 2009* (NCES 2009-083). Washington, DC: U.S. Department of Education.

Punch, M. (1994). Politics and ethics in qualitative research. In N. K. Denzin & Y. S. Lincoln (Eds.). *Handbook of qualitative research* (pp. 83–97). Thousand Oaks, CA: Sage.

Putnam, I. (1977). Poverty thresholds: Their history and future development. In M. Orshansky (Ed.), *The measure of poverty. Technical paper I: Documentation of background information and rationale for current poverty matrix* (pp. 272–283). Washington, DC: U.S. Department of Health, Education, and Welfare.

Pyrczak, F. (2005). *Evaluating research in academic journals: A practical guide to realistic evaluation* (3rd ed.). Glendale, CA: Pyrczak Publishing.

Radloff, L. (1977). The CES-D scale: A self-report depression scale for research in the general population. *Applied Psychological Measurement, 1,* 385–401.

Ragin, C. C. (1994). *Constructing social research.* Thousand Oaks, CA: Pine Forge.

Ravitch, S., & Wirth, K. (2007). Developing a pedagogy of opportunity for students and their teachers: Navigations and negotiations in insider action research. *Action Research, 5*(1), 75–91.

Reissman, C. K. (2002). Narrative analysis. In A. M. Huberman & M. B. Miles (Eds.), *The qualitative researcher's companion* (pp. 217–270). Thousand Oaks, CA: Sage.

Reissman, C. K. (2008). *Narrative methods for the human sciences.* Thousand Oaks, CA: Sage.

Rex, L. A., Steadman, S. C., & Graciano, M. K. (2006). Researching the complexity of classroom interaction. In J. L. Green, G. Camilli, & P. B. Elmore (Eds.), *Handbook of complementary methods in education research* (pp. 727–771).Mahwah, NJ: American Educational Research Association.

Reynolds, A. J., Temple, J. A., Robertson, D. L., & Mann, E. A. (2001). Long-term effects of an early childhood intervention on educational achievement and juvenile arrest: A 15-year follow-up of low-income children in public schools. *Journal of the American Medical Association, 285*(18), 2339–2346.

Reynolds, P. D. (1979). *Ethical dilemmas and social science research.* San Francisco: Jossey-Bass.

Richards, T. J., & Richards, L. (1994). Using computers in qualitative research. In N. K. Denzin & Y. S. Lincoln (Eds.), *Handbook of qualitative research* (pp. 445–462). Thousand Oaks, CA: Sage.

Roosa, M. W., Deng, S., Nair, R. L., & Burrell, G. L. (2005). Measures for studying poverty in family and child research. *Journal of Marriage and Family, 67,* 971–988.

Rosen, A. (2003). Evidence-based social work practice: Challenges and promise. *Social Work Research, 27*(4), 197–208.

Rosenberg, S. L., Heck, D. J., & Banilower, E. R. (2005). *Does teacher content preparation moderate the impacts of professional development? A longitudinal analysis of LSC teacher questionnaire data.* Chapel Hill, NC: Horizon Research, Inc.

Rossi, P. H., & Freeman, H. E. (1989). *Evaluation: A systematic approach* (4th ed.). Newbury Park, CA: Sage.

Rossman, G. B., & Rallis, S. F. (1998). *Learning in the field: An introduction to qualitative research.* Thousand Oaks, CA: Sage.

Rubin, H. J., & Rubin, I. S. (1995). *Qualitative interviewing: The art of hearing data.* Thousand Oaks, CA: Sage.

Ruggles, P. (1990). *Drawing the line: Alternative poverty measures and their implications for public policy.* Washington, DC: Urban Institute Press.

Sampson, R. J., & Laub, J. H. (1994). Urban poverty and the family context of delinquency: A new look at structure and process in a classic study. *Child Development, 65,* 523–540.

Sampson, R. J., & Wilson, W. J. (1995). Toward a theory of race, crime, and urban inequality. In J. Hagan & R. Peterson (Eds.), *Crime and inequality* (pp. 37–56). Stanford, CA: Stanford University Press.

Schanzenbach, D. (2006). What have researchers learned from Project STAR? In *Brookings Papers on Education Policy 2007.* Washington, DC: Brookings Institution.

Schober, M. F. (1999). Making sense of survey questions. In M. G. Sirken, D. J. Hermann, S. Schechter, N. Schwartz, J. M. Tanur, & R. Tourangeau (Eds.), *Cognition and survey research* (pp. 77–94). New York: John Wiley.

Schofield, J. W. (2002). Increasing the generalizability of qualitative research. In A. M. Huberman & M. B. Miles (Eds.), *The qualitative researcher's companion* (pp. 171–203). Thousand Oaks, CA: Sage.

Schon, D. (1983). *The reflective practitioner: How professionals think in action.* New York: Basic Books.

Schon, D. (1987). *Educating the reflective practitioner.* San Francisco: Jossey-Bass.

Schottelkorb, A., & Ray, D. (2009). ADHD symptom reduction in elementary students: A single-case effectiveness design. *Professional School Counseling, 13*(1), 11–22.

Schutt, R. K. (2009). *Investigating the social world* (6th ed.). Thousand Oaks, CA: Pine Forge.

Schutt, R. K. (2012). *Investigating the social world* (7th ed.). Thousand Oaks, CA: Pine Forge.

Schwandt, T. A. (1994). Constructivist, interpretivist approaches to human inquiry. In N. K. Denzin & Y. S. Lincoln (Eds.), *Handbook of qualitative research* (pp. 118–137). Thousand Oaks, CA: Sage.

Scriven, M. (1972). Prose and cons about goal-free evaluation. *Evaluation Comment, 3,* 1–7.

Sechrest, L., & Sidani, S. (1995). Quantitative and qualitative methods: Is there an alternative? *Evaluation and Program Planning, 18,* 77–87.

Selm, M. V., & Jankowski, N. W. (2006). Conducting online surveys. *Quality and Quantity, 40*, 435–456.

Shadish, W. R., Cook, T. D., & Leviton, L. C. (Eds.). (1991). *Foundations of program evaluation: Theories of practice.* Thousand Oaks, CA: Sage.

Shepherd, J., Hill, D., Bristor, J., & Montalvan, P. (1996). Converting an ongoing health study to CAPI: Findings from the National Health and Nutrition Study. In R. B. Warnecke (Ed.), *Health survey research methods conference proceedings* (pp. 159–164). Hyattsville, MD: U.S. Department of Health and Human Services.

Short, K. S. (2011). *Who is poor? A new look with the supplemental poverty measure* (SEHSD Working Paper 2010-15). Washington, DC: U.S. Census Bureau.

Sieber, J. E. (1992). *Planning ethically responsible research: A guide for students and internal review boards.* Thousand Oaks, CA: Sage.

Sjoberg, G. (Ed.). (1967). *Ethics, politics, and social research.* Cambridge, MA: Schenkman.

Skinner, K. (2009). *Charter school success or selective out-migration of low-achievers? Effects of enrollment management on student achievement.* Boston: Massachusetts Association of Teachers.

Smith, J. (1991). A methodology for twenty-first century sociology. *Social Forces, 70*, 1–7.

Smith, M. L. (2006). Multiple methodology in education research. In J. Green, G. Camilli, & P. B. Elmore (Eds.), *Handbook of complementary research methods in education* (pp. 457–476). Mahwah, NJ: Lawrence Erlbaum.

Smith, P. S., Banilower, E. R., McMahon, K. C., & Weiss, I. R. (2002). *National survey of science and mathematics education: Trends from 1977–2000.* Chapel Hill, NC: Horizon Research.

Smith, T. W. (1987). That which we call welfare by any other name would smell sweeter: An analysis of the impact of question wording on response patterns. *Public Opinion Quarterly, 51*(1), 75–83.

Smyth, J. D., Dillman, D. A., Christian, L. M., & Stern, M. J. (2004, May). *How visual grouping influences answers to internet surveys.* Extended version of paper presented at the annual meeting of the American Association for Public Opinion Research, Phoenix, AZ. Retrieved July 5, 2005, from http://survey.sesrc.wsu.edu/dillman/papers.htm

South, S. J., & Spitze, G. (1994). Housework in marital and non-marital households. *American Sociological Review, 59*, 327–347.

Spicer, Y. (2004). *"Our experience says we know something: We are still here." An autoethnographic study of African American women principals in Massachusetts K–12 public schools.* Unpublished doctoral dissertation, University of Massachusetts, Boston.

Stake, R. E. (1995). *The art of case study research.* Thousand Oaks, CA: Sage.

Stark, D. R. (2003). *Early Head Start: Celebrating success and ensuring its future.* Washington, DC: ZERO TO THREE: National Center for Infants, Toddlers and Families.

Stenhouse, L. (1975). *An introduction to curriculum research and development.* London: Heinemann.

Stephen, J. M., Young, M. F., & Calabrese, T. (2007). Does moral judgment go offline when students are online? A comparative analysis of undergraduates' beliefs and behaviors related to conventional and digital cheating. *Ethics and Behavior, 17*, 233–254.

Strike, K. A., Anderson, M. L., Curren, R., van Geel, T., Pritchard, I., & Robertson, E. (2002). *Ethical standards of the American Educational Research Association: Cases and commentary.* Washington, DC: AERA.

Sudman, S. (1976). *Applied sampling.* New York: Academic Press.

Sunderland, A. (2005). *Children, families and welfare reform: A three-city study.* Princeton, NJ: The Robert Wood Johnson Foundation. Retrieved October 5, 2005, from www.rwjf.org/reports/grr/037218.htm

Sylva, K., Melhuishi, E., Sammons, P., Siraj-Blatchford, I., & Taggart, B. (2008). *Effective pre-school and primary education 3–11 project (EPPE 3-11) final report from the primary phase: Pre-school, school and family influences on children's development during key stage 2 (age 7–11)* (Research Report DCSF-RR061). London: Department for Education.

Tashakkori, A., & Teddlie, C. (2010). Putting the human back in "human research methodology": The researcher in mixed methods research. *Journal of Mixed Methods Research, 4*(4), 271–277.

Thorne, B. (1993). *Gender play: Girls and boys in school.* New Brunswick, NJ: Rutgers University Press.

Tillman, L. C. (2004). African American principals and the legacy of *Brown. Review of Research in Education, 28*, 101–146.

Tourangeau, R. (1999). Context effects. In M. G. Sirken, D. J. Herrmann, S. Schechter, N. Schwartz, J. M. Tanur, & R. Tourangeau (Eds.), *Cognition and survey research* (pp. 111–132). New York: John Wiley.

Tourangeau, R. (2004). Survey research and societal change. *Annual Review of Psychology, 55,* 775–801.

Tripodi, T. (1994). *A primer on single-subject design for clinical social workers.* Washington, DC: National Association of Social Workers.

Tufte, E. R. (1983). *The visual display of quantitative information.* Cheshire, CT: Graphics Press.

Turner, C. F., & Martin, E. (Eds.). (1984). *Surveying subjective phenomena* (Vols. 1–2). New York: Russell Sage Foundation.

Uchitelle, L. (1999, October 16). Devising new math to define poverty. *The New York Times,* pp. A1, A14.

U.S. Census Bureau. (2009). *Income, poverty, and health insurance coverage in the United States: 2009* (Report P60, n. 238, Table B–2, 62–7). Washington, DC: U.S. Department of Commerce, Census Bureau.

U.S. Census Bureau. (2011). *Statistical abstract of the United States.* Washington, DC: Government Printing Office. http://www.census.gov/statab/www/

U.S. Department of Health and Human Services, Administration for Children and Families. (2002). *Making a difference in the lives of infants and toddlers and their families: The impacts of early Head Start.* Washington, DC: Author.

Valadez, J. R. (2008). Shaping the educational decisions of Mexican immigrant high school students. *American Educational Research Journal, 45,* 834–860.

Van Maanen, J. (1995). An end to innocence: The ethnography of ethnography. In J. Van Maanen (Ed.), *Representation in ethnography* (pp. 1–35). Thousand Oaks, CA: Sage.

Van Maanen, J. (2002). The fact of fiction in organizational ethnography. In A. M. Huberman & M. B. Miles (Eds.), *The qualitative researcher's companion* (pp. 101–117). Thousand Oaks, CA: Sage.

Viswanathan, M. (2005). *Measurement error and research design.* Thousand Oaks, CA: Sage.

W. K. Kellogg Foundation. (2004). *Logic model development guide program implementation template.* http://www.wkkf.org

Wallace, W. L. (1983). *Principles of scientific sociology.* New York: Aldine de Gruyter.

Wallgren, A., Wallgren, B., Persson, R., Jorner, U., & Haaland, J.-A. (1996). *Graphing statistics and data: Creating better charts.* Thousand Oaks, CA: Sage.

Walters, P. B., & Lareau, A. (2009). Introduction. In P. B. Walters, A. Lareau, & S. Ramis (Eds.), *Education research on trial: Policy reform and the call for scientific rigor* (pp. 1–14). New York: Routledge.

Waters-Adams, S. (2006). *Action research in education.* Retrieved October 13, 2009, from http://www.edu.plymouth.ac.uk/RESINED/actionresearch/arhome.htm

Wazana, A., Bresnahan, M., & Kline, J. (2007).The autism epidemic: Fact or artifact? *Journal of the American Academy of Child and Adolescent Psychiatry, 46*(6), 721–730.

Webb, E. J., Campbell, D. T., Schwartz, R. D., & Sechrest, L. (2000). *Unobtrusive measures* (Rev. ed.). Thousand Oaks, CA: Sage.

Weber, M. (1949). *The methodology of the social sciences* (E. A. Shils & H. A. Finch, Trans.). New York: Free Press.

Wechsler, H., Lee, J. E., Kuo M., Seibring, M., Nelson, T. F., & Lee, H. (2002). Trends in college binge drinking during a period of increased prevention efforts. *Journal of American College Health, 50,* 203–217.

Weiss, I. R., Banilower, E. R., McMahon, K. C., & Smith, P. S. (2001). *Report of the 2000 national survey of science and mathematics education.* Chapel Hill, NC: Horizon Research, Inc.

Wengraf, T. (2001). *Qualitative research interviewing: Biographic narrative and semi-structured methods.* Thousand Oaks, CA: Sage.

Whipple, J. (2004). Music in intervention for children and adolescents with autism: A meta-analysis. *Journal of Music Therapy, 41*(2), 90–106.

Whittington, D. (2002). *2000 National survey of science and mathematics education: Status of high school mathematics teaching.* Chapel Hill, NC: Horizon Research.

Whyte, W. F. (1955). *Street corner society.* Chicago: University of Chicago Press.

Wilson, W. J. (1987). *The truly disadvantaged: The inner city, the underclass, and public policy.* Chicago: University of Chicago Press.

Wilson, W. J. (1998). Engaging publics in sociological dialogue through the media. *Contemporary Sociology, 27,* 435–438.

Wolcott, H. F. (1995). *The art of fieldwork.* Walnut Creek, CA: AltaMira Press.

Author Index

Subject Index

About the Authors

Joseph W. Check, PhD, is Associate Professor and Director of the Leadership in Urban Schools EdD program in the College of Education and Human Development, University of Massachusetts, Boston. He completed his BA at Boston College and his MA and PhD at Tufts University. His prior publications include *Politics, Language, and Culture: A Critical Look at Urban School Reform* (2002); co-editorship of *Writing Within School Reform,* a monograph series of the Annenberg Institute for School Reform at Brown University; and book chapters and articles on literacy, practitioner inquiry, and urban school reform. He has supervised dissertations in school reform, professional development, literacy, home/school interactions, and special education. He has served as principal or co-principal investigator for numerous grant-funded professional development programs, including a 4-year, $4 million practitioner inquiry project in 14 urban school districts funded by the DeWitt-Wallace Reader's Digest Foundation. He regularly teaches graduate-level research courses.

Russell K. Schutt, PhD, is Professor and Chair of Sociology at the University of Massachusetts, Boston and Lecturer on Sociology in the Department of Psychiatry (Beth Israel-Deaconess Medical Center) at the Harvard Medical School. He completed his BA, MA, and PhD (1977) degrees at the University of Illinois at Chicago and was a Postdoctoral Fellow in the Sociology of Social Control Training Program at Yale University (1977–1979). In addition to *Investigating the Social World: The Process and Practice of Research* (6th ed.), *Making Sense of the Social World* (3rd ed.; with Dan Chambliss), and adaptations for the fields of social work (with Ray Engel) and criminology/criminal justice (with Ronet Bachman), he is the author of *Organization in a Changing Environment,* co-editor of *The Organizational Response to Social Problems,* and co-author of *Responding to the Homeless: Policy and Practice.* He has authored and co-authored numerous journal articles, book chapters, and research reports on homelessness, service preferences and satisfaction, mental health, organizations, law, and teaching research methods. His recent funded research experience includes a National Cancer Institute–funded study of community health workers and recruitment for cancer clinical trials and a National Institute of Mental Health–funded study of housing alternatives for homeless persons diagnosed with severe mental illness. His publications in peer-reviewed journals range in focus from the effect of social context on cognition, satisfaction, and functioning to the service preferences of homeless persons and service personnel, the admission practices of craft unions, and the social factors in legal decisions.

SAGE Research Methods Online

The essential tool for researchers

**Sign up now at
www.sagepub.com/srmo
for more information.**

An expert research tool

- An **expertly designed taxonomy** with more than 1,400 unique terms for social and behavioral science research methods

- **Visual and hierarchical search tools** to help you discover material and link to related methods

- Easy-to-use navigation tools
- Content organized by complexity
- Tools for citing, printing, and downloading content with ease
- Regularly updated content and features

A wealth of essential content

- The most comprehensive picture of quantitative, qualitative, and mixed methods available today

- More than **100,000 pages of SAGE book and reference material** on research methods as well as editorially selected material from SAGE journals

- More than **600 books** available in their entirety online

Launching 2011!

§SAGE research methods online